THE COMPLETE PERSONAL ESSAYS
OF ROBERT LOUIS STEVENSON

For all of Robert Louis Stevenson's achievements in fiction, many of his contemporaries thought of him primarily as an essayist. His essays, known for their intellectual substance, emotional force, and stylistic vitality, were widely considered the best of their time. Despite the importance of Stevenson's nonfiction, his personal essays—70 in total—have never been printed together in a single volume until now.

Stevenson's essays explore a range of topics from illness and evolution to marriage and dreams, and from literal and literary travel to the behavior of children and the character of dogs. Grappling with many of the cultural, ethical, and existential questions of his age, he resists dogma to draw fresh conclusions. Stevenson examines beggars and university students, immigrants and engineers, invalids and nurses, outlining his own colorful life story and unique approach to "the art of living" along the way.

Whereas the most common and widely available versions of these texts were modified after Stevenson's death, this volume gathers his personal essays, many of which have never appeared in any modern edition, in their authorized versions. These essays are still considered classic models of the form, and in this volume, the Editor presents them alongside an introduction and notes to assist in a rereading and reappreciation that is long overdue.

Trenton B. Olsen is Associate Professor of English at Brigham Young University–Idaho, USA. He is the author of *Wordsworth and Evolution in Victorian Literature: Entangled Influence* (2019).

D1568915

THE COMPLETE PERSONAL ESSAYS OF ROBERT LOUIS STEVENSON

Edited by Trenton B. Olsen

Routledge
Taylor & Francis Group

LONDON AND NEW YORK

First published 2021
by Routledge
4 Park Square, Milton Park, Abingdon, Oxon OX14 4RN
605 Third Avenue, New York, NY 10017

First issued in paperback 2023

Routledge is an imprint of the Taylor & Francis Group, an informa business

British Library Cataloguing-in-Publication Data
A catalogue record for this book is available from the British Library

Library of Congress Cataloging-in-Publication Data
A catalog record for this book has been requested

ISBN: 978-1-03-257070-9 (pbk)
ISBN: 978-0-367-18048-5 (hbk)
ISBN: 978-0-429-05930-8 (ebk)

DOI: 10.4324/9780429059308

Typeset in Times New Roman
by Apex CoVantage, LLC

Publisher's Note
The publisher has gone to great lengths to ensure the quality of this reprint but points out that some imperfections in the original copies may be apparent.

Stevenson's essays are not mine to dedicate. In fact, he already dedicated half of them in published collections: *Virginibus Puerisque and Other Papers* to William Ernest Henley, *Memories and Portraits* to his mother, Margaret Stevenson, and *Across the Plains with Other Memories and Essays* to the French writer Paul Bourget. But my part in producing this volume—the work of gathering, transcribing, annotating, and introducing the essays—I dedicate with love to my children: Austin, Trudy, Logan, and Calvin.

CONTENTS

CONTENTS

CONTENTS

ACKNOWLEDGMENTS

I first encountered Stevenson's essays as a graduate student and was immediately struck by their intellectual substance, emotional force, and stylistic vibrancy. I was surprised to learn that no complete collection of his personal essays had been published, and I am grateful to the editors at Routledge, particularly Kimberley Smith and Simon Alexander, for helping me change that. Many people assisted in this work, and it is a pleasure to thank them here.

I wish to thank the general and volume editors of the indispensable *New Edinburgh Edition of the Works of Robert Louis Stevenson*—Stephen Arata, Richard Dury, Penny Fielding, Anthony Mandal, and Lesley Graham—for generously sharing their transcripts of nine of Stevenson's unpublished essays. These transcripts, painstakingly decoded and copied from Stevenson's manuscripts, saved me countless hours and headaches. I owe special thanks to Richard Dury for suggesting and facilitating the assistance of *The New Edinburgh Edition*, answering several questions on the essays from his own notes, and for his kind and thoughtful review of this volume's introduction. His expertise, generosity, and encouragement have been remarkable gifts.

I have been fortunate to share Stevenson's essays with many students, who helped me think through them in class discussions and assignments. I am grateful for the significant contributions of a talented group of undergraduate research assistants: Dylan Hansen, Olivia Fisher, Hannah Herring, Michelle Grooms, Marnae Kelley, Noelle Streadbeck, and Adam Penrod, who formatted documents and helped me confirm that my transcript matched the copy text through long, careful read-aloud sessions. Their thoroughness, insight, and enthusiasm improved both the process and the final product. Thanks also to the editing students at Brigham Young University (BYU)–Idaho, who helped copy-edit my notes and assist with transcription, and to their professors Scott Cameron, Janine Gilbert, and Tom Ballard. I am grateful for the assistance of librarians at Yale University's Beinecke Library, the University of Edinburgh's Centre for Research Collections, the Huntington Library, the Princeton University Library, and the Harry Ransom Center at the University of Texas for digital reproductions. I am especially indebted to Sam Nielson of the David O. McKay Library at BYU–Idaho for helping me track down the original periodical versions of many of these essays and acquiring books for this project.

Producing a scholarly edition raises many questions, and I thank Roderick Watson, Andrew Elfenbein, Mark Farnsworth, Darin Merrill, and Jackie Harris for answering some of them. Thanks to Eric d'Evegnee for his assistance with the French translations and to Jason Williams, Jefferson Slagle, and Quinn Grover for reviewing my introductory essay. I am grateful for the support of Mark Bennion, chair of BYU–Idaho's Department of English, and Eric Waltz, dean of the College of Language and Letters.

Finally, my heartfelt thanks to my wife, Mandy, for her companionship on our "one illogical adventure" and to our children, Austin, Trudy, Logan, and Calvin: fine students and better teachers of the "Art of Living" (39, 65).

INTRODUCTION

On summer break from his university studies in 1868 and a few months before his eighteenth birthday, Robert Louis Stevenson worked late into the night. Stevenson was considered "the pattern of an idler," and his industrious vigils would have surprised those who knew him (143). He rarely attended class at the University of Edinburgh and had no interest in his current career training: a sort of summer internship in the family business of marine and lighthouse engineering in the coastal villages near Edinburgh and the remote far north of Scotland. In his essay "The Education of an Engineer," he recalled, "my one genuine pre-occupation lay elsewhere, and my only industry was in the hours when I was not on duty." He had already made his "own private determination to be an author" and spent his nights working on a historical novel and poetry collection that would never see the light of day. Later that fall, he would write his first essay—"Night Outside the Wick Mail"—a draft that he circulated to his cousin about his return trip to Edinburgh. Over the next few years, he began publishing essays: first in an obscure college magazine and then in major periodicals. By the time his famous novels *Treasure Island* (1883) and *Strange Case of Dr. Jekyll and Mr. Hyde* (1886) appeared, Stevenson had been making a name for himself in nonfiction for more than a decade. But before all of this, he spent his nights at a desk. Sickly and ambitious, entirely unknown and "with intimations of early death and immortality," he traded sleep for writing, "toiling to leave a memory behind" him (252).

On immortality and neglect: reception histories

When Stevenson did suffer an early death, 26 years later at 44 and a world away in Samoa, his contemporaries debated whether he would be best remembered for his fiction or essays. Stevenson wrote more than 100 essays in his lifetime, and while they range from biographical portraits and political arguments to travel narratives and literary criticism, most of them are best described as personal: informal, intimate essays that attempt to reveal the writer through dramatized thought and experience. It was Stevenson's personal essays, Edmond Gosse argued, that "reveal him in his best character" (775). Richard Le Gallienne concurred that for all the merits of his novels and short stories, "Stevenson's final fame will be that

1

of an essayist" (Maixner 391–92).[1] In fact, Gosse insisted, "if Stevenson is not the most exquisite of the English essayists, we know not to whom that praise is due" (775). He was widely considered the most successful essayist of his generation. *The Cambridge History of English Literature* (1916) presented Stevenson as the "foremost essayist since Lamb," and William Lyon Phelps's 1906 selection of Stevenson's essays made him a ubiquitous model for college composition courses in the early twentieth century (161).

Victorian reviewers recognized that Stevenson was reinvigorating an old genre, and while they almost unanimously praised his essays' style, they also valued their ideas. Robert-Louis Abrahamson explains the particular philosophical appeal of Stevenson's essays in his time:

> Caught in the late Victorian conflict between science and religious truths, between material progress and aesthetic pleasure, between bourgeois respectability and decadent rebellion, this generation found a guide in Stevenson's non-dogmatic call to discover values, not in religious or social conventions but within oneself, and to find joy and meaning, not by denying or avoiding the dangers and failures of life, but by embracing them.
>
> (lxxxvi)

The values upheld in his essays include kindness, cheerfulness, and courage even and especially in the face of uncertainty and despair, values that resonated in an age of intellectual, social, and spiritual anxiety.

Though Stevenson's contemporaries were certainly interested in his discussion of the aesthetic, ethical, and existential questions of his time, it was the personal element of his essays—their revelation of the man himself—that they prized most highly. Stevenson's obituary in *The Times* strikes a notably personal tone:

> The world has lost, not only a great writer, but a most attractive personality. For his readers everywhere regarded Stevenson, not merely as a writer of books, but as a singularly charming, interesting, attractive, personal friend. . . . He had won us all to himself by his self-revelations, made as they were with an art that was consummate, and bringing before us a personality of the most delightful, the most lovable kind.
>
> (*Times*, Dec. 18, 774)

The obituary's writer singled out Stevenson's personal essays as the medium of this interchange, observing that "chiefly it is . . . in the Essays that we find this self-portraiture." In 1895, Alice Brown made a similar point: "He who reads the novels without reference to the essays . . . does not know the temper of Stevenson, the man" (42). The high position Gosse assigned Stevenson's essays in literary history also centered on the personality they revealed: "After Montaigne, who is there to be named who has expressed in more exquisite abandonment a nature more ingenious and more human?" (775).

Despite the importance of Stevenson's nonfiction in his own career and in literary history, his personal essays—70 in total—have never been printed all together in a single volume until now. The two primary reasons for this absence relate to the historical fluctuations of both Stevenson's critical reputation and the academic status of the essay form. As Lesley Graham has demonstrated, these two developments overlap and interrelate. The need for this edition grows from the critical neglect of Stevenson's essays in particular and the essay form in general. It is past time for a rereading and reappreciation of Stevenson's essays, which, in Graham's words, still "lie little-read, and too long under-examined for their own intrinsic merits" (335). Similarly, Carl H. Klaus urges, "a methodology for understanding the essay is long overdue" (xxvi). I would argue that the personal elements and popularity of both Stevenson's work and the essay form have contributed to the twentieth-century decline in status and corresponding critical neglect of both Stevenson and the genre.

Once a leading literary celebrity, Stevenson was dismissed by early twentieth-century critics. As Richard Dury has outlined, Modernists devalued Stevenson for a number of reasons: his novels departed from the realism that now defined the genre, his style so admired by Victorians seemed to them superficial and insincere, and his association with children's literature contributed to a later sense that he was beneath serious critical attention. The self-revelation of his essays provided ammunition for the reaction. Their intimacy, combined with his early death in the romanticized Pacific, contributed to a sentimental, reverent admiration for Stevenson the man, which Modernists rejected. Andrew Lang noted at Stevenson's death that "his admirers were enthusiastic worshippers," and they congregated at the altar of his personal essays (775). Readers' emotional connection with the essays reinforced E.M. Forster's charge of "sentimentality" and "quaintness" (83). Stevenson's popularity now worked against him, as he became a literary monument to tear down. In 1931, Edwin Muir observed, "Stevenson has simply fallen out of the procession. He is still read by the vulgar, but he has joined the band of writers on whom, by tacit consent, the serious critics have nothing to say" (377).[2]

The resurgence of critical interest in Stevenson that began in the 1980s, accelerated in the 1990s, and shown no signs of slowing down since has focused much more on his fiction than his essays. Anticipating this boom in scholarly interest, now evident in continual book publications and the successful *Journal of Stevenson Studies*, David Daiches observed in *Robert Louis Stevenson: A Revaluation* (1947), "it has long been the fashion to esteem him as an essayist and dismiss the novels," and set out to "redirect attention to the novels as the most impressive expression of Stevenson's genius" (148). Though his position in the canon is securely reestablished, most modern Stevenson scholarship has tacitly accepted this reversal of interest, turning to the essays to illuminate his fiction but rarely studying them for their own sake. This tendency, however, is beginning to change: in 2012,

3

the *Journal of Stevenson Studies* published a volume of scholarly articles devoted exclusively to the essays, and in the introduction to *Essays I: Virginibus Puerisque and Other Papers* (2018) in *The New Edinburgh Edition*, Abrahamson, Dury, Graham, and Alex Thomson offer the longest, most thorough discussion of Stevenson's critical and creative essays to date.

This shift in attention from Stevenson's essays to his fiction has occurred in part because scholars began to reexamine his work when the essay itself was falling from critical favor: a recurring pattern in the genre's history. The critical neglect of the personal essay, punctuated by periodic rounds of dismissal, seems to correlate very little with its popularity and vitality. The implied inferiority is evident in Samuel Johnson's definition of *essay* in his *Dictionary of the English Language* (1755): "a loose sally of the mind; an irregular, indigested piece, not a regular, orderly performance." Despite this codified devaluing of the genre, Johnson was writing during what has been called "the Great Age of the English Essay" and was himself one of its preeminent practitioners. Before Stevenson's literary reputation was resuscitated, critics were also pronouncing the essay dead in publications like Elizabeth Drew's "The Lost Art of the Essay" (1935), W.P. Eaton's "On Burying the Essay" (1948), and Clifton Fadiman's "A Gentle Dirge for the Familiar Essay" (1955). Of course, the period when Virginia Woolf, George Orwell, F. Scott Fitzgerald, E.B. White, and James Baldwin were writing and publishing personal essays is a strange time to hold a funeral for the form. Over the past 30 years, following Lee Gutkind's lead at the University of Pittsburgh, graduate programs in creative nonfiction—now the most widely published literary genre—have proliferated internationally. The rise of the personal essay on the internet has further contributed to this increasing popularity but also led to another cycle of dismissals such as Laura Bennett's "The First Person Industrial Complex" (2015) and Jia Tolentino's "The Personal Essay Boom is Over" (2017), which appeared in *The New Yorker*: a premier venue for personal essays.[3]

This disconnect relates to a lack of research focus on the essay genre. As Phillip Lopate notes, "the personal essay has rarely been isolated and studied as such" (xxiii). When the personal essay is studied, it is often by its practitioners, such as Lopate and Klaus.[4] Creative writers have contributed some of the most useful commentaries on the form. Whereas academic journals like *Novel: A Forum on Fiction* and *Contemporary Literature* are edited by literary scholars, rather than novelists and poets, virtually all of the editors and advisory board members of *Assay: A Journal of Nonfiction Studies* are creative writers.[5] In the absence of significant scholarly attention on the genre, contemporary essayists bear the double duty of creative and critical writing. The same pattern holds true for Stevenson's work. While some scholars are beginning to focus on Stevenson's essays, many creative writers and general readers have long considered them classic models of the form. Lopate's best-selling collection *The Art of the Personal Essay: An Anthology from the Classical Era to the Present* (1995) features three of Stevenson's essays, and, despite the lack of scholarly attention, *The Literary*

Hub recently included Stevenson in a published list of essayists most widely anthologized in the past 25 years (Temple).

The critical neglect of the form says little about its value or the quality of individual texts but rather reflects a tension between scholarly writing and personal essays. As the *New Edinburgh Edition* editors note, "increasingly professionalized critics had difficulty in finding an approach" to the genre (lviii). The essay's popularity, traditional lack of prestige, essayists' long-standing tendency to define their work against scholarly writing, and the genre's inherently analytical mode, which seems to do some of the critic's work for them, are all likely reasons for this scholarly resistance.

While these factors have played a role in the relative dearth of scholarship, perhaps the most significant barrier between modern criticism and the essay lies in its personal element. Influential literary theory, from New Criticism's "intentional fallacy" in the mid-twentieth century to Post-Structuralism's later "Death of the Author," has distanced writers from texts and made scholars reluctant to read literature biographically. This separation is easier with fiction, poetry, and drama than the personal essay. While recognizing the essay as a self-contained literary text and acknowledging the distinction between the narrative "I" character at the essay's center and its actual author, fully detaching personal essays from their authors' lives is neither possible nor desirable.[6]

Stevenson and the art of life

Whereas later critics discounted the personal element in Stevenson's work, rejecting Victorians' fascination with the man revealed on the page, Stevenson himself insisted on the link between literature and life in his essays. In addition to "the mechanical side of his trade," he wrote, the artist must learn the "Art of Living" (65). For Stevenson, the essayist must be both "a lover and artificer of words" and "a lover and forger of experience" with not only a "sense of poetry in letters" but also "poetry of life" (279–280). He admired the lives as well as the work of nonfiction writers: asserting that readers of Montaigne "will end by seeing that this old gentleman was in a dozen ways a finer fellow, and held in a dozen ways a nobler view of life, than they or their contemporaries." He finds in the *Meditations* of Marcus Aurelius the "memory of the man himself . . . as though you had touched a loyal hand, looked into brave eyes, and made a noble friend" (395–396). Stevenson not only declares, with the French critic Sainte-Beuve, that "all experience [is] a single great book" but that the essayist must "be a living book," blurring the distinction between the writer's life and art (64, 505).

While Stevenson's personal essays are much more than autobiographical anecdotes, taken together they vividly outline his colorful life story. Stevenson was born in Edinburgh on 13 November 1850 to Thomas and Margaret Stevenson. An only child and frequently ill, Stevenson often had to amuse himself, though he played with his many cousins when healthy. While Stevenson's powerful imagination enlivened his play and love of story, as seen in his essays "Child's Play," "A Penny Plain and Twopence Coloured," and "Reminiscences of Colinton Manse," it also gave him night terrors, described in "A Chapter on Dreams" and "Nuits Blanches." Both the nightmares, which inspired *Jekyll and Hyde*, and the imaginative play, which launched *Treasure Island*, continued into his adulthood. His nurse, Alison Cunningham or "Cummy," raised him with affection, pious lessons, stories of Scottish martyrs, and images of hell. If Cummy's talk animated his nightmares, she also helped him through long nights and childhood illnesses. Stevenson paid tribute to her in his essay "Nurses" and dedicated *A Child's Garden of Verses* (1885) to her.

Stevenson enrolled at the University of Edinburgh in November of 1867 and reflected on student life in "The Modern Student Considered Generally" and "Some College Memories." With little interest in formal studies or career preparation, Stevenson practiced the art of inactivity celebrated in "An Apology for Idlers." He developed a close circle of friends at the university, whose portraits as conversationalists appear in his essay "Talk and Talkers." He joined the debating club the Speculative Society: a formative experience described in "Debating Societies." While apparently shirking his responsibilities, Stevenson was learning how to write, as narrated in "Books which Have Influenced Me." Along with his friends, he founded *Edinburgh University Magazine*: an exciting and ultimately failed venture, recounted in "A College Magazine," where he published five of the essays printed here. Sharing in the monetary risk of the short-lived publication, Stevenson quipped, "It was a comfortable thought to me that I had a father," who financially supported him until his early thirties (147). His sensitivity to the injustice of his own unmerited good fortune compared to his poorer and more studious classmates prompted the deep ethical reflection of "Lay Morals." He finally told his father in April of 1871 that he had no interest in engineering or anything but literature—experience he would draw on in the essays "The Morality of the Profession of Letters," "On the Choice of a Profession," and "A Letter to a Young Gentleman who Proposes to Embrace the Career of Art." In a compromise, Stevenson agreed to study law for the Scottish Bar.

There would be other difficult news to tell his parents, such as his loss of faith in the Christian religion, which he announced in January of 1873 after what he described as a "very hard reading" of Charles Darwin and Herbert Spencer (*Letters* 1:249). He grappled with the moral implications of this disbelief in "Pulvis et Umbra," which he called his "Darwinian sermon," and continued to value and explore Christian ethics, if not doctrine, in essays like "Lay Morals," "A Christmas Sermon," and "Old Mortality" (*Letters* 6:60). The resulting strain on his loving but difficult relationship with his parents likely contributed to his essay "Crabbed Age and Youth" and his statement in "Truth of Intercourse" that "between parent and child intercourse is apt to degenerate into a verbal fencing bout, and misapprehensions to become ingrained" (50).

When healthy, he walked considerable distances, described in "Walking Tours," "Roads," and essays on specific journeys, such as "Epilogue to *An Inland Voyage*" and "Cockermouth and Keswick." When ill, Stevenson sought climates where he could recover in France ("Ordered South"), Switzerland ("The Stimulation of the Alps," "Davos in Winter" and "Health and Mountains"), and ultimately in Samoa. Repeatedly throughout his life, he felt that he was "under the very dart of death" and had to maintain his spirits and his work in severe illness, as seen in "Æs Triplex" and "The Misgivings of Convalescence" (252). Poor health notwithstanding, he sought to be "a true lover of living," and in his essays, we find him sea diving, alpine sledding, inadvertently starting a forest fire in California, having his fortune told, getting arrested, and befriending beggars, painters, children, scholars, gardeners, donkeys, and dogs (83).

Though he was first "Ordered South" to France by his doctor in 1873, Stevenson repeatedly returned from 1874 to 1878, visiting Paris ("In the Latin Quarter" and "The Paris Bourse") and immersing himself in the artist colonies around Barbizon ("Forest Notes" and "Fontainebleau"). It was there at Grez-sur-Loing in September of 1876 that he met Fanny Osbourne, who was in France with her children to study painting and distance herself from an unfaithful husband in California. Within two months, Stevenson had finished an essay "On Falling in Love," which he would pair with the "Virginibus Puerisque" essays on marriage. In less than three years, he was on a boat for New York and then a train for California (where he wrote "The Old Pacific Capital" and "A Modern Cosmopolis") to propose to Fanny, ten years his senior and, much to the chagrin of his parents, still married. She divorced her husband, Sam Osborne, and married Stevenson on 19 May 1880 in San Francisco. With his new family, Stevenson would live in California, France, Scotland, England, Davos, New York's Adirondacks, Australia, and the Pacific Islands.

With the publication of *Treasure Island*, first serially in 1881 and as a book in 1883, Stevenson the essayist and memoirist became a novelist. But the 1886 success of *Dr. Jekyll and Mr. Hyde* made him a celebrity. Having written that "no young man ought to be at peace till he is self-supporting," Stevenson was for the first time financially independent of his father, who died the following year (481). He accepted a lucrative but grueling contract to write a monthly essay for *Scribner's* magazine in 1888. Completing the final three essays in May, he left for the South Seas the following month. Exhausted by the series, he would write only two more personal essays: "Rosa Quo Locorum" in 1890 and "My First Book: *Treasure Island*," which was published three months before his death in 1894. Despite taxing Pacific cruises, Stevenson's health generally improved in Samoa, where he focused on writing fiction and South Sea chronicles. Raised on stories of Scottish uprisings and having witnessed imperialist exploitation in his travels, he advocated for Samoans' peace and political interests. He lived on a large estate called Vailima with Fanny, her children, son-in-law, grandson, and Stevenson's mother. On 3 December 1894, he died suddenly of a cerebral hemorrhage and was buried on the nearby summit of Mount Vaea.

Stevenson's life experience not only provided content for his essays but also shaped his approach to the genre. He compares writing to his earliest pastimes in "Child's Play," and his irony and humor suit the essay form—defined by Cynthia Ozick as "the movement of a free mind at play" (162). Lopate uses Stevenson's "An Apology for Idlers" to illustrate the essayist's traditional position as an "idler figure" whose "curiosity, openness, appetite for pleasure, willingness to reflect. . . [and] capacity for perception" embody the genre's virtues (xxxiv). Stevenson, who by all accounts was a remarkable talker, not only strikes a conversational tone in his essays but sometimes calls them "gossips" or "chats," and uses intimate markers like "let us talk it over between friends" (*Letters* 6: 31, 116; 26). We can also see traces of the college debater in the contrarianism of the essayist. With "a cry from the opposite party," he argues against popular opinion, conventional wisdom, and traditional morality (62). Stevenson especially valued the debating society's requirement to argue against one's own position: "to argue out—to feel with—to elaborate completely—the case as it stands against yourself," and this self-interrogation is evident in his essays (458). The personal essay's generic freedom from dogma was a good fit for a writer who lost his faith in early life and embraced doubt and uncertainty, maintaining that "a dogma learned is only a new error" (397). While "questing after elements of truth," which he considered hard to learn and harder to communicate, he acknowledged, "there is no such thing as the whole truth" (179, 59).

For Stevenson, this imperfect pursuit of an elusive and often illusory truth characterized both the essay and life itself. He contradicts his earlier positions on the virtues of idleness, the false wisdom of age, and other topics over his career and sometimes within a single essay.[7] In his notes for an early essay collection to be called "Life at Twenty Five," Stevenson chose an epigraph from Walt Whitman: "Do I contradict myself? Very well, then I contradict myself."[8] Stevenson recognized from the beginning that the personal essayist is large and contains multitudes. He considered this self-contradiction and internal debate central not only to the personal essay but to life, as we "grow to love things we hated and hate things we loved" (55).

Stevenson's essays on walking reflect the crooked life journey. Physical travel mirrors an inward exploration as "you sink into yourself," and the road itself reflects the winding track of the mind (109). In Stevensonian essays and walking tours, "freedom is of the essence," and it is the journey, the attempt, or the *essay*—the genre's original meaning—that is privileged over the destination or conclusion (107). "We shall never reach the goal," Stevenson acknowledges, and "it is even more than probable that there is no such place." Since "failure is the fate allotted" both in literature and in life, "to travel hopefully is a better thing than to arrive" (298, 87–88). The one sure destination in Stevenson's essays is death, which haunts them. Several, such as "Æs Triplex," "The Misgivings of Convalescence," "The Wreath of Immortelles," and "Old Mortality," are devoted to the subject of death. Others, including "Virginibus Puerisque III," "Ordered South," "El Dorado," and

"A Christmas Sermon," reflect the life course by turning toward death at their conclusions.

The Lantern Bearer

Stevenson's own death, mourned around the world, brings us back to the image of the desperate, ailing teenager writing through the night in "The Education of an Engineer." The young Stevenson, who had no interest in building lighthouses but "loved the art of words and the appearances of life," sat "between his candles" at the desk as night wore on and the darkness of uncertainty, fear, and failure deepened around him. From the open window, he wrote, "my literary tapers beaconed forth more brightly." Eventually, the moths came thick to the candles and began to "fall in agonies upon [his] paper" until "flesh and blood could not endure" to continue (252–253). Far from the towering lighthouses, monuments of his family's achievement, that illuminated Scotland's rocky coastline, Stevenson was sending out a different sort of beacon: small "literary tapers" which at the moment were extinguishing insect lives rather than saving countless people. The contrast reflects Stevenson's insecurity about his relationship to the family business, lamenting even late in life, "I ought to have been able to build lighthouses and write *David Balfour* too" (*Letters* 8: 235). In an untitled poem in *Underwoods* (1887), Stevenson muses, "I declined / The labours of my sires, and fled the sea, / The towers we founded and the lamps we lit, / To play at home with paper like a child" (1–4).

While rejecting his ancestral trade, Stevenson represents lighthouse engineering and literature in similar terms. In his father's obituary, "Thomas Stevenson: Civil Engineer," Stevenson shines a light on the light-maker, praising his father as one of "mankind's benefactors" and honoring his "unwearied search after perfection": the struggle Stevenson wanted his essays both to elevate and embody. Soon to set sail for the Pacific, Stevenson reflected that because of his father's lighthouse designs "in all parts of the world a safer landfall awaits the mariner" (172). In "A Plea for Gas Lamps," Stevenson asserts a preference for the old street lamps of his ancestor's design over the new electric lighting.[9] As in his famous poem "The Lamplighter," Stevenson celebrates those who "took to their heels every evening, and ran with a good heart" to illuminate the streets by nightfall and light the way for others. "Though perfection was not absolutely reached," Stevenson praises the lamplighter "speeding up the street and, at measured intervals, knocking another luminous hole into the dusk" (118).

Stevenson's personal essays are attempts to knock holes of light through the darkness. In "Cockermouth and Keswick," he reflects, "I find myself facing as stoutly as I can a hard, combative existence, full of doubt, difficulties, defeats, disappointments and dangers" (467). Stevenson's tendency to dwell on this darkness, his refusal to minimize or ignore it, is what makes many of the essays' luminous, transcendent conclusions so compelling. In "The Morality of

the Profession of Letters," Stevenson asserts that while the writer "should tell
of the kind and wholesome and beautiful elements of our life; he should tell
unsparingly of the evil and sorrow" (382). Maintaining that the suffering, injustice, and cruelty of the world "cannot be too darkly drawn," he also sought "to
find out where joy resides, and give it a voice" (293, 265). "On the Enjoyment
of Unpleasant Places" offers more than a mode of engaging with the natural
world but a philosophy of life, which Stevenson carried out in his essays. He
concludes "Virginibus Puerisque II," for instance, by elevating marriage precisely because of its inevitable failure, rather than in spite of it. Similarly, in
"Pulvis et Umbra," the world's indifferent brutality and humanity's "invincible"
moral "frailties" make our "ineffectual efforts" to do right all the more important
and remarkable (291). These concluding beams of light appear at the essays'
darkest points. The honest, unflinching presentation of immense conflict make
the partial, clear-eyed, and hard-won resolutions all the more meaningful. "We
must reach some solution," Stevenson insisted, "but we do not wish to reach it
cheaply, or quickly" (179). The light depends on the darkness, as "we do not
wish to see . . . triumph without some honourable toil" (312).

Stevenson portrays the interiority of the essayist as a literary light. In "The
Lantern Bearers," he recounts childhood holidays when he and his playmates hid
bull's-eye lanterns under their coats:

> The essence of this bliss was to walk by yourself in the black night; the
> slide shut, the top-coat buttoned; not a ray escaping, whether to conduct
> your footsteps or to make your glory public: a mere pillar of darkness in
> the dark; and all the while, deep down in the privacy of your fool's heart,
> to know you had a bull's-eye at your belt, and to exult and sing over the
> knowledge.
>
> (262)

The essay likens this hidden lantern to the inner life, proclaiming there is a
secret poet and "golden chamber at the heart" of every person: "for as dark as
his pathway seems to the observer, he will have some kind of a bull's-eye at
his belt" (262). While Stevenson applies this insight to readers of fiction, the
metaphor also reflects the personal essay. The "best teachers," he wrote, "climb
beyond teaching to the plane of art; it is themselves, and what is best in themselves, that they communicate" (397). This "central self," however, "fades and
grows clear again . . . like a revolving Pharos [or lighthouse] in the night." If
the "inner consciousness" is a "lantern alternately obscured and shining," then
the work of the personal essayist is "to discover, even dimly . . . this veiled
prophet of ourselves" and reveal it to others (496–497). It is Stevenson's illuminated and illuminating inner life, revealed through his essays, that resonated
so deeply with his contemporaries. By uncovering the light of their interior life
on the page, the essayist reminds the reader of their own through what Lopate

calls "the shiver of self-recognition" (xxvi). Stevenson conveys this idea in "Lay Morals":

> If, as teachers, we are to say anything to the purpose, we must say what will remind the pupil of his soul. . . . In short, say to him anything that he has once thought, or been upon the point of thinking, or show him any view of life that he has once clearly seen, or been upon the point of clearly seeing; and you have done your part and may leave him to complete the education for himself.
>
> (499)

The personal essay addresses the personal reader. If an essay lights the reader's path, it is by helping them remember and uncover their own lantern because, as Stevenson's great influence Montaigne asserted, "Every man has within himself the entire human condition" (qtd. in Lopate xxiii). In the words of the late Brian Doyle, an essayist of Stevensonian verve and humanity, who counted the "lean amused Scotchman" his favorite author and chief influence, Robert Louis Stevenson "[brought] light against the darkness . . . as well as any man who ever set pen to paper" (8).

About this edition

This collection's primary contribution is to present all of Stevenson's personal essays for the first time in a single volume. Erring on the side of inclusion, I have sought to collect all of Stevenson's essays that could be categorized as personal, including unpublished and unfinished pieces and excluding book-length travel narratives or chapters from memoirs in favor of self-contained essays. Some of the essays' personal or autobiographical content takes the form of narrated first-hand experience and observation. In others, personal tastes, sensibilities, and feeling come through cultural analysis or moral reflection. Stevenson himself distinguished his personal or "familiar essays" from "studies" or "critical essays," including reviews, literary criticism, and biographical portraits (*Letters* 2: 165, 5:217, 6:142). Of course, there is some overlap across categories. Some of the personal essays also have critical content on fiction and the art of writing, such as "The Lantern-Bearers," "The Morality of the Profession of Letters," or "Child's Play," but there are also central personal elements. Similarly, Stevenson's critical work retains stylistic qualities of the personal essay and explores idiosyncratic perspectives. The distinction between the genres is a matter of emphasis. Stevenson frequently turns to historical and literary examples in his personal essays to develop an insight or illuminate an experience, but the primary purpose of these essays is to reveal something about or from the self, whereas the critical essay's first aim is to reveal something about the object of study. Stevenson's obituary for his father, "Thomas Stevenson: Civil

Engineer," is similar to his biographical studies, but his intimate knowledge of his father and his autobiographically revealing portrait gives it a place in this collection.

In addition to this overdue gathering of Stevenson's personal essays, part of this edition's purpose is to help recover an accurate and reliable version of his text. Many of the most widely available versions of the essays online and in print use the 28-volume *Works of Robert Louis Stevenson* (1894–1898): a version of the text that was edited and altered by Stevenson's friend Sidney Colvin after the author's death. The result is that accurate editions of Stevenson's essays are now the exception rather than the rule. *The New Edinburgh Edition of the Collected Works of Robert Louis Stevenson*, which will publish all of the critical and personal essays over five volumes, is leading this recovery effort for Stevenson's entire canon in what will ultimately be a comprehensive 39-volume collection. My hope is that assembling all of Stevenson's personal essays, many of which have never been annotated in any modern edition, for the first time in a single volume will complement this landmark series and offer these under-appreciated essays not only to scholars but also to students, creative writers, and general readers.

Notes

1 From Le Gallienne's review of *Across the Plains* in *The Academy*, 14 May 1892.
2 While Stevenson fell from critical favor in this period, it would be a mistake to think that this was a universal response or that Modernism itself somehow invalidated his work. T.S. Eliot considered Stevenson "a writer of primary importance," W.B. Yeats admired his writing, and there is extensive scholarship on Stevenson as a proto-Modernist (Maixner 43). See, for instance, Alan Sandison's *Robert Louis Stevenson and the Appearance of Modernism* (Palgrave, 1996).
3 Tolentino, a prominent essayist herself, focuses on the decline of "a specific sort of ultra-confessional essay, written by a person you've never heard of and published online"—a genre she argues has "essentially disappeared."
4 See also Patricia Foster and Jeff Porter's edited volume *Understanding the Essay* (2012).
5 While *Contemporary Literature* considers scholarly submissions on multiple genres, they have two editors assigned to fiction, one to poetry, and none to creative nonfiction.
6 More recent theoretical approaches centered on identity, including race and ethnic studies, gender and queer theory, and disability studies may elevate the personal essay for its ability to illuminate the experience and perspectives of marginalized people.
7 Rejecting the claim of elders to superior wisdom in "Crabbed Age and Youth," Stevenson notes in "Talk and Talkers II," "the best teachers are the aged." Praising idleness early on, he later writes, "restfulness is a quality for cattle. All the virtues are active." He rages against the illness that confines him to be "idle among spiritless idlers; not perhaps dying, yet hardly living either." Reflecting that "a slightly greater age teaches a slightly different wisdom," he added a note to his republished version of "Ordered South" that reversed the essay's conclusion.
8 Stevenson's note "Life at Twenty Five," transcribed by Graham Balfour, is at the National Library of Scotland (MS 9900, Notebook 1895, f. 15).

9 Thomas Smith (1752–1815), step-father to Stevenson's grandfather Robert Stevenson, designed the street lighting for Edinburgh's New Town at the end of the eighteenth century. His system of parabolic reflectors focused oil-lit lamps and quadrupled their power (Harman 3).

Works Cited

Abrahamson, Robert-Louis. "Introduction." *Essays I: Virginibus Puerisque and Other Papers. The New Edinburgh Edition of the Works of Robert Louis Stevenson*, edited by Robert-Louis Abrahamson, Richard Dury, Lesley Graham, Alex Thomson. General editors, Penny Fielding, Richard Dury, Stephen D. Arata, and Anthony A. Mandal, Edinburgh UP, 2018, pp. lxix–cviii.

Abrahamson, Robert-Louis, Richard Dury, Lesley Graham, and Alex Thomson. "Stevenson as Essayist." *Essays I: Virginibus Puerisque and Other Papers. The New Edinburgh Edition of the Works of Robert Louis Stevenson*, edited by Robert-Louis Abrahamson, Richard Dury, Lesley Graham, Alex Thomson. General editors, Penny Fielding, Richard Dury, Stephen D. Arata, and Anthony A. Mandal, Edinburgh UP, 2018, pp. xxxiii–lxviii.

Barthes, Roland. "The Death of the Author." *Image, Music, Text*, translated by Stephen Heath, Hill and Wang, 1978, pp. 142–48.

Bennett, Laura. "The First Person Industrial Complex." *Slate*, 14 Sept. 2015, www.slate.com. Accessed 29 Oct. 2020.

Brown, Alice. *Robert Louis Stevenson: A Study*. Copeland and Day, 1895.

Daiches, David. *Robert Louis Stevenson: A Revaluation*. Maclellan, 1947.

"Death of Robert Louis Stevenson." *Public Opinion: A Comprehensive Summary of the Press Throughout the World on All Important Topics*, vol. LXVI, July–Dec. 1894, pp. 774–75.

Doyle, Brian. *A Book of Uncommon Prayer: 100 Celebrations of the Miracle & Muddle of the Ordinary*. Sorin Books, 2014.

Drew, Elizabeth. "The Lost Art of the Essay." *Saturday Review of Literature*, 16 Feb. 1935.

Dury, Richard. "Robert Louis Stevenson's Critical Reception." www.robert-louis-stevenson.org/richard-dury-archive. "The Richard Dury Archive." *RLS Website*. Accessed 29 Oct. 2020.

Eaton, W. P. "On Burying the Essay." *Virginia Quarterly Review*, vol. 24, 1948.

Fadiman, Clifton. "A Gentle Dirge for the Familiar Essay." *Party of One*. The World Publishing Co., 1955.

Forster, E. M. "Anonymity: An Inquiry." *Two Cheers for Democracy*. Edward Arnold, 1951.

Foster, Patricia, and Jeff Porter, editors. *Understanding the Essay*. Broadview Press, 2012.

Gigante, Denise, editor. *The Great Age of the English Essay: An Anthology*. Yale UP, 2008.

Gosse, Edmund. "Mr. Edmund Gosse in *The St. James's Gazette*." *Public Opinion*, 21 Dec. 1894.

Graham, Lesley. "The Reception of Stevenson's Essays." *Journal of Stevenson Studies*, vol. 9, 2012, pp. 313–42.

Harman, Claire. *Myself and the Other Fellow: A Life of Robert Louis Stevenson*. Harper Perennial, 2006.

Johnson, Samuel. *A Dictionary of the English Language*. W. Strahan, 1755.

Klaus, Carl H. "Toward a Collective Poetics of the Essay." *Essayists on the Essay: Montaigne to Our Time*, edited by Carl H. Klaus and Ned Stuckey-French, U of Iowa P, 2012, pp. xv–xxvii.

Lang, Andrew. "Mr. Andrew Lang in *The Daily News*, Dec. 18." *Public Opinion*, 21 Dec. 1894.

Le Gallienne, Richard. "Across the Plains." *The Academy*, vol. 41, no. 1045, 14 May 1892, p. 462.

Lopate, Phillip, editor. *The Art of the Personal Essay: An Anthology from the Classical Era to the Present*. Anchor Books, 1995.

Maixner, Paul, editor. *Robert Louis Stevenson: The Critical Heritage*. Routledge, 1981.

Muir, Edwin. "Robert Louis Stevenson." *The Bookman*, Sept. 1931, p. 55.

Ozick, Cynthia. "She: Portrait of the Essay as a Warm Body." *Essayists on the Essay*, edited by Patricia Foster and Jeff Porter, Broadview Press, 2012, pp. 162–69.

Sandison, Alan. *Robert Louis Stevenson and the Appearance of Modernism*. Palgrave, 1996.

Stevenson, Robert Louis. *A Child's Garden of Verses*. Longmans, 1885.

———. "Say Not of Me that Weakly I Declined." *Underwoods*. Chatto, 1887, p. 73.

———. *Strange Case of Dr. Jekyll and Mr. Hyde*, Longmans, 1886.

———. *The Letters of Robert Louis Stevenson*, edited by Bradford A Booth and Ernest Mehew, Yale UP, 1995, 8 vols.

———. *The Works of Robert Louis Stevenson. Edinburgh Edition*, edited by Sidney Colvin, Chatto & Windus, 1894–1898, 28 vols.

———. *Treasure Island*. Cassell, 1883.

Temple, Emily. "The Most Anthologized Essays of the Last 25 Years." *The Literary Hub*, 31 July 2017, lithub.com. Accessed 29 Oct. 2020.

"*Times*, Dec. 18." *Public Opinion*, 21 Dec. 1894, p. 774.

Tolentino, Jia. "The Personal Essay Boom is Over." *The New Yorker*, 18 May 2017.

Walker, Hugh. "Critical and Miscellaneous Prose." *The Cambridge History of English and American Literature*. Vol. 14: The Victorian Age, Part Two, Cambridge UP, 1907–21.

A NOTE ON THE TEXT AND ANNOTATIONS

This edition organizes Stevenson's personal essays in three main categories: essays that appeared in published collections in Stevenson's lifetime, uncollected pieces he published in periodicals, and his early work and other essays unpublished before his death. The first 38 essays are grouped as they were in collected volumes, with the omission of the critical essays and "Across the Plains," which is a separately published part of Stevenson's memoir *The Amateur Emigrant* (1895). I have used the first book editions of *Virginibus Puerisque* (1881) and *Memories and Portraits* (1887), which Stevenson actively prepared for publication by revising the earlier magazine versions. *Across the Plains with Other Memories and Essays* (1892) was more Sidney Colvin's publishing project than Stevenson's, but I have opted to keep the collection's grouping. While Colvin proposed the volume, Stevenson suggested most of its personal essays in an 1891 letter (7:154). What's more, he signed off on the selection and communicated to Colvin how pleased he was with the final product (7:309–10). While retaining the collection's organization, I have used the earlier periodical versions of the essays as copy texts since Stevenson was more heavily involved in their publication. I have chosen periodical publications as copy texts of the uncollected published essays and manuscripts for the unpublished ones, kindly supplied by the editors of *The New Edinburgh Edition of the Works of Robert Louis Stevenson*. Both the uncollected essays and early and unpublished essays are organized chronologically within the sections. With the exception of "The Old Scotch Gardener," which Stevenson revised for publication in *Memories and Portraits*, I have placed the essays which appeared in *Edinburgh University Magazine* under "Unpublished and Early Essays." Stevenson himself considered the essays self-published rather than published: "the main point of the concern. . . [was] to print our own works" (147). For all their considerable merits, he clearly considered them part of his juvenilia: the work of a "manuscript student" rather than a "printed author" (148).

Roughly half of this volume's essays have appeared in other recently edited collections. I am indebted to four collections in particular: Glenda Norquay's *R.L. Stevenson on Fiction: An Anthology of Literary and Critical Essays* (Edinburgh UP, 1999), Kenneth Gelder's *Robert Louis Stevenson: The Scottish Stories and Essays* (Edinburgh UP, 1989), Matthew Kaiser's *An Apology for Idlers and Other*

Essays (Cognella, 2018), and Robert-Louis Abrahamson's *Essays I: Virginibus Puerisque and Other Papers* (Edinburgh UP, 2018) from *The New Edinburgh Edition of the Works of Robert Louis Stevenson*. I have relied on these editors' excellent annotations.

All definitions, unless otherwise noted, are based on *The Oxford English Dictionary*. Notes do not distinguish between Stevenson's exact quotations, misquotations, and paraphrases of other sources. Stevenson's original notes are prefaced by "**RLS**" and a colon.

Cross references are indicated by note and page numbers. *Letters* refers to Bradford A. Booth and Ernest Mehew's *The Letters of Robert Louis Stevenson*, 8 vols (Yale UP, 1995).

Below are the publication and manuscript details of the texts used in this edition.

Virginibus Puerisque and Other Papers. London, Kegan Paul, 1881.

1) "Virginibus Puerisque" (1–26).
2) "Virginibus Puerisque II" (27–46).
3) "Virginibus Puerisque III. On Falling in Love" (47–67).
4) "Virginibus Puerisque IV. Truth of Intercourse" (68–86).
5) "Crabbed Age and Youth" (87–114).
6) "An Apology for Idlers" (115–16).
7) "Ordered South" (137–63).
8) "Æs Triplex" (164–83).
9) "El Dorado" (184–90).
10) "The English Admirals" (191–218).
11) "Child's Play" (237–60).
12) "Walking Tours" (261–78).
13) "Pan's Pipes" (279–87).
14) "A Plea for Gas Lamps" (288–96).

Memories and Portraits. New York, Charles Scribner's Sons, 1887.

15) "The Foreigner at Home" (1–23).
16) "Some College Memories" (24–37).
17) "Old Mortality" (38–56).
18) "A College Magazine" (57–76).
19) "An Old Scotch Gardener" (77–89).
20) "Pastoral" (90–105).
21) "The Manse" (106–19).
22) "Memoirs of an Islet" (120–31).
23) "Thomas Stevenson: Civil Engineer" (132–43).

24) "Talk and Talkers" (144–68).
25) "Talk and Talkers II" (169–90).
26) "The Character of Dogs" (191–212).
27) "A Penny Plain and Twopence Coloured" (213–27).

Across the Plains with other Memories and Essays (1892)
Periodical Versions

28) "The Old Pacific Capital." *Fraser's Magazine*, 131, Nov. 1880, pp. 647–57.
29) "Fontainebleau: Village Communities of Painters." *The Magazine of Art*, vol. 7, May–June 1884, pp. 253–72.
30) "Epilogue to *An Inland Voyage*." *Scribner's Magazine*, vol. 4, Aug. 1888, pp. 250–56.
31) "Contributions to the History of Fife." *Scribner's Magazine*, vol. 4, Oct. 1888, pp. 507–12.
32) "The Education of an Engineer." *Scribner's Magazine*, vol. 4, Nov. 1888, pp. 636–40.
33) "The Lantern-Bearers." *Scribner's Magazine*, vol. 3. Feb. 1888, pp. 251–56.
34) "A Chapter on Dreams." *Scribner's Magazine*, vol. 3, Jan. 1888, pp. 122–28.
35) "Beggars." *Scribner's Magazine*, vol. 3, Mar. 1888, pp. 380–84.
36) "A Letter to a Young Gentleman Who Proposes to Embrace the Career of Art." *Scribner's Magazine*, vol. 4, Sep. 1888, pp. 377–81.
37) "Pulvis et Umbra." *Scribner's Magazine*, vol. 3, Apr. 1888, pp. 509–12.
38) "A Christmas Sermon." *Scribner's Magazine*, vol. 4, Dec. 1888, pp. 764–68.

Published Periodical Essays

39) "Roads." *The Portfolio*, 4, Dec. 1873, pp. 185–88.
40) "Notes on the Movement of Young Children." *The Portfolio*, 5, Aug. 1874, pp. 115–17.
41) "On the Enjoyment of Unpleasant Places." *The Portfolio*, 5, Aug. 1874, pp. 173–76.
42) "An Autumn Effect." *The Portfolio*, 6, Apr. 1875, pp. 53–58, 70–75.
43) "Forest Notes." *Cornhill Magazine*, 33, May 1876, pp. 545–61.
44) "In the Latin Quarter I: A Ball at Mr. Elsinare's." *London: A Magazine of Art*, Feb. 17, 1877.
45) "In the Latin Quarter II: A Studio of Ladies." *London: A Magazine of Art*, Feb. 17, 1877.
46) "The Paris Bourse." *London: A Magazine of Art*, vol. 4, p. 88.
47) "Health and Mountains." *Pall Mall Gazette*, 17 Feb. 1881, pp. 10–11.
48) "Davos in Winter." *Pall Mall Gazette*, 21 Feb. 1881, pp. 689–90.
49) "Alpine Diversions." *Pall Mall Gazette*, 26 Feb. 1881.
50) "The Stimulation of the Alps." *Pall Mall Gazette*, 5 Mar. 1881, p. 10.

51) "The Misgivings of Convalescence." *Pall Mall Gazette*, 17 Mar. 1881, p. 10.

52) "The Morality of the Profession of Letters." *Fortnightly Review*, Apr. 1881, pp. 513–20.

53) "A Modern Cosmopolis." *The Magazine of Art*, vol. 6, May 1883, pp. 272–76.

54) "Books which Have Influenced Me." *British Weekly Extras. No. 1. Books Which Have Influenced Me*. London, British Weekly, 1887, pp. 3–16.

55) "Gentlemen." *Scribner's Magazine*, vol. 3, May 1888, pp. 635–40.

56) "My First Book: *Treasure Island*." *The Idler Magazine*, vol. 6, Aug. 1894, pp. 3–11.

Unpublished and Early Essays

57) "Night Outside the Wick Mail"

Reprinted in "To Bob Stevenson, 17 November 1868." *The Letters of Robert Louis Stevenson*. Edited by Bradford A. Booth and Ernest Mehew. Yale UP, 1994. Vol. 1, pp. 169–72.

58) "Reminiscences of Colinton Manse"

"Reminiscences of Colinton Manse." Beinecke Rare Book and Manuscript Library, Yale U, GEN MSS 664, box 74, folder 1812.

59) "Sketches" ("The Satirist," "Nuits Blanches," "The Wreath of Immortelles," "Nurses").

The Beinecke Rare Book and Manuscript Library, Yale U, GEN MSS 664, box 42, folder 936.

60) "A Retrospect"

"Dunoon. Visit in 1870 at a house where R.L.S. had spent a week in childhood." Beinecke Rare Book and Manuscript Library, Yale U, GEN MSS 664, box 29, folder 669.

61) "The Philosophy of Umbrellas"

Edinburgh University Magazine, no. 2, Feb. 1871, pp. 46–48.
"College Papers-No. 1 & 2." Centre for Research Collections, Edinburgh University Library, JA 2411.

62) "The Modern Student Considered Generally"

Edinburgh University Magazine, no. 2, Feb. 1871, pp. 25–29.
"College Papers-No. 1 & 2." Centre for Research Collections, Edinburgh University Library, JA 2411.

63) "Debating Societies"

Edinburgh University Magazine, no. 3, Mar. 1871, pp. 59–62.

"College Papers-No. 1 & 2." Centre for Research Collections, Edinburgh University Library, JA 2411.

64) "The Philosophy of Nomenclature"

Edinburgh University Magazine, 1871, pp. 106–8.
Beinecke Rare Book and Manuscript Library, Yale U, call no. Ip St48 871E.

65) "Cockermouth and Keswick"

"Cockermouth and Keswick (A fragment: 1871)." Beinecke Rare Book and Manuscript Library, Yale U, GEN MSS 664, box 27, folder 641.

66) "A Winter's Walk in Carrick and Galloway"

Beinecke Rare Book and Manuscript Library, Yale U, GEN MSS 664, box 39, folder 859.

67) "On the Choice of a Profession, in a Letter to a Young Gentleman"

MS, Huntington Library, HM 401, f. 1, 6 p.

68) "Lay Morals"

"Lay Morals." Beinecke Rare Book and Manuscript Library, Yale U, GEN MSS 664, box 32, folder, 766.

69) "The Ideal House"

"The ideal house, handwritten manuscript." The Harry Ransom Center, U of Texas, MS 4035, Container 1.4.

70) "Rosa Quo Locorum"

"Random Memories: Rosa Quo Locorum" 1894. Princeton University Library, Morris L. Parrish Collection of Victorian Novelists, MS. CO171, No. 125, AM 15045.

VIRGINIBUS PUERISQUE AND OTHER PAPERS

1

VIRGINIBUS PUERISQUE[1]

With the single exception of Falstaff, all Shakespeare's characters are what we call marrying men. Mercutio, as he was own cousin to Benedick and Biron, would have come to the same end in the long run. Even Iago had a wife, and, what is far stranger, he was jealous. People like Jacques and the Fool in *Lear*, although we can hardly imagine they would ever marry, kept single out of a cynical humour or for a broken heart, and not, as we do nowadays, from a spirit of incredulity and preference for the single state. For that matter, if you turn to George Sand's French version of *As You Like It* (and I think I can promise you will like it but little), you will find Jacques marries Celia just as Orlando marries Rosalind.[2]

At least there seems to have been much less hesitation over marriage in Shakespeare's days; and what hesitation there was was of a laughing sort, and not much more serious, one way or the other, than that of Panurge.[3] In modern comedies the heroes are mostly of Benedick's way of thinking, but twice as much in earnest, and not one quarter so confident. And I take this diffidence as a proof of how sincere their terror is. They know they are only human after all; they know what gins and pitfalls lie about their feet; and how the shadow of matrimony waits, resolute and awful, at the cross-roads. They would wish to keep their liberty; but if that may not be, why, God's will be done! "What, are you afraid of marriage?" asks Cécile, in *Maître Guérin*.[4] "Oh, mon Dieu, non!"[5] replies Arthur; "I should take chloroform." They look forward to marriage much in the same way as they prepare themselves for death: each seems inevitable; each is a great Perhaps, and a leap into the dark, for which, when a man is in the blue devils, he has specially to harden his heart. That splendid scoundrel, Maxime de Trailles, took the news of marriages much as an old man hears the deaths of his contemporaries. "C'est désespérant," he cried, throwing himself down in the armchair at Madame Schontz's; "c'est désespérant, nous nous marions tous!"[6] Every marriage was like another grey hair on his head; and the jolly church bells seemed to taunt him with his fifty years and fair round belly.[7]

The fact is, we are much more afraid of life than our ancestors, and cannot find it in our hearts either to marry or not to marry. Marriage is terrifying, but so is a cold and forlorn old age. The friendships of men are vastly agreeable, but they are insecure. You know all the time that one friend will marry and put you to the door; a second accept a situation in China, and become no more to you than a name, a reminiscence, and an occasional crossed letter,[8] very laborious to read; a third will take up with some religious crotchet and treat you to sour looks thenceforward. So, in one way or another, life forces men apart and breaks up the goodly fellowships for ever. The very flexibility and ease which make men's friendships so agreeable while they endure, make them the easier to destroy and forget. And a man who has a few friends, or one who has a dozen (if there be any one so wealthy on this earth), cannot forget on how precarious a base his happiness reposes; and how by a stroke or two of fate—a death, a few light words, a piece of stamped paper, a woman's bright eyes—he may be left, in a month, destitute of all. Marriage is certainly a perilous remedy. Instead of on two or three, you stake your happiness on one life only. But still, as the bargain is more explicit and complete on your part, it is more so on the other; and you have not to fear so many contingencies; it is not every wind that can blow you from your anchorage; and, so long as Death withholds his sickle, you will always have a friend at home. People who share a cell in the Bastille, or are thrown together on an uninhabited isle, if they do not immediately fall to fisticuffs, will find some possible ground of compromise. They will learn each other's ways and humours, so as to know where they must go warily, and where they may lean their whole weight. The discretion of the first years becomes the settled habit of the last; and so, with wisdom and patience, two lives may grow indissolubly into one.

But marriage, if comfortable, is not at all heroic. It certainly narrows and damps the spirits of generous men. In marriage, a man becomes slack and selfish, and undergoes a fatty degeneration of his moral being. It is not only when Lydgate misallies himself with Rosamond Vincy, but when Ladislaw marries above him with Dorothea, that this may be exemplified.[9] The air of the fireside withers out all the fine wildings of the husband's heart. He is so comfortable and happy that he begins to prefer comfort and happiness to everything else on earth, his wife included. Yesterday he would have shared his last shilling; to-day "his first duty is to his family," and is fulfilled in large measure by laying down vintages and husbanding the health of an invaluable parent. Twenty years ago this man was equally capable of crime or heroism; now he is fit for neither. His soul is asleep, and you may speak without constraint; you will not wake him. It is not for nothing that Don Quixote was a bachelor and Marcus Aurelius married ill.[10] For women, there is less of this danger. Marriage is of so much use to a woman, opens out to her so much more of life, and puts her in the way of so much more freedom and usefulness, that, whether she marry ill or well, she can hardly miss some benefit. It is true, however, that some of the merriest and most genuine of women are old maids; and that those old maids, and wives who are unhappily married, have often most of the true motherly touch. And this would seem to show, even for women, some narrowing influence in comfortable married life. But the rule is none the less certain: if you wish the pick of men and women, take a good bachelor and a good wife.

I am often filled with wonder that so many marriages are passably successful, and so few come to open failure, the more so as I fail to understand the principle on which people regulate their choice. I see women marrying indiscriminately with staring burgesses and ferret-faced, white-eyed boys, and men dwell in contentment with noisy scullions, or taking into their lives acidulous vestals.[11] It is a common answer to say the good people marry because they fall in love; and of course you may use and misuse a word as much as you please, if you have the world along with you. But love is at least a somewhat hyperbolical expression for such lukewarm preference. It is not here, anyway, that Love employs his golden shafts; he cannot be said, with any fitness of language, to reign here and revel. Indeed, if this be love at all, it is plain the poets have been fooling with mankind since the foundation of the world. And you have only to look these happy couples in the face, to see they have never been in love, or in hate, or in any other high passion, all their days. When you see a dish of fruit at dessert, you sometimes set your affections upon one particular peach or nectarine, watch it with some anxiety as it comes round the table, and feel quite a sensible disappointment when it is taken by some one else. I have used the phrase "high passion." Well, I should say this was about as high a passion as generally leads to marriage. One husband hears after marriage that some poor fellow is dying of his wife's love. "What a pity!" he exclaims; "you know I could so easily have got another!" And yet that is a very happy union. Or again: A young man was telling me the sweet story of his loves. "I like it well enough as long as her sisters are there," said this amorous swain; "but I don't know what to do when we're alone." Once more: A married lady was debating the subject with another lady. "You know, dear," said the first, "after ten years of marriage, if he is nothing else, your husband is always an old friend." "I have many old friends," returned the other, "but I prefer them to be nothing more." "Oh, perhaps I might *prefer* that also!" There is a common note in these three illustrations of the modern idyll; and it must be owned the god goes among us with a limping gait and blear eyes. You wonder whether it was so always; whether desire was always equally dull and spiritless, and possession equally cold. I cannot help fancying most people make, ere they marry, some such table of recommendations as Hannah Godwin wrote to her brother William anent her friend, Miss Gay.[12] It is so charmingly comical, and so pat to the occasion, that I must quote a few phrases. "The young lady is in every sense formed to make one of your disposition really happy. She has a pleasing voice, with which she accompanies her musical instrument with judgment. She has an easy politeness in her manners, neither free nor reserved. She is a good housekeeper and a good economist, and yet of a generous disposition. As to her internal accomplishments, I have reason to speak still more highly of them: good sense without vanity, a penetrating judgment without a disposition to satire, with about as much religion as my William likes, struck me with a wish that she was my William's wife." That is about the tune: pleasing voice, moderate good looks, unimpeachable internal accomplishments after the style of the copy-book, with about as much religion as my William likes; and then, with all speed, to church.

To deal plainly, if they only married when they fell in love, most people would die unwed; and, among the others, there would be not a few tumultuous households. The Lion is the King of Beasts, but he is scarcely suitable for a domestic pet. In the same way, I suspect love is rather too violent a passion to make, in all cases, a good domestic sentiment. Like other violent excitements, it throws up not only what is best, but what is worst and smallest, in men's characters. Just as some people are malicious in drink, or brawling and virulent under the influence of religious feeling, some are moody, jealous, and exacting when they are in love, who are honest, downright, good-hearted fellows enough in the everyday affairs and humours of the world.

How then, seeing we are driven to the hypothesis that people choose in comparatively cold blood, how is it they choose so well? One is almost tempted to hint that it does not much matter whom you marry; that, in fact, marriage is a subjective affection, and if you have made up your mind to it, and once talked yourself fairly over, you could "pull it through" with anybody. But even if we take matrimony at its lowest, even if we regard it as no more than a sort of friendship recognized by the police, there must be degrees in the freedom and sympathy realized, and some principle to guide simple folk in their selection. Now what should this principle be? Are there no more definite rules than are to be found in the Prayer-book?[13] Law and religion forbid the bans on the ground of propinquity or consanguinity; society steps in to separate classes; and in all this most critical matter, has common sense, has wisdom, never a word to say? In the absence of more magisterial teaching, let us talk it over between friends: even a few guesses may be of interest to youths and maidens.

In all that concerns eating and drinking, company, climate, and ways of life, community of taste[14] is to be sought for. It would be trying, for instance, to keep bed and board with an early riser or a vegetarian. In matters of art and intellect, I believe it is of no consequence. Certainly it is of none in the companionships of men, who will dine more readily with one who has a good heart, a good cellar, and a humorous tongue, than with another who shares all their favourite hobbies and is melancholy withal. If your wife likes Tupper,[15] that is no reason why you should hang your head. She thinks with the majority, and has the courage of her opinions. I have always suspected public taste to be a mongrel product, out of affectation by dogmatism; and felt sure, if you could only find an honest man of no special literary bent, he would tell you he thought much of Shakespeare bombastic and most absurd, and all of him written in very obscure English and wearisome to read. And not long ago I was able to lay by my lantern in content, for I found the honest man. He was a fellow of parts,[16] quick, humorous, a clever painter, and with an eye for certain poetical effects of sea and ships. I am not much of a judge of that kind of thing, but a sketch of his comes before me sometimes at night. How strong, supple, and living the ship seems upon the billows! With what a dip and rake she shears the flying sea! I cannot fancy the man who saw this effect, and took it on the wing with so much force and spirit, was what you call commonplace in the last recesses of the heart. And yet he thought, and was not ashamed to have it known of him, that Ouida[17] was better in every way than William Shakespeare. If there were more people of his honesty, this would be about the staple of lay criticism. It is not taste that is plentiful, but courage that is rare. And what have we in place? How many, who think no otherwise than the young painter, have we not heard disbursing second-hand hyperboles? Have you never turned sick at heart, O best of critics! when some of your own sweet adjectives were returned on you before a gaping audience? Enthusiasm about art is become a function of the average female being, which she performs with precision and a sort of haunting sprightliness, like an ingenious and well-regulated machine. Sometimes, alas! the calmest man is carried away in the torrent, bandies adjectives with the best, and out-Herods Herod[18] for some shameful moments. When you remember that, you will be tempted to put things strongly, and say you will marry no one who is not like George the Second,[19] and cannot state openly a distaste for poetry and painting.

The word "facts" is, in some ways, crucial. I have spoken with Jesuits and Plymouth Brethren,[20] mathematicians and poets, dogmatic republicans and dear old gentlemen in bird's-eye neckcloths; and each understood the word "facts" in an occult sense of his own. Try as I might, I could get no nearer the principle of their division. What was essential to them, seemed to me trivial or untrue. We could come to no compromise as to what was, or what was not, important in the life of man. Turn as we pleased, we all stood back to back in a big ring, and saw another quarter of the heavens, with different mountain-tops along the sky-line, and different constellations overhead. We had each of us some whimsy in the brain, which we believed more than anything else, and which discoloured all experience to its own shade. How would you have people agree, when one is deaf and the other blind? Now this is where there should be community between man and wife. They should be agreed on their catchword in *"facts of religion,"* or *"facts of science,"* or *"society, my dear;"* for without such an agreement all intercourse is a painful strain upon the mind. "About as much religion as my William likes," in short, that is what is necessary to make a happy couple of any William and his spouse. For there are differences which no habit nor affection can reconcile, and the Bohemian must not intermarry with the Pharisee. Imagine Consuelo as Mrs. Samuel Budgett,[21] the wife of the successful merchant! The best of men and the best of women may sometimes live together all their lives, and, for want of some consent on fundamental questions, hold each other lost spirits to the end.

A certain sort of talent is almost indispensable for people who would spend years together and not bore themselves to death. But the talent, like the agreement, must be for and about life. To dwell happily together, they should be versed in the niceties of the heart, and born with a faculty for willing compromise. The woman must be talented as a woman, and it will not much matter although she is talented in nothing else. She must know her *métier de femme,*[22] and have a fine touch for the affections. And it is more important that a person should be a good gossip, and talk pleasantly and smartly of common friends and the thousand and one nothings of the day and hour, than that she should speak with the tongues of men and angels;[23] for a while together by the fire, happens more frequently in marriage than the presence of a distinguished foreigner to dinner. That people should laugh over the same sort of jests, and have many a story of "grouse in the gun-room,"[24] many an old joke between them which time cannot wither nor custom stale,[25] is a better preparation for life, by your leave, than many other things higher and better sounding in the world's ears. You could read Kant by yourself, if you wanted; but you must share a joke with some one else. You can forgive people who do not follow you through a philosophical disquisition; but to find your wife laughing when you had tears in your eyes, or staring when you were in a fit of laughter, would go some way towards a dissolution of the marriage.

I know a woman who, from some distaste or disability, could never so much as understand the meaning of the word *politics*, and has given up trying to distinguish Whigs from Tories; but take her on her own politics, ask her about other men or women and the chicanery of everyday existence—the rubs, the tricks, the vanities on which life turns—and you will not find many more shrewd, trenchant, and humorous. Nay, to make plainer what I have in mind, this same woman has a share of the higher and more poetical understanding, frank interest in things for their own sake, and enduring astonishment at the most common. She is not to be deceived by custom, or made to think a mystery solved when it is repeated. I have heard her say she could wonder herself crazy over the human eyebrow. Now in a world where most of us walk very contentedly in the little lit circle of their own reason, and have to be reminded of what lies without by specious and clamant exceptions—earthquakes, eruptions of Vesuvius, banjos floating in mid-air at a *séance*, and the like—a mind so fresh and unsophisticated is no despicable gift. I will own I think it a better sort of mind than goes necessarily with the clearest views on public business. It will wash. It will find something to say at an odd moment. It has in it the spring of pleasant and quaint fancies. Whereas I can imagine myself yawning all night long until my jaws ached and the tears came into my eyes, although my companion on the other side of the hearth held the most enlightened opinions on the franchise or the ballot.

The question of professions, in as far as they regard marriage, was only interesting to women until of late days, but it touches all of us now. Certainly, if I could help it, I would never marry a wife who wrote. The practice of letters is miserably harassing to the mind; and after an hour or two's work, all the more human portion of the author is extinct; he will bully, backbite, and speak daggers. Music, I hear, is not much better. But painting, on the contrary, is often highly sedative; because so much of the labour, after your picture is once begun, is almost entirely manual, and of that skilled sort of manual labour which offers a continual series of successes, and so tickles a man, through his vanity, into good humour. Alas! in letters there is nothing of this sort. You may write as beautiful a hand as you will, you have always something else to think of, and cannot pause to notice your loops and flourishes; they are beside the mark, and the first law stationer could put you to the blush. Rousseau, indeed, made some account of penmanship, even made it a source of livelihood, when he copied out the *Héloïse* for *dilettante* ladies;[26] and therein showed that strange eccentric prudence which guided him among so many thousand follies and insanities. It would be well for all of the *genus irritabile*[27] thus to add something of skilled labour to intangible brainwork. To find the right word is so doubtful a success and lies so near to failure, that there is no satisfaction in a year of it; but we all know when we have formed a letter perfectly; and a stupid artist, right or wrong, is almost equally certain he has found a right tone or a right colour, or made a dexterous stroke with his brush. And, again, painters may work out of doors; and the fresh air, the deliberate seasons, and the "tranquillizing influence" of the green earth, counterbalance the fever of thought, and keep them cool, placable, and prosaic.

A ship captain is a good man to marry if it is a marriage of love, for absences are a good influence in love and keep it bright and delicate; but he is just the worst man if the feeling is more pedestrian, as habit is too frequently torn open and the solder has never time to set. Men who fish, botanize, work with the turning-lathe, or gather sea-weeds will make admirable husbands; and a little amateur painting in water-colour shows the innocent and quiet mind. Those who have a few intimates are to be avoided; while those who swim loose, who have their hat in their hand all along the street, who can number an infinity of acquaintances and are not chargeable with any one friend, promise an easy disposition and no rival to the wife's influence. I will not say they are the best of men, but they are the stuff out of which adroit and capable women manufacture the best of husbands. It is to be noticed that those who have loved once or twice already are so much the better educated to a woman's hand; the bright boy of fiction is an odd and most uncomfortable mixture of shyness and coarseness, and needs a deal of civilizing. Lastly (and this is, perhaps, the golden rule), no woman should marry a teetotaller, or a man who does not smoke. It is not for nothing that this "ignoble tabagie," as Michelet calls it, spreads over all the world.[28] Michelet rails against it because it renders you happy apart from thought or work; to provident women this will seem no evil influence in married life. Whatever keeps a man in the front garden, whatever checks wandering fancy and all inordinate ambition, whatever makes for lounging and contentment, makes just so surely for domestic happiness.

These notes, if they amuse the reader at all, will probably amuse him more when he differs than when he agrees with them; at least they will do no harm, for nobody will follow my advice. But the last word is of more concern. Marriage is a step so grave and decisive that it attracts light-headed, variable men by its very awfulness. They have been so tried among the inconstant squalls and currents, so often sailed for islands in the air or lain becalmed with burning heart, that they will risk all for solid ground below their feet. Desperate pilots, they run their seasick, weary bark upon the dashing rocks.[29] It seems as if marriage were the royal road through life, and realized, on the instant, what we have all dreamed on summer Sundays when the bells ring, or at night when we cannot sleep for the desire of living. They think it will sober and change them. Like those who join a brotherhood, they fancy it needs but an act to be out of the coil and clamour for ever. But this is a wile of the devil's. To the end, spring winds will sow disquietude, passing faces leave a regret behind them, and the whole world keep calling and calling in their ears. For marriage is like life in this—that it is a field of battle, and not a bed of roses.

Notes

1 "Virginibus puerisque canto" (Latin): I sing to maids and boys (Horace, *Odes*, 3.1).
2 Characters in Shakespeare: Falstaff (*1 and 2 Henry IV* and *The Merry Wives of Windsor*), Mercutio (*Romeo and Juliet*), Benedick (*Much Ado about Nothing*), Iago (*Othello*), Jacques (*As You Like It*, adapted into French by George Sand in 1856), and the Fool (*King Lear*).
3 Panurge—character in François Rabelais's fictional series *Gargantua and Pantagruel* (1532–1564), who never decides whether or not he should marry.
4 Comedy by Émile Augier (1864).
5 Oh, my God, no!
6 Maxime de Trailles—Character in several of Honoré de Balzac's *Comédie humaine* novels. The French quotation ("It's depressing; every one of us is getting married!") is from *Le Député d'Arcis* (1854).
7 Shakespeare, *As You Like It*, 2.7.152–3.
8 A letter written horizontally and vertically to save on postage.
9 Characters in George Eliot's *Middlemarch* (1872).
10 Protagonist of Miguel de Cervantes's novel *Don Quixote* (1605–1616). The Roman philosopher and emperor Marcus Aurelius (121–180 AD) was not close with his wife.
11 The Vestal Virgins: six maidens barred from marriage who tended the sacred fire in the Roman Forum.
12 29 June 1784 letter in Charles Kegan Paul's *William Godwin: His Friends and Contemporaries* (1876).
13 *The Book of Common Prayer* forbids relatives to marry each other.
14 A translation of the Enlightenment aesthetic term *sensus communis* or "common sense" from Immanuel Kant's *Gemeinsinn*.
15 Martin Tupper (1810–1889), a moralizing poet known for his popular *Proverbial Philosophies*.
16 Talents.
17 Penname of the popular novelist Maria Louise Ramé (1839–1908).
18 "It offends me to the soul to hear a robustious periwig-pated fellow tear a passion to tatters . . . It out-Herods Herod" (Shakespeare, *Hamlet*, 3.2. 7–12). Herod was traditionally characterized by exaggerated raving in medieval miracle plays.
19 The British King George II (1683–1760) reportedly disdained literature and the arts.
20 Jesuits—A Catholic religious order founded by Ignatius of Loyola in 1540. The Plymouth Brethren—a strict sect of evangelical Protestants.
21 The romantic heroine of George Sand's *Consuelo* (1842) and Samuel Budgett (1794–1851), considered the model of a respectable Christian businessman and the subject of William Arthur's popular book *The Successful Merchant: Sketches of the Life of Mr. Samuel Budgett* (1852).
22 Womanly duties (French).
23 1 Corinthians 13:1.
24 In Oliver Goldsmith's *She Stoops to Conquer* (1773), the servant Diggory cannot help laughing when his master tells guests the oft-repeated story of the grouse in the gun-room (3.1).
25 Shakespeare, *Antony and Cleopatra*, 2.2.240–1.

26 Jean-Jacques Rousseau made a fair copy of the first two parts of *Julie; or, The New Heloise* (1761) on gilt-paper for his mistress Thérèse Levasseur and copied an extract for his admirer Madame de Luxembourg (*Confessions* 9–10).
27 The irritable species of poets (Latin). Horace, *Epistles*, II.2.
28 Base habit of smoking (French).—Jules Michelet, *Histoire de France* (1871–1874), XII. 9.
29 Shakespeare, *Romeo and Juliet*, 5.3.117–118.

2

VIRGINIBUS PUERISQUE[1] II

Hope, they say, deserts us at no period of our existence. From first to last, and in the face of smarting disillusions, we continue to expect good fortune, better health, and better conduct; and that so confidently, that we judge it needless to deserve them. I think it improbable that I shall ever write like Shakespeare, conduct an army like Hannibal,[2] or distinguish myself like Marcus Aurelius in the paths of virtue; and yet I have my by-days, hope prompting, when I am very ready to believe that I shall combine all these various excellences in my own person, and go marching down to posterity with divine honours. There is nothing so monstrous but we can believe it of ourselves. About ourselves, about our aspirations and delinquencies, we have dwelt by choice in a delicious vagueness from our boyhood up. No one will have forgotten Tom Sawyer's aspiration: "Ah, if he could only die *temporarily*!" Or, perhaps, better still, the inward resolution of the two pirates, that "so long as they remained in that business, their piracies should not again be sullied with the crime of stealing."[3] Here we recognize the thoughts of our boyhood; and our boyhood ceased—well, when?—not, I think, at twenty; nor, perhaps, altogether at twenty-five; nor yet at thirty; and possibly, to be quite frank, we are still in the thick of that arcadian[4] period. For as the race of man, after centuries of civilization, still keeps some traits of their barbarian fathers, so man the individual is not altogether quit of youth, when he is already old and honoured, and Lord Chancellor of England. We advance in years somewhat in the manner of an invading army in a barren land; the age that we have reached, as the phrase goes, we but hold with an outpost, and still keep open our communications with the extreme rear and first beginnings of the march. There is our true base—that is not only the beginning, but the perennial spring of our faculties; and grandfather William[5] can retire upon occasion into the green, enchanted forest of his boyhood.

The unfading boyishness of hope and its vigorous irrationality are nowhere better displayed than in questions of conduct. There is a character in the *Pilgrim's Progress*, one Mr. *Linger-after-Lust*[6] with whom I fancy we are all on speaking terms; one famous among the famous for ingenuity of hope up to and beyond the moment of defeat; one who, after eighty years of contrary experience, will believe it possible to continue in the business of piracy and yet avoid the guilt of theft. Every sin is our last; every 1st of January a remarkable turning-point in our career. Any overt act, above all, is felt to be alchemic in its power to change. A drunkard takes the pledge;[7] it will be strange if that does not help him. For how many years did Mr. Pepys continue to make and break his little vows?[8] And yet I have not heard that he was discouraged in the end. By such steps we think to fix a momentary resolution; as a timid fellow hies him to the dentist's while the tooth is stinging.

But, alas, by planting a stake at the top of flood, you can neither prevent nor delay the inevitable ebb. There is no hocus-pocus in morality; and even the "sanctimonious ceremony"[9] of marriage leaves the man unchanged. This is a hard saying, and has an air of paradox. For there is something in marriage so natural and inviting, that the step has an air of great simplicity and ease; it offers to bury for ever many aching preoccupations; it is to afford us unfailing and familiar company through life; it opens up a smiling prospect of the blest and passive kind of love, rather than the blessing and active; it is approached not only through the delights of courtship, but by a public performance and repeated legal signatures. A man naturally thinks it will go hard with him if he cannot be good and fortunate and happy within such august circumvallations.

And yet there is probably no other act in a man's life so hot-headed and foolhardy as this one of marriage. For years, let us suppose, you have been making the most indifferent business of your career. Your experience has not, we may dare to say, been more encouraging than Paul's or Horace's; like them, you have seen and desired the good that you were not able to accomplish; like them, you have done the evil that you loathed.[10] You have waked at night in a hot or a cold sweat, according to your habit of body, remembering, with dismal surprise, your own unpardonable acts and sayings. You have been sometimes tempted to withdraw entirely from this game of life; as a man who makes nothing but misses withdraws from that less dangerous one of billiards. You have fallen back upon the thought that you yourself most sharply smarted for your misdemeanours, or, in the old, plaintive phrase, that you were nobody's enemy but your own. And then you have been made aware of what was beautiful and amiable, wise and kind, in the other part of your behaviour; and it seemed as if nothing could reconcile the contradiction, as indeed nothing can. If you are a man, you have shut your mouth hard and said nothing; and if you are only a man in the making, you have recognised that yours was quite a special case, and you yourself not guilty of your own pestiferous career.

Granted, and with all my heart. Let us accept these apologies; let us agree that you are nobody's enemy but your own; let us agree that you are a sort of moral cripple, impotent for good; and let us regard you with the unmingled pity due to such a fate. But there is one thing to which, on these terms, we can never agree;— we can never agree to have you marry. What! you have had one life to manage, and have failed so strangely, and now can see nothing wiser than to conjoin with it the management of some one else's? Because you have been unfaithful in a very little, you propose yourself to be a ruler over ten cities.[11] You strip yourself by such a step of all remaining consolations and excuses. You are no longer content to be your own enemy; you must be your wife's also. You have been hitherto in a mere subaltern attitude; dealing cruel blows about you in life, yet only half responsible, since you came there by no choice or movement of your own. Now, it appears, you must take things on your own authority: God made you, but you marry yourself; and for all that your wife suffers no one is responsible but you. A man must be very certain of his knowledge ere he undertakes to guide a ticket-of-leave man[12] through a dangerous pass; you have eternally missed your way in life, with consequences that you still deplore, and yet you masterfully seize your wife's hand, and, blindfold, drag her after you to ruin. It is your wife, you observe, whom you select. She, whose happiness you most desire, you choose to be your victim. You would earnestly warn her from a tottering bridge or bad investment. If she were to marry some one else, how you would tremble for her fate! If she were only your sister, and you thought half as much of her, how doubtfully would you entrust her future to a man no better than yourself!

Times are changed with him who marries; there are no more by-path meadows,[13] where you may innocently linger, but the road lies long and straight and dusty to the grave. Idleness, which is often becoming and even wise in the bachelor, begins to wear a different aspect when you have a wife to support. Suppose, after you are married, one of those little slips were to befall you. What happened last November might surely happen February next. They may have annoyed you at the time, because they were not what you had meant; but how will they annoy you in the future, and how will they shake the fabric of your wife's confidence and peace! A thousand things unpleasing went on in the *chiaroscuro*[14] of a life that you shrank from too particularly realizing; you did not care, in these days, to make a fetish of your conscience; you would recognize your failures with a nod, and so, good day. But the time for these reserves is over. You have wilfully introduced a witness into your life, the scene of these defeats, and can no longer close the mind's eye upon uncomely passages, but must stand up straight and put a name upon your actions. And your witness is not only the judge, but the victim of your sins; not only can she condemn you to the sharpest penalties, but she must herself share feelingly in their endurance. And observe, once more, with what temerity you have chosen precisely *her* to be your spy, whose esteem you value highest, and whom you have already taught to think you better than you are. You may think you had a conscience, and believed in God; but what is a conscience to a wife? Wise men of yore erected statues of their deities, and consciously performed their part in life before those marble eyes. A god watched them at the board, and stood by their bedside in the morning when they woke; and all about their ancient cities, where they bought and sold, or where they piped and wrestled, there would stand some symbol of the things that are outside of man. These were lessons, delivered in the quiet dialect of art, which told their story faithfully, but gently. It is the same lesson, if you will—but how harrowingly taught!—when the woman you respect shall weep from your unkindness or blush with shame at your misconduct. Poor girls in Italy turn their painted Madonnas to the wall: you cannot set aside your wife.[15] To marry is to domesticate the

Recording Angel.[16] Once you are married, there is nothing left for you, not even suicide, but to be good.

And goodness in marriage is a more intricate problem than mere single virtue; for in marriage there are two ideals to be realized. A girl, it is true, has always lived in a glass house among reproving relatives, whose word was law; she has been bred up to sacrifice her judgments and take the key submissively from dear papa; and it is wonderful how swiftly she can change her tune into the husband's. Her morality has been, too often, an affair of precept and conformity. But in the case of a bachelor who has enjoyed some measure both of privacy and freedom, his moral judgments have been passed in some accordance with his nature. His sins were always sins in his own sight; he could then only sin when he did some act against his clear conviction; the light that he walked by was obscure, but it was single.[17] Now, when two people of any grit and spirit put their fortunes into one, there succeeds to this comparative certainty, a huge welter of competing jurisdictions. It no longer matters so much how life appears to one; one must consult another: one, who may be strong, must not offend the other, who is weak.[18] The only weak brother I am willing to consider is (to make a bull for once)[19] my wife. For her, and for her only, I must waive my righteous judgments, and go crookedly about my life. How, then, in such an atmosphere of compromise, to keep honour bright and abstain from base capitulations? How are you to put aside love's pleadings? How are you, the apostle of laxity, to turn suddenly about into the rabbi of precision; and, after these years of ragged practice, pose for a hero to the lackey who has found you out? In this temptation to mutual indulgence lies the particular peril to morality in married life. Daily they drop a little lower from the first ideal, and for a while continue to accept these changelings with a gross complacency. At last Love wakes and looks about him; finds his hero sunk into a stout old brute, intent on brandy pawnee; finds his heroine divested of her angel brightness; and in the flash of that first disenchantment, flees for ever.

Again, the husband, in these unions, is usually a man, and the wife commonly enough a woman; and when this is the case, although it makes the firmer marriage, a thick additional veil of misconception hangs above the doubtful business. Women, I believe, are somewhat rarer than men; but then, if I were a woman myself, I daresay I should hold the reverse; and at least we all enter more or less wholly into one or other of these camps. A man who delights women by his feminine perceptions, will often scatter his admirers by a chance explosion of the under side of man; and the most masculine and direct of women will some day, to your dire surprise, draw out like a telescope into successive lengths of personation. Alas! for the man, knowing her to be at heart more candid than himself, who shall flounder, panting, through these mazes in the quest for truth. The proper qualities of each sex are, indeed, eternally surprising to the other. Between the Latin and the Teuton races there are similar divergences, not to be bridged by the most liberal sympathy. And in the good, plain, cut-and-dry explanations of this life, which pass current among us as the wisdom of the elders, this difficulty has been turned with the aid of pious lies.[20] Thus, when a young lady has angelic

features, eats nothing to speak of, plays all day long on the piano, and sings rav-
ishingly in church, it requires a rough infidelity, falsely called cynicism, to believe
that she may be a little devil after all. Yet so it is: she may be a tale-bearer, a
liar, and a thief; she may have a taste for brandy, and no heart. My compliments
to George Eliot for her Rosamond Vincy; the ugly work of satire she has transmuted to the ends of art, by the companion figure of Lydgate;[21] and the satire was
much wanted for the education of young men. That doctrine of the excellence of
women, however chivalrous, is cowardly as well as false. It is better to face the
fact, and know, when you marry, that you take into your life a creature of equal, if
of unlike, frailties; whose weak human heart beats no more tunefully than yours.

But it is the object of a liberal education, not only to obscure the knowledge of
one sex by another, but to magnify the natural differences between the two. Man
is a creature who lives not upon bread alone,[22] but principally by catchwords; and
the little rift between the sexes is astonishingly widened by simply teaching one
set of catchwords to the girls and another to the boys. To the first, there is shown
but a very small field of experience, and taught a very trenchant principle for
judgment and action; to the other, the world of life is more largely displayed, and
their rule of conduct is proportionally widened. They are taught to follow different
virtues, to hate different vices, to place their ideal, even for each other, in different
achievements. What should be the result of such a course? When a horse has run
away, and the two flustered people in the gig have each possessed themselves of
a rein, we know the end of that conveyance will be in the ditch. So, when I see a
raw youth and a green girl, fluted and fiddled in a dancing measure into that most
serious contract, and setting out upon life's journey with ideas so monstrously
divergent, I am not surprised that some make shipwreck, but that any come to
port. What the boy does almost proudly, as a manly peccadillo, the girl will shudder at as a debasing vice; what is to her the mere common sense of tactics, he
will spit out of his mouth as shameful. Through such a sea of contrarieties must
this green couple steer their way; and contrive to love each other; and to respect,
forsooth; and be ready, when the time arrives, to educate the little men and women
who shall succeed to their places and perplexities.

And yet, when all has been said, the man who should hold back from marriage
is in the same case with him who runs away from battle. To avoid an occasion for
our virtues is a worse degree of failure than to push forward pluckily and make a
fall. It is lawful to pray God that we be not led into temptation;[23] but not lawful to
skulk from those that come to us. The noblest passage in one of the noblest books
of this century, is where the old pope glories in the trial, nay, in the partial fall
and but imperfect triumph, of the younger hero.[24] Without some such manly note,
it were perhaps better to have no conscience at all. But there is a vast difference
between teaching flight, and showing points of peril that a man may march the
more warily. And the true conclusion of this paper is to turn our back on apprehensions, and embrace that shining and courageous virtue, Faith. Hope is the boy,
a blind, headlong, pleasant fellow, good to chase swallows with the salt; Faith
is the grave, experienced, yet smiling man. Hope lives on ignorance; open-eyed

36

Faith is built upon a knowledge of our life, of the tyranny of circumstance, and the frailty of human resolution. Hope looks for unqualified success; but Faith counts certainly on failure, and takes honourable defeat to be a form of victory. Hope is a kind old pagan; but Faith grew up in Christian days, and early learnt humility. In the one temper, a man is indignant that he cannot spring up in a clap to heights of elegance and virtue; in the other, out of a sense of his infirmities, he is filled with confidence because a year has come and gone, and he has still preserved some rags of honour. In the first, he expects an angel for a wife; in the last, he knows that she is like himself—erring, thoughtless, and untrue; but like himself also, filled with a struggling radiancy of better things, and adorned with ineffective qualities. You may safely go to school with hope; but ere you marry, should have learned the mingled lesson of the world: that dolls are stuffed with sawdust, and yet are excellent play-things; that hope and love address themselves to a perfection never realized, and yet, firmly held, become the salt and staff of life; that you yourself are compacted of infirmities, perfect, you might say, in imperfection, and yet you have a something in you lovable and worth preserving; and that, while the mass of mankind lies under this scurvy condemnation, you will scarce find one but, by some generous reading, will become to you a lesson, a model, and a noble spouse through life. So thinking, you will constantly support your own unworthiness, and easily forgive the failings of your friend. Nay, you will be wisely glad that you retain the sense of blemishes; for the faults of married people continually spur up each of them, hour by hour, to do better and to meet and love upon a higher ground. And ever, between the failures, there will come glimpses of kind virtues to encourage and console.

Notes

1 "Virginibus puerisque canto" (Latin): I sing to maids and boys (Horace, *Odes*, 3.1).
2 Hannibal (247–182 BC), great Carthaginian general in the Second Punic War.
3 Quotations from chapters 8 and 13 of Mark Twain's *The Adventures of Tom Sawyer* (1876).
4 Idyllic, utopian.
5 Generic name for a foolish old man.
6 A character in Bunyan's *Pilgrim's Progress* (1678) who seeks to divert pilgrims from the path to God.
7 The Total Abstinence Society, established in 1838, encouraged people to make one enduring pledge to avoid alcohol for life.
8 Samuel Pepys (1633–1703), English naval administrator and MP whose famous *Diary and Correspondence* was published in 1825. In his biographical essay "Samuel Pepys" (1881), Stevenson writes, "the story of his oaths, so often broken, so courageously renewed, is worthy rather of admiration than the contempt it has received."—*The Works of Robert Louis Stevenson. Tusitala Edition* 27:198–9 (Longman, 1923–27).
9 Shakespeare, *The Tempest*, 4.1.15–17.
10 Paul wrote, "For the good that I would I do not: but the evil which I would not, that I do" (Romans 7:19). Horace confesses to running away from battle (*Odes*, 2. 7). Stevenson may be confusing Horace with Ovid's *Metamorphoses*: "I see better things and approve, but I follow the worse" (7.20–21).

11 Luke 19:17.
12 A convict on parole to seek employment.
13 A pleasant, easy divergence from the path in *Pilgrim's Progress*.
14 A contrast of darkness and light in painting.
15 See George Sand's *Consuelo* (1843, ch. 20).
16 The Recording Angel tallies each person's good deeds and sins.
17 Matthew 6:22–23.
18 Romans 14:21; 1 Corinthians 8:11.
19 An illogical statement, often revealing a hidden truth.
20 Falsehoods permitted by the state for social stability in Plato's *The Republic* (Book III).
21 Characters in George Eliot's *Middlemarch* (1872).
22 Luke 4:4.
23 The Lord's Prayer (Matthew 6:13).
24 Pope Innocent XII's monologue on the appeal of the convict Guido Franceschini in Book X of Robert Browning's *The Ring and the Book* (1869).

3

VIRGINIBUS PUERISQUE III.
ON FALLING IN LOVE[1]

"Lord, what fools these mortals be!"[2]

There is only one event in life which really astonishes a man and startles him out of his prepared opinions. Everything else befalls him very much as he expected. Event succeeds to event, with an agreeable variety indeed, but with little that is either startling or intense; they form together no more than a sort of background, or running accompaniment to the man's own reflections; and he falls naturally into a cool, curious, and smiling habit of mind, and builds himself up in a conception of life which expects to-morrow to be after the pattern of to-day and yesterday. He may be accustomed to the vagaries of his friends and acquaintances under the influence of love. He may sometimes look forward to it for himself with an incomprehensible expectation. But it is a subject in which neither intuition nor the behaviour of others will help the philosopher to the truth. There is probably nothing rightly thought or rightly written on this matter of love that is not a piece of the person's experience. I remember an anecdote of a well-known French theorist, who was debating a point eagerly in his *cénacle*.[3] It was objected against him that he had never experienced love. Whereupon he arose, left the society, and made it a point not to return to it until he considered that he had supplied the defect. "Now," he remarked, on entering, "now I am in a position to continue the discussion." Perhaps he had not penetrated very deeply into the subject after all; but the story indicates right thinking, and may serve as an apologue to readers of this essay.

When at last the scales fall from his eyes, it is not without something of the nature of dismay that the man finds himself in such changed conditions. He has to deal with commanding emotions instead of the easy dislikes and preferences in which he has hitherto passed his days; and he recognizes capabilities for pain and pleasure of which he had not yet suspected the existence.

Falling in love is the one illogical adventure, the one thing of which we are tempted to think as supernatural, in our trite and reasonable world. The effect is out of all proportion with the cause. Two persons, neither of them, it may be, very amiable or very beautiful, meet, speak a little, and look a little into each other's eyes. That has been done a dozen or so of times in the experience of either

39

with no great result. But on this occasion all is different. They fall at once into that state in which another person becomes to us the very gist and centrepoint of God's creation, and demolishes our laborious theories with a smile; in which our ideas are so bound up with the one master-thought that even the trivial cares of our own person become so many acts of devotion, and the love of life itself is translated into a wish to remain in the same world with so precious and desirable a fellow-creature. And all the while their acquaintances look on in stupor, and ask each other, with almost passionate emphasis, what so-and-so can see in that woman, or such-an-one in that man? I am sure, gentlemen, I cannot tell you. For my part, I cannot think what the women mean. It might be very well, if the Apollo Belvedere[4] should suddenly glow all over into life, and step forward from the pedestal with that godlike air of his. But of the misbegotten changelings who call themselves men, and prate intolerably over dinner-tables, I never saw one who seemed worthy to inspire love—no, nor read of any, except Leonardo da Vinci, and perhaps Goethe in his youth.[5] About women I entertain a somewhat different opinion; but there, I have the misfortune to be a man.

There are many matters in which you may waylay Destiny, and bid him stand and deliver.[6] Hard work, high thinking,[7] adventurous excitement, and a great deal more that forms a part of this or the other person's spiritual bill of fare, are within the reach of almost any one who can dare a little and be patient. But it is by no means in the way of every one to fall in love. You know the difficulty Shakespeare was put into when Queen Elizabeth asked him to show Falstaff in love.[8] I do not believe that Henry Fielding was ever in love. Scott, if it were not for a passage or two in *Rob Roy*, would give me very much the same effect.[9] These are great names and (what is more to the purpose) strong, healthy, high-strung, and generous natures, of whom the reverse might have been expected. As for the innumerable army of anæmic and tailorish persons who occupy the face of this planet with so much propriety, it is palpably absurd to imagine them in any such situation as a love-affair. A wet rag goes safely by the fire; and if a man is blind, he cannot expect to be much impressed by romantic scenery. Apart from all this, many lovable people miss each other in the world, or meet under some unfavourable star. There is the nice and critical moment of declaration to be got over. From timidity or lack of opportunity a good half of possible love cases never get so far, and at least another quarter do there cease and determine. A very adroit person, to be sure, manages to prepare the way and out with his declaration in the nick of time. And then there is a fine solid sort of man, who goes on from snub to snub; and if he has to declare forty times, will continue imperturbably declaring, amid the astonished consideration of men and angels, until he has a favourable answer. I daresay, if one were a woman, one would like to marry a man who was capable of doing this, but not quite one who had done so. It is just a little bit abject, and somehow just a little bit gross; and marriages in which one of the parties has been thus battered into consent scarcely form agreeable subjects for meditation. Love should run out to meet love with open arms. Indeed, the ideal story is that of two people who go into love step for step, with a fluttered consciousness, like a pair of children venturing together into a dark room. From the first moment when they see each other, with a pang of curiosity, through stage after stage of growing pleasure and embarrassment, they can read the expression of their own trouble in each other's eyes. There is here no declaration properly so called; the feeling is so plainly shared, that as soon as the man knows what it is in his own heart, he is sure of what it is in the woman's.

This simple accident of falling in love is as beneficial as it is astonishing. It arrests the petrifying influence of years, disproves cold-blooded and cynical conclusions, and awakens dormant sensibilities. Hitherto the man had found it a good policy to disbelieve the existence of any enjoyment which was out of his reach; and thus he turned his back upon the strong sunny parts of nature, and accustomed himself to look exclusively on what was common and dull. He accepted a prose ideal, let himself go blind of many sympathies by disuse; and if he were young and witty, or beautiful, wilfully forewent these advantages. He joined himself to the following of what, in the old mythology of love, was prettily called *nonchaloir*;[10] and in an odd mixture of feelings, a fling of self-respect, a preference for selfish liberty, and a great dash of that fear with which good people regard serious interests, kept himself back from the straightforward course of life among certain selected activities. And now, all of a sudden, he is unhorsed, like St. Paul,[11] from his infidel affectation. His heart, which has been ticking accurate seconds for the last year, gives a bound and begins to beat high and irregularly in his breast. It seems as if he had never heard or felt or seen until that moment; and by the report of his memory, he must have lived his past life between sleep and waking, or with the preoccupied attention of a brown study. He is practically incommoded by the generosity of his feelings, smiles much when he is alone, and develops a habit of looking rather blankly upon the moon and stars. But it is not at all within the province of a prose essayist to give a picture of this hyperbolical frame of mind; and the thing has been done already, and that to admiration. In *Adelaide*, in Tennyson's *Maud*, and in some of Heine's songs, you get the absolute expression of this midsummer spirit.[12] Romeo and Juliet were very much in love; although they tell me some German critics are of a different opinion, probably the same who would have us think Mercutio a dull fellow. Poor Antony was in love, and no mistake.[13] That lay figure Marius, in *Les Misérables*, is also a genuine case in his own way, and worth observation. A good many of George Sand's people are thoroughly in love; and so are a good many of George Meredith's.[14] Altogether, there is plenty to read on the subject. If the root of the matter be in him, and if he has the requisite chords to set in vibration, a young man may occasionally enter, with the key of art, into that land of Beulah which is upon the borders of Heaven and within sight of the City of Love.[15] There let him sit awhile to hatch delightful hopes and perilous illusions.

One thing that accompanies the passion in its first blush is certainly difficult to explain. It comes (I do not quite see how) that from having a very supreme sense of pleasure in all parts of life—in lying down to sleep, in waking, in motion, in breathing, in continuing to be—the lover begins to regard his happiness as beneficial for the rest of the world, and highly meritorious in himself. Our race has never been able contentedly to suppose that the noise of its wars, conducted by a few young gentlemen in a corner of an inconsiderable star, does not re-echo among the courts of Heaven with quite a formidable effect. In much the same taste, when people find a great to-do in their own breasts, they imagine it must have some influence in their neighbourhood. The presence of the two lovers is so enchanting to each other that it seems as if it must be the best thing possible for everybody else. They are half inclined to fancy it is because of them and their love that the sky is blue and the sun shines. And certainly the weather is usually fine while people are courting. . . . In point of fact, although the happy man feels very kindly towards others of his own sex, there is apt to be something too much of the magnifico in his demeanour. If people grow presuming and self-important over such matters as a dukedom or the Holy See, they will scarcely support the dizziest elevation in life without some suspicion of a strut; and the dizziest elevation is to love and be loved in return. Consequently, accepted lovers are a trifle condescending in their address to other men. An overweening sense of the passion and importance of life hardly conduces to simplicity of manner. To women, they feel very nobly, very purely, and very generously, as if they were so many Joan-of-Arc's; but this does not come out in their behaviour; and they treat them to Grandisonian airs[16] marked with a suspicion of fatuity. I am not quite certain that women do not like this sort of thing; but really, after having bemused myself over *Daniel Deronda*,[17] I have given up trying to understand what they like.

If it did nothing else, this sublime and ridiculous superstition, that the pleasure of the pair is somehow blessed to others, and everybody is made happier in their happiness, would serve at least to keep love generous and great-hearted. Nor is it quite a baseless superstition after all. Other lovers are hugely interested. They strike the nicest balance between pity and approval, when they see people aping the greatness of their own sentiments. It is an understood thing in the play, that while the young gentlefolk are courting on the terrace, a rough flirtation is being carried on, and a light, trivial sort of love is growing up, between the footman and the singing chambermaid. As people are generally cast for the leading parts in their own imaginations, the reader can apply the parallel to real life without much chance of going wrong. In short, they are quite sure this other love-affair is not so deep-seated as their own, but they like dearly to see it going forward. And love, considered as a spectacle, must have attractions for many who are not of the confraternity. The sentimental old maid is a commonplace of the novelists; and he must be rather a poor sort of human being, to be sure, who can look on at this pretty madness without indulgence and sympathy. For nature commends itself to people with a most insinuating art; the busiest is now and again arrested by a great sunset; and you may be as pacific or as cold-blooded as you will, but you cannot help some emotion when you read of well-disputed battles, or meet a pair of lovers in the lane.

Certainly, whatever it may be with regard to the world at large, this idea of benef-icent pleasure is true as between the sweethearts. To do good and communicate[18] is the lover's grand intention. It is the happiness of the other that makes his own most intense gratification. It is not possible to disentangle the different emotions, the pride, humility, pity and passion, which are excited by a look of happy love or an unexpected caress. To make oneself beautiful, to dress the hair, to excel in talk, to do anything and all things that puff out the character and attributes and make them imposing in the eyes of others, is not only to magnify one's self, but to offer the most delicate homage at the same time. And it is in this latter intention that they are done by lovers; for the essence of love is kindness; and indeed it may be best defined as passionate kindness: kindness, so to speak, run mad and become importunate and violent. Vanity in a merely personal sense exists no longer. The lover takes a perilous pleasure in privately displaying his weak points and having them, one after another, accepted and condoned. He wishes to be assured that he is not loved for this or that good quality, but for himself, or something as like himself as he can contrive to set forward. For, although it may have been a very difficult thing to paint the marriage of Cana,[19] or write the fourth act of *Antony and Cleopatra*, there is a more difficult piece of art before every one in this world who cares to set about explaining his own character to others. Words and acts are easily wrenched from their true significance; and they are all the language we have to come and go upon. A pitiful job we make of it, as a rule. For better or worse, people mistake our meaning and take our emotions at a wrong valuation. And generally we rest pretty content with our failures; we are content to be misapprehended by cackling flirts; but when once a man is moonstruck with this affection of love, he makes it a point of honour to clear such dubieties away. He cannot have the Best of her Sex misled upon a point of this importance; and his pride revolts at being loved in a mistake.

He discovers a great reluctance to return on former periods of his life. To all that has not been shared with her, rights and duties, bygone fortunes and dispositions, he can look back only by a difficult and repugnant effort of the will. That he should have wasted some years in ignorance of what alone was really important, that he may have entertained the thought of other women with any show of complacency, is a burthen almost too heavy for his self-respect. But it is the thought of another past that rankles in his spirit like a poisoned wound. That he himself made a fashion of being alive in the bald, beggarly days before a certain meeting, is deplorable enough in all good conscience. But that She should have permitted herself the same liberty seems inconsistent with a Divine providence.

A great many people run down jealousy, on the score that it is an artificial feeling, as well as practically inconvenient. This is scarcely fair; for the feeling on which it merely attends, like an ill-humoured courtier, is itself artificial in exactly the same sense and to the same degree. I suppose what is meant by that objection is that jealousy has not always been a character of man; formed no part of that very modest kit of sentiments with which he is supposed to have begun the world; but waited to make its appearance in better days and among richer natures. And this is equally true of love, and friendship, and love of country, and delight in what they call the beauties of nature, and most other things worth having. Love, in particular, will not endure any historical scrutiny: to all who have fallen across it, it is one of the most incontestable facts in the world; but if you begin to ask what it was in other periods and countries, in Greece for instance, the strangest doubts begin to spring up, and everything seems so vague and changing that a dream is logical in comparison. Jealousy, at any rate, is one of the consequences of love; you may like it or not, at pleasure; but there it is.

It is not exactly jealousy, however, that we feel when we reflect on the past of those we love. A bundle of letters found after years of happy union creates no sense of insecurity in the present; and yet it will pain a man sharply. The two people entertain no vulgar doubt of each other: but this pre-existence of both occurs to the mind as something indelicate. To be altogether right, they should have had twin birth together, at the same moment with the feeling that unites them. Then indeed it would be simple and perfect and without reserve or afterthought. Then they would understand each other with a fulness impossible otherwise. There would be no barrier between them of associations that cannot be imparted. They would be led into none of those comparisons that send the blood back to the heart. And they would know that there had been no time lost, and they had been together as much as was possible. For besides terror for the separation that must follow some time or other in the future, men feel anger, and something like remorse, when they think of that other separation which endured until they met. Some one has written that love makes people believe in immortality,[20] because there seems not to be room enough in life for so great a tenderness, and it is inconceivable that the most masterful of our emotions should have no more than the spare moments of a few years. Indeed, it seems strange; but if we call to mind analogies, we can hardly regard it as impossible.

"The blind bow-boy," who smiles upon us from the end of terraces in old Dutch gardens, laughingly hails his bird-bolts among a fleeting generation.[21] But for as fast as ever he shoots, the game dissolves and disappears into eternity from under his falling arrows; this one is gone ere he is struck; the other has but time to make one gesture and give one passionate cry; and they are all the things of a moment. When the generation is gone, when the play is over, when the thirty years' panorama has been withdrawn in tatters from the stage of the world, we may ask what has become of these great, weighty, and undying loves, and the sweethearts who despised mortal conditions in a fine credulity; and they can only show us a few songs in a bygone taste, a few actions worth remembering, and a few children who have retained some happy stamp from the disposition of their parents.

Notes

1 "Virginibus puerisque canto" (Latin): I sing to maids and boys (Horace, *Odes*, 3.1). Stevenson began work on this essay a month after meeting his future wife, Fanny Osbourne. See n. 1, p. 231.
2 Puck's statement on human lovers in Shakespeare's *A Midsummer Night's Dream* (3.2.115).
3 Small social group of artists or intellectuals.

4 Ancient Greek statue celebrated as the standard of male beauty.
5 Both Leonardo da Vinci and Goethe were admired for their good looks.
6 "Stand and deliver" was the highwayman's command to his victims to stop and sur-render their belongings.
7 William Wordsworth, "Written in London. September, 1802" (11).
8 John Dennis recorded this theatrical tradition in *Comical Gallant* (1702).
9 Fielding treats romantic love ironically in *Tom Jones* (1749). In Walter Scott's *Rob Roy* (1818), the hero Frank Osbaldistone bursts into tears upon leaving his beloved forever.
10 Neglect, disregard.
11 Paul "fell to the earth" and was often depicted falling off a horse upon conversion (Acts 9:4).
12 "Adelaide": a poem of unattainable love by Friedrich von Matthisson and set to music by Beethoven. The lovers in Alfred Tennyson's "Maud" (1855) are kept apart. Maud dies broken-hearted and the narrator goes insane. German poet Heinrich Heine (1797–1856).
13 Characters in Shakespeare. Mercutio is known for his wit. Marc Antony gave up his position and empire for Cleopatra.
14 George Sand, penname of French novelist Amantine Dupin (1804–76). English novelist George Meredith (1828–1909).
15 A pleasant country bordering heaven in Bunyan's *Pilgrim's Progress*.
16 The eponymous romantic hero of Samuel Richardson's *Sir Charles Grandison* (1754) known for his formality and eloquence.
17 George Eliot's novel *Daniel Deronda* (1876). Stevenson called its title character a "melancholy puppy and humbug. . . [an] abomination of Desolation in the way of manhood" (*Letters* 2:228).
18 Hebrews 13:16.
19 Many paintings depict this biblical event (John 2:1–11). Stevenson likely refers to Paolo Veronese's "The Wedding at Cana" (1563) in the Louvre.
20 "Love is the desire that good be forever present to us. Of necessity Love must also be the desire of immortality."—Percy Bysshe Shelley, "The Banquet of Plato" (1840).
21 Cupid in *Romeo and Juliet* (2.3.14–15). Hails: rains down like hail; bolts: crossbow arrows.

4

VIRGINIBUS PUERISQUE[1] IV.
TRUTH OF INTERCOURSE

Among sayings that have a currency in spite of being wholly false upon the face of them for the sake of a half-truth upon another subject which is accidentally combined with the error, one of the grossest and broadest conveys the monstrous proposition that it is easy to tell the truth and hard to tell a lie. I wish heartily it were. But the truth is one; it has first to be discovered, then justly and exactly uttered. Even with instruments specially contrived for such a purpose—with a foot rule, a level or a theodolite—it is not easy to be exact; it is easier, alas! to be inexact. From those who mark the divisions on a scale to those who measure the boundaries of empires or the distance of the heavenly stars it is by careful method and minute, unwearying attention that men rise even to material exactness or to sure knowledge even of external and constant things. But it is easier to draw the outline of a mountain than the changing appearance of a face; and truth in human relations is of this more intangible and dubious order: hard to seize, harder to communicate. Veracity to facts in a loose, colloquial sense—not to say that I have been in Malabar when as a matter of fact I was never out of England, not to say that I have read Cervantes in the original when as a matter of fact I know not one syllable of Spanish—this, indeed, is easy and to the same degree unimportant in itself. Lies of this sort, according to circumstances, may or may not be important; in a certain sense even they may or may not be false. The habitual liar may be a very honest fellow, and live truly with his wife and friends; while another man who never told a formal falsehood in his life may yet be himself one lie—heart and face, from top to bottom. This is the kind of lie which poisons intimacy. And, vice versâ, veracity to sentiment, truth in a relation, truth to your own heart and your friends, never to feign or falsify emotion—that is the truth which makes love possible and mankind happy.

L'art de bien dire[2] is but a drawing-room accomplishment unless it be pressed into the service of the truth. The difficulty of literature is not to write, but to write what you mean; not to affect your reader, but to affect him precisely as you wish. This is commonly understood in the case of books or set orations; even in making your will, or writing an explicit letter, some difficulty is admitted by the world. But one thing you can never make Philistine[3] natures understand; one thing, which yet lies on the surface, remains as unseizable to their wits as a high flight of metaphysics—namely, that the business of life is mainly carried on by means of this difficult art of literature, and according to a man's proficiency in that art shall be the freedom and the fulness of his intercourse with other men. Anybody, it is supposed, can say what he means; and, in spite of their notorious experience to the contrary, people so continue to suppose.

Now, I simply open the last book I have been reading—Mr. Leland's captivating *English Gipsies*.[4] "It is said," I find on p. 7, "that those who can converse with Irish peasants in their own native tongue form far higher opinions of their appreciation of the beautiful, and of *the elements of humour and pathos in their hearts*, than do those who know their thoughts only through the medium of English. I know from my own observations that this is quite the case with the Indians of North America, and it is unquestionably so with the gipsy." In short, where a man has not a full possession of the language, the most important, because the most amiable, qualities of his nature have to lie buried and fallow; for the pleasure of comradeship, and the intellectual part of love, rest upon these very "elements of humour and pathos." Here is a man opulent in both, and for lack of a medium he can put none of it out to interest in the market of affection! But what is thus made plain to our apprehensions in the case of a foreign language is partially true even with the tongue we learned in childhood. Indeed, we all speak different dialects; one shall be copious and exact, another loose and meagre; but the speech of the ideal talker shall correspond and fit upon the truth of fact—not clumsily, obscuring lineaments, like a mantle, but cleanly adhering, like an athlete's skin. And what is the result? That the one can open himself more clearly to his friends, and can enjoy more of what makes life truly valuable—intimacy with those he loves.

An orator makes a false step; he employs some trivial, some absurd, some vulgar phrase; in the turn of a sentence he insults, by a side wind, those whom he is labouring to charm; in speaking to one sentiment he unconsciously ruffles another in parenthesis; and you are not surprised, for you know his task to be delicate and filled with perils. "O frivolous mind of man, light ignorance!"[5] As if yourself, when you seek to explain some misunderstanding or excuse some apparent fault, speaking swiftly and addressing a mind still recently incensed, were not harnessing for a more perilous adventure; as if yourself required less tact and eloquence; as if an angry friend or a suspicious lover were not more easy to offend than a meeting of indifferent politicians! Nay, and the orator treads in a beaten round; the matters he discusses have been discussed a thousand times before; language is ready-shaped to his purpose; he speaks out of a cut and dry vocabulary. But you—may it not be that your defence reposes on some subtlety of feeling, not so much as touched upon in Shakespeare, to express which, like a pioneer, you must venture forth into zones of thought still unsurveyed, and become yourself a literary innovator? For even in love there are unlovely humours; ambiguous acts, unpardonable words, may yet have sprung from a kind sentiment. If the injured one could read your heart, you may be sure that he would understand and pardon; but, alas! the heart cannot be shown—it has to be demonstrated in words. Do you think it is a hard thing to write poetry? Why, that is to write poetry, and of a high, if not the highest, order.

I should even more admire "the lifelong and heroic literary labours"[6] of my fellow-men, patiently clearing up in words their loves and their contentions, and speaking their autobiography daily to their wives, were it not for a circumstance which lessens their difficulty and my admiration by equal parts. For life, though largely, is not entirely carried on by literature. We are subject to physical passions and contortions; the voice breaks and changes, and speaks by unconscious and winning inflections; we have legible countenances, like an open book; things that cannot be said look eloquently through the eyes; and the soul, not locked into the body as a dungeon, dwells ever on the threshold with appealing signals. Groans and tears, looks and gestures, a flush or a paleness, are often the most clear report-ers of the heart, and speak more directly to the hearts of others. The message flies by these interpreters in the least space of time, and the misunderstanding is averted in the moment of its birth. To explain in words takes time and a just and patient hearing; and in the critical epochs of a close relation, patience and justice are not qualities on which we can rely. But the look or the gesture explains things in a breath; they tell their message without ambiguity; unlike speech, they cannot stumble, by the way, on a reproach or an allusion that should steel your friend against the truth; and then they have a higher authority, for they are the direct expression of the heart, not yet transmitted through the unfaithful and sophisti-cating brain. Not long ago I wrote a letter to a friend which came near involving us in quarrel; but we met, and in personal talk I repeated the worst of what I had written, and added worse to that; and with the commentary of the body it seemed not unfriendly either to hear or say. Indeed, letters are in vain for the purposes of intimacy; an absence is a dead break in the relation; yet two who know each other fully and are bent on perpetuity in love, may so preserve the attitude of their affec-tions that they may meet on the same terms as they had parted.

Pitiful is the case of the blind, who cannot read the face; pitiful that of the deaf, who cannot follow the changes of the voice. And there are others also to be pitied; for there are some of an inert, uneloquent nature, who have been denied all the symbols of communication, who have neither a lively play of facial expression, nor speaking gestures, nor a responsive voice, nor yet the gift of frank, explanatory speech. People truly made of clay, people tied for life into a bag which no one can undo. They are poorer than the gipsy, for their heart can speak no language under heaven. Such people we must learn slowly by the tenor of their acts, or through yea and nay communications; or we take them on trust on the strength of a gen-eral air, and now and again, when we see the spirit breaking through in a flash, correct or change our estimate. But these will be uphill intimacies, without charm or freedom, to the end; and freedom is the chief ingredient in confidence. Some minds, romantically dull, despise physical endowments. That is a doctrine for a misanthrope; to those who like their fellow-creatures it must always be meaning-less; and, for my part, I can see few things more desirable, after the possession of such radical qualities as honour and humour and pathos, than to have a lively and not a stolid countenance; to have looks to correspond with every feeling; to be elegant and delightful in person, so that we shall please even in the intervals of active pleasing, and may never discredit speech with uncouth manners and become unconsciously our own burlesques. But of all unfortunates there is one creature (for I will not call him man) conspicuous in misfortune. This is he who has forfeited his birthright of expression, who has cultivated artful intonations, who has taught his face tricks, like a pet monkey, and on every side perverted or cut off his means of communication with his fellow-men. The body is a house of many windows: there we all sit, showing ourselves and crying on the passers-by to come and love us. But this fellow has filled his windows with opaque glass, elegantly coloured. His house may be admired for its design, the crowd may pause before the stained windows, but meanwhile the poor proprietor must lie languishing within, uncomforted, unchangeably alone.

Truth of intercourse is something more difficult than to refrain from open lies. It is possible to avoid falsehood and yet not tell the truth. It is not enough to answer formal questions. To reach the truth by yea and nay communications implies a questioner with a share of inspiration, such as is often found in mutual love. *Yea* and *nay* mean nothing; the meaning must have been related in the question. Many words are often necessary to convey a very simple statement; for in this sort of exercise we never hit the gold;[7] the most that we can hope is by many arrows, more or less far off on different sides, to indicate, in the course of time, for what target we are aiming, and after an hour's talk, back and forward, to convey the purport of a single principle or a single thought. And yet while the curt, pithy speaker misses the point entirely, a wordy, prolegomenous babbler will often add three new offences in the process of excusing one. It is really a most delicate affair. The world was made before the English language, and seemingly upon a different design. Suppose we held our converse not in words, but in music; those who have a bad ear would find themselves cut off from all near commerce, and no better than foreigners in this big world. But we do not consider how many have "a bad ear" for words, nor how often the most eloquent find nothing to reply. I hate questioners and questions; there are so few that can be spoken to without a lie. "*Do you forgive me?*" Madam and sweetheart, so far as I have gone in life I have never yet been able to discover what forgiveness means. "*Is it still the same between us?*" Why, how can it be? It is eternally different; and yet you are still the friend of my heart. "*Do you understand me?*" God knows; I should think it highly improbable.

The cruellest lies are often told in silence. A man may have sat in a room for hours and not opened his teeth, and yet come out of that room a disloyal friend or a vile calumniator. And how many loves have perished because, from pride, or spite, or diffidence, or that unmanly shame which withholds a man from daring to betray emotion, a lover, at the critical point of the relation, has but hung his head and held his tongue? And, again, a lie may be told by a truth, or a truth conveyed through a lie. Truth to facts is not always truth to sentiment; and part of the truth, as often happens in answer to a question, may be the foulest calumny. A fact may be an exception; but the feeling is the law, and it is that which you must neither garble nor belie. The whole tenor of a conversation is a part of the meaning of each separate statement; the beginning and the end define and travesty the intermediate conversation. You never speak to God; you address a fellow-man, full of his own tempers; and to tell truth, rightly understood, is not to state the true facts, but to convey a true impression; truth in spirit, not truth to letter, is the true veracity. To reconcile averted friends a Jesuitical[8] discretion is often needful, not so much to gain a kind hearing as to communicate sober truth. Women have an ill name in this connection; yet they live in as true relations; the lie of a good woman is the true index of her heart.

"It takes," says Thoreau, in the noblest and most useful passage I remember to have read in any modern author, "two to speak truth—one to speak and another to hear."[9] He must be very little experienced, or have no great zeal for truth, who does not recognize the fact. A grain of anger or a grain of suspicion produces strange acoustical effects, and makes the ear greedy to remark offence. Hence we find those who have once quarrelled carry themselves distantly, and are ever ready to break the truce. To speak truth there must be moral equality or else no respect; and hence between parent and child intercourse is apt to degenerate into a verbal fencing bout, and misapprehensions to become ingrained. And there is another side to this, for the parent begins with an imperfect notion of the child's character, formed in early years or during the equinoctial gales[10] of youth; to this he adheres, noting only the facts which suit with his preconception; and wherever a person fancies himself unjustly judged, he at once and finally gives up the effort to speak truth. With our chosen friends, on the other hand, and still more between lovers (for mutual understanding is love's essence), the truth is easily indicated by the one and aptly comprehended by the other. A hint taken, a look understood, conveys the gist of long and delicate explanations; and where the life is known even *yea* and *nay* become luminous. In the closest of all relations—that of a love well founded and equally shared—speech is half discarded, like a roundabout, infantile process or a ceremony of formal etiquette; and the two communicate directly by their presences, and with few looks and fewer words contrive to share their good and evil and uphold each other's hearts in joy. For love rests upon a physical basis; it is a familiarity of nature's making and apart from voluntary choice. Understanding has in some sort outrun knowledge, for the affection, perhaps, began with the acquaintance; and as it was not made like other relations, so it is not, like them, to be perturbed or clouded. Each knows more than can be uttered; each lives by faith, and believes by a natural compulsion; and between man and wife the language of the body is largely developed and grown strangely eloquent. The thought that prompted and was conveyed in a caress would only lose to be set down in words—aye, although Shakespeare himself should be the scribe.

Yet it is in these dear intimacies, beyond all others, that we must strive and do battle for the truth. Let but a doubt arise, and alas! all the previous intimacy and confidence is but another charge against the person doubted. "*What a monstrous dishonesty is this if I have been deceived so long and so completely!*" Let but that thought gain entrance, and you plead before a deaf tribunal. Appeal to the past;

why, that is your crime! Make all clear, convince the reason; alas! speciousness is but a proof against you. "*If you can abuse me now, the more likely that you have abused me from the first.*"

For a strong affection such moments are worth supporting, and they will end well; for your advocate is in your lover's heart and speaks her own language; it is not you but she herself who can defend and clear you of the charge. But in slighter intimacies, and for a less stringent union? Indeed, is it worth while? We are all *incompris*,[11] only more or less concerned for the mischance; all trying wrongly to do right; all fawning at each other's feet like dumb, neglected lap-dogs. Sometimes we catch an eye—this is our opportunity in the ages—and we wag our tail with a poor smile. "*Is that all?*" All? If you only knew! But how can they know? They do not love us; the more fools we to squander life on the indifferent.

But the morality of the thing, you will be glad to hear, is excellent; for it is only by trying to understand others that we can get our own hearts understood; and in matters of human feeling the clement judge is the most successful pleader.

Notes

1 "Virginibus puerisque canto" (Latin): I sing to maids and boys (Horace, *Odes*, 3.1).
2 The art of speaking well (French).
3 Middle-class people more concerned with materialism than culture or art—a term popularized by Matthew Arnold's *Culture and Anarchy* (1869).
4 Charles G. Leland, *The English Gipsies and their Language* (1874).
5 Matthew Arnold, "Fragment of Chorus of a *Dejaneira*" (1867, 1–2).
6 Henry David Thoreau, *Walden* (1878, "Reading").
7 Center of an archery target.
8 Carefully argued tactfulness.
9 **RLS:** *A Week on the Concord and Merrimack Rivers*, Wednesday, p. 283.
10 Referring to the popular but mistaken belief that storms are more common during the spring and fall equinox.
11 Misunderstood, underappreciated (French).

5

CRABBED AGE AND YOUTH[1]

"You know my mother now and then argues very notably; always
very warmly at least. I happen often to differ from her; and we both
think so well of our own arguments, that we very seldom are so
happy as to convince one another. A pretty common case, I believe,
in all *vehement* debatings. She says, I am *too witty*; Anglicè,[2] *too
pert*; I, that she is *too wise*; that is to say, being likewise put into
English, *not so young as she has been*."
                    – Miss Howe to Miss Harlowe, *Clarissa*, vol. ii. Letter xiii.[3]

There is a strong feeling in favour of cowardly and prudential proverbs. The sentiments of a man while he is full of ardour and hope are to be received, it is
supposed, with some qualification. But when the same person has ignominiously
failed and begins to eat up his words, he should be listened to like an oracle. Most
of our pocket wisdom is conceived for the use of mediocre people, to discourage
them from ambitious attempts, and generally console them in their mediocrity.
And since mediocre people constitute the bulk of humanity, this is no doubt very
properly so. But it does not follow that the one sort of proposition is any less
true than the other, or that Icarus[4] is not to be more praised, and perhaps more
envied, than Mr. Samuel Budgett the Successful Merchant.[5] The one is dead, to
be sure, while the other is still in his counting-house counting out his money;[6]
and doubtless this is a consideration. But we have, on the other hand, some bold
and magnanimous sayings common to high races and natures, which set forth the
advantage of the losing side, and proclaim it better to be a dead lion than a living dog.[7] It is difficult to fancy how the mediocrities reconcile such sayings with
their proverbs. According to the latter, every lad who goes to sea is an egregious
ass; never to forget your umbrella through a long life would seem a higher and
wiser flight of achievement than to go smiling to the stake; and so long as you
are a bit of a coward and inflexible in money matters, you fulfil the whole duty
of man. It is a still more difficult consideration for our average men, that while
all their teachers, from Solomon down to Benjamin Franklin and the infamous
Budgett, have inculcated the same ideal of manners, caution, and respectability,

52

those characters in history who have most notoriously flown in the face of such precepts are spoken of in hyperbolical terms of praise, and honoured with public monuments in the streets of our commercial centres. This is very bewildering to the moral sense. You have Joan of Arc, who left a humble but honest and reputable livelihood under the eyes of her parents, to go a-colonelling, in the company of rowdy soldiers, against the enemies of France; surely a melancholy example for one's daughters! And then you have Columbus, who may have pioneered America, but when all is said, was a most imprudent navigator. His life is not the kind of thing one would like to put into the hands of young people; rather, one would do one's utmost to keep it from their knowledge, as a red flag of adventure and disintegrating influence in life. The time would fail me if I were to recite all the big names in history whose exploits are perfectly irrational and even shocking to the business mind. The incongruity is speaking; and I imagine it must engender among the mediocrities a very peculiar attitude towards the nobler and showier sides of national life. They will read of the Charge of Balaclava[8] in much the same spirit as they assist at a performance of the *Lyons Mail*.[9] Persons of substance take in the *Times* and sit composedly in pit or boxes according to the degree of their prosperity in business. As for the generals who go galloping up and down among bomb-shells in absurd cocked hats—as for the actors who raddle[10] their faces and demean themselves for hire upon the stage—they must belong, thank God! to a different order of beings, whom we watch as we watch the clouds careering in the windy, bottomless inane, or read about like characters in ancient and rather fabulous annals. Our offspring would no more think of copying their behaviour, let us hope, than of doffing their clothes and painting themselves blue in consequence of certain admissions in the first chapter of their school history of England.[11]

Discredited as they are in practice, the cowardly proverbs hold their own in theory; and it is another instance of the same spirit, that the opinions of old men about life have been accepted as final. All sorts of allowances are made for the illusions of youth; and none, or almost none, for the disenchantments of age. It is held to be a good taunt, and somehow or other to clinch the question logically, when an old gentleman waggles his head and says: "Ah, so I thought when I was your age." It is not thought an answer at all, if the young man retorts: "My venerable sir, so I shall most probably think when I am yours." And yet the one is as good as the other: pass for pass, tit for tat, a Roland for an Oliver.[12]

"Opinion in good men," says Milton, "is but knowledge in the making."[13] All opinions, properly so called, are stages on the road to truth. It does not follow that a man will travel any further; but if he has really considered the world and drawn a conclusion, he has travelled as far. This does not apply to formulæ got by rote, which are stages on the road to nowhere but second childhood and the grave. To have a catchword in your mouth is not the same thing as to hold an opinion; still less is it the same thing as to have made one for yourself. There are too many of these catchwords in the world for people to rap out upon you like an oath and by way of an argument. They have a currency as intellectual counters; and many respectable persons pay their way with nothing else. They seem to stand for vague bodies of theory in the background. The imputed virtue of folios full of knockdown arguments is supposed to reside in them, just as some of the majesty of the British Empire dwells in the constable's truncheon. They are used in pure superstition, as old clodhoppers spoil Latin by way of an exorcism.[14] And yet they are vastly serviceable for checking unprofitable discussion and stopping the mouths of babes and sucklings.[15] And when a young man comes to a certain stage of intellectual growth, the examination of these counters forms a gymnastic at once amusing and fortifying to the mind.

Because I have reached Paris, I am not ashamed of having passed through Newhaven and Dieppe. They were very good places to pass through, and I am none the less at my destination. All my old opinions were only stages on the way to the one I now hold, as itself is only a stage on the way to something else. I am no more abashed at having been a red-hot Socialist with a panacea of my own than at having been a sucking infant. Doubtless the world is quite right in a million ways; but you have to be kicked about a little to convince you of the fact. And in the meanwhile you must do something, be something, believe something. It is not possible to keep the mind in a state of accurate balance and blank; and even if you could do so, instead of coming ultimately to the right conclusion, you would be very apt to remain in a state of balance and blank to perpetuity. Even in quite intermediate stages, a dash of enthusiasm is not a thing to be ashamed of in the retrospect: if St. Paul had not been a very zealous Pharisee, he would have been a colder Christian.[16] For my part, I look back to the time when I was a Socialist with something like regret. I have convinced myself (for the moment) that we had better leave these great changes to what we call great blind forces: their blindness being so much more perspicacious than the little, peering, partial eyesight of men. I seem to see that my own scheme would not answer; and all the other schemes I ever heard propounded would depress some elements of goodness just as much as they encouraged others. Now I know that in thus turning Conservative with years, I am going through the normal cycle of change and travelling in the common orbit of men's opinions. I submit to this, as I would submit to gout or grey hair, as a concomitant of growing age or else of failing animal heat; but I do not acknowledge that it is necessarily a change for the better—I daresay it is deplorably for the worse. I have no choice in the business, and can no more resist this tendency of my mind than I could prevent my body from beginning to totter and decay. If I am spared (as the phrase runs) I shall doubtless outlive some troublesome desires; but I am in no hurry about that; nor, when the time comes, shall I plume myself on the immunity. Just in the same way, I do not greatly pride myself on having outlived my belief in the fairy tales of Socialism. Old people have faults of their own; they tend to become cowardly, niggardly, and suspicious. Whether from the growth of experience or the decline of animal heat, I see that age leads to these and certain other faults; and it follows, of course, that while in one sense I hope I am journeying towards the truth, in another I am indubitably posting towards these forms and sources of error.

As we go catching and catching at this or that corner of knowledge, now getting a foresight of generous possibilities, now chilled with a glimpse of prudence,
we may compare the headlong course of our years to a swift torrent in which a
man is carried away; now he is dashed against a boulder, now he grapples for a
moment to a trailing spray; at the end, he is hurled out and overwhelmed in a dark
and bottomless ocean. We have no more than glimpses and touches; we are torn
away from our theories; we are spun round and round and shown this or the other
view of life, until only fools or knaves can hold to their opinions. We take a sight
at a condition in life, and say we have studied it; our most elaborate view is no
more than an impression. If we had breathing space, we should take the occasion
to modify and adjust; but at this breakneck hurry, we are no sooner boys than
we are adult, no sooner in love than married or jilted, no sooner one age than we
begin to be another, and no sooner in the fulness of our manhood than we begin
to decline towards the grave. It is in vain to seek for consistency or expect clear
and stable views in a medium so perturbed and fleeting. This is no cabinet science,
in which things are tested to a scruple; we theorize with a pistol to our head; we
are confronted with a new set of conditions on which we have not only to pass
a judgment, but to take action, before the hour is at an end. And we cannot even
regard ourselves as a constant; in this flux of things, our identity itself seems in a
perpetual variation; and not infrequently we find our own disguise the strangest in
the masquerade. In the course of time, we grow to love things we hated and hate
things we loved. Milton is not so dull as he once was, nor perhaps Ainsworth[17]
so amusing. It is decidedly harder to climb trees, and not nearly so hard to sit
still. There is no use pretending; even the thrice royal game of hide and seek has
somehow lost in zest. All our attributes are modified or changed; and it will be a
poor account of us if our views do not modify and change in a proportion. To hold
the same views at forty as we held at twenty is to have been stupefied for a score
of years, and take rank, not as a prophet, but as an unteachable brat, well birched
and none the wiser. It is as if a ship captain should sail to India from the Port of
London; and having brought a chart of the Thames on deck at his first setting out,
should obstinately use no other for the whole voyage.

And mark you, it would be no less foolish to begin at Gravesend with a chart of
the Red Sea. *Si Jeunesse savait, si Vieillesse pouvait,*[18] is a very pretty sentiment,
but not necessarily right. In five cases out of ten, it is not so much that the young
people do not know, as that they do not choose. There is something irreverent
in the speculation, but perhaps the want of power has more to do with the wise
resolutions of age than we are always willing to admit. It would be an instructive experiment to make an old man young again and leave him all his *savoir.*[19]
I scarcely think he would put his money in the Savings Bank after all; I doubt if he
would be such an admirable son as we are led to expect; and as for his conduct in
love, I believe firmly he would out-Herod Herod,[20] and put the whole of his new
compeers to the blush. Prudence is a wooden Juggernaut,[21] before whom Benjamin Franklin walks with the portly air of a high priest, and after whom dances
many a successful merchant in the character of Atys.[22] But it is not a deity to

cultivate in youth. If a man lives to any considerable age, it cannot be denied that he laments his imprudences, but I notice he often laments his youth a deal more bitterly and with a more genuine intonation.

It is customary to say that age should be considered, because it comes last. It seems just as much to the point, that youth comes first. And the scale fairly kicks the beam,[23] if you go on to add that age, in a majority of cases, never comes at all. Disease and accident make short work of even the most prosperous persons; death costs nothing, and the expense of a headstone is an inconsiderable trifle to the happy heir. To be suddenly snuffed out in the middle of ambitious schemes, is tragical enough at best; but when a man has been grudging himself his own life in the meanwhile, and saving up everything for the festival that was never to be, it becomes that hysterically moving sort of tragedy which lies on the confines of farce. The victim is dead—and he has cunningly overreached himself; a combination of calamities none the less absurd for being grim. To husband a favourite claret until the batch turns sour, is not at all an artful stroke of policy; and how much more with a whole cellar—a whole bodily existence! People may lay down their lives with cheerfulness in the sure expectation of a blessed immortality; but that is a different affair from giving up youth with all its admirable pleasures, in the hope of a better quality of gruel in a more than problematical, nay, more than improbable, old age. We should not compliment a hungry man, who should refuse a whole dinner and reserve all his appetite for the dessert, before he knew whether there was to be any dessert or not. If there be such a thing as imprudence in the world, we surely have it here. We sail in leaky bottoms and on great and perilous waters; and to take a cue from the dolorous old naval ballad, we have heard the mermaidens singing, and know that we shall never see dry land any more.[24] Old and young, we are all on our last cruise. If there is a fill of tobacco among the crew, for God's sake pass it round, and let us have a pipe before we go!

Indeed, by the report of our elders, this nervous preparation for old age is only trouble thrown away. We fall on guard, and after all it is a friend who comes to meet us. After the sun is down and the west faded, the heavens begin to fill with shining stars. So, as we grow old, a sort of equable jog-trot of feeling is substituted for the violent ups and downs of passion and disgust; the same influence that restrains our hopes, quiets our apprehensions; if the pleasures are less intense, the troubles are milder and more tolerable; and in a word, this period for which we are asked to hoard up everything as for a time of famine, is, in its own right, the richest, easiest, and happiest of life.

Nay, by managing its own work and following its own happy inspiration, youth is doing the best it can to endow the leisure of age. A full, busy youth is your only prelude to a self-contained and independent age; and the muff[25] inevitably develops into the bore. There are not many Doctor Johnsons, to set forth upon their first romantic voyage at sixty-four.[26] If we wish to scale Mont Blanc or visit a thieves' kitchen in the East End, to go down in a diving dress or up in a balloon, we must be about it while we are still young. It will not do to delay until we are clogged with prudence and limping with rheumatism, and people begin to ask us:

"What does Gravity out of bed?"[27] Youth is the time to go flashing from one end of the world to the other both in mind and body; to try the manners of different nations; to hear the chimes at midnight;[28] to see sunrise in town and country; to be converted at a revival; to circumnavigate the metaphysics, write halting verses, run a mile to see a fire, and wait all day long in the theatre to applaud *Hernani*.[29] There is some meaning in the old theory about wild oats; and a man who has not had his greensickness[30] and got done with it for good, is as little to be depended on as an unvaccinated infant. "It is extraordinary," says Lord Beaconsfield, one of the brightest and best preserved of youths up to the date of his last novel, "it is extraordinary how hourly and how violently change the feelings of an inexperienced young man."[31] And this mobility is a special talent entrusted to his care; a sort of indestructible virginity; a magic armour, with which he can pass unhurt through great dangers and come unbedaubed out of the miriest passages. Let him voyage, speculate, see all that he can, do all that he may; his soul has as many lives as a cat; he will live in all weathers, and never be a halfpenny the worse. Those who go to the devil in youth, with anything like a fair chance, were probably little worth saving from the first; they must have been feeble fellows—creatures made of putty and packthread, without steel or fire, anger or true joyfulness, in their composition; we may sympathize with their parents, but there is not much cause to go into mourning for themselves; for to be quite honest, the weak brother is the worst of mankind.

When the old man waggles his head and says, "Ah, so I thought when I was your age," he has proved the youth's case. Doubtless, whether from growth of experience or decline of animal heat, he thinks so no longer; but he thought so while he was young; and all men have thought so while they were young, since there was dew in the morning or hawthorn in May; and here is another young man adding his vote to those of previous generations and rivetting another link to the chain of testimony. It is as natural and as right for a young man to be imprudent and exaggerated, to live in swoops and circles, and beat about his cage like any other wild thing newly captured, as it is for old men to turn grey, or mothers to love their offspring, or heroes to die for something more valuable than their lives.

By way of an apologue for the aged, when they feel more than usually tempted to offer their advice, let me recommend the following little tale. A child who had been remarkably fond of toys (and in particular of lead soldiers) found himself growing to the level of acknowledged boyhood without any abatement of this childish taste. He was thirteen; already he had been taunted for dallying overlong about the playbox; he had to blush if he was found among his lead soldiers; the shades of the prison-house[32] were closing about him with a vengeance. There is nothing more difficult than to put the thoughts of children into the language of their elders; but this is the effect of his meditations at this juncture: "Plainly," he said, "I must give up my playthings, in the meanwhile, since I am not in a position to secure myself against idle jeers. At the same time, I am sure that playthings are the very pick of life; all people give them up out of the same pusillanimous respect for those who are a little older; and if they do not return to them as soon as they can, it is only because they grow stupid and forget. I shall be wiser; I shall conform for a little to the ways of their foolish world; but so soon as I have made enough money, I shall retire and shut myself up among my playthings until the day I die." Nay, as he was passing in the train along the Estrelles mountains between Cannes and Fréjus, he remarked a pretty house in an orange garden at the angle of a bay, and decided that this should be his Happy Valley.[33] Astrea Redux;[34] childhood was to come again! The idea has an air of simple nobility to me, not unworthy of Cincinnatus.[35] And yet, as the reader has probably antici-pated, it is never likely to be carried into effect. There was a worm i' the bud,[36] a fatal error in the premises. Childhood must pass away, and then youth, as surely as age approaches. The true wisdom is to be always seasonable, and to change with a good grace in changing circumstances. To love playthings well as a child, to lead an adventurous and honourable youth, and to settle when the time arrives, into a green and smiling age, is to be a good artist in life and deserve well of yourself and your neighbour.

You need repent none of your youthful vagaries. They may have been over the score on one side, just as those of age are probably over the score on the other. But they had a point; they not only befitted your age and expressed its attitude and pas-sions, but they had a relation to what was outside of you, and implied criticisms on the existing state of things, which you need not allow to have been undeserved, because you now see that they were partial. All error, not merely verbal, is a strong way of stating that the current truth is incomplete. The follies of youth have a basis in sound reason, just as much as the embarrassing questions put by babes and sucklings. Their most antisocial acts indicate the defects of our society. When the torrent sweeps the man against a boulder, you must expect him to scream, and you need not be surprised if the scream is sometimes a theory. Shelley, chaf-ing at the Church of England, discovered the cure of all evils in universal athe-ism.[37] Generous lads irritated at the injustices of society, see nothing for it but the abolishment of everything and Kingdom Come of anarchy. Shelley was a young fool; so are these cocksparrow revolutionaries. But it is better to be a fool than to be dead. It is better to emit a scream in the shape of a theory than to be entirely insensible to the jars and incongruities of life and take everything as it comes in a forlorn stupidity. Some people swallow the universe like a pill; they travel on through the world, like smiling images pushed from behind. For God's sake give me the young man who has brains enough to make a fool of himself! As for the others, the irony of facts shall take it out of their hands, and make fools of them in downright earnest, ere the farce be over. There shall be such a mopping and a mowing[38] at the last day, and such blushing and confusion of countenance for all those who have been wise in their own esteem, and have not learnt the rough les-sons that youth hands on to age. If we are indeed here to perfect and complete our own natures, and grow larger, stronger, and more sympathetic against some nobler career in the future, we had all best bestir ourselves to the utmost while we have the time. To equip a dull, respectable person with wings would be but to make a parody of an angel.

CRABBED AGE AND YOUTH

In short, if youth is not quite right in its opinions, there is a strong probability that age is not much more so. Undying hope is co-ruler of the human bosom with infallible credulity. A man finds he has been wrong at every preceding stage of his career, only to deduce the astonishing conclusion that he is at last entirely right. Mankind, after centuries of failure, are still upon the eve of a thoroughly constitutional millennium. Since we have explored the maze so long without result, it follows, for poor human reason, that we cannot have to explore much longer; close by must be the centre, with a champagne luncheon and a piece of ornamental water. How if there were no centre at all, but just one alley after another, and the whole world a labyrinth without end or issue?

I overheard the other day a scrap of conversation, which I take the liberty to reproduce. "What I advance is true," said one. "But not the whole truth," answered the other. "Sir," returned the first (and it seemed to me there was a smack of Dr. Johnson in the speech), "Sir, there is no such thing as the whole truth!" Indeed, there is nothing so evident in life as that there are two sides to a question. History is one long illustration. The forces of nature are engaged, day by day, in cudgelling it into our backward intelligences. We never pause for a moment's consideration, but we admit it as an axiom. An enthusiast sways humanity exactly by disregarding this great truth, and dinning it into our ears that this or that question has only one possible solution; and your enthusiast is a fine florid fellow, dominates things for a while and shakes the world out of a doze; but when once he is gone, an army of quiet and uninfluential people set to work to remind us of the other side and demolish the generous imposture. While Calvin is putting everybody exactly right in his *Institutes* and hot-headed Knox is thundering in the pulpit, Montaigne is already looking at the other side in his library in Perigord, and predicting that they will find as much to quarrel about in the Bible as they had found already in the Church.[39] Age may have one side, but assuredly Youth has the other. There is nothing more certain than that both are right, except perhaps that both are wrong. Let them agree to differ; for who knows but what agreeing to differ may not be a form of agreement rather than a form of difference?

I suppose it is written that any one who sets up for a bit of a philosopher, must contradict himself to his very face. For here have I fairly talked myself into thinking that we have the whole thing before us at last; that there is no answer to the mystery, except that there are as many as you please; that there is no centre to the maze because, like the famous sphere, its centre is everywhere;[40] and that agreeing to differ with every ceremony of politeness, is the only "one undisturbed song of pure concent"[41] to which we are ever likely to lend our musical voices.

Notes

1 "Crabbed age and youth cannot live together" (Shakespeare, *The Passionate Pilgrim*, 12.1).
2 As the English would say.
3 Richardson's epistolary novel *Clarissa: Or the History of a Young Lady* (1748).

4 The youth in Greek mythology who died after flying too close to the sun, melting his wax wings.

5 Samuel Budgett (1794–1851), considered the model of a respectable Christian businessman and the subject of William Arthur's popular book *The Successful Merchant: Sketches of the Life of Mr. Samuel Budgett* (1852).

6 From the nursery rhyme "Sing a Song of Sixpence."

7 A reversal of Ecclesiastes 9:4: "a living dog is better than a dead lion."

8 The Battle of Balaclava, 25 Oct. 1854, was a Russian Victory over British allied forces in the Crimean War (1853–1856), commemorated in Tennyson's "The Charge of the Light Brigade" (1854).

9 Charles Reade's English adaptation of Paul Siraudin's and Eugène Moreau's French melodrama *Le Courrier de Lyons* (1850) based on a famous case of highway robbery and murder.

10 Paint with rouge.

11 The Picts: ancient British warriors who painted themselves blue before battle.

12 To give as good as one gets, referring to champion knights who fought under Charlemagne.

13 Milton, *Areopagitica* (1644).

14 Clodhopper: a country bumpkin. The incantation "hocus pocus" was thought to be a corruption of the phrase "hoc est corpus meum" (this is my body) in the Latin Mass.

15 Psalms 8:2; Matthew 21:16.

16 Philippians 3:5–8.

17 William Harrison Ainsworth (1805–82) wrote popular historical novels about the highwayman Dick Turpin.

18 If youth only knew, if age only could (French).

19 Knowing (French).

20 King Herod had nine concubines. Shakespeare, *Hamlet*, 3.2.12. See also n. 18, p. 30.

21 A heavy, sacred wagon bearing the image of a Hindu god.

22 Attis: Greek god of vegetation who castrated himself.

23 The argument comes down decisively on that side.

24 In English sea ballads, mermaids often signaled impending disaster. The refrain of "The Mermaid Song" is "For you'll never see dry land."

25 Bumbler; stupid or incompetent person.

26 Samuel Johnson (1709–1784) narrated his 1773 travels in the Scottish Highlands and outer islands at age 63 in *A Journey to the Western Islands of Scotland* (1775).

27 Shakespeare, *1 Henry IV*, 2.5.270.

28 "We have heard the chimes at midnight" or stayed out late with friends (Shakespeare, *2 Henry IV*, 3.2.197).

29 Victor Hugo's Romantic tragedy *Hernani* (1830).

30 "The disease of virgins": anemia, commonly attributed to young women's lovesickness. In Shakespeare's *2 Henry IV*, Falstaff says Prince John has "a kind of male greensickness" (4.2.83–84).

31 From *The Young Duke* (1831) by Benjamin Disraeli, Earl of Beaconsfield (1804–1881), Prime Minister, historian, and novelist most recently of *Lothair* (1870).

32 Wordsworth, "Ode: Intimations of Immortality" (68).

33 The idyllic setting of the royal palace in Samuel Johnson's *Rasselas* (1759).

34 The restoration of Astraea (Latin): Greek goddess of purity, innocence, and justice.

35 Lucius Quinctius Cincinnatus (520–430 BC), a Roman aristocrat who twice left his rural retirement to serve his country.

36 Shakespeare, *Twelfth Night*, 2.4.110.

37 Romantic poet Percy Shelley was expelled from Oxford for writing *The Necessity of Atheism* (1811).

38 Pulling faces; pouting (Shakespeare, *King Lear*, 4.1.58–60).
39 Michel de Montaigne (1533–1592), French author of the *Essais*, which established the essay form. Stevenson refers to Montaigne's "On Experience." John Knox (1513–1572), leader of the Scottish Protestant Reformation and founder of the Presbyterian Church of Scotland. (See Stevenson's 1875 essay "John Knox and His Relations to Women.") John Calvin (1509–1564), French pastor and Protestant reformer best known for the theological system named for him and its doctrine of predestination.
40 An ancient definition of God: a sphere whose center is everywhere.
41 Milton, "At a Solemn Music" (1645), l.6.

6

AN APOLOGY FOR IDLERS

"BOSWELL: We grow weary when idle.

"JOHNSON: That is, sir, because others being busy, we want company; but if we were idle, there would be no growing weary; we should all entertain one another."[1]

Just now, when every one is bound, under pain of a decree in absence convicting them of *lèse*-respectability,[2] to enter on some lucrative profession, and labour therein with something not far short of enthusiasm, a cry from the opposite party who are content when they have enough, and like to look on and enjoy in the meanwhile, savours a little of bravado and gasconade. And yet this should not be. Idleness so called, which does not consist in doing nothing, but in doing a great deal not recognized in the dogmatic formularies of the ruling class, has as good a right to state its position as industry itself. It is admitted that the presence of people who refuse to enter in the great handicap race for sixpenny pieces, is at once an insult and a disenchantment for those who do. A fine fellow (as we see so many) takes his determination, votes for the sixpences, and, in the emphatic Americanism, "goes for" them. And while such an one is ploughing distressfully up the road, it is not hard to understand his resentment, when he perceives cool persons in the meadows by the wayside, lying with a handkerchief over their ears and a glass at their elbow. Alexander is touched in a very delicate place by the disregard of Diogenes.[3] Where was the glory of having taken Rome for these tumultuous barbarians, who poured into the Senate house, and found the Fathers sitting silent and unmoved by their success?[4] It is a sore thing to have laboured along and scaled the arduous hill-tops, and when all is done, find humanity indifferent to your achievement. Hence physicists condemn the unphysical; financiers have only a superficial toleration for those who know little of stocks; literary persons despise the unlettered; and people of all pursuits combine to disparage those who have none.

But though this is one difficulty of the subject, it is not the greatest. You could not be put in prison for speaking against industry, but you can be sent to Coventry[5] for speaking like a fool. The greatest difficulty with most subjects is to do them well; therefore, please to remember this is an apology. It is certain that much may be judiciously argued in favour of diligence; only there is something to be said against it, and that is what, on the present occasion, I have to say. To state one argument is not necessarily to be deaf to all others, and that a man has written a book of travels in Montenegro, is no reason why he should never have been to Richmond.

It is surely beyond a doubt that people should be a good deal idle in youth. For though here and there a Lord Macaulay may escape from school honours with all his wits about him, most boys pay so dear for their medals that they never afterwards have a shot in their locker,[6] and begin the world bankrupt.[7] And the same holds true during all the time a lad is educating himself, or suffering others to educate him. It must have been a very foolish old gentleman who addressed Johnson at Oxford in these words: "Young man, ply your book diligently now, and acquire a stock of knowledge; for when years come upon you, you will find that poring upon books will be but an irksome task."[8] The old gentleman seems to have been unaware that many other things besides reading grow irksome, and not a few become impossible, by the time a man has to use spectacles and cannot walk without a stick. Books are good enough in their own way, but they are a mighty bloodless substitute for life. It seems a pity to sit, like the Lady of Shalott, peering into a mirror, with your back turned on all the bustle and glamour of reality.[9] And if a man reads very hard, as the old anecdote reminds us, he will have little time for thought.

If you look back on your own education, I am sure it will not be the full, vivid, instructive hours of truantry that you regret; you would rather cancel some lacklustre periods between sleep and waking in the class. For my own part, I have attended a good many lectures in my time. I still remember that the spinning of a top is a case of Kinetic Stability. I still remember that Emphyteusis is not a disease, nor Stillicide a crime.[10] But though I would not willingly part with such scraps of science, I do not set the same store by them as by certain other odds and ends that I came by in the open street while I was playing truant. This is not the moment to dilate on that mighty place of education, which was the favourite school of Dickens and of Balzac,[11] and turns out yearly many inglorious masters in the Science of the Aspects of Life. Suffice it to say this: if a lad does not learn in the streets, it is because he has no faculty of learning. Nor is the truant always in the streets, for if he prefers, he may go out by the gardened suburbs into the country. He may pitch on some tuft of lilacs over a burn,[12] and smoke innumerable pipes to the tune of the water on the stones. A bird will sing in the thicket. And there he may fall into a vein of kindly thought, and see things in a new perspective. Why, if this be not education, what is? We may conceive Mr. Worldly Wiseman[13] accosting such an one, and the conversation that should thereupon ensue:—

"How now, young fellow, what dost thou here?"

"Truly, sir, I take mine ease."

"Is not this the hour of the class? and should'st thou not be plying thy Book with diligence, to the end thou mayest obtain knowledge?"

"Nay, but thus also I follow after Learning, by your leave."

"Learning, quotha![14] After what fashion, I pray thee? Is it mathematics?"

"No, to be sure."

"Is it metaphysics?"

"Nor that."

"Is it some language?"

"Nay, it is no language."

"Is it a trade?"

"Nor a trade neither."

"Why, then, what is't?"

"Indeed, sir, as a time may soon come for me to go upon Pilgrimage, I am desirous to note what is commonly done by persons in my case, and where are the ugliest Sloughs and Thickets on the Road; as also, what manner of Staff is of the best service. Moreover, I lie here, by this water, to learn by root-of-heart a lesson which my master teaches me to call Peace, or Contentment."

Hereupon Mr. Worldly Wiseman was much commoved with passion, and shaking his cane with a very threatful countenance, broke forth upon this wise: "Learning, quotha!" said he; "I would have all such rogues scourged by the Hangman!"

And so he would go his way, ruffling out his cravat with a crackle of starch, like a turkey when it spread its feathers.

Now this, of Mr. Wiseman's, is the common opinion. A fact is not called a fact, but a piece of gossip, if it does not fall into one of your scholastic categories. An inquiry must be in some acknowledged direction, with a name to go by; or else you are not inquiring at all, only lounging; and the workhouse is too good for you. It is supposed that all knowledge is at the bottom of a well, or the far end of a telescope. Sainte-Beuve,[15] as he grew older, came to regard all experience as a single great book, in which to study for a few years ere we go hence; and it seemed all one to him whether you should read in Chapter xx., which is the differential calculus, or in Chapter xxxix., which is hearing the band play in the gardens. As a matter of fact, an intelligent person, looking out of his eyes and hearkening in his ears, with a smile on his face all the time, will get more true education than many another in a life of heroic vigils. There is certainly some chill and arid knowledge to be found upon the summits of formal and laborious science; but it is all round about you, and for the trouble of looking, that you will acquire the warm and palpitating facts of life. While others are filling their memory with a lumber[16] of words, one-half of which they will forget before the week be out, your truant may learn some really useful art: to play the fiddle, to know a good cigar, or to speak with ease and opportunity[17] to all varieties of men. Many who have "plied their book diligently," and know all about some one branch or another of accepted lore, come out of the study with an ancient and owl-like demeanour, and prove dry, stockish, and dyspeptic in all the better and brighter parts of life. Many make a large fortune, who remain underbred and pathetically stupid to the last. And meantime there goes the idler, who began life along with them—by your leave, a different picture. He has had time to take care of his health and his spirits; he has been a great deal in the open air, which is the most salutary of all things for both body and mind; and if he has never read the great Book in very recondite places, he has dipped into it and skimmed it over to excellent purpose. Might not the student afford some Hebrew roots, and the business man some of his half-crowns, for a share of the idler's knowledge of life at large, and Art of Living? Nay, and the idler has another and more important quality than these. I mean his wisdom. He who has much looked on at the childish satisfaction of other people in their hobbies, will regard his own with only a very ironical indulgence. He will not be heard among the dogmatists. He will have a great and cool allowance for all sorts of people and opinions. If he finds no out-of-the-way truths, he will identify himself with no very burning falsehood. His way takes him along a by-road, not much frequented, but very even and pleasant, which is called Commonplace Lane, and leads to the Belvedere[18] of Commonsense. Thence he shall command an agreeable, if no very noble prospect; and while others behold the East and West, the Devil and the Sunrise, he will be contentedly aware of a sort of morning hour upon all sublunary things, with an army of shadows running speedily and in many different directions into the great daylight of Eternity. The shadows and the generations, the shrill doctors and the plangent wars, go by into ultimate silence and emptiness; but underneath all this, a man may see, out of the Belvedere windows, much green and peaceful landscape; many firelit parlours; good people laughing, drinking, and making love, as they did before the Flood or the French Revolution; and the old shepherd telling his tale under the hawthorn.[19]

Extreme *busyness*, whether at school or college, kirk or market, is a symptom of deficient vitality; and a faculty for idleness implies a catholic appetite and a strong sense of personal identity. There is a sort of dead-alive, hackneyed people about, who are scarcely conscious of living except in the exercise of some conventional occupation. Bring these fellows into the country, or set them aboard ship, and you will see how they pine for their desk or their study. They have no curiosity; they cannot give themselves over to random provocations; they do not take pleasure in the exercise of their faculties for its own sake; and unless Necessity lays about them with a stick, they will even stand still. It is no good speaking to such folk: they *cannot* be idle, their nature is not generous enough; and they pass those hours in a sort of coma, which are not dedicated to furious moiling in the gold-mill. When they do not require to go to the office, when they are not hungry and have no mind to drink, the whole breathing world is a blank to them.[20] If they have to wait an hour or so for a train, they fall into a stupid trance with their eyes open. To see them, you would suppose there was nothing to look at and no one to speak with; you would imagine they were paralyzed or alienated;[21] and yet very possibly they are hard workers in their own way, and have good eyesight for a flaw in a deed or a turn of the market. They have been to school and college, but all the time they had their eye on the medal; they have gone about in the world and mixed with clever people, but all the time they were thinking of their own affairs.

65

As if a man's soul were not too small to begin with, they have dwarfed and narrowed theirs by a life of all work and no play; until here they are at forty, with a listless attention, a mind vacant of all material of amusement, and not one thought to rub against another, while they wait for the train. Before he was breeched, he might have clambered on the boxes; when he was twenty, he would have stared at the girls; but now the pipe is smoked out, the snuff-box empty, and my gentleman sits bolt upright upon a bench, with lamentable eyes. This does not appeal to me as being Success in Life.

But it is not only the person himself who suffers from his busy habits, but his wife and children, his friends and relations, and down to the very people he sits with in a railway carriage or an omnibus. Perpetual devotion to what a man calls his business, is only to be sustained by perpetual neglect of many other things. And it is not by any means certain that a man's business is the most important thing he has to do. To an impartial estimate it will seem clear that many of the wisest, most virtuous, and most beneficent parts that are to be played upon the Theatre of Life are filled by gratuitous performers, and pass, among the world at large, as phases of idleness. For in that Theatre, not only the walking gentlemen, singing chambermaids, and diligent fiddlers in the orchestra, but those who look on and clap their hands from the benches, do really play a part and fulfil important offices towards the general result. You are no doubt very dependent on the care of your lawyer and stockbroker, of the guards and signalmen who convey you rapidly from place to place, and the policemen who walk the streets for your protection; but is there not a thought of gratitude in your heart for certain other benefactors who set you smiling when they fall in your way, or season your dinner with good company? Colonel Newcome helped to lose his friend's money; Fred Bayham had an ugly trick of borrowing shirts; and yet they were better people to fall among than Mr. Barnes.[22] And though Falstaff was neither sober nor very honest, I think I could name one or two long-faced Barabbases whom the world could better have done without.[23] Hazlitt mentions that he was more sensible of obligation to Northcote, who had never done him anything he could call a service, than to his whole circle of ostentatious friends;[24] for he thought a good companion emphatically the greatest benefactor.

I know there are people in the world who cannot feel grateful unless the favour has been done them at the cost of pain and difficulty. But this is a churlish disposition. A man may send you six sheets of letter-paper covered with the most entertaining gossip, or you may pass half an hour pleasantly, perhaps profitably, over an article of his; do you think the service would be greater, if he had made the manuscript in his heart's blood, like a compact with the devil? Do you really fancy you should be more beholden to your correspondent, if he had been damning you all the while for your importunity? Pleasures are more beneficial than duties because, like the quality of mercy, they are not strained, and they are twice blest.[25] There must always be two to a kiss, and there may be a score in a jest; but wherever there is an element of sacrifice, the favour is conferred with pain, and, among generous people, received with confusion.

There is no duty we so much underrate as the duty of being happy. By being happy, we sow anonymous benefits upon the world, which remain unknown even to ourselves, or when they are disclosed, surprise nobody so much as the benefactor. The other day, a ragged, barefoot boy ran down the street after a marble, with so jolly an air that he set every one he passed into a good humour; one of these persons, who had been delivered from more than usually black thoughts, stopped the little fellow and gave him some money with this remark: "You see what sometimes comes of looking pleased." If he had looked pleased before, he had now to look both pleased and mystified. For my part, I justify this encouragement of smiling rather than tearful children; I do not wish to pay for tears anywhere but upon the stage; but I am prepared to deal largely in the opposite commodity. A happy man or woman is a better thing to find than a five-pound note. He or she is a radiating focus of good will; and their entrance into a room is as though another candle had been lighted. We need not care whether they could prove the forty-seventh proposition;[26] they do a better thing than that, they practically demonstrate the great Theorem of the Liveableness of Life. Consequently, if a person cannot be happy without remaining idle, idle he should remain. It is a revolutionary precept; but, thanks to hunger and the workhouse, one not easily to be abused, and, within practical limits, it is one of the most incontestable truths in the whole Body of Morality. Look at one of your industrious fellows for a moment, I beseech you. He sows hurry and reaps indigestion; he puts a vast deal of activity out to interest, and receives a large measure of nervous derangement in return. Either he absents himself entirely from all fellowship, and lives a recluse in a garret, with carpet slippers and a leaden inkpot; or he comes among people swiftly and bitterly, in a contraction of his whole nervous system, to discharge some temper before he returns to work. I do not care how much or how well he works, this fellow is an evil feature in other people's lives. They would be happier if he were dead. They could easier do without his services in the Circumlocution Office,[27] than they can tolerate his fractious spirits. He poisons life at the well-head. It is better to be beggared out of hand by a scapegrace nephew, than daily hag-ridden by a peevish uncle.

And what, in God's name, is all this pother about? For what cause do they embitter their own and other people's lives? That a man should publish three or thirty articles a year, that he should finish or not finish his great allegorical picture, are questions of little interest to the world. The ranks of life are full; and although a thousand fall, there are always some to go into the breach. When they told Joan of Arc she should be at home minding women's work, she answered there were plenty to spin and wash. And so, even with your own rare gifts! When nature is "so careless of the single life,"[28] why should we coddle ourselves into the fancy that our own is of exceptional importance? Suppose Shakespeare had been knocked on the head some dark night in Sir Thomas Lucy's preserves,[29] the world would have wagged on better or worse, the pitcher gone to the well, the scythe to the corn, and the student to his book; and no one been any the wiser of the loss.

There are not many works extant, if you look the alternative all over, which are worth the price of a pound of tobacco to a man of limited means. This is a sobering reflection for the proudest of our earthly vanities. Even a tobacconist may, upon consideration, find no great cause for personal vainglory in the phrase; for although tobacco is an admirable sedative, the qualities necessary for retailing it are neither rare nor precious in themselves. Alas and alas! you may take it how you will, but the services of no single individual are indispensable. Atlas was just a gentleman with a protracted nightmare![30] And yet you see merchants who go and labour themselves into a great fortune and thence into the bankruptcy court; scribblers who keep scribbling at little articles until their temper is a cross to all who come about them, as though Pharaoh should set the Israelites to make a pin instead of a pyramid; and fine young men who work themselves into a decline, and are driven off in a hearse with white plumes upon it.[31] Would you not suppose these persons had been whispered, by the Master of the Ceremonies, the promise of some momentous destiny? and that this lukewarm bullet on which they play their farces was the bull's-eye and centrepoint of all the universe? And yet it is not so. The ends for which they give away their priceless youth, for all they know, may be chimerical or hurtful; the glory and riches they expect may never come, or may find them indifferent; and they and the world they inhabit are so inconsiderable that the mind freezes at the thought.

Notes

1 Boswell, *Life of Johnson*, 26 Oct. 1769.
2 *Lèse-majesté*, the treasonous crime of demeaning the monarch's dignity, wryly recast to mean insulting middle-class values.
3 According to Plutarch, Alexander the Great went to Corinth to meet the philosopher Diogenes of Sinope (412–323 BC) and found him sunbathing. Alexander asked Diogenes how he could be of service, and the philosopher answered, "Stand a little out of my sun."
4 The Gauls invaded Rome around 389 BC. According to Livy, the elderly senators sat in front of their houses in ceremonial dress to show their pride and contempt.
5 Ostracized.
6 Ammunition.
7 Thomas Babington Macaulay (1800–1859), English politician and historian, who won many academic prizes as a boy and later at Cambridge.
8 Boswell, *Life of Johnson*, 21 Jul. 1763.
9 Tennyson, "The Lady of Shalott" (1833).
10 Emphyteusis: a perpetual right in another person's land. Stillicide: the right to collect water dripping from a neighbor's roof onto one's property.
11 Novelists whose characters often develop through adversity with few educational or economic opportunities.
12 A creek.
13 A character in Bunyan's *Pilgrim's Progress* who advocates legality and civility over Christian morality.
14 A sarcastic "indeed!" used after a quotation.
15 Charles Augustin Sainte-Beuve (1804–1869), French literary critic.
16 Useless odds and ends.

17 Aptitude or competence.
18 An elevated pavilion commanding an expansive view.
19 Milton, *L'Allegro* (1645, 67–8).
20 Probably an allusion to Robert Browning's "Fra Lippo Lippi" (1855): "This world's no blot for us, / Nor blank; it means intensely, and means good: / To find its meaning is my meat and drink" (313–315).
21 Deranged, mentally unstable.
22 Characters in Thackeray's *The Newcomes* (1855).
23 The thief whom Pontius Pilate spared from crucifixion in place of Jesus (John 18:39–40).
24 English essayist William Hazlitt's impressions of the charismatic painter James Northcote (1746–1831) appear in his *Conversations with Northcote* (1830).
25 Shakespeare, *The Merchant of Venice*, 4.1.179, 181.
26 The forty-seventh proposition or Pythagorean Theorem from Euclid's *Elements*: a foundational geometry text written around 300 B.C. and commonly taught in the 19th century.
27 A fictitious, unhelpful government agency in Charles Dickens's *Little Dorrit* (1857).
28 Tennyson, *In Memoriam* (1840), 55.7–8.
29 Shakespeare was prosecuted for poaching in Sir Thomas Lucy's park at Charlecote near Stratford.
30 The Titan condemned by Zeus to hold the sky on his shoulders forever.
31 Signifying the death of a young person.

7

ORDERED SOUTH

By a curious irony of fate, the places to which we are sent when health deserts us are often singularly beautiful.[1] Often, too, they are places we have visited in former years, or seen briefly in passing by, and kept ever afterwards in pious memory; and we please ourselves with the fancy that we shall repeat many vivid and pleasurable sensations, and take up again the thread of our enjoyment in the same spirit as we let it fall. We shall now have an opportunity of finishing many pleasant excursions, interrupted of yore before our curiosity was fully satisfied. It may be that we have kept in mind, during all these years, the recollection of some valley into which we have just looked down for a moment before we lost sight of it in the disorder of the hills; it may be that we have lain awake at night, and agreeably tantalized ourselves with the thought of corners we had never turned, or summits we had all but climbed: we shall now be able, as we tell ourselves, to complete all these unfinished pleasures, and pass beyond the barriers that confined our recollections.

The promise is so great, and we are all so easily led away when hope and memory are both in one story, that I dare say the sick man is not very inconsolable when he receives sentence of banishment, and is inclined to regard his ill-health as not the least fortunate accident of his life. Nor is he immediately undeceived. The stir and speed of the journey, and the restlessness that goes to bed with him as he tries to sleep between two days of noisy progress, fever him, and stimulate his dull nerves into something of their old quickness and sensibility. And so he can enjoy the faint autumnal splendour of the landscape, as he sees hill and plain, vineyard and forest, clad in one wonderful glory of fairy gold, which the first great winds of winter will transmute, as in the fable, into withered leaves.[2] And so too he can enjoy the admirable brevity and simplicity of such little glimpses of country and country ways as flash upon him through the windows of the train; little glimpses that have a character all their own; sights seen as a travelling swallow might see them from the wing, or Iris as she went abroad over the land on some Olympian errand.[3] Here and there, indeed, a few children huzzah and wave their hands to the express; but for the most part, it is an interruption too brief and isolated to attract much notice; the sheep do not cease from browsing; a girl sits balanced on the projecting tiller of a canal boat, so precariously that it seems as if a fly or the splash of a leaping fish would be enough to overthrow the dainty equilibrium, and yet all these hundreds of tons of coal and wood and iron have been precipitated roaring past her very ear, and there is not a start, not a tremor, not a turn of the averted head, to indicate that she has been even conscious of its passage.

Herein, I think, lies the chief attraction of railway travel. The speed is so easy, and the train disturbs so little the scenes through which it takes us, that our heart becomes full of the placidity and stillness of the country; and while the body is borne forward in the flying chain of carriages, the thoughts alight, as the humour moves them, at unfrequented stations; they make haste up the poplar alley that leads toward the town; they are left behind with the signalman as, shading his eyes with his hand, he watches the long train sweep away into the golden distance.

Moreover, there is still before the invalid the shock of wonder and delight with which he will learn that he has passed the indefinable line that separates South from North. And this is an uncertain moment; for sometimes the consciousness is forced upon him early, on the occasion of some slight association, a colour, a flower, or a scent; and sometimes not until, one fine morning, he wakes up with the southern sunshine peeping through the *persiennes*,[4] and the southern patois confusedly audible below the windows. Whether it come early or late, however, this pleasure will not end with the anticipation, as do so many others of the same family. It will leave him wider awake than it found him, and give a new significance to all he may see for many days to come. There is something in the mere name of the South that carries enthusiasm along with it. At the sound of the word, he pricks up his ears; he becomes as anxious to seek out beauties and to get by heart the permanent lines and character of the landscape, as if he had been told that it was all his own—an estate out of which he had been kept unjustly, and which he was now to receive in free and full possession. Even those who have never been there before feel as if they had been; and everybody goes comparing, and seeking for the familiar, and finding it with such ecstasies of recognition, that one would think they were coming home after a weary absence, instead of travelling hourly farther abroad.

It is only after he is fairly arrived and settled down in his chosen corner, that the invalid begins to understand the change that has befallen him. Everything about him is as he had remembered, or as he had anticipated. Here, at his feet, under his eyes, are the olive gardens and the blue sea. Nothing can change the eternal magnificence of form of the naked Alps behind Mentone; nothing, not even the crude curves of the railway, can utterly deform the suavity of contour of one bay after another along the whole reach of the Riviera. And of all this, he has only a cold head knowledge that is divorced from enjoyment. He recognizes with his intelligence that this thing and that thing is beautiful, while in his heart of hearts he has to confess that it is not beautiful for him. It is in vain that he spurs his discouraged spirit; in vain that he chooses out points of view, and stands there, looking with all his eyes, and waiting for some return of the pleasure that he remembers in other days, as the sick folk may have awaited the coming of the angel at the pool of Bethesda.[5] He is like an enthusiast leading about with him a stolid, indifferent tourist. There is some one by who is out of sympathy with the scene, and is not moved up to the measure of the occasion; and that some one is himself. The world is disenchanted for him. He seems to himself to touch things with muffled hands, and to see them through a veil. His life becomes a palsied fumbling after notes that are silent when he has found and struck them. He cannot recognize that this phlegmatic and unimpressionable body with which he now goes burthened, is the same that he knew heretofore so quick and delicate and alive.

He is tempted to lay the blame on the very softness and amenity of the climate, and to fancy that in the rigours of the winter at home, these dead emotions would revive and flourish. A longing for the brightness and silence of fallen snow seizes him at such times. He is homesick for the hale rough weather; for the tracery of the frost upon his window-panes at morning, the reluctant descent of the first flakes, and the white roofs relieved against the sombre sky. And yet the stuff of which these yearnings are made, is of the flimsiest: if but the thermometer fall a little below its ordinary Mediterranean level, or a wind come down from the snow-clad Alps behind, the spirit of his fancies changes upon the instant, and many a doleful vignette of the grim wintry streets at home returns to him, and begins to haunt his memory. The hopeless, huddled attitude of tramps in doorways; the flinching gait of barefoot children on the icy pavement; the sheen of the rainy streets towards afternoon; the meagre anatomy of the poor defined by the clinging of wet garments; the high canorous note of the North-easter on days when the very houses seem to stiffen with cold: these, and such as these, crowd back upon him, and mockingly substitute themselves for the fanciful winter scenes with which he had pleased himself a while before. He cannot be glad enough that he is where he is. If only the others could be there also; if only those tramps could lie down for a little in the sunshine, and those children warm their feet, this once, upon a kindlier earth; if only there were no cold anywhere, and no nakedness, and no hunger; if only it were as well with all men as it is with him!

For it is not altogether ill with the invalid, after all. If it is only rarely that anything penetrates vividly into his numbed spirit, yet, when anything does, it brings with it a joy that is all the more poignant for its very rarity. There is something pathetic in these occasional returns of a glad activity of heart. In his lowest hours he will be stirred and awakened by many such; and they will spring perhaps from very trivial sources; as a friend once said to me, the "spirit of delight"[6] comes often on small wings. For the pleasure that we take in beautiful nature is essentially capricious. It comes sometimes when we least look for it; and sometimes, when we expect it most certainly, it leaves us to gape joylessly for days together, in the very home-land of the beautiful. We may have passed a place a thousand times and one; and on the thousand and second it will be transfigured, and stand forth in a certain splendour of reality from the dull circle of surroundings; so that we see it "with a child's first pleasure," as Wordsworth saw the daffodils by the lake side.[7] And if this falls out capriciously with the healthy, how much more so with the invalid. Some day he will find his first violet, and be lost in pleasant

72

wonder, by what alchemy the cold earth of the clods, and the vapid air and rain, can be transmuted into colour so rich and odour so touchingly sweet. Or perhaps he may see a group of washerwomen relieved, on a spit of shingle, against the blue sea, or a meeting of flower-gatherers in the tempered daylight of an olive-garden; and something significant or monumental in the grouping, something in the harmony of faint colour that is always characteristic of the dress of these southern women, will come home to him unexpectedly, and awake in him that satisfaction with which we tell ourselves that we are the richer by one more beau-tiful experience. Or it may be something even slighter: as when the opulence of the sunshine, which somehow gets lost and fails to produce its effect on the large scale, is suddenly revealed to him by the chance isolation—as he changes the posi-tion of his sunshade—of a yard or two of roadway with its stones and weeds. And then, there is no end to the infinite variety of the olive-yards themselves. Even the colour is indeterminate and continually shifting: now you would say it was green, now grey, now blue; now tree stands above tree, like "cloud on cloud,"[8] massed into filmy indistinctness; and now, at the wind's will, the whole sea of foliage is shaken and broken up with little momentary silverings and shadows. But every one sees the world in his own way. To some the glad moment may have arrived on other provocations; and their recollection may be most vivid of the stately gait of women carrying burthens on their heads; of tropical effects, with canes and naked rock and sunlight; of the relief of cypresses; of the troubled, busy-looking groups of sea-pines, that seem always as if they were being wielded and swept together by a whirlwind; of the air coming, laden with virginal perfumes, over the myrtles and the scented underwood; of the empurpled hills standing up, solemn and sharp, out of the green-gold air of the east at evening.

There go many elements, without doubt, to the making of one such moment of intense perception; and it is on the happy agreement of these many elements, on the harmonious vibration of many nerves, that the whole delight of the moment must depend. Who can forget how, when he has chanced upon some attitude of complete restfulness, after long uneasy rolling to and fro on grass or heather, the whole fashion of the landscape has been changed for him, as though the sun had just broken forth, or a great artist had only then completed, by some cunning touch, the composition of the picture? And not only a change of posture—a snatch of perfume, the sudden singing of a bird, the freshness of some pulse of air from an invisible sea, the light shadow of a travelling cloud, the merest nothing that sends a little shiver along the most infinitesimal nerve of a man's body—not one of the least of these but has a hand somehow in the general effect, and brings some refinement of its own into the character of the pleasure we feel.

And if the external conditions are thus varied and subtle, even more so are those within our own bodies. No man can find out the world, says Solomon, from beginning to end, because the world is in his heart;[9] and so it is impossible for any of us to understand, from beginning to end, that agreement of harmonious circum-stances that creates in us the highest pleasure of admiration, precisely because some of these circumstances are hidden from us for ever in the constitution of our

73

own bodies. After we have reckoned up all that we can see or hear or feel, there still remains to be taken into account some sensibility more delicate than usual in the nerves affected, or some exquisite refinement in the architecture of the brain, which is indeed to the sense of the beautiful as the eye or the ear to the sense of hearing or sight. We admire splendid views and great pictures; and yet what is truly admirable is rather the mind within us, that gathers together these scattered details for its delight, and makes out of certain colours, certain distributions of graduated light and darkness, that intelligible whole which alone we call a picture or a view. Hazlitt, relating in one of his essays how he went on foot from one great man's house to another's in search of works of art, begins suddenly to triumph over these noble or wealthy owners, because he was more capable of enjoying their costly possessions than they were; because they had paid the money and he had received the pleasure.[10] And the occasion is a fair one for self-complacency. While the one man was working to be able to buy the picture, the other was work-ing to be able to enjoy the picture. An inherited aptitude will have been diligently improved in either case; only the one man has made for himself a fortune, and the other has made for himself a living spirit.

It is a fair occasion for self-complacency, I repeat, when the event shows a man to have chosen the better part,[11] and laid out his life more wisely, in the long run, than those who have credit for most wisdom.

And yet even this is not a good unmixed; and like all other possessions, although in a less degree, the possession of a brain that has been thus improved and cultivated, and made into the prime organ of a man's enjoyment, brings with it certain inevitable cares and disappointments. The happiness of such an one comes to depend greatly upon those fine shades of sensation that heighten and harmonize the coarser elements of beauty. And thus a degree of nervous prostra-tion, that to other men would be hardly disagreeable, is enough to overthrow for him the whole fabric of his life, to take, except at rare moments, the edge off his pleasures, and to meet him wherever he goes with failure, and the sense of want, and disenchantment of the world and life.

It is not in such numbness of spirit only that the life of the invalid resembles a premature old age. Those excursions that he had promised himself to finish, prove too long or too arduous for his feeble body; and the barrier-hills are as impassable as ever. Many a white town that sits far out on the promontory, many a comely fold of wood on the mountain side, beckons and allures his imagination day after day, and is yet as inaccessible to his feet as the clefts and gorges of the clouds. The sense of distance grows upon him wonderfully; and after some feverish efforts and the fretful uneasiness of the first few days, he falls contentedly in with the restrictions of his weakness. His narrow round becomes pleasant and familiar to him as the cell to a contented prisoner. Just as he has fallen already out of the mid race of active life, he now falls out of the little eddy that circulates in the shallow waters of the sanatorium. He sees the country people come and go about their eve-ryday affairs, the foreigners stream out in goodly pleasure parties; the stir of man's activity is all about him, as he suns himself inertly in some sheltered corner; and he looks on with a patriarchal impersonality of interest, such as a man may feel when he pictures to himself the fortunes of his remote descendants, or the robust old age of the oak he has planted over-night.

In this falling aside, in this quietude and desertion of other men, there is no inharmonious prelude to the last quietude and desertion of the grave; in this dulness of the senses there is a gentle preparation for the final insensibility of death. And to him the idea of mortality comes in a shape less violent and harsh than is its wont, less as an abrupt catastrophe than as a thing of infinitesimal gradation, and the last step on a long decline of way. As we turn to and fro in bed, and every moment the movements grow feebler and smaller and the attitude more restful and easy, until sleep overtakes us at a stride and we move no more, so desire after desire leaves him; day by day his strength decreases, and the circle of his activity grows ever narrower; and he feels, if he is to be thus tenderly weaned from the passion of life, thus gradually inducted into the slumber of death, that when at last the end comes, it will come quietly and fitly. If anything is to reconcile poor spirits to the coming of the last enemy, surely it should be such a mild approach as this; not to hale us forth with violence, but to persuade us from a place we have no further pleasure in. It is not so much, indeed, death that approaches as life that withdraws and withers up from round about him. He has outlived his own usefulness, and almost his own enjoyment; and if there is to be no recovery; if never again will he be young and strong and passionate, if the actual present shall be to him always like a thing read in a book or remembered out of the far-away past; if, in fact, this be veritably nightfall, he will not wish greatly for the continuance of a twilight that only strains and disappoints the eyes, but steadfastly await the perfect darkness. He will pray for Medea: when she comes, let her either rejuvenate or slay.[12]

And yet the ties that still attach him to the world are many and kindly. The sight of children has a significance for him such as it may have for the aged also, but not for others. If he has been used to feel humanely, and to look upon life somewhat more widely than from the narrow loophole of personal pleasure and advancement, it is strange how small a portion of his thoughts will be changed or embittered by this proximity of death. He knows that already, in English counties, the sower follows the ploughman up the face of the field, and the rooks follow the sower; and he knows also that he may not live to go home again and see the corn spring and ripen, and be cut down at last, and brought home with gladness. And yet the future of this harvest, the continuance of drought or the coming of rain unseasonably, touch him as sensibly as ever. For he has long been used to wait with interest the issue of events in which his own concern was nothing; and to be joyful in a plenty, and sorrowful for a famine, that did not increase or diminish, by one half loaf, the equable sufficiency of his own supply.

Thus there remain unaltered all the disinterested hopes for mankind and a better future which have been the solace and inspiration of his life. These he has set beyond the reach of any fate that only menaces himself; and it makes small difference whether he die five thousand years, or five thousand and fifty years, before the good epoch for which he faithfully labours. He has not deceived himself; he has known from the beginning that he followed the pillar of fire and cloud, only to perish himself in the wilderness, and that it was reserved for others to enter joyfully into possession of the land.[13] And so, as everything grows greyer and quieter about him, and slopes towards extinction, these unfaded visions accompany his sad decline, and follow him, with friendly voices and hopeful words, into the very vestibule of death. The desire of love or of fame scarcely moved him, in his days of health, more strongly than these generous aspirations move him now; and so life is carried forward beyond life, and a vista kept open for the eyes of hope, even when his hands grope already on the face of the impassable.

Lastly, he is bound tenderly to life by the thought of his friends; or shall we not say rather, that by their thought for him, by their unchangeable solicitude and love, he remains woven into the very stuff of life, beyond the power of bodily dissolution to undo? In a thousand ways will he survive and be perpetuated. Much of Etienne de la Boetie survived during all the years in which Montaigne continued to converse with him on the pages of the ever-delightful essays.[14] Much of what was truly Goethe was dead already when he revisited places that knew him no more, and found no better consolation than the promise of his own verses, that soon he too would be at rest.[15] Indeed, when we think of what it is that we most seek and cherish, and find most pride and pleasure in calling ours, it will sometimes seem to us as if our friends, at our decease, would suffer loss more truly than ourselves. As a monarch who should care more for the outlying colonies he knows on the map or through the report of his vicegerents, than for the trunk of his empire under his eyes at home, are we not more concerned about the shadowy life that we have in the hearts of others, and that portion in their thoughts and fancies which, in a certain far-away sense, belongs to us, than about the real knot of our identity—that central metropolis of self, of which alone we are immediately aware—or the diligent service of arteries and veins, and infinitesimal activity of ganglia, which we know (as we know a proposition in Euclid) to be the source and substance of the whole? At the death of every one whom we love, some fair and honourable portion of our existence falls away, and we are dislodged from one of these dear provinces; and they are not, perhaps, the most fortunate who survive a long series of such impoverishments, till their life and influence narrow gradually into the meagre limit of their own spirits, and death, when he comes at last, can destroy them at one blow.

NOTE.—To this essay I must in honesty append a word or two of qualification; for this is one of the points on which a slightly greater age teaches us a slightly different wisdom:

A youth delights in generalities, and keeps loose from particular obligations; he jogs on the footpath way, himself pursuing butterflies, but courteously lending his applause to the advance of the human species and the coming of the kingdom of justice and love. As he grows older, he begins to think more narrowly of man's action in the general, and perhaps more arrogantly of his own in the particular. He has not that same unspeakable trust in what he would have done had he been spared, seeing finally that that would have been little; but he has a far higher notion of the blank that he will make by dying. A young man feels himself one too many in the world; his is a painful situation: he has no calling; no obvious utility; no ties, but to his parents, and these he is sure to disregard. I do not think that a proper allowance has been made for this true cause of suffering in youth; but by the mere fact of a prolonged existence, we outgrow either the fact or else the feeling. Either we become so callously accustomed to our own useless figure in the world, or else—and this, thank God, in the majority of cases—we so collect about us the interest or the love of our fellows, so multiply our effective part in the affairs of life, that we need to entertain no longer the question of our right to be.

And so in the majority of cases, a man who fancies himself dying, will get cold comfort from the very youthful view expressed in this essay. He, as a living man, has some to help, some to love, some to correct; it may be, some to punish. These duties cling, not upon humanity, but upon the man himself. It is he, not another, who is one woman's son and a second woman's husband and a third woman's father. That life which began so small, has now grown, with a myriad filaments, into the lives of others. It is not indispensable; another will take the place and shoulder the discharged responsibility; but the better the man and the nobler his purposes, the more will he be tempted to regret the extinction of his powers and the deletion of his personality. To have lived a generation, is not only to have grown at home in that perplexing medium, but to have assumed innumerable duties. To die at such an age, has, for all but the entirely base, something of the air of a betrayal. A man does not only reflect upon what he might have done in a future that is never to be his; but beholding himself so early a deserter from the fight, he eats his heart for the good he might have done already. To have been so useless and now to lose all hope of being useful any more—there it is that death and memory assail him. And even if mankind shall go on, founding heroic cities, practising heroic virtues, rising steadily from strength to strength; even if his work shall be fulfilled, his friends consoled, his wife remarried by a better than he; how shall this alter, in one jot, his estimation of a career which was his only business in this world, which was so fitfully pursued, and which is now so ineffectively to end?

Notes

1 Stevenson was sent by doctor's orders to Mentone, France for the winter of 1873–1874.
2 In the *Arabian Nights* tale "The History of the Barber's Fourth Brother," a magician pays with coins that turn into leaves.
3 Iris, goddess of the rainbow and messenger of the gods.
4 Louvered exterior window shutters.
5 John 5:2–4.
6 "Rarely, rarely, comest thou, / Spirit of Delight"—P.B. Shelley, "Song" (1820), 1–2.
7 See William Wordsworth's "I wandered lonely as a cloud" and "My heart leaps up."
8 John Keats, *Hyperion* (1820) 1.7.
9 Ecclesiastes 3:11.

10 Hazlitt's "On the Pleasure of Painting" (1821).

11 Luke 10:42.

12 Medea, a witch in Ovid's Metamorphoses who kills an old ram and restores it as a young lamb (7.312–321).

13 Moses led the Israelites through the wilderness, guided by a cloud by day and a pillar of fire by night, but was ultimately kept from the Promised Land himself (Exodus 13:21, Deuteronomy 32:50).

14 Étienne de La Boétie (1530–1563), French judge and Montaigne's intimate friend, celebrated in his essay "On Friendship" (1580).

15 The final lines of Goethe's "Wandrers Nachtlied II" (1780). According to G.H. Lewes's *Life of Goethe* (1855), Goethe wrote these lines on the wall of a mountain hut in his youth and wept to return and reread the line months before his death.

8

ÆS TRIPLEX[1]

The changes wrought by death are in themselves so sharp and final, and so terrible and melancholy in their consequences, that the thing stands alone in man's experience, and has no parallel upon earth. It outdoes all other accidents because it is the last of them. Sometimes it leaps suddenly upon its victims, like a Thug;[2] sometimes it lays a regular siege and creeps upon their citadel during a score of years. And when the business is done, there is sore havoc made in other people's lives, and a pin knocked out by which many subsidiary friendships hung together. There are empty chairs, solitary walks, and single beds at night. Again, in taking away our friends, death does not take them away utterly, but leaves behind a mocking, tragical, and soon intolerable residue, which must be hurriedly concealed. Hence a whole chapter of sights and customs striking to the mind, from the pyramids of Egypt to the gibbets and dule trees[3] of mediæval Europe. The poorest persons have a bit of pageant going towards the tomb; memorial stones are set up over the least memorable; and, in order to preserve some show of respect for what remains of our old loves and friendships, we must accompany it with much grimly ludicrous ceremonial, and the hired undertaker parades before the door. All this, and much more of the same sort, accompanied by the eloquence of poets, has gone a great way to put humanity in error; nay, in many philosophies the error has been embodied and laid down with every circumstance of logic; although in real life the bustle and swiftness, in leaving people little time to think, have not left them time enough to go dangerously wrong in practice.

As a matter of fact, although few things are spoken of with more fearful whisperings than this prospect of death, few have less influence on conduct under healthy circumstances. We have all heard of cities in South America built upon the side of fiery mountains, and how, even in this tremendous neighbourhood, the inhabitants are not a jot more impressed by the solemnity of mortal conditions than if they were delving gardens in the greenest corner of England. There are serenades and suppers and much gallantry among the myrtles overhead; and meanwhile the foundation shudders underfoot, the bowels of the mountain growl, and at any moment living ruin may leap sky-high into the moonlight, and tumble man and his merry-making in the dust. In the eyes of very young people, and very dull old ones, there is something indescribably reckless and desperate in such a picture. It seems not credible that respectable married people, with umbrellas, should find appetite for a bit of supper within quite a long distance of a fiery mountain; ordinary life begins to smell of high-handed debauch when it is carried on so close to a catastrophe; and even cheese and salad, it seems, could hardly be relished in such circumstances without something like a defiance of the Creator. It should be a place for nobody but hermits dwelling in prayer and maceration, or mere born-devils drowning care in a perpetual carouse.

And yet, when one comes to think upon it calmly, the situation of these South American citizens forms only a very pale figure for the state of ordinary mankind. This world itself, travelling blindly and swiftly in overcrowded space, among a million other worlds travelling blindly and swiftly in contrary directions, may very well come by a knock that would set it into explosion like a penny squib. And what, pathologically looked at, is the human body with all its organs, but a mere bagful of petards? The least of these is as dangerous to the whole economy as the ship's powder-magazine to the ship; and with every breath we breathe, and every meal we eat, we are putting one or more of them in peril. If we clung as devotedly as some philosophers pretend we do to the abstract idea of life, or were half as frightened as they make out we are, for the subversive accident that ends it all, the trumpets might sound by the hour and no one would follow them into battle—the blue-peter might fly at the truck,[4] but who would climb into a sea-going ship? Think (if these philosophers were right) with what a preparation of spirit we should affront the daily peril of the dinner-table: a deadlier spot than any battle-field in history; where the far greater proportion of our ancestors have miserably left their bones! What woman would ever be lured into marriage, so much more danger-ous than the wildest sea? And what would it be to grow old? For, after a certain distance, every step we take in life we find the ice growing thinner below our feet, and all around us and behind us we see our contemporaries going through. By the time a man gets well into the seventies, his continued existence is a mere miracle; and when he lays his old bones in bed for the night, there is an overwhelming prob-ability that he will never see the day. Do the old men mind it, as a matter of fact? Why, no. They were never merrier; they have their grog at night, and tell the raciest stories; they hear of the death of people about their own age, or even younger, not as if it was a grisly warning, but with a simple childlike pleasure at having outlived some one else; and when a draught might puff them out like a guttering candle, or a bit of a stumble shatter them like so much glass, their old hearts keep sound and unaffrighted, and they go on, bubbling with laughter, through years of man's age compared to which the valley at Balaklava[5] was as safe and peaceful as a village cricket-green on Sunday. It may fairly be questioned (if we look to the peril only) whether it was a much more daring feat for Curtius to plunge into the gulf,[6] than for any old gentleman of ninety to doff his clothes and clamber into bed.

Indeed, it is a memorable subject for consideration, with what unconcern and gaiety mankind pricks on along the Valley of the Shadow of Death.[7] The whole way is one wilderness of snares, and the end of it, for those who fear the last pinch, is irrevocable ruin. And yet we go spinning through it all, like a party for the Derby.[8] Perhaps the reader remembers one of the humorous devices of the deified Caligula: how he encouraged a vast concourse of holiday-makers on to his bridge over Baiæ bay; and when they were in the height of their enjoyment, turned loose the Prætorian guards among the company, and had them tossed into the sea.[9] This is no bad miniature of the dealings of nature with the transitory race of man. Only, what a chequered picnic we have of it, even while it lasts! and into what great waters, not to be crossed by any swimmer, God's pale Praetorian throws us over in the end!

We live the time that a match flickers; we pop the cork of a ginger-beer bottle, and the earthquake swallows us on the instant. Is it not odd, is it not incongruous, is it not, in the highest sense of human speech, incredible, that we should think so highly of the ginger-beer, and regard so little the devouring earthquake? The love of Life and the fear of Death are two famous phrases that grow harder to understand the more we think about them. It is a well-known fact that an immense proportion of boat accidents would never happen if people held the sheet in their hands instead of making it fast; and yet, unless it be some martinet of a profes-sional mariner or some landsman with shattered nerves, every one of God's crea-tures makes it fast.[10] A strange instance of man's unconcern and brazen boldness in the face of death!

We confound ourselves with metaphysical phrases, which we import into daily talk with noble inappropriateness. We have no idea of what death is, apart from its circumstances and some of its consequences to others; and although we have some experience of living, there is not a man on earth who has flown so high into abstraction as to have any practical guess at the meaning of the word *life*. All literature, from Job and Omar Khayam to Thomas Carlyle or Walt Whitman,[11] is but an attempt to look upon the human state with such largeness of view as shall enable us to rise from the consideration of living to the Definition of Life. And our sages give us about the best satisfaction in their power when they say that it is a vapour, or a show, or made out of the same stuff with dreams.[12] Philosophy, in its more rigid sense, has been at the same work for ages; and after a myriad bald heads have wagged over the problem, and piles of words have been heaped one upon another into dry and cloudy volumes without end, philosophy has the hon-our of laying before us, with modest pride, her contribution towards the subject: that life is a Permanent Possibility of Sensation.[13] Truly a fine result! A man may very well love beef, or hunting, or a woman; but surely, surely, not a Permanent Possibility of Sensation! He may be afraid of a precipice, or a dentist, or a large enemy with a club, or even an undertaker's man; but not certainly of abstract death. We may trick with the word life in its dozen senses until we are weary of tricking; we may argue in terms of all the philosophies on earth, but one fact remains true throughout—that we do not love life, in the sense that we are greatly preoccupied about its conservation; that we do not, properly speaking, love life at all, but living.

Into the views of the least careful there will enter some degree of providence;[14] no man's eyes are fixed entirely on the passing hour; but although we have some anticipation of good health, good weather, wine, active employment, love, and self-approval, the sum of these anticipations does not amount to anything like a general view of life's possibilities and issues; nor are those who cherish them most vividly, at all the most scrupulous of their personal safety. To be deeply interested in the accidents of our existence, to enjoy keenly the mixed texture of human experience, rather leads a man to disregard precautions, and risk his neck against a straw. For surely the love of living is stronger in an Alpine climber roping over a peril, or a hunter riding merrily at a stiff fence, than in a creature who lives upon a diet and walks a measured distance in the interest of his constitution.

There is a great deal of very vile nonsense talked upon both sides of the matter: tearing divines reducing life to the dimensions of a mere funeral procession, so short as to be hardly decent; and melancholy unbelievers yearning for the tomb as if it were a world too far away. Both sides must feel a little ashamed of their performances now and again when they draw in their chairs to dinner. Indeed, a good meal and a bottle of wine is an answer to most standard works upon the question. When a man's heart warms to his viands, he forgets a great deal of sophistry, and soars into a rosy zone of contemplation. Death may be knocking at the door, like the Commander's statue;[15] we have something else in hand, thank God, and let him knock. Passing bells[16] are ringing all the world over. All the world over, and every hour, some one is parting company with all his aches and ecstasies. For us also the trap is laid. But we are so fond of life that we have no leisure to entertain the terror of death. It is a honeymoon with us all through, and none of the longest. Small blame to us if we give our whole hearts to this glowing bride of ours, to the appetites, to honour, to the hungry curiosity of the mind, to the pleasure of the eyes in nature, and the pride of our own nimble bodies.

We all of us appreciate the sensations; but as for caring about the Permanence of the Possibility, a man's head is generally very bald, and his senses very dull, before he comes to that. Whether we regard life as a lane leading to a dead wall— a mere bag's end,[17] as the French say—or whether we think of it as a vestibule or gymnasium, where we wait our turn and prepare our faculties for some more noble destiny; whether we thunder in a pulpit, or pule in little atheistic poetry-books, about its vanity and brevity; whether we look justly for years of health and vigour, or are about to mount into a bath-chair,[18] as a step towards the hearse; in each and all of these views and situations there is but one conclusion possible: that a man should stop his ears against paralyzing terror, and run the race that is set before him with a single mind. No one surely could have recoiled with more heartache and terror from the thought of death than our respected lexicographer;[19] and yet we know how little it affected his conduct, how wisely and boldly he walked, and in what a fresh and lively vein he spoke of life. Already an old man, he ventured on his Highland tour;[20] and his heart, bound with triple brass, did not recoil before twenty-seven individual cups of tea. As courage and intelligence are the two qualities best worth a good man's cultivation, so it is the first part of intelligence to recognize our precarious estate in life, and the first part of courage to be not at all abashed before the fact. A frank and somewhat headlong carriage, not looking too anxiously before, not dallying in maudlin regret over the past, stamps the man who is well armoured for this world.

And not only well armoured for himself, but a good friend and a good citizen to boot. We do not go to cowards for tender dealing; there is nothing so cruel as panic; the man who has least fear for his own carcase, has most time to consider others. That eminent chemist[21] who took his walks abroad in tin shoes, and subsisted wholly upon tepid milk, had all his work cut out for him in considerate dealings with his own digestion. So soon as prudence has begun to grow up in the brain, like a dismal fungus, it finds its first expression in a paralysis of generous acts. The victim begins to shrink spiritually; he develops a fancy for parlours with a regulated temperature, and takes his morality on the principle of tin shoes and tepid milk. The care of one important body or soul becomes so engrossing, that all the noises of the outer world begin to come thin and faint into the parlour with the regulated temperature; and the tin shoes go equably forward over blood and rain. To be overwise is to ossify; and the scruple-monger ends by standing stockstill. Now the man who has his heart on his sleeve, and a good whirling weathercock of a brain, who reckons his life as a thing to be dashingly used and cheerfully hazarded, makes a very different acquaintance of the world, keeps all his pulses going true and fast, and gathers impetus as he runs, until, if he be running towards anything better than wildfire,[22] he may shoot up and become a constellation in the end. Lord look after his health, Lord have a care of his soul, says he; and he has at the key of the position, and swashes through incongruity and peril towards his aim. Death is on all sides of him with pointed batteries, as he is on all sides of all of us; unfortunate surprises gird him round; mim-mouthed[23] friends and relations hold up their hands in quite a little elegiacal synod about his path: and what cares he for all this? Being a true lover of living, a fellow with something pushing and spontaneous in his inside, he must, like any other soldier, in any other stirring, deadly warfare, push on at his best pace until he touch the goal. "A peerage or Westminster Abbey!" cried Nelson in his bright, boyish, heroic manner.[24] These are great incentives; not for any of these, but for the plain satisfaction of living, of being about their business in some sort or other, do the brave, serviceable men of every nation tread down the nettle danger,[25] and pass flyingly over all the stumbling-blocks of prudence. Think of the heroism of Johnson, think of that superb indifference to mortal limitation that set him upon his dictionary, and carried him through triumphantly until the end! Who, if he were wisely considerate of things at large, would ever embark upon any work much more considerable than a halfpenny post card? Who would project a serial novel, after Thackeray and Dickens had each fallen in mid-course?[26] Who would find heart enough to begin to live, if he dallied with the consideration of death?

And, after all, what sorry and pitiful quibbling all this is! To forego all the issues of living in a parlour with a regulated temperature—as if that were not to die a hundred times over, and for ten years at a stretch! As if it were not to die in one's own lifetime, and without even the sad immunities of death! As if it were not to die, and yet be the patient spectators of our own pitiable change! The Permanent

Possibility is preserved, but the sensations carefully held at arm's length, as if one kept a photographic plate in a dark chamber. It is better to lose health like a spendthrift than to waste it like a miser. It is better to live and be done with it, than to die daily in the sick-room. By all means begin your folio; even if the doctor does not give you a year, even if he hesitates about a month, make one brave push and see what can be accomplished in a week. It is not only in finished undertakings that we ought to honour useful labour. A spirit goes out of the man who means execution, which outlives the most untimely ending. All who have meant good work with their whole hearts, have done good work, although they may die before they have the time to sign it. Every heart that has beat strong and cheerfully has left a hopeful impulse behind it in the world, and bettered the tradition of mankind. And even if death catch people, like an open pitfall, and in mid-career, laying out vast projects, and planning monstrous foundations, flushed with hope, and their mouths full of boastful language, they should be at once tripped up and silenced: is there not something brave and spirited in such a termination? And does not life go down with a better grace, foaming in full body over a precipice, than miserably straggling to an end in sandy deltas?

When the Greeks made their fine saying that those whom the gods love die young, I cannot help believing they had this sort of death also in their eye. For surely, at whatever age it overtake the man, this is to die young. Death has not been suffered to take so much as an illusion from his heart. In the hot-fit of life, a-tiptoe on the highest point of being, he passes at a bound on to the other side. The noise of the mallet and chisel is scarcely quenched, the trumpets are hardly done blowing, when, trailing with him clouds of glory,[27] this happy-starred, full-blooded spirit shoots into the spiritual land.

Notes

1 Triple brass (Latin). Horace, *Odes*, I.3. "Illi robur et *aes* triplex / Circa pectus erat": "Strong oak and triple brass / Armored his heart."
2 Thugs: originally an Indian cult of robbers and assassins.
3 Trees historically used in Scotland as gallows.
4 Blue-peter: a blue flag with a white square signaling immediate sailing; truck: platform on top of a mast.
5 The Battle of Balaclava, 25 Oct. 1854, was a Russian Victory over British allied forces in the Crimean War (1853–1856), commemorated in Tennyson's "The Charge of the Light Brigade" (1854).
6 In mythology, Marcus Curtius rode into a giant crevice in the Roman Forum, sacrificing himself to appease the gods.
7 Psalms 23:4.
8 Annual horse race at Epsom near London.
9 The Roman emperor Caligula (AD 12–41) declared himself a god and built a three-mile bridge across the Baiae Bay near Naples. Praetorian Guard: the emperor's elite security force.
10 "Sheet": the rope directing a small vessel's sail. It is safer, though less convenient, to hold it in case of sudden wind change than to "make it fast" or tie the rope in place.

11 The biblical Book of Job explores God's role in human suffering; *Rubaiyat* is a materialist Persian poem by Omar Khayyam (1048–1131) translated by Edward FitzGerald (1809–1883); English historian and essayist Thomas Carlyle (1795–1881) stresses moral duty; Walt Whitman's (1819–1892) poetry celebrates physical sensation and openness to experience.

12 Shakespeare, *The Tempest*, 4.1.156–157.

13 John Stuart Mill's definition of matter in *Sir William Hamilton's Philosophy* (1865).

14 Careful management.

15 In Mozart's *Don Giovanni* (1787), the statue of the dead Commendatore Don Pedro knocks at Don Giovanni's door and carries him to hell.

16 Funeral bells.

17 A cul-de-sac: "bottom of the bag."

18 A covered wheelchair.

19 Samuel Johnson (1709–1784) compiled the authoritative *Dictionary of the English Language* (1755).

20 Johnson narrated his 1773 travels in the Scottish Highlands and outer islands at age 63 in *A Journey to the Western Islands of Scotland* (1775).

21 Scottish chemist Joseph Black (1728–1799), known for his frail health and careful living.

22 A will-o'-the-wisp, an illusion.

23 Prim or demure.

24 Nelson reportedly said this on the eve of the Battle of the Nile (1 Aug. 1798), meaning survival and a title or a hero's death.

25 Shakespeare, *1 Henry IV*, 2.4.8–9.

26 Both Thackeray and Dickens died before completing their final novels: *Denis Duval* (1863) and *The Mystery of Edwin Drood* (1870), respectively. Stevenson was writing his last novel, the ambitious and unfinished *Weir of Hermiston* (1896), the morning of his death.

27 Wordsworth, "Ode: Intimations" (65).

9

EL DORADO[1]

It seems as if a great deal were attainable in a world where there are so many marriages and decisive battles, and where we all, at certain hours of the day, and with great gusto and despatch, stow a portion of victuals finally and irretrievably into the bag which contains us. And it would seem also, on a hasty view, that the attainment of as much as possible was the one goal of man's contentious life. And yet, as regards the spirit, this is but a semblance. We live in an ascending scale when we live happily, one thing leading to another in an endless series. There is always a new horizon for onward-looking men, and although we dwell on a small planet, immersed in petty business and not enduring beyond a brief period of years, we are so constituted that our hopes are inaccessible, like stars, and the term of hoping is prolonged until the term of life. To be truly happy is a question of how we begin and not of how we end, of what we want and not of what we have. An aspiration is a joy for ever,[2] a possession as solid as a landed estate, a fortune which we can never exhaust and which gives us year by year a revenue of pleasurable activity. To have many of these is to be spiritually rich. Life is only a very dull and ill-directed theatre unless we have some interests in the piece; and to those who have neither art nor science, the world is a mere arrangement of colours, or a rough footway where they may very well break their shins. It is in virtue of his own desires and curiosities that any man continues to exist with even patience, that he is charmed by the look of things and people, and that he wakens every morning with a renewed appetite for work and pleasure. Desire and curiosity are the two eyes through which he sees the world in the most enchanted colours: it is they that make women beautiful or fossils interesting: and the man may squander his estate and come to beggary, but if he keeps these two amulets he is still rich in the possibilities of pleasure. Suppose he could take one meal so compact and comprehensive that he should never hunger any more; suppose him, at a glance, to take in all the features of the world and allay the desire for knowledge; suppose him to do the like in any province of experience—would not that man be in a poor way for amusement ever after?

One who goes touring on foot with a single volume in his knapsack reads with circumspection, pausing often to reflect, and often laying the book down to contemplate the landscape or the prints in the inn parlour; for he fears to come to an end of his entertainment, and be left companionless on the last stages of his journey. A young fellow recently finished the works of Thomas Carlyle, winding up, if we remember aright, with the ten note-books upon Frederick the Great.[3] "What!" cried the young fellow, in consternation, "is there no more Carlyle? Am I left to the daily papers?" A more celebrated instance is that of Alexander, who wept bitterly because he had no more worlds to subdue.[4] And when Gibbon had finished the *Decline and Fall*, he had only a few moments of joy; and it was with a "sober melancholy" that he parted from his labours.[5]

Happily we all shoot at the moon with ineffectual arrows; our hopes are set on inaccessible El Dorado; we come to an end of nothing here below. Interests are only plucked up to sow themselves again, like mustard. You would think, when the child was born, there would be an end to trouble; and yet it is only the beginning of fresh anxieties; and when you have seen it through its teething and its education and at last its marriage, alas! it is only to have new fears, new quivering sensibilities, with every day; and the health of your children's children grows as touching a concern as that of your own. Again, when you have married your wife, you would think you were got upon a hill-top, and might begin to go downward by an easy slope. But you have only ended courting to begin marriage. Falling in love and winning love are often difficult tasks to overbearing and rebellious spirits; but to keep in love is also a business of some importance, to which both man and wife must bring kindness and goodwill. The true love story commences at the altar, when there lies before the married pair a most beautiful contest of wisdom and generosity, and a life-long struggle towards an unattainable ideal. Unattainable? Aye, surely unattainable, from the very fact that they are two instead of one.

"Of making books there is no end,"[6] complained the Preacher; and did not perceive how highly he was praising letters as an occupation. There is no end, indeed, to making books or experiments, or to travel, or to gathering wealth. Problem gives rise to problem. We may study for ever, and we are never as learned as we would. We have never made a statue worthy of our dreams. And when we have discovered a continent, or crossed a chain of mountains, it is only to find another ocean or another plain upon the further side. In the infinite universe there is room for our swiftest diligence and to spare. It is not like the works of Carlyle, which can be read to an end. Even in a corner of it, in a private park, or in the neighbourhood of a single hamlet, the weather and the seasons keep so deftly changing that although we walk there for a lifetime there will be always something new to startle and delight us.

There is only one wish realizable on the earth; only one thing that can be perfectly attained: Death. And from a variety of circumstances we have no one to tell us whether it be worth attaining.

A strange picture we make on our way to our chimæras, ceaselessly marching, grudging ourselves the time for rest; indefatigable, adventurous pioneers. It is true that we shall never reach the goal; it is even more than probable that there is no such place; and if we lived for centuries and were endowed with the powers of a god, we should find ourselves not much nearer what we wanted at the end. O toiling hands of mortals![7] O unwearied feet, travelling ye know not whither! Soon, soon, it seems to you, you must come forth on some conspicuous[8] hilltop, and but a little way further, against the setting sun, descry the spires of El Dorado. Little do ye know your own blessedness; for to travel hopefully is a better thing than to arrive, and the true success is to labour.

Notes

1 The legendary golden city Spanish conquistadores sought in vain, symbolizing an unattainable or illusory ideal.
2 "A thing of beauty is a joy forever"—Keats, *Endymion* (1818), 1.1.
3 Chapman & Hall's ten-volume edition of Thomas Carlyle's *History of Frederick the Great* (1873).
4 According to Plutarch, Alexander the Great (356–323 BC) asked Anaxarchus, "Is it not a matter for tears that, when the number of worlds is infinite, I have not conquered one?"
5 Edward Gibbon's six-volume *The History of the Decline and Fall of the Roman Empire* (1776–89).
6 Ecclesiastes 12:12.
7 *Sophocles, with English Notes*, 2 vols. (1859), II, 292.
8 With extensive views.

10

THE ENGLISH ADMIRALS

"Whether it be wise in men to do such actions or no, I am sure it is
so in States to honour them."
— Sir William Temple.[1]

There is one story of the wars of Rome which I have always very much envied for England. Germanicus was going down at the head of the legions into a dangerous river—on the opposite bank the woods were full of Germans—when there flew out seven great eagles which seemed to marshal the Romans on their way; they did not pause or waver, but disappeared into the forest where the enemy lay concealed.[2] "Forward!" cried Germanicus, with a fine rhetorical inspiration. "Forward! and follow the Roman birds." It would be a very heavy spirit that did not give a leap at such a signal, and a very timorous one that continued to have any doubt of success. To appropriate the eagles as fellow-countrymen was to make imaginary allies of the forces of nature; the Roman Empire and its military fortunes, and along with these the prospects of those individual Roman legionaries now fording a river in Germany, looked altogether greater and more hopeful. It is a kind of illusion easy to produce. A particular shape of cloud, the appearance of a particular star, the holiday of some particular saint, anything in short to remind the combatants of patriotic legends or old successes, may be enough to change the issue of a pitched battle;[3] for it gives to the one party a feeling that Right and the larger interests are with them.

If an Englishman wishes to have such a feeling, it must be about the sea. The lion[4] is nothing to us; he has not been taken to the hearts of the people, and naturalized as an English emblem. We know right well that a lion would fall foul of us as grimly as he would of a Frenchman or a Moldavian Jew, and we do not carry him before us in the smoke of battle. But the sea is our approach and bulwark; it has been the scene of our greatest triumphs and dangers; and we are accustomed in lyrical strains to claim it as our own. The prostrating experiences of foreigners between Calais and Dover have always an agreeable side to English prepossessions. A man from Bedfordshire, who does not know one end of the ship from the other until she begins to move, swaggers among such persons with a sense of hereditary nautical experience. To suppose yourself endowed with natural parts for the sea because you are the countryman of Blake and mighty Nelson,[5] is perhaps just as unwarrantable as to imagine Scotch extraction a sufficient guarantee that you will look well in a kilt. But the feeling is there, and seated beyond the reach of argument. We should consider ourselves unworthy of our descent if we did not share the arrogance of our progenitors, and please ourselves with the pretension that the sea is English. Even where it is looked upon by the guns and battlements of another nation we regard it as a kind of English cemetery, where the bones of our seafaring fathers take their rest until the last trumpet;[6] for I suppose no other nation has lost as many ships, or sent as many brave fellows to the bottom.

There is nowhere such a background for heroism as the noble, terrifying, and picturesque conditions of some of our sea fights. Hawke's battle in the tempest,[7] and Aboukir at the moment when the French Admiral blew up,[8] reach the limit of what is imposing to the imagination. And our naval annals owe some of their interest to the fantastic and beautiful appearance of old war-ships and the romance that invests the sea and everything sea-going in the eyes of English lads on a half-holiday at the coast. Nay, and what we know of the misery between decks enhances the bravery of what was done by giving it something for contrast. We like to know that these bold and honest fellows contrived to live, and to keep bold and honest, among absurd and vile surroundings.

No reader can forget the description of the *Thunder* in *Roderick Random*:[9] the disorderly tyranny; the cruelty and dirt of officers and men; deck after deck, each with some new object of offence; the hospital, where the hammocks were huddled together with but fourteen inches space for each; the cockpit, far under water, where, "in an intolerable stench," the spectacled steward kept the accounts of the different messes; and the canvas enclosure, six feet square, in which Morgan made flip and salmagundi,[10] smoked his pipe, sang his Welsh songs, and swore his queer Welsh imprecations. There are portions of this business on board the *Thunder* over which the reader passes lightly and hurriedly, like a traveller in a malarious country. It is easy enough to understand the opinion of Dr. Johnson: "Why, sir," he said, "no man will be a sailor who has contrivance enough to get himself into a jail."[11] You would fancy any one's spirit would die out under such an accumulation of darkness, noisomeness, and injustice, above all when he had not come there of his own free will, but under the cutlasses and bludgeons of the press-gang. But perhaps a watch on deck in the sharp sea air put a man on his mettle again; a battle must have been a capital relief; and prize-money, bloodily earned and grossly squandered, opened the doors of the prison for a twinkling. Somehow or other, at least, this worst of possible lives could not overlie the spirit and gaiety of our sailors; they did their duty as though they had some interest in the fortune of that country which so cruelly oppressed them, they served their guns merrily when it came to fighting, and they had the readiest ear for a bold, honourable sentiment, of any class of men the world ever produced.

Most men of high destinies have high-sounding names.[12] Pym and Habakkuk may do pretty well, but they must not think to cope with the Cromwells and

Isaiahs. And you could not find a better case in point than that of the English Admirals. Drake and Rooke and Hawke are picked names for men of execution. Frobisher, Rodney, Boscawen, Foul-Weather Jack Byron, are all good to catch the eye in a page of a naval history. Cloudesley Shovel is a mouthful of quaint and sounding syllables. Benbow has a bulldog quality that suits the man's character, and it takes us back to those English archers who were his true comrades for plainness, tenacity, and pluck. Raleigh is spirited and martial, and signifies an act of bold conduct in the field.[13] It is impossible to judge of Blake or Nelson, no names current among men being worthy of such heroes. But still it is odd enough, and very appropriate in this connection, that the latter was greatly taken with his Sicilian title. "The signification, perhaps, pleased him," says Southey; "Duke of Thunder was what in Dahomey would have been called a *strong name*; it was to a sailor's taste, and certainly to no man could it be more applicable."[14] Admiral in itself is one of the most satisfactory of distinctions, it has a noble sound and a very proud history; and Columbus thought so highly of it, that he enjoined his heirs to sign themselves by that title as long as the house should last.[15]

But it is the spirit of the men, and not their names, that I wish to speak about in this paper. That spirit is truly English; they, and not Tennyson's cotton-spinners[16] or Mr. D'Arcy Thompson's Abstract Bagman,[17] are the true and typical Englishmen. There may be more *head* of bagmen in the country, but human beings are reckoned by number only in political constitutions. And the Admirals are typical in the full force of the word. They are splendid examples of virtue, indeed, but of a virtue in which most Englishmen can claim a moderate share; and what we admire in their lives is a sort of apotheosis of ourselves. Almost everybody in our land, except humanitarians[18] and a few persons whose youth has been depressed by exceptionally æsthetic surroundings, can understand and sympathize with an Admiral or a prize-fighter. I do not wish to bracket Benbow and Tom Cribb; but, depend upon it, they are practically bracketed for admiration in the minds of many frequenters of ale-houses. If you told them about Germanicus and the eagles, or Regulus going back to Carthage,[19] they would very likely fall asleep; but tell them about Harry Pearce and Jem Belcher, or about Nelson and the Nile, and they put down their pipes to listen. I have by me a copy of *Boxiana*,[20] on the fly-leaves of which a youthful member of the fancy[21] kept a chronicle of remarkable events and an obituary of great men. Here we find piously chronicled the demise of jockeys, watermen,[22] and pugilists—Johnny Moore, of the Liverpool Prize Ring; Tom Spring,[23] aged fifty-six; "Pierce Egan, senior, writer of *Boxiana* and other sporting works"—and among all these, the Duke of Wellington![24] If Benbow had lived in the time of this annalist, do you suppose his name would not have been added to the glorious roll? In short, we do not all feel warmly towards Wesley or Laud, we cannot all take pleasure in *Paradise Lost*;[25] but there are certain common sentiments and touches of nature by which the whole nation is made to feel kinship. A little while ago everybody, from Hazlitt and John Wilson[26] down to the imbecile creature who scribbled his register on the fly-leaves of *Boxiana*, felt a more or less shamefaced satisfaction in the exploits of prize-fighters. And the exploits of the Admirals are popular to the same degree, and tell in all ranks of society. Their sayings and doings stir English blood like the sound of a trumpet; and if the Indian Empire, the trade of London, and all the outward and visible ensigns of our greatness should pass away, we should still leave behind us a durable monument of what we were in these sayings and doings of the English Admirals.

Duncan, lying off the Texel with his own flagship, the *Venerable*, and only one other vessel, heard that the whole Dutch fleet was putting to sea. He told Captain Hotham to anchor alongside of him in the narrowest part of the channel, and fight his vessel till she sank. "I have taken the depth of the water," added he, "and when the *Venerable* goes down, my flag will still fly."[27] And you observe this is no naked Viking in a prehistoric period; but a Scotch member of Parliament, with a smattering of the classics, a telescope, a cocked hat of great size, and flannel underclothing. In the same spirit, Nelson went into Aboukir with six colours flying; so that even if five were shot away, it should not be imagined he had struck. He too must needs wear his four stars outside his Admiral's frock, to be a butt for sharpshooters. "In honour I gained them," he said to objectors, adding with sublime illogicality, "in honour I will die with them." Captain Douglas of the *Royal Oak*, when the Dutch fired his vessel in the Thames, sent his men ashore, but was burned along with her himself rather than desert his post without orders. Just then, perhaps the Merry Monarch[28] was chasing a moth round the supper-table with the ladies of his court. When Raleigh sailed into Cadiz, and all the forts and ships opened fire on him at once, he scorned to shoot a gun, and made answer with a flourish of insulting trumpets. I like this bravado better than the wisest dispositions to insure victory; it comes from the heart and goes to it. God has made nobler heroes, but he never made a finer gentleman than Walter Raleigh. And as our Admirals were full of heroic superstitions, and had a strutting and vainglorious style of fight, so they discovered a startling eagerness for battle, and courted war like a mistress. When the news came to Essex before Cadiz that the attack had been decided, he threw his hat into the sea. It is in this way that a schoolboy hears of a half-holiday; but this was a bearded man of great possessions who had just been allowed to risk his life. Benbow could not lie still in his bunk after he had lost his leg;[29] he must be on deck in a basket to direct and animate the fight. I said they loved war like a mistress; yet I think there are not many mistresses we should continue to woo under similar circumstances. Trowbridge went ashore with the *Culloden*, and was able to take no part in the battle of the Nile. "The merits of that ship and her gallant captain," wrote Nelson to the Admiralty, "are too well known to benefit by anything I could say. Her misfortune was great in getting aground, *while her more fortunate companions were in the full tide of happiness*."[30] This is a notable expression, and depicts the whole great-hearted, big-spoken stock of the English Admirals to a hair. It was to be "in the full tide of happiness" for Nelson to destroy five thousand five hundred and twenty-five of his fellow-creatures, and have his own scalp torn open by a piece of langridge shot. Hear him again at Copenhagen: "A shot through the mainmast knocked the splinters about; and he observed to one of his officers with a smile, "It is warm work, and this day may be the last to any of us at a moment;" and then, stopping short at the gangway, added, with emotion, *"But, mark you—I would not be elsewhere for thousands."*

I must tell one more story, which has lately been made familiar to us all, and that in one of the noblest ballads[31] in the English language. I had written my tame prose abstract, I shall beg the reader to believe, when I had no notion that the sacred bard designed an immortality for Greenville. Sir Richard Greenville was Vice-Admiral to Lord Thomas Howard, and lay off the Azores with the English squadron in 1591. He was a noted tyrant to his crew: a dark, bullying fellow apparently; and it is related of him that he would chew and swallow wineglasses, by way of con-vivial levity, till the blood ran out of his mouth.[32] When the Spanish fleet of fifty sail came within sight of the English, his ship, the *Revenge*, was the last to weigh anchor, and was so far circumvented by the Spaniards, that there were but two courses open—either to turn her back upon the enemy or sail through one of his squadrons. The first alternative Greenville dismissed as dishonourable to himself, his country, and her Majesty's ship. Accordingly, he chose the latter, and steered into the Spanish armament. Several vessels he forced to luff and fall under his lee; until, about three o'clock of the afternoon, a great ship of three decks of ordnance took the wind out of his sails, and immediately boarded. Thenceforward, and all night long, the *Revenge* held her own single-handed against the Spaniards. As one ship was beaten off, another took its place. She endured, according to Raleigh's computation, "eight hundred shot of great artillery, besides many assaults and entries." By morning the powder was spent, the pikes all broken, not a stick was standing, "nothing left overhead either for flight or defence;" six feet of water in the hold; almost all the men hurt; and Greenville himself in a dying condition. To bring them to this pass, a fleet of fifty sail had been mauling them for fifteen hours, the *Admiral of the Hulks* and the *Ascension* of Seville had both gone down alongside, and two other vessels had taken refuge on shore in a sinking state. In Hawke's words, they had "taken a great deal of drubbing." The captain and crew thought they had done about enough; but Greenville was not of this opinion; he gave orders to the master gunner, whom he knew to be a fellow after his own stamp, to scuttle the *Revenge* where she lay. The others, who were not mortally wounded like the Admiral, interfered with some decision, locked the master gun-ner in his cabin, after having deprived him of his sword, for he manifested an intention to kill himself if he were not to sink the ship; and sent to the Spaniards to demand terms. These were granted. The second or third day after, Greenville died of his wounds aboard the Spanish flag-ship, leaving his contempt upon the "traitors and dogs"[33] who had not chosen to do as he did, and engage fifty vessels, well found and fully manned, with six inferior craft ravaged by sickness and short of stores. He at least, he said, had done his duty as he was bound to do, and looked for everlasting fame.

Some one said to me the other day that they considered this story to be of a pes-tilent example. I am not inclined to imagine we shall ever be put into any practical difficulty from a superfluity of Greenvilles. And besides, I demur to the opinion. The worth of such actions is not a thing to be decided in a quaver of sensibility or a flush of righteous commonsense. The man who wished to make the ballads of his country,[34] coveted a small matter compared to what Richard Greenville accomplished. I wonder how many people have been inspired by this mad story, and how many battles have been actually won for England in the spirit thus engendered. It is only with a measure of habitual foolhardiness that you can be sure, in the common run of men, of courage on a reasonable occasion. An army or a fleet, if it is not led by quixotic fancies, will not be led far by terror of the Provost Marshal. Even German warfare, in addition to maps and telegraphs, is not above employing the *Wacht am Rhein*.[35] Nor is it only in the profession of arms that such stories may do good to a man. In this desperate and gleeful fighting, whether it is Greenville or Benbow, Hawke or Nelson, who flies his colours in the ship, we see men brought to the test and giving proof of what we call heroic feeling. Prosperous humanitarians tell me, in my club smoking-room, that they are a prey to prodigious heroic feelings, and that it costs them more nobility of soul to do nothing in particular, than would carry on all the wars, by sea or land, of bellicose humanity. It may very well be so, and yet not touch the point in question. For what I desire is to see some of this nobility brought face to face with me in an inspiriting achievement. A man may talk smoothly over a cigar in my club smoking-room from now to the Day of Judgment, without adding anything to mankind's treasury of illustrious and encouraging examples. It is not over the virtues of a curate-and-tea-party novel, that people are abashed into high resolutions. It may be because their hearts are crass, but to stir them properly they must have men entering into glory with some pomp and circumstance. And that is why these stories of our sea-captains, printed, so to speak, in capitals, and full of bracing moral influence, are more valuable to England than any material benefit in all the books of political economy between Westminster and Birmingham. Greenville chewing wineglasses at table makes no very pleasant figure, any more than a thousand other artists when they are viewed in the body, or met in private life; but his work of art, his finished tragedy, is an eloquent performance; and I contend it ought not only to enliven men of the sword as they go into battle, but send back merchant clerks with more heart and spirit to their book-keeping by double entry.

There is another question which seems bound up in this; and that is Temple's problem: whether it was wise of Douglas to burn with the *Royal Oak*? and by implication, what it was that made him do so? Many will tell you it was the desire of fame.

"To what do Cæsar and Alexander owe the infinite grandeur of their renown, but to fortune? How many men has she extinguished in the beginning of their progress, of whom we have no knowledge; who brought as much courage to the work as they, if their adverse hap had not cut them off in the first sally of their arms? Amongst so many and so great dangers, I do not remember to have anywhere read that Caesar was ever wounded; a thousand have fallen in less dangers than the least of these he went through. A great many brave actions must be expected to be performed without witness, for one that comes to some notice. A man is not always at the top of a breach, or at the head of an army in the sight of his general, as upon a platform. He is often surprised between the hedge and the ditch; he must run the hazard of his life against a henroost; he must dislodge four rascally musketeers out of a barn; he must prick out single from his party, as necessity arises, and meet adventures alone."

Thus far Montaigne, in a characteristic essay on *Glory*. Where death is certain, as in the cases of Douglas or Greenville, it seems all one from a personal point of view. The man who lost his life against a henroost, is in the same pickle with him who lost his life against a fortified place of the first order. Whether he has missed a peerage or only the corporal's stripes, it is all one if he has missed them and is quietly in the grave. It was by a hazard that we learned the conduct of the four marines of the *Wager*.[36] There was no room for these brave fellows in the boat, and they were left behind upon the island to a certain death. They were soldiers, they said, and knew well enough it was their business to die; and as their comrades pulled away, they stood upon the beach, gave three cheers, and cried "God bless the king!" Now, one or two of those who were in the boat escaped, against all likelihood, to tell the story. That was a great thing for us; but surely it cannot, by any possible twisting of human speech, be construed into anything great for the marines. You may suppose, if you like, that they died hoping their behaviour would not be forgotten; or you may suppose they thought nothing on the subject, which is much more likely. What can be the signification of the word "fame" to a private of marines, who cannot read and knows nothing of past history beyond the reminiscences of his grandmother? But whichever supposition you make, the fact is unchanged. They died while the question still hung in the balance; and I suppose their bones were already white, before the winds and the waves and the humour of Indian chiefs and Spanish governors had decided whether they were to be unknown and useless martyrs or honoured heroes. Indeed, I believe this is the lesson: if it is for fame that men do brave actions, they are only silly fellows after all.

It is at best but a pettifogging, pickthank business to decompose actions into little personal motives, and explain heroism away. The Abstract Bagman will grow like an Admiral at heart, not by ungrateful carping, but in a heat of admiration. But there is another theory of the personal motive in these fine sayings and doings, which I believe to be true and wholesome. People usually do things, and suffer martyrdoms, because they have an inclination that way. The best artist is not the man who fixes his eye on posterity, but the one who loves the practice of his art. And instead of having a taste for being successful merchants and retiring at thirty, some people have a taste for high and what we call heroic forms of excitement. If the Admirals courted war like a mistress; if, as the drum beat to quarters, the sailors came gaily out of the forecastle; it is because a fight is a period of multiplied and intense experiences, and, by Nelson's computation, worth "thousands" to any one who has a heart under his jacket. If the marines of the *Wager* gave three cheers and cried "God bless the king," it was because they liked to do things nobly for their own satisfaction. They were giving their lives, there was no help for that; and they made it a point of self-respect to give them handsomely. And there were never four happier marines in God's world than these four at that moment.

If it was worth thousands to be at the Baltic, I wish a Benthamite arithmetician[37] would calculate how much it was worth to be one of these four marines; or how much their story is worth to each of us who read it. And mark you, undemonstrative men would have spoiled the situation. The finest action is the better for a piece of purple. If the soldiers of the *Birkenhead* had not gone down in line,[38] or these marines of the *Wager* had walked away simply into the island, like plenty of other brave fellows in the like circumstances, my Benthamite arithmetician would assign a far lower value to the two stories. We have to desire a grand air in our heroes; and such a knowledge of the human stage as shall make them put the dots on their own i's, and leave us in no suspense as to when they mean to be heroic. And hence, we should congratulate ourselves upon the fact that our Admirals were not only great-hearted but big-spoken.

The heroes themselves say, as often as not, that fame is their object; but I do not think that is much to the purpose. People generally say what they have been taught to say; that was the catchword they were given in youth to express the aims of their way of life; and men who are gaining great battles are not likely to take much trouble in reviewing their sentiments and the words in which they were told to express them. Almost every person, if you will believe himself, holds a quite different theory of life from the one on which he is patently acting. And the fact is, fame may be a forethought and an afterthought, but it is too abstract an idea to move people greatly in moments of swift and momentous decision. It is from something more immediate, some determination of blood to the head, some trick of the fancy, that the breach is stormed or the bold word spoken. I am sure a fellow shooting an ugly weir in a canoe has exactly as much thought about fame as most commanders going into battle; and yet the action, fall out how it will, is not one of those the muse delights to celebrate. Indeed it is difficult to see why the fellow does a thing so nameless and yet so formidable to look at, unless on the theory that he likes it. I suspect that is why; and I suspect it is at least ten per cent. of why Lord Beaconsfield and Mr. Gladstone[39] have debated so much in the House of Commons, and why Burnaby rode to Khiva[40] the other day, and why the Admirals courted war like a mistress.

Notes

1 Temple, in a letter to Lord Lisle (Aug. 1667) on the actions of Captain Douglas in the Battle of Medway.—*The Works of William Temple, Bart*, 4 vols. (1814), I, 284.
2 Tacitus mentions eight eagles, symbol of the Roman military standard (*Annals*, 2.10.17).
3 King Angus saw a vision of the saltire cross in the clouds, leading his army of Scots and Picts to victory over an invading English army in 735. The Bayeux Tapestry includes Haley's Comet before the Battle of Hastings in 1066. King Henry V's St. Crispin's Day speech at Agincourt in Shakespeare's *Henry V* (4.3.18–67).
4 The British royal coat of arms features a lion.
5 Robert Blake (1598–1657), the Father of the Royal Navy. Horatio Nelson (1758–1805), British naval hero in the Napoleonic Wars.
6 1 Corinthians 15:52.

7 Edward Hawke (1705–81) defeated the French in the Battle of Quiberon Bay on 20 Nov. 1759 in severe storms.

8 Nelson blew up the French flagship *Orient* in his victory at the Battle of the Nile at Aboukir Bay on 1 Aug. 1798.

9 *Roderick Random* (1748): a historical novel by Tobias Smollett.

10 Morgan, first mate of the man-of-war *Thunder* in *Roderick Random*. Flip: a heated drink made of beer, spirit, and sugar; salmagundi: a dish of chopped meat, anchovies, and eggs.

11 Boswell, *Journal of a Tour to the Hebrides*, 31 Aug. 1773.

12 See "The Philosophy of Nomenclature" (p. 460).

13 Famous English naval heroes: Sir Francis Drake (1540–96), Sir George Rooke (1650–1709), George Brydges Rodney (1718–92), Edward Boscawen (1711–61), John Byron (1723–86), Sir Cloudesley Shovell (1650–1707), and John Benbow (1653–1702).

14 Southey, *Life of Nelson*, 189. The Sicilian title was Duke of Bronte, Greek for "thunder."

15 A condition in Columbus's will and testament.

16 "We are not cotton-spinners all, / But some love England and her honour yet"—Tennyson, "The Third of February, 1852" (45–6).

17 D'Arcy Thompson (1829–1902), Stevenson's classics master at Edinburgh Academy in 1861–1862. His "Abstract Bagman" was a type of person consumed by business and insensible to beauty.

18 Implied excessive sentimentality in the 19th century.

19 Marcus Atilius Regulus, a Roman general and Carthaginian prisoner of war in 255 BC, was reportedly sent to Rome to plead for peace. Instead, he urged continued war and returned to Carthage to honor his parole and be tortured to death.

20 Pierce Egan (1772–1849) published a six-volume collection of his articles on boxing: *Boxiana; or, Sketches of Ancient and Modern Pugilism* (1829).

21 The prize-ring or those who frequent it.

22 Watermen operated ferries on the Thames and competed in boat races.

23 Champion English bare-knuckle prize-fighters: Tom Cribb (1781–1848), Henry Pearce (1777–1809), Jem Belcher (1781–1811), John Moore (dates unknown), and Tom Spring (1791–1851).

24 Arthur Wellesley, 1st Duke of Wellington (1769–1852), British military commander and Prime Minister best known for defeating French Emperor Napoleon Bonaparte (1769–1821) at Waterloo in 1815.

25 John Wesley (1703–1791), founder of the Methodist movement; William Laud (1573–1645), Archbishop of Canterbury, who promoted the High Anglican liturgy over Puritanism.

26 William Hazlitt's "The Fight" (1822); John Wilson (1785–1854) wrote articles on boxing for *Blackwood's Edinburgh Magazine*.

27 Adam Duncan (1731–1804), Admiral of the North Sea, won the Battle of Camperdown off the Dutch island of Texel in 1797.

28 King Charles II (1630–85).

29 Inspired the opening setting of Stevenson's *Treasure Island*: the Admiral Benbow Inn.

30 Southey, *Life of Nelson*, 150.

31 Tennyson, "The Revenge: A Ballad of the Fleet" (1878).

32 Sir Walter Raleigh, *Report of the Truth concerning the Last Sea-Fight of the Revenge* (1591).

33 Southey, *Lives of the British Admirals*, 3, 337.

34 "If a man were permitted to make all the ballads, he need not care who should make the laws of a nation"—Andrew Fletcher, *An Account of a Conversation concerning Right Regulation of Government* (1703).

35 "The Watch on the Rhine," a patriotic German poem by Max Schneckenburger on defending the Rhine, which was popular in the Franco-Prussian War.

36 HMS *Wager*, a warship under Captain Cheap, wrecked off the coast of southern Chile in October 1741.

37 Follower of Utilitarianism, a philosophy championed by Jeremy Bentham (1748–1832), which calculates morality according to the greatest happiness for the greatest number of people.

38 In the HMS *Birkenhead* wreck off South Africa in 1852, the crew allowed the women and children to board the few available lifeboats, establishing the code of "women and children first" or the Birkenhead Drill.

39 Benjamin Disraeli or Lord Beaconsfield (1804–1881) and William Gladstone (1809–1898): Members of Parliament and Prime Ministers.

40 Frederick Burnaby (1842–85), British Army officer sent on a dangerous unofficial intelligence mission to Khiva (Uzbekistan), described in his *A Ride to Khiva* (1876).

11

CHILD'S PLAY

The regret we have for our childhood is not wholly justifiable: so much a man
may lay down without fear of public ribaldry; for although we shake our heads
over the change, we are not unconscious of the manifold advantages of our new
state. What we lose in generous impulse, we more than gain in the habit of generously watching others; and the capacity to enjoy Shakespeare may balance a lost
aptitude for playing at soldiers. Terror is gone out of our lives, moreover; we no
longer see the devil in the bed-curtains nor lie awake to listen to the wind. We
go to school no more; and if we have only exchanged one drudgery for another
(which is by no means sure), we are set free for ever from the daily fear of chas-
tisement. And yet a great change has overtaken us; and although we do not enjoy
ourselves less, at least we take our pleasure differently. We need pickles nowadays
to make Wednesday's cold mutton please our Friday's appetite; and I can remember the time when to call it red venison, and tell myself a hunter's story, would
have made it more palatable than the best of sauces. To the grown person, cold
mutton is cold mutton all the world over; not all the mythology ever invented by
man will make it better or worse to him; the broad fact, the clamant reality, of the
mutton carries away before it such seductive figments. But for the child it is still
possible to weave an enchantment over eatables; and if he has but read of a dish
in a story-book, it will be heavenly manna to him for a week.

If a grown man does not like eating and drinking and exercise, if he is not something positive[1] in his tastes, it means he has a feeble body and should have some
medicine; but children may be pure spirits, if they will, and take their enjoyment
in a world of moonshine. Sensation does not count for so much in our first years
as afterwards; something of the swaddling numbness of infancy clings about us;
we see and touch and hear through a sort of golden mist. Children, for instance,
are able enough to see, but they have no great faculty for looking; they do not use
their eyes for the pleasure of using them, but for by-ends of their own; and the
things I call to mind seeing most vividly, were not beautiful in themselves, but
merely interesting or enviable to me as I thought they might be turned to practical
account in play. Nor is the sense of touch so clean and poignant in children as it
is in a man. If you will turn over your old memories, I think the sensations of this
sort you remember will be somewhat vague, and come to not much more than a

blunt, general sense of heat on summer days, or a blunt, general sense of well-being in bed. And here, of course, you will understand pleasurable sensations; for overmastering pain—the most deadly and tragical element in life, and the true commander of man's soul and body—alas! pain has its own way with all of us; it breaks in, a rude visitant,[2] upon the fairy garden where the child wanders in a dream, no less surely than it rules upon the field of battle, or sends the immortal war-god whimpering to his father;[3] and innocence, no more than philosophy, can protect us from this sting. As for taste, when we bear in mind the excesses of unmitigated sugar which delight a youthful palate, "it is surely no very cynical asperity"[4] to think taste a character of the maturer growth. Smell and hearing are perhaps more developed; I remember many scents, many voices, and a great deal of spring singing in the woods. But hearing is capable of vast improvement as a means of pleasure; and there is all the world between gaping wonderment at the jargon of birds, and the emotion with which a man listens to articulate music.

At the same time, and step by step with this increase in the definition and intensity of what we feel which accompanies our growing age, another change takes place in the sphere of intellect, by which all things are transformed and seen through theories and associations as through coloured windows. We make to ourselves day by day, out of history, and gossip, and economical speculations, and God knows what, a medium in which we walk and through which we look abroad. We study shop windows with other eyes than in our childhood, never to wonder,[5] not always to admire, but to make and modify our little incongruous theories about life. It is no longer the uniform of a soldier that arrests our attention; but perhaps the flowing carriage of a woman, or perhaps a countenance that has been vividly stamped with passion and carries an adventurous story written in its lines. The pleasure of surprise is passed away; sugar-loaves and water-carts[6] seem mighty tame to encounter; and we walk the streets to make romances and to sociologise. Nor must we deny that a good many of us walk them solely for the purposes of transit or in the interest of a livelier digestion. These, indeed, may look back with mingled thoughts upon their childhood, but the rest are in a better case; they know more than when they were children, they understand better, their desires and sympathies answer more nimbly to the provocation of the senses, and their minds are brimming with interest as they go about the world.

According to my contention, this is a flight to which children cannot rise. They are wheeled in perambulators or dragged about by nurses in a pleasing stupor. A vague, faint, abiding wonderment possesses them. Here and there some specially remarkable circumstance, such as a water-cart or a guardsman, fairly penetrates into the seat of thought and calls them, for half a moment, out of themselves; and you may see them, still towed forward sideways by the inexorable nurse as by a sort of destiny, but still staring at the bright object in their wake. It may be some minutes before another such moving spectacle reawakens them to the world in which they dwell. For other children, they almost invariably show some intelligent sympathy. "There is a fine fellow making mud pies," they seem to say; "that I can understand, there is some sense in mud pies." But the doings of their elders, unless where they are speakingly[7] picturesque or recommend them-selves by the quality of being easily imitable, they let them go over their heads (as we say) without the least regard. If it were not for this perpetual imitation, we should be tempted to fancy they despised us outright, or only considered us in the light of creatures brutally strong and brutally silly; among whom they conde-scended to dwell in obedience like a philosopher at a barbarous court. At times they display an arrogance of disregard that is truly staggering. Once, when I was groaning aloud with physical pain, a young gentleman came into the room and nonchalantly inquired if I had seen his bow and arrow. He made no account of my groans, which he accepted, as he had to accept so much else, as a piece of the inexplicable conduct of his elders; and, like a wise young gentleman, he would waste no wonder on the subject. Those elders, who care so little for rational enjoy-ment, and are even the enemy of rational enjoyment for others, he had accepted without understanding and without complaint, as the rest of us accept the scheme of the universe.

We grown people can tell ourselves a story, give and take strokes until the buck-lers ring, ride far and fast, marry, fall, and die; all the while sitting quietly by the fire or lying prone in bed. This is exactly what a child cannot do, or does not do, at least, when he can find anything else. He works all with lay figures and stage properties. When his story comes to the fighting, he must rise, get something by way of a sword and have a set-to with a piece of furniture, until he is out of breath. When he comes to ride with the king's pardon, he must bestride a chair, which he will so hurry and belabour and on which he will so furiously demean himself, that the messenger will arrive, if not bloody with spurring, at least fiery red with haste. If his romance involves an accident upon a cliff, he must clamber in person about the chest of drawers and fall bodily upon the carpet, before his imagination is satisfied. Lead soldiers, dolls, all toys, in short, are in the same category and answer the same end. Nothing can stagger a child's faith; he accepts the clumsiest substitutes and can swallow the most staring incongruities. The chair he has just been besieging as a castle, or valiantly cutting to the ground as a dragon, is taken away for the accommodation of a morning visitor, and he is nothing abashed; he can skirmish by the hour with a stationary coal-scuttle; in the midst of the enchanted pleasance, he can see, without sensible shock, the gardener soberly digging potatoes for the day's dinner. He can make abstraction of whatever does not fit into his fable; and he puts his eyes into his pocket, just as we hold our noses in an unsavoury lane. And so it is, that although the ways of children cross with those of their elders in a hundred places daily, they never go in the same direction nor so much as lie in the same element. So may the telegraph wires intersect the line of the high-road, or so might a landscape painter and a bagman[8] visit the same country, and yet move in different worlds.

People struck with these spectacles, cry aloud about the power of imagination in the young. Indeed there may be two words to that. It is, in some ways, but a pedestrian fancy that the child exhibits. It is the grown people who make the nursery stories; all the children do, is jealously to preserve the text. One out of a dozen reasons why *Robinson Crusoe*[9] should be so popular with youth, is that it hits their level in this matter to a nicety; Crusoe was always at makeshifts and had, in so many words, to *play* at a great variety of professions; and then the book is all about tools, and there is nothing that delights a child so much. Hammers and saws belong to a province of life that positively calls for imitation. The juvenile lyrical drama,[10] surely of the most ancient Thespian[11] model, wherein the trades of mankind are successively simulated to the running burthen "On a cold and frosty morning,"[12] gives a good instance of the artistic taste in children. And this need for overt action and lay figures testifies to a defect in the child's imagination which prevents him from carrying out his novels in the privacy of his own heart. He does not yet know enough of the world and men. His experience is incomplete. That stage-wardrobe and scene-room that we call the memory is so ill provided, that he can overtake few combinations and body out few stories, to his own content, without some external aid. He is at the experimental stage; he is not sure how one would feel in certain circumstances; to make sure, he must come as near trying it as his means permit.

And so here is young heroism with a wooden sword, and mothers practice their kind vocation over a bit of jointed stick. It may be laughable enough just now; but it is these same people and these same thoughts, that not long hence, when they are on the theatre of life, will make you weep and tremble. For children think very much the same thoughts, and dream the same dreams, as bearded men and marriageable women. No one is more romantic. Fame and honour, the love of young men and the love of mothers, the business man's pleasure in method, all these and others they anticipate and rehearse in their play hours. Upon us, who are further advanced and fairly dealing with the threads of destiny, they only glance from time to time to glean a hint for their own mimetic reproduction. Two children playing at soldiers are far more interesting to each other than one of the scarlet beings whom both are busy imitating. This is perhaps the greatest oddity of all. "Art for art"[13] is their motto; and the doings of grown folk are only interesting as the raw material for play. Not Théophile Gautier, not Flaubert,[14] can look more callously upon life, or rate the reproduction more highly over the reality; and they will parody an execution, a death-bed, or the funeral of the young man of Nain,[15] with all the cheerfulness in the world.

The true parallel for play is not to be found, of course, in conscious art, which, though it be derived from play, is itself an abstract, impersonal thing, and depends largely upon philosophical interests beyond the scope of childhood. It is when we make castles in the air and personate the leading character in our own romances, that we return to the spirit of our first years. Only, there are several reasons why the spirit is no longer so agreeable to indulge.

Nowadays, when we admit this personal element into our divagations we are apt to stir up uncomfortable and sorrowful memories, and remind ourselves sharply of old wounds. Our day-dreams can no longer lie all in the air like a story in the *Arabian Nights*;[16] they read to us rather like the history of a period in which we ourselves had taken part, where we come across many unfortunate passages and find our own conduct smartly reprimanded. And then the child, mind you, acts his parts. He does not merely repeat them to himself; he leaps, he runs, and sets the blood agog over all his body. And so his play breathes him; and he no sooner assumes a passion than he gives it vent. Alas! when we betake ourselves to our intellectual form of play, sitting quietly by the fire or lying prone in bed, we rouse many hot feelings for which we can find no outlet. Substitutes are not acceptable to the mature mind, which desires the thing itself; and even to rehearse a triumphant dialogue with one's enemy, although it is perhaps the most satisfactory piece of play still left within our reach, is not entirely satisfying, and is even apt to lead to a visit and an interview which may be the reverse of triumphant after all.

In the child's world of dim sensation, play is all in all. "Making believe" is the gist of his whole life, and he cannot so much as take a walk except in character. I could not learn my alphabet without some suitable *mise-en-scène*,[17] and had to act a business man in an office before I could sit down to my book. Will you kindly question your memory, and find out how much you did, work or pleasure, in good faith and soberness, and for how much you had to cheat yourself with some invention? I remember, as though it were yesterday, the expansion of spirit, the dignity and self-reliance, that came with a pair of mustachios in burnt cork, even when there was none to see. Children are even content to forego what we call the realities, and prefer the shadow to the substance. When they might be speaking intelligibly together, they chatter senseless gibberish by the hour, and are quite happy because they are making believe to speak French. I have said already how even the imperious appetite of hunger suffers itself to be gulled and led by the nose with the fag end of an old song. And it goes deeper than this: when children are together even a meal is felt as an interruption in the business of life; and they must find some imaginative sanction, and tell themselves some sort of story, to account for, to colour, to render entertaining, the simple processes of eating and drinking. What wonderful fancies I have heard evolved out of the pattern upon tea-cups!—from which there followed a code of rules and a whole world of excitement, until tea-drinking began to take rank as a game. When my cousin[18] and I took our porridge of a morning, we had a device to enliven the course of the meal. He ate his with sugar, and explained it to be a country continually buried under snow. I took mine with milk, and explained it to be a country suffering gradual inundation. You can imagine us exchanging bulletins; how here was an island still unsubmerged, here a valley not yet covered with snow; what inventions were made; how his population lived in cabins on perches and travelled on stilts, and how mine was always in boats; how the interest grew furious, as the last corner of safe ground was cut off on all sides and grew smaller every moment; and how, in fine, the food was of altogether secondary importance, and might even have been nauseous, so long as we seasoned it with these dreams. But perhaps the most exciting moments I ever had over a meal, were in the case of calves' feet jelly. It was hardly possible not to believe—and you may be sure, so far from trying, I did all I could to favour the illusion—that some part of it was hollow, and that sooner or later my spoon would lay open the secret tabernacle of the golden rock. There, might some miniature *Red Beard*[19] await his hour; there might one find the treasures of the *Forty Thieves*, and bewildered Cassim beating about the walls.[20] And so I quarried on slowly, with bated breath, savouring the interest. Believe me, I had little palate left for the jelly; and though I preferred the taste when I took cream with it, I used often to go without, because the cream dimmed the transparent fractures.

Even with games, this spirit is authoritative with right-minded children. It is thus that hide-and-seek has so pre-eminent a sovereignty, for it is the well-spring of romance, and the actions and the excitement to which it gives rise lend themselves to almost any sort of fable. And thus cricket, which is a mere matter of dexterity, palpably about nothing and for no end, often fails to satisfy infantile craving. It is a game, if you like, but not a game of play. You cannot tell yourself a story about cricket; and the activity it calls forth can be justified on no rational theory.

Even football, although it admirably simulates the tug and the ebb and flow of battle, has presented difficulties to the mind of young sticklers after verisimilitude; and I knew at least one little boy who was mightily exercised about the presence of the ball, and had to spirit himself up, whenever he came to play, with an elaborate story of enchantment, and take the missile as a sort of talisman bandied about in conflict between two Arabian nations.

To think of such a frame of mind, is to become disquieted about the bringing up of children. Surely they dwell in a mythological epoch, and are not the contemporaries of their parents. What can they think of them? what can they make of these bearded or petticoated giants who look down upon their games? who move upon a cloudy Olympus, following unknown designs apart from rational enjoyment? who profess the tenderest solicitude for children, and yet every now and again reach down out of their altitude and terribly vindicate the prerogatives of age? Off goes the child, corporally smarting, but morally rebellious. Were there ever such unthinkable deities as parents? I would give a great deal to know what, in nine cases out of ten, is the child's unvarnished feeling. A sense of past cajolery; a sense of personal attraction, at best very feeble; above all, I should imagine, a sense of terror for the untried residue of mankind: go to make up the attraction that he feels. No wonder, poor little heart, with such a weltering world in front of him, if he clings to the hand he knows! The dread irrationality of the whole affair, as it seems to children, is a thing we are all too ready to forget. "Oh, why," I remember passionately wondering, "why can we not all be happy and devote ourselves to play?" And when children do philosophize, I believe it is usually to very much the same purpose.

One thing, at least, comes very clearly out of these considerations; that whatever we are to expect at the hands of children, it should not be any peddling[21] exactitude about matters of fact. They walk in a vain show,[22] and among mists and rainbows; they are passionate after dreams and unconcerned about realities; speech is a difficult art not wholly learned; and there is nothing in their own tastes or purposes to teach them what we mean by abstract truthfulness. When a bad writer is inexact, even if he can look back on half a century of years, we charge him with incompetence and not with dishonesty. And why not extend the same allowance to imperfect speakers? Let a stockbroker be dead stupid about poetry, or a poet inexact in the details of business, and we excuse them heartily from blame. But show us a miserable, unbreeched human entity, whose whole profession it is to take a tub for a fortified town and a shaving-brush for the deadly stiletto, and who passes three-fourths of his time in a dream and the rest in open self-deception; and we expect him to be as nice upon a matter of fact as a scientific expert bearing evidence. Upon my heart, I think it less than decent. You do not consider how little the child sees, or how swift he is to weave what he has seen into bewildering fiction; and that he cares no more for what you call truth, than you for a gingerbread dragoon.

I am reminded, as I write, that the child is very inquiring as to the precise truth of stories. But indeed this is a very different matter, and one bound up with the subject of play, and the precise amount of playfulness, or playability, to be looked for in the world. Many such burning questions must arise in the course of nursery education. Among the fauna of this planet, which already embraces the pretty soldier and the terrifying Irish beggarman, is, or is not, the child to expect a Bluebeard or a Cormoran?[23] Is he, or is he not, to look out for magicians, kindly and potent? May he, or may he not, reasonably hope to be cast away upon a desert island, or turned to such diminutive proportions that he can live on equal terms with his lead soldiery, and go a cruise in his own toy schooner? Surely all these are practical questions to a neophyte entering upon life with a view to play. Precision upon such a point, the child can understand. But if you merely ask him of his past behaviour, as to who threw such a stone, for instance, or struck such and such a match; or whether he had looked into a parcel or gone by a forbidden path; why, he can see no moment in the inquiry, and it is ten to one, he has already half forgotten and half bemused himself with subsequent imaginings.

It would be easy to leave them in their native cloudland, where they figure so prettily—pretty like flowers and innocent like dogs. They will come out of their gardens soon enough, and have to go into offices and the witness-box. Spare them yet a while, O conscientious parent! Let them doze among their playthings yet a little! for who knows what a rough, war-faring existence lies before them in the future?

Notes

1 Physical.
2 A description of death in Edward Young's 1745 poem *Night-Thoughts* (5.728).
3 Ares, god of war, is wounded by Diomedes in the *Iliad* and runs to Zeus.
4 An allusion to Samuel Johnson's 7 Feb. 1755 letter to the Earl of Chesterfield, mentioned in Boswell's *The Life of Dr. Johnson* (1791), declining a belated offer of patronage: "I hope it is no very cynical asperity, not to confess obligations where no benefit has been received."

5 Never wonder—a central tenet of the Gradgrind school, taught by Mr. M'Choakumchild in opposition to imagination and feeling in Dickens's *Hard Times* (1854).
6 Horse-drawn cart for delivering water.
7 Obviously.
8 Traveling salesman.
9 Daniel Defoe's novel *Robinson Crusoe* (1791).
10 Pantomime.
11 Thespis, father of Greek drama in the 6th century BC.
12 From the nursery rhyme "Here We Go Round the Mullberry Bush."
13 A phrase ("l'art pour l'art") coined by the French philosopher Victor Cousin (1792–1867).
14 Théophile Gautier (1811–1872) and Gustave Flaubert (1821–1880): French writers who valued aesthetics over ethics.
15 A man Jesus raised from the dead (Luke 7:12–16).
16 A collection of Middle-Eastern folk tales unified by a framing narrative that was first translated into English in the early 18th century.
17 The staging of a play.
18 Bob Stevenson (1847–1900), Stevenson's cousin and lifelong friend.
19 Frederick I or "Redbeard" (1112–1190), Roman emperor fabled to have escaped death by hibernating in a hidden Bavarian mountain chamber.
20 In *The Arabian Nights*, Ali Baba discovers treasure in a secret cave, where his brother Kasim gets trapped after attempting to steal it.
21 Trifling, paltry.
22 Psalms 39:6.
23 Bluebeard, wealthy nobleman in a French folktale who murders a series of wives. Cormoran, a Cornish giant of English folklore.

12

WALKING TOURS

It must not be imagined that a walking tour, as some would have us fancy, is merely a better or worse way of seeing the country. There are many ways of seeing landscape quite as good; and none more vivid, in spite of canting dilettantes, than from a railway train. But landscape on a walking tour is quite accessory. He who is indeed of the brotherhood does not voyage in quest of the picturesque, but of certain jolly humours—of the hope and spirit with which the march begins at morning, and the peace and spiritual repletion of the evening's rest. He cannot tell whether he puts his knapsack on, or takes it off, with more delight. The excitement of the departure puts him in key for that of the arrival. Whatever he does is not only a reward in itself, but will be further rewarded in the sequel; and so pleasure leads on to pleasure in an endless chain. It is this that so few can understand; they will either be always lounging or always at five miles an hour; they do not play off the one against the other, prepare all day for the evening, and all evening for the next day. And, above all, it is here that your overwalker fails of comprehension. His heart rises against those who drink their curaçoa in liqueur glasses, when he himself can swill it in a brown john.[1] He will not believe that the flavour is more delicate in the smaller dose. He will not believe that to walk this unconscionable distance is merely to stupefy and brutalize himself, and come to his inn, at night, with a sort of frost on his five wits, and a starless night of darkness in his spirit. Not for him the mild luminous evening of the temperate walker! He has nothing left of man but a physical need for bedtime and a double nightcap; and even his pipe, if he be a smoker, will be savourless and disenchanted. It is the fate of such an one to take twice as much trouble as is needed to obtain happiness, and miss the happiness in the end; he is the man of the proverb, in short, who goes further and fares worse.

Now, to be properly enjoyed, a walking tour should be gone upon alone. If you go in a company, or even in pairs, it is no longer a walking tour in anything but name; it is something else and more in the nature of a picnic. A walking tour should be gone upon alone, because freedom is of the essence; because you should be able to stop and go on, and follow this way or that, as the freak takes you; and because you must have your own pace, and neither trot alongside a champion walker, nor mince in time with a girl. And then you must be open to all impressions and let your thoughts take colour from what you see. You should be as a pipe for any wind to play upon. "I cannot see the wit," says Hazlitt, "of walking and talking at the same time. When I am in the country I wish to vegetate like the country."[2] Which is the gist of all that can be said upon the matter. There should be no cackle of voices at your elbow, to jar on the meditative silence of the morning. And so long as a man is reasoning he cannot surrender himself to that fine intoxication that comes of much motion in the open air, that begins in a sort of dazzle and sluggishness of the brain, and ends in a peace that passes comprehension.[3]

During the first day or so of any tour there are moments of bitterness, when the traveller feels more than coldly towards his knapsack, when he is half in a mind to throw it bodily over the hedge and, like Christian on a similar occasion, "give three leaps and go on singing."[4] And yet it soon acquires a property of easiness. It becomes magnetic; the spirit of the journey enters into it. And no sooner have you passed the straps over your shoulder than the lees of sleep are cleared from you, you pull yourself together with a shake, and fall at once into your stride. And surely, of all possible moods, this, in which a man takes the road, is the best. Of course, if he *will* keep thinking of his anxieties, if he *will* open the merchant Abudah's chest and walk arm-in-arm with the hag—why, wherever he is, and whether he walk fast or slow, the chances are that he will not be happy.[5] And so much the more shame to himself! There are perhaps thirty men setting forth at that same hour, and I would lay a large wager there is not another dull face among the thirty. It would be a fine thing to follow, in a coat of darkness,[6] one after another of these wayfarers, some summer morning, for the first few miles upon the road. This one, who walks fast, with a keen look in his eyes, is all concentrated in his own mind; he is up at his loom, weaving and weaving, to set the landscape to words. This one peers about, as he goes, among the grasses; he waits by the canal to watch the dragon-flies; he leans on the gate of the pasture, and cannot look enough upon the complacent kine. And here comes another, talking, laughing, and gesticulating to himself. His face changes from time to time, as indignation flashes from his eyes or anger clouds his forehead. He is composing articles, delivering orations, and conducting the most impassioned interviews, by the way. A little farther on, and it is as like as not he will begin to sing. And well for him, supposing him to be no great master in that art, if he stumble across no stolid peasant at a corner; for, on such an occasion, I scarcely know which is the more troubled, or whether it is worse to suffer the confusion of your troubadour, or the unfeigned alarm of your clown. A sedentary population, accustomed, besides, to the strange mechanical bearing of the common tramp, can in no wise explain to itself the gaiety of these passers-by. I knew one man who was arrested as a runaway lunatic, because, although a full-grown person with a red beard,[7] he skipped as he went like a child. And you would be astonished if I were to tell you all the grave and learned heads who have confessed to me that, when on walking tours, they sang—and sang very ill—and had a pair of red ears when, as described above, the inauspicious peasant plumped into their arms from round a corner. And here, lest you should think I am exaggerating, is Hazlitt's own confession, from his essay *On Going a Journey* which is so good that there should be a tax levied on all who have not read it:—

Give me the clear blue sky over my head," says he, "and the green turf beneath my feet, a winding road before me, and a three hours' march to dinner—and then to thinking! It is hard if I cannot start some game on these lone heaths. I laugh, I run, I leap, I sing for joy.

Bravo! After that adventure of my friend with the policeman, you would not have cared, would you, to publish that in the first person? But we have no bravery nowadays, and, even in books, must all pretend to be as dull and foolish as our neighbours. It was not so with Hazlitt. And notice how learned he is (as, indeed, throughout the essay) in the theory of walking tours. He is none of your athletic men in purple stockings, who walk their fifty miles a day: three hours' march is his ideal. And then he must have a winding road, the epicure!

Yet there is one thing I object to in these words of his, one thing in the great master's practice that seems to me not wholly wise. I do not approve of that leaping and running. Both of these hurry the respiration; they both shake up the brain out of its glorious open-air confusion; and they both break the pace. Uneven walking is not so agreeable to the body, and it distracts and irritates the mind. Whereas, when once you have fallen into an equable stride, it requires no conscious thought from you to keep it up, and yet it prevents you from thinking earnestly of anything else. Like knitting, like the work of a copying clerk, it gradually neutralizes and sets to sleep the serious activity of the mind. We can think of this or that, lightly and laughingly, as a child thinks, or as we think in a morning doze; we can make puns or puzzle out acrostics, and trifle in a thousand ways with words and rhymes; but when it comes to honest work, when we come to gather ourselves together for an effort, we may sound the trumpet as loud and long as we please; the great barons of the mind will not rally to the standard, but sit, each one, at home, warming his hands over his own fire and brooding on his own private thought!

In the course of a day's walk, you see, there is much variance in the mood. From the exhilaration of the start, to the happy phlegm[8] of the arrival, the change is certainly great. As the day goes on, the traveller moves from the one extreme towards the other. He becomes more and more incorporated with the material landscape, and the open-air drunkenness grows upon him with great strides, until he posts along the road, and sees everything about him, as in a cheerful dream. The first is certainly brighter, but the second stage is the more peaceful. A man does not make so many articles towards the end, nor does he laugh aloud; but the purely animal pleasures, the sense of physical well-being, the delight of every inhalation, of every time the muscles tighten down the thigh, console him for the absence of the others, and bring him to his destination still content.

Nor must I forget to say a word on bivouacs.[9] You come to a milestone on a hill, or some place where deep ways meet under trees; and off goes the knapsack, and down you sit to smoke a pipe in the shade. You sink into yourself, and the birds come round and look at you; and your smoke dissipates upon the afternoon under the blue dome of heaven; and the sun lies warm upon your feet, and the cool air visits your neck and turns aside your open shirt. If you are not happy, you must have an evil conscience. You may dally as long as you like by the roadside. It is almost as if the millennium[10] were arrived, when we shall throw our clocks and watches over the housetop, and remember time and seasons no more. Not to keep hours for a lifetime is, I was going to say, to live for ever. You have no idea, unless you have tried it, how endlessly long is a summer's day, that you measure out only by hunger, and bring to an end only when you are drowsy. I know a village where there are hardly any clocks, where no one knows more of the days of the week than by a sort of instinct for the fête on Sundays, and where only one person can tell you the day of the month, and she is generally wrong; and, if people were aware how slow Time journeyed in that village, and what armfuls of spare hours he gives, over and above the bargain, to its wise inhabitants, I believe there would be a stampede out of London, Liverpool, Paris, and a variety of large towns, where the clocks lose their heads, and shake the hours out each one faster than the other, as though they were all in a wager. And all these foolish pilgrims would each bring his own misery along with him, in a watch-pocket! It is to be noticed, there were no clocks and watches in the much-vaunted days before the flood. It follows, of course, there were no appointments, and punctuality was not yet thought upon. "Though ye take from a covetous man all his treasure," says Milton, "he has yet one jewel left; ye cannot deprive him of his covetousness."[11] And so I would say of a modern man of business, you may do what you will for him, put him in Eden, give him the elixir of life[12]—he has still a flaw at heart, he still has his business habits. Now, there is no time when business habits are more mitigated than on a walking tour. And so during these halts, as I say, you will feel almost free.

But it is at night, and after dinner, that the best hour comes. There are no such pipes to be smoked as those that follow a good day's march; the flavour of the tobacco is a thing to be remembered, it is so dry and aromatic, so full and so fine. If you wind up the evening with grog, you will own there was never such grog; at every sip a jocund tranquillity spreads about your limbs, and sits easily in your heart. If you read a book—and you will never do so save by fits and starts—you find the language strangely racy and harmonious; words take a new meaning; single sentences possess the ear for half an hour together; and the writer endears himself to you, at every page, by the nicest coincidence of sentiment. It seems as if it were a book you had written yourself in a dream. To all we have read on such occasions we look back with special favour. "It was on the 10th of April, 1798," says Hazlitt, with amorous precision, "that I sat down to a volume of the *New Héloïse*,[13] at the Inn at Llangollen, over a bottle of sherry and a cold chicken." I should wish to quote more, for though we are mighty fine fellows nowadays, we cannot write like Hazlitt. And, talking of that, a volume of Hazlitt's essays would be a capital pocket-book on such a journey; so would a volume of Heine's songs; and for *Tristram Shandy* I can pledge a fair experience.[14]

110

If the evening be fine and warm, there is nothing better in life than to lounge before the inn door in the sunset, or lean over the parapet of the bridge, to watch the weeds and the quick fishes. It is then, if ever, that you taste Joviality to the full significance of that audacious word. Your muscles are so agreeably slack, you feel so clean and so strong and so idle, that whether you move or sit still, whatever you do is done with pride and a kingly sort of pleasure. You fall in talk with any one, wise or foolish, drunk or sober. And it seems as if a hot walk purged you, more than of anything else, of all narrowness and pride, and left curiosity to play its part freely, as in a child or a man of science. You lay aside all your own hobbies, to watch provincial humours develop themselves before you, now as a laughable farce, and now grave and beautiful like an old tale.

Or perhaps you are left to your own company for the night, and surly weather imprisons you by the fire. You may remember how Burns, numbering past pleasures, dwells upon the hours when he has been "happy thinking."[15] It is a phrase that may well perplex a poor modern, girt about on every side by clocks and chimes, and haunted, even at night, by flaming dial-plates.[16] For we are all so busy, and have so many far-off projects to realize, and castles in the fire to turn into solid habitable mansions on a gravel soil, that we can find no time for pleasure trips into the Land of Thought and among the Hills of Vanity. Changed times, indeed, when we must sit all night, beside the fire, with folded hands; and a changed world for most of us, when we find we can pass the hours without discontent, and be happy thinking. We are in such haste to be doing, to be writing, to be gathering gear,[17] to make our voice audible a moment in the derisive silence of eternity, that we forget that one thing, of which these are but the parts—namely, to live. We fall in love, we drink hard, we run to and fro upon the earth like frightened sheep.

And now you are to ask yourself if, when all is done, you would not have been better to sit by the fire at home, and be happy thinking. To sit still and contemplate,—to remember the faces of women without desire, to be pleased by the great deeds of men without envy, to be everything and everywhere in sympathy, and yet content to remain where and what you are—is not this to know both wisdom and virtue, and to dwell with happiness? After all, it is not they who carry flags, but they who look upon it from a private chamber, who have the fun of the procession. And once you are at that, you are in the very humour of all social heresy. It is no time for shuffling, or for big, empty words. If you ask yourself what you mean by fame, riches, or learning, the answer is far to seek; and you go back into that kingdom of light imaginations, which seem so vain in the eyes of Philistines perspiring after wealth, and so momentous to those who are stricken with the disproportions of the world, and, in the face of the gigantic stars, cannot stop to split differences between two degrees of the infinitesimally small, such as a tobacco pipe or the Roman Empire, a million of money or a fiddle-stick's end.

You lean from the window, your last pipe reeking whitely into the darkness, your body full of delicious pains, your mind enthroned in the seventh circle of content; when suddenly the mood changes, the weather-cock goes about, and you ask yourself one question more: whether, for the interval, you have been the wisest philosopher or the most egregious of donkeys? Human experience is not yet able to reply; but at least you have had a fine moment, and looked down upon all the kingdoms of the earth.[18] And whether it was wise or foolish, to-morrow's travel will carry you body and mind, into some different parish of the infinite.

Notes

1 "Apparently a confusion of 'brown george,' a large earthenware vessel, and 'demi-john,' a large glass or earthenware bottle"—W. G. Bryan and R. S. Crane, *The English Familiar Essay: Representative Texts* (Ginn & Co., 1916, 466).
2 This essay's Hazlitt quotations are from "On Going on a Journey."
3 Philippians 4:7.
4 Christian's response after his burden falls from his back at the Cross in Bunyan's *Pilgrim's Progress*.
5 In James Ridley's *The Tales of the Genii: or, the Delightful Lessons of Horam* (1764), the Merchant Abudah opens a box to find an old woman who disturbs his nights and drives him to seek out illusory sources of contentment.
6 The invisibility cloak worn by Jack the Giant Slayer in the fairytale.
7 Most likely W.E. Henley. See n. 12, p. 184.
8 Johann Winckelmann, *Geschichte der Kunst des Alterthums* (1764).
9 Encampment or resting place.
10 Christ's reign in the first resurrection outside of time at the end of the world (Revelation 20:3).
11 Milton, *Areopagitica* (1644).
12 An immortality potion.
13 Jean-Jacques Rousseau, *Julie, or the New Heloise* (1761).
14 Laurence Sterne's novel *Tristram Shandy* (1759); German poet Heinrich Heine (1797–1856).
15 Robert Burns, "The Rigs o' Barley" (1782) 31–32.
16 Gas-illuminated outdoor clock faces.
17 Robert Burns, "The Rigs o' Barley" (33).
18 Matthew 4:1–11.

13

PAN'S PIPES

The world in which we live has been variously said and sung[1] by the most ingenious poets and philosophers: these reducing it to formulæ and chemical ingredients, those striking the lyre in high-sounding measures for the handiwork of God. What experience supplies is of a mingled tissue, and the choosing mind has much to reject before it can get together the materials of a theory. Dew and thunder, destroying Atilla and the Spring lambkins, belong to an order of contrasts which no repetition can assimilate. There is an uncouth, outlandish strain throughout the web of the world,[2] as from a vexatious planet in the house of life. Things are not congruous and wear strange disguises: the consummate flower is fostered out of dung, and after nourishing itself awhile with heaven's delicate distillations, decays again into indistinguishable soil; and with Cæsar's ashes, Hamlet tells us, the urchins make dirt pies and filthily besmear their countenance.[3] Nay, the kindly shine of summer, when tracked home with the scientific spyglass, is found to issue from the most portentous nightmare of the universe—the great, conflagrant sun: a world of hell's squibs, tumultuary, roaring aloud, inimical to life. The sun itself is enough to disgust a human being of the scene which he inhabits; and you would not fancy there was a green or habitable spot in a universe thus awfully lighted up. And yet it is by the blaze of such a conflagration, to which the fire of Rome was but a spark, that we do all our fiddling, and hold domestic tea-parties at the arbour door.[4]

The Greeks figured Pan, the god of Nature, now terribly stamping his foot, so that armies were dispersed;[5] now by the woodside on a summer noon trolling on his pipe until he charmed the hearts of upland ploughmen. And the Greeks, in so figuring, uttered the last word of human experience. To certain smoke-dried spirits matter and motion and elastic aethers,[6] and the hypothesis of this or that other spectacled professor, tell a speaking story; but for youth and all ductile and congenial minds, Pan is not dead,[7] but of all the classic hierarchy alone survives in triumph; goat-footed, with a gleeful and an angry look, the type of the shaggy world: and in every wood, if you go with a spirit properly prepared, you shall hear the note of his pipe.

For it is a shaggy world, and yet studded with gardens; where the salt and tumbling sea receives clear rivers running from among reeds and lilies; fruitful and austere; a rustic world; sunshiny, lewd, and cruel. What is it the birds sing among the trees in pairing-time? What means the sound of the rain falling far and wide upon the leafy forest? To what tune does the fisherman whistle, as he hauls in his net at morning, and the bright fish are heaped inside the boat? These are all airs upon Pan's pipe; he it was who gave them breath in the exultation of his heart, and gleefully modulated their outflow with his lips and fingers. The coarse mirth of herdsmen, shaking the dells with laughter and striking out high echoes from the rock; the tune of moving feet in the lamplit city, or on the smooth ball-room floor; the hooves of many horses, beating the wide pastures in alarm; the song of hurrying rivers; the colour of clear skies; and smiles and the live touch of hands; and the voice of things, and their significant look, and the renovating influence they breathe forth—these are his joyful measures, to which the whole earth treads in choral harmony. To this music the young lambs bound as to a tabor,[8] and the London shop-girl skips rudely in the dance. For it puts a spirit of gladness in all hearts; and to look on the happy side of nature is common, in their hours, to all created things. Some are vocal under a good influence, are pleasing whenever they are pleased, and hand on their happiness to others, as a child who, looking upon lovely things, looks lovely. Some leap to the strains with unapt foot, and make a halting figure in the universal dance. And some, like sour spectators at the play, receive the music into their hearts with an unmoved countenance, and walk like strangers through the general rejoicing. But let him feign never so carefully, there is not a man but has his pulses shaken when Pan trolls out a stave of ecstasy and sets the world a-singing.

Alas if that were all! But oftentimes the air is changed; and in the screech of the night wind, chasing navies, subverting the tall ships and the rooted cedar of the hills; in the random deadly levin[9] or the fury of headlong floods, we recognize the "dread foundation"[10] of life and the anger in Pan's heart. Earth wages open war against her children, and under her softest touch hides treacherous claws. The cool waters invite us in to drown; the domestic hearth burns up in the hour of sleep, and makes an end of all. Everything is good or bad, helpful or deadly, not in itself, but by its circumstances. For a few bright days in England the hurricane must break forth and the North Sea pay a toll of populous ships.

And when the universal music has led lovers into the paths of dalliance, confident of Nature's sympathy, suddenly the air shifts into a minor, and death makes a clutch from his ambuscade below the bed of marriage. For death is given in a kiss; the dearest kindnesses are fatal; and into this life, where one thing preys upon another, the child too often makes its entrance from the mother's corpse. It is no wonder, with so traitorous a scheme of things, if the wise people who created for us the idea of Pan thought that of all fears the fear of him was the most terrible, since it embraces all. And still we preserve the phrase: a panic terror. To reckon dangers too curiously, to hearken too intently for the threat that runs through all the winning music of the world, to hold back the hand from the rose because of the thorn, and from life because of death: this it is to be afraid of Pan. Highly respectable citizens who flee life's pleasures and responsibilities and keep, with upright hat, upon the midway of custom, avoiding the right hand and the left, the ecstasies and the agonies, how surprised they would be if they could hear their attitude mythologically expressed, and knew themselves as tooth-chattering ones, who flee from Nature because they fear the hand of Nature's God! Shrilly sound Pan's pipes; and behold the banker instantly concealed in the bank parlour! For to distrust one's impulses is to be recreant to Pan.

There are moments when the mind refuses to be satisfied with evolution, and demands a ruddier presentation of the sum of man's experience. Sometimes the mood is brought about by laughter at the humorous side of life, as when, abstracting ourselves from earth, we imagine people plodding on foot, or seated in ships and speedy trains, with the planet all the while whirling in the opposite direction, so that, for all their hurry, they travel back-foremost through the universe of space. Sometimes it comes by the spirit of delight,[11] and sometimes by the spirit of terror. At least, there will always be hours when we refuse to be put off by the feint of explanation, nicknamed science; and demand instead some palpitating image of our estate, that shall represent the troubled and uncertain element in which we dwell, and satisfy reason by the means of art. Science writes of the world as if with the cold finger of a starfish; it is all true; but what is it when compared to the reality of which it discourses? where hearts beat high in April, and death strikes, and hills totter in the earthquake, and there is a glamour over all the objects of sight, and a thrill in all noises for the ear, and Romance herself has made her dwelling among men? So we come back to the old myth, and hear the goat-footed piper making the music which is itself the charm and terror of things; and when a glen invites our visiting footsteps, fancy that Pan leads us thither with a gracious tremolo; or when our hearts quail at the thunder of the cataract, tell ourselves that he has stamped his hoof in the nigh thicket.[12]

Notes

1 "Then shall be said or sung the Apostles' Creed by the Minister and the people, standing" (*Book of Common Prayer*).
2 Possibly an allusion to Charles Darwin's description of nature's "inextricable web of affinities" and "web of complex relations" in *On the Origin of Species* (1859, ch. 13, ch. 3).
3 "Imperious Caesar, dead and turn'd to clay, / Might stop a hole to keep the wind away" (Shakespeare, *Hamlet*, 5. 1.196–7). Stevenson is apparently also remembering a passage from Dickens's *The Mystery of Edwin Drood* (1870, ch. 3): "the Cloisterham children grow small salad in the dust of abbots and abbesses, and make dirt-pies of nuns and friars."
4 According to Suetonius, Nero played his lyre during the Great Fire of Rome in AD 64 or proverbially "fiddled while Rome burned."
5 In legend, Pan advised Bacchus to have his men shout in the night. Thinking they were surrounded because of the echoes, the superior enemy forces fled.
6 Victorian physicists hypothesized that "aether," which ancients believed pervaded space, was the medium through which light travelled like a wave.

7 Elizabeth Barrett Browning's poem "The Dead Pan" (1845), with the refrain "Pan, Pan is dead," cites a tradition that during Christ's agony in Gethsemane a cry of "Great Pan is dead!" rang out and the oracles ceased.
8 Wordsworth, "Ode: Intimations" (20–1).
9 Lightning.
10 Wordsworth, "In my mind's eye a Temple, like a cloud" (10–11).
11 P.B. Shelley, "Song" (2).
12 "While, hidden in the thicket nigh, / Puck should brood o'er his frolic sly"—Walter Scott, *Rokeby* (1813), 4.2.17–18.

14

A PLEA FOR GAS LAMPS[1]

Cities given, the problem was to light them. How to conduct individual citizens about the burgess-warren, when once heaven had withdrawn its leading luminary? or—since we live in a scientific age—when once our spinning planet has turned its back upon the sun? The moon, from time to time, was doubtless very helpful; the stars had a cheery look among the chimney-pots; and a cresset[2] here and there, on church or citadel, produced a fine pictorial effect, and, in places where the ground lay unevenly, held out the right hand of conduct to the benighted. But sun, moon, and stars abstracted or concealed, the night-faring inhabitant had to fall back—we speak on the authority of old prints—upon stable lanthorns, two stories in height.[3] Many holes, drilled in the conical turret-roof of this vagabond Pharos,[4] let up spouts of dazzlement into the bearer's eyes; and as he paced forth in the ghostly darkness, carrying his own sun by a ring about his finger, day and night swung to and fro and up and down about his footsteps. Blackness haunted his path; he was beleaguered by goblins as he went; and, curfew being struck, he found no light but that he travelled in throughout the township.

Closely following on this epoch of migratory lanthorns in a world of extinction, came the era of oil-lights, hard to kindle, easy to extinguish, pale and wavering in the hour of their endurance. Rudely puffed the winds of heaven; roguishly clomb up the all-destructive urchin; and, lo! in a moment night re-established her void empire, and the cit[5] groped along the wall, suppered but bedless, occult from guidance,[6] and sorrily wading in the kennels.[7] As if gamesome winds and gamesome youths were not sufficient, it was the habit to sling these feeble luminaries from house to house above the fairway. There, on invisible cordage, let them swing! And suppose some crane-necked general to go speeding by on a tall charger, spurring the destiny of nations, red-hot in expedition, there would indubitably be some effusion of military blood, and oaths, and a certain crash of glass; and while the chieftain rode forward with a purple coxcomb,[8] the street would be left to original darkness, unpiloted, unvoyageable, a province of the desert night.

The conservative, looking before and after, draws from each contemplation the matter for content. Out of the age of gas lamps he glances back slightingly at the mirk and glimmer in which his ancestors wandered; his heart waxes jocund at the contrast; nor do his lips refrain from a stave, in the highest style of poetry, lauding progress and the golden mean. When gas first spread along a city, mapping it forth about evenfall for the eye of observant birds, a new age had begun for sociality and corporate pleasure-seeking, and begun with proper circumstance, becoming its own birthright. The work of Prometheus[9] had advanced by another stride. Mankind and its supper parties were no longer at the mercy of a few miles of sea-fog; sundown no longer emptied the promenade; and the day was lengthened out to every man's fancy. The city-folk had stars of their own; biddable, domesticated stars.

It is true that these were not so steady, nor yet so clear, as their originals; nor indeed was their lustre so elegant as that of the best wax candles. But then the gas stars, being nearer at hand, were more practically efficacious than Jupiter himself. It is true, again, that they did not unfold their rays with the appropriate spontaneity of the planets, coming out along the firmament one after another, as the need arises. But the lamplighters[10] took to their heels every evening, and ran with a good heart. It was pretty to see man thus emulating the punctuality of heaven's orbs; and though perfection was not absolutely reached, and now and then an individual may have been knocked on the head by the ladder of the flying functionary, yet people commended his zeal in a proverb,[11] and taught their children to say, "God bless the lamplighter!" And since his passage was a piece of the day's programme, the children were well pleased to repeat the benediction, not, of course, in so many words, which would have been improper, but in some chaste circumlocution, suitable for infant lips.

God bless him, indeed! For the term of his twilight diligence is near at hand; and for not much longer shall we watch him speeding up the street and, at measured intervals, knocking another luminous hole into the dusk. The Greeks would have made a noble myth of such an one; how he distributed starlight, and, as soon as the need was over, re-collected it; and the little bull's-eye,[12] which was his instrument, and held enough fire to kindle a whole parish, would have been fitly commemorated in the legend. Now, like all heroic tasks, his labours draw towards apotheosis, and in the light of victory himself shall disappear. For another advance has been effected. Our tame stars are to come out in future, not one by one, but all in a body and at once. A sedate electrician somewhere in a back office touches a spring—and behold! from one end to another of the city, from east to west, from the Alexandra to the Crystal Palace,[13] there is light! *Fiat Lux*,[14] says the sedate electrician. What a spectacle, on some clear, dark nightfall, from the edge of Hampstead Hill, when in a moment, in the twinkling of an eye,[15] the design of the monstrous city flashes into vision—a glittering hieroglyph many square miles in extent; and when, to borrow and debase an image, all the evening street-lamps burst together into song![16] Such is the spectacle of the future, preluded the other day by the experiment in Pall Mall.[17] Star-rise by electricity, the most romantic flight of civilization; the compensatory benefit for an innumerable array of factories and bankers' clerks. To the artistic spirit exercised about Thirlmere,[18] here is a crumb of consolation; consolatory, at least, to such of them as look out upon the world through seeing eyes, and contentedly accept beauty where it comes.

But the conservative, while lauding progress, is ever timid of innovation; his is the hand upheld to counsel pause; his is the signal advising slow advance. The word *electricity* now sounds the note of danger. In Paris, at the mouth of the Passage des Princes, in the place before the Opera portico, and in the Rue Drouot at the *Figaro* office, a new sort of urban star now shines out nightly, horrible, unearthly, obnoxious to the human eye; a lamp for a nightmare! Such a light as this should shine only on murders and public crime, or along the corridors of lunatic asylums, a horror to heighten horror. To look at it only once is to fall in love with gas, which gives a warm domestic radiance fit to eat by. Mankind, you would have thought, might have remained content with what Prometheus stole for them and not gone fishing the profound heaven with kites[19] to catch and domesticate the wild-fire of the storm. Yet here we have the levin[20] brand at our doors, and it is proposed that we should henceforward take our walks abroad in the glare of permanent lightning. A man need not be very superstitious if he scruple to follow his pleasures by the light of the Terror that Flieth,[21] nor very epicurean if he prefer to see the face of beauty more becomingly displayed. That ugly blinding glare may not improperly advertise the home of slanderous *Figaro*,[22] which is a back-shop to the infernal regions; but where soft joys prevail, where people are convoked to pleasure and the philosopher looks on smiling and silent, where love and laughter and deifying wine abound, there, at least, let the old mild lustre shine upon the ways of man.

Notes

1 Before electric lighting, Edinburgh street lights were illuminated by reflective oil-lit lamps, originally designed by Thomas Smith, stepfather to RLS's grandfather Robert Stevenson. See Claire Harman's *Myself and the Other Fellow: A Life of Robert Louis Stevenson* (Harper, 2005, p. 3).
2 An iron vessel, usually suspended from a roof, containing fuel to be burned for light.
3 A square glass lantern whose conical top resembles a roofed house.
4 Lighthouse (Greek).
5 Citizen or townsman.
6 "Invisible, so that no one could guide him"—A. F. Shuster (ed.), *A Book of English Essays: 1600–1900* (H. Frowde, 1913, n. 559).
7 Gutters.
8 Head.
9 A Titan who stole fire for humanity from the gods.
10 See Stevenson's poem "The Lamplighter" in *A Child's Garden of Verses* (1885).
11 Running "like a lamplighter" meant with all possible speed.
12 Bull's-eye lantern, which shone light through a thick glass disc in the front. See "The Lantern-Bearers" (p. 259).
13 The Crystal Palace was moved from Hyde Park to Sydenham in south London after the Great Exhibition closed in 1854. The north London counterpart Alexandra Palace was built in 1873.
14 "Let there be light" (Latin, Genesis 1:3).
15 1 Corinthians 15:52.
16 Job 38:7.
17 Electrical lighting was tested in Pall Mall on 13 April 1878.

18 In 1879 the Manchester Corporation turned Lake Thirlmere in the English Lake District into a reservoir. The unsuccessful opposition of the Thirlmere Defence Association, led by Hardwicke Rawnsley and other members of the Wordsworth Society, ultimately led to the establishment of the National Trust in 1895.
19 Benjamin Franklin flew a kite into a thundercloud to demonstrate lightning's electricity in 1752.
20 Lightning.
21 Psalm 91:5.
22 *Le Figaro*: a sensational Parisian daily newspaper.

MEMORIES AND PORTRAITS

15

THE FOREIGNER AT HOME

"This is no my ain house; I ken by the biggin' o't."[1]

Two recent books, one by Mr. Grant White on England, one on France by the diabolically clever Mr. Hillebrand,[2] may well have set people thinking on the divisions of races and nations. Such thoughts should arise with particular congruity and force to inhabitants of that United Kingdom, peopled from so many different stocks, babbling so many different dialects, and offering in its extent such singular contrasts, from the busiest over-population to the unkindliest desert, from the Black Country to the Moor of Rannoch. It is not only when we cross the seas that we go abroad; there are foreign parts of England; and the race that has conquered so wide an empire has not yet managed to assimilate the islands whence she sprang. Ireland, Wales, and the Scottish mountains still cling, in part, to their old Gaelic speech. It was but the other day that English triumphed in Cornwall, and they still show in Mousehole, on St. Michael's Bay, the house of the last Cornish-speaking woman. English itself, which will now frank the traveller through the most of North America, through the greater South Sea Islands, in India, along much of the coast of Africa, and in the ports of China and Japan, is still to be heard, in its home country, in half a hundred varying stages of transition. You may go all over the States, and—setting aside the actual intrusion and influence of foreigners, negro, French, or Chinese—you shall scarce meet with so marked a difference of accent as in the forty miles between Edinburgh and Glasgow, or of dialect as in the hundred miles between Edinburgh and Aberdeen. Book English has gone round the world, but at home we still preserve the racy idioms of our fathers, and every county, in some parts every dale, has its own quality of speech, vocal or verbal. In like manner, local custom and prejudice, even local religion and local law, linger on into the latter end of the nineteenth century—*imperia in imperio*,[3] foreign things at home.

In spite of these promptings to reflection, ignorance of his neighbours is the character of the typical John Bull. His is a domineering nature, steady in fight, imperious to command, but neither curious nor quick about the life of others. In French colonies, and still more in the Dutch, I have read that there is an immediate and lively contact between the dominant and the dominated race, that a certain sympathy is begotten, or at the least a transfusion of prejudices, making life easier for both. But the Englishman sits apart, bursting with pride and ignorance. He figures among his vassals in the hour of peace with the same disdainful air that led him on to victory. A passing enthusiasm for some foreign art or fashion may deceive the world, it cannot impose upon his intimates. He may be amused by a foreigner as by a monkey, but he will never condescend to study him with any patience. Miss Bird,[4] an authoress with whom I profess myself in love, declares all the viands of Japan to be uneatable—a staggering pretension. So, when the Prince of Wales's marriage was celebrated at Mentone by a dinner to the Mentonese, it was proposed to give them solid English fare—roast beef and plum pudding, and no tomfoolery. Here we have either pole of the Britannic folly. We will not eat the food of any foreigner; nor, when we have the chance, will we suffer him to eat of it himself. The same spirit inspired Miss Bird's American missionaries, who had come thousands of miles to change the faith of Japan, and openly professed their ignorance of the religions they were trying to supplant.

I quote an American in this connection without scruple. Uncle Sam is better than John Bull, but he is tarred with the English stick. For Mr. Grant White the States are the New England States and nothing more. He wonders at the amount of drinking in London; let him try San Francisco. He wittily reproves English ignorance as to the status of women in America; but has he not himself forgotten Wyoming? The name Yankee, of which he is so tenacious, is used over the most of the great Union as a term of reproach. The Yankee States, of which he is so staunch a subject, are but a drop in the bucket. And we find in his book a vast virgin ignorance of the life and prospects of America; every view partial, parochial, not raised to the horizon; the moral feeling proper, at the largest, to a clique of States; and the whole scope and atmosphere not American, but merely Yankee. I will go far beyond him in reprobating the assumption and the incivility of my countryfolk to their cousins from beyond the sea; I grill in my blood over the silly rudeness of our newspaper articles; and I do not know where to look when I find myself in company with an American and see my countrymen unbending to him as to a performing dog. But in the case of Mr. Grant White example were better than precept. Wyoming is, after all, more readily accessible to Mr. White than Boston to the English, and the New England self-sufficiency no better justified than the Britannic.

It is so, perhaps, in all countries; perhaps in all, men are most ignorant of the foreigners at home. John Bull is ignorant of the States; he is probably ignorant of India; but considering his opportunities, he is far more ignorant of countries nearer his own door. There is one country, for instance—its frontier not so far from London, its people closely akin, its language the same in all essentials with the English—of which I will go bail he knows nothing. His ignorance of the sister kingdom cannot be described; it can only be illustrated by anecdote. I once travelled with a man of plausible manners and good intelligence,—a University man, as the phrase goes,—a man, besides, who had taken his degree in life and knew a thing or two about the age we live in. We were deep in talk, whirling between Peterborough and London; among other things, he began to describe some piece of legal injustice he had recently encountered, and I observed in my innocence that things were not so in Scotland. "I beg your pardon," said he, "this is a matter of law." He had never heard of the Scots law; nor did he choose to be informed. The law was the same for the whole country, he told me roundly; every child knew that. At last, to settle matters, I explained to him that I was a member of a Scottish legal body, and had stood the brunt of an examination in the very law in question. Thereupon he looked me for a moment full in the face and dropped the conversation. This is a monstrous instance, if you like, but it does not stand alone in the experience of Scots.

England and Scotland differ, indeed, in law, in history, in religion, in education, and in the very look of nature and men's faces, not always widely, but always trenchantly. Many particulars that struck Mr. Grant White, a Yankee, struck me, a Scot, no less forcibly; he and I felt ourselves foreigners on many common provocations. A Scotchman may tramp the better part of Europe and the United States, and never again receive so vivid an impression of foreign travel and strange lands and manners as on his first excursion into England. The change from a hilly to a level country strikes him with delighted wonder. Along the flat horizon there arise the frequent venerable towers of churches. He sees at the end of airy vistas the revolution of the windmill sails. He may go where he pleases in the future; he may see Alps, and Pyramids, and lions; but it will be hard to beat the pleasure of that moment. There are, indeed, few merrier spectacles than that of many windmills bickering together in a fresh breeze over a woody country; their halting alacrity of movement, their pleasant business, making bread all day with uncouth gesticulations, their air, gigantically human, as of a creature half alive, put a spirit of romance into the tamest landscape. When the Scotch child sees them first he falls immediately in love; and from that time forward windmills keep turning in his dreams. And so, in their degree, with every feature of the life and landscape. The warm, habitable age of towns and hamlets, the green, settled, ancient look of the country; the lush hedgerows, stiles, and privy pathways in the fields; the sluggish, brimming rivers; chalk and smock-frocks; chimes of bells and the rapid, pertly-sounding English speech—they are all new to the curiosity; they are all set to English airs in the child's story that he tells himself at night. The sharp edge of novelty wears off; the feeling is scotched, but I doubt whether it is ever killed. Rather it keeps returning, ever the more rarely and strangely, and even in scenes to which you have been long accustomed suddenly awakes and gives a relish to enjoyment or heightens the sense of isolation.

One thing especially continues unfamiliar to the Scotchman's eye—the domestic architecture, the look of streets and buildings; the quaint, venerable age of many, and the thin walls and warm colouring of all. We have, in Scotland, far fewer ancient buildings, above all in country places; and those that we have are all of hewn or harled masonry. Wood has been sparingly used in their construction; the window-frames are sunken in the wall, not flat to the front, as in England; the roofs are steeper-pitched; even a hill farm will have a massy, square, cold and permanent appearance. English houses, in comparison, have the look of cardboard toys, such as a puff might shatter. And to this the Scotchman never becomes used. His eye can never rest consciously on one of these brick houses—rickles of brick, as he might call them—or on one of these flat-chested streets, but he is instantly reminded where he is, and instantly travels back in fancy to his home. "This is no my ain house; I ken by the biggin' o't." And yet perhaps it is his own, bought with his own money, the key of it long polished in his pocket; but it has not yet, and never will be, thoroughly adopted by his imagination; nor does he cease to remember that, in the whole length and breadth of his native country, there was no building even distantly resembling it.

But it is not alone in scenery and architecture that we count England foreign. The constitution of society, the very pillars of the empire, surprise and even pain us. The dull, neglected peasant, sunk in matter, insolent, gross and servile, makes a startling contrast with our own long-legged, long-headed, thoughtful, Bible-quoting ploughman. A week or two in such a place as Suffolk leaves the Scotch-man gasping. It seems incredible that within the boundaries of his own island a class should have been thus forgotten. Even the educated and intelligent, who hold our own opinions and speak in our own words, yet seem to hold them with a difference or from another reason, and to speak on all things with less interest and conviction. The first shock of English society is like a cold plunge. It is possible that the Scot comes looking for too much, and to be sure his first experiment will be in the wrong direction. Yet surely his complaint is grounded; surely the speech of Englishmen is too often lacking in generous ardour, the better part of the man too often withheld from the social commerce, and the contact of mind with mind evaded as with terror. A Scotch peasant will talk more liberally out of his own experience. He will not put you by with conversational counters and small jests; he will give you the best of himself, like one interested in life and man's chief end. A Scotchman is vain, interested in himself and others, eager for sympathy, setting forth his thoughts and experience in the best light. The egoism of the Englishman is self-contained. He does not seek to proselytise. He takes no interest in Scotland or the Scotch, and, what is the unkindest cut of all,[5] he does not care to justify his indifference. Give him the wages of going on and being an Englishman, that is all he asks; and in the meantime, while you continue to associate, he would rather not be reminded of your baser origin. Compared with the grand, tree-like self-sufficiency of his demeanour, the vanity and curiosity of the Scot seem uneasy, vulgar and immodest. That you should continually try to establish human and serious relations, that you should actually feel an interest in John Bull, and desire and invite a return of interest from him, may argue something more awake and lively in your mind, but it still puts you in the attitude of a suitor and a poor relation. Thus even the lowest class of the educated English towers over a Scotchman by the head and shoulders.

Different indeed is the atmosphere in which Scotch and English youth begin to look about them, come to themselves in life, and gather up those first apprehensions

126

which are the material of future thought and, to a great extent, the rule of future conduct. I have been to school in both countries, and I found, in the boys of the North, something at once rougher and more tender, at once more reserve and more expansion, a greater habitual distance chequered by glimpses of a nearer intimacy, and on the whole wider extremes of temperament and sensibility. The boy of the South seems more wholesome, but less thoughtful; he gives himself to games as to a business, striving to excel, but is not readily transported by imagination; the type remains with me as cleaner in mind and body, more active, fonder of eating, endowed with a lesser and a less romantic sense of life and of the future, and more immersed in present circumstances. And certainly, for one thing, English boys are younger for their age. Sabbath observance makes a series of grim, and perhaps serviceable, pauses in the tenor of Scotch boyhood—days of great stillness and solitude for the rebellious mind, when in the dearth of books and play, and in the intervals of studying the Shorter Catechism, the intellect and senses prey upon and test each other. The typical English Sunday, with the huge midday dinner and the plethoric afternoon, leads perhaps to different results. About the very cradle of the Scot there goes a hum of metaphysical divinity; and the whole of two divergent systems is summed up, not merely speciously, in the two first questions of the rival catechisms, the English tritely inquiring, "What is your name?" the Scottish striking at the very roots of life with, "What is the chief end of man?" and answering nobly, if obscurely, "To glorify God and to enjoy Him for ever."[6] I do not wish to make an idol of the Shorter Catechism; but the fact of such a question being asked opens to us Scotch a great field of speculation; and the fact that it is asked of all of us, from the peer to the ploughboy, binds us more nearly together. No Englishman of Byron's age, character and history, would have had patience for long theological discussions on the way to fight for Greece; but the daft Gordon blood and the Aberdonian schooldays kept their influence to the end.[7] We have spoken of the material conditions; nor need much more be said of these: of the land lying everywhere more exposed, of the wind always louder and bleaker, of the black, roaring winters, of the gloom of high-lying, old stone cities, imminent on the windy seaboard; compared with the level streets, the warm colouring of the brick, the domestic quaintness of the architecture, among which English children begin to grow up and come to themselves in life. As the stage of the University approaches, the contrast becomes more express. The English lad goes to Oxford or Cambridge; there, in an ideal world of gardens, to lead a semi-scenic life, costumed, disciplined and drilled by proctors. Nor is this to be regarded merely as a stage of education; it is a piece of privilege besides, and a step that separates him further from the bulk of his compatriots. At an earlier age the Scottish lad begins his greatly different experience of crowded class-rooms, of a gaunt quadrangle, of a bell hourly booming over the traffic of the city to recall him from the public-house where he has been lunching, or the streets where he has been wandering fancy-free. His college life has little of restraint, and nothing of necessary gentility. He will find no quiet clique of the exclusive, studious and cultured; no rotten borough of the arts. All classes rub shoulders on the greasy benches. The raffish young gentleman in gloves must measure his scholarship with the plain, clownish laddie from the parish school. They separate, at the session's end, one to smoke cigars about a watering-place, the other to resume the labours of the field beside his peasant family. The first muster of a college class in Scotland is a scene of curious and painful interest; so many lads, fresh from the heather, hang round the stove in cloddish embarrassment, ruffled by the presence of their smarter comrades, and afraid of the sound of their own rustic voices. It was in these early days, I think, that Professor Blackie[8] won the affection of his pupils, putting these uncouth, umbrageous students at their ease with ready human geniality. Thus, at least, we have a healthy democratic atmosphere to breathe in while at work; even when there is no cordiality there is always a juxtaposition of the different classes, and in the competition of study the intellectual power of each is plainly demonstrated to the other. Our tasks ended, we of the North go forth as freemen into the humming, lamplit city. At five o'clock you may see the last of us hiving from the college gates, in the glare of the shop windows, under the green glimmer of the winter sunset. The frost tingles in our blood; no proctor lies in wait to intercept us; till the bell sounds again, we are the masters of the world; and some portion of our lives is always Saturday, *la trêve de Dieu*.[9]

Nor must we omit the sense of the nature of his country and his country's history gradually growing in the child's mind from story and from observation. A Scottish child hears much of shipwreck, outlying iron skerries, pitiless breakers, and great sea-lights; much of heathery mountains, wild clans, and hunted Covenanters.[10] Breaths come to him in song of the distant Cheviots and the ring of foraying hoofs. He glories in his hard-fisted forefathers, of the iron girdle and the handful of oatmeal, who rode so swiftly and lived so sparely on their raids. Poverty, ill-luck, enterprise, and constant resolution are the fibres of the legend of his country's history. The heroes and kings of Scotland have been tragically fated; the most marking incidents in Scottish history—Flodden, Darien, or the Forty-five—were still either failures or defeats; and the fall of Wallace and the repeated reverses of the Bruce combine with the very smallness of the country to teach rather a moral than a material criterion for life.[11] Britain is altogether small, the mere taproot of her extended empire; Scotland, again, which alone the Scottish boy adopts in his imagination, is but a little part of that, and avowedly cold, sterile and unpopulous. It is not so for nothing. I once seemed to have perceived in an American boy a greater readiness of sympathy for lands that are great, and rich, and growing, like his own. It proved to be quite otherwise: a mere dumb piece of boyish romance, that I had lacked penetration to divine. But the error serves the purpose of my argument; for I am sure, at least, that the heart of young Scotland will be always touched more nearly by paucity of number and Spartan poverty of life.

So we may argue, and yet the difference is not explained. That Shorter Catechism which I took as being so typical of Scotland, was yet composed in the city of Westminster. The division of races is more sharply marked within the borders of Scotland itself than between the countries. Galloway and Buchan,

Lothian and Lochaber, are like foreign parts; yet you may choose a man from any of them, and, ten to one, he shall prove to have the headmark of a Scot. A century and a half ago the Highlander wore a different costume, spoke a different language, worshipped in another church, held different morals, and obeyed a different social constitution from his fellow-countrymen either of the south or north. Even the English, it is recorded, did not loathe the Highlander and the Highland costume as they were loathed by the remainder of the Scotch. Yet the Highlander felt himself a Scot. He would willingly raid into the Scotch lowlands; but his courage failed him at the border, and he regarded England as a perilous, unhomely land. When the Black Watch,[12] after years of foreign service, returned to Scotland, veterans leaped out and kissed the earth at Port Patrick. They had been in Ireland, stationed among men of their own race and language, where they were well liked and treated with affection; but it was the soil of Galloway that they kissed at the extreme end of the hostile lowlands, among a people who did not understand their speech, and who had hated, harried, and hanged them since the dawn of history. Last, and perhaps most curious, the sons of chieftains were often educated on the continent of Europe. They went abroad speaking Gaelic; they returned speaking, not English, but the broad dialect of Scotland. Now, what idea had they in their minds when they thus, in thought, identified themselves with their ancestral enemies? What was the sense in which they were Scotch and not English, or Scotch and not Irish? Can a bare name be thus influential on the minds and affections of men, and a political aggregation blind them to the nature of facts? The story of the Austrian Empire would seem to answer, No;[13] the far more galling business of Ireland clenches the negative from nearer home. Is it common education, common morals, a common language or a common faith, that join men into nations? There were practically none of these in the case we are considering.

The fact remains: in spite of the difference of blood and language, the Lowlander feels himself the sentimental countryman of the Highlander. When they meet abroad, they fall upon each other's necks in spirit; even at home there is a kind of clannish intimacy in their talk. But from his compatriot in the south the Lowlander stands consciously apart. He has had a different training; he obeys different laws; he makes his will in other terms, is otherwise divorced and married; his eyes are not at home in an English landscape or with English houses; his ear continues to remark the English speech; and even though his tongue acquire the Southern knack, he will still have a strong Scotch accent of the mind.

Notes

1 "This is not my own house; I know by the building of it" from the Scottish song "This is no mine ain House."
2 Richard Grant White's *England Without and Within* (1881) and Karl Hillebrand's *France and the French in the Second Half of the Nineteenth Century* (1880).
3 "A realm within a realm" (Latin).

4 Isabella Bird (1831–1904), English explorer, naturalist, and author of *Unbeaten Tracks in Japan* (1880).
5 Shakespeare, *Julius Caesar*, 3.2.177.
6 The Presbyterian Westminster Shorter Catechism was approved by England's Parliament in 1648 and abandoned with the restoration of the monarchy in 1660. The Church of Scotland adopted it in 1648 and the Scottish Parliament authorized it in 1649.
7 Byron died of disease in 1824 while fighting in the Greek War of Independence against the Ottoman Empire.
8 John Stuart Blackie (1809–1895), professor at the University of Edinburgh, poet, and scholar of classics and Scottish culture.
9 "The truce of God" (French); a ceasefire, a holiday.
10 Scottish Presbyterians of the 19th century who pledged and fought to maintain their church government. See n. 22, p. 439.
11 In the War of the League of Cambrai's Battle of Flodden (9 Sept. 1513), the English army defeated Scotland and killed King James IV. The Darien Scheme: a failed attempt at Scottish colonization in Panama, which devastated Scotland's economy and facilitated the Act of Union with England in 1707. Sir William Wallace (1270–1305), celebrated leader in the First War of Scottish Independence who was captured and brutally executed under King Edward I. Robert I, or Robert the Bruce, King of Scotland (1306–1329), successfully led the First War of Scottish Independence.
12 The 42nd Royal Highland Regiment of Foot, a Scottish infantry regiment of the British Army, which fought in a series of wars abroad, including the American War of Independence and the Peninsular War.
13 A great central European power, the Austrian Empire (1804–1867) was dissolved after the defeat of Austria in the Austro-Prussian War: the German Confederation's civil war.

16

SOME COLLEGE MEMORIES

I am asked to write something (it is not specifically stated what) to the profit and glory of my *Alma Mater*;[1] and the fact is I seem to be in very nearly the same case with those who addressed me, for while I am willing enough to write something, I know not what to write. Only one point I see, that if I am to write at all, it should be of the University itself and my own days under its shadow; of the things that are still the same and of those that are already changed: such talk, in short, as would pass naturally between a student of to-day and one of yesterday, supposing them to meet and grow confidential.

The generations pass away swiftly enough on the high seas of life; more swiftly still in the little bubbling backwater of the quadrangle; so that we see there, on a scale startlingly diminished, the flight of time and the succession of men. I looked for my name the other day in last year's case book of the Speculative.[2] Naturally enough I looked for it near the end; it was not there, nor yet in the next column, so that I began to think it had been dropped at press; and when at last I found it, mounted on the shoulders of so many successors, and looking in that posture like the name of a man of ninety, I was conscious of some of the dignity of years. This kind of dignity of temporal precession is likely, with prolonged life, to become more familiar, possibly less welcome; but I felt it strongly then, it is strongly on me now, and I am the more emboldened to speak with my successors in the tone of a parent and a praiser of things past.

For, indeed, that which they attend is but a fallen University; it has doubtless some remains of good, for human institutions decline by gradual stages; but decline, in spite of all seeming embellishments, it does; and what is perhaps more singular, began to do so when I ceased to be a student. Thus, by an odd chance, I had the very last of the very best of *Alma Mater*; the same thing, I hear (which makes it the more strange), had previously happened to my father; and if they are good and do not die, something not at all unsimilar will be found in time to have befallen my successors of to-day. Of the specific points of change, of advantage in the past, of shortcoming in the present, I must own that, on a near examination, they look wondrous cloudy. The chief and far the most lamentable change is the absence of a certain lean, ugly, idle, unpopular student, whose presence was for me the gist and heart of the whole matter; whose changing humours,

131

fine occasional purposes of good, flinching acceptance of evil, shiverings on wet, east-windy, morning journeys up to class, infinite yawnings during lecture and unquenchable gusto in the delights of truantry, made up the sunshine and shadow of my college life. You cannot fancy what you missed in missing him; his virtues, I make sure, are inconceivable to his successors, just as they were apparently concealed from his contemporaries, for I was practically alone in the pleasure I had in his society. Poor soul, I remember how much he was cast down at times, and how life (which had not yet begun) seemed to be already at an end, and hope quite dead, and misfortune and dishonour, like physical presences, dogging him as he went. And it may be worth while to add that these clouds rolled away in their season, and that all clouds roll away at last, and the troubles of youth in particular are things but of a moment. So this student, whom I have in my eye, took his full share of these concerns, and that very largely by his own fault; but he still clung to his fortune, and in the midst of much misconduct, kept on in his own way learning how to work; and at last, to his wonder, escaped out of the stage of studentship not openly shamed; leaving behind him the University of Edinburgh shorn of a good deal of its interest for myself.

But while he is (in more senses than one) the first person, he is by no means the only one whom I regret, or whom the students of to-day, if they knew what they had lost, would regret also. They have still Tait,[3] to be sure—long may they have him!—and they have still Tait's class-room, cupola and all; but think of what a different place it was when this youth of mine (at least on roll days) would be present on the benches, and, at the near end of the platform, Lindsay senior was airing his robust old age.[4] It is possible my successors may have never even heard of Old Lindsay; but when he went, a link snapped with the last century. He had something of a rustic air, sturdy and fresh and plain; he spoke with a ripe east-country accent, which I used to admire; his reminiscences were all of journeys on foot or highways busy with post-chaises—a Scotland before steam; he had seen the coal fire on the Isle of May,[5] and he regaled me with tales of my own grandfather. Thus he was for me a mirror of things perished; it was only in his memory that I could see the huge shock of flames of the May beacon stream to leeward, and the watchers, as they fed the fire, lay hold unscorched of the windward bars of the furnace; it was only thus that I could see my grandfather driving swiftly in a gig along the seaboard road from Pittenweem to Crail, and for all his business hurry, drawing up to speak good-humouredly with those he met. And now, in his turn, Lindsay is gone also; inhabits only the memories of other men, till these shall follow him; and figures in my reminiscences as my grandfather figured in his.

To-day, again, they have Professor Butcher, and I hear he has a prodigious deal of Greek; and they have Professor Chrystal, who is a man filled with the mathematics.[6] And doubtless these are set-offs. But they cannot change the fact that Professor Blackie has retired, and that Professor Kelland is dead.[7] No man's education is complete or truly liberal who knew not Kelland. There were unutterable lessons in the mere sight of that frail old clerical gentleman, lively as a boy, kind like a fairy godfather, and keeping perfect order in his class by the spell of that very kindness. I have heard him drift into reminiscences in class time, though not for long, and give us glimpses of old-world life in out-of-the-way English parishes when he was young; thus playing the same part as Lindsay—the part of the surviving memory, signalling out of the dark backward and abysm of time the images of perished things. But it was a part that scarce became him; he somehow lacked the means: for all his silver hair and worn face, he was not truly old; and he had too much of the unrest and petulant fire of youth, and too much invincible innocence of mind, to play the veteran well. The time to measure him best, to taste (in the old phrase) his gracious nature, was when he received his class at home. What a pretty simplicity would he then show, trying to amuse us like children with toys; and what an engaging nervousness of manner, as fearing that his efforts might not succeed! Truly he made us all feel like children, and like children embarrassed, but at the same time filled with sympathy for the conscientious, troubled elder-boy who was working so hard to entertain us. A theorist has held the view that there is no feature in man so tell-tale as his spectacles; that the mouth may be compressed and the brow smoothed artificially, but the sheen of the barnacles is diagnostic. And truly it must have been thus with Kelland; for as I still fancy I behold him frisking actively about the platform, pointer in hand, that which I seem to see most clearly is the way his glasses glittered with affection. I never knew but one other man who had (if you will permit the phrase) so kind a spectacle; and that was Dr. Appleton.[8] But the light in his case was tempered and passive; in Kelland's it danced, and changed, and flashed vivaciously among the students, like a perpetual challenge to goodwill.

I cannot say so much about Professor Blackie, for a good reason. Kelland's class I attended, once even gained there a certificate of merit, the only distinction of my University career. But although I am the holder of a certificate of attendance in the professor's own hand, I cannot remember to have been present in the Greek class above a dozen times. Professor Blackie was even kind enough to remark (more than once) while in the very act of writing the document above referred to, that he did not know my face. Indeed, I denied myself many opportunities; acting upon an extensive and highly rational system of truantry, which cost me a great deal of trouble to put in exercise—perhaps as much as would have taught me Greek—and sent me forth into the world and the profession of letters with the merest shadow of an education. But they say it is always a good thing to have taken pains, and that success is its own reward, whatever be its nature; so that, perhaps, even upon this I should plume myself, that no one ever played the truant with more deliberate care, and none ever had more certificates for less education. One consequence, however, of my system is that I have much less to say of Professor Blackie than I had of Professor Kelland; and as he is still alive, and will long, I hope, continue to be so, it will not surprise you very much that I have no intention of saying it.

Meanwhile, how many others have gone—Jenkin, Hodgson, and I know not who besides;[9] and of that tide of students that used to throng the arch and blacken the quadrangle, how many are scattered into the remotest parts of the earth, and how many more have lain down beside their fathers in their "resting-graves"![10] And again, how many of these last have not found their way there, all too early, through the stress of education! That was one thing, at least, from which my truantry protected me. I am sorry indeed that I have no Greek, but I should be sorrier still if I were dead; nor do I know the name of that branch of knowledge which is worth acquiring at the price of a brain fever. There are many sordid tragedies in the life of the student, above all if he be poor, or drunken, or both; but nothing more moves a wise man's pity than the case of the lad who is in too much hurry to be learned. And so, for the sake of a moral at the end, I will call up one more figure, and have done. A student, ambitious of success by that hot, intemperate manner of study that now grows so common, read night and day for an examination. As he went on, the task became more easy to him, sleep was more easily banished, his brain grew hot and clear and more capacious, the necessary knowledge daily fuller and more orderly. It came to the eve of the trial and he watched all night in his high chamber, reviewing what he knew, and already secure of success. His window looked eastward, and being (as I said) high up, and the house itself standing on a hill, commanded a view over dwindling suburbs to a country horizon. At last my student drew up his blind, and still in quite a jocund humour, looked abroad. Day was breaking, the east was tinging with strange fires, the clouds breaking up for the coming of the sun; and at the sight, nameless terror seized upon his mind. He was sane, his senses were undisturbed; he saw clearly, and knew what he was seeing, and knew that it was normal; but he could neither bear to see it nor find the strength to look away, and fled in panic from his chamber into the enclosure of the street. In the cool air and silence, and among the sleeping houses, his strength was renewed. Nothing troubled him but the memory of what had passed, and an abject fear of its return.

> Gallo canente, spes redit,
> Aegris salus refunditur,
> Lapsis fides revertitur,[11]

as they sang of old in Portugal in the Morning Office. But to him that good hour of cockcrow, and the changes of the dawn, had brought panic, and lasting doubt, and such terror as he still shook to think of. He dared not return to his lodging; he could not eat; he sat down, he rose up, he wandered; the city woke about him with its cheerful bustle, the sun climbed overhead; and still he grew but the more absorbed in the distress of his recollection and the fear of his past fear. At the appointed hour, he came to the door of the place of examination; but when he was asked, he had forgotten his name. Seeing him so disordered, they had not the heart to send him away, but gave him a paper and admitted him, still nameless, to the Hall. Vain kindness, vain efforts. He could only sit in a still growing horror, writing nothing, ignorant of all, his mind filled with a single memory of the breaking day and his own intolerable fear. And that same night he was tossing in a brain fever.

134

People are afraid of war and wounds and dentists, all with excellent reason; but these are not to be compared with such chaotic terrors of the mind as fell on this young man, and made him cover his eyes from the innocent morning. We all have by our bedsides the box of the Merchant Abudah, thank God, securely enough shut; but when a young man sacrifices sleep to labour, let him have a care, for he is playing with the lock.[12]

Notes

1 The University of Edinburgh.
2 The Speculative Society is a debate club of students at the University of Edinburgh founded in 1764. Stevenson was elected to the Society on 16 Feb. 1869.
3 Peter Tait (1831–1901), Edinburgh professor, physicist, and pioneer in thermodynamics.
4 James Lindsay served from 1814 to 1872 as the experimental assistant to successive professors of natural philosophy, including Peter Tait. His son, Tom Lindsay, succeeded him.
5 A continually manned, coal-fired beacon constructed in 1635 and replaced by Stevenson's grandfather Robert Stevenson with a lighthouse in 1816.
6 Samuel Butcher (1850–1910), Cambridge classicist and later MP. George Crystal (1851–1911), mathematician who studied seiches (inland wave patterns).
7 John Stuart Blackie (1809–1895), poet and scholar of classics and Scottish culture. Philip Kelland (1808–1879), mathematician and educational reformer.
8 Charles Edward Cutts Birchall Appleton (1841–1879), professor of philosophy and founder of the journal *The Academy: A Monthly Record of Literature, Learning, Science, and Art.*
9 Fleeming Jenkin (1833–1885), engineering professor best known for inventing electric cable cars. Stevenson participated in amateur theatricals at Jenkin's house. His fondness and respect for his professor and friend led him to write *Memoir of Fleeming Jenkin* (1888). William Ballantyne Hodgson (1815–1880), professor of political economy and educational reformer.
10 Patrick Walker, *Biographia Presbyteriana*, vol. 1 (1827, 285).
11 From St. Ambrose's Latin liturgical hymn "Aeterne rerum conditor" ("Maker of all, eternal King): "New hope his clarion note awakes, / Sickness the feeble frame forsakes, / The Robber sheathes his lawless sword, / Faith to fallen is restored" (Trans. W. J. Copeland).
12 In James Ridley's *The Tales of the Genii: or, the Delightful Lessons of Horam* (1764), the Merchant Abudah opens a box to find an old woman who disturbs his nights and drives him to seek out illusory sources of contentment.

17

OLD MORTALITY[1]

There is a certain graveyard, looked upon on the one side by a prison, on the other by the windows of a quiet hotel; below, under a steep cliff, it beholds the traffic of many lines of rail, and the scream of the engine and the shock of meeting buffers mount to it all day long.[2] The aisles are lined with the inclosed sepulchres of families, door beyond door, like houses in a street; and in the morning the shadow of the prison turrets, and of many tall memorials, fall upon the graves. There, in the hot fits of youth, I came to be unhappy. Pleasant incidents are woven with my memory of the place. I here made friends with a certain plain old gentleman, a visitor on sunny mornings, gravely cheerful, who, with one eye upon the place that awaited him, chirped about his youth like winter sparrows; a beautiful housemaid of the hotel once, for some days together, dumbly flirted with me from a window and kept my wild heart flying; and once—she possibly remembers—the wise Eugenia followed me to that austere inclosure. Her hair came down, and in the shelter of the tomb my trembling fingers helped her to repair the braid. But for the most part I went there solitary and, with irrevocable emotion, pored on the names of the forgotten. Name after name, and to each the conventional attributions and the idle dates: a regiment of the unknown that had been the joy of mothers, and had thrilled with the illusions of youth, and at last, in the dim sick-room, wrestled with the pangs of old mortality. In that whole crew of the silenced there was but one of whom my fancy had received a picture; and he, with his comely, florid countenance, bewigged and habited in scarlet, and in his day combining fame and popularity, stood forth, like a taunt,[3] among that company of phantom appellations. It was then possible to leave behind us something more explicit than these severe, monotonous and lying epitaphs; and the thing left, the memory of a painted picture and what we call the immortality of a name, was hardly more desirable than mere oblivion. Even David Hume, as he lay composed beneath that "circular idea," was fainter than a dream;[4] and when the housemaid, broom in hand, smiled and beckoned from the open window, the fame of that bewigged philosopher melted like a raindrop in the sea.

And yet in soberness I cared as little for the housemaid as for David Hume. The interests of youth are rarely frank; his passions, like Noah's dove, come home to roost.[5] The fire, sensibility, and volume of his own nature, that is all that he has learned to recognise. The tumultuary and gray tide of life, the empire of routine, the unrejoicing faces of his elders, fill him with contemptuous surprise; there also he seems to walk among the tombs of spirits; and it is only in the course of years, and after much rubbing with his fellow-men, that he begins by glimpses to see himself from without and his fellows from within: to know his own for one among the thousand undenoted countenances of the city street, and to divine in others the throb of human agony and hope. In the meantime he will avoid the hospital doors, the pale faces, the cripple, the sweet whiff of chloroform—for there, on the most thoughtless, the pains of others are burned home; but he will continue to walk, in a divine self-pity, the aisles of the forgotten graveyard. The length of man's life, which is endless to the brave and busy, is scorned by his ambitious thought. He cannot bear to have come for so little, and to go again so wholly. He cannot bear, above all, in that brief scene, to be still idle, and by way of cure, neglects the little that he has to do. The parable of the talent[6] is the brief epitome of youth. To believe in immortality is one thing, but it is first needful to believe in life. Denunciatory preachers seem not to suspect that they may be taken gravely and in evil part; that young men may come to think of time as of a moment, and with the pride of Satan wave back the inadequate gift. Yet here is a true peril; this it is that sets them to pace the graveyard alleys and to read, with strange extremes of pity and derision, the memorials of the dead.

Books were the proper remedy: books of vivid human import, forcing upon their minds the issues, pleasures, busyness, importance and immediacy of that life in which they stand; books of smiling or heroic temper, to excite or to console; books of a large design, shadowing the complexity of that game of consequences to which we all sit down, the hanger-back not least. But the average sermon flees the point, disporting itself in that eternity of which we know, and need to know, so little; avoiding the bright, crowded, and momentous fields of life where destiny awaits us. Upon the average book a writer may be silent; he may set it down to his ill-hap that when his own youth was in the acrid fermentation, he should have fallen and fed upon the cheerless fields of Obermann. Yet to Mr. Arnold, who led him to these pastures, he still bears a grudge.[7] The day is perhaps not far off when people will begin to count *Moll Flanders*, ay, or *The Country Wife*, more wholesome and more pious diet than these guide-books to consistent egoism.[8]

But the most inhuman of boys soon wearies of the inhumanity of Obermann. And even while I still continued to be a haunter of the graveyard, I began insensibly to turn my attention to the grave-diggers, and was weaned out of myself to observe the conduct of visitors. This was dayspring, indeed, to a lad in such great darkness. Not that I began to see men, or to try to see them, from within, nor to learn charity and modesty and justice from the sight; but still stared at them externally from the prison windows of my affectation. Once I remember to have observed two working-women with a baby halting by a grave; there was something monumental in the grouping, one upright carrying the child, the other with bowed face crouching by her side. A wreath of immortelles under a glass dome had thus attracted them;[9] and, drawing near, I overheard their judgment on that

wonder. "Eh! what extravagance!" To a youth afflicted with the callosity of sentiment, this quaint and pregnant saying appeared merely base.

My acquaintance with grave-diggers, considering its length, was unremarkable.
One, indeed, whom I found plying his spade in the red evening, high above Allan
Water and in the shadow of Dunblane Cathedral, told me of his acquaintance with
the birds that still attended on his labours; how some would even perch about him,
waiting for their prey; and in a true Sexton's Calendar, how the species varied
with the season of the year. But this was the very poetry of the profession. The
others whom I knew were somewhat dry. A faint flavour of the gardener hung
about them, but sophisticated and disbloomed. They had engagements to keep,
not alone with the deliberate series of the seasons, but with mankind's clocks and
hour-long measurement of time. And thus there was no leisure for the relishing
pinch, or the hour-long gossip, foot on spade. They were men wrapped up in their
grim business; they liked well to open long-closed family vaults, blowing in the
key and throwing wide the grating; and they carried in their minds a calendar of
names and dates. It would be "in fifty-twa"[10] that such a tomb was last opened
for "Miss Jemimy." It was thus they spoke of their past patients—familiarly but
not without respect, like old family servants. Here is indeed a servant, whom we
forget that we possess; who does not wait at the bright table, or run at the bell's
summons, but patiently smokes his pipe beside the mortuary fire, and in his faithful memory notches the burials of our race. To suspect Shakespeare in his matu-
rity of a superficial touch savours of paradox; yet he was surely in error when he
attributed insensibility to the digger of the grave. But perhaps it is on Hamlet that
the charge should lie; or perhaps the English sexton differs from the Scotch.[11] The
"goodman delver,"[12] reckoning up his years of office, might have at least suggested other thoughts. It is a pride common among sextons. A cabinet-maker does
not count his cabinets, nor even an author his volumes, save when they stare upon
him from the shelves; but the grave-digger numbers his graves. He would indeed
be something different from human if his solitary open-air and tragic labours left
not a broad mark upon his mind. There, in his tranquil aisle, apart from city clamour, among the cats and robins and the ancient effigies and legends of the tomb,
he waits the continual passage of his contemporaries, falling like minute drops
into eternity. As they fall, he counts them; and this enumeration, which was at
first perhaps appalling to his soul, in the process of years and by the kindly influence of habit grows to be his pride and pleasure. There are many common stories
telling how he piques himself on crowded cemeteries. But I will rather tell of the
old grave-digger of Monkton, to whose unsuffering bedside the minister was summoned. He dwelt in a cottage built into the wall of the churchyard; and through a
bull's-eye pane above his bed he could see, as he lay dying, the rank grasses and
the upright and recumbent stones. Dr. Laurie was, I think, a Moderate: 'tis certain,
at least, that he took a very Roman view of deathbed dispositions; for he told the
old man that he had lived beyond man's natural years, that his life had been easy
and reputable, that his family had all grown up and been a credit to his care, and
that it now behoved him unregretfully to gird his loins and follow the majority.

The grave-digger heard him out; then he raised himself upon one elbow, and with the other hand pointed through the window to the scene of his life-long labours. "Doctor," he said, "I ha'e laid three hunner and fower-score in that kirkyaird; an it had been His wull," indicating Heaven, "I would ha'e likit weel to ha'e made out the fower hunner."[13] But it was not to be; this tragedian of the fifth act had now another part to play; and the time had come when others were to gird and carry him.[14]

II

I would fain strike a note that should be more heroical; but the ground of all youth's suffering, solitude, hysteria, and haunting of the grave, is nothing else than naked, ignorant selfishness. It is himself that he sees dead; those are his virtues that are forgotten; his is the vague epitaph. Pity him but the more, if pity be your cue; for where a man is all pride, vanity, and personal aspiration, he goes through fire unshielded. In every part and corner of our life, to lose oneself is to be gainer; to forget oneself is to be happy; and this poor, laughable and tragic fool has not yet learned the rudiments; himself, giant Prometheus, is still ironed on the peaks of Caucasus.[15] But by and by his truant interests will leave that tortured body, slip abroad and gather flowers. Then shall death appear before him in an altered guise; no longer as a doom peculiar to himself, whether fate's crowning injustice or his own last vengeance upon those who fail to value him; but now as a power that wounds him far more tenderly, not without solemn compensations, taking and giving, bereaving and yet storing up.

The first step for all is to learn to the dregs our own ignoble fallibility. When we have fallen through storey after storey of our vanity and aspiration, and sit rueful among the ruins, then it is that we begin to measure the stature of our friends: how they stand between us and our own contempt, believing in our best; how, linking us with others, and still spreading wide the influential circle, they weave us in and in with the fabric of contemporary life; and to what petty size they dwarf the virtues and the vices that appeared gigantic in our youth. So that at the last, when such a pin falls out—when there vanishes in the least breath of time one of those rich magazines of life on which we drew for our supply—when he who had first dawned upon us as a face among the faces of the city, and, still growing, came to bulk on our regard with those clear features of the loved and living man, falls in a breath to memory and shadow, there falls along with him a whole wing of the palace of our life.

III

One such face I now remember; one such blank some half a dozen of us labour to dissemble. In his youth he was most beautiful in person, most serene and genial by disposition; full of racy words and quaint thoughts.[16] Laughter attended on his coming. He had the air of a great gentleman, jovial and royal with his equals, and to the poorest student gentle and attentive. Power seemed to reside in him exhaust-less; we saw him stoop to play with us, but held him marked for higher destinies; we loved his notice; and I have rarely had my pride more gratified than when he sat at my father's table, my acknowledged friend. So he walked among us, both hands full of gifts, carrying with nonchalance the seeds of a most influential life.

The powers and the ground of friendship is a mystery; but, looking back, I can discern that, in part, we loved the thing he was, for some shadow of what he was to be. For with all his beauty, power, breeding, urbanity and mirth, there was in those days something soulless in our friend. He would astonish us by sallies, witty, innocent and inhumane; and by a misapplied Johnsonian pleasantry,[17] demolish honest sentiment. I can still see and hear him, as he went his way along the lamplit streets, *Là ci darem la mano*[18] on his lips, a noble figure of a youth, but following vanity and incredulous of good;[19] and sure enough, somewhere on the high seas of life, with his health, his hopes, his patrimony and his self-respect, miserably went down.

From this disaster, like a spent swimmer, he came desperately ashore, bankrupt of money and consideration; creeping to the family he had deserted; with broken wing, never more to rise. But in his face there was a light of knowledge that was new to it. Of the wounds of his body he was never healed; died of them gradually, with clear-eyed resignation; of his wounded pride, we knew only from his silence. He returned to that city where he had lorded it in his ambitious youth; lived there alone, seeing few; striving to retrieve the irretrievable; at times still grappling with that mortal frailty that had brought him down; still joying in his friend's suc-cesses; his laugh still ready but with kindlier music; and over all his thoughts the shadow of that unalterable law which he had disavowed and which had brought him low. Lastly, when his bodily evils had quite disabled him, he lay a great while dying, still without complaint, still finding interests; to his last step gentle, urbane and with the will to smile.

The tale of this great failure is, to those who remained true to him, the tale of a success. In his youth he took thought for no one but himself; when he came ashore again, his whole armada lost,[20] he seemed to think of none but others. Such was his tenderness for others, such his instinct of fine courtesy and pride, that of that impure passion of remorse he never breathed a syllable; even regret was rare with him, and pointed with a jest. You would not have dreamed, if you had known him then, that this was that great failure, that beacon to young men, over whose fall a whole society had hissed and pointed fingers. Often have we gone to him, red-hot with our own hopeful sorrows, railing on the rose-leaves in our princely bed of life, and he would patiently give ear and wisely counsel; and it was only upon some return of our own thoughts that we were reminded what manner of man this was to whom we disembosomed: a man, by his own fault, ruined; shut out of the garden of his gifts; his whole city of hope both ploughed and salted; silently await-ing the deliverer. Then something took us by the throat; and to see him there, so gentle, patient, brave and pious, oppressed but not cast down, sorrow was so swal-lowed up in admiration that we could not dare to pity him. Even if the old fault flashed out again, it but awoke our wonder that, in that lost battle, he should have still the energy to fight. He had gone to ruin with a kind of kingly *abandon*, like one who condescended; but once ruined, with the lights all out, he fought as for a kingdom. Most men, finding themselves the authors of their own disgrace, rail the louder against God or destiny. Most men, when they repent, oblige their friends to share the bitterness of that repentance. But he had held an inquest and passed sentence: *mene, mene*;[21] and condemned himself to smiling silence. He had given trouble enough; had earned misfortune amply, and foregone the right to murmur.

Thus was our old comrade, like Samson, careless in his days of strength;[22] but on the coming of adversity, and when that strength was gone that had betrayed him—"for our strength is weakness"[23]—he began to blossom and bring forth. Well, now, he is out of the fight: the burden that he bore thrown down before the great deliverer. We

in the vast cathedral leave him;
God accept him,
Christ receive him![24]

IV

If we go now and look on these innumerable epitaphs, the pathos and the irony are strangely fled. They do not stand merely to the dead, these foolish monuments; they are pillars and legends set up to glorify the difficult but not desperate life of man. This ground is hallowed by the heroes of defeat.

I see the indifferent pass before my friend's last resting-place; pause, with a shrug of pity, marvelling that so rich an argosy had sunk. A pity, now that he is done with suffering, a pity most uncalled for, and an ignorant wonder. Before those who loved him, his memory shines like a reproach; they honour him for silent lessons; they cherish his example; and in what remains before them of their toil, fear to be unworthy of the dead. For this proud man was one of those who prospered in the valley of humiliation;—of whom Bunyan wrote that, "Though Christian had the hard hap to meet in the valley with Apollyon, yet I must tell you, that in former times men have met with angels here; have found pearls here; and have in this place found the words of life."[25]

Notes

1 The historical figure Robert Paterson (1715–1801) or "Old Mortality," featured in Walter Scott's novel *Old Mortality* (1816), was a stonemason who traveled the Scottish Lowlands carving inscriptions on Covenanter martyrs' unmarked graves.
2 Old Calton Cemetery above the east end of Princes Street in Edinburgh.
3 David Hume (1711–1776), Scottish Enlightenment philosopher of empiricism and naturalism, as he appears in Allan Ramsay's well-known 1766 portrait.
4 An Edinburgh student wrote the following lines on Hume's prominent, circular tomb: "Beneath the circular idea, / Vulgarly called a tomb, / Ideas and impressions rest, / Which

constituted Hume." The lines satirize Hume's belief that our perceptions were ideas rather than objective realities and link the circular tomb with circular reasoning, which Hume considered an inherent problem with induction.

5 Genesis 8: 8–11.

6 Matthew 25:14–30.

7 *Obermann* (1804), Romantic French novel by Étienne Pivert de Senancour, popularized in English by the poet and critic Matthew Arnold.

8 Daniel Defoe's *Moll Flanders* (1722) in which the title character has twelve children with seven different men; William Wycherley's sexually explicit comedy *The Country Wife* (1675).

9 See "Sketches III. The Wreath of Immortelles" (p. 434).

10 1852.

11 A reference to the gravedigging scene in Shakespeare's *Hamlet* 5.1.

12 Digger.

13 He buried 300 and four score (380) people and hoped to reach 400.

14 John 21:18.

15 Prometheus, who stole fire from the gods, was nailed to a mountain in Caucasus where an eagle ate his self-regenerating liver every day until he was freed by Hercules.

16 James Walter Ferrier (1850–1883), Stevenson's close friend and collaborator as a student, died of alcoholism in 1883. Stevenson wrote this essay in the months following his death with the blessing of Ferrier's sister (*Letters* 4.283, 285). See also n. 1, p. 438.

17 Samuel Johnson (1709–1784), famously witty English poet, critic, and lexicographer.

18 A duet in Mozart's 1787 opera *Don Giovanni* (1.3).

19 See "The Satirist" in "Sketches" (p. 431). See also n. 1, p. 438.

20 King Philip II's naval fleet, the Spanish Armada, was soundly defeated and almost entirely lost after attacking England in 1588.

21 "MENE, MENE, TEKEL, UPHARSIN": the message on the wall of the temple after Belshazzar desecrated the temple, interpreted by Daniel as, "God hath numbered thy kingdom, and finished it. Thou art weighed in the balances, and art found wanting" (Daniel 5:24–28).

22 Judges 13–16.

23 2 Corinthians 12:9.

24 Tennyson, "Ode on the Death of the Duke of Wellington" (280–281).

25 John Bunyan, *The Pilgrim's Progress* (1678, Part 2, ch. 6).

18

A COLLEGE MAGAZINE

I

All through my boyhood and youth, I was known and pointed out for the pattern of an idler; and yet I was always busy on my own private end, which was to learn to write. I kept always two books in my pocket, one to read, one to write in. As I walked, my mind was busy fitting what I saw with appropriate words; when I sat by the roadside, I would either read, or a pencil and a penny version-book would be in my hand, to note down the features of the scene or commemorate some halting stanzas. Thus I lived with words. And what I thus wrote was for no ulterior use, it was written consciously for practice. It was not so much that I wished to be an author (though I wished that too) as that I had vowed that I would learn to write. That was a proficiency that tempted me; and I practised to acquire it, as men learn to whittle, in a wager with myself. Description was the principal field of my exercise; for to any one with senses there is always something worth describing, and town and country are but one continuous subject. But I worked in other ways also; often accompanied my walks with dramatic dialogues, in which I played many parts; and often exercised myself in writing down conversations from memory.

This was all excellent, no doubt; so were the diaries I sometimes tried to keep, but always and very speedily discarded, finding them a school of posturing and melancholy self-deception. And yet this was not the most efficient part of my training. Good though it was, it only taught me (so far as I have learned them at all) the lower and less intellectual elements of the art, the choice of the essential note and the right word: things that to a happier constitution had perhaps come by nature. And regarded as training, it had one grave defect; for it set me no standard of achievement. So that there was perhaps more profit, as there was certainly more effort, in my secret labours at home. Whenever I read a book or a passage that particularly pleased me, in which a thing was said or an effect rendered with propriety, in which there was either some conspicuous force or some happy distinction in the style, I must sit down at once and set myself to ape that quality. I was unsuccessful, and I knew it; and tried again, and was again unsuccessful and always unsuccessful; but at least in these vain bouts, I got some practice in rhythm, in harmony, in construction and the co-ordination of parts. I have thus played the sedulous ape to Hazlitt, to Lamb, to Wordsworth, to Sir Thomas Browne, to Defoe, to Hawthorne, to Montaigne, to Baudelaire and to Obermann.[1] I remember one of these monkey tricks, which was called *The Vanity of Morals*: it was to have had a second part, *The Vanity of Knowledge*; and as I had neither morality nor scholarship, the names were apt; but the second part was never attempted, and the first part was written (which is my reason for recalling it, ghostlike, from its ashes) no less than three times: first in the manner of Hazlitt, second in the manner of Ruskin,[2] who had cast on me a passing spell, and third, in a laborious pasticcio of Sir Thomas Browne. So with my other works: *Cain*, an epic, was (save the mark!) an imitation of *Sordello*[3]: *Robin Hood*, a tale in verse, took an eclectic middle course among the fields of Keats, Chaucer and Morris[4]: in *Monmouth*, a tragedy, I reclined on the bosom of Mr. Swinburne;[5] in my innumerable gouty-footed lyrics, I followed many masters; in the first draft of *The King's Pardon*, a tragedy, I was on the trail of no lesser man than John Webster; in the second draft of the same piece, with staggering versatility, I had shifted my allegiance to Congreve, and of course conceived my fable in a less serious vein—for it was not Congreve's verse, it was his exquisite prose, that I admired and sought to copy.[6] Even at the age of thirteen I had tried to do justice to the inhabitants of the famous city of Peebles in the style of the *Book of Snobs*.[7] So I might go on for ever, through all my abortive novels, and down to my later plays, of which I think more tenderly, for they were not only conceived at first under the bracing influence of old Dumas,[8] but have met with resurrections: one, strangely bettered by another hand, came on the stage itself and was played by bodily actors;[9] the other, originally known as *Semiramis: a Tragedy*, I have observed on bookstalls under the *alias* of *Prince Otto*.[10] But enough has been said to show by what arts of impersonation, and in what purely ventriloquial efforts I first saw my words on paper.

That, like it or not, is the way to learn to write; whether I have profited or not, that is the way. It was so Keats learned, and there was never a finer temperament for literature than Keats's; it was so, if we could trace it out, that all men have learned; and that is why a revival of letters is always accompanied or heralded by a cast back to earlier and fresher models. Perhaps I hear some one cry out: But this is not the way to be original! It is not; nor is there any way but to be born so. Nor yet, if you are born original, is there anything in this training that shall clip the wings of your originality. There can be none more original than Montaigne, neither could any be more unlike Cicero;[11] yet no craftsman can fail to see how much the one must have tried in his time to imitate the other. Burns is the very type of a prime force in letters: he was of all men the most imitative.[12] Shakespeare himself, the imperial, proceeds directly from a school. It is only from a school that we can expect to have good writers; it is almost invariably from a school that great writers, these lawless exceptions, issue. Nor is there anything here that should astonish the considerate. Before he can tell what cadences he truly prefers, the student should have tried all that are possible; before he can choose and preserve a fitting key of words, he should long have practised the literary scales; and it is only after years of such gymnastic that he can sit down at last, legions of words swarming to his call, dozens of turns of phrase simultaneously bidding for his choice, and he himself knowing what he wants to do and (within the narrow limit of a man's ability) able to do it.

And it is the great point of these imitations that there still shines beyond the student's reach his inimitable model. Let him try as he please, he is still sure of failure; and it is a very old and a very true saying that failure is the only highroad to success. I must have had some disposition to learn; for I clear-sightedly condemned my own performances. I liked doing them indeed; but when they were done, I could see they were rubbish. In consequence, I very rarely showed them even to my friends; and such friends as I chose to be my confidants I must have chosen well, for they had the friendliness to be quite plain with me. "Padding," said one. Another wrote: "I cannot understand why you do lyrics so badly." No more could I! Thrice I put myself in the way of a more authoritative rebuff, by sending a paper to a magazine. These were returned; and I was not surprised nor even pained. If they had not been looked at, as (like all amateurs) I suspected was the case, there was no good in repeating the experiment; if they had been looked at—well, then I had not yet learned to write, and I must keep on learning and living. Lastly, I had a piece of good fortune which is the occasion of this paper, and by which I was able to see my literature in print, and to measure experimentally how far I stood from the favour of the public.

II

The Speculative Society is a body of some antiquity, and has counted among its members Scott, Brougham, Jeffrey, Horner, Benjamin Constant, Robert Emmet, and many a legal and local celebrity besides.[13] By an accident, variously explained, it has its rooms in the very buildings of the University of Edinburgh: a hall, Turkey-carpeted, hung with pictures, looking, when lighted up at night with fire and candle, like some goodly dining-room; a passage-like library, walled with books in their wire cages; and a corridor with a fireplace, benches, a table, many prints of famous members, and a mural tablet to the virtues of a former secretary. Here a member can warm himself and loaf and read; here, in defiance of Senatus-consults,[14] he can smoke. The Senatus looks askance at these privileges; looks even with a somewhat vinegar aspect on the whole society; which argues a lack of proportion in the learned mind, for the world, we may be sure, will prize far higher this haunt of dead lions than all the living dogs of the professorate.

I sat one December morning in the library of the Speculative; a very humble-minded youth, though it was a virtue I never had much credit for; yet proud of my privileges as a member of the Spec.; proud of the pipe I was smoking in the teeth of the Senatus; and in particular, proud of being in the next room to three very distinguished students,[15] who were then conversing beside the corridor fire. One of these has now his name on the back of several volumes, and his voice, I learn, is influential in the law courts. Of the death of the second, you have just

145

been reading what I had to say. And the third also has escaped out of that battle of life in which he fought so hard, it may be so unwisely. They were all three, as I have said, notable students; but this was the most conspicuous. Wealthy, handsome, ambitious, adventurous, diplomatic, a reader of Balzac, and of all men that I have known, the most like to one of Balzac's characters, he led a life, and was attended by an ill fortune, that could be properly set forth only in the *Comédie Humaine*.[16] He had then his eye on Parliament; and soon after the time of which I write, he made a showy speech at a political dinner, was cried up to heaven next day in the *Courant*, and the day after was dashed lower than earth with a charge of plagiarism in the *Scotsman*.[17] Report would have it (I daresay, very wrongly) that he was betrayed by one in whom he particularly trusted, and that the author of the charge had learned its truth from his own lips. Thus, at least, he was up one day on a pinnacle, admired and envied by all; and the next, though still but a boy, he was publicly disgraced.[18] The blow would have broken a less finely tempered spirit; and even him I suppose it rendered reckless; for he took flight to London, and there, in a fast club, disposed of the bulk of his considerable patrimony in the space of one winter. For years thereafter he lived I know not how; always well dressed, always in good hotels and good society, always with empty pockets. The charm of his manner may have stood him in good stead; but though my own manners are very agreeable, I have never found in them a source of livelihood; and to explain the miracle of his continued existence, I must fall back upon the theory of the philosopher, that in his case, as in all of the same kind, "there was a suffering relative in the background." From this genteel eclipse he reappeared upon the scene, and presently sought me out in the character of a generous editor. It is in this part that I best remember him; tall, slender, with a not ungraceful stoop; looking quite like a refined gentleman, and quite like an urbane adventurer; smiling with an engaging ambiguity; cocking at you one peaked eyebrow with a great appearance of finesse; speaking low and sweet and thick, with a touch of burr; telling strange tales with singular deliberation and, to a patient listener, excellent effect. After all these ups and downs, he seemed still, like the rich student that he was of yore, to breathe of money; seemed still perfectly sure of himself and certain of his end. Yet he was then upon the brink of his last overthrow. He had set himself to found the strangest thing in our society: one of those periodical sheets from which men suppose themselves to learn opinions; in which young gentlemen from the universities are encouraged, at so much a line, to garble facts, insult foreign nations and calumniate private individuals; and which are now the source of glory, so that if a man's name be often enough printed there, he becomes a kind of demigod; and people will pardon him when he talks back and forth, as they do for Mr. Gladstone;[19] and crowd him to suffocation on railway platforms, as they did the other day to General Boulanger;[20] and buy his literary works, as I hope you have just done for me. Our fathers, when they were upon some great enterprise, would sacrifice a life; building, it may be, a favourite slave into the foundations of their palace. It was with his own life that my companion disarmed the envy of the gods. He fought his paper single-handed; trusting no one, for he was something of a cynic; up early and down late, for he was nothing of a sluggard; daily ear-wigging influential men, for he was a master of ingratiation. In that slender and silken fellow there must have been a rare vein of courage, that he should thus have died at his employment; and doubtless ambition spoke loudly in his ear, and doubtless love also, for it seems there was a marriage in his view had he succeeded. But he died, and his paper died after him; and of all this grace, and tact, and courage, it must seem to our blind eyes as if there had come literally nothing.

These three students sat, as I was saying, in the corridor, under the mural tablet that records the virtues of Macbean, the former secretary.[21] We would often smile at that ineloquent memorial, and thought it a poor thing to come into the world at all and leave no more behind one than Macbean. And yet of these three, two are gone and have left less; and this book, perhaps, when it is old and foxy, and some one picks it up in a corner of a book-shop, and glances through it, smiling at the old, graceless turns of speech, and perhaps for the love of *Alma Mater* (which may be still extant and flourishing) buys it, not without haggling, for some pence—this book may alone preserve a memory of James Walter Ferrier and Robert Glasgow Brown.

Their thoughts ran very differently on that December morning; they were all on fire with ambition; and when they had called me in to them, and made me a sharer in their design, I too became drunken with pride and hope. We were to found a University magazine. A pair of little, active brothers—Livingstone by name, great skippers on the foot, great rubbers of the hands, who kept a book-shop over against the University building—had been debauched to play the part of publishers.[22] We four were to be conjunct editors and, what was the main point of the concern, to print our own works;[23] while, by every rule of arithmetic—that flatterer of credulity—the adventure must succeed and bring great profit. Well, well: it was a bright vision. I went home that morning walking upon air. To have been chosen by these three distinguished students was to me the most unspeakable advance; it was my first draught of consideration; it reconciled me to myself and to my fellow-men; and as I steered round the railings at the Tron,[24] I could not withhold my lips from smiling publicly. Yet, in the bottom of my heart, I knew that magazine would be a grim fiasco; I knew it would not be worth reading; I knew, even if it were, that nobody would read it; and I kept wondering how I should be able, upon my compact income of twelve pounds per annum, payable monthly, to meet my share in the expense. It was a comfortable thought to me that I had a father.

The magazine appeared, in a yellow cover which was the best part of it, for at least it was unassuming; it ran four months in undisturbed obscurity, and died without a gasp. The first number was edited by all four of us with prodigious bustle; the second fell principally into the hands of Ferrier and me; the third I edited alone; and it has long been a solemn question who it was that edited the fourth. It would perhaps be still more difficult to say who read it. Poor yellow sheet, that looked so hopefully in the Livingstones' window! Poor, harmless paper, that might have gone to print a *Shakespeare* on, and was instead so clumsily defaced with nonsense! And, shall I say, Poor Editors? I cannot pity myself, to whom it was all pure gain. It was no news to me, but only the wholesome confirmation of my judgment, when the magazine struggled into half-birth, and instantly sickened and subsided into night. I had sent a copy to the lady with whom my heart was at that time somewhat engaged, and who did all that in her lay to break it; and she, with some tact, passed over the gift and my cherished contributions in silence. I will not say that I was pleased at this; but I will tell her now, if by any chance she takes up the work of her former servant, that I thought the better of her taste. I cleared the decks after this lost engagement; had the necessary interview with my father, which passed off not amiss; paid over my share of the expense to the two little, active brothers, who rubbed their hands as much, but methought skipped rather less than formerly, having perhaps, these two also, embarked upon the enterprise with some graceful illusions; and then, reviewing the whole episode, I told myself that the time was not yet ripe, nor the man ready; and to work I went again with my penny version-books, having fallen back in one day from the printed author to the manuscript student.

III

From this defunct periodical I am going to reprint one of my own papers. The poor little piece is all tail-foremost. I have done my best to straighten its array, I have pruned it fearlessly, and it remains invertebrate and wordy. No self-respecting magazine would print the thing; and here you behold it in a bound volume, not for any worth of its own, but for the sake of the man whom it purports dimly to represent and some of whose sayings it preserves; so that in this volume of *Memories and Portraits*, Robert Young, the Swanston gardener, may stand alongside of John Todd, the Swanston shepherd.[25] Not that John and Robert drew very close together in their lives; for John was rough, he smelt of the windy brae; and Robert was gentle, and smacked of the garden in the hollow. Perhaps it is to my shame that I liked John the better of the two; he had grit and dash, and that salt of the Old Adam that pleases men with any savage inheritance of blood; and he was a wayfarer besides, and took my gipsy fancy. But however that may be, and however Robert's profile may be blurred in the boyish sketch that follows, he was a man of a most quaint and beautiful nature, whom, if it were possible to recast a piece of work so old, I should like well to draw again with a maturer touch. And as I think of him and of John, I wonder in what other country two such men would be found dwelling together, in a hamlet of some twenty cottages, in the woody fold of a green hill.

Notes

1 William Hazlitt (1778–1830), English Romantic essayist. Charles Lamb (1775–1834), English essayist and critic. Michel de Montaigne (1533–1592), French author of the *Essais*, which established the essay form. William Wordsworth (1770–1850), eminent English Romantic poet. Sir Thomas Browne (1605–1682), scholar of science, religion, and the occult. Daniel Defoe (1660–1731), English author of *Robinson Crusoe* (1791). Nathaniel Hawthorne (1804–1864), American Romantic fiction writer. Charles

Baudelaire (1821–1867), proto-Modernist French poet and critic. *Obermann* (1804), Romantic French novel by Étienne Pivert de Senancour.

2 John Ruskin (1819–1900), most prominent English art critic of the Victorian period.

3 Robert Browning's *Sordello* (1840), a narrative poem about 13th-century Italian troubadour Sordello da Goito. "(God) save the mark"—originally an incantation against evil, now an exclamatory phrase used to apologize, often ironically for something mentioned: Stevenson's imitation of *Sordello* in this case because of its notorious convolution. See also Stevenson's review essay "Mr. Browning Again!" (1875).

4 John Keats (1795–1821), English Romantic lyric poet. Geoffrey Chaucer (1343–1400), leading English poet of the Middle Ages. William Morris (1834–1896), British poet, novelist, designer, and socialist activist.

5 Algernon Charles Swinburne (1837–1909), English poet and critic known for prosodic innovation and controversial content.

6 English dramatists John Webster (1580–1632) and William Congreve (1670–1729).

7 William Makepeace Thackeray's satirical collection *The Book of Snobs* (1848).

8 Alexandre Dumas (1802–1870), French historical novelist.

9 Stevenson's *Deacon Brodie*, co-authored with W.E. Henley, privately printed in 1880, first performed in 1882, and published in 1888.

10 Stevenson's *Prince Otto: A Romance* (1885).

11 Cicero (106–43 BC), famous Roman statesman, orator, and philosopher.

12 See Stevenson's essay "Some Aspects of Robert Burns" (1879).

13 The Speculative Society: a student debating club Stevenson joined at the University of Edinburgh; Sir Walter Scott (1771–1832), eminent Scottish novelist and poet; Henry Brougham (1778–1868), Lord High Chancellor; Francis Jeffrey (1773–1850), Scottish judge and literary critic; Francis Horner (1778–1817), Whig MP, journalist, and political economist; Benjamin Constant (1767–1830), Swiss-French writer and political activist; Robert Emmet (1729–1802), Irish state physician and father of the Irish nationalist leader.

14 *Senatus academicus*: the university's governing body.

15 George William Thomson Omond (1846–1929), advocate and prolific historian, James Walter Ferrier (1850–1883, n. 16, p. 142), and Robert Glasgow Caldwell Brown (died 1878).

16 Honoré de Balzac (1799–1850), French novelist and playwright, author of the novel series *Comedie Humaine* (The Human Comedy). See also Stevenson's essay "Balzac's Correspondence" (1877).

17 *The Edinburgh Evening Courant* (1718–1871) and *The Scotsman* (est. 1817).

18 See "Old Mortality" (136).

19 William Gladstone (1809–1898), Liberal politician and four-time British Prime Minister between 1868 and 1894.

20 Georges Ernest Jean-Marie Boulanger (1837–1891), French General and popular politician.

21 William Macbean, former secretary of the Speculative Society, died at 19 in 1842.

22 E. & S. (Edward and Stuart Moodie) Livingstone, Edinburgh booksellers and publishers from 1863 to 1905.

23 Stevenson published "The Philosophy of Umbrellas," "The Modern Student Considered Generally," "Debating Societies," "An Old Scotch Gardener," and "The Philosophy of Nomenclature" in *Edinburgh University Magazine* (Jan.–Apr. 1871).

24 Tron Kirk: a 17th-century church and prominent landmark on Edinburgh's Royal Mile.

25 "An Old Scotch Gardener" and "Pastoral." Thomas Stevenson leased Swanston Cottage in the Pentland Hills as the family's country home from 1867 to 1880.

19

AN OLD SCOTCH GARDENER

I think I might almost have said the last: somewhere, indeed, in the utter-most glens of the Lammermuir or among the south-western hills there may yet linger a decrepid representative of this bygone good fellowship; but as far as actual experience goes, I have only met one man in my life who might fitly be quoted in the same breath with Andrew Fairservice,[1]—though without his vices. He was a man whose very presence could impart a savour of quaint antiquity to the baldest and most modern flower-plots. There was a dignity about his tall stooping form, and an earnestness in his wrinkled face that recalled Don Quixote; but a Don Quixote who had come through the training of the Covenant, and been nourished in his youth on *Walker's Lives* and *The Hind Let Loose*.[2]

Now, as I could not bear to let such a man pass away with no sketch preserved of his old-fashioned virtues, I hope the reader will take this as an excuse for the present paper, and judge as kindly as he can the infirmities of my description.[3] To me, who find it so difficult to tell the little that I know, he stands essentially as a *genius loci*. It is impossible to separate his spare form and old straw hat from the garden in the lap of the hill, with its rocks overgrown with clematis, its shadowy walks, and the splendid breadth of champaign that one saw from the north-west corner. The garden and gardener seem part and parcel of each other. When I take him from his right surroundings and try to make him appear for me on paper, he looks unreal and phantasmal: the best that I can say may convey some notion to those that never saw him, but to me it will be ever impotent.

The first time that I saw him, I fancy Robert was pretty old already: he had certainly begun to use his years as a stalking horse. Latterly he was beyond all the impudencies of logic, considering a reference to the parish register worth all the reasons in the world. "*I am old and well stricken in years,*" he was wont to say; and I never found any one bold enough to answer the argument. Apart from this vantage that he kept over all who were not yet octogenarian, he had some other drawbacks as a gardener. He shrank the very place he cultivated. The dignity and reduced gentility of his appearance made the small garden cut a sorry figure. He was full of tales of greater situations in his younger days. He spoke of castles and parks with a humbling familiarity. He told of places where under-gardeners had trembled at his looks, where there were meres and swanneries, labyrinths of walk and wildernesses of sad shrubbery in his control, till you could not help feeling that it was condescension on his part to dress your humbler garden plots. You were thrown at once into an invidious position. You felt that you were profiting by the needs of dignity, and that his poverty and not his will consented to your vulgar rule. Involuntarily you compared yourself with the swineherd that made Alfred watch his cakes, or some bloated citizen who may have given his sons and his condescension to the fallen Dionysius.[4] Nor were the disagreeables purely fanciful and metaphysical, for the sway that he exercised over your feelings he extended to your garden, and, through the garden, to your diet. He would trim a hedge, throw away a favourite plant, or fill the most favoured and fertile section of the garden with a vegetable that none of us could eat, in supreme contempt for our opinion. If you asked him to send you in one of your own artichokes, "*that I wull, mem,*" he would say, "*with pleasure, for it is mair blessed to give than to receive.*" Ay, and even when, by extra twisting of the screw, we prevailed on him to prefer our commands to his own inclination, and he went away, stately and sad, professing that "*our wull was his pleasure,*" but yet reminding us that he would do it "*with feelin's,*"—even then, I say, the triumphant master felt humbled in his triumph, felt that he ruled on sufferance only, that he was taking a mean advantage of the other's low estate, and that the whole scene had been one of those "slights that patient merit of the unworthy takes."[5]

In flowers his taste was old-fashioned and catholic; affecting sunflowers and dahlias, wallflowers and roses, and holding in supreme aversion whatsoever was fantastic, new-fashioned or wild. There was one exception to this sweeping ban. Fox-gloves, though undoubtedly guilty on the last count, he not only spared, but loved; and when the shrubbery was being thinned, he stayed his hand and dexterously manipulated his bill in order to save every stately stem. In boyhood, as he told me once, speaking in that tone that only actors and the old-fashioned common folk can use nowadays, his heart grew "*proud*" within him when he came on a burn-course among the braes of Manor that shone purple with their graceful trophies; and not all his apprentice-ship and practice for so many years of precise gardening had banished these boyish recollections from his heart. Indeed, he was a man keenly alive to the beauty of all that was bygone. He abounded in old stories of his boyhood, and kept pious account of all his former pleasures; and when he went (on a holiday) to visit one of the fabled great places of the earth where he had served before, he came back full of little pre-Raphaelite reminiscences that showed real passion for the past, such as might have shaken hands with Hazlitt or Jean-Jacques.[6]

But however his sympathy with his old feelings might affect his liking for the fox-gloves, the very truth was that he scorned all flowers together. They were but garnishings, childish toys, trifling ornaments for the ladies' chimney-shelves. It was towards his cauliflowers and peas and cabbage that his heart grew warm. His preference for the more useful growths was such that cabbages were found invading the flower-plots, and an outpost of savoys was once discovered in the centre of the lawn. He would prelect over some thriving plant with wonderful enthusiasm, piling

151

reminiscence on reminiscence of former and perhaps yet finer specimens. Yet even then he did not let the credit leave himself. He had, indeed, raised "*finer o' them;*" but it seemed that no one else had been favoured with a like success. All other gardeners, in fact, were mere foils to his own superior attainments; and he would recount, with perfect soberness of voice and visage, how so and so had wondered, and such another could scarcely give credit to his eyes. Nor was it with his rivals only that he parted praise and blame. If you remarked how well a plant was looking, he would gravely touch his hat and thank you with solemn unction; all credit in the matter falling to him. If, on the other hand, you called his attention to some back-going vegetable, he would quote Scripture: "*Paul may plant and Apollos may water;*"[7] all blame being left to Providence, on the score of deficient rain or untimely frosts.

There was one thing in the garden that shared his preference with his favourite cabbages and rhubarb, and that other was the bee-hive. Their sound, their industry, perhaps their sweet product also, had taken hold of his imagination and heart, whether by way of memory or no I cannot say, although perhaps the bees too were linked to him by some recollection of Manor braes and his country childhood. Nevertheless, he was too chary of his personal safety or (let me rather say) his personal dignity to mingle in any active office towards them. But he could stand by while one of the contemned rivals did the work for him, and protest that it was quite safe in spite of his own considerate distance and the cries of the distressed assistant. In regard to bees, he was rather a man of word than deed, and some of his most striking sentences had the bees for text. "*They are indeed wonderfu'* creatures, mem,*" he said once. "*They just mind me o' what the Queen of Sheba said to Solomon—and I think she said it wi' a sigh,— 'The half of it hath not been told unto me.'*"[8]

As far as the Bible goes, he was deeply read. Like the old Covenanters, of whom he was the worthy representative, his mouth was full of sacred quotations; it was the book that he had studied most and thought upon most deeply. To many people in his station the Bible, and perhaps Burns, are the only books of any vital literary merit that they read, feeding themselves, for the rest, on the draff of country newspapers, and the very instructive but not very palatable pabulum of some cheap educational series. This was Robert's position. All day long he had dreamed of the Hebrew stories, and his head had been full of Hebrew poetry and Gospel ethics; until they had struck deep root into his heart, and the very expressions had become a part of him; so that he rarely spoke without some antique idiom or Scripture mannerism that gave a raciness to the merest trivialities of talk. But the influence of the Bible did not stop here. There was more in Robert than quaint phrase and ready store of reference. He was imbued with a spirit of peace and love: he interposed between man and wife: he threw himself between the angry, touching his hat the while with all the ceremony of an usher: he protected the birds from everybody but himself, seeing, I suppose, a great difference between official execution and wanton sport. His mistress telling him one day to put some ferns into his master's particular corner, and adding, "Though, indeed, Robert, he doesn't deserve them, for he wouldn't help me to gather them,"

"*Eh, mem,*" replies Robert, "*but I wouldnae say that, for I think he's just a most deservin' gentleman.*" Again, two of our friends, who were on intimate terms, and accustomed to use language to each other, somewhat without the bounds of the parliamentary, happened to differ about the position of a seat in the garden. The discussion, as was usual when these two were at it, soon waxed tolerably insulting on both sides. Every one accustomed to such controversies several times a day was quietly enjoying this prize-fight of somewhat abusive wit—every one but Robert, to whom the perfect good faith of the whole quarrel seemed unquestionable, and who, after having waited till his conscience would suffer him to wait no more, and till he expected every moment that the disputants would fall to blows, cut suddenly in with tones of almost tearful entreaty: "*Eh, but, gentlemen, I wad hae nae mair words about it!*" One thing was noticeable about Robert's religion: it was neither dogmatic nor sectarian. He never expatiated (at least, in my hearing) on the doctrines of his creed, and he never condemned anybody else. I have no doubt that he held all Roman Catholics, Atheists, and Mahometans as considerably out of it; I don't believe he had any sympathy for Prelacy; and the natural feelings of man must have made him a little sore about Free-Churchism; but at least, he never talked about these views, never grew controversially noisy, and never openly aspersed the belief or practice of anybody. Now all this is not generally characteristic of Scotch piety; Scotch sects being churches militant with a vengeance, and Scotch believers perpetual crusaders the one against the other, and missionaries the one to the other. Perhaps Robert's originally tender heart was what made the difference; or, perhaps, his solitary and pleasant labour among fruits and flowers had taught him a more sunshiny creed than those whose work is among the tares of fallen humanity; and the soft influences of the garden had entered deep into his spirit,

> Annihilating all that's made
> To a green thought in a green shade.[9]

But I could go on for ever chronicling his golden sayings or telling of his innocent and living piety. I had meant to tell of his cottage, with the German pipe hung reverently above the fire, and the shell box that he had made for his son, and of which he would say pathetically: "*He was real pleased wi' it at first, but I think he's got a kind o' tired o' it now*"—the son being then a man of about forty. But I will let all these pass. "'*Tis more significant: he's dead.*"[10] The earth, that he had digged so much in his life, was dug out by another for himself; and the flowers that he had tended drew their life still from him, but in a new and nearer way. A bird flew about the open grave, as if it too wished to honour the obsequies of one who had so often quoted Scripture in favour of its kind: "Are not two sparrows sold for one farthing, and yet not one of them falleth to the ground."[11]

Yes, he is dead. But the kings did not rise in the place of death to greet him "with taunting proverbs" as they rose to greet the haughty Babylonian;[12] for in his life he was lowly, and a peacemaker and a servant of God.

Notes

1 The gardener in Scott's *Rob Roy* (1817).
2 Covenanters were Scottish Presbyterians of the seventeenth century who pledged and fought to maintain their church government (n. 22, p. 439). Covenanting histories: Patrick Walker's *Biographia Presbyteriana* (1732) and Alexander Shield's *A Hind Let Loose* (1687).
3 Robert Young, the gardener at Swanston Cottage, died on 22 Feb. 1870, aged 72. See p. 148.
4 According to legend, Alfred the Great disguised himself and took shelter in a swineherd's house in Somerset during a Viking invasion in 878. The swineherd asked Alfred, who was distracted by his kingdom's peril, to watch some cakes baking, and scolded him after he let them burn. Dionysius: Greek god of wine.
5 *Hamlet* 3.1.73–74.
6 The Pre-Raphaelite Brotherhood, a group of Victorian painters led by Dante Gabriel Rossetti, William Holman Hunt, and John Everett Millais, who sought a return to 14th- and 15th-century Italian art's direct, detailed, and vibrant representation of nature. William Hazlitt (1778–1830), English Romantic essayist. Jean-Jacque Rousseau (1712–1778), Genevan writer and philosopher influential in Romanticism and the French Revolution.
7 1 Corinthians 3:6.
8 1 Kings 10:7.
9 Andrew Marvell, "The Garden" (1681, 47–48).
10 Andrew Marvell, "An Epitaph upon—" (18).
11 Matthew 10:29.
12 Isaiah 14:4–21.

20

PASTORAL

To leave home in early life is to be stunned and quickened with novelties; but when years have come, it only casts a more endearing light upon the past. As in those composite photographs of Mr. Galton's,[1] the image of each new sitter brings out but the more clearly the central features of the race; when once youth has flown, each new impression only deepens the sense of nationality and the desire of native places. So may some cadet of Royal Écossais or the Albany Regiment,[2] as he mounted guard about French citadels, so may some officer marching his company of the Scots-Dutch among the polders, have felt the soft rains of the Hebrides[3] upon his brow, or started in the ranks at the remembered aroma of peat-smoke. And the rivers of home are dear in particular to all men. This is as old as Naaman, who was jealous for Abana and Pharpar;[4] it is confined to no race nor country, for I know one of Scottish blood but a child of Suffolk, whose fancy still lingers about the lilied lowland waters of that shire. But the streams of Scotland are incomparable in themselves—or I am only the more Scottish to suppose so—and their sound and colour dwell for ever in the memory. How often and willingly do I not look again in fancy on Tummel, or Manor, or the talking Airdle, or Dee swirling in its Lynn; on the bright burn of Kinnaird, or the golden burn that pours and sulks in the den behind Kingussie! I think shame to leave out one of these enchantresses, but the list would grow too long if I remembered all; only I may not forget Allan Water, nor birch-wetting Rogie, nor yet Almond; nor, for all its pollutions, that Water of Leith of the many and well-named mills—Bell's Mills, and Canon Mills, and Silver Mills; nor Redford Burn of pleasant memories; nor yet, for all its smallness, that nameless trickle that springs in the green bosom of Allermuir, and is fed from Halkerside with a perennial teacupful, and threads the moss under the Shearer's Knowe,[5] and makes one pool there, overhung by a rock, where I loved to sit and make bad verses, and is then kidnapped in its infancy by subterranean pipes for the service of the sea-beholding city in the plain. From many points in the moss you may see at one glance its whole course and that of all its tributaries; the geographer of this Lilliput[6] may visit all its corners without sitting down, and not yet begin to be breathed; Shearer's Knowe and Halker-side are but names of adjacent cantons on a single shoulder of a hill, as names are squandered (it would seem to the inexpert, in superfluity) upon these upland sheepwalks; a bucket would receive the whole discharge of the toy river; it would take it an appreciable time to fill your morning bath; for the most part, besides, it soaks unseen through the moss; and yet for the sake of auld lang syne,[7] and the figure of a certain *genius loci*, I am condemned to linger awhile in fancy by its shores; and if the nymph (who cannot be above a span in stature) will but inspire my pen, I would gladly carry the reader along with me.

John Todd,[8] when I knew him, was already "the oldest herd on the Pentlands," and had been all his days faithful to that curlew-scattering, sheep-collecting life. He remembered the droving days, when the drove roads, that now lie green and solitary through the heather, were thronged thoroughfares. He had himself often marched flocks into England, sleeping on the hillsides with his caravan; and by his account it was a rough business not without danger. The drove roads lay apart from habitation; the drovers met in the wilderness, as to-day the deep-sea fishers meet off the banks in the solitude of the Atlantic; and in the one as in the other case rough habits and fist-law were the rule. Crimes were committed, sheep filched, and drovers robbed and beaten; most of which offences had a moorland burial and were never heard of in the courts of justice. John, in those days, was at least once attacked,—by two men after his watch,—and at least once, betrayed by his habitual anger, fell under the danger of the law and was clapped into some rustic prison-house, the doors of which he burst in the night and was no more heard of in that quarter. When I knew him, his life had fallen in quieter places, and he had no cares beyond the dulness of his dogs and the inroads of pedestrians from town. But for a man of his propensity to wrath these were enough; he knew neither rest nor peace, except by snatches; in the gray of the summer morning, and already from far up the hill, he would wake the "toun" with the sound of his shoutings; and in the lambing time, his cries were not yet silenced late at night. This wrathful voice of a man unseen might be said to haunt that quarter of the Pentlands, an audible bogie; and no doubt it added to the fear in which men stood of John a touch of something legendary. For my own part, he was at first my enemy, and I, in my character of a rambling boy, his natural abhorrence. It was long before I saw him near at hand, knowing him only by some sudden blast of bellowing from far above, bidding me "c'way oot amang the sheep." The quietest recesses of the hill harboured this ogre; I skulked in my favourite wilderness like a Cameronian of the Killing Time, and John Todd was my Claverhouse,[9] and his dogs my questing dragoons. Little by little we dropped into civilities; his hail at sight of me began to have less of the ring of a war-slogan; soon, we never met but he produced his snuff-box, which was with him, like the calumet[10] with the Red Indian, a part of the heraldry of peace; and at length, in the ripeness of time, we grew to be a pair of friends, and when I lived alone in these parts in the winter, it was a settled thing for John to "give me a cry" over the garden wall as he set forth upon his evening round, and for me to overtake and bear him company.

That dread voice of his that shook the hills when he was angry, fell in ordinary talk very pleasantly upon the ear, with a kind of honied, friendly whine, not far off singing, that was eminently Scottish. He laughed not very often, and when he did, with a sudden, loud haw-haw, hearty but somehow joyless, like an echo from a rock. His face was permanently set and coloured; ruddy and stiff with weathering; more like a picture than a face; yet with a certain strain and a threat of latent anger in the expression, like that of a man trained too fine and harassed with perpetual vigilance. He spoke in the richest dialect of Scotch I ever heard; the words in themselves were a pleasure and often a surprise to me, so that I often came back from one of our patrols with new acquisitions; and this vocabulary he would handle like a master, stalking a little before me, "beard on shoulder," the plaid hanging loosely about him, the yellow staff clapped under his arm, and guiding me uphill by that devious, tactical ascent which seems peculiar to men of his trade. I might count him with the best talkers; only that talking Scotch and talking English seem incomparable acts. He touched on nothing at least, but he adorned it; when he narrated, the scene was before you; when he spoke (as he did mostly) of his own antique business, the thing took on a colour of romance and curiosity that was surprising. The clans of sheep with their particular territories on the hill, and how, in the yearly killings and purchases, each must be proportionally thinned and strengthened; the midnight busyness of animals, the signs of the weather, the cares of the snowy season, the exquisite stupidity of sheep, the exquisite cunning of dogs: all these he could present so humanly, and with so much old experience and living gusto, that weariness was excluded. And in the midst he would suddenly straighten his bowed back, the stick would fly abroad in demonstration, and the sharp thunder of his voice roll out a long itinerary for the dogs, so that you saw at last the use of that great wealth of names for every knowe and howe[11] upon the hillside; and the dogs, having hearkened with lowered tails and raised faces, would run up their flags again to the masthead and spread themselves upon the indicated circuit. It used to fill me with wonder how they could follow and retain so long a story. But John denied these creatures all intelligence; they were the constant butt of his passion and contempt; it was just possible to work with the like of them, he said,—not more than possible. And then he would expand upon the subject of the really good dogs that he had known, and the one really good dog that he had himself possessed. He had been offered forty pounds for it; but a good collie was worth more than that, more than anything, to a "herd;" he did the herd's work for him. "As for the like of them!" he would cry, and scornfully indicate the scouring tails of his assistants.

Once—I translate John's Lallan,[12] for I cannot do it justice, being born *Britannis in montibus*, indeed, but alas! *inerudito sæculo*[13]—once, in the days of his good dog, he had bought some sheep in Edinburgh, and on the way out, the road being crowded, two were lost. This was a reproach to John, and a slur upon the dog; and both were alive to their misfortune. Word came, after some days, that a farmer about Braid had found a pair of sheep; and thither went John and the dog to ask for restitution. But the farmer was a hard man and stood upon his rights. "How were they marked?" he asked; and since John had bought right and left from many sellers and had no notion of the marks—"Very well," said the farmer, "then it's only right that I should keep them."—"Well," said John, "it's a fact that

I cannae tell the sheep; but if my dog can, will ye let me have them?" The farmer was honest as well as hard, and besides I daresay he had little fear of the ordeal; so he had all the sheep upon his farm into one large park, and turned John's dog into their midst. That hairy man of business knew his errand well; he knew that John and he had bought two sheep and (to their shame) lost them about Borough-muirhead; he knew besides (the Lord knows how, unless by listening) that they were come to Braid for their recovery; and without pause or blunder singled out, first one and then another, the two waifs. It was that afternoon the forty pounds were offered and refused. And the shepherd and his dog—what do I say? the true shepherd and his man—set off together by Fairmilehead in jocund humour, and "smiled to ither"[14] all the way home, with the two recovered ones before them. So far, so good; but intelligence may be abused. The dog, as he is by little man's inferior in mind, is only by little his superior in virtue; and John had another collie tale of quite a different complexion. At the foot of the moss behind Kirk Yetton (Caer Ketton, wise men say) there is a scrog of low wood and a pool with a dam for washing sheep. John was one day lying under a bush in the scrog, when he was aware of a collie on the far hillside skulking down through the deepest of the heather with obtrusive stealth. He knew the dog; knew him for a clever, rising practitioner from quite a distant farm; one whom perhaps he had coveted as he saw him masterfully steering flocks to market. But what did the practitioner so far from home? and why this guilty and secret manœuvring towards the pool?—for it was towards the pool that he was heading. John lay the closer under his bush, and presently saw the dog come forth upon the margin, look all about to see if he were anywhere observed, plunge in and repeatedly wash himself over head and ears, and then (but now openly and with tail in air) strike homeward over the hills. That same night word was sent his master, and the rising practitioner, shaken up from where he lay, all innocence before the fire, was had out to a dykeside and promptly shot; for alas! he was that foulest of criminals under trust, a sheep-eater; and it was from the maculation of sheep's blood that he had come so far to cleanse himself in the pool behind Kirk Yetton.

A trade that touches nature, one that lies at the foundations of life, in which we have all had ancestors employed, so that on a hint of it ancestral memories revive, lends itself to literary use, vocal or written. The fortune of a tale lies not alone in the skill of him that writes, but as much, perhaps, in the inherited experience of him who reads; and when I hear with a particular thrill of things that I have never done or seen, it is one of that innumerable army of my ancestors rejoicing in past deeds. Thus novels begin to touch not the fine *dilettanti* but the gross mass of mankind, when they leave off to speak of parlours and shades of manner and still-born niceties of motive, and begin to deal with fighting, sailoring, adventure, death or child-birth; and thus ancient outdoor crafts and occupations, whether Mr. Hardy wields the shepherd's crook or Count Tolstoi swings the scythe,[15] lift romance into a near neighbourhood with epic. These aged things have on them the dew of man's morning; they lie near, not so much to us, the semi-artificial flowerets, as to the trunk and aboriginal taproot of the race. A thousand interests spring up in the process of the ages, and a thousand perish; that is now an eccentricity or a lost art which was once the fashion of an empire; and those only are perennial matters that rouse us today, and that roused men in all epochs of the past. There is a certain critic, not indeed of execution but of matter, whom I dare be known to set before the best: a certain low-browed, hairy gentleman, at first a percher in the fork of trees, next (as they relate) a dweller in caves, and whom I think I see squatting in cave-mouths, of a pleasant afternoon, to munch his berries—his wife, that accomplished lady, squatting by his side: his name I never heard, but he is often described as Probably Arboreal,[16] which may serve for recognition. Each has his own tree of ancestors, but at the top of all sits Probably Arboreal; in all our veins there run some minims of his old, wild, tree-top blood; our civilised nerves still tingle with his rude terrors and pleasures; and to that which would have moved our common ancestor, all must obediently thrill.

We have not so far to climb to come to shepherds; and it may be I had one for an ascendant who has largely moulded me. But yet I think I owe my taste for that hillside business rather to the art and interest of John Todd. He it was that made it live for me, as the artist can make all things live. It was through him the simple strategy of massing sheep upon a snowy evening, with its attendant scampering of earnest, shaggy aides-de-camp, was an affair that I never wearied of seeing, and that I never weary of recalling to mind: the shadow of the night darkening on the hills, inscrutable black blots of snow shower moving here and there like night already come, huddles of yellow sheep and dartings of black dogs upon the snow, a bitter air that took you by the throat, unearthly harpings of the wind along the moors; and for centre piece to all these features and influences, John winding up the brae, keeping his captain's eye upon all sides, and breaking, ever and again, into a spasm of bellowing that seemed to make the evening bleaker. It is thus that I still see him in my mind's eye, perched on a hump of the declivity not far from Halkerside, his staff in airy flourish, his great voice taking hold upon the hills and echoing terror to the lowlands; I, meanwhile, standing somewhat back, until the fit should be over, and, with a pinch of snuff, my friend relapse into his easy, even conversation.

Notes

1 Francis Galton (1822–1911), father of eugenics and cousin of Charles Darwin. Galton developed composite photography, featured in his *Inquiries into Human Faculty and its Development* (1883), which combined different subjects in a single blended image to supposedly reveal physiognomic traits indicating health, disease, beauty, or criminality.

2 The Jacobite Royal Scots or the Royal Écossais: a French military regiment of Scottish exiles that served in the Seven Years' War and during the Jacobite rising of 1745. The 72nd Regiment or the Duke of Albany's Own Highlanders: a British Army Highland Infantry regiment, which fought in the Napoleonic Wars among other conflicts.

3 Polders: Dutch lowlands reclaimed from the sea and protected by dikes.

4 Elisha told the leprous Naaman to wash seven times in the River Jordan to be healed. He objected, "Are not Abana and Pharpar, rivers of Damascus, better than all the waters of Israel?" (2 Kings 5:12).

5 Rivers and streams in Scotland.

6 Lilliput—the kingdom of tiny people in Jonathan Swift's *Gulliver's Travels* (1726).

7 For *auld lang syne*: in consideration or regard for old friendship or loyalty, for old time's sake. Literal Scottish translation: times long past.

8 See the final paragraph of "A College Magazine" (p. 148).

9 John Graham of Claverhouse, first Viscount Dundee (1649–1689), an enemy of the Covenanters who led a Jacobite army for the Stuarts against William of Orange and ordered the executions of some 100 Cameronians: Covenanters led by Rev. Richard Cameron (1648–1680).

10 Native American ceremonial pipe.

11 A hollow or valley (Scottish).

12 Lowland Scottish dialect.

13 Being born in the mountains of Britain (i.e. Scotland), indeed, but alas! Of an ignorant century (Latin).

14 Ither: each other (Scottish).

15 Novelists who depicted rural characters: Thomas Hardy (1840–1928) and Leo Tolstoy (1828–1910).

16 "We thus learn that man is descended from a hairy quadruped, furnished with a tail and pointed ears, probably arboreal in its habits."—Charles Darwin, *Descent of Man* (1871, 2:389).

21

THE MANSE[1]

I have named, among many rivers that make music in my memory, that dirty Water of Leith. Often and often I desire to look upon it again; and the choice of a point of view is easy to me. It should be at a certain water-door, embowered in shrubbery. The river is there dammed back for the service of the flour-mill just below, so that it lies deep and darkling, and the sand slopes into brown obscurity with a glint of gold; and it has but newly been recruited by the borrowings of the snuff-mill just above, and these, tumbling merrily in, shake the pool to its black heart, fill it with drowsy eddies, and set the curded froth of many other mills solemnly steering to and fro upon the surface. Or so it was when I was young; for change, and the masons, and the pruning-knife, have been busy; and if I could hope to repeat a cherished experience, it must be on many and impossible conditions. I must choose, as well as the point of view, a certain moment in my growth, so that the scale may be exaggerated, and the trees on the steep opposite side may seem to climb to heaven, and the sand by the water-door, where I am standing, seem as low as Styx.[2] And I must choose the season also, so that the valley may be brimmed like a cup with sunshine and the songs of birds;—and the year of grace, so that when I turn to leave the riverside I may find the old manse and its inhabitants unchanged.

It was a place in that time like no other: the garden cut into provinces by a great hedge of beech, and overlooked by the church and the terrace of the churchyard, where the tombstones were thick, and after nightfall "spunkies"[3] might be seen to dance, at least by children; flower-plots lying warm in sunshine; laurels and the great yew making elsewhere a pleasing horror of shade; the smell of water rising from all round, with an added tang of paper-mills; the sound of water everywhere, and the sound of mills—the wheel and the dam singing their alternate strain; the birds on every bush and from every corner of the overhanging woods pealing out their notes until the air throbbed with them; and in the midst of this, the manse. I see it, by the standard of my childish stature, as a great and roomy house. In truth, it was not so large as I supposed, nor yet so convenient, and, standing where it did, it is difficult to suppose that it was healthful. Yet a large family of stalwart sons and tall daughters was housed and reared, and came to man and womanhood in that nest of little chambers; so that the face of the earth was peppered with the children of the manse, and letters with outlandish stamps became familiar to the local postman, and the walls of the little chambers brightened with the wonders of the East. The dullest could see this was a house that had a pair of hands in divers foreign places: a well-beloved house—its image fondly dwelt on by many travellers.

Here lived an ancestor of mine, who was a herd of men. I read him, judging with older criticism the report of childish observation, as a man of singular simplicity of nature; unemotional, and hating the display of what he felt; standing contented on the old ways; a lover of his life and innocent habits to the end. We children admired him: partly for his beautiful face and silver hair, for none more than children are concerned for beauty and, above all, for beauty in the old; partly for the solemn light in which we beheld him once a week, the observed of all observers, in the pulpit. But his strictness and distance, the effect, I now fancy, of old age, slow blood, and settled habit, oppressed us with a kind of terror. When not abroad, he sat much alone, writing sermons or letters to his scattered family in a dark and cold room with a library of bloodless books—or so they seemed in those days, although I have some of them now on my own shelves and like well enough to read them; and these lonely hours wrapped him in the greater gloom for our imaginations. But the study had a redeeming grace in many Indian pictures, gaudily coloured and dear to young eyes. I cannot depict (for I have no such passions now) the greed with which I beheld them; and when I was once sent in to say a psalm to my grandfather, I went, quaking indeed with fear, but at the same time glowing with hope that, if I said it well, he might reward me with an Indian picture.

> Thy foot He'll not let slide, nor will
> He slumber that thee keeps,[4]

it ran: a strange conglomerate of the unpronounceable, a sad model to set in childhood before one who was himself to be a versifier, and a task in recitation that really merited reward. And I must suppose the old man thought so too, and was either touched or amused by the performance; for he took me in his arms with most unwonted tenderness, and kissed me, and gave me a little kindly sermon for my psalm; so that, for that day, we were clerk and parson. I was struck by this reception into so tender a surprise that I forgot my disappointment. And indeed the hope was one of those that childhood forges for a pastime, and with no design upon reality. Nothing was more unlikely than that my grandfather should strip himself of one of those pictures, love-gifts and reminders of his absent sons; nothing more unlikely than that he should bestow it upon me. He had no idea of spoiling children, leaving all that to my aunt; he had fared hard himself, and blubbered under the rod in the last century; and his ways were still Spartan for the young. The last word I heard upon his lips was in this Spartan key. He had over-walked in the teeth of an east wind, and was now near the end of his many days. He sat by the dining-room fire, with his white hair, pale face and bloodshot eyes, a somewhat awful figure; and my aunt had given him a dose of our good old Scotch medicine, Dr. Gregory's powder. Now that remedy, as the work of a near kinsman of Rob Roy himself, may have a savour of romance for the imagination;[5] but it comes uncouthly to the palate. The old gentleman had taken it with a wry face; and that being accomplished, sat with perfect simplicity, like a child's, munching a "barley-sugar kiss." But when my aunt, having the canister open in her hands, proposed to let me share in the sweets, he interfered at once. I had had no Gregory; then I should have no barley-sugar kiss: so he decided with a touch of irritation. And just then the phaeton coming opportunely to the kitchen door—for such was our unlordly fashion—I was taken for the last time from the presence of my grandfather.

Now I often wonder what I have inherited from this old minister. I must suppose, indeed, that he was fond of preaching sermons, and so am I, though I never heard it maintained that either of us loved to hear them. He sought health in his youth in the Isle of Wight, and I have sought it in both hemispheres; but whereas he found and kept it, I am still on the quest. He was a great lover of Shakespeare, whom he read aloud, I have been told, with taste; well, I love my Shakespeare also, and am persuaded I can read him well, though I own I never have been told so. He made embroidery, designing his own patterns; and in that kind of work I never made anything but a kettle-holder in Berlin wool, and an odd garter of knitting, which was as black as the chimney before I had done with it. He loved port, and nuts, and porter; and so do I, but they agreed better with my grandfather, which seems to me a breach of contract. He had chalk-stones in his fingers; and these, in good time, I may possibly inherit, but I would much rather have inherited his noble presence. Try as I please, I cannot join myself on with the reverend doctor; and all the while, no doubt, and even as I write the phrase, he moves in my blood, and whispers words to me, and sits efficient in the very knot and centre of my being. In his garden, as I played there, I learned the love of mills—or had I an ancestor a miller?—and a kindness for the neighbourhood of graves, as homely things not without their poetry—or had I an ancestor a sexton? But what of the garden where he played himself?—for that, too, was a scene of my education. Some part of me played there in the eighteenth century, and ran races under the green avenue at Pilrig; some part of me trudged up Leith Walk, which was still a country place, and sat on the High School benches, and was thrashed, perhaps, by Dr. Adam. The house where I spent my youth was not yet thought upon; but we made holiday parties among the cornfields on its site, and ate strawberries and cream near by at a gardener's. All this I had forgotten; only my grandfather remembered and once reminded me. I have forgotten, too, how we grew up, and took orders, and went to our first Ayrshire parish, and fell in love with and married a daughter of Burns's Dr. Smith—"Smith opens out his cauld harangues."[6] I have forgotten, but I was there all the same, and heard stories of Burns at first hand.

And there is a thing stranger than all that; for this *homunculus*[7] or part-man of mine that walked about the eighteenth century with Dr. Balfour in his youth, was in the way of meeting other *homunculos* or part-men, in the persons of my other ancestors. These were of a lower order, and doubtless we looked down upon them duly. But as I went to college with Dr. Balfour, I may have seen the lamp and oil man taking down the shutters from his shop beside the Tron;—we may have had a rabbit-hutch or a bookshelf made for us by a certain carpenter in I know not what wynd of the old, smoky city; or, upon some holiday excursion, we may have looked into the windows of a cottage in a flower-garden and seen a certain weaver plying his shuttle. And these were all kinsmen of mine upon the other side; and from the eyes of the lamp and oil man one-half of my unborn father, and one-quarter of myself, looked out upon us as we went by to college. Nothing of all this would cross the mind of the young student, as he posted up the Bridges with trim, stockinged legs, in that city of cocked hats and good Scotch still unadulterated. It would not cross his mind that he should have a daughter; and the lamp and oil man, just then beginning, by a not unnatural metastasis, to bloom into a lighthouse-engineer, should have a grandson; and that these two, in the fulness of time, should wed; and some portion of that student himself should survive yet a year or two longer in the person of their child.

But our ancestral adventures are beyond even the arithmetic of fancy; and it is the chief recommendation of long pedigrees, that we can follow backward the careers of our *homunculos* and be reminded of our antenatal lives. Our conscious years are but a moment in the history of the elements that build us. Are you a bank-clerk, and do you live at Peckham? It was not always so. And though to-day I am only a man of letters, either tradition errs or I was present when there landed at St. Andrews a French barber-surgeon, to tend the health and the beard of the great Cardinal Beaton; I have shaken a spear in the Debateable Land and shouted the slogan of the Elliots;[8] I was present when a skipper, plying from Dundee, smuggled Jacobites to France after the'15;[9] I was in a West India merchant's office, perhaps next door to Bailie Nichol Jarvie's,[10] and managed the business of a plantation in St. Kitt's;[11] I was with my engineer-grandfather (the son-in-law of the lamp and oil man)[12] when he sailed north about Scotland on the famous cruise that gave us the *Pirate* and the *Lord of the Isles*;[13] I was with him, too, on the Bell Rock, in the fog, when the *Smeaton* had drifted from her moorings, and the Aberdeen men, pick in hand, had seized upon the only boats, and he must stoop and lap sea-water before his tongue could utter audible words;[14] and once more with him when the Bell Rock beacon took a "thrawe," and his workmen fled into the tower, then nearly finished, and he sat unmoved reading in his Bible—or affecting to read—till one after another slunk back with confusion of countenance to their engineer. Yes, parts of me have seen life, and met adventures, and sometimes met them well. And away in the still cloudier past, the threads that make me up can be traced by fancy into the bosoms of thousands and millions of ascendants: Picts who rallied round Macbeth and the old (and highly preferable) system of descent by females, fleërs from before the legions of Agricola, marchers in Pannonian morasses, star-gazers on Chaldæan plateaus; and, furthest of all, what face is this that fancy can see peering through the disparted branches? What sleeper in green tree-tops, what muncher of nuts, concludes my pedigree? Probably arboreal in his habits. . . .

And I know not which is the more strange, that I should carry about with me some fibres of my minister-grandfather; or that in him, as he sat in his cool study, grave, reverend, contented gentleman, there was an aboriginal frisking of the blood that was not his; tree-top memories, like undeveloped negatives, lay dormant in his mind; tree-top instincts awoke and were trod down; and Probably Arboreal (scarce to be distinguished from a monkey) gambolled and chattered in the brain of the old divine.

Notes

1 The manse was the home of Stevenson's grandfather Reverend Lewis Balfour (1777–1860), minister of the village Colinton southwest of Edinburgh. Stevenson visited the manse often as a child and played there with his many cousins.

2 Mythological river crossed by the dead in the underworld Hades.

3 A will-o'-the-wisp or *ignis fatuus*: a phosphorescent light seen flickering over marshy ground at night. In folklore, a misleading ghost light.

4 Metrical Psalm 121.

5 In his introduction to *Rob Roy*, Scott writes about a family connection between the MacGregors and the Gregorys.

6 Robert Burns mentions Stevenson's great-grandfather Dr. Smith of Galston in "The Holy Fair": "Smith opens up his cold harangues, / On practice and on morals" (verse 14).

7 A microscopic, fully formed person that was believed to grow into the fetus.

8 Stevenson refers to a remote connection to "Sir John Elphinstone of Logie and . . . Sir Gilbert Elliot, known as Lord Minto, a judge of the Court of Sessions" (Graham Balfour, *The Life of Robert Louis Stevenson*, I, 11).

9 Stevenson, *Records of a Family of Engineers* (165).

10 A merchant in Scott's *Rob Roy*.

11 Stevenson's great-grandfather Alan Stevenson (1752–1774).

12 Robert Stevenson (1772–1850), son of Alan Stevenson. Robert's widowed mother later married the oil lamp developer and early lighthouse engineer Thomas Smith (1752–1815).

13 Robert Stevenson and his colleagues sailed to the northern islands of Scotland and down the west coast with Sir Walter Scott in 1814. The trip inspired Scott's *The Pirate* (1822) and his poem *Lord of the Isles* (1815).

14 From Robert Stevenson's experience supervising the building of the Bell Rock lighthouse. See n. 6, p. 174.

22

MEMOIRS OF AN ISLET

Those who try to be artists use, time after time, the matter of their recollections, setting and resetting little coloured memories of men and scenes, rigging up (it may be) some especial friend in the attire of a buccaneer, and decreeing armies to manœuvre, or murder to be done, on the playground of their youth. But the memories are a fairy gift which cannot be worn out in using. After a dozen services in various tales, the little sunbright pictures of the past still shine in the mind's eye with not a lineament defaced, not a tint impaired. *Glück und unglück wird gesang*, if Goethe pleases;[1] yet only by endless avatars, the original re-embodying after each. So that a writer, in time, begins to wonder at the perdurable life of these impressions; begins, perhaps, to fancy that he wrongs them when he weaves them in with fiction; and looking back on them with ever-growing kindness, puts them at last, substantive jewels, in a setting of their own.

One or two of these pleasant spectres I think I have laid. I used one but the other day: a little eyot of dense, freshwater sand, where I once waded deep in butterburrs, delighting to hear the song of the river on both sides, and to tell myself that I was indeed and at last upon an island. Two of my puppets lay there a summer's day, hearkening to the shearers at work in riverside fields and to the drums of the gray old garrison upon the neighbouring hill. And this was, I think, done rightly: the place was rightly peopled—and now belongs not to me but to my puppets—for a time at least. In time, perhaps, the puppets will grow faint; the original memory swim up instant as ever; and I shall once more lie in bed, and see the little sandy isle in Allan Water as it is in nature, and the child (that once was me) wading there in butterburrs; and wonder at the instancy and virgin freshness of that memory; and be pricked again, in season and out of season, by the desire to weave it into art.

There is another isle in my collection, the memory of which besieges me. I put a whole family there, in one of my tales;[2] and later on, threw upon its shores, and condemned to several days of rain and shellfish on its tumbled boulders, the hero of another.[3] The ink is not yet faded; the sound of the sentences is still in my mind's ear; and I am under a spell to write of that island again.

I

The little isle of Earraid lies close in to the south-west corner of the Ross of Mull: the sound of Iona on one side, across which you may see the isle and church of Columba; the open sea to the other, where you shall be able to mark, on a clear, surfy day, the breakers running white on many sunken rocks. I first saw it, or first remember seeing it,[4] framed in the round bull's-eye of a cabin port, the sea lying smooth along its shores like the waters of a lake, the colourless, clear light of the early morning making plain its heathery and rocky hummocks. There stood upon it, in these days, a single rude house of uncemented stones, approached by a pier of wreckwood. It must have been very early, for it was then summer, and in summer, in that latitude, day scarcely withdraws; but even at that hour the house was making a sweet smoke of peats which came to me over the bay, and the bare-legged daughters of the cotter were wading by the pier. The same day we visited the shores of the isle in the ship's boats; rowed deep into Fiddler's Hole, sounding as we went; and having taken stock of all possible accommodation, pitched on the northern inlet as the scene of operations. For it was no accident that had brought the lighthouse steamer to anchor in the Bay of Earraid. Fifteen miles away to sea-ward, a certain black rock stood environed by the Atlantic rollers, the outpost of the Torran reefs. Here was a tower to be built, and a star lighted, for the conduct of seamen. But as the rock was small, and hard of access, and far from land, the work would be one of years; and my father was now looking for a shore station, where the stones might be quarried and dressed, the men live, and the tender, with some degree of safety, lie at anchor.

I saw Earraid next from the stern thwart of an Iona lugger, Sam Bough[5] and I sitting there cheek by jowl, with our feet upon our baggage, in a beautiful, clear, northern summer eve. And behold! there was now a pier of stone, there were rows of sheds, railways, travelling-cranes, a street of cottages, an iron house for the resident engineer, wooden bothies for the men, a stage where the courses of the tower were put together experimentally, and behind the settlement a great gash in the hillside where granite was quarried. In the bay, the steamer lay at her moorings. All day long there hung about the place the music of chinking tools; and even in the dead of night, the watchman carried his lantern to and fro in the dark settlement, and could light the pipe of any midnight muser. It was, above all, strange to see Earraid on the Sunday, when the sound of the tools ceased and there fell a crystal quiet. All about the green compound men would be sauntering in their Sunday's best, walking with those lax joints of the reposing toiler, thoughtfully smoking, talking small, as if in honour of the stillness, or hearkening to the wailing of the gulls. And it was strange to see our Sabbath services, held, as they were, in one of the bothies, with Mr. Brebner reading at a table, and the congregation perched about in the double tier of sleeping bunks; and to hear the singing of the psalms, "the chapters," the inevitable Spurgeon's sermon, and the old, eloquent lighthouse prayer.

In fine weather, when by the spy-glass on the hill the sea was observed to run low upon the reef, there would be a sound of preparation in the very early morning; and before the sun had risen from behind Ben More, the tender would steam out of the bay. Over fifteen sea-miles of the great blue Atlantic rollers she ploughed her way, trailing at her tail a brace of wallowing stone-lighters. The open ocean widened upon either board, and the hills of the mainland began to go down on the horizon, before she came to her unhomely destination, and lay-to at last where the rock clapped its black head above the swell, with the tall iron barrack on its spider legs, and the truncated tower, and the cranes waving their arms, and the smoke of the engine-fire rising in the mid-sea. An ugly reef is this of the Dhu Heartach; no pleasant assemblage of shelves, and pools, and creeks, about which a child might play for a whole summer without weariness, like the Bell Rock or the Skerryvore, but one oval nodule of black-trap, sparsely bedabbled with an inconspicuous fucus, and alive in every crevice with a dingy insect between a slater and a bug. No other life was there but that of sea-birds, and of the sea itself, that here ran like a mill-race, and growled about the outer reef for ever, and ever and again, in the calmest weather, roared and spouted on the rock itself. Times were different upon Dhu-Heartach when it blew, and the night fell dark, and the neighbour lights of Skerryvore and Rhu-val were quenched in fog, and the men sat prisoned high up in their iron drum, that then resounded with the lashing of the sprays. Fear sat with them in their sea-beleaguered dwelling; and the colour changed in anxious faces when some greater billow struck the barrack, and its pillars quivered and sprang under the blow. It was then that the foreman builder, Mr. Goodwillie, whom I see before me still in his rock-habit of undecipherable rags, would get his fiddle down and strike up human minstrelsy amid the music of the storm. But it was in sunshine only that I saw Dhu-Heartach; and it was in sunshine, or the yet lovelier summer afterglow, that the steamer would return to Earraid, ploughing an enchanted sea; the obedient lighters, relieved of their deck cargo, riding in her wake more quietly; and the steersman upon each, as she rose on the long swell, standing tall and dark against the shining west.

II

But it was in Earraid itself that I delighted chiefly. The lighthouse settlement scarce encroached beyond its fences; over the top of the first brae the ground was all virgin, the world all shut out, the face of things unchanged by any of man's doings. Here was no living presence, save for the limpets on the rocks, for some old, gray, rain-beaten ram that I might rouse out of a ferny den betwixt two boulders, or for the haunting and the piping of the gulls. It was older than man; it was found so by incoming Celts, and seafaring Norsemen, and Columba's priests. The earthy savour of the bog plants, the rude disorder of the boulders, the inimitable seaside brightness of the air, the brine and the iodine, the lap of the billows among the weedy reefs, the sudden springing up of a great run of dashing surf along the

168

sea-front of the isle, all that I saw and felt my predecessors must have seen and felt with scarce a difference. I steeped myself in open air and in past ages.

> Delightful would it be to me to be in *Uchd Ailiun*
> On the pinnacle of a rock,
> That I might often see
> The face of the ocean;
> That I might hear the song of the wonderful birds,
> Source of happiness;
> That I might hear the thunder of the crowding waves
> Upon the rocks:
> At times at work without compulsion—
> This would be delightful;
> At times plucking dulse from the rocks;
> At times at fishing.

So, about the next island of Iona, sang Columba himself twelve hundred years before.[6] And so might I have sung of Earraid.

And all the while I was aware that this life of sea-bathing and sun-burning was for me but a holiday. In that year cannon were roaring for days together on French battlefields;[7] and I would sit in my isle (I call it mine, after the use of lovers) and think upon the war, and the loudness of these far-away battles, and the pain of the men's wounds, and the weariness of their marching. And I would think too of that other war which is as old as mankind, and is indeed the life of man: the unsparing war, the grinding slavery of competition; the toil of seventy years, dear-bought bread, precarious honour, the perils and pitfalls, and the poor rewards. It was a long look forward; the future summoned me as with trumpet calls, it warned me back as with a voice of weeping and beseeching; and I thrilled and trembled on the brink of life, like a childish bather on the beach.

There was another young man on Earraid in these days, and we were much together, bathing, clambering on the boulders, trying to sail a boat and spinning round instead in the oily whirlpools of the roost. But the most part of the time we spoke of the great uncharted desert of our futures; wondering together what should there befall us; hearing with surprise the sound of our own voices in the empty vestibule of youth. As far, and as hard, as it seemed then to look forward to the grave, so far it seems now to look backward upon these emotions; so hard to recall justly that loath submission, as of the sacrificial bull, with which we stooped our necks under the yoke of destiny. I met my old companion but the other day; I cannot tell of course what he was thinking; but, upon my part, I was wondering to see us both so much at home, and so composed and sedentary in the world; and how much we had gained, and how much we had lost, to attain to that composure; and which had been upon the whole our best estate: when we sat there prating sensibly like men of some experience, or when we shared our timorous and hopeful counsels in a western islet.

169

Notes

1 "Happiness and unhappiness become song."
2 Stevenson's "The Merry Men."
3 David Balfour in *Kidnapped* (1886).
4 Stevenson was in Erraid in Aug. 1870 for his engineering training. See n. 1. p. 257.
5 Sam Bough (1822–1878), British landscape painter. See Stevenson's "The Late Sam Bough, R.S.A." (1878).
6 Poem by St. Columba (521–597), Irish Catholic missionary who established an abbey on Iona and is credited with spreading Christianity in Scotland.
7 The Franco-Prussian War (1870–1871).

23

THOMAS STEVENSON

Civil Engineer

The death of Thomas Stevenson[1] will mean not very much to the general reader. His service to mankind took on forms of which the public knows little and understands less. He came seldom to London, and then only as a task, remaining always a stranger and a convinced provincial; putting up for years at the same hotel where his father had gone before him; faithful for long to the same restaurant, the same church, and the same theatre, chosen simply for propinquity; steadfastly refusing to dine out. He had a circle of his own, indeed, at home; few men were more beloved in Edinburgh, where he breathed an air that pleased him; and wherever he went, in railway carriages or hotel smoking-rooms, his strange, humorous vein of talk, and his transparent honesty, raised him up friends and admirers. But to the general public and the world of London, except about the parliamentary committee-rooms, he remained unknown. All the time, his lights were in every part of the world, guiding the mariner; his firm were consulting engineers to the Indian, the New Zealand, and the Japanese Lighthouse Boards, so that Edinburgh was a world centre for that branch of applied science; in Germany, he had been called "the Nestor of lighthouse illumination;"[2] even in France, where his claims were long denied, he was at last, on the occasion of the late Exposition, recognised and medalled.[3] And to show by one instance the inverted nature of his reputation, comparatively small at home, yet filling the world, a friend of mine was this winter on a visit to the Spanish main, and was asked by a Peruvian if he "knew Mr. Stevenson the author, because his works were much esteemed in Peru?" My friend supposed the reference was to the writer of tales; but the Peruvian had never heard of Dr. Jekyll; what he had in his eye, what was esteemed in Peru, were the volumes of the engineer.[4]

Thomas Stevenson was born at Edinburgh in the year 1818, the grandson of Thomas Smith, first engineer to the Board of Northern Lights, son of Robert Stevenson, brother of Alan and David; so that his nephew, David Alan Stevenson, joined with him at the time of his death in the engineership, is the sixth of the family who has held, successively or conjointly, that office.[5] The Bell Rock,[6] his father's great triumph, was finished before he was born; but he served under his brother Alan in the building of Skerryvore,[7] the noblest of all extant deep-sea lights; and, in conjunction with his brother David, he added two—the Chickens

171

and Dhu Heartach[8]—to that small number of man's extreme outposts in the ocean. Of shore lights, the two brothers last named erected no fewer than twenty-seven; of beacons,[9] about twenty-five. Many harbours were successfully carried out: one, the harbour of Wick, the chief disaster of my father's life, was a failure; the sea proved too strong for man's arts; and after expedients hitherto unthought of, and on a scale hyper-cyclopean, the work must be deserted, and now stands a ruin in that bleak, God-forsaken bay, ten miles from John-o'-Groat's.[10] In the improvement of rivers the brothers were likewise in a large way of practice over both England and Scotland, nor had any British engineer anything approaching their experience.

It was about this nucleus of his professional labours that all my father's scientific inquiries and inventions centred; these proceeded from, and acted back upon, his daily business. Thus it was as a harbour engineer that he became interested in the propagation and reduction of waves; a difficult subject in regard to which he has left behind him much suggestive matter and some valuable approximate results. Storms were his sworn adversaries, and it was through the study of storms that he approached that of meteorology at large. Many who knew him not otherwise, knew—perhaps have in their gardens—his louvre-boarded screen for instruments.[11] But the great achievement of his life was, of course, in optics as applied to lighthouse illumination. Fresnel[12] had done much; Fresnel had settled the fixed light apparatus on a principle that still seems unimprovable; and when Thomas Stevenson stepped in and brought to a comparable perfection the revolving light, a not unnatural jealousy and much painful controversy rose in France. It had its hour; and, as I have told already, even in France it has blown by. Had it not, it would have mattered the less, since all through his life my father continued to justify his claim by fresh advances. New apparatus for lights in new situations was continually being designed with the same unwearied search after perfection, the same nice ingenuity of means; and though the holophotal revolving light[13] perhaps still remains his most elegant contrivance, it is difficult to give it the palm over the much later condensing system, with its thousand possible modifications. The number and the value of these improvements entitle their author to the name of one of mankind's benefactors. In all parts of the world a safer landfall awaits the mariner. Two things must be said: and, first, that Thomas Stevenson was no mathematician. Natural shrewdness, a sentiment of optical laws, and a great intensity of consideration led him to just conclusions; but to calculate the necessary formulæ for the instruments he had conceived was often beyond him, and he must fall back on the help of others, notably on that of his cousin and lifelong intimate friend, *emeritus* Professor Swan, of St. Andrews, and his later friend, Professor P. G. Tait.[14] It is a curious enough circumstance, and a great encouragement to others, that a man so ill equipped should have succeeded in one of the most abstract and arduous walks of applied science. The second remark is one that applies to the whole family, and only particularly to Thomas Stevenson from the great number and importance of his inventions: holding as the Stevensons did a Government appointment, they regarded their original work as something due already to the nation, and none of them has ever taken out a patent. It is another cause of the comparative obscurity of the name: for a patent not only brings in money, it infallibly spreads reputation; and my father's instruments enter anonymously into a hundred light-rooms, and are passed anonymously over in a hundred reports, where the least considerable patent would stand out and tell its author's story.

But the life-work of Thomas Stevenson remains; what we have lost, what we now rather try to recall, is the friend and companion. He was a man of a somewhat antique strain: with a blended sternness and softness that was wholly Scottish and at first somewhat bewildering; with a profound essential melancholy of disposition and (what often accompanies it) the most humorous geniality in company; shrewd and childish; passionately attached, passionately prejudiced; a man of many extremes, many faults of temper, and no very stable foothold for himself among life's troubles. Yet he was a wise adviser; many men, and these not inconsiderable, took counsel with him habitually. "I sat at his feet," writes one of these, "when I asked his advice, and when the broad brow was set in thought and the firm mouth said his say, I always knew that no man could add to the worth of the conclusion." He had excellent taste, though whimsical and partial; collected old furniture and delighted specially in sunflowers long before the days of Mr. Wilde;[15] took a lasting pleasure in prints and pictures; was a devout admirer of Thomson of Duddingston[16] at a time when few shared the taste; and though he read little, was constant to his favourite books. He had never any Greek; Latin he happily re-taught himself after he had left school, where he was a mere consistent idler: happily, I say, for Lactantius, Vossius, and Cardinal Bona were his chief authors.[17] The first he must have read for twenty years uninterruptedly, keeping it near him in his study, and carrying it in his bag on journeys. Another old theologian, Brown of Wamphray, was often in his hands.[18] When he was indisposed, he had two books, *Guy Mannering* and *The Parent's Assistant*, of which he never wearied.[19] He was a strong Conservative, or, as he preferred to call himself, a Tory; except in so far as his views were modified by a hot-headed chivalrous sentiment for women. He was actually in favour of a marriage law under which any woman might have a divorce for the asking, and no man on any ground whatever; and the same sentiment found another expression in a Magdalen Mission in Edinburgh,[20] founded and largely supported by himself. This was but one of the many channels of his public generosity; his private was equally unstrained. The Church of Scotland, of which he held the doctrines (though in a sense of his own) and to which he bore a clansman's loyalty, profited often by his time and money; and though, from a morbid sense of his own unworthiness, he would never consent to be an office-bearer, his advice was often sought, and he served the Church on many committees. What he perhaps valued highest in his work were his contributions to the defence of Christianity; one of which, in particular, was praised by Hutchinson Stirling and reprinted at the request of Professor Crawford.[21]

His sense of his own unworthiness I have called morbid; morbid, too, were his sense of the fleetingness of life and his concern for death. He had never accepted the conditions of man's life or his own character; and his inmost thoughts were ever tinged with the Celtic melancholy. Cases of conscience were sometimes grievous to him, and that delicate employment of a scientific witness cost him many qualms. But he found respite from these troublesome humours in his work, in his lifelong study of natural science, in the society of those he loved, and in his daily walks, which now would carry him far into the country with some congenial friend, and now keep him dangling about the town from one old book-shop to another, and scraping romantic acquaintance with every dog that passed. His talk, compounded of so much sterling sense and so much freakish humour, and clothed in language so apt, droll, and emphatic, was a perpetual delight to all who knew him before the clouds began to settle on his mind. His use of language was both just and picturesque; and when at the beginning of his illness he began to feel the ebbing of this power, it was strange and painful to hear him reject one word after another as inadequate, and at length desist from the search and leave his phrase unfinished rather than finish it without propriety. It was perhaps another Celtic trait that his affections and emotions, passionate as these were, and liable to passionate ups and downs, found the most eloquent expression both in words and gestures. Love, anger, and indignation shone through him and broke forth in imagery, like what we read of Southern races. For all these emotional extremes, and in spite of the melancholy ground of his character, he had upon the whole a happy life; nor was he less fortunate in his death, which at the last came to him unaware.

Notes

1 Robert Louis Stevenson's father, Thomas Stevenson (1818–1887).
2 A wise old man or leader in a field, alluding to the Greeks' counselor at Troy in the *Iliad*.
3 The 1878 World's Fair in Paris. Thomas Stevenson's medals are at the Huntington Library in California.
4 Thomas Stevenson wrote *The Design and Construction of Harbors: A Treatise on Maritime Engineering* (1864), *Lighthouse Construction and Illumination* (1881), and *Tides and Coast Works* (1885).
5 Stevenson's grandfather Robert Stevenson (1772–1850) was a famous lighthouse engineer. Thomas's brothers Alan Stevenson (1807–1865) and David Stevenson (1815–1886) also continued their father's legacy. In his final years, Robert Louis Stevenson was writing the posthumously published *Records of a Family of Engineers* (1896).
6 Famous lighthouse built between 1807 and 1811 on Bell Rock: an almost completely submerged sandstone reef in the North Sea off the coast of Angus, Scotland. The Scottish Engineer John Rennie (1761–1821) was named chief engineer and was involved in early designs, but Robert Stevenson did most of the work and received most of the credit.
7 Skerryvore was built between 1838 and 1844 on a remote island off the west coast of Scotland near Tiree. At 156 feet, it is Scotland's tallest lighthouse.
8 The Chicken Rock Lighthouse was completed in 1874 off the Isle of Man. Dhu Heartach, as it was commonly known, is actually spelled Dubh Artach, meaning "the black rock" in Scottish Gaelic. It was designed by Thomas Stevenson and built between 1867 and 1872 off Scotland's west coast near the Ross of Mull.
9 **RLS:** "In Dr. Murray's admirable new dictionary, I have remarked a flaw *sub voce* Beacon. In its express, technical sense, a beacon may be defined as 'a founded, artificial sea-mark, not lighted.'"

10 Thomas Stevenson began construction on the breakwater at Wick in 1863. After repairing and rebuilding it after it was repeatedly destroyed by storms, he abandoned it in 1877.

11 In 1864, Thomas Stevenson developed a screen with louvered walls with slats angled to admit light and air but to keep rain and direct sunshine out in order to protect meteorological instruments from the elements and provide a standardized environment for accurate measurement. Though the original design has since been slightly modified, it is still called a Stevenson screen and used in modern weather stations.

12 Augustin-Jean Fresnel (1788–1827), French engineer and physicist who helped establish the wave theory of light and invented the Fresnel lens for lighthouses: a composite compact lens making light visible from greater distances.

13 Thomas Stevenson's improvement on Fresnel's design, which intensifies light by reflecting all or nearly all of it outward.

14 William Swan (1818–1894), Scottish mathematician, astronomer, and physicist. Peter Tait (1831–1901), Scottish physicist and pioneer in thermodynamics.

15 Oscar Wilde (1854–1900), Irish poet, playwright, and novelist. A leader of the aesthetic movement promoting art for art's sake, which was symbolically associated with sunflowers.

16 John Thomson of Duddingston (1778–1840), Church of Scotland minister and landscape painter.

17 Lactantius (250–325), early Christian author and advisor to Constantine I, best known for his defense of Christianity against paganism *Institutiones Divinae* or "The Divine Institutes." Gerardus Vossius (1577–1649), Dutch classical scholar and Protestant theologian. Giovanni Bona (1609–1674), Italian cardinal and devotional author.

18 John Brown of Wamphray (1610–1679), Scottish minister.

19 Maria Edgeworth's children's stories collection *The Parent's Assistant* (1796) and Walter Scott's novel *Guy Mannering* (1815).

20 A refuge for former prostitutes and "fallen" women, often partially funded by sewing and laundry services, designed to provide Christian instruction and foster moral reform.

21 Thomas Stevenson wrote *Christianity Confirmed by Jewish and Heathen Testimony and the Deductions from Physical Science* (1877) and several religious articles. James Hutchison Stirling (1820–1909), Scottish physician and philosopher best known for *The Secret of Hegel* (1865). Thomas Jackson Crawford (1812–1875), Professor of Divinity and Moderator of the General Assembly of the Church of Scotland.

24

TALK AND TALKERS I

Sir, we had a good talk.

– Johnson.[1]

As we must account for every idle word, so we must for every idle silence.

– Franklin[2]

I

There can be no fairer ambition than to excel in talk; to be affable, gay, ready, clear and welcome; to have a fact, a thought, or an illustration, pat to every subject; and not only to cheer the flight of time among our intimates, but bear our part in that great international congress, always sitting, where public wrongs are first declared, public errors first corrected, and the course of public opinion shaped, day by day, a little nearer to the right. No measure comes before Parliament but it has been long ago prepared by the grand jury of the talkers; no book is written that has not been largely composed by their assistance. Literature in many of its branches is no other than the shadow of good talk; but the imitation falls far short of the original in life, freedom and effect. There are always two to a talk, giving and taking, comparing experience and according conclusions. Talk is fluid, tentative, continually "in further search and progress;"[3] while written words remain fixed, become idols even to the writer, found wooden dogmatisms, and preserve flies of obvious error in the amber of the truth. Last and chief, while literature, gagged with linsey-woolsey, can only deal with a fraction of the life of man, talk goes fancy free and may call a spade a spade. Talk has none of the freezing immunities of the pulpit. It cannot, even if it would, become merely æsthetic or merely classical like literature. A jest intervenes, the solemn humbug is dissolved in laughter, and speech runs forth out of the contemporary groove into the open fields of nature, cheery and cheering, like schoolboys out of school. And it is in talk alone that we can learn our period and ourselves. In short, the first duty of a man is to speak; that is his chief business in this world; and talk, which is the harmonious speech of two or more, is by far the most accessible of pleasures. It costs nothing in money; it is all profit; it completes our education, founds and fosters our friendships, and can be enjoyed at any age and in almost any state of health.

The spice of life is battle; the friendliest relations are still a kind of contest; and if we would not forego all that is valuable in our lot, we must continually face some other person, eye to eye, and wrestle a fall whether in love or enmity. It is still by force of body, or power of character or intellect, that we attain to worthy pleasures. Men and women contend for each other in the lists of love, like rival mesmerists; the active and adroit decide their challenges in the sports of the body; and the sedentary sit down to chess or conversation. All sluggish and pacific pleasures are, to the same degree, solitary and selfish; and every durable bond between human beings is founded in or heightened by some element of competition. Now, the relation that has the least root in matter is undoubtedly that airy one of friendship; and hence, I suppose, it is that good talk most commonly arises among friends. Talk is, indeed, both the scene and instrument of friendship. It is in talk alone that the friends can measure strength, and enjoy that amicable counter-assertion of personality which is the gauge of relations and the sport of life.

A good talk is not to be had for the asking. Humours must first be accorded in a kind of overture or prologue; hour, company and circumstance be suited; and then, at a fit juncture, the subject, the quarry of two heated minds, spring up like a deer out of the wood. Not that the talker has any of the hunter's pride, though he has all and more than all his ardour. The genuine artist follows the stream of conversation as an angler follows the windings of a brook, not dallying where he fails to "kill." He trusts implicitly to hazard; and he is rewarded by continual variety, continual pleasure, and those changing prospects of the truth that are the best of education. There is nothing in a subject, so called, that we should regard it as an idol, or follow it beyond the promptings of desire. Indeed, there are few subjects; and so far as they are truly talkable, more than the half of them may be reduced to three: that I am I, that you are you, and that there are other people dimly understood to be not quite the same as either. Wherever talk may range, it still runs half the time on these eternal lines. The theme being set, each plays on himself as on an instrument; asserts and justifies himself; ransacks his brain for instances and opinions, and brings them forth new-minted, to his own surprise and the admiration of his adversary. All natural talk is a festival of ostentation; and by the laws of the game each accepts and fans the vanity of the other. It is from that reason that we venture to lay ourselves so open, that we dare to be so warmly eloquent, and that we swell in each other's eyes to such a vast proportion. For talkers, once launched, begin to overflow the limits of their ordinary selves, tower up to the height of their secret pretensions, and give themselves out for the heroes, brave, pious, musical and wise, that in their most shining moments they aspire to be. So they weave for themselves with words and for a while inhabit a palace of delights, temple at once and theatre, where they fill the round of the world's dignities, and feast with the gods, exulting in Kudos. And when the talk is over, each goes his way, still flushed with vanity and admiration, still trailing clouds of glory;[4] each declines from the height of his ideal orgie, not in a moment, but by slow declension. I remember, in the *entr'acte*[5] of an afternoon performance, coming forth into the sunshine, in a beautiful green, gardened corner of a romantic city; and as I sat and smoked, the music moving in my blood, I seemed to sit there and evaporate *The Flying Dutchman*[6] (for it was that I had been hearing) with a wonderful sense of life, warmth, well-being and pride; and the noises of the city, voices, bells and marching feet, fell together in my ears like a symphonious orchestra. In the same way, the excitement of a good talk lives for a long while after in the blood, the heart still hot within you, the brain still simmering, and the physical earth swimming around you with the colours of the sunset.

Natural talk, like ploughing, should turn up a large surface of life, rather than dig mines into geological strata. Masses of experience, anecdote, incident, cross-lights, quotation, historical instances, the whole flotsam and jetsam of two minds forced in and in upon the matter in hand from every point of the compass, and from every degree of mental elevation and abasement—these are the material with which talk is fortified, the food on which the talkers thrive. Such argument as is proper to the exercise should still be brief and seizing. Talk should proceed by instances; by the apposite, not the expository. It should keep close along the lines of humanity, near the bosoms and businesses of men, at the level where history, fiction and experience intersect and illuminate each other. I am I, and You are You, with all my heart; but conceive how these lean propositions change and brighten when, instead of words, the actual you and I sit cheek by jowl, the spirit housed in the live body, and the very clothes uttering voices to corroborate the story in the face. Not less surprising is the change when we leave off to speak of generalities— the bad, the good, the miser, and all the characters of Theophrastus[7]—and call up other men, by anecdote or instance, in their very trick and feature; or trading on a common knowledge, toss each other famous names, still glowing with the hues of life. Communication is no longer by words, but by the instancing of whole biographies, epics, systems of philosophy, and epochs of history, in bulk. That which is understood excels that which is spoken in quantity and quality alike; ideas thus figured and personified, change hands, as we may say, like coin; and the speakers imply without effort the most obscure and intricate thoughts. Strangers who have a large common ground of reading will, for this reason, come the sooner to the grapple of genuine converse. If they know Othello and Napoleon, Consuelo and Clarissa Harlowe, Vautrin and Steenie Steenson,[8] they can leave generalities and begin at once to speak by figures.

Conduct and art are the two subjects that arise most frequently and that embrace the widest range of facts. A few pleasures bear discussion for their own sake, but only those which are most social or most radically human; and even these can only be discussed among their devotees. A technicality is always welcome to the expert, whether in athletics, art or law; I have heard the best kind of talk on technicalities from such rare and happy persons as both know and love their business.

No human being ever spoke of scenery for above two minutes at a time, which makes me suspect we hear too much of it in literature. The weather is regarded as the very nadir and scoff of conversational topics. And yet the weather, the dramatic element in scenery, is far more tractable in language, and far more human both in import and suggestion than the stable features of the landscape. Sailors and shepherds, and the people generally of coast and mountain, talk well of it; and it is often excitingly presented in literature. But the tendency of all living talk draws it back and back into the common focus of humanity. Talk is a creature of the street and marketplace, feeding on gossip; and its last resort is still in a discussion on morals. That is the heroic form of gossip; heroic in virtue of its high pretensions; but still gossip, because it turns on personalities. You can keep no men long, nor Scotchmen at all, off moral or theological discussion. These are to all the world what law is to lawyers; they are everybody's technicalities; the medium through which all consider life, and the dialect in which they express their judgments. I knew three young men who walked together daily for some two months in a solemn and beautiful forest and in cloudless summer weather; daily they talked with unabated zest, and yet scarce wandered that whole time beyond two subjects—theology and love. And perhaps neither a court of love nor an assembly of divines would have granted their premises or welcomed their conclusions.

Conclusions, indeed, are not often reached by talk any more than by private thinking. That is not the profit. The profit is in the exercise, and above all in the experience; for when we reason at large on any subject, we review our state and history in life. From time to time, however, and specially, I think, in talking art, talk becomes effective, conquering like war, widening the boundaries of knowledge like an exploration. A point arises; the question takes a problematical, a baffling, yet a likely air; the talkers begin to feel lively presentiments of some conclusion near at hand; towards this they strive with emulous ardour, each by his own path, and struggling for first utterance; and then one leaps upon the summit of that matter with a shout, and almost at the same moment the other is beside him; and behold they are agreed. Like enough, the progress is illusory, a mere cat's cradle having been wound and unwound out of words. But the sense of joint discovery is none the less giddy and inspiriting. And in the life of the talker such triumphs, though imaginary, are neither few nor far apart; they are attained with speed and pleasure, in the hour of mirth; and by the nature of the process, they are always worthily shared.

There is a certain attitude, combative at once and deferential, eager to fight yet most averse to quarrel, which marks out at once the talkable man. It is not eloquence, not fairness, not obstinacy, but a certain proportion of all of these that I love to encounter in my amicable adversaries. They must not be pontiffs holding doctrine, but huntsmen questing after elements of truth. Neither must they be boys to be instructed, but fellow-teachers with whom I may wrangle and agree on equal terms. We must reach some solution, some shadow of consent; for without that, eager talk becomes a torture. But we do not wish to reach it cheaply, or quickly, or without the tussle and effort wherein pleasure lies.

The very best talker, with me, is one whom I shall call Spring-Heel'd Jack.[9] I say so, because I never knew any one who mingled so largely the possible ingredients of converse. In the Spanish proverb, the fourth man necessary to compound a salad, is a madman to mix it: Jack is that madman. I know not which is more remarkable; the insane lucidity of his conclusions, the humorous eloquence of his language, or his power of method, bringing the whole of life into the focus of the subject treated, mixing the conversational salad like a drunken god. He doubles like the serpent, changes and flashes like the shaken kaleidoscope, transmigrates bodily into the views of others, and so, in the twinkling of an eye and with a heady rapture, turns questions inside out and flings them empty before you on the ground, like a triumphant conjuror. It is my common practice when a piece of conduct puzzles me, to attack it in the presence of Jack with such grossness, such partiality and such wearing iteration, as at length shall spur him up in its defence. In a moment he transmigrates, dons the required character, and with moonstruck philosophy justifies the act in question. I can fancy nothing to compare with the *vim* of these impersonations, the strange scale of language, flying from Shakespeare to Kant, and from Kant to Major Dyngwell—[10]

As fast as a musician scatters sounds
Out of an instrument—[11]

the sudden, sweeping generalisations, the absurd irrelevant particularities, the wit, wisdom, folly, humour, eloquence and bathos, each startling in its kind, and yet all luminous in the admired disorder of their combination. A talker of a different calibre, though belonging to the same school, is Burly.[12] Burly is a man of a great presence; he commands a larger atmosphere, gives the impression of a grosser mass of character than most men. It has been said of him that his presence could be felt in a room you entered blindfold; and the same, I think, has been said of other powerful constitutions condemned to much physical inaction. There is something boisterous and piratic in Burly's manner of talk which suits well enough with this impression. He will roar you down, he will bury his face in his hands, he will undergo passions of revolt and agony; and meanwhile his attitude of mind is really both conciliatory and receptive; and after Pistol has been out-Pistol'd,[13] and the welkin[14] rung for hours, you begin to perceive a certain subsidence in these spring torrents, points of agreement issue, and you end arm-in-arm, and in a glow of mutual admiration. The outcry only serves to make your final union the more unexpected and precious. Throughout there has been perfect sincerity, perfect intelligence, a desire to hear although not always to listen, and an unaffected eagerness to meet concessions. You have, with Burly, none of the dangers that attend debate with Spring-Heel'd Jack; who may at any moment turn his powers of transmigration on yourself, create for you a view you never held, and then furiously fall on you for holding it. These, at least, are my two favourites, and both are loud, copious, intolerant talkers. This argues that I myself am in the same category; for if we love talking at all, we love a bright, fierce adversary,

180

who will hold his ground, foot by foot, in much our own manner, sell his attention dearly, and give us our full measure of the dust and exertion of battle. Both these men can be beat from a position, but it takes six hours to do it; a high and hard adventure, worth attempting. With both you can pass days in an enchanted country of the mind, with people, scenery and manners of its own; live a life apart, more arduous, active and glowing than any real existence; and come forth again when the talk is over, as out of a theatre or a dream, to find the east wind still blowing and the chimney-pots of the old battered city still around you. Jack has the far finer mind, Burly the far more honest; Jack gives us the animated poetry, Burly the romantic prose, of similar themes; the one glances high like a meteor and makes a light in darkness; the other, with many changing hues of fire, burns at the sea-level, like a conflagration; but both have the same humour and artistic interests, the same unquenched ardour in pursuit, the same gusts of talk and thunderclaps of contradiction.

Cockshot[15] is a different article, but vastly entertaining, and has been meat and drink to me for many a long evening. His manner is dry, brisk and pertinacious, and the choice of words not much. The point about him is his extraordinary readiness and spirit. You can propound nothing but he has either a theory about it ready-made, or will have one instantly on the stocks, and proceed to lay its timbers and launch it in your presence. "Let me see," he will say. "Give me a moment. I *should* have some theory for that." A blither spectacle than the vigour with which he sets about the task, it were hard to fancy. He is possessed by a demoniac energy, welding the elements for his life, and bending ideas, as an athlete bends a horseshoe, with a visible and lively effort. He has, in theorising, a compass, an art; what I would call the synthetic gusto; something of a Herbert Spencer,[16] who should see the fun of the thing. You are not bound, and no more is he, to place your faith in these brand-new opinions. But some of them are right enough, durable even for life; and the poorest serve for a cock-shy—as when idle people, after picnics, float a bottle on a pond and have an hour's diversion ere it sinks. Whichever they are, serious opinions or humours of the moment, he still defends his ventures with indefatigable wit and spirit, hitting savagely himself, but taking punishment like a man. He knows and never forgets that people talk, first of all, for the sake of talking; conducts himself in the ring, to use the old slang, like a thorough "glutton," and honestly enjoys a telling facer from his adversary. Cockshot is bottled effervescency, the sworn foe of sleep. Three-in-the-morning Cockshot, says a victim. His talk is like the driest of all imaginable dry champagnes. Sleight of hand and inimitable quickness are the qualities by which he lives. Athelred,[17] on the other hand, presents you with the spectacle of a sincere and somewhat slow nature thinking aloud. He is the most unready man I ever knew to shine in conversation. You may see him sometimes wrestle with a refractory jest for a minute or two together, and perhaps fail to throw it in the end. And there is something singularly engaging, often instructive, in the simplicity with which he thus exposes the process as well as the result, the works as well as the dial of the clock. Withal he has his hours of inspiration. Apt words come to him as if by accident, and, coming from deeper down, they smack the more personally, they have the more of fine old crusted humanity, rich in sediment and humour. There are sayings of his in which he has stamped himself into the very grain of the language; you would think he must have worn the words next his skin and slept with them. Yet it is not as a sayer of particular good things that Athelred is most to be regarded, rather as the stalwart woodman of thought. I have pulled on a light cord often enough, while he has been wielding the broad-axe; and between us, on this unequal division, many a specious fallacy has fallen. I have known him to battle the same question night after night for years, keeping it in the reign of talk, constantly applying it and re-applying it to life with humorous or grave intention, and all the while, never hurrying, nor flagging, nor taking an unfair advantage of the facts. Jack at a given moment, when arising, as it were, from the tripod, can be more radiantly just to those from whom he differs; but then the tenor of his thoughts is even calumnious; while Athelred, slower to forge excuses, is yet slower to condemn, and sits over the welter of the world, vacillating but still judicial, and still faithfully contending with his doubts.

Both the last talkers deal much in points of conduct and religion studied in the "dry light" of prose.[18] Indirectly and as if against his will the same elements from time to time appear in the troubled and poetic talk of Opalstein.[19] His various and exotic knowledge, complete although unready sympathies, and fine, full, discriminative flow of language, fit him out to be the best of talkers; so perhaps he is with some, not *quite* with me—*proxime accessit*,[20] I should say. He sings the praises of the earth and the arts, flowers and jewels, wine and music, in a moonlight, serenading manner, as to the light guitar; even wisdom comes from his tongue like singing; no one is, indeed, more tuneful in the upper notes. But even while he sings the song of the Sirens, he still hearkens to the barking of the Sphinx. Jarring Byronic notes interrupt the flow of his Horatian humours.[21] His mirth has something of the tragedy of the world for its perpetual background; and he feasts like Don Giovanni[22] to a double orchestra, one lightly sounding for the dance, one pealing Beethoven in the distance. He is not truly reconciled either with life or with himself; and this instant war in his members sometimes divides the man's attention. He does not always, perhaps not often, frankly surrender himself in conversation. He brings into the talk other thoughts than those which he expresses; you are conscious that he keeps an eye on something else, that he does not shake off the world, nor quite forget himself. Hence arise occasional disappointments; even an occasional unfairness for his companions, who find themselves one day giving too much, and the next, when they are wary out of season, giving perhaps too little. Purcel[23] is in another class from any I have mentioned. He is no debater, but appears in conversation, as occasion rises, in two distinct characters, one of which I admire and fear, and the other love. In the first, he is radiantly civil and rather silent, sits on a high, courtly hilltop, and from that vantage-ground drops you his remarks like favours. He seems not to share in our sublunary contentions; he wears no sign of interest; when on a sudden there falls in a crystal of wit, so polished that the dull do not perceive it, but so right that the sensitive are silenced. True talk should have more body and blood, should be louder, vainer and more declaratory of the man; the true talker should not hold so steady an advantage over whom he speaks with; and that is one reason out of a score why I prefer my Purcel in his second character, when he unbends into a strain of graceful gossip, singing like the fireside kettle. In these moods he has an elegant homeliness that rings of the true Queen Anne.[24] I know another person[25] who attains, in his moments, to the insolence of a Restoration comedy, speaking, I declare, as Congreve wrote; but that is a sport of nature, and scarce falls under the rubric, for there is none, alas! to give him answer.

One last remark occurs: It is the mark of genuine conversation that the sayings can scarce be quoted with their full effect beyond the circle of common friends. To have their proper weight they should appear in a biography, and with the portrait of the speaker. Good talk is dramatic; it is like an impromptu piece of acting where each should represent himself to the greatest advantage; and that is the best kind of talk where each speaker is most fully and candidly himself, and where, if you were to shift the speeches round from one to another, there would be the greatest loss in significance and perspicuity. It is for this reason that talk depends so wholly on our company. We should like to introduce Falstaff and Mercutio, or Falstaff and Sir Toby; but Falstaff in talk with Cordelia seems even painful.[26] Most of us, by the Protean[27] quality of man, can talk to some degree with all; but the true talk, that strikes out all the slumbering best of us, comes only with the peculiar brethren of our spirits, is founded as deep as love in the constitution of our being, and is a thing to relish with all our energy, while yet we have it, and to be grateful for for ever.

Notes

1 In *The Life of Samuel Johnson* (1791), James Boswell describes Johnson, "highly satisfied with his colloquial prowess the preceding evening," saying, "we had good talk," to which Boswell replied, "Yes, sir; you tossed and gored several persons" (ch. 7).
2 Benjamin Franklin, *Poor Richard's Almanack* (1738).
3 William Hazlitt, "On the Difference Between Writing and Speaking" (1826).
4 William Wordsworth, "Ode: Intimations" (65).
5 Intermission (French).
6 Richard Wagner's 1843 opera.
7 Theophrastus (371–287 BC), Greek philosopher and author of the influential *Characters* on negative types of people in Athens.
8 Title characters in George Sand's *Consuelo* (1842) and Richardson's *Clarissa* (1748); Vautrin or Jacques Collin in Balzac's novel series *La Comédie humaine*; Steenie Steenson—a character in "Wandering Willie's Tale" in Walter Scott's novel *Redgauntlet* (1824).
9 Stevenson's cousin Bob Stevenson (1847–1900). Stevenson used aliases for his friends in this essay, identifying them in a letter to his mother (*Letters* III.314).
10 Captain Dyngwell—a character in the satirical magazine *Punch*.
11 Wordsworth, *The Excursion* (4.524–525).

12 William Ernest Henley (1849–1903), playwright, journalist, and poet best remembered for "Invictus." He had a leg amputated and was the model for Stevenson's Long John Silver in *Treasure Island*. Henley and Stevenson had a close but volatile relationship.
13 Blustering character in Shakespeare's *2 Henry IV*, *The Merry Wives of Windsor*, and *Henry V*.
14 Sky; loud sounds make the welkin ring.
15 Fleeming Jenkin (1833–1885), Stevenson's professor and friend (n. 9, p. 135).
16 Herbert Spencer (1820–1913), philosopher and evolutionary biologist.
17 Sir Walter Grindlay Simpson (1843–1898, n. 1, p. 242).
18 "The most perfect soul is a dry light, which flies out of the body as lightning breaks from a cloud" ("Romulus," *Plutarch's Lives*).
19 John Addington Symonds (1840–1893), critic, translator, historian, and biographer.
20 Runner-up or coming very near to it (Latin).
21 Relating to the poets Horace and Byron. Stevenson contrasts Byron's brooding tragedy with Horace's friendly Epicureanism.
22 Title character in Mozart's 1787 opera *Don Giovanni* based on the Spanish dramatist Tirso de Molina's fictional character Don Juan.
23 Sir Edmund William Gosse (1849–1928), critic, poet, and memoirist.
24 Queen Anne (1665–1714), the last monarch of the Scottish Stuart line.
25 Charles Baxter (1848–1919), lawyer and Stevenson's close friend since 1871.
26 Characters in Shakespeare.
27 Versatile, mutable, referring to the Greek god of sea change, Proteus.

25

TALK AND TALKERS II

In the last paper[1] there was perhaps too much about mere debate; and there was nothing said at all about that kind of talk which is merely luminous and restful, a higher power of silence, the quiet of the evening shared by ruminating friends. There is something, aside from personal preference, to be alleged in support of this omission. Those who are no chimney-cornerers, who rejoice in the social thunderstorm, have a ground in reason for their choice. They get little rest indeed; but restfulness is a quality for cattle; the virtues are all active, life is alert, and it is in repose that men prepare themselves for evil. On the other hand, they are bruised into a knowledge of themselves and others; they have in a high degree the fencer's pleasure in dexterity displayed and proved; what they get they get upon life's terms, paying for it as they go; and once the talk is launched, they are assured of honest dealing from an adversary eager like themselves. The aboriginal man within us, the cave-dweller, still lusty as when he fought tooth and nail for roots and berries, scents this kind of equal battle from afar; it is like his old primæval days upon the crags, a return to the sincerity of savage life from the comfortable fictions of the civilised. And if it be delightful to the Old Man, it is none the less profitable to his younger brother, the conscientious gentleman. I feel never quite sure of your urbane and smiling coteries; I fear they indulge a man's vanities in silence, suffer him to encroach, encourage him on to be an ass,[2] and send him forth again, not merely contemned for the moment, but radically more contemptible than when he entered. But if I have a flushed, blustering fellow for my opposite, bent on carrying a point, my vanity is sure to have its ears rubbed, once at least, in the course of the debate. He will not spare me when we differ; he will not fear to demonstrate my folly to my face.

For many natures there is not much charm in the still, chambered society, the circle of bland countenances, the digestive silence, the admired remark, the flutter of affectionate approval. They demand more atmosphere and exercise; "a gale upon their spirits," as our pious ancestors would phrase it;[3] to have their wits well breathed in an uproarious Valhalla.[4] And I suspect that the choice, given their character and faults, is one to be defended. The purely wise are silenced by facts; they talk in a clear atmosphere, problems lying around them like a view in nature; if they can be shown to be somewhat in the wrong, they digest the reproof like a thrashing, and make better intellectual blood. They stand corrected by a whisper; a word or a glance reminds them of the great eternal law. But it is not so with all. Others in conversation seek rather contact with their fellow-men than increase of knowledge or clarity of thought. The drama, not the philosophy, of life is the sphere of their intellectual activity. Even when they pursue truth, they desire as much as possible of what we may call human scenery along the road they follow. They dwell in the heart of life; the blood sounding in their ears, their eyes laying hold of what delights them with a brutal avidity that makes them blind to all besides, their interest riveted on people, living, loving, talking, tangible people. To a man of this description, the sphere of argument seems very pale and ghostly. By a strong expression, a perturbed countenance, floods of tears, an insult which his conscience obliges him to swallow, he is brought round to knowledge which no syllogism would have conveyed to him. His own experience is so vivid, he is so superlatively conscious of himself, that if, day after day, he is allowed to hector and hear nothing but approving echoes, he will lose his hold on the soberness of things and take himself in earnest for a god. Talk might be to such an one the very way of moral ruin; the school where he might learn to be at once intolerable and ridiculous.

This character is perhaps commoner than philosophers suppose. And for persons of that stamp to learn much by conversation, they must speak with their superiors, not in intellect, for that is a superiority that must be proved, but in station. If they cannot find a friend to bully them for their good, they must find either an old man, a woman, or some one so far below them in the artificial order of society, that courtesy may he particularly exercised.

The best teachers are the aged. To the old our mouths are always partly closed; we must swallow our obvious retorts and listen. They sit above our heads, on life's raised daïs, and appeal at once to our respect and pity. A flavour of the old school, a touch of something different in their manner—which is freer and rounder, if they come of what is called a good family, and often more timid and precise if they are of the middle class—serves, in these days, to accentuate the difference of age and add a distinction to gray hairs. But their superiority is founded more deeply than by outward marks or gestures. They are before us in the march of man; they have more or less solved the irking problem; they have battled through the equinox of life; in good and evil they have held their course; and now, without open shame, they near the crown and harbour. It may be we have been struck with one of fortune's darts; we can scarce be civil, so cruelly is our spirit tossed. Yet long before we were so much as thought upon, the like calamity befell the old man or woman that now, with pleasant humour, rallies us upon our inattention, sitting composed in the holy evening of man's life, in the clear shining after rain. We grow ashamed of our distresses, new and hot and coarse, like villainous roadside brandy; we see life in aerial perspective, under the heavens of faith; and out of the worst, in the mere presence of contented elders, look forward and take patience. Fear shrinks before them "like a thing reproved,"[5] not the flitting and ineffectual fear of death, but the instant, dwelling terror of the responsibilities and revenges of life. Their speech, indeed, is timid; they report lions in the path; they counsel a meticulous footing; but their serene, marred faces are more eloquent and tell another story. Where they have gone, we will go also, not very greatly fearing; what they have endured unbroken, we also, God helping us, will make a shift to bear.

Not only is the presence of the aged in itself remedial, but their minds are stored with antidotes, wisdom's simple, plain considerations overlooked by youth. They have matter to communicate, be they never so stupid. Their talk is not merely literature, it is great literature; classic in virtue of the speaker's detachment, studded, like a book of travel, with things we should not otherwise have learnt. In virtue, I have said, of the speaker's detachment,—and this is why, of two old men, the one who is not your father speaks to you with the more sensible authority; for in the paternal relation the oldest have lively interests and remain still young. Thus I have known two young men great friends; each swore by the other's father; the father of each swore by the other lad; and yet each pair of parent and child were perpetually by the ears. This is typical: it reads like the germ of some kindly comedy.

The old appear in conversation in two characters: the critically silent and the garrulous anecdotic. The last is perhaps what we look for; it is perhaps the more instructive. An old gentleman, well on in years, sits handsomely and naturally in the bow-window of his age, scanning experience with reverted eye; and chirping and smiling, communicates the accidents and reads the lesson of his long career. Opinions are strengthened, indeed, but they are also weeded out in the course of years. What remains steadily present to the eye of the retired veteran in his hermitage, what still ministers to his content, what still quickens his old honest heart—these are "the real long-lived things" that Whitman tells us to prefer.[6] Where youth agrees with age, not where they differ, wisdom lies; and it is when the young disciple finds his heart to beat in tune with his gray-bearded teacher's that a lesson may be learned. I have known one old gentleman, whom I may name, for he in now gathered to his stock—Robert Hunter, Sheriff of Dumbarton, and author of an excellent law-book still re-edited and republished.[7] Whether he was originally big or little is more than I can guess. When I knew him he was all fallen away and fallen in; crooked and shrunken; buckled into a stiff waistcoat for support; troubled by ailments, which kept him hobbling in and out of the room; one foot gouty; a wig for decency, not for deception, on his head; close shaved, except under his chin—and for that he never failed to apologise, for it went sore against the traditions of his life. You can imagine how he would fare in a novel by Miss Mather;[8] yet this rag of a Chelsea veteran lived to his last year in the plenitude of all that is best in man, brimming with human kindness, and staunch as a Roman soldier under his manifold infirmities. You could not say that he had lost his memory, for he would repeat Shakespeare and Webster and Jeremy Taylor and Burke by the page together; but the parchment was filled up, there was no room for fresh inscriptions, and he was capable of repeating the same anecdote on many successive visits.[9] His voice survived in its full power, and he took a pride in using it. On his last voyage as Commissioner of Lighthouses, he hailed a ship at sea and made himself clearly audible without a speaking trumpet, ruffling the while with a proper vanity in his achievement. He had a habit of eking out his words with interrogative hems, which was puzzling and a little wearisome, suited ill with his appearance, and seemed a survival from some former stage of bodily portliness. Of yore, when he was a great pedestrian and no enemy to good claret, he may have pointed with these minute guns his allocutions to the bench. His humour was perfectly equable, set beyond the reach of fate; gout, rheumatism, stone and gravel might have combined their forces against that frail tabernacle, but when I came round on Sunday evening, he would lay aside Jeremy Taylor's *Life of Christ*[10] and greet me with the same open brow, the same kind formality of manner. His opinions and sympathies dated the man almost to a decade. He had begun life, under his mother's influence, as an admirer of Junius,[11] but on maturer knowledge had transferred his admiration to Burke. He cautioned me, with entire gravity, to be punctilious in writing English; never to forget that I was a Scotchman, that English was a foreign tongue, and that if I attempted the colloquial, I should certainly be shamed: the remark was apposite, I suppose, in the days of David Hume.[12] Scott[13] was too new for him; he had known the author—known him, too, for a Tory; and to the genuine classic a contemporary is always something of a trouble. He had the old, serious love of the play; had even, as he was proud to tell, played a certain part in the history of Shakespearian revivals, for he had successfully pressed on Murray, of the old Edinburgh Theatre,[14] the idea of producing Shakespeare's fairy pieces with great scenic display. A moderate in religion, he was much struck in the last years of his life by a conversation with two young lads, revivalists.[15] "H'm," he would say—"new to me. I have had—h'm—no such experience." It struck him, not with pain, rather with a solemn philosophic interest, that he, a Christian as he hoped, and a Christian of so old a standing, should hear these young fellows talking of his own subject, his own weapons that he had fought the battle of life with,—"and—h'm—not understand." In this wise and graceful attitude he did justice to himself and others, reposed unshaken in his old beliefs, and recognised their limits without anger or alarm. His last recorded remark, on the last night of his life, was after he had been arguing against Calvinism with his minister and was interrupted by an intolerable pang. "After all," he said, "of all the 'isms, I know none so bad as rheumatism." My own last sight of him was some time before, when we dined together at an inn; he had been on circuit, for he stuck to his duties like a chief part of his existence; and I remember it as the only occasion on which he ever soiled his lips with slang—a thing he loathed. We were both Roberts; and as we took our places at table, he addressed me with a twinkle: "We are just what you would call two bob."[16] He offered me port, I remember, as the proper milk of youth; spoke of "twenty-shilling notes;" and throughout the meal was full of old-world pleasantry and quaintness, like an ancient boy on a holiday. But what I recall chiefly was his confession that he had never read *Othello* to an end. Shakespeare was his continual study. He loved nothing better than to display his knowledge and memory by adducing parallel passages from Shakespeare, passages where the same word was employed, or the same idea differently treated.

But *Othello* had beaten him. "That noble gentleman and that noble lady—h'm—too painful for me." The same night the hoardings were covered with posters, "Burlesque of *Othello*," and the contrast blazed up in my mind like a bonfire. An unforgettable look it gave me into that kind man's soul. His acquaintance was indeed a liberal and pious education. All the humanities were taught in that bare dining-room beside his gouty footstool. He was a piece of good advice; he was himself the instance that pointed and adorned his various talk. Nor could a young man have found elsewhere a place so set apart from envy, fear, discontent, or any of the passions that debase; a life so honest and composed; a soul like an ancient violin, so subdued to harmony, responding to a touch in music—as in that dining-room, with Mr. Hunter chatting at the eleventh hour, under the shadow of eternity, fearless and gentle.

The second class of old people are not anecdotic; they are rather hearers than talkers, listening to the young with an amused and critical attention. To have this sort of intercourse to perfection, I think we must go to old ladies. Women are better hearers than men, to begin with; they learn, I fear in anguish, to bear with the tedious and infantile vanity of the other sex; and we will take more from a woman than even from the oldest man in the way of biting comment. Biting comment is the chief part, whether for profit or amusement, in this business. The old lady that I have in my eye is a very caustic speaker, her tongue, after years of practice, in absolute command, whether for silence or attack. If she chance to dislike you, you will be tempted to curse the malignity of age. But if you chance to please even slightly, you will be listened to with a particular laughing grace of sympathy, and from time to time chastised, as if in play, with a parasol as heavy as a pole-axe. It requires a singular art, as well as the vantage-ground of age, to deal these stunning corrections among the coxcombs of the young. The pill is disguised in sugar of wit; it is administered as a compliment—if you had not pleased, you would not have been censured; it is a personal affair—a hyphen, a *trait d'union*,[17] between you and your censor; age's philandering, for her pleasure and your good. Incontestably the young man feels very much of a fool; but he must be a perfect Malvolio,[18] sick with self-love, if he cannot take an open buffet and still smile. The correction of silence is what kills; when you know you have transgressed, and your friend says nothing and avoids your eye. If a man were made of gutta-percha,[19] his heart would quail at such a moment. But when the word is out, the worst is over; and a fellow with any good-humour at all may pass through a perfect hail of witty criticism, every bare place on his soul hit to the quick with a shrewd missile, and reappear, as if after a dive, tingling with a fine moral reaction, and ready, with a shrinking readiness, one-third loath, for a repetition of the discipline.

There are few women, not well sunned and ripened, and perhaps toughened, who can thus stand apart from a man and say the true thing with a kind of genial cruelty. Still there are some—and I doubt if there be any man who can return the compliment. The class of man represented by Vernon Whitford in *The Egoist* says, indeed, the true thing, but he says it stockishly. Vernon is a noble fellow, and makes, by the way, a noble and instructive contrast to Daniel Deronda; his conduct is the conduct of a man of honour; but we agree with him, against our consciences, when he remorsefully considers "its astonishing dryness."[20] He is the best of men, but the best of women manage to combine all that and something more. Their very faults assist them; they are helped even by the falseness of their position in life. They can retire into the fortified camp of the proprieties. They can touch a subject and suppress it. The most adroit employ a somewhat elaborate reserve as a means to be frank, much as they wear gloves when they shake hands. But a man has the full responsibility of his freedom, cannot evade a question, can scarce be silent without rudeness, must answer for his words upon the moment, and is not seldom left face to face with a damning choice, between the more or less dishonourable wriggling of Deronda and the downright woodenness of Vernon Whitford.

But the superiority of women is perpetually menaced; they do not sit throned on infirmities like the old; they are suitors as well as sovereigns; their vanity is engaged, their affections are too apt to follow; and hence much of the talk between the sexes degenerates into something unworthy of the name. The desire to please, to shine with a certain softness of lustre and to draw a fascinating picture of oneself, banishes from conversation all that is sterling and most of what is humorous. As soon as a strong current of mutual admiration begins to flow, the human interest triumphs entirely over the intellectual, and the commerce of words, consciously or not, becomes secondary to the commercing of eyes. But even where this ridiculous danger is avoided, and a man and woman converse equally and honestly, something in their nature or their education falsifies the strain. An instinct prompts them to agree; and where that is impossible, to agree to differ. Should they neglect the warning, at the first suspicion of an argument, they find themselves in different hemispheres. About any point of business or conduct, any actual affair demanding settlement, a woman will speak and listen, hear and answer arguments, not only with natural wisdom, but with candour and logical honesty. But if the subject of debate be something in the air, an abstraction, an excuse for talk, a logical Aunt Sally, then may the male debater instantly abandon hope; he may employ reason, adduce facts, be supple, be smiling, be angry, all shall avail him nothing; what the woman said first, that (unless she has forgotten it) she will repeat at the end. Hence, at the very junctures when a talk between men grows brighter and quicker and begins to promise to bear fruit, talk between the sexes is menaced with dissolution. The point of difference, the point of interest, is evaded by the brilliant woman, under a shower of irrelevant conversational rockets; it is bridged by the discreet woman with a rustle of silk, as she passes smoothly forward to the nearest point of safety. And this sort of prestidigitation, juggling the dangerous topic out of sight until it can be reintroduced with safety in an altered shape, is a piece of tactics among the true drawing-room queens.

The drawing-room is, indeed, an artificial place; it is so by our choice and for our sins. The subjection of women; the ideal imposed upon them from the cradle, and worn, like a hair-shirt, with so much constancy; their motherly, superior tenderness to man's vanity and self-importance; their managing arts—the arts of a civilised slave among good-natured barbarians—are all painful ingredients and all help to falsify relations. It is not till we get clear of that amusing artificial scene that genuine relations are founded, or ideas honestly compared. In the garden, on the road or the hillside, or *tête-à-tête* and apart from interruptions, occasions arise when we may learn much from any single woman; and nowhere more often than in married life. Marriage is one long conversation, chequered by disputes. The disputes are valueless; they but ingrain the difference; the heroic heart of woman prompting her at once to nail her colours to the mast. But in the intervals, almost unconsciously and with no desire to shine, the whole material of life is turned over and over, ideas are struck out and shared, the two persons more and more adapt their notions one to suit the other, and in process of time, without sound of trumpet, they conduct each other into new worlds of thought.

Notes

1 "Talk and Talkers" was published in Apr. 1882 in *Cornhill Magazine*. This "sequel" appeared in August.

2 Shakespeare, *Twelfth Night*, 5.1.10–18.

3 A common phrase in Scottish Covenanter writing.

4 The heavenly afterlife of fighting and feasting for slain warriors in Norse mythology.

5 Percy Shelley, "Adonais: An Elegy on the Death of John Keats" (45.9).

6 Walt Whitman, "Preface," *Leaves of Grass*.

7 Robert Hunter, *A Treatise on the Law of Landlord and Tenant* (1833).

8 Helen Mathers, penname of the popular novelist Ellen Buckingham Mathews (1853–1920).

9 John Webster (1580–1632), English dramatist. Edmund Burke (1729–1797), influential conservative MP and philosopher best known for his works *The Sublime and the Beautiful* (1757) and *Reflections on the Revolution in France* (1790). Jeremy Taylor (1613–1667), Anglican theologian known for his prose style.

10 *The Great Exemplar: Or, the Life of Jesus Christ* (1649).

11 The pseudonym of an unidentified Whig satirical writer for the *Public Advertiser* (1769–1772).

12 David Hume (1711–1776), Scottish Enlightenment philosopher.

13 Sir Walter Scott (1771–1832), eminent Scottish novelist and poet.

14 William Henry Wood Murray (1790–1852), actor and owner of Edinburgh's Theatre Royal known for dramatizing Walter Scott's *Waverley* novels.

15 Proselyting Evangelicals who separated from the Church of Scotland.

16 "Bob" is slang for the British shilling.

17 A connection between otherwise unattached parties; a mark of connection or hyphen (French).

18 The antagonist of Shakespeare's *Twelfth Night*.

19 The juice of trees found in Malaysia and used for electric cables and various products.

20 Characters in George Meredith's *The Egoist* (1879) and George Eliot's *Daniel Deronda* (1876). Jules Michelet, *The Insect* (1857).

26

THE CHARACTER OF DOGS

The civilisation, the manners, and the morals of dog-kind are to a great extent subordinated to those of his ancestral master, man. This animal, in many ways so superior, has accepted a position of inferiority, shares the domestic life, and humours the caprices of the tyrant. But the potentate, like the British in India, pays small regard to the character of his willing client, judges him with listless glances, and condemns him in a byword. Listless have been the looks of his admirers, who have exhausted idle terms of praise, and buried the poor soul below exaggerations. And yet more idle and, if possible, more unintelligent has been the attitude of his express detractors; those who are very fond of dogs "but in their proper place"; who say "poo' fellow, poo' fellow," and are themselves far poorer; who whet the knife of the vivisectionist[1] or heat his oven; who are not ashamed to admire "the creature's instinct"; and flying far beyond folly, have dared to resuscitate the theory of animal machines.[2] The "dog's instinct" and the "automaton-dog,"[3] in this age of psychology and science, sound like strange anachronisms. An automaton he certainly is; a machine working independently of his control, the heart like the mill-wheel, keeping all in motion, and the consciousness, like a person shut in the mill garret, enjoying the view out of the window and shaken by the thunder of the stones; an automaton in one corner of which a living spirit is confined: an automaton like man. Instinct again he certainly possesses. Inherited aptitudes are his, inherited frailties. Some things he at once views and understands, as though he were awakened from a sleep, as though he came "trailing clouds of glory."[4] But with him, as with man, the field of instinct is limited; its utterances are obscure and occasional; and about the far larger part of life both the dog and his master must conduct their steps by deduction and observation.

The leading distinction between dog and man, after and perhaps before the different duration of their lives, is that the one can speak and that the other cannot. The absence of the power of speech confines the dog in the development of his intellect. It hinders him from many speculations, for words are the beginning of metaphysic. At the same blow it saves him from many superstitions, and his silence has won for him a higher name for virtue than his conduct justifies. The faults of the dog are many. He is vainer than man, singularly greedy of notice, singularly intolerant of ridicule, suspicious like the deaf, jealous to the degree of frenzy, and radically devoid of truth. The day of an intelligent small dog is passed in the manufacture and the laborious communication of falsehood; he lies with his tail, he lies with his eye, he lies with his protesting paw; and when he rattles his dish or scratches at the door his purpose is other than appears. But he has some apology to offer for the vice. Many of the signs which form his dialect have come to bear an arbitrary meaning, clearly understood both by his master and himself; yet when a new want arises he must either invent a new vehicle of meaning or wrest an old one to a different purpose; and this necessity frequently recurring must tend to lessen his idea of the sanctity of symbols. Meanwhile the dog is clear in his own conscience, and draws, with a human nicety, the distinction between formal and essential truth. Of his punning perversions, his legitimate dexterity with symbols, he is even vain; but when he has told and been detected in a lie, there is not a hair upon his body but confesses guilt. To a dog of gentlemanly feeling theft and falsehood are disgraceful vices. The canine, like the human, gentleman demands in his misdemeanours Montaigne's *"je ne sais quoi de généreux."*[5] He is never more than half ashamed of having barked or bitten; and for those faults into which he has been led by the desire to shine before a lady of his race, he retains, even under physical correction, a share of pride. But to be caught lying, if he understands it, instantly uncurls his fleece.

Just as among dull observers he preserves a name for truth, the dog has been credited with modesty. It is amazing how the use of language blunts the faculties of man—that because vainglory finds no vent in words, creatures supplied with eyes have been unable to detect a fault so gross and obvious. If a small spoiled dog were suddenly to be endowed with speech, he would prate interminably, and still about himself; when we had friends, we should be forced to lock him in a garret; and what with his whining jealousies and his foible for falsehood, in a year's time he would have gone far to weary out our love. I was about to compare him to Sir Willoughby Patterne,[6] but the Patternes have a manlier sense of their own merits; and the parallel, besides, is ready. Hans Christian Andersen, as we behold him in his startling memoirs, thrilling from top to toe with an excruciating vanity,[7] and scouting even along the street for shadows of offence—here was the talking dog.

It is just this rage for consideration that has betrayed the dog into his satellite position as the friend of man. The cat, an animal of franker appetites, preserves his independence. But the dog, with one eye ever on the audience, has been wheedled into slavery, and praised and patted into the renunciation of his nature. Once he ceased hunting and became man's plate-licker, the Rubicon was crossed. Thenceforth he was a gentleman of leisure; and except the few whom we keep working, the whole race grew more and more self-conscious, mannered and affected. The number of things that a small dog does naturally is strangely small. Enjoying better spirits and not crushed under material cares, he is far more theatrical than average man. His whole life, if he be a dog of any pretension to gallantry, is spent in a vain show, and in the hot pursuit of admiration. Take out your puppy for a walk, and you will find the little ball of fur clumsy, stupid, bewildered, but natural. Let but a few months pass, and when you repeat the process you will find nature buried in convention. He will do nothing plainly; but the simplest processes of our material life will all be bent into the forms of an elaborate and mysterious etiquette. Instinct, says the fool, has awakened. But it is not so. Some dogs—some, at the very least—if they be kept separate from others, remain quite natural; and these, when at length they meet with a companion of experience, and have the game explained to them, distinguish themselves by the severity of their devotion to its rules. I wish I were allowed to tell a story which would radiantly illuminate the point; but men, like dogs, have an elaborate and mysterious etiquette. It is their bond of sympathy that both are the children of convention.

The person, man or dog, who has a conscience is eternally condemned to some degree of humbug; the sense of the law in their members[8] fatally precipitates either towards a frozen and affected bearing. And the converse is true; and in the elaborate and conscious manners of the dog, moral opinions and the love of the ideal stand confessed. To follow for ten minutes in the street some swaggering, canine cavalier, is to receive a lesson in dramatic art and the cultured conduct of the body; in every act and gesture you see him true to a refined conception; and the dullest cur, beholding him, pricks up his ear and proceeds to imitate and parody that charming ease. For to be a high-mannered and high-minded gentleman, careless, affable, and gay, is the inborn pretension of the dog. The large dog, so much lazier, so much more weighed upon with matter, so majestic in repose, so beautiful in effort, is born with the dramatic means to wholly represent the part. And it is more pathetic and perhaps more instructive to consider the small dog in his conscientious and imperfect efforts to outdo Sir Philip Sidney.[9] For the ideal of the dog is feudal and religious; the ever-present polytheism, the whip-bearing Olympus of mankind, rules them on the one hand; on the other, their singular difference of size and strength among themselves effectually prevents the appearance of the democratic notion. Or we might more exactly compare their society to the curious spectacle presented by a school—ushers, monitors,[10] and big and little boys—qualified by one circumstance, the introduction of the other sex. In each, we should observe a somewhat similar tension of manner, and somewhat similar points of honour. In each the larger animal keeps a contemptuous good humour; in each the smaller annoys him with wasp-like impudence, certain of practical immunity; in each we shall find a double life producing double characters, and an excursive and noisy heroism combined with a fair amount of practical timidity. I have known dogs, and I have known school heroes that, set aside the fur, could hardly have been told apart; and if we desire to understand the chivalry of old, we must turn to the school playfields or the dungheap where the dogs are trooping.

Woman, with the dog, has been long enfranchised. Incessant massacre of female innocents has changed the proportions of the sexes and perverted their relations. Thus, when we regard the manners of the dog, we see a romantic and monogamous animal, once perhaps as delicate as the cat, at war with impossible conditions. Man has much to answer for; and the part he plays is yet more damnable and parlous than Corin's in the eyes of Touchstone.[11] But his intervention has at least created an imperial situation for the rare surviving ladies. In that society they reign without a rival: conscious queens; and in the only instance of a canine wife-beater that has ever fallen under my notice, the criminal was somewhat excused by the circumstances of his story. He is a little, very alert, well-bred, intelligent Skye,[12] as black as a hat, with a wet bramble for a nose and two cairngorms[13] for eyes. To the human observer, he is decidedly well-looking; but to the ladies of his race he seems abhorrent. A thorough elaborate gentleman, of the plume and sword-knot order,[14] he was born with a nice sense of gallantry to women. He took at their hands the most outrageous treatment; I have heard him bleating like a sheep, I have seen him streaming blood, and his ear tattered like a regimental banner; and yet he would scorn to make reprisals. Nay more, when a human lady upraised the contumelious whip against the very dame who had been so cruelly misusing him, my little great-heart gave but one hoarse cry and fell upon the tyrant tooth and nail. This is the tale of a soul's tragedy.[15] After three years of unavailing chivalry, he suddenly, in one hour, threw off the yoke of obligation; had he been Shakespeare he would then have written *Troilus and Cressida*[16] to brand the offending sex; but being only a little dog, he began to bite them. The surprise of the ladies whom he attacked indicated the monstrosity of his offence; but he had fairly beaten off his better angel, fairly committed moral suicide; for almost in the same hour, throwing aside the last rags of decency, he proceeded to attack the aged also. The fact is worth remark, showing, as it does, that ethical laws are common both to dogs and men; and that with both a single deliberate violation of the conscience loosens all. "But while the lamp holds on to burn," says the paraphrase, "the greatest sinner may return."[17] I have been cheered to see symptoms of effectual penitence in my sweet ruffian; and by the handling that he accepted uncomplainingly the other day from an indignant fair one, I begin to hope the period of *Sturm und Drang*[18] is closed.

All these little gentlemen are subtle casuists. The duty to the female dog is plain; but where competing duties rise, down they will sit and study them out, like Jesuit confessors. I knew another little Skye, somewhat plain in manner and appearance, but a creature compact of amiability and solid wisdom. His family going abroad for a winter, he was received for that period by an uncle in the same city. The winter over, his own family home again, and his own house (of which he was very proud) reopened, he found himself in a dilemma between two conflicting duties of loyalty and gratitude. His old friends were not to be neglected, but it seemed hardly decent to desert the new. This was how he solved the problem. Every morning, as soon as the door was opened, off posted Coolin[19] to his uncle's, visited the children in the nursery, saluted the whole family, and was back at home in time for breakfast and his bit of fish. Nor was this done without a sacrifice on his part, sharply felt; for he had to forego the particular honour and jewel of his day—his morning's walk with my father. And, perhaps from this cause, he gradually wearied of and relaxed the practice, and at length returned entirely to his ancient habits. But the same decision served him in another and more distressing case of divided duty, which happened not long after. He was not at all a kitchen dog, but the cook had nursed him with unusual kindness during the distemper;

and though he did not adore her as he adored my father—although (born snob) he was critically conscious of her position as "only a servant"—he still cherished for her a special gratitude. Well, the cook left, and retired some streets away to lodgings of her own; and there was Coolin in precisely the same situation with any young gentleman who has had the inestimable benefit of a faithful nurse. The canine conscience did not solve the problem with a pound of tea at Christmas. No longer content to pay a flying visit, it was the whole forenoon that he dedicated to his solitary friend. And so, day by day, he continued to comfort her solitude until (for some reason which I could never understand and cannot approve) he was kept locked up to break him of the graceful habit. Here, it is not the similarity, it is the difference, that is worthy of remark; the clearly marked degrees of gratitude and the proportional duration of his visits. Anything further removed from instinct it were hard to fancy; and one is even stirred to a certain impatience with a character so destitute of spontaneity, so passionless in justice, and so priggishly obedient to the voice of reason.

There are not many dogs like this good Coolin, and not many people. But the type is one well marked, both in the human and the canine family. Gallantry was not his aim, but a solid and somewhat oppressive respectability. He was a sworn foe to the unusual and the conspicuous, a praiser of the golden mean, a kind of city uncle modified by Cheeryble.[20] And as he was precise and conscientious in all the steps of his own blameless course, he looked for the same precision and an even greater gravity in the bearing of his deity, my father. It was no sinecure to be Coolin's idol: he was exacting like a rigid parent; and at every sign of levity in the man whom he respected, he announced loudly the death of virtue and the proximate fall of the pillars of the earth.

I have called him a snob; but all dogs are so, though in varying degrees. It is hard to follow their snobbery among themselves; for though I think we can perceive distinctions of rank, we cannot grasp what is the criterion. Thus in Edinburgh, in a good part of the town, there were several distinct societies or clubs that met in the morning to—the phrase is technical—to "rake the backets"[21] in a troop. A friend of mine, the master of three dogs, was one day surprised to observe that they had left one club and joined another; but whether it was a rise or a fall, and the result of an invitation or an expulsion, was more than he could guess. And this illustrates pointedly our ignorance of the real life of dogs, their social ambitions and their social hierarchies. At least, in their dealings with men they are not only conscious of sex, but of the difference of station. And that in the most snobbish manner; for the poor man's dog is not offended by the notice of the rich, and keeps all his ugly feeling for those poorer or more ragged than his master. And again, for every station they have an ideal of behaviour, to which the master, under pain of derogation, will do wisely to conform. How often has not a cold glance of an eye informed me that my dog was disappointed; and how much more gladly would he not have taken a beating than to be thus wounded in the seat of piety!

I knew one disrespectable dog. He was far liker a cat; cared little or nothing for men, with whom he merely coexisted as we do with cattle, and was entirely devoted to the art of poaching. A house would not hold him, and to live in a town was what he refused. He led, I believe, a life of troubled but genuine pleasure, and perished beyond all question in a trap. But this was an exception, a marked reversion to the ancestral type; like the hairy human infant. The true dog of the nineteenth century, to judge by the remainder of my fairly large acquaintance, is in love with respectability. A street-dog was once adopted by a lady. While still an Arab, he had done as Arabs do, gambolling in the mud, charging into butchers' stalls, a cat-hunter, a sturdy beggar, a common rogue and vagabond; but with his rise into society he laid aside these inconsistent pleasures. He stole no more, he hunted no more cats; and conscious of his collar, he ignored his old companions. Yet the canine upper class was never brought to recognise the upstart, and from that hour, except for human countenance, he was alone. Friendless, shorn of his sports and the habits of a lifetime, he still lived in a glory of happiness, content with his acquired respectability, and with no care but to support it solemnly. Are we to condemn or praise this self-made dog? We praise his human brother. And thus to conquer vicious habits is as rare with dogs as with men. With the more part, for all their scruple-mongering and moral thought, the vices that are born with them remain invincible throughout; and they live all their years, glorying in their virtues, but still the slaves of their defects. Thus the sage Coolin was a thief to the last; among a thousand peccadilloes, a whole goose and a whole cold leg of mutton lay upon his conscience; but Woggs,[22] whose soul's shipwreck in the matter of gallantry I have recounted above, has only twice been known to steal, and has often nobly conquered the temptation. The eighth is his favourite commandment. There is something painfully human in these unequal virtues and mortal frailties of the best. Still more painful is the bearing of those "stammering professors"[23] in the house of sickness and under the terror of death. It is beyond a doubt to me that, somehow or other, the dog connects together, or confounds, the uneasiness of sickness and the consciousness of guilt. To the pains of the body he often adds the tortures of the conscience; and at these times his haggard protestations form, in regard to the human deathbed, a dreadful parody or parallel.

I once supposed that I had found an inverse relation between the double etiquette which dogs obey; and that those who were most addicted to the showy street life among other dogs were less careful in the practice of home virtues for the tyrant man. But the female dog, that mass of carneying affections, shines equally in either sphere; rules her rough posse of attendant swains with unwearying tact and gusto; and with her master and mistress pushes the arts of insinuation to their crowning point. The attention of man and the regard of other dogs flatter (it would thus appear) the same sensibility; but perhaps, if we could read the canine heart, they would be found to flatter it in very different degrees. Dogs live with man as courtiers round a monarch, steeped in the flattery of his notice and enriched with sinecures. To push their favour in this world of pickings and caresses is, perhaps, the business of their lives; and their joys may lie outside. I am in despair at our persistent ignorance. I read in the lives of our companions the same processes of reason, the same antique and fatal conflicts of the right against the wrong, and of unbitted nature with too rigid custom; I see them with our weaknesses, vain, false, inconstant against appetite, and with our one stalk of virtue, devoted to the dream of an ideal; and yet, as they hurry by me on the street with tail in air, or come singly to solicit my regard, I must own the secret purport of their lives is still inscrutable to man. Is man the friend, or is he the patron only? Have they indeed forgotten nature's voice? or are those moments snatched from courtiership when they touch noses with the tinker's mongrel, the brief reward and pleasure of their artificial lives? Doubtless, when man shares with his dog the toils of a profession and the pleasures of an art, as with the shepherd or the poacher, the affection warms and strengthens till it fills the soul. But doubtless, also, the masters are, in many cases, the object of a merely interested cultus, sitting aloft like Louis Quatorze,[24] giving and receiving flattery and favour; and the dogs, like the majority of men, have but foregone their true existence and become the dupes of their ambition.

Notes

1 Vivisection: the controversial Victorian practice of dissecting living animals for physiological and medical research. Stevenson corresponded with the anti-vivisectionist activist Frances Power Cobbe (1822–1904, *Letters* 2.244). According to Graham Balfour, Stevenson stopped a dog fight in Samoa and saved a dog from being beaten in Pitlochry (361).

2 René Descartes's idea that animals are purely physical machines without intelligence or emotion. Descartes, who famously wrote, "I think, therefore I am" in *Discourse on the Method* (1637), believed that these qualities fundamentally distinguished humans from animals, whereas Darwin argued differences of degree rather than kind (*Descent of Man*, ch. 6).

3 A moving device, typically fashioned as a human or animal, with a concealed mechanism that appears to operate spontaneously.

4 Wordsworth, "Ode: Intimations" (65).

5 A certain generosity (French); Michel de Montaigne (1533–1592), French author of the *Essais*, which established the essay form.

6 The self-centered main character of Meredith's novel *The Egoist*.

7 Popular Danish children's author Hans Christian Andersen's *The Story of My Life* (1871).

8 Romans 7:23.

9 Sir Philip Sidney (1554–1586), English poet, scholar, courtier, and soldier. He was reportedly wounded in the thigh at the Battle of Zutphen after removing his thigh armor so he would not be better protected than his men. Before dying some weeks later, he gave his water to another injured soldier. Sidney was celebrated as the heroic ideal of British manhood.

10 Usher: an assistant to a schoolmaster or head-teacher; monitor: a student assigned to teach junior pupils.

11 "Sin is damnation: Thou art in a parlous state, shepherd" (Shakespeare, *As You Like It*, 3.2.43–44).

12 Stevenson's dog "Woggs" or "Bogue" was a black Skye terrier.

13 Brown quartz from Scotland's Cairngorms, used as ornaments of Highland dress.

14 Describes formal military dress uniform.

15 Title of Robert Browning's play *A Soul's Tragedy* (1846).

16 Shakespeare's 1602 problem comedy set in the Trojan War. After swearing faithfulness to her Trojan lover, Troilus, Cressida promptly succumbs to the advances of the Greek Diomedes.

17 Isaac Watts, "Life is the Time to Serve the Lord."

18 Proto-Romantic German literary movement *Sturm und Drang* (storm and stress) associated with Goethe.

19 Coolin was Stevenson's Skye terrier from 1857 to 1869. Stevenson had Coolin's tomb moved from Swanston Cottage to Skerryvore (*Letters* 5:392).

20 The Cheeryble Brothers are noble, charitable characters in Charles Dickens's *Nicholas Nickleby* (1839).

21 Backet: a small, wooden trough typically used to carry ashes or waste.

22 **RLS:** "Walter, Watty, Woggy, Woggs, Wogg, and lastly Bogue; under which last name he fell in battle some twelve months ago. Glory was his aim and he attained it; for his icon, by the hand of Caldecott, now lies among the treasures of the nation." Bogue was injured in a fight with another dog in 1886 and treated in a dogs' infirmary, but he escaped, attacked a bigger dog, and died. This essay was originally published in *The English Illustrated Magazine* in Feb. 1884 and illustrated by Randolph Caldecott (1846–1886). Caldecott's drawings are held at the British Museum.

23 Professing Christians.

24 Louis XIV (1638–1715).

27

"A PENNY PLAIN AND TWOPENCE COLOURED"

These words will be familiar to all students of Skelt's Juvenile Drama.[1] That national monument, after having changed its name to Park's, to Webb's, to Redington's, and last of all to Pollock's,[2] has now become, for the most part, a memory. Some of its pillars, like Stonehenge, are still afoot, the rest clean vanished. It may be the Museum numbers a full set; and Mr. Ionides[3] perhaps, or else her gracious Majesty, may boast their great collections; but to the plain private person they are become, like Raphaels, unattainable. I have, at different times, possessed *Aladdin, The Red Rover, The Blind Boy, The Old Oak Chest, The Wood Dæmon, Jack Sheppard, The Miller and his Men, Der Freischütz, The Smuggler, The Forest of Bondy, Robin Hood, The Waterman, Richard I., My Poll and my Partner Joe, The Inchcape Bell* (imperfect), and *Three-Fingered Jack, the Terror of Jamaica*; and I have assisted others in the illumination of *The Maid of the Inn* and *The Battle of Waterloo*.[4] In this roll-call of stirring names you read the evidences of a happy childhood; and though not half of them are still to be procured of any living stationer, in the mind of their once happy owner all survive, kaleidoscopes of changing pictures, echoes of the past.

There stands, I fancy, to this day (but now how fallen!) a certain stationer's shop at a corner of the wide thoroughfare that joins the city of my childhood with the sea. When, upon any Saturday, we made a party to behold the ships, we passed that corner; and since in those days I loved a ship as a man loves Burgundy or daybreak, this of itself had been enough to hallow it. But there was more than that. In the Leith Walk window, all the year round, there stood displayed a theatre in working order, with a "forest set," a "combat," and a few "robbers carousing" in the slides; and below and about, dearer tenfold to me! the plays themselves, those budgets of romance, lay tumbled one upon another. Long and often have I lingered there with empty pockets. One figure, we shall say, was visible in the first plate of characters, bearded, pistol in hand, or drawing to his ear the clothyard arrow; I would spell the name: was it Macaire, or Long Tom Coffin, or Grindoff, 2d dress? O, how I would long to see the rest! how—if the name by chance were hidden—I would wonder in what play he figured, and what immortal legend justified his attitude and strange apparel! And then to go within, to announce yourself as an intending purchaser, and, closely watched, be suffered to undo those bundles and breathlessly devour those pages of gesticulating villains, epileptic combats, bosky forests, palaces and war-ships, frowning fortresses and prison vaults—it was a giddy joy. That shop, which was dark and smelt of Bibles, was a loadstone rock for all that bore the name of boy. They could not pass it by, nor, having entered, leave it. It was a place besieged; the shopmen, like the Jews rebuilding Salem, had a double task. They kept us at the stick's end, frowned us down, snatched each play out of our hand ere we were trusted with another; and, inceditable as it may sound, used to demand of us upon our entrance, like banditti, if we came with money or with empty hand. Old Mr. Smith himself, worn out with my eternal vacillation, once swept the treasures from before me, with the cry: "I do not believe, child, that you are an intending purchaser at all!" These were the dragons of the garden; but for such joys of paradise we could have faced the Terror of Jamaica himself. Every sheet we fingered was another lightning glance into obscure, delicious story; it was like wallowing in the raw stuff of story-books. I know nothing to compare with it save now and then in dreams, when I am privileged to read in certain unwrit stories of adventure, from which I awake to find the world all vanity. The *crux* of Buridan's donkey[5] was as nothing to the uncertainty of the boy as he handled and lingered and doated on these bundles of delight; there was a physical pleasure in the sight and touch of them which he would jealously prolong; and when at length the deed was done, the play selected, and the impatient shopman had brushed the rest into the gray portfolio, and the boy was forth again, a little late for dinner, the lamps springing into light in the blue winter's even, and *The Miller*, or *The Rover*, or some kindred drama clutched against his side—on what gay feet he ran, and how he laughed aloud in exultation! I can hear that laughter still. Out of all the years of my life, I can recall but one homecoming to compare with these, and that was on the night when I brought back with me the *Arabian Entertainments* in the fat, old, double-columned volume with the prints. I was just well into the story of the Hunchback, I remember, when my clergyman-grandfather (a man we counted pretty stiff) came in behind me. I grew blind with terror. But instead of ordering the book away, he said he envied me. Ah, well he might!

The purchase and the first half-hour at home, that was the summit. Thenceforth the interest declined by little and little. The fable, as set forth in the play-book, proved to be not worthy of the scenes and characters: what fable would not? Such passages as: "Scene 6. The Hermitage. Night set scene. Place back of scene I, No. 2, at back of stage and hermitage, Fig. 2, out of set piece, R. H. in a slanting direction"—such passages, I say, though very practical, are hardly to be called good reading. Indeed, as literature, these dramas did not much appeal to me. I forget the very outline of the plots. Of *The Blind Boy*, beyond the fact that he was a most injured prince and once, I think, abducted, I know nothing. And *The Old Oak Chest*, what was it all about? that proscript (1st dress), that prodigious number of banditti, that old woman with the broom, and the magnificent kitchen in the third act (was it in the third?)—they are all fallen in a deliquium, swim faintly in my brain, and mix and vanish.

I cannot deny that joy attended the illumination; nor can I quite forget that child who, wilfully foregoing pleasure, stoops to "twopence coloured." With crimson lake (hark to the sound of it—crimson lake!—the horns of elf-land are not richer on the ear)—with crimson lake and Prussian blue a certain purple is to be compounded which, for cloaks especially, Titian[6] could not equal. The latter colour with gamboge, a hated name although an exquisite pigment, supplied a green of such a savoury greenness that today my heart regrets it. Nor can I recall without a tender weakness the very aspect of the water where I dipped my brush. Yes, there was pleasure in the painting. But when all was painted, it is needless to deny it, all was spoiled. You might, indeed, set up a scene or two to look at; but to cut the figures out was simply sacrilege; nor could any child twice court the tedium, the worry, and the long-drawn disenchantment of an actual performance. Two days after the purchase the honey had been sucked. Parents used to complain; they thought I wearied of my play. It was not so: no more than a person can be said to have wearied of his dinner when he leaves the bones and dishes; I had got the marrow of it and said grace.

Then was the time to turn to the back of the play-book and to study that enticing double file of names, where poetry, for the true child of Skelt, reigned happy and glorious like her Majesty the Queen. Much as I have travelled in these realms of gold,[7] I have yet seen, upon that map or abstract, names of El Dorados that still haunt the ear of memory, and are still but names. *The Floating Beacon*—why was that denied me? or *The Wreck Ashore? Sixteen-String Jack*, whom I did not even guess to be a highwayman, troubled me awake and haunted my slumbers; and there is one sequence of three from that enchanted calender[8] that I still at times recall, like a loved verse of poetry: *Lodoiska, Silver Palace, Echo of Westminster Bridge.*[9] Names, bare names, are surely more to children than we poor, grown-up, obliterated fools remember.

The name of Skelt itself has always seemed a part and parcel of the charm of his productions. It may be different with the rose, but the attraction of this paper drama sensibly declined when Webb had crept into the rubric: a poor cuckoo, flaunting in Skelt's nest. And now we have reached Pollock, sounding deeper gulfs. Indeed, this name of Skelt appears so stagey and piratic, that I will adopt it boldly to design these qualities. Skeltery, then, is a quality of much art. It is even to be found, with reverence be it said, among the works of nature. The stagey is its generic name; but it is an old, insular, home-bred staginess; not French, domestically British; not of to-day, but smacking of O. Smith, Fitzball,[10] and the great age of melodrama: a peculiar fragrance haunting it; uttering its unimportant message in a tone of voice that has the charm of fresh antiquity. I will not insist upon the art of Skelt's purveyors. These wonderful characters that once so thrilled our soul with their bold attitude, array of deadly engines and incomparable costume, to-day look somewhat pallidly; the extreme hard favour of the heroine strikes me, I had almost said with pain; the villain's scowl no longer thrills me like a trumpet; and the scenes themselves, those once unparalleled landscapes, seem the efforts of a prentice hand. So much of fault we find; but on the other side the impartial critic rejoices to remark the presence of a great unity of gusto; of those direct clap-trap appeals, which a man is dead and buriable when he fails to answer; of the footlight glamour, the ready-made, bare-faced, transpontine[11] picturesque, a thing not one with cold reality, but how much dearer to the mind!

The scenery of Skeltdom—or, shall we say, the kingdom of Transpontus?— had a prevailing character. Whether it set forth Poland as in *The Blind Boy*, or Bohemia with *The Miller and his Men*, or Italy with *The Old Oak Chest*, still it was Transpontus. A botanist could tell it by the plants. The hollyhock was all pervasive, running wild in deserts; the dock was common, and the bending reed; and overshadowing these were poplar, palm, potato tree, and *Quercus Skeltica*— brave growths. The caves were all embowelled in the Surreyside formation; the soil was all betrodden by the light pump of T. P. Cooke.[12] Skelt, to be sure, had yet another, an oriental string: he held the gorgeous east in fee; and in the new quarter of Hyères, say, in the garden of the Hotel des Iles d'Or, you may behold these blessed visions realised. But on these I will not dwell; they were an out-work; it was in the occidental scenery that Skelt was all himself. It had a strong flavour of England; it was a sort of indigestion of England and drop-scenes, and I am bound to say was charming. How the roads wander, how the castle sits upon the hill, how the sun eradiates from behind the cloud, and how the congregated clouds themselves uproll, as stiff as bolsters! Here is the cottage interior, the usual first flat, with the cloak upon the nail, the rosaries of onions, the gun and powder-horn and corner-cupboard; here is the inn (this drama must be nautical, I fore-see Captain Luff and Bold Bob Bowsprit) with the red curtain, pipes, spittoons, and eight-day clock; and there again is that impressive dungeon with the chains, which was so dull to colour. England, the hedgerow elms, the thin brick houses, windmills, glimpses of the navigable Thames—England, when at last I came to visit it, was only Skelt made evident: to cross the border was, for the Scotsman, to come home to Skelt; there was the inn-sign and there the horse-trough, all foreshadowed in the faithful Skelt. If, at the ripe age of fourteen years, I bought a certain cudgel, got a friend to load it, and thenceforward walked the tame ways of the earth my own ideal, radiating pure romance—still I was but a puppet in the hand of Skelt; the original of that regretted bludgeon, and surely the antitype of all the bludgeon kind, greatly improved from Cruikshank, had adorned the hand of Jonathan Wild, pl. I.[13] "This is mastering me," as Whitman cries, upon some lesser provocation.[14] What am I? what are life, art, letters, the world, but what my Skelt has made them? He stamped himself upon my immaturity. The world was plain before I knew him, a poor penny world; but soon it was all coloured with romance. If I go to the theatre to see a good old melodrama, 'tis but Skelt a little faded. If I visit a bold scene in nature, Skelt would have been bolder; there had been certainly a castle on that mountain, and the hollow tree—that set piece— I seem to miss it in the foreground. Indeed, out of this cut-and-dry, dull, swag-gering, obtrusive and infantile art, I seem to have learned the very spirit of my life's enjoyment; met there the shadows of the characters I was to read about and love in a late future; got the romance of *Der Freischütz* long ere I was to hear of

Weber[15] or the mighty Formes; acquired a gallery of scenes and characters with which, in the silent theatre of the brain, I might enact all novels and romances; and took from these rude cuts an enduring and transforming pleasure. Reader— and yourself?

A word of moral: it appears that B. Pollock, late J. Redington, No. 73 Hoxton Street, not only publishes twenty-three of these old stage favourites, but owns the necessary plates and displays a modest readiness to issue other thirty-three. If you love art, folly, or the bright eyes of children, speed to Pollock's, or to Clarke's of Garrick Street. In Pollock's list of publicanda I perceive a pair of my ancient aspirations: *Wreck Ashore* and *Sixteen-String Jack*; and I cherish the belief that when these shall see once more the light of day, B. Pollock will remember this apologist. But, indeed, I have a dream at times that is not all a dream. I seem to myself to wander in a ghostly street—E. W., I think, the postal district—close below the fool's-cap of St. Paul's, and yet within easy hearing of the echo of the Abbey bridge. There in a dim shop, low in the roof and smelling strong of glue and footlights, I find myself in quaking treaty with great Skelt himself, the aboriginal, all dusty from the tomb. I buy, with what a choking heart—I buy them all, all but the pantomimes; I pay my mental money, and go forth; and lo! the packets are dust.

Notes

1 The English illustrator G. Skelt (1835–1872) was a leading producer of juvenile dramas: toy or model theaters for children made of paperboard.

2 Publishers who produced toy theater sheets.

3 Alexander Ionides (1810–1890), a wealthy Greek patron and art collector in London.

4 Titles of popular melodramas. Authorship and performance dates according to Donald Mullin's *Victorian Plays: A Record of Significant Productions on the London Stage, 1837–90* (Greenwood, 1987): *Aladdin* (1844), E. Fitzball's *The Red Rover* (1837), J. Kenney's *The Blind Boy* (1839), J.M. Scott's *The Old Oak Chest* (1842), J.B. Buckstone's *Jack Sheppard* (1839), I. Pocock's *The Miller and His Men* (1813), *Der Freischütz, or The Smuggler* (1838), W. Barrymore's *The Forest of Bondy* (1838), *Robin Hood* (1838), C. Dibdin's *The Waterman* (1774), J.T. Hawes's *My Poll and My Partner Joe* (1837), E. Fitzball's *The Inchcape Bell* (1837). *The Maid of the Inn*, *The Battle of Waterloo*, and *Three-Fingered Jack, The Terror of Jamaica* were performed in 1842.

5 A philosophical illustration that imagines a donkey, equally hungry and thirsty precisely midway between water and hay, who is unable to decide between the two and dies. The thought experiment favors free will over the determinism of the 14th-century philosopher Jean Buridan.

6 Titian (1490–1576), leading Italian Renaissance painter of the Venetian school.

7 Keats, "On First Looking into Chapman's Homer" (1).

8 A machine that uses rollers to press paper for smoothing or glazing.

9 E. Fitzball's *The Floating Beacon* (1838), J.B. Buckstone's *The Wreck Ashore* (1837), *Lodoiska* (1839), *Silver Palace* (1838), and *The Echo of Westminster Bridge* (1838). *Sixteen-String Jack* was performed in various versions in the 1840s.

10 O. Smith, a melodramatic actor and leading villain at the Adelphi Theatre. Edward Fitzball (1792–1873), prolific English author of melodramas.

11 Transpontus, transpontine: literally "over the bridge"—a sensationalistic and melodramatic style of theater popular south of the Thames.

12 Thomas "Tippy" Potter Cooke (1786–1864), successful English melodrama actor.

13 George Cruikshank (1792–1878), caricaturist and illustrator; Jonathan Wild (1683–1725), English criminal, portrayed in Henry Fielding's satire *Jonathan Wild* (1743). Pl. I–Plate 1, or the first illustration in Skelt's toy theater of *Jonathan Wild*.

14 Walt Whitman, "Song of Myself" (1855, 37.1).

15 Carl Maria von Weber's opera *Der Freischütz* (1821) or *The Marksman*.

ACROSS THE PLAINS WITH OTHER MEMORIES AND ESSAYS[1]

28

THE OLD PACIFIC CAPITAL[2]

The Woods and the Pacific

The Bay of Monterey has been compared by no less a person than General Sherman[3] to a bent fishing-hook; and the comparison, if less important than the march through Georgia, still shows the eye of a soldier for topography. Santa Cruz sits exposed at the shank; the mouth of the Salinas river is at the middle of the bend; and Monterey itself is cosily ensconced beside the barb. Thus the ancient capital of California faces across the bay, while the Pacific Ocean, though hidden by low hills and forest, bombards her left flank and rear with never-dying surf. In front of the town, the long line of sea-beach trends north and north-west, and then westward to enclose the bay. The waves which lap so quietly about the jetties of Monterey grow louder and larger in the distance; you can see the breakers leaping high and white by day; at night the outline of the shore is traced in transparent silver by the moonlight and the flying foam; and from all round, even in quiet weather, the low, the distant, thrilling roar of the Pacific hangs over the coast and the adjacent country like smoke above a battle.

These long beaches are enticing to the idle man. It would be hard to find a walk more solitary and at the same time more exciting to the mind. Crowds of ducks and seagulls hover over the sea. Sandpipers trot in and out by troops after the retiring waves, trilling together in a chorus of infinitesimal song. Strange sea-tangles, new to the European eye, the bones of whales, or sometimes a whole whale's carcase, white with carrion-gulls and poisoning the wind, lie scattered here and there along the sands. The waves come in slowly, vast and green, curve their translucent necks, and burst with a surprising uproar, that runs, waxing and waning, up and down the long key-board of the beach. The foam of these great ruins mounts in an instant to the ridge of the sand glacis, swiftly fleets back again, and is met and buried by the next breaker. The interest is perpetually fresh. On no other coast that I know shall you enjoy, in calm, sunny weather, such a spectacle of Ocean's greatness, such beauty of changing colour, or such degrees of thunder in the sound. The very air is more than usually salt by this Homeric[4] deep.

In shore, a tract of sand-hills borders on the beach. Here and there a lagoon, more or less brackish, attracts the birds and hunters. A rough, spotty undergrowth partially conceals the sand. The crouching, hardy, live-oaks flourish singly or in thickets—the kind of wood for murderers to crawl among—and here and there the skirts of the forest extend downward from the hills, with a floor of turf and long aisles of pine-trees hung with Spaniard's Beard.[5] Through this quaint desert the railway cars drew near to Monterey from the junction at Salinas City—though that and so many other things are now for ever altered—and it was from here that you had your first view of the old township lying in the sands, its white windmills bickering in the chill, perpetual wind, and the first fogs of the evening drawing drearily around it from the sea.

The one common note of all this country is the haunting presence of the ocean. A great faint sound of breakers follows you high up into the inland canyons; the roar of water dwells in the clean, empty rooms of Monterey as in a shell upon the chimney; go where you will, you have but to pause and listen to hear the voice of the Pacific. You pass out of the town to the south-west, and mount the hill among pine woods. Glade, thicket, and grove surround you. You follow winding sandy tracts that lead nowhither. You see a deer; a multitude of quail arises. But the sound of the sea still follows you as you advance, like that of wind among the trees, only harsher and stranger to the ear; and when at length you gain the summit, out breaks on every hand and with freshened vigour that same unending, distant, whispering rumble of the ocean; for now you are on the top of Monterey peninsula, and the noise no longer only mounts to you from behind along the beach towards Santa Cruz, but from your right also, round by Chinatown and Pinos lighthouse, and from down before you to the mouth of the Carmello river. The whole woodland is begirt with thundering surges. The silence that immediately surrounds you where you stand is not so much broken as it is haunted by this distant, circling rumour. It sets your senses upon edge; you strain your attention; you are clearly and unusually conscious of small sounds near at hand; you walk listening like an Indian hunter; and that voice of the Pacific is a sort of disquieting company to you in your walk.

When once I was in these woods I found it difficult to turn homeward. All woods lure a rambler onward; but in those of Monterey it was the surf that particularly invited me to prolong my walks. I would push straight for the shore where I thought it to be nearest. Indeed, there was scarce a direction that would not, sooner or later, have brought me forth on the Pacific. The emptiness of the woods gave me a sense of freedom and discovery in these excursions. I never, in all my visits, met but one man. He was a Mexican, very dark of hue, but smiling and fat, and he carried an axe, though his true business at that moment was to seek for straying cattle. I asked him what o'clock it was, but he seemed neither to know nor care; and when he in his turn asked me for news of his cattle, I showed myself equally indifferent. We stood and smiled upon each other for a few seconds, and then turned without a word and took our several ways across the forest.

One day—I shall never forget it—I had taken a trail that was new to me. After a while the woods began to open, the sea to sound nearer hand. I came upon a road, and, to my surprise, a stile. A step or two further, and, without leaving the woods,

I found myself among trim houses. I walked through street after street, parallel and at right angles, paved with sward and dotted with trees, but still undeniable streets, and each with its name posted at the corner, as in a real town. Facing down the main thoroughfare—"Central Avenue," as it was ticketed—I saw an open-air temple, with benches and sounding-board, as though for an orchestra. The houses were all tightly shuttered; there was no smoke, no sound but of the waves, no moving thing. I have never been in any place that seemed so dream-like. Pompeii is all in a bustle with visitors, and its antiquity and strangeness deceive the imagination; but this town had plainly not been built above a year or two, and perhaps had been deserted overnight. Indeed, it was not so much like a deserted town as like a scene upon the stage by daylight and with no one on the boards. The barking of a dog led me at last to the only house still occupied, where a Scotch pastor and his wife pass the winter alone in this empty theatre. The place was "The Pacific Camp Grounds, the Christian Seaside Resort." Thither, in the warm season, crowds come to enjoy a life of teetotalism,[6] religion, and flirtation, which I am willing to think blameless and agreeable. The neighbourhood at least is well selected. The Pacific booms in front. Westward is Point Pinos, with the lighthouse in a wilderness of sand,[7] where you will find the lightkeeper play-ing the piano, making models and bows and arrows, studying dawn and sunrise in amateur oil-painting, and with a dozen other elegant pursuits and interests to surprise his brave, old-country rivals. To the east, and still nearer, you will come upon a space of open down, a hamlet, a haven among rocks, a world of surge and screaming seagulls. Such scenes are very similar in different climates; they appear homely to the eyes of all; to me this was like a dozen spots in Scot-land. And yet the boats that ride in the haven are of strange outlandish design; and if you walk into the hamlet you will behold costumes and faces and hear a tongue that are unfamiliar to the memory. The joss-stick burns, the opium-pipe is smoked, the floors are strewn with slips of coloured paper—prayers, you would say, that had somehow missed their destination—and a man, guiding his upright pencil from right to left across the sheet, writes home the news of Monterey to the Celestial Empire.[8]

The woods and the Pacific rule between them the climate of this seaboard region. On the streets of Monterey, when the air does not smell salt from the one, it will be blowing perfumed from the resinous tree-tops of the other. For days together a hot dry air will overhang the town, close as from an oven, yet healthful and aromatic in the nostrils. The cause is not far to seek, for the woods are afire, and the hot wind is blowing from the hills. These fires are one of the great dangers of California. I have seen from Monterey as many as three at the same time, by day a cloud of smoke, by night a red coal of conflagration in the distance. A lit-tle thing will start them, and if the wind be favourable they gallop over miles of country faster than a horse. The inhabitants must turn out and work like demons, for it is not only the pleasant groves that are destroyed; the climate and the soil are equally at stake, and these fires prevent the rains of the next winter, and dry up perennial fountains. California has been a land of promise in its time, like

Palestine; but if the woods continue so swiftly to perish, it may become, like Palestine, a land of desolation.

To visit the woods while they are languidly burning, is a strange piece of experience. The fire passes through the underbrush at a run. Every here and there a tree flares up instantaneously from root to summit, scattering tufts of flame; and is quenched, it seems, as quickly. But this last is only in semblance. For after this first squib-like conflagration of the dry moss and twigs, there remains behind a deep-rooted and consuming fire in the very entrails of the tree. The resin of the pitch pine is principally condensed at the base of the bole and in the spreading roots. Thus, after the light, showy, skirmishing flames, which are only as the match to the explosion, have already scampered down the wind into the distance, the true harm is but beginning for this giant of the woods. You may approach the tree from one side, and see it, scorched indeed from top to bottom, but apparently survivor of the peril. Make the circuit, and there, on the other side of the column, is a clear mass of living coal, spreading like an ulcer; while underground, to their most extended fibre, the roots are being eaten out by fire, and the smoke is rising through the fissures to the surface. A little while, and, without a nod of warning, the huge pine-tree snaps off short across the ground and falls prostrate with a crash. Meanwhile the fire continues its silent business; the roots are reduced to a fine ash; and long afterwards, if you pass by, you will find the earth pierced with radiating galleries, and preserving the design of all these subterranean spurs, as though it were the mould for a new tree instead of the print of an old one. These pitch pines of Monterey are, with the single exception of the Monterey cypress, the most fantastic of forest trees. No words can give an idea of the contortion of their growth; they might figure without change in a circle of the nether hell as Dante pictured it; and at the rate at which trees grow, and at which forest fires spring up and gallop through the hills of California, we may look forward to a time when there will not be one of them left standing in that land of their nativity. At least they have not so much to fear from the axe, but perish by what may be called a natural, although a violent death; while it is man in his short-sighted greed that robs the country of the nobler red-wood. Yet a little while and perhaps all the hills of seaboard California may be as bald as Tamalpais.

I have an interest of my own in these forest fires, for I came so near to lynching on one occasion, that a braver man might have retained a thrill from the experience. I wished to be certain whether it was the moss, that quaint funereal ornament of Californian forests, which blazed up so rapidly when the flame first touched the tree. I suppose I must have been under the influence of Satan; for instead of plucking off a piece for my experiment, what should I do but walk up to a great pine tree in a portion of the wood which had escaped so much as scorching, strike a match, and apply the flame gingerly to one of the tassels. The tree went off simply like a rocket; in three seconds it was a roaring pillar of fire. Close by I could hear the shouts of those who were at work combating the original conflagration. I could see the waggon that had brought them tied to a live oak in a piece of open; I could even catch the flash of an axe as it swung up through the underwood into the sunlight. Had any one observed the result of my experiment my neck was literally not worth a pinch of snuff; after a few minutes of passionate expostulation I should have been run up to a convenient bough.

> To die for faction is a common evil;
> But to be hanged for nonsense is the devil.[9]

I have run repeatedly, but never as I ran that day. At night I went out of town, and there was my own particular fire, quite distinct from the other, and burning as I thought with even greater spirit.

But it is the Pacific that exercises the most direct and obvious power upon the climate. At sunset, for months together, vast, wet, melancholy fogs arise and come shoreward from the ocean. From the hill top above Monterey the scene is often noble, although it is always sad. The upper air is still bright with sunlight; a glow still rests upon the Gabelano Peak; but the fogs are in possession of the lower levels; they crawl in scarves among the sand-hills; they float, a little higher, in clouds of a gigantic size and often of a wild configuration; to the south, where they have struck the seaward shoulder of the mountains of Santa Lucia, they double back and spire up skyward like smoke. Where their shadow touches, colour dies out of the world. The air grows chill and deadly as they advance. The trade-wind freshens, the trees begin to sigh, and all the windmills in Monterey are whirling and creaking and filling their cisterns with the brackish water of the sands. It takes but a little while till the invasion is complete. The sea, in its lighter order, has submerged the earth. Monterey is curtained in for the night in thick, wet, salt, and frigid clouds; so to remain till day returns; and before the sun's rays they slowly disperse and retreat in broken squadrons to the bosom of the sea. And yet often when the fog is thickest and most chill, a few steps out of the town and up the slope, the night will be dry and warm and full of inland perfume.

Mexicans, Americans, and Indians

The history of Monterey has yet to be written. Founded by Catholic missionaries, a place of wise beneficence to Indians, a place of arms, a Mexican capital continually wrested by one faction from another, an American capital when the first House of Representatives held its deliberations, and then falling lower and lower from the capital of the State to the capital of a county, and from that again, by the loss of its charter and town lands, to a mere bankrupt village, its rise and decline is typical of that of all Mexican institutions and even Mexican families in California.[10] Nothing is stranger in that strange State than the rapidity with which the soil has changed hands. The Mexicans, you may say, are all poor and landless, like their former capital; and yet both it and they hold themselves apart and preserve their ancient customs and something of their ancient air.

The town, when I was there, was a place of two or three streets, economically paved with sea sand, and two or three lanes, which were watercourses in the rainy

213

season, and were, at all times, rent up by fissures four or five feet deep. There were no street lights. Short sections of wooden sidewalk only added to the dangers of the night, for they were often high above the level of the roadway, and no one could tell where they would be likely to begin or end. The houses were, for the most part, built of unbaked adobe brick, many of them old for so new a country, some of very elegant proportions, with low, spacious, shapely rooms, and walls so thick that the heat of summer never dried them to the heart. At the approach of the rainy season a deathly chill and a graveyard smell began to hang about the lower floors; and diseases of the chest are common and fatal among house-keeping people of either sex.

There was no activity but in and around the saloons, where people sat almost all day long playing cards. The smallest excursion was made on horseback. You would scarcely ever see the main street without a horse or two tied to posts, and making a fine figure with their Mexican housings. It struck me oddly to come across some of the "Cornhill" illustrations to Mr. Blackmore's "Erema," and see all the characters astride on English saddles.[11] As a matter of fact, an English saddle is a rarity even in San Francisco, and, you may say, a thing unknown in all the rest of California. In a place so exclusively Mexican as Monterey, you saw not only Mexican saddles but true Vaquero[12] riding—men always at the hand-gallop up hill and down dale, and round the sharpest corner, urging their horses with cries and gesticulations and cruel rotatory spurs, checking them dead with a touch, or wheeling them right-about-face in a square yard. The type of face and character of bearing is surprisingly un-American. The first ranged from something like the pure Spanish, to something, in its sad fixity, not unlike the pure Indian, although I do not suppose there was one pure blood of either race in all the country. As for the second, it was a matter of perpetual surprise to find, in that world of absolutely mannerless Americans, a people full of deportment, solemnly courteous, and doing all things with grace and decorum. In dress they ran to colour and bright sashes. Not even the most Americanised could always resist the temptation to stick a red rose into his hatband. Not even the most Americanised would condescend to wear the vile dress hat of civilisation. Spanish was the language of the streets. It was difficult to get along without a word or two of that language for an occasion. The only communications in which the population joined were with a view to amusement. A weekly public ball took place with great etiquette, in addition to the numerous fandangoes[13] in private houses. There was a really fair amateur brass band. Night after night serenaders would be going about the street, sometimes in a company and with several instruments and voices together, sometimes severally, each guitar before a different window. It was a strange thing to lie awake in nineteenth century America, and hear the guitar accompany, and one of these old, heart-breaking Spanish love songs mount into the night air, perhaps in a deep baritone, perhaps in that high-pitched, pathetic, womanish alto which is so common among Mexican men, and which strikes on the unaccustomed ear as something not entirely human but altogether sad.

The town, then, was essentially and wholly Mexican; and yet almost all the land in the neighbourhood was held by Americans, and it was from the same class, numerically so small, that the principal officials were selected. This Mexican and that Mexican would describe to you his old family estates, not one rood[14] of which remained to him. You would ask him how that came about, and elicit some tangled story back-foremost, from which you gathered that the Americans had been greedy like designing men, and the Mexicans greedy like children, but no other certain fact. Their merits and their faults contributed alike to the ruin of the former landholders. It is true they were improvident, and easily dazzled with the sight of ready money; but they were gentlefolk besides, and that in a way which curiously unfitted them to combat Yankee craft. Suppose they have a paper to sign, they would think it a reflection on the other party to examine the terms with any great minuteness; nay, suppose them to observe some doubtful clause, it is ten to one they would refuse from delicacy to object to it. I know I am speaking within the mark, for I have seen such a case occur, and the Mexican, in spite of the advice of his lawyer, has signed the imperfect paper like a lamb. To have spoken in the matter, he said, above all to have let the other party guess that he had seen a lawyer, would have "been like doubting his word." The scruple sounds oddly to one of ourselves, who has been brought up to understand all business as a competition in fraud, and honesty itself to be a virtue which regards the carrying out but not the creation of agreements. This single unworldly trait will account for much of that revolution of which we are speaking. The Mexicans have the name of being great swindlers, but certainly the accusation cuts both ways. In a contest of this sort, the entire booty would scarcely have passed into the hands of the more scrupulous race.

Physically the Americans have triumphed; but it is not yet entirely seen how far they have themselves been morally conquered. This is, of course, but a part of a part of an extraordinary problem now in the course of being solved in the various States of the American Union. I am reminded of an anecdote. Some years ago, at a great sale of wine, all the odd lots were purchased by a grocer in a small way in the old town of Edinburgh. The agent had the curiosity to visit him some time after and inquire what possible use he could have for such material. He was shown, by way of answer, a huge vat where all the liquors, from humble Gladstone to imperial Tokay, were fermenting together. "And what," he asked, "do you propose to call this?" "I'm no very sure," replied the grocer, "but I think it's going to turn out port." In the older Eastern States, I think we may say that this hotch-potch of races is going to turn out English, or thereabout. But the problem is indefinitely varied in other zones. The elements are differently mingled in the south, in what we may call the Territorial belt,[15] and in the group of States on the Pacific coast. Above all, in these last, we may look to see some monstrous hybrid—whether good or evil, who shall forecast? but certainly original and all its own. In my little restaurant at Monterey, we have sat down to table day after day, a Frenchman, two Portuguese, an Italian, a Mexican, and a Scotchman: we had for common visitors an American from Illinois, a nearly pure blood Indian woman, and a naturalised Chinese; and from time to time a Switzer and a German came down from country ranches for the night. No wonder that the Pacific coast is a foreign land to visitors from the Eastern States, for each race contributes something of its own. Even the despised Chinese have taught the youth of California, none indeed of their virtues, but the debasing use of opium. And chief among these influences is that of the Mexicans.

The Mexicans, although in the State, are out of it. They still preserve a sort of international independence, and keep their affairs snug and to themselves. Only four or five years ago Vasquez,[16] the bandit, his troop being dispersed and the hunt too hot for him in other parts of California, returned to his native Monterey, and was seen publicly in her streets and saloons, fearing no man. The year that I was there there occurred two reputed murders. As the Montereyans are exceptionally vile speakers of each other and of every one behind his back, it is not possible for me to judge how much truth there may have been in these reports; but in the one case every one believed, and in the other some suspected, that there had been foul play; and nobody dreamed for an instant of taking the authorities into their counsel. Now this is, of course, characteristic enough of the Mexicans; but it is a noteworthy feature that all the Americans in Monterey acquiesced without a word in this inaction. Even when I spoke to them upon the subject, they seemed not to understand my surprise: they had forgotten the traditions of their own race and upbringing, and become, in a word, wholly Mexicanised.

Again, the Mexicans, having no ready money to speak of, rely almost entirely in their business transactions upon each other's worthless paper. Pedro the penniless pays you with an I O U from the equally penniless Miguel. It is a sort of local currency by courtesy. Credit in these parts has passed into a superstition. I have seen a strong, violent man struggling for months to recover a debt, and getting nothing but an exchange of waste paper. The very storekeepers are averse to asking for cash payments, and are more surprised than pleased when they are offered. They fear there must be something under it, and that you mean to withdraw from them your custom. I have seen the enterprising chemist and stationer begging me with fervour to let my account run on, although I had my purse open in my hand; and partly from the commonness of the case, partly from some remains of that generous old Mexican tradition which made all men welcome to their tables, a person may be notoriously both unwilling and unable to pay, and still find credit for the necessaries of life in the stores of Monterey. Now this villainous habit of living upon "tick" has grown into Californian nature. I do not only mean that the American and European storekeepers of Monterey are as lax as Mexicans; I mean that American farmers in many parts of the State expect unlimited credit, and profit by it in the meanwhile, without a thought for consequences. Jew storekeepers have already learned the advantage to be gained from this; they lead on the farmer into irretrievable indebtedness, and keep him ever after as their bond-slave, hopelessly grinding in the mill. So the whirligig of time brings in its revenges, and except that the Jew knows better than to foreclose, you may see Americans bound in the same chains with which they themselves had formerly bound the Mexican. It seems as if certain sorts of follies, like certain sorts of grain, were natural to the soil rather than to the race that holds and tills it for the moment.

In the meantime, however, the Americans rule in Monterey County. The new county seat, Salinas City, in the bald, corn-bearing plain under the Gabelano Peak, is a town of a purely American character. The land is held, for the most part, in those enormous tracts which are another legacy of Mexican days, and form the present chief danger and disgrace of California; and the holders are mostly of American or British birth. We have here in England no idea of the troubles and inconveniences which flow from the existence of these large landholders—land thieves, land sharks, or land-grabbers, they are more commonly and plainly called. Thus the townlands of Monterey are all in the hands of a single man. How they came there is an obscure, vexatious question, and, rightly or wrongly, the man is hated with a great hatred. His life has been repeatedly in danger. Not very long ago, I was told, the stage was stopped and examined three evenings in succession by disguised horsemen thirsting for his blood. A certain house on the Salinas road, they say, he always passes in his buggy at full speed, for the squatter sent him warning long ago. But a year since he was publicly pointed out for death by no less a man than Mr. Dennis Kearney.[17] Kearney is a man too well known in California, but a word of explanation is required for English readers. Originally an Irish drayman,[18] he rose, by his command of bad language, to almost dictatorial authority in the State; throned it there for six months or so, his mouth full of oaths, gallowses, and conflagrations; was first snuffed out last winter by Mr. Coleman,[19] backed by his San Francisco Vigilantes and three Gatling guns; completed his own ruin by throwing in his lot with the grotesque Greenbacker party;[20] and had at last to be rescued by his old enemies, the police, out of the hands of his rebellious followers. It was while he was at the top of his fortune that Kearney visited Monterey with his battle-cry against Chinese labour, the railroad monopolists, and the land thieves; and his one articulate counsel to the Montereyans was to "hang David Jacks."[21] Had the town been American, in my private opinion this would have been done years ago. Land is a subject on which there is no jesting in the West, and I have seen my friend the lawyer drive out of Monterey to adjust a competition of titles with the face of a captain going into battle and his Smith-and-Wesson convenient to his hand.

On the ranche of another of these landholders you may find our old friend, the truck system,[22] in full operation. Men live there, year in year out, to cut timber for a nominal wage, which is all consumed in supplies. The longer they remain in this desirable service the deeper they will fall in debt—a burlesque injustice in a new country, where labour should be precious, and one of those typical instances which explains the prevailing discontent and the success of the demagogue Kearney.

In a comparison between what was and what is in California, the praisers of times past will fix upon the Indians of Carmello. The valley drained by the river so named is a true Californian valley, bare, dotted with chaparal, overlooked by quaint, unfinished hills. The Carmel runs by many pleasant farms, a clear and shallow river, loved by wading kine; and at last, as it is falling towards a quicksand

and the great Pacific, passes a ruined mission on a hill. From the mission church the eye embraces a great field of ocean, and the ear is filled with a continuous sound of distant breakers on the shore. But[23] the day of the Jesuit has gone by, the day of the Yankee has succeeded, and there is no one left to care for the converted savage. The mission church is roofless and ruinous; sea breezes and sea fogs, and the alternation of the rain and sunshine, daily widening the breaches and casting the crockets from the wall. As an antiquity in this new land, a quaint specimen of missionary architecture, and a memorial of good deeds, it had a triple claim to preservation from all thinking people; but neglect and abuse have been its portion. There is no sign of American interference, save where a headboard has been torn from a grave to be a mark for pistol bullets. So it is with the Indians for whom it was erected. Their lands, I was told, are being yearly encroached upon by the neighbouring American proprietor, and with that exception no man troubles his head for the Indians of Carmel. Only one day in the year, the day before our Guy Faux,[24] the *padre* drives over the hill from Monterey; the little sacristy, which is the only covered portion of the church, is filled with seats and decorated for the service; the Indians troop together, their bright dresses contrasting with their dark and melancholy faces; and there, among a crowd of somewhat unsympathetic holiday makers, you may hear God served with perhaps more touching circumstances than in any other temple under heaven. An Indian, stone blind and about eighty years of age, conducts the singing; other Indians compose the choir; yet they have the Gregorian music at their finger ends, and pronounce the Latin so correctly that I could follow the meaning as they sang. The pronunciation was odd and nasal, the singing hurried and staccato. "In sæcula sæculo-ho-horum,"[25] they went, with a vigorous aspirate to every additional syllable. I have never seen faces more vividly lit up with joy than the faces of these Indian singers. It was to them not only the worship of God, nor an act by which they recalled and commemorated better days, but was besides an exercise of culture, where all they knew of art and letters was united and expressed. And it made a man's heart sorry for the good fathers of yore, who had taught them to dig and to reap, to read and to sing, who had given them European mass-books which they still preserve and study in their cottages, and who had now passed away from all authority and influence in that land—to be succeeded by greedy land thieves and sacrilegious pistol-shots. So ugly a thing our Anglo-Saxon Protestantism may appear beside the doings of the Society of Jesus.

But revolution in this world succeeds to revolution. All that I say in this paper is in a paulo-past tense.[26] The Monterey of last year exists no longer. A huge hotel has sprung up in the desert by the railway. Three sets of diners sit down successively to table. Invaluable toilettes figure along the beach and between the live oaks; and Monterey is advertised in the newspapers, and posted in the waiting-rooms at railway stations, as a resort for wealth and fashion. Alas for the little town! it is not strong enough to resist the influence of the flaunting caravanserai,[27] and the poor, quaint, penniless native gentlemen of Monterey must perish, like a lower race, before the millionaire vulgarians of the Big Bonanza.[28]

Notes

1 While the essays in this section are grouped as they are in *Across the Plains with Other Memories and Essays* (1892), which Stevenson approved, the text comes from the earlier periodical versions since Stevenson was not heavily involved in preparing the volume for publication.
2 Stevenson lived in California (Monterey, San Francisco, and Napa Valley) from 30 Aug. 1879 to 29 July 1880. He went in pursuit of the still married Fanny Osbourne, who divorced her husband in Dec. 1879 and married Stevenson on 19 May 1880.
3 William Tecumseh Sherman (1820–1891), key Union general in the American Civil War.
4 Relating to Homer's *The Odyssey*.
5 Spanish moss.
6 Total abstinence from alcohol.
7 Built in 1855, Monterey Bay's Point Pinos Lighthouse is the oldest continually operating lighthouse on America's Pacific coast.
8 China.
9 John Dryden, *Absalom and Achitophel* (1681, Part 2, 498–499).
10 Founded in 1770, Monterey was the capital of Alta, California under both Spain and Mexico and the site of California's first constitutional convention in 1849 following the Mexican-American War.
11 R. D. Blackmore's novel *Erema; or, my father's sin* (1876–1877), set in California and England and serialized in *Cornhill Magazine*.
12 Colonial Spanish horsemen and cattle herders—the first western cowboys.
13 A lively dance in ¾ time popular in Spain and Spanish America.
14 A 7- or 8-yard measurement of land, originally *rod* (16.5 feet).
15 At the time of publication in 1880, Montana, Idaho, Wyoming, Utah, New Mexico, and Arizona were not yet states but U.S. territories.
16 Tiburcio Vásquez (1835–1875).
17 Denis Kearney (1847–1907), California labor leader known for his violent hostility toward Chinese immigrants, which hostility led to the Chinese Exclusion Act of 1882.
18 Driver of a dray: a flat-bed wagon generally used for transporting beer.
19 William Tell Coleman (1824–1893), California businessman who mobilized a citizen's militia to assist police after one of Kearney's labor protests became an anti-Asian riot. In the 1850s, Coleman's Committee of Vigilance drove out the Democratic Party machine through secret trials, extra legal deportations, and lynchings.
20 The Greenback Party (1874–1889), an independent, anti-monopoly, pro-labor, agrarian U.S. political party that advocated currency reform.
21 David Jacks (1822–1909), Scottish immigrant and powerful Monterey businessman and landowner.
22 Exploitative "in kind" payment of commodities, vouchers, or company credit as wages.
23 Stevenson added the material between the first and fifth sentences of the paragraph to *Across the Plains* (1892).
24 Guy Fawkes Day—Nov. 5: A British holiday celebrating the failure of the 1605 Gunpowder Plot on Parliament.
25 "Unto the ages of ages" (Latin) describes God's eternal nature in the Catholic mass.
26 About to be or a little after (Latin).
27 Roadside inns along commercial trade routes in the Eastern world.
28 A massive gold and silver ore deposit in Virginia City, Nevada found by Irish-American investors in 1873.

29

FONTAINEBLEAU
Village Communities of Painters[1]

The forest of Fontainebleau is the great *al-fresco*[2] school of art of modern France. It has the prestige of the great names, Rousseau and Millet;[3] through the palace, its artistic history mounts as high as the days of the Renaissance; and the singular charm which it exerts upon the minds of men still leads the casual visitor to return.

The charm of Fontainebleau is a thing apart. It is a place that people love even more than they admire. The vigorous forest air, the silence, the majestic avenues of highway, the wilderness of tumbled boulders, the great age and dignity of certain groves—these are but ingredients, they are not the secret of the philtre. The place is sanative; the air, the light, the perfumes, and the shapes of things concord in happy harmony. The artist may be idle and not fear the "blues." He may dally with his life. Mirth, lyric mirth, and a vivacious classical contentment are of the very essence of the better kind of art; and these, in that most smiling forest, he has the chance to learn or to remember. Even on the plain of Bière, where the Angelus of Millet still tolls upon the ear of fancy[4] a larger air, a higher heaven, something ancient and healthy in the face of nature, purify the mind alike from dulness and hysteria. There is no place where the young are more gladly conscious of their youth, or the old better contented with their age.

The fact of its great and special beauty further recommends this country to the artist. The field was chosen by men in whose blood there still raced some of the gleeful or solemn exultation of great art—Millet who loved dignity like Michelangelo, Rousseau whose modern brush was dipped in the glamour of the ancients. It was chosen before the day of that strange turn in the history of art, of which we now perceive the culmination in impressionistic[5] tales and pictures—that voluntary aversion of the eye from all speciously strong and beautiful effects—that disinterested love of dulness which has set so many Peter Bells to paint the riverside primrose.[6] It was then chosen for its proximity to Paris. And for the same cause, and by the force of tradition, the painter of to-day continues to inhabit and to paint it. There is in France scenery incomparable for romance and harmony. Provence, and the valley of the Rhone from Vienne to Tarascon, are one succession of masterpieces waiting for the brush. The beauty is not merely beauty; it tells, besides, a tale to the imagination, and surprises while it charms. Here you shall see castellated towns that would befit the scenery of dreamland; streets that glow with colour like cathedral windows; hills of the most exquisite proportions; flowers of every precious colour, growing thick like grass. All these, by the grace of railway travel, are brought to the very door of the modern painter; yet he does not seek them; he remains faithful to Fontainebleau, to the eternal bridge of Gretz, to the watering-pot cascade in Cernay valley. And perhaps, as a story of romantic incident stands forth more boldly in the achromatic outlines of Dumas or Scott than overlaid with the peering preciosity of Gautier, these large and distant land-scapes are unsuited to the painting of to-day;[7] perhaps the art of our contemporary painters is indeed more at home among the gentler attractions of the north. Even Fontainebleau was chosen for him; even in Fontainebleau, he shrinks from what is sharply charactered. But one thing, at least, is certain, whatever he may choose to paint and in whatever manner, it is good for the artist to dwell among grace-ful shapes. Fontainebleau, if it be but quiet scenery, is classically graceful; and though the student may look for different qualities, this quality, silently present, will educate his hand and eye.

But, before all its other advantages—charm, loveliness, or proximity to Paris—comes the great fact that it is already colonised. The institution of a painters' colony is a work of time and tact. The population must be conquered. The inn-keeper has to be taught, and he soon learns, the lesson of unlimited credit; he must be taught to welcome as a favoured guest a young gentleman in a very greasy coat, and with little baggage beyond a box of colours and a canvas; and he must learn to preserve his faith in customers who will eat heartily and drink of the best, borrow money to buy tobacco, and perhaps not pay a stiver for a year. A colour merchant has next to be attracted. A certain vogue must be given to the place, lest the painter, most gregarious of animals, should find himself alone. And no sooner are these first difficulties overcome, than fresh perils spring up upon the other side; and the bourgeois and the tourist are knocking at the gate. This is the crucial moment for the colony. If these intruders gain a footing, they not only banish freedom and amenity; pretty soon, by means of their long purses, they will have undone the education of the innkeeper; prices will rise and credit shorten; and the poor painter must fare farther on and find another hamlet. "Not here, O Apollo!"[8] will become his song. Thus Trouville and, the other day, St. Raphael were lost to the arts.[9] Curious and not always edifying are the shifts that the French student uses to defend his lair; like the cuttlefish, he must sometimes blacken the waters of his chosen pool; but at such a time and for so practical a purpose Mrs. Grundy[10] must allow him licence. Where his own purse and credit are not threatened, he will do the honours of his village generously. Any artist is made welcome, through whatever medium he may seek expression; science is respected; even the idler, if he prove, as he so rarely does, a gentleman, will soon begin to find himself at home. And when that essentially modern creature, the English or American girl-student, began to walk calmly into his favourite inns as if into a drawing-room at home, the French painter owned himself defenceless; he submitted or he fled. His French respectability, quite as precise as ours, though covering different provinces of life, recoiled aghast before the innovation. But the girls were painters; there was nothing to be done; and Barbizon, when I last saw it and for the time at least, was practically ceded to the fair invader. Paterfamilias,[11] on the other hand, the common tourist, the holiday shopman, and the cheap young gentleman upon the spree, he hounded from his villages with every circumstance of contumely.

This purely artistic society is excellent for the young artist. The lads are mostly fools; they hold the latest orthodoxy in its crudeness; they are at that stage of education, for the most part, when a man is too much occupied with style to be aware of the necessity for any matter; and this, above all for the Englishman, is excellent. To work grossly at the trade, to forget sentiment, to think of his material and nothing else, is, for a while at least, the king's highway of progress. Here, in England, too many painters and writers dwell dispersed, unshielded, among the intelligent bourgeois. These, when they are not merely indifferent, prate to him about the lofty aims and moral influence of art. And this is the lad's ruin. For art is, first of all and last of all, a trade. The love of words and not a desire to publish new discoveries, the love of form and not a novel reading of historical events, mark the vocation of the writer and the painter. The arabesque,[12] properly speaking, and even in literature, is the first fancy of the artist; he first plays with his material as a child plays with a kaleidoscope; and he is already in a second stage when he begins to use his pretty counters for the end of representation. In that, he must pause long and toil faithfully; that is his apprenticeship; and it is only the few who will really grow beyond it, and go forward, fully equipped, to do the business of real art—to give life to abstractions and significance and charm to facts. In the meanwhile, let him dwell much among his fellow-craftsmen. They alone can take a serious interest in the childish tasks and pitiful successes of these years. They alone can behold with equanimity this fingering of the dumb keyboard, this polishing of empty sentences, this dull and literal painting of dull and insignificant subjects. Outsiders will spur him on. They will say, "Why do you not write a great book? paint a great picture?" If his guardian angel fail him, they may even persuade him to the attempt, and, ten to one, his hand is coarsened and his style falsified for life.

And this brings me to a warning. The life of the apprentice to any art is both unstrained and pleasing; it is strewn with small successes in the midst of a career of failure, patiently supported; the heaviest scholar is conscious of a certain progress; and if he come not appreciably nearer to the art of Shakespeare, grows letter-perfect in the domain of A-B, ab. But the time comes when a man should cease prelusory gymnastic, stand up, put a violence upon his will, and for better or worse, begin the business of creation. This evil day, there is a tendency continually to postpone: above all with painters. They have made so many studies that it has become a habit; they make more, the walls of exhibitions blush with them; and death finds these aged students still busy with their horn-book. This class of man finds a congenial home in artist villages; in the slang of the English colony at Barbizon we used to call them "Snoozers." Continual returns to the city, the society of men further advanced, the study of great works, a sense of humour or, if such a thing is to be had, a little religion or philosophy, are the means of treatment.

It will be time enough to think of curing the malady after it has been caught; for to catch it is the very thing for which you seek that dream-land of the painters' village. "Snoozing" is a part of the artistic education; and the rudiments must be learned stupidly, all else being forgotten, as if they were an object in themselves.

Lastly, there is something, or there seems to be something, in the very air of France that communicates the love of style. Precision, clarity, the cleanly and crafty employment of material, a grace in the handling, apart from any value in the thought, seem to be acquired by the mere residence; or if not acquired, become at least the more appreciated. The air of Paris is alive with this technical inspiration. And to leave that airy city and awake next day upon the borders of the forest is but to change externals. The same spirit of dexterity and finish breathes from the long alleys and the lofty groves, from the wildernesses that are still pretty in their confusion, and the great plain that contrives to be decorative in its emptiness.

II

In spite of its really considerable extent, the forest of Fontainebleau is hardly anywhere tedious. I know the whole western side of it with what, I suppose, I may call thoroughness; well enough at least to testify that there is no square mile without some special character and charm. Such quarters, for instance, as the Long Rocher, the Bas-Bréau, and the Reine Blanche, might be a hundred miles apart; they have scarce a point in common beyond the silence of the birds. The two last are really conterminous; and in both are tall and ancient trees that have outlived a thousand political vicissitudes. But in the one the great oaks prosper placidly upon an even floor; they beshadow a great field; and the air and the light are very free below their stretching boughs. In the other the trees find difficult footing; castles of white rock lie tumbled one upon another, the foot slips, the crooked viper slumbers, the moss clings in the crevice; and above it all the great beech goes spiring and casting forth her arms, and, with a grace beyond church architecture, canopies this rugged chaos. Meanwhile, dividing the two cantons, the broad white causeway of the Paris road runs in an avenue: a road conceived for pageantry and for triumphal marches, an avenue for an army;[13] but its days of glory over, it now lies grilling in the sun between cool groves, and only at intervals the vehicle of the cruising tourist is seen far away and faintly audible during its ample sweep. A little upon one side, and you find a district of sand and birch and boulder; a little upon the other lies the valley of Apremont, all juniper and heather; and close beyond that you may walk into a zone of pine-trees. So artfully are the ingredients mingled. Nor must it be forgotten that, in all this part, you come continually forth upon a hill-top, and behold the plain, northward and westward, like an unrefulgent sea; nor that all day long the shadows keep changing; and at last, to the red fires of sunset, night succeeds, and with the night a new forest, full of whisper, gloom, and fragrance. There are few things more renovating than to leave Paris, the lamplit arches of the Carrousel, and the long alignment of the glittering streets, and to bathe the senses in this fragrant darkness of the wood.

In this continual variety the mind is kept vividly alive. It is a changeful place to paint, a stirring place to live in. As fast as your foot carries you, you pass from scene to scene, each endeared with sylvan charm, each vigorously painted in the colours of the sun. The air, which is cooled all day in crypts of underwood, the incense of the resin, the listening silence of the groves, the unbroken solitude, the sunlit distance, the scurrying of woodland animals, the shadowy flitting of deer, and that hereditary spell of forests on the mind of man who still remembers and salutes the ancient refuge of his race—legend and sight, sound and silence, alike gratify and stimulate the heart.

And yet the forest has been civilised throughout. The most savage corners bear a name, and have been cherished like antiquities; in the most remote, nature has prepared and balanced her effects as if with conscious art; and man, with his guiding arrows of blue paint,[14] has countersigned the picture. After your farthest wandering, you are never surprised to come forth upon the vast avenue of highway, to strike the centre point of branching alleys, or to find the aqueduct trailing, thousand-footed, through the brush. It is not a wilderness; it is rather a preserve. And, fitly enough, the centre of the maze is not a hermit's cavern. In the midst, a little mirthful town lies sunlit, humming with the business of pleasure; and the palace, breathing distinction and peopled by historic names, stands smokeless among gardens.

Perhaps the last attempt at savage life was that of the harmless humbug who called himself the hermit. In a great tree, close by the high-road, he had built himself a little cabin after the manner of the Swiss Family Robinson;[15] thither he mounted at night, by the romantic aid of a rope ladder; and if dirt be any proof of sincerity, the man was as savage as a Sioux. I had the pleasure of his acquaintance; he appeared grossly stupid, not in his perfect wits, and interested in nothing but small change; for that he had a great avidity. In the course of time, he proved to be a chicken stealer, and vanished from his perch; and perhaps from the first he was no true votary of forest freedom, but an ingenious, theatrically-minded beggar, and his cabin in the tree was only stock-in-trade to beg withal. The choice of his position would seem to indicate so much; for if in the forest there are no places still to be discovered, there are many that have been forgotten, and that lie unvisited. There, to be sure, are the blue arrows waiting to reconduct you, now blazed upon a tree, now posted in the corner of a rock. But your security from interruption is complete; you might camp for weeks, if there were only water, and not a soul suspect your presence; and if I may suppose the reader to have committed some great crime and come to me for aid, I think I could still find my way to a small cavern, fitted with a hearth and chimney, where he might lie perfectly concealed. A confederate landscape-painter might daily supply him with food; for water, he would have to make a nightly tramp as far as to the nearest pond; and at last, when the hue and cry began to blow over, he might get gently on the train at some side station, work round by a series of junctions, and be quietly captured at the frontier.

Thus Fontainebleau, although it is truly but a pleasure-ground, and although, in favourable weather, and in the more celebrated quarters, it literally buzzes with the tourist, yet has some of the immunities and offers some of the repose of natural forests. And the solitary, although he must return at night to his frequented inn, may yet pass the day with his own thoughts in the companionable silence of the trees. The demands of the imagination vary; some can be alone in a back garden looked upon by windows; others, like the ostrich, are content with a solitude that meets the eye; and others, again, expand in fancy to the very borders of their desert, and are irritably conscious of a hunter's camp in an adjacent county. To these last, of course, Fontainebleau will seem but an extended tea-garden: a Rosherville[16] on a by-day. But to the plain man it offers solitude: an excellent thing in itself, and a good whet for company.

III

I was for some time a consistent Barbizonian; *et ego in Arcadia vixi*,[17] it was a pleasant season; and that noiseless hamlet lying close among the borders of the wood is for me, as for so many others, a green spot in memory. The great Millet was just dead, the green shutters of his modest house were closed; his daughters were in mourning. The date of my first visit was thus an epoch in the history of art: in a lesser way, it was an epoch in the history of the Latin Quarter.[18] The "Petit Cénacle"[19] was dead and buried; Murger and his crew of sponging vagabonds were all at rest from their expedients; the tradition of their real life was nearly lost; and the prettified legend of the "Vie de Bohème"[20] had become a sort of gospel, and still gave the cue to zealous imitators. But if the book be written in rose-water, the imitation was still further expurgated; honesty was the rule; the innkeepers gave, as I have said, almost unlimited credit; they suffered the seediest painter to depart, to take all his belongings, and to leave his bill unpaid; and if they sometimes lost, it was by English and Americans alone. At the same time, the great influx of Anglo-Saxons had begun to affect the life of the studios. There had been disputes; and in one instance, at least, the English and the Americans had made common cause to prevent a cruel pleasantry. It would be well if nations and races could communicate their qualities; but in practice, when they look upon each other, they have an eye to nothing but defects. The Anglo-Saxon is essentially dishonest; the French is devoid by nature of the principle that we call "Fair Play." The Frenchman marvelled at the scruples of his guest, and, when that defender of innocence retired over-seas and left his bills unpaid, he marvelled once again; the good and evil were, in his eyes, part and parcel of the same eccentricity; a shrug expressed his judgment upon both.

At Barbizon there was no master, no pontiff in the arts. Palizzi[21] bore rule at Gretz—urbane, superior rule—his memory rich in anecdotes of the great men of yore, his mind fertile in theories; sceptical, composed, and venerable to the eye; and yet beneath these outworks, all twittering with Italian superstition, his eye scouting for omens, and the whole fabric of his manners giving way on the appearance of a hunchback. Cernay has Pelouse, the admirable, placid Pelouse, smilingly critical of youth, who, when a full-blown commercial traveller, suddenly threw down his samples, bought a colour box, and became the master whom we have all admired. Marlotte, for a central figure, boasts Olivier de Penne. Only Barbizon, since the death of Millet, is a headless commonwealth. Even its secondary lights, and those who in my day made the stranger welcome, have since deserted it. The good Lachèvre has departed,[22] carrying his household gods; and long before that Gaston Lafenestre was taken from our midst by an untimely death.[23] He died before he had deserved success; it may be, he would never have deserved it; but his kind, comely, modest countenance still haunts the memory of all who knew him. Another—whom I will not name—has moved further on, pursuing the strange Odyssey of his decadence. His days of royal favour had departed even then; but he still retained, in his narrower life at Barbizon, a certain stamp of conscious importance, hearty, friendly, filling the room, the occupant of several chairs; nor had he yet ceased his losing battle, still labouring upon great canvases that none would buy, still waiting the return of fortune. But these days also were too good to last; and the former favourite of two sovereigns fled, if I heard the truth, by night. There was a time when he was counted a great man, and Millet but a dauber; behold, how the whirligig of time brings in his revenges! To pity Millet is a piece of arrogance; if life be hard for such resolute and pious spirits, it is harder still for us, had we the wit to understand it; but we may pity his unhappier rival, who, for no apparent merit, was raised to opulence and momentary fame, and, through no apparent fault, was suffered step by step to sink again to nothing. No misfortune can exceed the bitterness of such back-foremost progress, even bravely supported as it was; but to those also who were taken early from the easel, a regret is due. From all the young men of this period, one stood out by the vigour of his promise; he was in the age of fermentation, enamoured of eccentricities. "Il faut faire de la peinture nouvelle,"[24] was his watchword; but if time and experience had continued his education, if he had been granted health to return from these excursions to the steady and the central, I must believe that the name of Hills[25] had become famous.

Siron's inn, that excellent artists' barrack, was managed upon easy principles. At any hour of the night, when you returned from wandering in the forest, you went to the billiard-room and helped yourself to liquors, or descended to the cellar and returned laden with beer or wine. The Sirons were all locked in slumber; there was none to check your inroads; only at the week's end a computation was made, the gross sum was divided, and a varying share set down to every lodger's name under the rubric: *estrats*.[26] Upon the more long-suffering the larger tax was levied; and your bill lengthened in a direct proportion to the easiness of your disposition. At any hour of the morning, again, you could get your coffee or cold milk, and set forth into the forest. The doves had perhaps wakened you, fluttering into your very chamber; and on the threshold of the inn you were met by the aroma of the forest. Close by were the great aisles, the mossy boulders, the interminable field of forest shadow. There you were free to dream and wander. And at noon, and again at six o'clock, a good meal awaited you on Siron's table. The whole of your accommodation, set aside that varying item of the *estrats*, cost you five francs a day; your bill was never offered you until you asked it; and if you were out of luck's way, you might depart for where you pleased and leave it pending.

IV

Theoretically, the house was open to all comers; practically, it was a kind of club. The guests protected themselves, and, in so doing, they protected Siron. Formal manners being laid aside, essential courtesy was the more rigidly exacted; the new arrival had to feel the pulse of the society; and a breach of its undefined obser- vances was promptly punished. A man might be as plain, as dull, as slovenly, as free of speech as he desired; but to a touch of presumption or a word of hectoring these free Barbizonians were as sensitive as a tea-party of maiden ladies. I have seen people driven forth from Barbizon; it would be difficult to say in words what they had done, but they deserved their fate. They had shown themselves unworthy to enjoy these corporate freedoms; they had pushed themselves; they had "made their head;"[27] they wanted tact to appreciate the "fine shades" of Barbizonian eti- quette. And once they were condemned, the process of extrusion was ruthless in its cruelty; after one evening with the formidable Bodmer,[28] the Baily of our commonwealth, the erring stranger was beheld no more; he rose exceeding early the next day, and the first coach conveyed him from the scene of his discomfiture. These sentences of banishment were never, in my knowledge, delivered against an artist; such would, I believe, have been illegal; but the odd and pleasant fact is this, that they were never needed. Painters, sculptors, writers, singers, I have seen all of these in Barbizon; and some were sulky, and some blatant and inane; but one and all entered at once into the spirit of the association. This singular society is purely French, a creature of French virtues, and possibly of French defects. It can- not be imitated by the English. The roughness, the impatience, the more obvious selfishness, and even the more ardent friendships of the Anglo-Saxon, speedily dismember such a commonwealth. But this random gathering of young French painters, with neither apparatus nor parade of government, yet kept the life of the place upon a certain footing, insensibly imposed their etiquette upon the docile, and by caustic speech enforced their edicts against the unwelcome. To think of it is to wonder the more at the strange failure of their race upon the larger theatre. This inbred civility—to use the word in its completest meaning—this natural and facile adjustment of contending liberties, seems all that is required to make a gov- ernable nation and a just and prosperous country.

Our society, thus purged and guarded, was full of high spirits, of laughter, and of the initiative of youth. The few elder men who joined us were still young at heart, and took the key from their companions. We returned from long stations in the fortifying air, our blood renewed by the sunshine, our spirits refreshed by the silence of the forest; the Babel[29] of loud voices sounded good; we fell to eat and play like the natural man; and in the high inn chamber, panelled with indifferent pictures and lit by candles guttering in the night air, the talk and laughter sounded far into the night. It was a good place and a good life for any naturally-minded youth; better yet for the student of painting, and perhaps best of all for the student of letters. He, too, was saturated in this atmosphere of style; he was shut out from the disturbing currents of the world, he might forget that there existed other and more pressing interests than that of art. But, in such a place, it was hardly possible to write; he could not drug his conscience, like the painter, by the production of listless studies; he saw himself idle among many who were apparently, and some who were really, employed; and what with the impulse of increasing health and the continual provocation of romantic scenes, he became tormented with the desire to work. He enjoyed a strenuous idleness full of visions; hearty meals, long, sweltering walks, mirth among companions; and still floating like music through his brain, foresights of great works that Shakespeare might be proud to have conceived, headless epics, glorious torsos of dramas, and words that were alive with import. So in youth, like Moses from the mountain, we have sights of that House Beautiful of art which we shall never enter.[30] They are dreams and unsubstantial; visions of style that repose upon no base of human meaning; the last heart-throbs of that excited amateur who has to die in all of us before the artist can be born. But they come to us in such a rainbow of glory that all subsequent achievement appears dull and earthy in comparison. We were all artists; almost all in the age of illusion, cultivating an imaginary genius, and walking to the strains of some deceiving Ariel;[31] small wonder, indeed, if we were happy! But art, of whatever nature, is a kind mistress; and though these dreams of youth fall by their own baselessness, others succeed, graver and more substantial; the symptoms change, the amiable malady endures; and still, at an equal distance, the House Beautiful shines upon its hill-top.

V

Gretz lies out of the forest, down by the bright river. It boasts a mill, an ancient church, a castle, and a bridge of many sterlings. And the bridge is a piece of public property; anonymously famous; beaming on the incurious dilettante from the walls of a hundred exhibitions. I have seen it in the Salon; I have seen it in the Academy; I have seen it in the last French Exposition,[32] excellently done by Bloomer;[33] here it is once more, illustrating this article.[34] Long-suffering bridge! And if you visit Gretz to-morrow, you shall find another generation, camped at the bottom of Chevillon's[35] garden under their white umbrellas, and doggedly painting it again.

The bridge taken for granted, Gretz is a less inspiring place than Barbizon. I give it the palm over Cernay. There is something ghastly in the great empty village square of Cernay, with the inn tables standing in one corner, as though the stage were set for rustic opera, and in the early morning all the painters breaking their fast upon white wine under the windows of the villagers. It is vastly different to awake in Gretz, to go down the green inn-garden, to find the river streaming through the bridge, and to see the dawn begin across the poplared level. The meals are laid in the cool arbour, under fluttering leaves. The splash of oars and bathers, the bathing costumes out to dry, the trim canoes beside the jetty, tell of a society that has an eye to pleasure. There is "something to do" at Gretz. Perhaps, for that very reason, I can recall no such enduring ardours, no such glories of exhilaration, as among the solemn groves and uneventful hours of Barbizon. This "something to do" is a great enemy to joy; it is a way out of it; you wreak your high spirits on some cut-and-dry employment, and behold them gone! But Gretz is a merry place after its kind: pretty to see merry to inhabit. The course of its pellucid river, whether up or down, is full of gentle attractions for the navigator: islanded reed-mazes where, in autumn, the red berries cluster; the mirrored and inverted images of trees; lilies, and mills, and the foam and thunder of weirs. And of all noble sweeps of roadway, none is nobler, on a windy dusk, than the high-road to Nemours between its lines of talking poplar.

But even Gretz is changed. The old inn, long shored and trussed and buttressed, fell at length under the mere weight of years, and the place as it was is but a fading image in the memory of former guests. They, indeed, recall the ancient wooden stair; they recall the rainy evening, the wide hearth, the blaze of the twig fire, and the company that gathered round the pillar in the kitchen. But the material fabric is now dust; soon, with the last of its inhabitants, its very memory shall follow; and they, in their turn, shall suffer the same law, and, both in name and lineament, vanish from the world of men. "For remembrance of the old house' sake," as Pepys once quaintly put it, let me tell one story.[36] When the tide of invasion swept over France,[37] two foreign painters were left stranded and penniless in Gretz; and there, until the war was over, the Chevillons ungrudgingly harboured them. It was difficult to obtain supplies; but the two waifs were still welcome to the best, sat down daily with the family to table, and at the due intervals were supplied with clean napkins, which they scrupled to employ. Madame Chevillon observed the fact and reprimanded them. But they stood firm; eat they must, but having no money they would soil no napkins.

VI

Nemours and Moret, for all they are so picturesque, have been little visited by painters. They are, indeed, too populous; they have manners of their own, and might resist the drastic process of colonisation. Montigny has been somewhat strangely neglected. I never knew it inhabited but once, when Will H. Low[38] installed himself there with a barrel of piquette, and entertained his friends in a leafy trellis above the weir, in sight of the green country, and to the music of the falling water. It was a most airy, quaint, and pleasant place of residence, just too rustic to be stagey; and from my memories of the place in general, and that garden trellis in particular—at morning, visited by birds, or at night, when the dew fell and the stars were of the party—I am inclined to think perhaps too favourably of the future of Montigny. Chailly-en-Bière has outlived all things, and lies dustily slumbering in the plain—the cemetery of itself. The great road remains to testify of its former bustle of postilions and carriage bells; and, like memorial tablets, there still hang in the inn room the paintings of a former generation, dead or deco-rated long ago. In my time, one man only, greatly daring, dwelt there. From time to time he would walk over to Barbizon, like a shade revisiting the glimpses of the moon, and after some communication with flesh and blood return to his austere hermitage. But even he, when I last revisited the forest, had come to Barbizon for good, and closed the roll of Chaillyites. It may revive—but I much doubt it. Achères and Recloses still wait a pioneer; Bourron is out of the question, being merely Gretz over again, without the river, the bridge, or the beauty; and of all the possible places on the western side, Marlotte alone remains to be discussed. I scarcely know Marlotte, and, very likely for that reason, am not much in love with it. It seems a glaring and unsightly hamlet. The inn of Mother Antonie is unattractive; and its more reputable rival, though comfortable enough, is com-monplace. Marlotte has a name; it is famous; if I were the young painter I would leave it alone in its glory.

VII

These are the words of an old stager; and though time is a good conservative in forest places, much may be untrue to-day. Many of us have passed Arcadian[39] days there and moved on, but yet left a portion of our souls behind us buried in the woods. I would not dig for these reliquiæ; they are incommunicable treasures that will not enrich the finder; and yet there they lie, interred below great oaks or scattered along forest paths, stores of youth's dynamite and dear remembrances. And as one generation passes on and renovates the field of tillage for the next, I entertain a fancy that when the young men of to-day go forth into the forest they shall find the air still vitalised by the spirits of their predecessors, and, like those "unheard melodies" that are the sweetest of all,[40] the memory of our laughter shall still haunt the field of trees. Those merry voices that in woods call the wanderer further, those thrilling silences and whispers of the groves, surely in Fontaine-bleau they must be vocal of me and my companions? We are not content to pass away entirely from the scenes of our delight; we would leave, if but in gratitude, a pillar and a legend.

One generation after another fall like honey-bees upon this memorable for-est, rifle its sweets, pack themselves with vital memories, and when the theft is consummated depart again into life richer, but poorer also. The forest, indeed, they have possessed, from that day forward it is theirs indissolubly, and they will return to walk in it at night in the fondest of their dreams, and use it for ever in their books and pictures. Yet when they made their packets, and put up their notes and sketches, something, it should seem, had been forgotten. A projection of themselves shall appear to haunt unfriended these scenes of happiness, a natu-ral child of fancy, begotten and forgotten unawares. Over the whole field of our wanderings such fetches are still travelling like indefatigable bagmen; but the imps of Fontainebleau, as of all beloved spots, are very long of life, and memory is piously unwilling to forget their orphanage. If anywhere about that wood you meet my airy bantling, greet him with tenderness. He was a pleasant lad, though now abandoned. And when it comes to your turn to quit the forest may you leave behind you such another; no Antony or Werther,[41] let us hope, no tearful whipster, but, as becomes this not uncheerful and most active age in which we figure, the child of happy hours.

No art, it may be said, was ever perfect, and not many noble, that has not been mirthfully conceived. And no man, it may be added, was ever anything but a wet blanket and a cross to his companions who boasted not a copious spirit of enjoyment. Whether as man or artist, let the youth make haste to Fontainebleau, and once there let him address himself to the spirit of the place; he will learn more from sketching than from studies,[42] although both are necessary; and if he can get into his heart the gaiety and inspiration of the woods he will have gone far to undo the evil of his sketches. A spirit once well strung up to the concert-pitch of the primeval out-of-doors will hardly dare to finish a study and magniloquently ticket it a picture. The incommunicable thrill of things, that is the tuning-fork by which we test the flatness of our art. Here it is that Nature teaches and condemns, and still spurs up to further effort and new failure. Thus it is that she sets us blushing at our ignorant and tepid works; and the more we find of these inspiring shocks the less shall we be apt to love the literal in our productions. In all sciences and senses the letter kills; and to-day, when cackling human geese express their ignorant condemnation of all studio pictures, it is a lesson most useful to be learnt. Let the young painter go to Fontainebleau, and while he stupefies himself with studies that teach him the mechanical side of his trade, let him walk in the great air, and be a servant of mirth, and not pick and botanise, but wait upon the moods of nature. So he will learn—or learn not to forget—the poetry of life and earth, which, when he has acquired his track, will save him from joyless reproduction.

Notes

1 Stevenson repeatedly visited France's Fontainebleau, Barbizon, and Grez-sur-Loing between 1875 and 1878. There he met Fanny van de Grift Osbourne (1840–1914), whom he would later marry, in September of 1876. "Fontainebleau" and "Forest Notes" are based on his time there. He stayed in Paris numerous times over the same period (1874–1877).
2 In the open air; outdoor (Italian).
3 Leaders of the Romantic Barbizon School of French landscape painting: Théodore Rousseau (1812–1867) and Jean-François Millet (1814–1875).
4 Millet's painting *The Angelus* depicts two peasants bowing in a field in ritual prayer as the Chailly-en-Bière church bells signal the end of the day's labor.
5 Impressionism: an artistic movement originating in 1870s French painting and named for Claude Monet's painting *Impression, Sunrise*, which attempted to accurately convey the impressions of light and movement.
6 William Wordsworth's *Peter Bell*: "In vain, through every changeful year, / Did nature lead him as before; / A primrose by a river's brim / A yellow primrose was to him, / And it was nothing more" (1.61–65).
7 Alexandre Dumas (1802–1870), French historical novelist. Sir Walter Scott (1771–1832), eminent Scottish novelist and poet. Théophile Gautier (1811–1872), French Romantic writer.

8 Matthew Arnold, "Apollo Musagetes" (5).

9 French tourist destinations.

10 Mrs. Grundy, fictional English character who exemplifies the way in which conventional opinion and the social pressure of respectability limit free expression. She first appears in Thomas Morton's 1798 play *Speed the Plough* in which Dame Ashfield constantly obsesses over what her neighbor Mrs. Grundy will say.

11 Male head of household (Latin).

12 A pattern consisting of interlacing, flowing lines.

13 Napoleon established a military school at the Palace of Fontainebleau in 1803.

14 Blue arrows are waymarking symbols denoting a bridleway or equestrian path.

15 Johann David Wyss, *The Swiss Family Robinson* (1812).

16 A 19th-century public pleasure garden in Kent, England.

17 Arcadia—region of Greece named for the mythic Arcas and traditionally celebrated as utopia: an unspoiled, rustic paradise. "Et in Arcadia ego"—*I have lived in Arcadia* (Latin)—the title of a 1638 painting by the French Baroque artist Nicolas Poussin, which depicts shepherds around a tomb.

18 The Latin Quarter is an intellectual and artistic hub near the former University of Paris, established in the 12th century, where students traditionally spoke Latin. See Stevenson's "In the Latin Quarter" I and II (pp. 352–359).

19 A group of leading French Romantic writers, including Victor Hugo (1802–1885), Charles Augustin Sainte-Beuve (1804–1869), and Théophile Gautier (1811–1872). See also Stevenson's essay "Victor Hugo's Romances" (1874).

20 French novelist Henri Murger's *Scènes de la vie de bohème* or *Scenes of Bohemian Life* (1851).

21 Giuseppe Palizzi (1812–1899), Italian painter who settled near Fontainebleau.

22 Henri Lachèvre. In *Chronicles of Friendships* (1908), Will H. Low describes spending evenings at his house with Stevenson, where Lachèvre worked for years on a large painting that he never finished. Low also notes that Stevenson modeled the character Anastasie in "The Treasure of Franchard" on Lachèvre's wife (105–107).

23 French landscape painters Léon Germain Pelouse (1838–1891), Olivier de Penne (1831–1897), and Gaston Ernest Lafenestre (1841–1877).

24 "We must paint in a new way" (French).

25 Carl Fredrik Hill (1849–1911), Swedish landscape painter who joined the Barbizon School in France in 1874. Following a psychotic breakdown in 1878, he stopped painting landscapes and produced fantastical drawings of his hallucinations.

26 Strata or layers.

27 Lamentations 2:10.

28 Karl Bodmer (1809–1893), Swiss-French painter and illustrator, known for his portraits of the American West, who joined the Barbizon School in France.

29 Biblical city where God confounded humanity's language (Genesis 11).

30 Deuteronomy 34:1–5. The "House Beautiful" is the palace built by God for the refreshment and renewal of Christian travelers in Bunyan's *Pilgrim's Progress*.

31 The singing spirit in Shakespeare's *The Tempest* traditionally associated with poetry and creativity, as in Percy Shelley's "With a Guitar, to Jane."

32 The Salon: the prestigious annual exhibit of the Academy of Fine Arts in Paris; Exposition: the French *Exposition Universelle* or World's Fair.

33 Hiram Reynolds Bloomer (1845–1911), an American landscape painter who lived in France from 1874 to 1879. The painting is *Old Bridge at Grez*.

34 "The Mill at Gretz" by Anthony Warton Henley (1851–1914), artist and brother of Stevenson's friend William Ernest Henley (n. 12, p. 184), editor of *London: The Magazine of Art*. In the periodical version, Stevenson includes a note on how his memory and impressions of the setting differed from the illustrations accompanying the essay.

35 The Chevillons ran a large, old stone inn on the river in Grez-sur-Loing.
36 *The Diary of Samuel Pepys* (25 Apr. 1663).
37 The Napoleonic Wars (1803–1815).
38 Will H. Low (1853–1932), American painter, art critic, and friend of Stevenson.
39 Idyllic, utopian.
40 John Keats, "Ode on a Grecian Urn" (11–12).
41 Marc Antony in Shakespeare's *Julius Caesar* and *Antony and Cleopatra* and Werther in Johann Wolfgang von Goethe's *The Sorrows of Young Werther* (1774).
42 In *Memories and Portraits*, this line reads, "he will learn more from exercise than from studies."

30

EPILOGUE TO *AN INLAND VOYAGE*[1]

The country where they journeyed, that green, breezy valley of the Loing, is one very attractive to cheerful and solitary people. The weather was superb; all night it thundered and lightened, and the rain fell in sheets; by day, the heavens were cloudless, the sun fervent, the air vigorous and pure. They walked separate: the Cigarette plodding behind with some philosophy, the lean Arethusa posting on ahead.[2] Thus each enjoyed his own reflections by the way; each had perhaps time to tire of them before he met his comrade at the designated inn; and the pleasures of society and solitude combined to fill the day. The Arethusa carried in his knapsack the works of Charles of Orleans,[3] and employed some of the hours of travel in the concoction of English roundels.[4] In this path, he must thus have preceded Mr. Lang, Mr. Dobson, Mr. Henley, and all contemporary roundeleers; but for good reasons, he will be the last to publish the result.[5] The Cigarette walked burthened with a volume of Michelet.[6] And both these books, it will be seen, played a part in the subsequent adventure.

The Arethusa was unwisely dressed. He is no precisian in attire; but by all accounts, he was never so ill inspired as on that tramp; having set forth indeed, upon a moment's notice, from the most unfashionable spot in Europe, Barbizon. On his head, he wore a smoking cap of Indian work, the gold lace pitifully frayed and tarnished. A flannel shirt of an agreeable dark hue, which the satirical called black; a light tweed coat, made by a good English tailor; ready-made cheap linen trousers and leathern gaiters completed his array. In person, he is exceptionally lean; and his face is not, like those of happier mortals, a certificate. For years he could not pass a frontier or visit a bank without suspicion; the police, everywhere but in his native city, looked askance upon him; and (though I am sure it will not be credited) he is actually denied admittance to the casino of Monte Carlo. If you will imagine him, dressed as above, stooping under his knapsack, walking nearly five miles an hour with the folds of the ready-made trousers fluttering about his spindle shanks, and still looking eagerly round him as if in terror of pursuit—the figure, when realized, is far from reassuring. When Villon journeyed (perhaps by the same pleasant valley) to his exile at Roussillon, I wonder if he had not something of the same appearance.[7] Something of the same preoccupation he had beyond a doubt, for he too must have tinkered verses as he walked, with more success than his successor. And if he had anything like the same inspiring weather, the same nights of uproar, men in armor rolling and resounding down the stairs of heaven, the rain hissing on the village streets, the wild bull's-eye of the storm flashing all night long into the bare inn-chamber—the same sweet return of day, the same unfathomable blue of noon, the same high-colored, halcyon eves—and above all if he had anything like as good a comrade, anything like as keen a relish for what he saw, and what he ate, and the rivers that he bathed in, and the rubbish that he wrote, I would exchange estates to-day with the poor exile, and count myself a gainer.

But there was another point of similarity between the two journeys, for which the Arethusa was to pay dear: both were gone upon in days of incomplete security. It was not long after the Franco-Prussian war. Swiftly as men forget, that country-side was still alive with tales of uhlans,[8] and outlying sentries, and hair-breadth 'scapes from the ignominious cord,[9] and pleasant momentary friendships between invader and invaded. A year, at the most two years later, you might have tramped all that country over and not heard one anecdote. And a year or two later, you would—if you were a rather ill-looking young man in nondescript array—have gone your rounds in greater safety; for along with more interesting matter, the Prussian spy would have somewhat faded from men's imaginations.

For all that, our voyager had got beyond Château Renard before he was conscious of arousing wonder. On the road between that place and Châtillon-sur-Loing, however, he encountered a rural postman; they fell together in talk, and spoke of a variety of subjects; but through one and all, the postman was still visibly preoccupied, and his eyes were faithful to the Arethusa's knapsack. At last, with mysterious roguishness, he inquired what it contained, and on being answered, shook his head with kindly incredulity. "*Non*," said he, "*non, vous avez des portraits*."[10] And then with a languishing appeal, "*Voyons*,[11] show me the portraits!" It was some little while before the Arethusa, with a shout of laughter, recognized his drift. By portraits he meant indecent photographs; and in the Arethusa, an austere and rising author, he thought to have identified a pornographic colporteur. When country folk in France have made up their minds as to a person's calling, argument is fruitless. Along all the rest of the way, the postman piped and fluted meltingly to get a sight of the collection; now he would upbraid, now he would reason—"*Voyons*, I will tell nobody;" then he tried corruption and insisted on paying for a glass of wine; and at last, when their ways separated—"*Non*," said he, "*ce n'est pas bien de votre part. O non, ce n'est pas bien*."[12] And shaking his head with quite a sentimental sense of injury, he departed unrefreshed.

On certain little difficulties encountered by the Arethusa at Châtillon-sur-Loing, I have not space to dwell; another Châtillon, of grislier memory, looms too near at hand.[13] But the next day, in a certain hamlet called La Jussière, he stopped to drink a glass of syrup in a very poor, bare drinking shop. The hostess, a comely woman, suckling a child, examined the traveller with kindly and pitying eyes. "You are not of this department?" she asked. The Arethusa told her he was English. "Ah!" she said, surprised. "We have no English. We have many Italians, however, and they do very well; they do not complain of the people of hereabouts. An English-man may do very well also; it will be something new." Here was a dark saying, over which the Arethusa pondered as he drank his grenadine; but when he rose and asked what was to pay, the light came upon him in a flash. "*O, pour vous,*"[14] replied the landlady—"a half-penny!" *Pour vous*? By heaven, she took him for a beggar! He paid his half-penny, feeling it were ungracious to correct her. But when he was forth again upon the road, he became vexed in spirit. The conscience is no gentleman, he is a rabbinical fellow; and his conscience told him he had stolen the syrup.

That night the travellers slept in Gien; the next day they passed the river and set forth (severally, as their custom was) on a short stage through the green plain upon the Berry side, to Châtillon-sur-Loire. It was the first day of the shooting; and the air rang with the report of firearms and the admiring cries of sportsmen. Overhead the birds were in consternation, wheeling in clouds, settling and re-arising. And yet with all this bustle on either hand, the road itself lay solitary. The Arethusa smoked a pipe beside a milestone, and I remember he laid down very exactly all he was to do at Châtillon: how he was to enjoy a cold plunge, to change his shirt, and to await the Cigarette's arrival, in sublime inaction, by the margin of the Loire. Fired by these ideas, he pushed the more rapidly forward, and came, early in the afternoon and in a breathing heat, to the entering-in of that ill-fated town. Childe Roland to the dark tower came.[15]

A polite gendarme[16] threw his shadow on the path.

"*Monsieur est voyageur?*" he asked.[17]

And the Arethusa, strong in his innocence, forgetful of his vile attire, replied—I had almost said with gayety: "So it would appear."

"His papers are in order?" said the gendarme. And when the Arethusa, with a slight change of voice, admitted he had none, he was informed (politely enough) that he must appear before the Commissary.

The Commissary sat at a table in his bedroom, stripped to the shirt and trou-sers, but still copiously perspiring; and when he turned upon the prisoner a large meaningless countenance, that was (like Bardolph's) "all whelks and bubuckles," the dullest might have been prepared for grief.[18] Here was a stupid man, sleepy with the heat and fretful at the interruption, whom neither appeal nor argument could reach.

THE COMMISSARY: You have no papers?

THE ARETHUSA: Not here.

THE COMMISSARY: Why?

THE ARETHUSA: I have left them behind in my valise.

THE COMMISSARY: You know, however, that it is forbidden to circulate without papers?

THE ARETHUSA: Pardon me: I am convinced of the contrary. I am here on my rights as an English subject by international treaty.

THE COMMISSARY *(with scorn)*: You call yourself an Englishman?

THE ARETHUSA: I do.

THE COMMISSARY: Humph.—What is your trade?

THE ARETHUSA: I am a Scotch Advocate.

THE COMMISSARY (*with singular annoyance*): A Scotch advocate! Do you then pretend to support yourself by that in this department?

The Arethusa modestly disclaimed the pretension. The Commissary had scored a point.

THE COMMISSARY: Why, then, do you travel?

THE ARETHUSA: I travel for pleasure.

THE COMMISSARY (*pointing to the knapsack, and with sublime incredulity*): *Avec ça? Voyez-vous, je suis un homme intelligent!* (With that? Look here, I am a person of intelligence!)

The culprit remaining silent under this home thrust, the Commissary relished his triumph for a while, and then demanded (like the postman, but with what different expectations!) to see the contents of the knapsack. And here the Arethusa, not yet sufficiently awake to his position, fell into a grave mistake. There was little or no furniture in the room except the commissary's chair and table; and to facilitate matters, the Arethusa (with all the innocence on earth) leant the knapsack on a corner of the bed. The Commissary fairly bounded from his seat; his face and neck flushed past purple, almost into blue; and he screamed to lay the desecrating object on the floor.

The knapsack proved to contain a change of shirts, of shoes, of socks and of linen trousers, a small dressing-case, a piece of soap in one of the shoes, two volumes of the *Collection Jannet* lettered *Poésies de Charles d'Orléans*,[19] a map, and a version book containing divers notes in prose and the remarkable English roundels of the voyager, still to this day unpublished: The Commissary of Châtillon is the only living man who has clapped an eye on these artistic trifles. He turned the assortment over with a contumelious finger; it was plain from his daintiness that he regarded the Arethusa and all his belongings as the very temple of infection. Still there was nothing suspicious but the map, nothing really criminal except the roundels; as for Charles of Orleans, to the ignorant mind of the prisoner, he seemed as good as a certificate; and it was supposed the farce was nearly over.

The inquisitor resumed his seat.

THE COMMISSARY (*after a pause*): *Eh bien, je vais vous dire ce que vous êtes. Vous êtes allemand et vous venez chanter à la foire.* (Well, then, I will tell you what you are. You are a German and have come to sing at the fair.)

THE ARETHUSA: Would you like to hear me sing? I believe I could convince you of the contrary.

THE COMMISSARY: *Pas de plaisanterie, monsieur!*[20]

THE ARETHUSA: Well, sir, oblige me at least by looking at this book. Here, I open it with my eyes shut. Read one of these songs—read this one—and tell me, you who are a man of intelligence, if it would be possible to sing it at a fair?

THE COMMISSARY (*critically*): *Mais oui. Très bien.*[21]

THE ARETHUSA: *Comment, monsieur!* What! But do you not observe it is antique. It is difficult to understand, even for you and me; but for the audience at a fair, it would be meaningless.

THE COMMISSARY (*taking a pen*): *Enfin, il faut en finir.*[22] What is your name?

THE ARETHUSA (*speaking with the swallowing vivacity of the English*): Robert-Louis-Stev'ns'n.

THE COMMISSARY (aghast): *Hé! Quoi?*[23]

THE ARETHUSA (*perceiving and improving his advantage*): Rob'rt-Lou's-Stev'ns'n.

THE COMMISSARY (*after several conflicts with his pen*): *Eh bien, il faut se passer du nom. Ça ne s'écrit pas.* (Well, we must do without the name: it is unspellable.)

The above is a rough summary of this momentous conversation, in which I have been chiefly careful to preserve the plums of the Commissary; but the remainder of the scene, perhaps because of his rising anger, has left but little definite in the memory of the Arethusa. The Commissary was not, I think, a practised literary man; no sooner, at least, had he taken pen in hand and embarked on the composition of the *procès-verbal*,[24] than he became distinctly more uncivil and began to show a predilection for that simplest of all forms of repartee: "You lie!" Several times the Arethusa let it pass, and then suddenly flared up, refused to accept more insults or to answer further questions, defied the Commissary to do his worst and promised him, if he did, that he should bitterly repent it. Perhaps if he had worn this proud front from the first, instead of beginning with a sense of entertainment and then going on to argue, the thing might have turned otherwise; for even at this eleventh hour, the Commissary was visibly staggered. But it was too late; he had been challenged; the *procès-verbal* was begun; and he again squared his elbows over his writing, and the Arethusa was led forth a prisoner.

A step or two down the hot road stood the gendarmerie. Thither was our unfortunate conducted, and there he was bidden to empty forth the contents of his pockets. A handkerchief, a pen, a pencil, a pipe and tobacco, matches, and some ten francs of change: that was all. Not a file, not a cipher, not a scrap of writing whether to identify or to condemn. The very gendarme was appalled before such destitution.

"I regret," he said, "that I arrested you, for I see that you are no *voyou*."[25] And he promised him every indulgence.

The Arethusa, thus encouraged, asked for his pipe. That he was told was impossible, but if he chewed, he might have some tobacco. He did not chew, however, and asked instead to have his handkerchief.

"*Non*," said the gendarme. "*Nous avons eu des histoires de gens qui se sont pendus.*" (No, we have had histories of people who hanged themselves.)

"What!" cried the Arethusa. "And is it for that you refuse me my handkerchief? But see how much more easily I could hang myself in my trousers!"

The man was struck by the novelty of the idea; but he stuck to his colors, and only continued to repeat vague offers of service.

"At least," said the Arethusa, "be sure that you arrest my comrade; he will follow me ere long on the same road, and you can tell him by the sack upon his shoulders."

This promised, the prisoner was led round into the back court of the building, a cellar door was opened, he was motioned down the stair, and bolts grated and chains clanged behind his descending person.

The philosophic and still more the imaginative mind is apt to suppose itself prepared for any mortal accident. Prison, among other ills, was one that had been often faced by the undaunted Arethusa. Even as he went down the stairs, he was telling himself that here was a famous occasion for a roundel, and that like the committed linnets of the tuneful cavalier, he too would make his prison musical. I will tell the truth at once: the roundel was never written, or it should be printed in this place, to raise a smile. Two reasons interfered: the first moral, the second physical.

It is one of the curiosities of human nature, that although all men are liars, they can none of them bear to be told so of themselves. To get and take the lie with equanimity is a stretch beyond the stoic; and the Arethusa, who had been surfeited upon that insult, was blazing inwardly with a white heat of smothered wrath. But the physical also had its part. The cellar in which he was confined was some feet underground, and it was only lighted by an unglazed, narrow aperture high up in the wall and smothered in the leaves of a green vine. The walls were of naked masonry, the floor of bare earth; by way of furniture there was an earthenware basin, a water jug, and a wooden bedstead with a blue-gray cloak for bedding. To be taken from the hot air of a summer's afternoon, the reverberation of the road and the stir of rapid exercise, and plunged into the gloom and damp of this receptacle for vagabonds, struck an instant chill upon the Arethusa's blood. Now see in how small a matter a hardship may consist: the floor was exceedingly uneven underfoot, with the very spade-marks, I suppose, of the laborers who dug the foundations of the barrack; and what with the poor twilight and the irregular surface, walking was impossible. The caged author resisted for a good while; but the chill of the place struck deeper and deeper; and at length, with such reluctance as you may fancy, he was driven to climb upon the bed and wrap himself in the public covering. There, then, he lay upon the verge of shivering, plunged in semi-darkness, wound in a garment whose touch he dreaded like the plague, and (in a spirit far removed from resignation) telling the roll of the insults he had just received. These are not circumstances favorable to the muse.

Meantime (to look at the upper surface where the sun was still shining and the guns of sportsmen were still noisy through the tufted plain) the Cigarette was drawing near at his more philosophic pace. In those days of liberty and health he was the constant partner of the Arethusa, and had ample opportunity to share in that gentleman's disfavor with the police. Many a bitter bowl had he partaken of with that disastrous comrade. He was himself a man born to float easily through life, his face and manner artfully recommending him to all. There was but one suspicious circumstance he could not carry off, and that was his companion. He will not readily forget the Commissary in what is ironically called the free town of Frankfort-on-the-Main; nor the Franco-Belgian frontier; nor the inn at La Fère; last, but not least, he is pretty certain to remember Châtillon-sur-Loire.

At the town entry, the gendarme culled him like a wayside flower; and a moment later, two persons, in a high state of surprise, were confronted in the Commissary's office. For if the Cigarette was surprised to be arrested, the Commissary was no less taken aback by the appearance and appointments of his captive. Here was a man about whom there could be no mistake: a man of an unquestionable and unassailable manner, in apple-pie order, dressed not with neatness merely but elegance, ready with his passport, at a word, and well supplied with money: a man the Commissary would have doffed his hat to on chance upon the highway; and this *beau cavalier*[26] unblushingly claimed the Arethusa for his comrade! The conclusion of the interview was foregone; of its humors, I remember only one. "Baronet?" demanded the magistrate, glancing up from the passport. "*Alors, monsieur, vous êtes le fils d'un baron?*"[27] And when the Cigarette (his one mistake throughout the interview) denied the soft impeachment, "*Alors,*" from the Commissary, "*ce n'est pas votre passeport!*"[28] But these were ineffectual thunders; he never dreamed of laying hands upon the Cigarette; presently he fell into a mood of unrestrained admiration, gloating over the contents of the knapsack, commending our friend's tailor. Ah, what an honored guest was the Commissary entertaining! what suitable clothes he wore for the warm weather! what beautiful maps, what an attractive work of history, he carried in his knapsack! You are to understand there was now but one point of difference between them: what was to be done with the Arethusa? the Cigarette demanding his release, the Commissary still claiming him as the dungeon's own. Now it chanced that the Cigarette had passed some years of his life in Egypt, where he had made acquaintance with two very bad things, cholera morbus[29] and pashas[30]; and in the eye of the Commissary, as he fingered the volume of Michelet, it seemed to our traveller there was something Turkish. I pass over this lightly; it is highly possible there was some misunderstanding, highly possible that the Commissary (charmed with his visitor) supposed the attraction to be mutual and took for an act of growing friendship what the Cigarette himself regarded as a bribe. And at any rate, was there ever a bribe more singular than an odd volume of Michelet's history? The work was promised him for the morrow, before our departure; and presently after, either because he had his price, or to show that he was not the man to be behind in friendly offices—"*Eh bien,*" he said, "*je suppose qu'il faut lâcher votre camarade.*"[31] And he tore up that feast of humor, the unfinished *procès-verbal*. Ah, if he had only torn up instead the Arethusa's roundels! There were many works burnt at Alexandria,[32] there are many treasured in the British Museum, that I could better spare than the *procès-verbal* of Châtillon. Poor bubuckled Commissary! I begin to be sorry that he never had his Michelet: perceiving in him fine human traits, a broad-based stupidity, a gusto in his magisterial functions, a taste for letters, a ready admiration for the admirable. And if he did not admire the Arethusa, he was not alone in that.

To the imprisoned one, shivering under the public covering, there came suddenly a noise of bolts and chains. He sprang to his feet, ready to welcome a companion in calamity; and instead of that, the door was flung wide, the friendly gendarme appeared above in the strong daylight, and with a magnificent gesture

240

(being probably a student of the drama)—"*Vous êtes libre!*"[33] he said. None too soon for the Arethusa. I doubt if he had been half an hour imprisoned; but by the watch in a man's brain (which was the only watch he carried) he should have been eight times longer; and he passed forth with ecstasy up the cellar stairs into the healing warmth of the afternoon sun; and the breath of the earth came as sweet as a cow's into his nostril; and he heard again (and could have laughed for pleasure) the concord of delicate noises that we call the hum of life.

And here it might be thought my history ended; but not so, this was an act-drop and not the curtain. Upon what followed in front of the barrack, since there was a lady in the case, I scruple to expatiate. The wife of the Maréchal-des-logis[34] was a handsome woman, and yet the Arethusa was not sorry to be gone from her society. Something of her image, cool as a peach on that hot afternoon, still lingers in his memory: yet more of her conversation. "You have there a very fine parlor," said the poor gentleman.—"Ah," said Madame la Maréchale (des-logis), "you are very well acquainted with such parlors!" And you should have seen with what a hard and scornful eye she measured the vagabond before her! I do not think he ever hated the Commissary; but before that interview was at an end, he hated Madame la Maréchale. His passion (as I am led to understand by one who was present) stood confessed in a burning eye, a pale cheek and a trembling utterance; Madame meanwhile tasting the joys of the matador,[35] goading him with barbed words and staring him coldly down.

It was certainly good to be away from this lady, and better still to sit down to an excellent dinner in the inn. Here, too, the despised travellers scraped acquaintance with their next neighbor, a gentleman of these parts, returned from the day's sport, who had the good taste to find pleasure in their society. The dinner at an end, the gentleman proposed the acquaintance should be ripened in the café.

The café was crowded with sportsmen, conclamantly explaining to each other and the world the smallness of their bags. About the centre of the room, the Cigarette and the Arethusa sat with their new acquaintance; a trio very well pleased, for the travellers (after their late experience) were greedy of consideration, and their sportsman rejoiced in a pair of patient listeners. Suddenly the glass door flew open with a crash; the Maréchal-des-logis appeared in the interval, gorgeously belted and befrogged, entered without salutation, strode up the room with a clang of spurs and weapons, and disappeared through a door at the far end. Close at his heels followed the Arethusa's gendarme of the afternoon, imitating, with a nice shade of difference, the imperial bearing of his chief; only, as he passed, he struck lightly with his open hand on the shoulder of his late captive, and with that ringing, dramatic utterance of which he had the secret—"*Suivez!*"[36] said he.

The arrest of the members,[37] the oath of the Tennis Court,[38] the signing of the declaration of independence,[39] Mark Antony's oration,[40] all the brave scenes of history, I conceive as having been not unlike that evening in the café at Châtillon. Terror breathed upon the assembly. A moment later, when the Arethusa had followed his recaptors into the further part of the house, the Cigarette found himself alone with his coffee in a ring of empty chairs and tables, all the lusty sportsmen huddled into corners, all their clamorous voices hushed in whispering, all their eyes shooting at him furtively as at a leper.

And the Arethusa? Well, he had a long, sometimes a trying, interview in the back kitchen. The Maréchal-des-logis, who was a very handsome man, and I believe both intelligent and honest, had no clear opinion on the case. He thought the Commissary had done wrong, but he did not wish to get his subordinates into trouble; and he proposed this, that, and the other, to all of which the Arethusa (with a growing sense of his position) demurred.

"In short," suggested the Arethusa, "you want to wash your hands of further responsibility? Well, then, let me go to Paris."

The Maréchal-des-logis looked at his watch.

"You may leave," said he, "by the ten o'clock train for Paris."

And at noon the next day the travellers were telling their misadventure in the dining-room at Siron's.[41]

Notes

1 *An Inland Voyage* (1878) recounts a canoe trip Stevenson took with his friend Sir Walter Grindlay Simpson (1843–1898) in 1876. The "Epilogue," published a decade after the memoir, narrates an experience on their walking tour of the Valley of Loing from Grez to Châtillion the previous year.

2 The Cigarette: Walter Simpson; The Arethusa: Stevenson. Arethusa was the nymph of Greek mythology who fled her home in Arcadia pursued by the river god Alpheus.

3 Charles of Orléans (1394–1465), Duke and last major courtly poet of France. See Stevenson's essay "Charles of Orleans" (1876).

4 Poems.

5 English poets and Stevenson's friends: Austin Dobson (1840–1921), Andrew Lang (1844–1912), and William Ernest Henley (1849–1903).

6 Jules Michelet (1798–1874), French philosopher, historian, and author of *Histoire de France* (1867).

7 François Villon (1431–1463), famous medieval French lyric poet. Repeatedly imprisoned or banished from Paris for burglary and once for murder, he went to Roussillon in 1456. See Stevenson's essays "Longnon's Villon" (1877) and "Francois Villon, Student, Poet, and Housebreaker" (1877).

8 Cavalrymen.

9 Hanging noose.

10 No, no, you have some portraits.

11 Let's see.

12 No, it's not right of you. O no, it's not right.

13 The Battle of Châtillon 13 Oct. 1870.

14 O, for you.

15 Robert Browning's 1852 poem, whose title comes from Edgar's song in Shakespeare's *King Lear* (3.4.163).

16 French police officer.

17 The gentleman is a traveler?

18 Shakespeare, *Henry V*, 3.6.104–106.

19 *Bibliothèque elzévirienne* (1853–1867): a multi-volume anthology of 16th-century French literature edited by French bibliographer and publisher Pierre Jannet (1820–1870); *The Poetry of Charles of Orléans*.

20 Don't make jokes, sir!
21 But yes, alright.
22 Finally, we must be done with it.
23 Hey! What?
24 Official written record.
25 Rogue.
26 Handsome gentleman.
27 So, sir, you're the son of a baron?
28 So, it's not your passport!
29 A gastrointestinal illness.
30 High-ranking Turkish government or military officers.
31 Well, I suppose that you have to let go of your comrade.
32 The Great Library of Alexandria in Egypt was accidentally burned by Julius Caesar in 48 BC.
33 You are free!
34 Sergeant
35 Bullfighter
36 Follow!
37 King Charles I's attempted arrest of five MPs in the House of Commons with armed soldiers on 4 Jan. 1642 helped incite the Civil War.
38 On 20 June 1789 at the beginning of the French Revolution, the Third Estate, representing most of the population and continually outvoted by the privileged class, moved to an indoor tennis court and vowed to stay until a written constitution was adopted.
39 The United States' Declaration of Independence from Great Britain, ratified 4 July 1776.
40 Roman general Mark Antony's (83–30 BC) eulogy of Julius Caesar helped turn the Roman people against his murderers, leading to civil wars, the fall of the republic, and the formation of the Roman Empire.
41 See "Fontainebleau: Village Communities of Painters" (p. 220).

31

CONTRIBUTIONS TO THE
HISTORY OF FIFE[1]

Many writers have vigorously described the pains of the first day or the first night at school; to a boy of any enterprise, I believe, they are more often agreeably exciting. Misery—or at least misery unrelieved—is confined to another period, to the days of suspense and the "dreadful looking-for" of departure; when the old life is running to an end, and the new life, with its new interests, not yet begun; and to the pain of an imminent parting, there is added the unrest of a state of conscious prëexistence. The area railings, the beloved shop-window, the smell of semi-suburban tanpits, the song of the church bells upon a Sunday, the thin, high voices of compatriot children in a playing field—what a sudden, what an over-powering pathos breathes to him from each familiar circumstance! The assaults of sorrow come not from within, as it seems to him, but from without. I was proud and glad to go to school; had I been let alone, I could have borne up like any hero; but there was around me, in all my native town, a conspiracy of lamentation: "Poor little boy, he is going away—unkind little boy, he is going to leave us;" so the unspoken burthen followed me as I went, with yearning and reproach. And at length, one melancholy afternoon in the early autumn, and at a place where it seems to me, looking back, it must be always autumn and generally Sunday, there came suddenly upon the face of all I saw—the long empty road, the lines of the tall houses, the church upon the hill, the woody hill-side garden—a look of such a piercing sadness that my heart died; and seating myself on a door-step, I shed tears of miserable sympathy. A benevolent cat cumbered me the while with con-solations—we two were alone in all that was visible of the London Road: two poor waifs who had each tasted sorrow—and she fawned upon the weeper, and gam-bolled for his entertainment, watching the effect, it seemed, with motherly eyes. Long ago has that small heart been quieted, that small body (then rigid and cold) buried in the end of a town garden, perhaps with some attendant children. She will never console another trembler on the brink of life: poor little mouse, bringing strength to the young elephant: poor little thing of a year or two ministering to the creature of near upon a century.

For the sake of the cat, God bless her! I confessed at home the story of my own weakness; and so it comes about that I owed a certain journey, and the reader owes the present paper, to a cat in the London Road. It was judged, if I had thus brimmed over on the public highway, some change of scene was (in the medical sense) indicated; my father at the time was visiting the harbor lights of Scotland; and it was decided he should take me along with him around a portion of the shores of Fife: my first professional tour, my first journey in the complete character of man, without the help of petticoats.[2]

The Kingdom of Fife (that royal province)[3] may be observed by the curious on the map, occupying a tongue of land between the firths of Forth and Tay. It may be continually seen from many parts of Edinburgh (among the rest, from the windows of my father's house) dying away into the distance and the easterly *haar* with one smoky sea-side town beyond another, or in winter printing on the gray heaven some glittering hill tops. It has no beauty to recommend it, being a low, sea-salted, wind-vexed promontory; trees very rare, except (as common on the east coast) along the dens of rivers; the fields well cultivated, I understand, but not lovely to the eye. It is of the coast I speak: the interior may be the garden of Eden. History broods over that part of the world like the easterly haar. Even on the map, its long row of Gaelic place-names bear testimony to an old and settled race. Of these little towns, posted along the shore as close as sedges, each with its bit of harbor, its old weather-beaten church or public building, its flavor of decayed prosperity and decaying fish, not one but has its legend, quaint or tragic: Dunfermline, in whose royal towers the king may be still observed (in the ballad) drinking the blood-red wine;[4] somnolent Inverkeithing, once the quarantine of Leith; Aberdour, hard by the monastic islet of Inchcolm, hard by Donibristle where the "bonny face was spoiled;"[5] Burntisland where, when Paul Jones was off the coast, the Reverend Mr. Shirra had a table carried between tide-marks, and publicly prayed against the rover at the pitch of his voice and his broad lowland dialect;[6] Kinghorn, where Alexander "brak's neckbane"[7] and left Scotland to the English wars; Kirkcaldy, where the witches once prevailed extremely and sunk tall ships and honest mariners in the North Sea;[8] Dysart, famous—well famous at least to me for the Dutch ships that lay in its harbor, painted like toys and with pots of flowers and cages of song-birds in the cabin windows, and for one particular Dutch skipper who would sit all day in slippers on the break of the poop, smoking a long German pipe; Wemyss (pronounce Weems) with its bat-haunted caves, where the Chevalier Johnstone, on his flight from Culloden, passed a night of superstitious terrors;[9] Leven, a bald, quite modern place, sacred to summer visitors, whence there has gone but yesterday the tall figure and the white locks of the last Englishman in Delhi, my uncle Dr. Balfour, who was still walking his hospital rounds, while the troopers from Meerut clattered and cried "Deen Deen" along the streets of the imperial city, and Willoughby mustered his handful of heroes at the magazine, and the nameless brave one in the telegraph office was perhaps already fingering his last despatch;[10] and just a little beyond Leven, Largo Law and the smoke of Largo town mounting about its feet, the town of Alexander Selkirk, better known under the name of Robinson Crusoe.[11] So on, the list might be pursued (only for private reasons, which the reader will shortly have an opportunity to guess) by St. Monance, and Pittenweem, and the two Anstruthers, and Cellardyke, and Crail where Primate Sharpe was once a humble and innocent country minister:[12] on to the heel of the land, to Fifeness, overlooked by a sea-wood of matted elders and the quaint old mansion of Balcomie, itself overlooking but the breach or the quiescence of the deep—the Carr Rock beacon rising close in front, and as night draws in, the star of the Inchcape reef springing up on the one hand, and the star of the May Island on the other, and further off yet a third and a greater on the craggy foreland of St. Abb's. And but a little way round the corner of the land, imminent itself above the sea, stands the gem of the province and the light of mediæval Scotland, St. Andrew's, where the great Cardinal Beaton held garrison against the world, and the second of the name and title perished (as you may read in Knox's jeering narrative) under the knives of true-blue Protestants,[13] and to this day (after so many centuries) the current voice of the professor is not hushed.

Here it was that my first tour of inspection began, early on a bleak easterly morning. There was a crashing run of sea upon the shore, I recollect, and my father and the man of the harbor light must sometimes raise their voices to be audible. Perhaps it is from this circumstance, that I always imagine St. Andrew's to be an ineffectual seat of learning, and the sound of the east wind and the bursting surf to linger in its drowsy class-rooms and confound the utterance of the professor, until teacher and taught are alike drowned in oblivion, and only the sea-gull beats on the windows and the draught of the sea-air rustles in the pages of the open lecture. But upon all this, and the romance of St. Andrew's in general, the reader must consult the works of Mr. Andrew Lang; who has written of it but the other day in his dainty prose and with his incommunicable humor, and long ago in one of his best poems, with grace, and local truth and a note of unaffected pathos.[14] Mr. Lang knows all about the romance, I say, and the educational advantages, but I doubt if he had turned his attention to the harbor lights; and it may be news even to him, that in the year 1863, their case was pitiable. Hanging about with the east wind humming in my teeth, and my hands (I make no doubt) in my pockets, I looked for the first time upon that tragi-comedy of the visiting engineer which I have seen so often reënacted on a more important stage. Eighty years ago, I find my grandfather writing: "It is the most painful thing that can occur to me to have a correspondence of this kind with any of the keepers, and when I come to the Light House, instead of having the satisfaction to meet them with approbation and welcome their Family, it is distressing when one is obliged to put on a most angry countenance and demeanor."[15] This painful obligation has been hereditary in my race. I have myself, on a perfectly amateur and unauthorized inspection of Turnberry Point, bent my brows upon the keeper on the question of storm-panes; and felt a keen pang of self-reproach, when we went down stairs again and I found he was making a coffin for his infant child; and then regained my equanimity with the thought that I had done the man a service, and when the proper inspector came, he would be readier with his panes. The human race is perhaps credited with more duplicity than it deserves. The visitation of a light-house at least is a business of the most transparent nature. As soon as the boat grates on the shore, and the keepers step forward in their uniformed coats, the very slouch of the fellows' shoulders tells their story and the engineer may begin at once to assume his "angry countenance." Certainly the brass of the handrail will be clouded; and if the brass be not immaculate, certainly all will be to match—the reflectors scratched, the spare lamp unready, the storm-panes in the storehouse. If a light is not rather more than middling good, it will be radically bad. Mediocrity (except in literature) appears to be unattainable by man. But of course the unfortunate of St. Andrew's was only an amateur, he was not in the Service, he had no uniform coat, he was (I believe) a plumber by his trade and stood (in the mediæval phrase) quite out of the danger of my father; but he had a painful interview for all that, and perspired extremely.

From St. Andrew's, we drove over Magus Muir. My father had announced we were "to post," and the phrase called up in my hopeful mind visions of top-boots and the pictures in Rowlandson's *Dance of Death*;[16] but it was only a jingling cab that came to the inn door, such as I had driven in a thousand times at the low price of one shilling on the streets of Edinburgh. Beyond this disappointment, I remember nothing of that drive. It is a road I have often travelled, and of not one of these journeys do I remember any single trait. The fact has not been supposed to encroach on the truth of the imagination. I still see Magus Muir two hundred years ago; a desert place, quite uninclosed; in the midst, the Primate's carriage fleeing at the gallop; the assassins loose reined in pursuit, Burley Balfour, pistol in hand, among the first. No scene of history has ever written itself so deeply on my mind; not because Balfour, that questionable zealot, was an ancestral cousin of my own;[17] not because of the pleadings of the victim and his daughter; not even because of the live bum-bee that flew out of Sharpe's 'bacco box, thus clearly indicating his complicity with Satan;[18] nor merely because, as it was after all a crime of a fine religious flavour, it figured in Sunday books and afforded a grateful relief from *Ministering Children* or the *Memoirs of Mrs. Katharine Winslowe*.[19] The figure that always fixed my attention is that of Hackston of Rathillet, sitting in the saddle with his cloak about his mouth, and through all that long, bungling, vociferous hurly-burly, revolving privately a case of conscience.[20] He would take no hand in the deed, because he had a private spite against the victim, and "that action" must be sullied with no suggestion of a worldly motive; on the other hand, "that action" in itself was highly justified, he had cast in his lot with "the actors," and he must stay there, inactive but publicly sharing the responsibility. "You are a gentleman—you will protect me!" cried the wounded old man, crawling towards him. "I will never lay a hand on you," said Hackston, and put his cloak about his mouth. It is an old temptation with me, to pluck away that cloak and see the face—to open that bosom and to read the heart. With incomplete romances about Hackston, the drawers of my youth were lumbered.[21] I read him up in every printed book that I could lay my hands on. I even dug among the Wodrow manuscripts,[22] sitting shame-faced in the very room where my hero had been tortured two centuries before, and keenly conscious of my youth in the midst of other and (as I fondly thought) more gifted students. All was vain: that he had passed a riotous nonage, that he was a zealot, that he twice displayed (compared with his grotesque companions) some tincture of soldierly resolution and even of military common sense, and that he figured memorably in the scene on Magus Muir, so much and no more could I expiscate. But whenever I cast my eyes backward, it is to see him like a landmark on the plains of history, sitting with his cloak about his mouth, inscrutable. How small a thing creates an immortality! I do not think he can have been a man entirely commonplace; but had he not thrown his cloak about his mouth, or had the witnesses forgot to chronicle the action, he would not thus have haunted the imagination of my boyhood, and to-day he would scarce delay me for a paragraph. An incident, at once romantic and dramatic, which at once awakes the judgment and makes a picture for the eye, how little do we realize its perdurable power! Perhaps no one does so but the author, just as none but he appreciates the influence of jingling words; so that he looks on upon life, with something of a covert smile, seeing people led by what they fancy to be thoughts and what are really the accustomed artifices of his own trade, or roused by what they take to be principles and are really picturesque effects. In a pleasant book about a school class club, Colonel Fergusson has recently told a little anecdote.[23] A "Philosophical Society" was formed by some Academy boys—among them, Colonel Fergusson himself, Fleeming Jenkin, and Andrew Wilson, the Christian Booddhist and author of *The Abode of Snow*.[24] Before these learned pundits, one member laid the following ingenious problem: "What would be the result of putting a pound of potassium in a pot of porter?" "I should think there would be a number of interesting bi-products," said a smatterer at my elbow; but for me the tale itself has a bi-product, and stands as a type of much that is most human. For this inquirer, who conceived himself to burn with a zeal entirely chemical, was really immersed in a design of a quite different nature; unconsciously to his own recently breached intelligence, he was engaged in literature. Putting, pound, potassium, pot, porter: initial p, mediant t—that was his idea, poor little boy! So with politics and that which excites men in the present, so with history and that which rouses them in the past: there lie at the root of what appears most serious unsuspected elements.

The triple town of Anstruther Wester, Anstruther Easter, and Cellardyke, all three Royal Burghs—or two Royal Burghs and a less distinguished suburb, I forget which—lies continuously along the sea-side, and boasts of either two or three separate parish churches, and either two or three separate harbors. These ambiguities are painful; but the fact is (although it argue me uncultured) I am but poorly posted upon Cellardyke. My business lay in the two Anstruthers. A tricklet of a stream divides them, spanned by a bridge; and over the bridge at the time of my knowledge, the celebrated Shell House stood outpost on the west. This had been the residence of an agreeable eccentric; during his fond tenancy, he had illustrated the outer walls, as high (if I remember rightly) as the roof, with elaborate patterns and pictures, and snatches of verse in the vein of *exegi monumentum*; shells and pebbles, artfully contrasted and conjoined, had been his medium; and I like to think of him standing back upon the bridge, when all was finished, drinking in the general effect and (like Gibbon) already lamenting his employ-ment. *Et ego artifex*, he may have thought; like Hayley over his poems or Haydon before his canvases.

The same bridge saw another sight in the seventeenth century. Mr. Thomson, the "curat" of Anstruther Easter, was a man highly obnoxious to the devout: in the first place because he was a "curat;" in the second place, because he was a person of irregular and scandalous life; and in the third place, because he was generally suspected of dealings with the Enemy of Man. These three disqualifications, in the popular literature of the time, go hand in hand; but the end of Mr. Thomson was a thing quite by itself, and in the proper phrase, a manifest judgment. He had been at a friend's house in Anstruther Wester, where (and elsewhere, I suspect) he had partaken of the bottle; indeed, to put the thing in our cold modern way, the reverend gentleman was on the brink of *delirium tremens*. It was a dark night, it seems; a little lassie came carrying a lantern to fetch the curate home; and away they went down the street of Anstruther Wester, the lantern swinging a bit in the child's hand, the barred lustre tossing up and down along the front of slumbering houses, and Mr. Thomson not altogether steady on his legs nor (to all appearance) easy in his mind. The pair had reached the middle of the bridge when (as I con-ceive the scene) the poor tippler started in some baseless fear and looked behind him; the child, already shaken by the minister's strange behavior, started also; in so doing, she would jerk the lantern; and for the space of a moment the lights and the shadows would be all confounded. Then it was that to the unhinged toper and the twittering child, a huge bulk of blackness seemed to sweep down, to pass them close by as they stood upon the bridge, and to vanish on the further side in the general darkness of the night. "Plainly the devil come for Mr. Thomson!" thought the child. What Mr. Thomson thought himself, we have no ground of knowledge; but he fell upon his knees in the midst of the bridge like a man praying. On the rest of the journey to the manse, history is silent; but when they came to the door, the poor caitiff, taking the lantern from the child, looked upon her with so lost a countenance that her little courage died within her, and she fled home screaming to her parents. Not a soul would venture out; all that night, the minister dwelt alone with his terrors in the manse; and when the day dawned, and men made bold to go about the streets, they found the devil had come indeed for Mr. Thomson.[25]

This manse of Anstruther Easter has another and a more cheerful association. It was early in the morning, about a century before the days of Mr. Thomson, that his predecessor was called out of bed to welcome a Grandee of Spain, the Duke of Medina Sidonia, just landed in the harbor underneath. But sure there was never seen a more decayed grandee; sure there was never a duke welcomed from a stranger place of exile. Half-way between Orkney and Shetland, there lies a certain isle; on the one hand the Atlantic, on the other the North Sea, bombard its pillared cliffs; sore-eyed, short-living, inbred fishers and their families herd in its few huts; in the graveyard, pieces of wreck-wood stand for monuments; there is nowhere a more inhospitable spot. *Belle-Isle-en-Mer*—Fair-Isle-at-Sea—that is a name that has always rung in my mind's ear like music; but the only "Fair Isle" on which I ever set my foot, was this unhomely, rugged turret-top of submarine sierras. Here, when his ship was broken, my lord Duke joyfully got ashore; here for long months he and certain of his men were harbored; and it was from this durance that he landed at last to be welcomed (as well as such a papist deserved, no doubt) by the godly incumbent of Anstruther Easter; and after the Fair Isle, what a fine city must that have appeared! and after the island diet, what a hospitable spot the minister's table! And yet he must have lived on friendly terms with his outlandish hosts. For to this day there still survives a relic of the long winter evenings when the sailors of the great Armada crouched about the hearths of the Fair-Islanders, the planks of their own lost galleon perhaps lighting up the scene, and the gale and the surf that beat about the coast contributing their melancholy voices. All the folk of the north isles are great artificers of knitting: the Fair-Islanders alone dye their fabrics in the Spanish manner. To this day, gloves and nightcaps, innocently decorated, may be seen for sale in the Shetland warehouse at Edinburgh, or on the Fair Isle itself in the catechist's house; and to this day, they tell the story of the Duke of Medina Sidonia's adventure.

It would seem as if the Fair Isle had some attraction for "persons of quality." When I landed there myself, an elderly gentleman, unshaved, poorly attired, his shoulders wrapped in a plaid, was seen walking to and fro, with a book in his hand, upon the beach. He paid no heed to our arrival, which we thought a strange thing in itself; but when one of the officers of the *Pharos*,[26] passing narrowly by him, observed his book to be a Greek Testament, our wonder and interest took a higher flight. The catechist was cross-examined; he said the gentleman had been put across some time before in Mr. Bruce of Sumburgh's schooner, the only link between the Fair Isle and the rest of the world; and that he held services and was doing "good." So much came glibly enough; but when pressed a little further, the catechist displayed embarrassment. A singular diffidence appeared upon his face: "They tell me," said he, in low tones, "that he's a lord." And a lord he was; a peer of the realm pacing that inhospitable beach with his Greek Testament, and his plaid about his shoulders, set upon doing good, as he understood it, worthy man! And his grandson, a good-looking little boy, much better dressed than the lordly evangelist, and speaking with a silken English accent very foreign to the scene, accompanied me for a while in my exploration of the island. I suppose this little fellow is now my lord, and wonder how much he remembers of the Fair Isle. Perhaps not much; for he seemed to accept very quietly his savage situation; and under such guidance, it is like that this was not his first nor yet his last adventure.

Notes

1 "Contributions to the History of Fife" and "The Education of an Engineer" appeared as a series called "Random Memories" in *Across the Plains with Other Memories and Essays* (1892).
2 Stevenson first visited Fife with his father at 12 years old in the summer of 1863.
3 A local appellation because of Fife's wealth and independence.

4 A reference to Alexander III in the ballad "Sir Patrick Spens": "The King sits in Dumferling toune, / Drinking the blude-red wine" (verse 1).
5 Refers to the ballad "The Bonnie Earl of Moray." Moray was murdered by the Earl of Huntly and his soldiers on 7 Feb. 1592 at Donibristle.
6 John Paul Jones (1747–1792), Scottish-American Naval commander in the American Revolution who raided Scotland in Sept. 1778. Kirkcaldy minister Rev. Shirra prayed for protection, and strong wind kept Jones's ships from landing.
7 Robert Burns, "Tam o' Shanter" (92). Alexander III fell from his horse and died while riding from Inverkeithing to Kinghorn in 1286.
8 In the late 16th century, Agnes Sampson and other alleged witches were believed to have caused a tempest that wrecked a cargo ship sailing from Brunt Island to Leith.
9 James Johnstone (1719–1791), soldier who participated in the Jacobite Rising, fled to France, and served in the French Colonial Army. He describes in his memoir the frightful sounds of birds in the caves where he hid.
10 In the Indian Rebellion of 1857, an armed uprising of Indian soldiers against the British East India Company, Lt. George Willoughby blew up a magazine, killing himself, the British soldiers barricaded with him, and hundreds of Indian fighters. Though the postmaster was dead, two young signalers relayed the crucial message.
11 The Scottish naval officer Alexander Selkirk, from Fife's Lower Largo, was marooned off the coast of Chile from 1704 to 1708 and was thought to be the inspiration for Defoe's *Robinson Crusoe*.
12 James Sharp (1613–1679) betrayed his fellow Covenanters and became Archbishop of St. Andrews.
13 Cardinal David Beaton was murdered at St. Andrews on 29 May 1546. John Knox described the murder in detail in *The History of the Reformation in Scotland*.
14 Andrew Lang's "Almae Matres" (1865), which begins, "St. Andrews by the northern sea, / A haunted town it is to me." Lang would later publish *St. Andrews* (1903)
15 *Records of a Family of Engineers* (204–205).
16 Thomas Rowlandson, *The English Dance of Death*, 2 vols. (1815–1816).
17 John Balfour of Kinloch lived in northern Fife and served as a commanding officer in the Covenanter battles at Drumclog and Bothwell Bridge in 1679. He may have been related to Stevenson.
18 James Sharp was murdered by Covenanters while travelling in a coach through Magus Muir in 1679. His assassins took his tobacco box and a live bee flew out of it. Someone called it Sharp's familiar—an assisting spirit often in the form of an animal—and some of the men understood the term to mean *devil*.
19 Maria Louisa Charlesworth's *Ministering Children: a tale dedicated to childhood* (1856) and Octavius Winslow's *Life in Jesus: A Memoir* (1865).
20 David Hackson of Rathillet, who fought at Drumclog and Bothwell Bridge in 1679, was one of Sharp's assassins and was executed the following year.
21 At 14, Stevenson began writing a novel called *Rathillet* on David Hackston.
22 Robert Wodrow, *The History of the Sufferings of the Church of Scotland* (1722).
23 Lt. Col. Alexander Fergusson, *Chronicles of the Cumming Club, and memories of old Academy Days* (1887).
24 Andrew Wilson (1831–1881), Scottish traveler and author of *The Abode of Snow: Observations on a Journey from Chinese Tibet to the Indian Caucasus, through the Upper Valleys of the Himalaya* (1875).
25 Thomson drowned himself in a river. His story was used as a cautionary tale about the fate of those who fall away from Covenanting beliefs.
26 Lighthouse.

32

THE EDUCATION OF AN ENGINEER[1]

Anstruther is a place sacred to the Muse; she inspired (really to a considerable extent) Tennant's vernacular poem *Anst'er Fair*;[2] and I have there waited on her myself with much devotion. This was when I came as a young man to glean engineering experience from the building of the breakwater. What I gleaned, I am sure I do not know; but indeed I had already my own private determination to be an author; I loved the art of words and the appearances of life; and *travellers*, and *headers*, and *rubble*, and *polished ashlar*, and *pierres perdues*, and even the thrilling question of the *string-course*,[3] interested me only (if they interested me at all) as properties for some possible romance or as words to add to my vocabulary. To grow a little catholic is the compensation of years; youth is one-eyed; and in those days, though I haunted the breakwater by day, and even loved the place for the sake of the sunshine, the thrilling sea-side air, the wash of waves on the sea-face, the green glimmer of the divers' helmets far below, and the musical chinking of the masons, my one genuine pre-occupation lay elsewhere, and my only industry was in the hours when I was not on duty. I lodged with a certain Bailie Brown, a carpenter by trade; and there as soon as dinner was despatched, in a chamber scented with dry rose-leaves, drew in my chair to the table and proceeded to pour forth literature, at such a speed and with such intimations of early death and immortality,[4] as I now look back upon with wonder. Then it was that I wrote *Voces Fidelium*,[5] a series of dramatic monologues in verse; then that I indited the bulk of a covenanting novel—like so many others, never finished.[6] Late I sat into the night, toiling (as I thought) under the very dart of death,[7] toiling to leave a memory behind me. I feel moved to thrust aside the curtain of the years, to hail that poor feverish idiot, to bid him go to bed and clap *Voces Fidelium* on the fire before he goes; so clear does he appear before me, sitting there between his candles in the rose-scented room and the late night; so ridiculous a picture (to my elderly wisdom) does the fool present! But he was driven to his bed at last without miraculous intervention; and the manner of his driving sets the last touch upon this eminently youthful business. The weather was then so warm that I must keep the windows open; the night without was populous with moths. As the late darkness deepened, my literary tapers beaconed forth more brightly; thicker and thicker came the dusty night-fliers, to gyrate for one brilliant instant round the

252

flame and fall in agonies upon my paper. Flesh and blood could not endure the spectacle; to capture immortality was doubtless a noble enterprise, but not to capture it at such a cost of suffering; and out would go the candles, and off would I go to bed in the darkness, raging to think that the blow might fall on the morrow, and there was *Voces Fidelium* still incomplete. Well, the moths are all gone, and *Voces Fidelium* along with them; only the fool is still on hand and practises new follies.

Only one thing in connection with the harbor tempted me; and that was the diving, an experience I burned to taste of. But this was not to be, at least in Anstruther; and the subject involves a change of scene to the sub-arctic town of Wick.[8] You can never have dwelt in a country more unsightly than that part of Caithness, the land faintly swelling, faintly falling, not a tree, not a hedgerow, the fields divided by single slate stones set upon their edge, the wind always singing in your ears and (down the long road that led nowhere) thrumming in the telegraph wires. Only as you approached the coast, was there anything to stir the heart. The plateau broke down to the North Sea in formidable cliffs, the tall out-stacks[9] rose like pillars ringed about with surf, the coves were over-brimmed with clamorous froth, the sea-birds screamed, the wind sang in the thyme on the cliff's edge; here and there, small ancient castles toppled on the brim; here and there, it was possible to dip into a dell of shelter, where you might lie and tell yourself you were a little warm, and hear (near at hand) the whin-pods[10] bursting in the afternoon sun, and (further off) the rumor of the turbulent sea. As for Wick itself, it is one of the meanest of man's towns, and situate certainly on the baldest of God's bays. It lives for herring, and a strange sight it is to see (of an afternoon) the heights of Pulteney blackened by seaward-looking fishers, as when a city crowds to a review—or, as when bees have swarmed, the ground is horrible with lumps and clusters; and a strange sight, and a beautiful, to see the fleet put silently out against a rising moon, the sea-line rough as a wood with sails, and ever and again and one after another, a boat flitting swiftly by the silver disk. This mass of fishers, this great fleet of boats, is out of all proportion to the town itself; and the oars are manned and the nets hauled by immigrants from the Long Island (as we call the outer Hebrides), who come for that season only and depart again, if "the take" be poor, leaving debts behind them. In a bad year, the end of the herring fishery is therefore an exciting time; fights are common, riots often possible; an apple knocked from a child's hand was once the signal for something like a war; and even when I was there, a gunboat lay in the bay to assist the authorities. To contrary interests, it should be observed, the curse of Babel[11] is here added; the Lews men are Gaelic speakers. Caithness has adopted English; an odd circumstance, if you reflect that both must be largely Norsemen by descent. I remember seeing one of the strongest instances of this division: a thing like a Punch-and-Judy box erected on the flat grave-stones of the churchyard; from the hutch or proscenium—I know not what to call it—an eldritch looking preacher laying down the law in Gaelic about some one of the name of *Powl*, whom I at last divined to be the apostle to the gentiles;[12] a large congregation of the Lews men very devoutly listening; and on the outskirts of the crowd, some of the town's children (to whom the whole affair was Greek and

Hebrew) profanely playing tigg.[13] The same descent, the same country, the same narrow sect of the same religion, and all these bonds made very largely nugatory by an accidental difference of dialect!

Into the bay of Wick stretched the dark length of the unfinished breakwater, in its cage of open staging; the travellers (like frames of churches) over-plumbing all; and away at the extreme end, the divers toiling unseen on the foundation. On a platform of loose planks, the assistants turned their air-mills;[14] a stone might be swinging between wind and water; underneath the swell ran gayly; and from time to time, a mailed dragon with a window glass snout came dripping up the ladder. Youth is a blessed season after all; my stay at Wick was in the year of *Voces Fidelium* and the rose-leaf room at Bailie Brown's; and already I did not care two straws for literary glory. Posthumous ambition perhaps requires an atmosphere of roses; and the more rugged excitant of Wick east winds had made another boy of me. To go down in the dress, that was my absorbing fancy; and with the countenance of a certain handsome scamp of a diver, Bob Bain by name, I gratified my whim.

It was gray, harsh, easterly weather, the swell ran pretty high, and out in the open there were "skipper's daughters,"[15] when I found myself at last on the diver's platform, twenty pounds of lead upon each foot and my whole person swollen with ply and ply of woollen underclothing. One moment, the salt wind was whistling round my night-capped head; the next, I was crushed almost double under the weight of the helmet. As that intolerable burthen was laid upon me, I could have found it in my heart (only for shame's sake) to cry off from the whole enterprise. But it was too late. The attendants began to turn the hurdy-gurdy[16] and the air to whistle through the tube; some one screwed in the barred window of the vizor; and I was cut off in a moment from my fellow-men; standing there in their midst, but quite divorced from intercourse: a creature deaf and dumb, pathetically looking forth upon them from a climate of his own. Except that I could move and feel, I was like a man fallen in a catalepsy. But time was scarce given me to realize my isolation; the weights were hung upon my back and breast, the signal rope was thrust into my unresisting hand; and setting a twenty-pound foot upon the ladder, I began ponderously to descend.

Some twenty rounds[17] below the platform, twilight fell. Looking up, I saw a low green heaven mottled with vanishing bells of white; looking around, except for the weedy spokes and shafts of the ladder, nothing but a green gloaming, somewhat opaque but very restful and delicious. Thirty rounds lower, I stepped off on the *pierres perdues* of the foundation; a dumb helmeted figure took me by the hand, and made a gesture (as I read it) of encouragement; and looking in at the creature's window, I beheld the face of Bain. There we were, hand to hand and (when it pleased us) eye to eye; and either might have burst himself with shouting, and not a whisper come to his companion's hearing. Each, in his own little world of air, stood incommunicably separate.

Bob had told me ere this a little tale, a five minutes' drama at the bottom of the sea, which at that moment possibly shot across my mind. He was down with

254

another, settling a stone of the sea-wall. They had it well adjusted, Bob gave the signal, the scissors[18] were slipped, the stone set home; and it was time to turn to something else. But still his companion remained bowed over the block like a mourner on a tomb, or only raised himself to make absurd contortions and mysterious signs unknown to the vocabulary of the diver. There, then, these two stood for a while, like the dead and the living; till there flashed a fortunate thought into Bob's mind, and he stooped, peered through the window of that other world, and beheld the face of its inhabitant wet with streaming tears. Ah! the man was in pain! And Bob glancing downward, saw what was the trouble: the block had been lowered on the foot of that unfortunate—he was caught alive at the bottom of the sea under fifteen tons of rock.

That two men should handle a stone so heavy, even swinging in the scissors, may appear strange to the inexpert. These must bear in mind the great density of the water of the sea, and the surprising results of transplantation to that medium. To understand a little what these are, and how a man's weight, so far from being an encumbrance, is the very ground of his agility, was the chief lesson of my submarine experience. The knowledge came upon me by degrees. As I began to go forward with the hand of my estranged companion, a world of tumbled stones was visible, pillared with the weedy uprights of the staging: overhead, a flat roof of green: a little in front, the sea-wall, like an unfinished rampart. And presently, in our upward progress, Bob motioned me to leap upon a stone; I looked to see if he were possibly in earnest, and he only signed to me the more imperiously. Now the block stood six feet high; it would have been quite a leap to me unencumbered; with the breast and back weights, and the twenty pounds upon each foot, and the staggering load of the helmet, the thing was out of reason. I laughed aloud in my tomb; and to prove to Bob how far he was astray, I gave a little impulse from my toes. Up I soared like a bird, my companion soaring at my side. As high as to the stone, and then higher, I pursued my impotent and empty flight. Even when the strong arm of Bob had checked my shoulders, my heels continued their ascent; so that I blew out sideways like an autumn leaf, and must be hauled in, hand over hand, as sailors haul in the slack of a sail, and propped upon my feet again like an intoxicated sparrow. Yet a little higher on the foundation, and we began to be affected by the bottom of the swell, running there like a strong breeze of wind. Or so I must suppose; for, safe in my cushion of air, I was conscious of no impact; only swayed idly like a weed, and was now borne helplessly abroad, and now swiftly—and yet with dream-like gentleness—impelled against my guide. So does a child's balloon divagate upon the currents of the air, and touch and slide off again from every obstacle. So must have ineffectually swung, so resented their inefficiency, those "light crowds" that followed the Star of Hades[19] and uttered "exiguous voices" in the land beyond Cocytus.[20]

There was something strangely exasperating, as well as strangely wearying, in these uncommanded evolutions. It is bitter to return to infancy, to be supported, and directed, and perpetually set upon your feet, by the hand of someone else. The air besides, as it is supplied to you by the busy millers on the platform, closes the eustachian tubes[21] and keeps the neophyte perpetually swallowing, till his throat is grown so dry that he can swallow no longer. And for all these reasons—although I had a fine, dizzy, muddle-headed joy in my surroundings, and longed, and tried, and always failed, to lay hands on the fish that darted here and there about me, swift as humming-birds—yet I fancy I was rather relieved than otherwise when Bain brought me back to the ladder and signed to me to mount. And there was one more experience before me even then. Of a sudden, my ascending head passed into the trough of a swell. Out of the green, I shot at once into a glory of rosy, almost of sanguine light—the multitudinous seas incarnadined, the heaven above a vault of crimson. And then the glory faded into the hard, ugly daylight of a Caithness autumn, with a low sky, a gray sea, and a whistling wind.

Bob Bain had five shillings for his trouble, and I had done what I desired. It was one of the best things I got from my education as an engineer: of which however, as a way of life, I wish to speak with sympathy. It takes a man into the open air; it keeps him hanging about harbor-sides, which is the richest form of idling; it carries him to wild islands; it gives him a taste of the genial dangers of the sea; it supplies him with dexterities to exercise; it makes demands upon his ingenuity; it will go far to cure him of any taste (if ever he had one) for the miserable life of cities. And when it has done so, it carries him back and shuts him in an office! From the roaring skerry and the wet thwart of the tossing boat, he passes to the stool and desk; and with a memory full of ships, and seas, and perilous headlands, and the shining pharos,[22] he must apply his long-sighted eyes to the petty niceties of drawing, or measure his inaccurate mind with several pages of consecutive figures. He is a wise youth, to be sure, who can balance one part of genuine life against two parts of drudgery between four walls, and for the sake of the one, manfully accept the other.

Wick was scarce an eligible place of stay. But how much better it was to hang in the cold wind upon the pier, to go down with Bob Bain among the roots of the staging, to be all day in a boat coiling a wet rope and shouting orders—not always very wise—than to be warm and dry, and dull, and dead-alive, in the most comfortable office. And Wick itself had in those days a note of originality. It may have still, but I misdoubt it much. The old minister of Keiss would not preach, in these degenerate times, for an hour and a half upon the clock. The gipsies must be gone from their cavern; where you might see, from the mouth, the women tending their fire, like Meg Merrilies,[23] and the men sleeping off their coarse potations; and where in winter gales, the surf would beleaguer them closely, bursting in their very door. A traveller to-day upon the Thurso coach would scarce observe a little cloud of smoke among the moorlands, and be told, quite openly, it marked a private still.[24] He would not indeed make that journey, for there is now no Thurso coach. And even if he could, one little thing that happened to me could never happen to him, or not with the same trenchancy of contrast.

We had been upon the road all evening; the coach top was crowded with Lews fishers going home, scarce anything but Gaelic had sounded in my ears; and our way had lain throughout over a moorish country very northern to behold. Latish at night, though it was still broad day in our subarctic latitude, we came down upon the shores of the roaring Pentland Firth, that grave of mariners; on one hand, the cliffs of Dunnet Head ran seaward; in front was the little bare, white town of Castleton, its streets full of blowing sand; nothing beyond, but the North Islands, the great deep, and the perennial ice-fields of the Pole. And here, in the last imaginable place, there sprang up young outlandish voices and a chatter of some foreign speech; and I saw, pursing the coach with its load of Hebridean fishers—as they had pursued *vetturini*[25] up the passes of the Apennines or perhaps along the grotto under Virgil's tomb[26]—two little dark-eyed, white-toothed Italian vagabonds, of twelve to fourteen years of age, one with a hurdy-gurdy, the other with a cage of white mice.[27] The coach passed on, and their small Italian chatter died in the distance; and I was left to marvel how they had wandered into that country, and how they fared in it, and what they thought of it, and when (if ever) they should see again the silver wind-breaks run among the olives, and the stone pine[28] stand guard upon Etruscan[29] sepulchres.

Upon any American, the strangeness of this incident is somewhat lost. For as far back as he goes in his own land, he will find some alien camping there; the Cornish miner, the French or Mexican half-blood, the negro in the South, these are deep in the woods and far among the mountains. But in an old, cold and rugged country such as mine, the days of immigration are long at an end; and away up there, which was at that time far beyond the northernmost extreme of railways, hard upon the shore of that ill-omened strait of whirlpools, in a land of moors where no stranger came, unless it should be a sportsman to shoot grouse or an antiquary to decipher runes, the presence of these small pedestrians struck the mind as though a bird-of-paradise had risen from the heather or an albatross come fishing in the bay of Wick. They were as strange to their surroundings as my lordly evangelist or the old Spanish grandee on the Fair Isle.[30] Years after, I read in the papers that some defaulting banker had been picked up by a yacht upon the coast of Wales; the two vagabonds of Castleton (I know not why) rose instantly before my fancy; and that same night I have made the framework of a blood-and-thunder tale, which perhaps the reader may have dipped through under the name of *The Pavilion on the Links*. But how far more picturesque is the plain fact!

Notes

1 As a university student, Stevenson spent his summers (1868–1870) training to follow the family profession of lighthouse engineering in the coastal villages and remote islands of Scotland: Anstruther, Wick, Orkney, the Shetland islands, and Erraid. See also "On the Enjoyment of Unpleasant Places," "Memoirs of an Islet," and "Night Outside the Wick Mail."

2 William Tennant's 1814 comic poem invokes the Muse's aid in glorifying "Anster's turnip-bearing vales."

3 Travellers: mechanisms for moving, lifting, or sliding construction material; headers: bricks or stone blocks placed with their ends to the face of the wall; rubble: rough pieces of undressed stone used to fill in cavities in walls; polished ashlar: finely cut

stones used as facing on walls; pierres perdues: blocks of stone piled in the water to form a seawall foundation; string-course: a raised horizontal band of bricks or stone on a structure.

4 Wordsworth, "Ode: Intimations of Immortality."

5 Voices of the faithful (Latin).

6 Stevenson published his research for his aborted novel as the historical essay: *The Pentland Rising: A Page of History, 1666* in 1866 at 16 years old. His father paid to have it privately printed.

7 Shakespeare, *Cymbeline*, 4.2.211.

8 Wick—a town in the far north of Scotland's eastern coast.

9 Rocky coastal outcrops.

10 Gorse seedpods.

11 After Noah's descendants tried to build a tower reaching heaven, God confounded their language (Genesis 11).

12 Paul.

13 Tag.

14 A manually operated pump supplying air to the diver's helmet through a hose.

15 Waves with white crests.

16 Stevenson compares the air-mill to a hurdy-gurdy: a stringed musical instrument with a hand crank.

17 Rungs on a ladder.

18 Grapple.

19 Lucifer (Revelation 12:4).

20 Mythological river in the underworld.

21 The auditory tube of the middle ear named for the 16th-century Italian anatomist Bartolomeo Eustachi.

22 Lighthouse.

23 Meg Merrilies is a gipsy woman in Walter Scott's *Guy Mannering* (1815) and the subject of Keats's eponymous 1818 poem.

24 An illegal whiskey distillery.

25 Coachmen.

26 In Naples.

27 Italians with white mice was a trope of the period often sympathetically associated with poor children. See Juliet McMaster's "Will Ladislaw and Other Italians with White Mice." *Victorian Review*, vol. 16, no. 2, 1990, pp. 1–7.

28 A Mediterranean pine with an umbrella-like canopy.

29 An ancient Italian civilization from the 8th to the 3rd century BC.

30 Stevenson's "Contributions to the History of Fife" describes two strangers who appear on Fair Isle: an unkempt lord he met there in 1869 and Alonso Pérez de Guzmán de Zuniga-Sotomayor, Commander of the Spanish Armada, who was shipwrecked there in 1588 after England defeated it.

33

THE LANTERN-BEARERS

I

These boys congregated every autumn about a certain easterly fisher village,[1] where they tasted in a high degree the glory of existence. The place was created seemingly on purpose for the diversion of young gentlemen. A street or two of houses, mostly red and many of them tiled; a number of fine trees clustered about the manse and the kirkyard, and turning the chief street into a shady alley; many little gardens more than usually bright with flowers; nets a-drying, and fisher-wives scolding in the backward parts; a smell of fish, a genial smell of seaweed; whiffs of blowing sand at the street-corners; shops with golf-balls and bottled lollipops; another shop with penny pickwicks (that remarkable cigar) and the *London Journal*,[2] dear to me for its startling pictures, and a few novels, dear for their suggestive names: such, as well as memory serves me, were the ingredients of the town. These, you are to conceive posted on a spit between two sandy bays, and sparsely flanked with villas—enough, for the boys to lodge in with their subsidiary parents, not enough (not yet enough) to cocknify the scene: a haven in the rocks in front: in front of that, a file of gray islets: to the left, endless links and sand wreaths, a wilderness of hiding-holes, alive with popping rabbits and soaring gulls: to the right, a range of seaward crags, one rugged brow beyond another; the ruins of a mighty and ancient fortress on the brink of one; coves between—now charmed into sunshine quiet, now whistling with wind and clamorous with bursting surges; the dens and sheltered hollows redolent of thyme and southernwood, the air at the cliff's edge brisk and clean and pungent of the sea—in front of all, the Bass Rock,[3] tilted seaward like a doubtful bather, the surf ringing it with white, the solan-geese hanging round its summit like a great and glittering smoke. This choice piece of seaboard was sacred, besides, to the wrecker; and the Bass, in the eye of fancy, still flew the colors of King James; and in the ear of fancy the arches of Tantallon still rang with horse-shoe iron, and echoed to the commands of Bell-the-Cat.

There was nothing to mar your days, if you were a boy summering in that part, but the embarrassment of pleasure. You might golf if you wanted; but I seem to have been better employed. You might secrete yourself in the Lady's Walk, a certain sunless dingle of elders, all mossed over by the damp as green as grass, and dotted here and there by the streamside with roofless walls, the cold homes of anchorites. To fit themselves for life, and with a special eye to acquire the art of smoking, it was even common for the boys to harbor there; and you might have seen a single penny pickwick, honestly shared in lengths with a blunt knife, bestrew the glen with these apprentices. Again, you might join our fishing parties, where we sat perched as thick as solan-geese, a covey of little anglers, boy and girl, angling over each other's heads, to the much entanglement of lines and loss of podleys and consequent shrill recrimination—shrill as the geese themselves. Indeed, had that been all, you might have done this often; but though fishing be a fine pastime, the podley is scarce to be regarded as a dainty for the table; and it was a point of honor that a boy should eat all that he had taken. Or again, you might climb the Law,[4] where the whale's jawbone stood landmark in the buzzing wind, and behold the face of many counties, and the smoke and spires of many towns, and the sails of distant ships. You might bathe, now in the flaws of fine weather that we pathetically call our summer, now in a gale of wind, with the sand scourging your bare hide, your clothes thrashing abroad from underneath their guardian stone, the froth of the great breakers casting you headlong ere it had drowned your knees. Or you might explore the tidal rocks, above all in the ebb of springs, when the very roots of the hills were for the nonce discovered; following my leader from one group to another, groping in slippery tangle for the wreck of ships, wading in pools after the abominable creatures of the sea, and ever with an eye cast backward on the march of the tide and the menaced line of your retreat. And then you might go Crusoeing, a word that covers all extempore eating in the open air: digging perhaps a house under the margin of the links, kindling a fire of the sea-ware, and cooking apples there—if they were truly apples, for I sometimes suppose the merchant must have played us off with some inferior and quite local fruit, capable of resolving, in the neighborhood of fire, into mere sand and smoke and iodine; or perhaps pushing to Tantallon, you might lunch on sandwiches and visions in the grassy court, while the wind hummed in the crumbling turrets; or clambering along the coast, eat geens[5] (the worst, I must suppose, in Christendom) from an adventurous geen-tree that had taken root under a cliff, where it was shaken with an ague of east wind, and silvered after gales with salt, and grew so foreign among its bleak surroundings that to eat of its produce was an adventure in itself.

There are mingled some dismal memories with so many that were joyous. Of the fisher-wife, for instance, who had cut her throat at Canty Bay; and of how I ran with the other children to the top of the Quadrant, and beheld a posse of silent people escorting a cart, and on the cart, bound in a chair, her throat bandaged, and the bandage all bloody—horror!—the fisher-wife herself, who continued thenceforth to hag-ride my thoughts, and even to-day (as I recall the scene) darkens daylight. She was lodged in the little old jail in the chief street; but whether or no she died there, with a wise terror of the worst, I never inquired. She had been tippling; it was but a dingy tragedy; and it seems strange and hard that, after all these years, the poor crazy sinner should be still pilloried on her cart in the scrap-book of my memory. Nor shall I readily forget a certain house in the Quadrant where a visitor died, and a dark old woman continued to dwell alone with the dead body; nor how this old woman conceived a hatred to myself and one of my cousins, and in the dread hour of the dusk, as we were clambering on the garden-walls, opened a window in that house of mortality and cursed us in a still voice and with a marrowy choice of language. It was a pair of very colorless urchins that fled down the lane from this remarkable experience! But I recall with a more doubtful sentiment, compounded out of fear and exultation, the coil of equinoctial tempests;[6] trumpeting squalls, scouring flaws of rain; the boats with their reefed lugsails scudding for the harbor mouth, where danger lay, for it was hard to make when the wind had any east in it; the wives clustered with blowing shawls at the pier-head, where (if fate was against them) they might see boat and husband and sons—their whole wealth and their whole family—engulfed under their eyes; and (what I saw but once) a troop of neighbors forcing such an unfortunate homeward, and she squalling and battling in their midst, a figure scarcely human, a tragic Mœnad.

These are things that I recall with interest; but what my memory dwells upon the most, I have been all this while withholding. It was a sport peculiar to the place, and indeed to a week or so of our two months' holiday there. Maybe it still flourishes in its native spot; for boys and their pastimes are swayed by periodic forces inscrutable to man; so that tops and marbles reappear in their due season, regular like the sun and moon; and the harmless art of knucklebones has seen the fall of the Roman empire and the rise of the United States. It may still flourish there, but nowhere else, I am persuaded; for I tried myself to introduce it on Tweedside, and was defeated lamentably; its charm being quite local, like a country wine that cannot be exported.

The idle manner of it was this:

Toward the end of September, when school-time was drawing near and the nights were already black, we would begin to sally from our respective villas, each equipped with a tin bull's-eye lantern. The thing was so well known that it had worn a rut in the commerce of Great Britain; and the grocers, about the due time, began to garnish their windows with our particular brand of luminary. We wore them buckled to the waist upon a cricket belt, and over them, such was the rigor of the game, a buttoned top-coat. They smelled noisomely of blistered tin; they never burned aright, though they would always burn our fingers; their use was naught; the pleasure of them merely fanciful; and yet a boy with a bull's-eye under his top-coat asked for nothing more. The fishermen used lanterns about their boats, and it was from them, I suppose, that we had got the hint; but theirs were not bull's-eyes, nor did we ever play at being fishermen. The police carried them at their belts, and we had plainly copied them in that; yet we did not pretend to be policemen. Burglars, indeed, we may have had some haunting thoughts of; and we had certainly an eye to past ages when lanterns were more common, and to certain story-books in which we had found them to figure very largely. But take it for all in all, the pleasure of the thing was substantive; and to be a boy with a bull's-eye under his top-coat was good enough for us.

When two of these asses met, there would be an anxious "Have you got your lantern?" and a gratified "Yes!" That was the shibboleth, and very needful too; for, as it was the rule to keep our glory contained, none could recognize a lantern-bearer, unless (like the pole-cat) by the smell. Four or five would sometimes climb into the belly of a ten-man lugger, with nothing but the thwarts above them—for the cabin was usually locked, or choose out some hollow of the links where the wind might whistle overhead. There the coats would be unbuttoned and the bull's-eyes discovered; and in the chequering glimmer, under the huge windy hall of the night, and cheered by a rich steam of toasting tinware, these fortunate young gentlemen would crouch together in the cold sand of the links or on the scaly bilges of the fishing-boat, and delight themselves with inappropriate talk. Woe is me that I may not give some specimens—some of their foresights of life, or deep inquiries into the rudiments of man and nature, these were so fiery and so innocent, they were so richly silly, so romantically young. But there is a kind of fool abroad, whose folly is not even laughable; and it is this fool who gives the note of literary decency. And the talk, at any rate, was but a condiment; and these gatherings themselves only accidents in the career of the lantern-bearer. The essence of this bliss was to walk by yourself in the black night; the slide shut, the top-coat buttoned; not a ray escaping, whether to conduct your footsteps or to make your glory public: a mere pillar of darkness in the dark; and all the while, deep down in the privacy of your fool's heart, to know you had a bull's-eye at your belt, and to exult and sing over the knowledge.

II

It is said that a poet has died young in the breast of the most stolid. It may be contended, rather, that this (somewhat minor) bard in almost every case survives, and is the spice of life to his possessor. Justice is not done to the versatility and the unplumbed childishness of man's imagination. His life from without may seem but a rude mound of mud; there will be some golden chamber at the heart of it, in which he dwells delighted; and for as dark as his pathway seems to the observer, he will have some kind of a bull's-eye at his belt. It would be hard to pick out a career more cheerless than that of Dancer,[7] as he figures in the "Old Bailey Reports," a prey to the most sordid persecutions, the butt of his neighborhood, betrayed by his hired man, his house beleaguered by the impish school-boy, and he himself grinding and fuming and impotently fleeing to the law against these pin-pricks. You marvel at first that any one should willingly prolong a life so destitute of charm and dignity; and then you call to memory that had he chosen, had he ceased to be a miser, he could have been freed at once from these trials, and might have built himself a castle and gone escorted by a squadron. For the love of more recondite joys, which we cannot estimate, which, it may be, we should envy, the man had willingly foregone both comfort and consideration. "His mind to him a kingdom was;"[8] and sure enough, digging into that mind, which seems at first a dust-heap, we unearth some priceless jewels. For Dancer must have had the love of power and the disdain of using it, a noble character in itself; disdain of many pleasures, a chief part of what is commonly called wisdom; disdain of the inevitable end, that finest trait of mankind; scorn of men's opinions, another element of virtue; and at the back of all, a conscience just like yours and mine, whining like a cur, swindling like a thimblerigger, but still pointing (there or thereabout) to some conventional standard. Here were a cabinet portrait to which Hawthorne[9] perhaps had done justice; and yet not Hawthorne either, for he was mildly minded, and it lay not in him to create for us that throb of the miser's pulse, his fretful energy of gusto, his vast arms of ambition clutching in he knows not what: insatiable, insane, a god with a muck-rake. Thus, at least, looking in the bosom of the miser, consideration detects the poet in the full tide of life, with more, indeed, of the poetic fire than usually goes to epics; and tracing that mean man about his cold hearth, and to and fro in his discomfortable house, spies within him a blazing bonfire of delight. And so with others, who do not live by bread alone,[10] but by some cherished and perhaps fantastic pleasure; who are meat salesmen to the external eye, and possibly to themselves are Shakespeares, Napoleons or Beethovens; who have not one virtue to rub against another in the field of active life, and yet perhaps, in the life of contemplation, sit with the saints. We see them on the street, and we can count their buttons; but heaven knows in what they pride themselves! heaven knows where they have set their treasure!

There is one fable that touches very near the quick of life: the fable of the monk who passed into the woods, heard a bird break into song, hearkened for a trill or two, and found himself on his return a stranger at his convent gates; for he had been absent fifty years, and of all his comrades there survived but one to recognize him. It is not only in the woods that this enchanter carols, though perhaps he is native there. He sings in the most doleful places. The miser hears him and chuckles, and the days are moments. With no more apparatus than an ill-smelling lantern I have evoked him on the naked links. All life that is not merely mechanical is spun out of two strands: seeking for that bird and hearing him. And it is just this that makes life so hard to value, and the delight of each so incommunicable. And just a knowledge of this, and a remembrance of those fortunate hours in which the bird has sung to us, that fills us with such wonder when we turn the pages of the realist. There, to be sure, we find a picture of life in so far as it consists of mud and of old iron, cheap desires and cheap fears, that which we are ashamed to remember and that which we are careless whether we forget; but of the note of that time-devouring nightingale we hear no news.

The case of these writers of romance is most obscure. They have been boys and youths; they have lingered outside the window of the beloved, who was then most probably writing to some one else; they have sat before a sheet of paper, and felt themselves mere continents of congested poetry, not one line of which would flow; they have walked alone in the woods, they have walked in cities under the countless lamps; they have been to sea, they have hated, they have feared, they have longed to knife a man, and maybe done it; the wild taste of life has stung their palate. Or, if you deny them all the rest, one pleasure at least they have tasted to the full—their books are there to prove it—the keen pleasure of successful literary composition. And yet they fill the globe with volumes, whose cleverness inspires me with despairing admiration, and whose consistent falsity to all I care to call existence, with despairing wrath. If I had no better hope than to continue to revolve among the dreary and petty businesses, and to be moved by the paltry hopes and fears with which they surround and animate their heroes, I declare I would die now. But there has never an hour of mine gone quite so dully yet; if it were spent waiting at a railway junction, I would have some scattering thoughts, I could count some grains of memory, compared to which the whole of one of these romances seems but dross. These writers would retort (if I take them properly) that this was very true; that it was the same with themselves and other persons of (what they call) the artistic temperament; that in this we were exceptional, and should apparently be ashamed of ourselves; but that our works must deal exclusively with (what they call) the average man, who was a prodigious dull fellow, and quite dead to all but the paltriest considerations. I accept the issue. We can only know others by ourselves. The artistic temperament (a plague on the expression!) does not make us different from our fellow-men, or it would make us incapable of writing novels; and the average man (a murrain on the word!) is just like you and me, or he would not be average. It was Whitman who stamped a kind of Birmingham sacredness upon the latter phrase; but Whitman knew very well, and showed very nobly, that the average man was full of joys and full of a poetry of his own.[11] And this harping on life's dulness and man's meanness is a loud profession of incompetence; it is one of two things: the cry of the blind eye, *I cannot see*, or the complaint of the dumb tongue, *I cannot utter*. To draw a life without delights is to prove I have not realized it. To picture a man without some sort of poetry—well, it goes near to prove my case, for it shows an author may have little enough. To see Dancer only as a dirty, old, small-minded, impotently fuming man, in a dirty house, besieged by Harrow boys, and probably beset by small attorneys, is to show myself as keen an observer as . . . the Harrow boys. But these young gentlemen (with a more becoming modesty) were content to pluck Dancer by the coat-tails; they did not suppose they had surprised his secret or could put him living in a book: and it is there my error would have lain. Or say that in the same romance—I continue to call these books romances, in the hope of giving pain—say that in the same romance, which now begins really to take shape, I should leave to speak of Dancer, and follow instead the Harrow boys; and say that I came on some such business as that of my lantern-bearers on the links; and described the boys as very cold, spat upon by flurries of rain, and drearily surrounded, all of which they were; and their talk as silly and indecent, which it certainly was. I might upon these lines, and had I Zola's genius, turn out, in a page or so, a gem of literary art, render the lanternlight with the touches of a master, and lay on the indecency with the ungrudging hand of love; and when all was done, what a triumph would my picture be of shallowness and dulness! how it would have missed the point! how it would have belied the boys![12] To the ear of the stenographer the talk is merely silly and indecent; but ask the boys themselves, and they are discussing (as it is highly proper they should) the possibilities of existence. To the eye of the observer they are wet and cold and drearily surrounded; but ask themselves, and they are in the heaven of a recondite pleasure, the ground of which is an ill-smelling lantern.

III

For, to repeat, the ground of a man's joy is often hard to hit. It may hinge at times upon a mere accessory, like the lantern. It may reside, like Dancer's, in the mysterious inwards of psychology. It may consist with perpetual failure, and find exercise in the continued chase. It has so little bond with externals (such as the observer scribbles in his note-book) that it may even touch them not; and the man's true life, for which he consents to live, lie altogether in the field of fancy. The clergyman, in his spare hours, may be winning battles, the farmer sailing ships, the banker reaping triumph in the arts: all leading another life, plying another trade from that they chose; like the poet's house-builder, who, after all is cased in stone,

By his fireside, as impotent fancy prompts,
Rebuilds it to his liking.[13]

In such a case the poetry runs underground. The observer (poor soul, with his documents!) is all abroad. For to look at the man is but to court deception. We shall see the trunk from which he draws his nourishment; but he himself is above and abroad in the green dome of foliage, hummed through by winds and nested in by nightingales. And the true realism were that of the poets, to climb up after him like a squirrel, and catch some glimpse of the heaven for which he lives. And the true realism, always and everywhere, is that of the poets: to find out where joy resides, and give it a voice far beyond singing.

For to miss the joy is to miss all. In the joy of the actors lies the sense of any action. That is the explanation, that the excuse. To one who has not the secret of the lanterns, the scene upon the links is meaningless. And hence the haunting and truly spectral unreality of realistic books. Hence, when we read the English realists, the incredulous wonder with which we observe the hero's constancy under the submerging tide of dulness, and how he bears up with his jibbing sweetheart, and endures the chatter of idiot girls, and stands by his whole unfeatured wilderness of an existence, instead of seeking relief in drink or foreign travel. Hence in the French, in that meat-market of middle-aged sensuality, the disgusted surprise with which we see the hero drift sidelong, and practically quite untempted, into every description of misconduct and dishonor. In each we miss the personal poetry, the enchanted atmosphere, that rainbow work of fancy that clothes what is naked and seems to ennoble what is base; in each, life falls dead like dough, instead of soaring away like a balloon into the colors of the sunset; each is true, each inconceivable; for no man lives in the external truth, among salts and acids, but in the warm, phantasmagoric chamber of his brain, with the painted windows and the storied walls.

Of this falsity we have had a recent example from a man who knows far better—Tolstoi's *Powers of Darkness*.[14] Here is a piece full of force and truth, yet quite untrue. For before Mikita was led into so dire a situation he was tempted, and temptations are beautiful at least in part; and a work which dwells on the ugliness of crime and gives no hint of any loveliness in the temptation, sins against the modesty of life, and even when a Tolstoi writes it, sinks to melodrama. The peasants are not understood; they saw their life in fairer colors; even the deaf girl was clothed in poetry for Mikita, or he had never fallen. And so, once again, even an Old Bailey melodrama, without some brightness of poetry and lustre of existence, falls into the inconceivable and ranks with fairy tales.

IV

In nobler books we are moved with something like the emotions of life; and this emotion is very variously provoked. We are so moved when Levine labors in the field, when André sinks beyond emotion, when Richard Feverel and Lucy Desborough meet beside the river, when Antony "not cowardly, puts off his helmet," when Kent has infinite pity on the dying Lear, when, in Dostoieffky's *Despised and Rejected*, the uncomplaining hero drains his cup of suffering and virtue.[15] These are notes that please the great heart of man. Not only love, and the fields, and the bright face of danger, but sacrifice and death and unmerited suffering humbly supported, touch in us the vein of the poetic. We love to think of them, we long to try them, we are humbly hopeful that we may prove heroes also.

We have heard, perhaps, too much of lesser matters. Here is the door, here is the open air. *Itur in antiquam silvam*.[16]

Notes

1 North Berwick, where Stevenson spent summers in the 1860s.
2 A popular periodical (1845–1912).
3 The Bass Rock would later feature in Stevenson's novel *Catriona* (1893).
4 Berwick Law, a local hill.
5 RLS: wild cherries.
6 Referring to the popular but mistaken belief that storms are more common during the spring and fall equinox.
7 Daniel Dancer (1716–94), a Pinner miser who lived cheaply and left a fortune, becoming the subject of popular narratives such as "The Strange and Unaccountable Life of Daniel Dancer" (1801).
8 "My mind to me a kingdom is" (1588). There is some dispute on the poem's authorship between Edward de Vere, Earl of Oxford and Sir Edward Dyer.
9 Nathaniel Hawthorne, *The House of Seven Gables* (ch. 11 "The Arched Window").
10 Luke 4:4.

11 See Stevenson's essay "The Gospel According to Walt Whitman" (1878).
12 Émile Zola (1840–1902), French novelist and leading figure of naturalism, which valued documenting everyday life in fiction over idealizing experience. See also Stevenson's essay "A Note on Realism" (1883).
13 Wordsworth, *The Prelude* (1850, VI.291–4).
14 Tolstoy's 1886 play.
15 Tolstoy's *Anna Karenina* and *War and Peace*, George Meredith's *The Ordeal of Richard Feverel*, Shakespeare's *Antony and Cleopatra* and *King Lear*.
16 From Virgil's *Aeneid* (VI.179), in which Aeneas and his men go "into the ancient forest" to gather wood for Misenus's funeral pyre.

34

A CHAPTER ON DREAMS

The past is all of one texture—whether feigned or suffered—whether acted out in three dimensions, or only witnessed in that small theatre of the brain which we keep brightly lighted all night long, after the jets[1] are down, and darkness and sleep reign undisturbed in the remainder of the body. There is no distinction on the face of our experiences; one is vivid indeed, and one dull, and one pleasant, and another agonizing to remember; but which of them is what we call true, and which a dream, there is not one hair to prove. The past stands on a precarious footing; another straw split in the field of metaphysic, and behold us robbed of it. There is scarce a family that can count four generations but lays a claim to some dormant title or some castle and estate: a claim not prosecutable in any court of law, but flattering to the fancy and a great alleviation of idle hours. A man's claim to his own past is yet less valid. A paper might turn up (in proper story-book fashion) in the secret drawer of an old ebony secretary, and restore your family to its ancient honors, and reinstate mine in a certain West Indian islet (not far from St. Kitt's, as beloved tradition hummed in my young ears) which was once ours, and is now unjustly someone else's, and for that matter (in the state of the sugar trade) is not worth anything to anybody. I do not say that these revolutions are likely; only no man can deny that they are possible; and the past, on the other hand, is lost forever: our old days and deeds, our old selves, too, and the very world in which these scenes were acted, all brought down to the same faint residuum as a last night's dream, to some incontinuous images, and an echo in the chambers of the brain. Not an hour, not a mood, not a glance of the eye, can we revoke; it is all gone, past conjuring. And yet conceive us robbed of it, conceive that little thread of memory that we trail behind us broken at the pocket's edge; and in what naked nullity should we be left! for we only guide ourselves, and only know ourselves, by these air-painted pictures of the past.

Upon these grounds, there are some among us who claim to have lived longer and more richly than their neighbors; when they lay asleep they claim they were still active; and among the treasures of memory that all men review for their amusement, these count in no second place the harvests of their dreams. There is one of this kind whom I have in my eye, and whose case is perhaps unusual enough to be described. He was from a child an ardent and uncomfortable dreamer. When he had a touch of fever at night, and the room swelled and shrank, and his clothes, hanging on a nail, now loomed up instant to the bigness of a church, and now drew away into a horror of infinite distance and infinite littleness, the poor soul was very well aware of what must follow, and struggled hard against the approaches of that slumber which was the beginning of sorrows. But his struggles were in vain; sooner or later the night-hag would have him by the throat, and pluck him, strangling and screaming, from his sleep. His dreams were at times commonplace enough, at times very strange: at times they were almost formless, he would be haunted, for instance, by nothing more definite than a certain hue of brown, which he did not mind in the least while he was awake, but feared and loathed while he was dreaming; at times, again, they took on every detail of circumstance, as when once he supposed he must swallow the populous world, and awoke screaming with the horror of the thought. The two chief troubles of his very narrow exist-ence—the practical and every-day trouble of school tasks and the ultimate and airy one of hell and judgment—were often confounded together into one appall-ing nightmare. He seemed to himself to stand before the Great White Throne;[2] he was called on, poor little devil, to recite some form of words, on which his destiny depended; his tongue stuck, his memory was blank, hell gaped for him; and he would awake, clinging to the curtain-rod with his knees to his chin.

These were extremely poor experiences, on the whole; and at that time of life my dreamer would have very willingly parted with his power of dreams. But pres-ently, in the course of his growth, the cries and physical contortions passed away, seemingly forever; his visions were still for the most part miserable, but they were more constantly supported; and he would awake with no more extreme symptom than a flying heart, a freezing scalp, cold sweats, and the speechless midnight fear. His dreams, too, as befitted a mind better stocked with particulars, became more circumstantial, and had more the air and continuity of life. The look of the world beginning to take hold on his attention, scenery came to play a part in his sleeping as well as in his waking thoughts, so that he would take long, uneventful journeys and see strange towns and beautiful places as he lay in bed. And, what is more sig-nificant, an odd taste that he had for the Georgian costume and for stories laid in that period of English history, began to rule the features of his dreams; so that he masqueraded there in a three-cornered hat, and was much engaged with Jacobite conspiracy between the hour for bed and that for breakfast. About the same time, he began to read in his dreams—tales, for the most part, and for the most part after the manner of G. P. R. James,[3] but so incredibly more vivid and moving than any printed book, that he has ever since been malcontent with literature.

And then, while he was yet a student, there came to him a dream-adventure which he has no anxiety to repeat; he began, that is to say, to dream in sequence and thus to lead a double life—one of the day, one of the night—one that he had every reason to believe was the true one, another that he had no means of proving to be false. I should have said he studied, or was by way of studying, at Edinburgh College, which (it may be supposed) was how I came to know him. Well, in his dream-life, he passed a long day in the surgical theatre, his heart in his mouth, his teeth on edge, seeing monstrous malformations and the abhorred dexterity of surgeons. In a heavy, rainy, foggy evening he came forth into the South Bridge, turned up the High Street, and entered the door of a tall *land*,[4] at the top of which he supposed himself to lodge. All night long, in his wet clothes, he climbed the stairs, stair after stair in endless series, and at every second flight a flaring lamp with a reflector. All night long, he brushed by single persons passing downward— beggarly women of the street, great, weary, muddy laborers, poor scarecrows of men, pale parodies of women—but all drowsy and weary like himself, and all single, and all brushing against him as they passed. In the end, out of a northern window, he would see day beginning to whiten over the Firth, give up the ascent, turn to descend, and in a breath be back again upon the streets, in his wet clothes, in the wet, haggard dawn, trudging to another day of monstrosities and opera- tions. Time went quicker in the life of dreams, some seven hours (as near as he can guess) to one; and it went, besides, more intensely, so that the gloom of these fancied experiences clouded the day, and he had not shaken off their shadow ere it was time to lie down and to renew them. I cannot tell how long it was that he endured this discipline; but it was long enough to leave a great black blot upon his memory, long enough to send him, trembling for his reason, to the doors of a certain doctor; whereupon with a simple draught he was restored to the common lot of man.

The poor gentleman has since been troubled by nothing of the sort; indeed, his nights were for some while like other men's, now blank, now checkered with dreams, and these sometimes charming, sometimes appalling, but except for an occasional vividness, of no extraordinary kind. I will just note one of these occa- sions, ere I pass on to what makes my dreamer truly interesting. It seemed to him that he was in the first floor of a rough hill-farm. The room showed some poor efforts at gentility, a carpet on the floor, a piano, I think, against the wall; but, for all these refinements, there was no mistaking he was in a moorland place, among hill-side people, and set in miles of heather. He looked down from the window upon a bare farm-yard, that seemed to have been long disused. A great, uneasy stillness lay upon the world. There was no sign of the farm folk or of any live stock, save for an old, brown, curly dog of the retriever breed, who sat close in against the wall of the house and seemed to be dozing. Something about this dog disquieted the dreamer; it was quite a nameless feeling, for the beast looked right enough—indeed, he was so old and dull and dusty and broken-down, that he should rather have awakened pity; and yet the conviction came and grew upon the dreamer that this was no proper dog at all, but something hellish. A great many dozing summer flies hummed about the yard; and presently the dog thrust forth his paw, caught a fly in his open palm, carried it to his mouth like an ape, and looking suddenly up at the dreamer in the window, winked to him with one eye. The dream went on, it matters not how it went; it was a good dream as dreams go; but there was nothing in the sequel worthy of that devilish brown dog. And the point of interest for me lies partly in that very fact: that having found so singular an incident, my imperfect dreamer should prove unable to carry the tale to a fit end and fall back on indescribable noises and indiscriminate horrors. It would be different now; he knows his business better!

For, to approach at last the point: This honest fellow had long been in the custom of setting himself to sleep with tales, and so had his father before him; but these were irresponsible inventions, told for the teller's pleasure, with no eye to the crass public or the thwart reviewer: Tales where a thread might be dropped, or one adventure quitted for another, on fancy's least suggestion. So that the little people who manage man's internal theatre had not as yet received a very rigorous training; and played upon their stage like children who should have slipped into the house and found it empty, rather than like drilled actors performing a set piece to a huge hall of faces. But presently my dreamer began to turn his former amusement of story-telling to (what is called) account; by which I mean that he began to write and sell his tales. Here was he, and here were the little people who did that part of his business, in quite new conditions. The stories must now be trimmed and pared and set upon all fours, they must run from a beginning to an end and fit (after a manner) with the laws of life; the pleasure, in one word, had become a business; and that not only for the dreamer, but for the little people of his theatre. These understood the change as well as he. When he lay down to prepare himself for sleep, he no longer sought amusement, but printable and profitable tales; and after he had dozed off in his box-seat, his little people continued their evolutions with the same mercantile design. All other forms of dream deserted him but two: he still occasionally reads the most delightful books, he still visits at times the most delightful places; and it is perhaps worthy of note that to these same places, and to one in particular, he returns at intervals of months and years, finding new field-paths, visiting new neighbors, beholding that happy valley under new effects of noon and dawn and sunset. But all the rest of the family of visions is quite lost to him: the common, mangled version of yesterday's affairs, the raw-head-and-bloody-bones nightmare, rumored to be the child of toasted cheese—these and their like are gone; and, for the most part, whether awake or asleep, he is simply occupied—he or his little people—in consciously making stories for the market. This dreamer (like many other persons) has encountered some trifling vicissitudes of fortune. When the bank begins to send letters and the butcher to linger at the back gate, he sets to belaboring his brains after a story, for that is his readiest money-winner; and, behold! at once the little people begin to bestir themselves in the same quest, and labor all night long, and all night long set before him truncheons of tales upon their lighted theatre. No fear of his being frightened now; the flying heart and the frozen scalp are things bygone; applause, growing applause, growing interest, growing exultation in his own cleverness (for he takes all the credit) and at last a jubilant leap to wakefulness, with the cry, "I have it, that'll do!" upon his lips: with such and similar emotions he sits at these nocturnal dramas, with such outbreaks, like Claudius in the play,[5] he scatters the performance in the midst. Often enough the waking is a disappointment: he has been too deep asleep, as I explain the thing; drowsiness has gained his little people, they have gone stumbling and maundering through their parts; and the play, to the awakened mind, is seen to be a tissue of absurdities. And yet how often have these sleepless Brownies[6] done him honest service, and given him, as he sat idly taking his pleasure in the boxes, better tales than he could fashion for himself.

Here is one, exactly as it came to him. It seemed he was the son of a very rich and wicked man, the owner of broad acres and a most damnable temper. The dreamer (and that was the son) had lived much abroad, on purpose to avoid his parent; and when at length he returned to England, it was to find him married again to a young wife, who was supposed to suffer cruelly and to loathe her yoke. Because of this marriage (as the dreamer indistinctly understood) it was desirable for father and son to have a meeting; and yet both being proud and both angry, neither would condescend upon a visit. Meet they did accordingly, in a desolate, sandy country by the sea; and there they quarrelled, and the son, stung by some intolerable insult, struck down the father dead. No suspicion was aroused; the dead man was found and buried, and the dreamer succeeded to the broad estates, and found himself installed under the same roof with his father's widow, for whom no provision had been made. These two lived very much alone, as people may after a bereavement, sat down to table together, shared the long evenings, and grew daily better friends; until it seemed to him of a sudden that she was prying about dangerous matters, that she had conceived a notion of his guilt, that she watched him and tried him with questions. He drew back from her company as men draw back from a precipice suddenly discovered; and yet so strong was the attraction that he would drift again and again into the old intimacy, and again and again be startled back by some suggestive question or some inexplicable meaning in her eye. So they lived at cross purposes, a life full of broken dialogue, challenging glances, and suppressed passion; until, one day, he saw the woman slipping from the house in a veil, followed her to the station, followed her in the train to the seaside country, and out over the sandhills to the very place where the murder was done. There she began to grope among the bents, he watching her, flat upon his face; and presently she had something in her hand—I cannot remember what it was, but it was deadly evidence against the dreamer—and as she held it up to look at it, perhaps from the shock of the discovery, her foot slipped, and she hung at some peril on the brink of the tall sand-wreaths. He had no thought but to spring up and rescue her; and there they stood face to face, she with that deadly matter openly in her hand—his very presence on the spot another link of proof. It was plain she was about to speak, but this was more than he could bear—he could bear to be lost, but not to talk of it with his destroyer; and he cut her short with trivial conversation. Arm in arm, they returned together to the train, talking he knew not what, made the journey back in the same carriage, sat down to dinner, and passed the evening in the drawing-room as in the past. But suspense and fear drummed in the dreamer's bosom. "She has not denounced me yet"—so his thoughts ran—"when will she denounce me? Will it be to-morrow?" And it was not to-morrow, nor the next day, nor the next; and their life settled back on the old terms, only that she seemed kinder than before, and that, as for him, the burthen of his suspense and wonder grew daily more unbearable, so that he wasted away like a man with a disease. Once, indeed,

he broke all bounds of decency, seized an occasion when she was abroad, ransacked her room, and at last, hidden away among her jewels, found the damning
evidence. There he stood, holding this thing, which was his life, in the hollow of
his hand, and marvelling at her inconsequent behavior, that she should seek, and
keep, and yet not use it; and then the door opened, and behold herself. So, once
more, they stood, eye to eye, with the evidence between them; and once more
she raised to him a face brimming with some communication; and once more he
shied away from speech and cut her off. But before he left the room, which he had
turned upside down, he laid back his death-warrant where he had found it; and at
that, her face lighted up. The next thing he heard, she was explaining to her maid,
with some ingenious falsehood, the disorder of her things. Flesh and blood would
bear the strain no longer; and I think it was the next morning (though chronology
is always hazy in the theatre of the mind) that he burst from his reserve. They had
been breakfasting together in one corner of a great, parquetted, sparely furnished
room of many windows; all the time of the meal she had tortured him with sly
allusions; and no sooner were the servants gone, and these two protagonists alone
together, than he leaped to his feet. She too sprang up, with a pale face; with a pale
face, she heard him as he raved out his complaint: Why did she torture him so?
she knew all, she knew he was no enemy to her; why did she not denounce him at
once? what signified her whole behavior? why did she torture him? and yet again,
why did she torture him? And when he had done, she fell upon her knees, and with
outstretched hands: "Do you not understand?" she cried. "I love you!"

Hereupon, with a pang of wonder and mercantile delight, the dreamer awoke.
His mercantile delight was not of long endurance; for it soon became plain that in
this spirited tale there were unmarketable elements; which is just the reason why
you have it here so briefly told. But his wonder has still kept growing; and I think
the reader's will also, if he consider it ripely. For now he sees why I speak of the
little people as of substantive inventors and performers. To the end they had kept
their secret. I will go bail for the dreamer (having excellent grounds for valuing
his candor) that he had no guess whatever at the motive of the woman—the hinge
of the whole well-invented plot—until the instant of that highly dramatic declaration. It was not his tale; it was the little people's! That he seemed himself to
play a part in it, to be and suffer in the person of the hero, is but an oddity of this
particular dream; at which, indeed, I wonder a little, and which I seek to explain
by analogy. In reading a plain tale, burthened with no psychology, and movingly
and truthfully told, we are sometimes deceived for a moment, and take the emotions of the hero for our own. It is our testimony to the spirit and truth of the performance. So, perhaps, was this illusion of the dreamer's; and as he was asleep,
he was doubtless the more easily and more perfectly deceived. But observe: not
only was the secret kept, the story was told with really guileful craftsmanship.
The conduct of both actors is (in the cant phrase) psychologically correct, and
the emotion aptly graduated up to the surprising climax. I am awake now, and
I know this trade; and yet I cannot better it. I am awake, and I live by this business; and yet I could not outdo—could not even equal—that crafty artifice (as of

some old, experienced carpenter of plays, some Dennery or Sardou)[7] by which the same situation is twice presented and the two actors twice brought face to face over the evidence, only once it is in her hand, once in his—and these in their due order, the least dramatic first. The more I think of it, the more I am moved to press upon the world my question: Who are the Little People? They are near connections of the dreamer's, beyond doubt; they share in his financial worries and have an eye to the bank-book; they share plainly in his training; they have plainly learned like him to build the scheme of a considerate story and to arrange emotion in progressive order; only I think they have more talent; and one thing is beyond doubt, they can tell him a story piece by piece, like a serial, and keep him all the while in ignorance of where they aim. Who are they, then? and who is the dreamer?

Well, as regards the dreamer, I can answer that, for he is no less a person than myself;—as I might have told you from the beginning, only that the critics murmur over my consistent egotism;—and as I am positively forced to tell you now, or I could advance but little further with my story. And for the Little People, what shall I say they are but just my Brownies, God bless them! who do one-half my work for me while I am fast asleep, and in all human likelihood, do the rest for me as well, when I am wide awake and fondly suppose I do it for myself. That part which is done while I am sleeping is the Brownies' part beyond contention; but that which is done when I am up and about is by no means necessarily mine, since all goes to show the Brownies have a hand in it even then. Here is a doubt that much concerns my conscience. For myself—what I call I, my conscious ego, the denizen of the pineal gland unless he has changed his residence since Descartes, the man with the conscience and the variable bank-account, the man with the hat and the boots, and the privilege of voting and not carrying his candidate at the general elections—I am sometimes tempted to suppose he is no story-teller at all, but a creature as matter of fact as any cheesemonger or any cheese, and a realist bemired up to the ears in actuality; so that, by that account, the whole of my published fiction should be the single-handed product of some Brownie, some Familiar, some unseen collaborator, whom I keep locked in a back garret, while I get all the praise and he but a share (which I cannot prevent him getting) of the pudding. I am an excellent adviser, something like Molière's servant; I pull back and I cut down; and I dress the whole in the best words and sentences that I can find and make; I hold the pen, too; and I do the sitting at the table, which is about the worst of it; and when all is done, I make up the manuscript and pay for the registration; so that, on the whole, I have some claim to share, though not so largely as I do, in the profits of our common enterprise.

I can but give an instance or so of what part is done sleeping and what part awake, and leave the reader to share what laurels there are, at his own nod, between myself and my collaborators; and to do this I will first take a book that a number of persons have been polite enough to read, the *Strange Case of Dr. Jekyll and Mr. Hyde*. I had long been trying to write a story on this subject, to find a body, a vehicle, for that strong sense of man's double being which must at times come in upon and overwhelm the mind of every thinking creature. I had even written one, *The Travelling Companion*, which was returned by an editor on the plea that it was a work of genius and indecent, and which I burned the other day on the ground that it was not a work of genius, and that *Jekyll* had supplanted it.[8] Then came one of those financial fluctuations to which (with an elegant modesty) I have hitherto referred in the third person. For two days I went about racking my brains for a plot of any sort; and on the second night I dreamed the scene at the window, and a scene afterward split in two, in which Hyde, pursued for some crime, took the powder and underwent the change in the presence of his pursuers. All the rest was made awake, and consciously, although I think I can trace in much of it the manner of my Brownies. The meaning of the tale is therefore mine, and had long pre-existed in my garden of Adonis, and tried one body after another in vain; indeed, I do most of the morality, worse luck! and my Brownies have not a rudiment of what we call a conscience. Mine, too, is the setting, mine the characters. All that was given me was the matter of three scenes, and the central idea of a voluntary change becoming involuntary. Will it be thought ungenerous, after I have been so liberally ladling out praise to my unseen collaborators, if I here toss them over, bound hand and foot, into the arena of the critics? For the business of the powders, which so many have censured, is, I am relieved to say, not mine at all but the Brownies'. Of another tale, in case the reader should have glanced at it, I may say a word: the not very defensible story of *Olalla*[9]. Here the court, the mother, the mother's niche, Olalla, Olalla's chamber, the meetings on the stair, the broken window, the ugly scene of the bite, were all given me in bulk and detail as I have tried to write them; to this I added only the external scenery (for in my dream I never was beyond the court), the portrait, the characters of Felipe and the priest, the moral, such as it is, and the last pages, such as, alas! they are. And I may even say that in this case the moral itself was given me; for it arose immediately on a comparison of the mother and the daughter, and from the hideous trick of atavism in the first. Sometimes a parabolic sense is still more undeniably present in a dream; sometimes I cannot but suppose my Brownies have been aping Bunyan, and yet in no case with what would possibly be called a moral in a tract; never with the ethical narrowness; conveying hints instead of life's larger limitations and that sort of sense which we seem to perceive in the arabesque of time and space.

For the most part, it will be seen, my Brownies are somewhat fantastic, like their stories hot and hot, full of passion and the picturesque, alive with animating incident; and they have no prejudice against the supernatural. But the other day they gave me a surprise, entertaining me with a love-story, a little April comedy, which I ought certainly to hand over to the author of *A Chance Acquaintance*, for he could write it as it should be written, and I am sure (although I mean to try) that I cannot.—But who would have supposed that a Brownie of mine should invent a tale for Mr. Howells?[10]

Notes

1 Contrivances.
2 Final judgment (Revelation 20:11–15).
3 George Payne Rainsford James (1799–1860), popular English author of historical romance novels.
4 A house of multiple storeys rented out as tenements.
5 Shakespeare, *Hamlet*.
6 Benevolent household sprites (*Dictionary of the Scots Language*).
7 Adolphe d'Ennery (1811–1899), author of various melodramas, translated into English in the 1860s; Victorien Sardou (1831–1908), prolific French dramatist.
8 A novel Stevenson wrote at Hyeres between 1882 and 1884 and later burned.
9 Written Nov.–Dec. 1885 and included in *The Merry Men and Other Tales* (1887).
10 William Dean Howells's novel, *A Chance Acquaintance* (1873). See also n. 15, p. 290.

35

BEGGARS

I

In a pleasant, airy, up-hill country, it was my fortune when I was young to make the acquaintance of a certain beggar. I call him beggar, though he usually allowed his coat and his shoes (which were open-mouthed, indeed) to beg for him. He was the wreck of an athletic man, tall, gaunt and bronzed; far gone in consumption,[1] with that disquieting smile of the mortally stricken on his face; but still active afoot, still with the brisk military carriage, the ready military salute. Three ways led through this piece of country; and as I was inconstant in my choice, I believe he must often have awaited me in vain. But often enough, he caught me; often enough, from some place of ambush by the roadside, he would spring suddenly forth in the regulation attitude, and launching at once into his inconsequential talk, fall into step with me upon my further course. "A fine morning, sir, though perhaps a trifle inclining to rain. I hope I see you well, sir. Why, no, sir, I don't feel as hearty myself as I could wish, but I am keeping about my ordinary. I am pleased to meet you on the road, sir. I assure you I quite look forward to one of our little conversations." He loved the sound of his own voice inordinately, and though (with something too off-hand to call servility) he would always hasten to agree with anything you said, yet he could never suffer you to say it to an end. By what transition he slid to his favorite subject I have no memory; but we had never been long together on the way before he was dealing, in a very military manner, with the English poets. "Shelley was a fine poet, sir, though a trifle atheistical in his opinions. His Queen Mab,[2] sir, is quite an atheistical work. Scott, sir, is not so poetical a writer. With the works of Shakespeare I am not so well acquainted, but he was a fine poet. Keats—John Keats, sir—he was a very fine poet." With such references, such trivial criticism, such loving parade of his own knowledge, he would beguile the road, striding forward up-hill, his staff now clapped to the ribs of his deep, resonant chest, now swinging in the air with the remembered jauntiness of the private soldier; and all the while his toes looking out of his boots, and his shirt looking out of his elbows, and death looking out of his smile, and his big, crazy frame shaken by accesses of cough.

He would often go the whole way home with me: often to borrow a book, and that book always a poet. Off he would march, to continue his mendicant rounds, with the volume slipped into the pocket of his ragged coat; and although he would sometimes keep it quite a while, yet it came always back again at last, not much the worse for its travels into beggardom. And in this way, doubtless, his knowledge grew and his glib, random criticism took a wider range. But my library was not the first he had drawn upon: at our first encounter, he was already brimful of Shelley and the atheistical Queen Mab, and "Keats—John Keats, sir."[3] And I have often wondered how he came by these acquirements; just as I often wondered how he fell to be a beggar. He had served through the Mutiny[4]—of which (like so many people) he could tell practically nothing beyond the names of places, and that it was "difficult work, sir," and very hot, or that so-and-so was "a very fine commander, sir." He was far too smart a man to have remained a private; in the nature of things, he must have won his stripes. And yet here he was without a pension. When I touched on this problem, he would content himself with diffidently offering me advice. "A man should be very careful when he is young, sir. If you'll excuse me saying so, a spirited young gentleman like yourself, sir, should be very careful. I was perhaps a trifle inclined to atheistical opinions myself." For (perhaps with a deeper wisdom than we are inclined in these days to admit) he plainly bracketed agnosticism with beer and skittles.[5]

Keats—John Keats, sir—and Shelley were his favorite bards. I cannot remember if I tried him with Rossetti;[6] but I know his taste to a hair, and if ever I did, he must have doted on that author. What took him was a richness in the speech; he loved the exotic, the unexpected word; the moving cadence of a phrase; a vague sense of emotion (about nothing) in the very letters of the alphabet: the romance of language. His honest head was very nearly empty, his intellect like a child's; and when he read his favorite authors, he can almost never have understood what he was reading. Yet the taste was not only genuine, it was exclusive; I tried in vain to offer him novels; he would none of them, he cared for nothing but romantic language that he could not understand. The case may be commoner than we suppose. I am reminded of a lad who was laid in the next cot to a friend of mine in a public hospital, and who was no sooner installed than he sent out (perhaps with his last pence) for a cheap Shakespeare. My friend pricked up his ears; fell at once in talk with his new neighbor, and was ready, when the book arrived, to make a singular discovery. For this lover of great literature understood not one sentence out of twelve, and his favorite part was that of which he understood the least—the inimitable, mouth-filling rodomontade of the ghost in Hamlet. It was a bright day in hospital when my friend expounded the sense of this beloved jargon: a task for which I am willing to believe my friend was very fit, though I can never regard it as an easy one. I know indeed a point or two, on which I would gladly question Mr. Shakespeare, that lover of big words, could he revisit the glimpses of the moon, or could I myself climb backward to the spacious days of Elizabeth. But in the second case, I should most likely pretermit these questionings, and take my place instead in the pit at the Blackfriars,[7] to hear the actor in his favorite part, playing up to Mr. Burbage,[8] and rolling out—as I seem to hear him—with a ponderous gusto,

Unhousel'd, disappointed, unanel'd.[9] What a pleasant chance, if we could go there in a party! and what a surprise for Mr. Burbage, when the ghost received the honors of the evening!

As for my old soldier, like Mr. Burbage and Mr. Shakespeare, he is long since dead; and now lies buried, I suppose, and nameless and quite forgotten, in some poor city graveyard.—But not for me, you brave heart, have you been buried! For me, you are still afoot, tasting the sun and air, and striding southward. By the groves of Comiston and beside the Hermitage of Braid, by the Hunters' Tryst, and where the curlews and plovers cry around Fairmilehead, I see and hear you, stalwartly carrying your deadly sickness, cheerfully discoursing of uncomprehended poets.

II

The thought of the old soldier recalls that of another tramp, his counterpart. This was a little, lean and fiery man, with the eyes of a dog and the face of a gypsy; whom I found one morning encamped with his wife and children and his grinder's wheel, beside the burn[10] of Kinnaird. To this beloved dell I went, at that time, daily; and daily the knife-grinder and I (for as long as his tent continued pleasantly to interrupt my little wilderness) sat on two stones, and smoked, and plucked grass, and talked to the tune of the brown water. His children were mere whelps, they fought and bit among the fern like vermin. His wife was a mere squaw; I saw her gather brush and tend the kettle, but she never ventured to address her lord while I was present. The tent was a mere gypsy hovel, like a sty for pigs. But the grinder himself had the fine self-sufficiency and grave politeness of the hunter and the savage; he did me the honors of this dell, which had been mine but the day before, took me far into the secrets of his life, and used me (I am proud to remember) as a friend.

Like my old soldier, he was far gone in the national complaint.[11] Unlike him, he had a vulgar taste in letters; scarce flying higher than the story papers; probably finding no difference, certainly seeking none, between Tannahill[12] and Burns; his noblest thoughts, whether of poetry or music, adequately embodied in that somewhat obvious ditty,

> Will ye gang, lassie, gang
> To the braes o' Balquidder:[13]

—which is indeed apt to echo in the ears of Scottish children, and to him, in view of his experience, must have found a special directness of address. But if he had no fine sense of poetry in letters, he felt with a deep joy the poetry of life. You should have heard him speak of what he loved; of the tent pitched beside the talking water; of the stars overhead at night; of the blest return of morning, the peep of day over the moors, the awaking birds among the birches; how he abhorred the long winter shut in cities; and with what delight, at the return of the spring, he once more pitched his camp in the living out-of-doors. But we were a pair of tramps; and to you, who are doubtless sedentary and a consistent first-class-passenger in life, he would scarce have laid himself so open;—to you, he might have been content to tell his story of a ghost—that of a buccaneer with his pistols as he lived—whom he had once encountered in a seaside cave near Buckie; and that would have been enough, for that would have shown you the mettle of the man. Here was a piece of experience solidly and livingly built up in words, here was a story created, *teres atque rotundus*.[14]

And to think of the old soldier, that lover of the literary bards! He had visited stranger spots than any seaside cave; encountered men more terrible than any spirit; done and dared and suffered in that incredible, unsung epic of the Mutiny War; played his part with the field force of Delhi, beleaguering and beleaguered; shared in that enduring, savage anger and contempt of death and decency that, for long months together, bedevil'd and inspired the army; was hurled to and fro in the battle-smoke of the assault; was there, perhaps, where Nicholson fell;[15] was there when the attacking column, with hell upon every side, found the soldier's enemy—strong drink,[16] and the lives of tens of thousands trembled in the scale, and the fate of the flag of England staggered. And of all this he had no more to say than "hot work, sir," or "the army suffered a great deal, sir," or "I believe General Wilson, sir, was not very highly thought of in the papers." His life was naught to him, the vivid pages of experience quite blank: in words his pleasure lay—melodious, agitated words—printed words, about that which he had never seen and was connatally incapable of comprehending. We have here two temperaments face to face; both untrained, unsophisticated, surprised (we may say) in the egg; both boldly charactered:—that of the artist, the lover and artificer of words; that of the maker, the seeër, the lover and forger of experience. If the one had a daughter and the other a son, and these married, might not some illustrious writer count descend from the beggar-soldier and the needy knife-grinder?

III

Everyone lives by selling something, whatever be his right to it. The burglar sells at the same time his own skill and courage and my silver plate (the whole at the most moderate figure) to a Jew receiver. The bandit sells the traveller an article of prime necessity: that traveller's life. And as for the old soldier, who stands for central mark to my capricious figures of eight, he dealt in a specialty; for he was the only beggar in the world who ever gave me pleasure for my money. He had learned a school of manners in the barracks and had the sense to cling to it, accosting strangers with a regimental freedom, thanking patrons with a merely regimental deference, sparing you at once the tragedy of his position and the embarrassment of yours. There was not one hint about him of the beggar's emphasis, the outburst of revolting gratitude, the rant and cant, the "God bless

you, Kind, Kind gentleman," which insults the smallness of your alms by dispro-
portional vehemence, which is so notably false, which would be so unbearable
if it were true. I am sometimes tempted to suppose this reading of the beggar's
part, a survival of the old days when Shakespeare was intoned upon the stage
and mourners keened beside the death-bed; to think that we cannot now accept
these strong emotions unless they be uttered in the just note of life; nor (save in
the pulpit) endure these gross conventions. They wound us, I am tempted to say,
like mockery; the high voice of keening (as it yet lingers on) strikes in the face of
sorrow like a buffet; and the rant and cant of the staled beggar stirs in us a shudder
of disgust. But the fact disproves these amateur opinions. The beggar lives by his
knowledge of the average man. He knows what he is about when he bandages his
head, and hires and drugs a babe, and poisons life with *Poor Mary Ann* or *Long,
long ago*;[17] he knows what he is about when he loads the critical ear and sickens
the nice conscience with intolerable thanks; they know what they are about, he
and his crew, when they pervade the slums of cities, ghastly parodies of suffering,
hateful parodies of gratitude. This trade can scarce be called an imposition; it has
been so blown upon with exposures; it flaunts its fraudulence so nakedly. We pay
them as we pay those who show us, in huge exaggeration, the monsters of our
drinking-water; or those who daily predict the fall of Britain. We pay them for the
pain they inflict, pay them, and wince, and hurry on. And truly there is nothing
that can shake the conscience like a beggar's thanks; and that polity in which such
protestations can be purchased for a shilling, seems no scene for an honest man.

Are there, then, we may be asked, no genuine beggars? And the answer is, Not
one. My old soldier was a humbug like the rest; his ragged boots were, in the
stage phrase, properties; whole boots were given him again and again, and always
gladly accepted; and the next day, there he was on the road as usual, with toes
exposed. His boots were his method; they were the man's trade; without his boots
he would have starved; he did not live by charity, but by appealing to a gross taste
in the public, which loves the limelight on the actor's face, and the toes out of
the beggar's boots. There is a true poverty, which no one sees: a false and merely
mimetic poverty, which usurps its place and dress, and lives, and above all drinks,
on the fruits of the usurpation. The true poverty does not go into the streets; the
banker may rest assured, he has never put a penny in its hand. The self-respecting
poor beg from each other; never from the rich. To live in the frock-coated ranks
of life, to hear canting scenes of gratitude rehearsed for twopence, a man might
suppose that giving was a thing gone out of fashion; yet it goes forward on a scale
so great as to fill me with surprise. In the houses of the working class, all day long
there will be a foot upon the stair; all day long there will be a knocking at the
doors; beggars come, beggars go, without stint, hardly with intermission, from
morning till night; and meanwhile, in the same city and but a few streets off, the
castles of the rich stand unsummoned. Get the tale of any honest tramp, you will
find it was always the poor who helped him; get the truth from any workman who
has met misfortunes, it was always next door that he would go for help, or only
with such exceptions as are said to prove a rule; look at the course of the mimetic

beggar, it is through the poor quarters that he trails his passage, showing his bandages to every window, piercing even to the attics with his nasal song. Here is a remarkable state of things in our Christian commonwealths, that the poor only should be asked to give.

IV

There is a pleasant tale of some worthless, phrasing Frenchman, who was taxed with ingratitude: "*Il faut savoir garder l'indépendance du cœur,*"[18] cried he. I own I feel with him. Gratitude without familiarity, gratitude otherwise than as a nameless element in a friendship, is a thing so near to hatred that I do not care to split the difference. Until I find a man who is pleased to receive obligations, I shall continue to question the tact of those who are eager to confer them. What an art it is, to give, even to our nearest friends! and what a test of manners, to receive! How, upon either side, we smuggle away the obligation, blushing for each other; how bluff and dull we make the giver; how hasty, how falsely cheerful, the receiver! And yet an act of such difficulty and distress between near friends, it is supposed we can perform to a total stranger and leave the man transfixed with grateful emotions. The last thing you can do to a man is to burthen him with an obligation, and it is what we propose to begin with! But let us not be deceived: unless he is totally degraded to his trade, anger jars in his inside, and he grates his teeth at our gratuity.

We should wipe two words from our vocabulary: gratitude and charity. In real life, help is given out of friendship, or it is not valued; it is received from the hand of friendship, or it is resented. We are all too proud to take a naked gift: we must seem to pay it, if in nothing else, then with the delights of our society. Here, then, is the pitiful fix of the rich man; here is that needle's eye in which he stuck already in the days of Christ,[19] and still sticks to-day, firmer, if possible, than ever: that he has the money and lacks the love which should make his money acceptable. Here and now, just as of old in Palestine, he has the rich to dinner, it is with the rich that he takes his pleasure: and when his turn comes to be charitable, he looks in vain for a recipient. His friends are not poor, they do not want; the poor are not his friends, they will not take. To whom is he to give? Where to find—note this phase—the Deserving Poor? Charity is (what they call) centralized; offices are hired; societies founded, with secretaries paid or unpaid: the hunt of the Deserving Poor goes merrily forward. I think it will take more than a merely human secretary to disinter that character. What! a class that is to be in want from no fault of its own, and yet greedily eager to receive from strangers; and to be quite respectable, and at the same time quite devoid of self-respect; and play the most delicate part of friendship, and yet never be seen; and wear the form of man, and yet fly in the face of all the laws of human nature:—and all this, in the hope of getting a belly-god Burgess through a needle's eye! O, let him stick, by all means; and let his polity tumble in the dust; and let his epitaph and all his literature (of which my own works begin to form no inconsiderable part) be abolished even from the history

282

of man! For a fool of this monstrosity of dulness, there can be no salvation: and the fool who looked for the elixir[20] of life was an angel of reason to the fool who looks for the Deserving Poor!

V

And yet there is one course which the unfortunate gentleman may take. He may subscribe to pay the taxes. There were the true charity, impartial and impersonal, cumbering none with obligation, helping all. There were a destination for loveless gifts; there were the way to reach the pocket of the deserving poor, and yet save the time of secretaries! But, alas! there is no color of romance in such a course; and people nowhere demand the picturesque so much as in their virtues.

Notes

1 Tuberculosis.
2 Percy Bysshe Shelley, *Queen Mab: A Philosophical Poem* (1813).
3 John Keats (1795–1821), English Romantic poet.
4 The Indian Rebellion of 1857—an armed uprising of Indian soldiers against the British East India Company lasting 18 months.
5 A game similar to bowling.
6 Dante Gabriel Rossetti (1828–1882), English Pre-Raphaelite poet and painter.
7 A sixteenth-century London theater.
8 Shakespeare was believed to play the Ghost in the first production of *Hamlet* in 1601. The Elizabethan actor Richard Burbage (1567–1619) played Hamlet.
9 *Hamlet* 1.5.77.
10 Creek.
11 Tuberculosis.
12 Robert Tannahill (1774–1810), Scottish working-class poet.
13 Tannahill, "Braes of Balquhidder" (1–2).
14 "Both smooth and round" (Latin). Horace, *Satires* 2.viii.
15 Famous British military officer John Nicholson (1821–1857) killed in the Siege of Delhi.
16 After British soldiers looted liquor stores en route to Delhi, General Archdale Wilson (1803–1874) ordered all alcohol destroyed.
17 Pathetic folk songs.
18 One must maintain an independent spirit (French). Theater director and magician Nestor Roqueplan (1805–1870).
19 Matthew 19:24.
20 An immortality potion.

36

A LETTER TO A YOUNG GENTLEMAN WHO PROPOSES TO EMBRACE THE CAREER OF ART

With the agreeable frankness of youth, you address me on a point of some practical importance to yourself and (it is even conceivable) of some gravity to the world: Should you or should you not become an artist? It is one which you must decide entirely for yourself; all that I can do is to bring under your notice some of the materials of that decision; and I will begin, as I shall probably conclude also, by assuring you that all depends on the vocation.

To know what you like is the beginning of wisdom and of old age. Youth is wholly experimental. The essence and charm of that unquiet and delightful epoch is ignorance of self as well as ignorance of life. These two unknowns the young man brings together again and again, now in the airiest touch, now with a bitter hug; now with exquisite pleasure, now with cutting pain; but never with indifference, to which he is a total stranger, and never with that near kinsman of indifference, contentment. If he be a youth of dainty senses or a brain easily heated, the interest of this series of experiments grows upon him out of all proportion to the pleasure he receives. It is not beauty that he loves, nor pleasure that he seeks, though he may think so; his design and his sufficient reward is to verify his own existence and taste the variety of human fate. To him, before the razor-edge of curiosity is dulled, all that is not actual living and the hot chase of experience wears a face of a disgusting dryness difficult to recall in later days; or if there be any exception—and here destiny steps in—it is in those moments when, wearied or surfeited of the primary activity of the senses, he calls up before memory the image of transacted pains and pleasures. Thus it is that such an one shies from all cut-and-dry professions, and inclines insensibly toward that career of art which consists only in the tasting and recording of experience.

This, which is not so much a vocation for art as an impatience of all other honest trades, frequently exists alone; and so existing, it will pass gently away in the course of years. Emphatically, it is not to be regarded; it is not a vocation, but a temptation; and when your father the other day so fiercely and (in my view) so properly discouraged your ambition, he was recalling not improbably some similar passage in his own experience. For the temptation is perhaps nearly as common as the vocation is rare. But again we have vocations which are imperfect; we have men whose minds are bound up, not so much in any art, as in the general *ars artium*[1] and common base of all creative work; who will now dip into painting, and now study counterpoint, and anon will be inditing a sonnet: all these with equal interest, all often with genuine knowledge. And of this temper, when it stands alone, I find it difficult to speak; but I should counsel such an one to take to letters, for in literature (which drags with so wide a net) all his information may be found some day useful, and if he should go on as he has begun, and turn at last into the critic, he will have learned to use the necessary tools. Lastly we come to those vocations which are at once decisive and precise; to the men who are born with the love of pigments, the passion of drawing, the gift of music, or the impulse to create with words, just as other and perhaps the same men are born with the love of hunting, or the sea, or horses, or the turning-lathe. These are predestined; if a man love the labor of any trade, apart from any question of success or fame, the gods have called him. He may have the general vocation too: he may have a taste for all the arts, and I think he often has; but the mark of his calling is this laborious partiality for one, this inextinguishable zest in its technical successes, and (perhaps above all) a certain candor of mind, to take his very trifling enterprise with a gravity that would befit the cares of empire, and to think the smallest improvement worth accomplishing at any expense of time and industry. The book, the statue, the sonata, must be gone upon with the unreasoning good faith and the unflagging spirit of children at their play. *Is it worth doing?*—when it shall have occurred to any artist to ask himself that question, it is implicitly answered in the negative. It does not occur to the child as he plays at being a pirate on the dining-room sofa, nor to the hunter as he pursues his quarry; and the candor of the one and the ardor of the other should be united in the bosom of the artist.

If you recognize in yourself some such decisive taste, there is no room for hesitation: follow your bent. And observe (lest I should too much discourage you) that the disposition does not usually burn so brightly at the first, or rather not so constantly. Habit and practice sharpen gifts; the necessity of toil grows less disgusting, grows even welcome, in the course of years; a small taste (if it be only genuine) waxes with indulgence into an exclusive passion. Enough, just now, if you can look back over a fair interval, and see that your chosen art has a little more than held its own among the thronging interests of youth. Time will do the rest, if devotion help it; and soon your every thought will be engrossed in that beloved occupation.

But even with devotion, you may remind me, even with unfaltering and delighted industry, many thousand artists spend their lives, if the result be regarded, utterly in vain: A thousand artists, and never one work of art. But the vast mass of mankind are incapable of doing anything reasonably well, art among the rest. The worthless artist would not improbably have been a quite incompetent baker. And the artist, even if he does not amuse the public, amuses himself; so that there will always be one man the happier for his vigils. This is the practical side of art: its inexpugnable fortress for the true practitioner. The direct returns—the wages of the trade—are small, but the indirect—the wages of the life—are incalculably great. No other business offers a man his daily bread upon such joyful terms. The soldier and the explorer have moments of a worthier excitement, but they are purchased by cruel hardships and periods of tedium that beggar language. In the life of the artist there need be no hour without its pleasure. I take the author, with whose career I am best acquainted; and it is true he works in a rebellious material, and that the act of writing is cramped and trying both to the eyes and the temper; but remark him in his study, when matter crowds upon him and words are not wanting—in what a continual series of small successes time flows by; with what a sense of power as of one moving mountains, he marshals his petty characters; with what pleasures both of the ear and eye, he sees his airy structure growing on the page; and how he labors in a craft to which the whole material of his life is tributary, and which opens a door to all his tastes, his loves, his hatreds and his convictions, so that what he writes is only what he longed to utter. He may have enjoyed many things in this big, tragic playground of the world; but what shall he have enjoyed more fully than a morning of successful work? Suppose it ill paid: the wonder is it should be paid at all. Other men pay, and pay dearly, for pleasures less desirable.

Nor will the practice of art afford you pleasure only; it affords besides an admirable training. For the artist works entirely upon honor. The public knows little or nothing of those merits in the quest of which you are condemned to spend the bulk of your endeavors. Merits of design, the merit of first-hand energy, the merit of a certain cheap accomplishment which a man of the artistic temper easily acquires—these they can recognize, and these they value. But to those more exquisite refinements of proficiency and finish, which the artist so ardently desires and so keenly feels, for which (in the vigorous words of Balzac) he must toil "like a miner buried in a landslip,"[2] for which, day after day, he recasts and revises and rejects—the gross mass of the public must be ever blind. To those lost pains, suppose you attain the highest pitch of merit, posterity may possibly do justice; suppose, as is so probable, you fail by even a hair's breadth of the highest, rest certain they shall never be observed. Under the shadow of this cold thought, alone in his studio, the artist must preserve from day to day his constancy to the ideal. It is this which makes his life noble; it is by this that the practice of his craft strengthens and matures his character; it is for this that even the serious countenance of the great emperor[3] was turned approvingly (if only for a moment) on the followers of Apollo,[4] and that sternly gentle voice bade the artist cherish his art.

And here there fall two warnings to be made. And first, if you are to continue to be a law to yourself, you must beware of the first signs of laziness. This idealism in honesty can only be supported by perpetual effort; the standard is easily lowered, the artist who says "*It will do*," is on the downward path; three or four pot-boilers[5] are enough at times (above all at wrong times) to falsify a talent, and by the practice of journalism a man runs the risk of becoming wedded to cheap finish. This is the danger on the one side; there is not less upon the other. The consciousness of how much the artist is (and must be) a law to himself, debauches the small heads. Perceiving recondite merits very hard to attain, making or swallowing artistic formulæ, or perhaps falling in love with some particular proficiency of his own, many artists forget the end of all art: to please. It is doubtless tempting to exclaim against the ignorant bourgeois; yet it should not be forgotten, it is he who is to pay us, and that (surely on the face of it) for services that he shall desire to have performed. Here also, if properly considered, there is a question of transcendental honesty. To give the public what they do not want, and yet expect to be supported: we have there a strange pretension, and yet not uncommon, above all with painters. The first duty in this world is for a man to pay his way; when that is quite accomplished, he may plunge into what eccentricity he likes; but emphatically not till then. Till then, he must pay assiduous court to the bourgeois who carries the purse. And if in the course of these capitulations he shall falsify his talent, it can never have been a strong one, and he will have preserved a better thing than talent—character. Or if he be of a mind so independent that he cannot stoop to this necessity, one course is yet open: he can desist from art, and follow some more manly way of life.

I speak of a more manly way of life, it is a point on which I must be frank. To live by a pleasure is not a high calling; it involves patronage, however veiled; it numbers the artist, however ambitious, along with dancing girls and billiard markers. The French have a romantic evasion for one employment, and call its practitioners the Daughters of Joy.[6] The artist is of the same family, he is of the Sons of Joy, chose his trade to please himself, gains his livelihood by pleasing others, and has parted with something of the sterner dignity of man. Journals but a little while ago declaimed against the Tennyson peerage;[7] and this Son of Joy was blamed for condescension when he followed the example of Lord Lawrence and Lord Cairns and Lord Clyde.[8] The poet was more happily inspired; with a better modesty he accepted the high honor; and anonymous journalists have not yet (if I am to believe them) recovered the vicarious disgrace to their profession. When it comes to their turn, these gentlemen can do themselves more justice; and I shall be glad to think of it; for to my barbarian eyesight, even Lord Tennyson looks somewhat out of place in that assembly. There should be no honors for the artist; he has already, in the practice of his art, more than his share of the rewards of life; the honors are pre-empted for other trades, more laborious and perhaps more useful.

But the devil in these trades of pleasing is to fail to please. In ordinary occupations, a man offers to do a certain thing or to produce a certain article with a merely conventional accomplishment, a design in which (we may almost say) it is difficult to fail. But the artist steps forth out of the crowd and proposes to delight: an impudent design, in which it is impossible to fail without odious circumstances. The poor Daughter of Joy, carrying her smiles and finery quite unregarded through the crowd, makes a figure which it is impossible to recall without a wounding pity. She is the type of the unsuccessful artist. The actor, the dancer, and the singer must appear like her in person, and drain publicly the cup of failure. But though the rest of us escape this crowning bitterness of the pillory, we all court in essence the same humiliation. We all profess to be able to delight. And how few of us are! We all pledge ourselves to be able to continue to delight. And the day will come to each, and even to the most admired, when the ardor shall have declined and the cunning shall be lost, and he shall sit by his deserted booth ashamed. Then shall he see himself condemned to do work for which he blushes to take payment. Then (as if his lot were not already cruel) he must lie exposed to the gibes of the wreckers of the press, who earn a little bitter bread by the condemnation of trash which they have not read, and the praise of excellence which they cannot understand.

And observe that this seems almost the necessary end at least of writers. *Les Blancs et les Bleus* (for instance) is of an order of merit very different from *Le Vicomte de Bragelonne*; *Denis Duval* is not written with the pen of *Esmond*; and if any gentleman can bear to spy upon the nakedness of *Castle Dangerous*, his name I think is Ham: let it be enough for the rest of us to read of it (not without tears) in the pages of Lockhart.[9] Thus in old age, when occupation and comfort are most needful, the writer must lay aside at once his pastime and his breadwinner. The painter indeed, if he succeed at all in engaging the attention of the public, gains great sums and can stand to his easel until a great age without dishonorable failure. The writer has the double misfortune to be ill-paid while he can work, and to be incapable of working when he is old. It is thus a way of life which conducts directly to a false position.

For the writer (in spite of notorious examples to the contrary) must look to be ill-paid. Tennyson and Montépin[10] make handsome livelihoods; but we cannot all hope to be Tennyson, and we do not all perhaps desire to be Montépin. If you adopt an art to be your trade, weed your mind at the outset of all desire of money. What you may decently expect, if you have some talent and much industry, is such an income as a clerk will earn with a tenth or perhaps a twentieth of your nervous output. Nor have you the right to look for more; in the wages of the life, not in the wages of the trade, lies your reward; the work is here the wages. It will be seen I have little sympathy with the common lamentations of the artist class. Perhaps they do not remember the hire of the field laborer;[11] or do they think no parallel will lie? Perhaps they have never observed what is the retiring allowance of a field officer; or do they suppose their contributions to the arts of pleasing more important than the services of a colonel? Perhaps they forget on how little Millet was content to live;[12] or do they think, because they have less genius, they stand excused from the display of equal virtues? But upon one point there should be no dubiety: if a man be not frugal, he has no business in the arts. If he be not frugal, he steers directly for that last tragic scene of *le vieux saltimbanque*;[13] if he be not frugal, he will find it hard to continue to be honest. Some day, when the butcher is knocking at the door, he may be tempted, he may be obliged, to turn out and sell a slovenly piece of work. If the obligation shall have arisen through no wantonness of his own, he is even to be commended; for words cannot describe how far more necessary it is that a man should support his family, than that he should attain to—or preserve—distinction in the arts. But if the pressure comes through his own fault, he has stolen, and stolen under trust, and stolen (which is the worst of all) in such a way that no law can reach him.

And now you may perhaps ask me, if the debutant artist is to have no thought of money, and if (as is implied) he is to expect no honors from the State, he may not at least look forward to the delights of popularity? Praise, you will tell me, is a savory dish. And in so far as you may mean the countenance of other artists, you would put your finger on one of the most essential and enduring pleasures of the career of art. But in so far as you should have an eye to the commendations of the public or the notice of the newspapers, be sure you would but be cherishing a dream. It is true that in certain esoteric journals the author (for instance) is duly criticised, and that he is often praised a great deal more than he deserves, sometimes for qualities which he prided himself on eschewing, and sometimes by ladies and gentlemen who have denied themselves the privilege of reading his work. But if a man be sensitive to this wild praise, we must suppose him equally alive to that which often accompanies and always follows it—wild ridicule. A man may have done well for years, and then he may fail; he will hear of his failure. Or he may have done well for years, and still do well, but the critics may have tired of praising him, or there may have sprung up some new idol of the instant, some "dust a little gilt,"[14] to whom they now prefer to offer sacrifice. I will be very bold and take a modern instance. A little while ago the name of Mr. Howells[15] was in every paper coupled with just laudations. And now it is the pleasure of the same journalists to pursue him daily with ineffective quips. Here is the obverse and the reverse of that empty and ugly thing called popularity. Will any man suppose it worth the gaining? Must not any man perceive that the reward of Mr. Howells lies in the practice of his fine and solid art, not in the perusal of paragraphs which are conceived in a spirit to-day of ignorant worship, and to-morrow of stupid injustice?

Notes

1 The art of arts: logic (Latin).
2 Balzac, *Cousin Bette* (1846).
3 Augustus (63 BC–19 AD), praised by Virgil and Horace.
4 Poets.
5 Works intended for profit rather than artistic merit.
6 Prostitutes.
7 Alfred Tennyson (1809–1892) was named Poet Laureate in 1850 and accepted the title of Baron from Queen Victoria in 1884 after declining it twice.
8 Lord John Lawrence (1811–1879), former Viceroy of India, was made a Baron in 1869; Lord Hugh McCalmont Cairns (1819–1885), Conservative politician, made Baron in 1867 and Viscount in 1878; Colin Campbell, Lord Clyde (1792–1863), British Field Marshal, made Baron in 1858.
9 Alexandre Dumas's novels *The Whites and the Blues* (1867) and *The Vicomte of Bragelonne: Ten Years Later* (1850). See Stevenson's essay "A Gossip on a Novel of Dumas's" (1887). William Makepeace Thackeray's novels *The History of Henry Esmond* (1852) and his final unfinished work *Denis Duval* (1863). Walter Scott's last, and arguably weakest, novel *Castle Dangerous* (1831). After Ham told his brothers that he had discovered his father, Noah, drunk and naked, his seed was cursed (Genesis 9:20–27). John Gibson Lockhart (1794–1854), Scott's son-in-law whose *Life of Sir*

Walter Scott (1837–39) describes the aging novelist's cognitive decline while writing *Castle Dangerous*.

10 Xavier de Montépin (1823–1902), popular French novelist.

11 In Christ's parable, the lord of the vineyard hires laborers throughout the day and pays them all equally, regardless of time worked (Matthew 20:1–16).

12 Jean-François Millet (1814–1875), French landscape painter of the Barbizon School.

13 Baudelaire's posthumously published prose-poem "Le vieux saltimbanque" (1869) ("The Old Mountebank") compares an old peddler of quack remedies to a forgotten artist too dependent on public approbation.

14 Shakespeare, *Troilus and Cressida*, 3.3.175–78.

15 William Dean Howells (1837–1920), an American novelist whose fiction shifted from comedies of manners to realistic portrayals of ethical dilemmas. Howells criticized Stevenson's romance fiction in print in *Harpers Monthly*, and Stevenson declined an opportunity to meet Howells with Fanny based on Howells's representation of divorce in *A Modern Instance* (1882).

37

PULVIS ET UMBRA[1]

We look for some reward of our endeavors and are disappointed; not success, not happiness, not even peace of conscience, crowns our ineffectual efforts to do well. Our frailties are invincible, our virtues barren; the battle goes sore against us to the going down of the sun.[2] The canting moralist tells us of right and wrong; and we look abroad, even on the face of our small earth, and find them change with every climate, and no country where some action is not honored for a virtue and none where it is not branded for a vice; and we look in our experience, and find no vital congruity in the wisest rules, but at the best a municipal fitness. It is not strange if we are tempted to despair of good. We ask too much. Our religions and moralities have been trimmed to flatter us, till they are all emasculate and sentimentalized, and only please and weaken. Truth is of a rougher strain. In the harsh face of life, faith can read a bracing gospel. The human race is a thing more ancient than the ten commandments; and the bones and revolutions of the Kosmos, in whose joints we are but moss and fungus, more ancient still.

I

Of the Kosmos in the last resort, science reports many doubtful things and all of them appalling. There seems no substance to this solid globe on which we stamp: nothing but symbols and ratios. Symbols and ratios carry us and bring us forth and beat us down; gravity that swings the incommensurable suns and worlds through space, is but a figment varying inversely as the squares of distances; and the suns and worlds themselves, imponderable figures of arithmetic, NH_3 and H_2O.[3] Consideration dares not dwell upon this view; that way madness lies;[4] science carries us into zones of speculation, where there is no habitable city for the mind of man.

But take the Kosmos with a grosser faith, as our senses give it us. We behold space sown with rotatory islands, suns and worlds and the shards and wrecks of systems: some, like the sun, still blazing; some rotting, like the earth; others, like the moon, stable in desolation. All of these we take to be made of something we call matter: a thing which no analysis can help us to conceive; to whose incredible properties, no familiarity can reconcile our minds. This stuff, when not purified by the lustration of fire, rots uncleanly into something we call life; seized through all

291

its atoms with a pediculous malady; swelling in tumors that become independent, sometimes even (by an abhorrent prodigy) locomotory; one splitting into millions, millions cohering into one, as the malady proceeds through varying stages. This vital putrescence of the dust, used as we are to it, yet strikes us with occasional disgust, and the profusion of worms in a piece of ancient turf, or the air of a marsh darkened with insects, will sometimes check our breathing so that we aspire for cleaner places. But none is clean: the moving sand is infected with lice; the pure spring, where it bursts out of the mountain, is a mere issue of worms; even in the hard rock, the crystal is forming.

In two main shapes this eruption covers the countenance of the earth: the animal and the vegetable: one in some degree the inversion of the other: the second rooted to the spot; the first coming detached out of its natal mud, and scurrying abroad with the myriad feet of insects or towering into heaven upon the wings of birds: a thing so inconceivable that, if it be well considered, the heart stops. To what passes with the anchored vermin, we have little clue: doubtless they have their joys and sorrows, their delights and killing agonies: it appears not how. But of the locomotory, to which we ourselves belong, we can tell more. These share with us a thousand miracles: the miracles of sight, of hearing, of the projection of sound, things that bridge space; the miracles of memory and reason, by which the present is conceived, and when it is gone, its image kept living in the brains of man and brute; the miracle of reproduction, with its imperious desires and staggering consequences. And to put the last touch upon this mountain mass of the revolting and the inconceivable, all these prey upon each other, tearing them in pieces, cramming them inside themselves, and by that summary process, growing fat: the vegetarian, the whale, perhaps the tree, not less than the lion of the desert; for the vegetarian is only the eater of the dumb.

Meanwhile our rotatory island loaded with viticidal life, and more drenched with blood, both animal and vegetable, than ever mutinied ship, scuds through space with unimaginable speed, and turns alternate cheeks to the reverberation of a blazing world, ninety million miles away.

II

What a monstrous spectre is this man, the disease of the agglutinated dust, lifting alternate feet or lying drugged with slumber; killing, feeding, growing, bringing forth small copies of himself; grown upon with hair like grass, fitted with eyes that move and glitter in his face; a thing to set children screaming;—and yet looked at nearlier, known as his fellows know him, how surprising are his attributes! Poor soul, here for so little, cast among so many hardships, filled with desires so incommensurate and so inconsistent, savagely surrounded, savagely fathered, irremediably condemned to prey upon his fellow lives: who should have blamed him had he been of a piece with his destiny and a being merely barbarous? And we look abroad and behold him instead filled with imperfect virtues: infinitely childish, often admirably valiant, often touchingly kind; sitting down, amidst his

292

momentary life, to debate of right and wrong and the attributes of deity; rising up to do battle for an egg or die for an idea; singling out his friends and his mate with the most cordial affection; bringing forth in pain, and rearing with long-suffering solicitude, his young. To touch at once the heart of his mystery, we find in him one thought, strange to the point of lunacy: the thought of duty; the thought of something owing to himself, to his neighbor, to his God: an ideal of decency, to which he would rise if it were possible; a limit of shame, below which, if it be possible, he will not stoop. The design in most men is one of conformity; here and there, in picked natures, it transcends itself and soars on the other side, arming martyrs with independence; but in all, in their degrees, it is a bosom thought:—Not in man alone, for we trace it in dogs and cats whom we know fairly well, and doubtless the like point of honor sways the elephant, the oyster and the louse, of whom we know so little:—But in man, at least, it sways with so complete an empire that merely selfish things come second, even with the selfish: that appetites are starved, fears conquered, pains supported; that almost the dullest shrinks from the reproval of a glance, although it were a child's; and all but the most cowardly stand their ground amid the risks of war; and the more noble, having strongly conceived an act as due to their ideal, affront and embrace death. Strange enough if, with their singular origin and perverted practice, they think rewards attend them in some future life: stranger still, if they are persuaded of the contrary, and think this blow, which they solicit, will strike them senseless for eternity. I shall be reminded what a tragedy of mis-conception and mis-conduct man at large presents: of organized injustice, cowardly violence and treacherous crime; and of the damning imperfections of the best. They cannot be too darkly drawn. Man is indeed marked for failure in his efforts to do right. But where the best consistently mis-carry, how tenfold more remarkable that all should continue to strive: and surely we should find it both touching and inspiriting, that in a field from which success is banished, the labors of our race should not be stayed.

If the first view of this creature, stalking in his rotatory isle, be a thing to shake the courage of the stoutest, on this nearer sight, he startles us with an admiring wonder. It matters not where we look, under what climate we observe him, in what stage of society, in what depth of ignorance, burthened with what erroneous morality: in the Navigator Islands[5], crowned with flowers and fabricating proverbs; by campfires in Assiniboia, the snow powdering his shoulders, the wind plucking his blanket, as he sits, passing the ceremonial calumet[6] and uttering his grave opinions like a Roman senator; in ships at sea, a man inured to hardship and vile pleasures, his brightest hope a fiddle in a tavern and a bedizened trull who sells herself to rob him, and he for all that simple, innocent, cheerful, kindly like a child, constant to toil, brave to drown, for others; in the slums of cities, moving among indifferent millions to mechanical employments, without hope of change in the future, with scarce a pleasure in the present, and yet true to his virtues, honest up to his lights, kind to his neighbors, tempted perhaps in vain by the bright gin-palace, perhaps long-suffering with the drunken wife that ruins him; in India (a woman this time) kneeling with broken cries and streaming tears, as she drowns her infant in the sacred river;[7] in the brothel, the discard of society, living mainly on strong drink, fed with affronts, a fool, a thief, the comrade of thieves, and even here keeping the point of honour and the touch of pity[8], often repaying the world's scorn with service, often standing firm upon a scruple, and at a certain cost, rejecting riches:—everywhere some virtue cherished or affected, everywhere some decency of thought and carriage, everywhere the ensign of man's ineffectual goodness:—ah! if I could show you this! if I could show these men and women, all the world over, in every stage of history, under every abuse of error, under every circumstance of failure, without hope, without help, without thanks, still obscurely fighting the lost fight of virtue, still clinging, in the brothel or on the scaffold, to some rag of honor, the poor jewel of their souls! They may seek to escape, and yet they cannot; it is not alone their privilege and glory, but their doom; they are condemned to some nobility; all their lives long, the desire of good is at their heels, the implacable hunter.

Of all earth's meteors, here at least is the most strange and consoling: that this ennobled lemur, this hair-crowned bubble of the dust, this inheritor of a few years and sorrows, should yet deny himself his rare delights, and add to his frequent pains, and live for an ideal, however mis-conceived. Nor can we stop with man. A new doctrine, received with screams a little while ago by canting moralists, and still not properly worked into the body of our thoughts,[9] lights us a step further into the heart of this rough but noble universe. For nowadays the pride of man denies in vain his kinship with the original dust. He stands no longer like a thing apart. Close at his heels we see the dog, prince of another genus: and in him too, we see dumbly testified the same cultus of an unattainable ideal, the same constancy in failure. Does it stop with the dog? We look at our feet where the ground is blackened with the swarming ant: a creature so small, so far from us in the hierarchy of brutes, that we can scarce trace and scarce comprehend his doings; and here also, in his ordered polities and rigorous justice, we see confessed the law of duty and the fact of individual sin. Does it stop, then, with the ant? Rather this desire of well-doing and this doom of frailty run through all the grades of life: rather is this earth, from the frosty top of Everest to the next margin of the internal fire, one stage of ineffectual virtues and one temple of pious tears and perseverance. The whole creation groaneth and travaileth together.[10] It is the common and the god-like law of life. The browsers, the biters, the barkers, the hairy coats of field and forest, the squirrel in the oak, the thousand footed scourer of the dust, as they share with us the gift of life, share with us the love of an ideal: strive like us—like us are tempted to grow weary of the struggle—to do well; like us receive at times unmerited refreshment, visitings of support, returns of courage; and are like us condemned to be crucified between that double law of the members and the will.[11] Are they like us, I wonder, in the timid hope of some reward, some sugar with the wholesome drug? do they, too, stand aghast at unrewarded virtues, at the sufferings of those whom, in our partiality, we take to be just, and the prosperity of such as, in our blindness, we call wicked? It may be; and yet God knows what they should look for. Even while they look, even while they repent, the foot of man treads them by thousands in the dust, the yelping hounds burst upon their trail, the bullet speeds, the knives are heating in the den of the vivisectionist; or the dew falls, and the generation of a day is blotted out. For these are creatures, compared with whom our weakness is consummate strength, our ignorance perfect wisdom, our brief span eternity.

And as we dwell, we living things, in our isle of terror and under the imminent hand of death, God forbid it should be man the erected, the reasoner, the wise in his own eyes—God forbid it should be man that wearies in well doing, that despairs of unrewarded effort, or utters the language of complaint.[12] Let it be enough for faith, that the whole creation groans in mortal frailty, strives with unconquerable constancy: Surely not all in vain.[13]

Notes

1 From Horace: "pulvis et umbra sumus": we are dust and ashes (*Odes* 4.7.16). Stevenson called this essay a "Darwinian sermon" (*Letters* 6.60).
2 Joshua 10:27.
3 Chemical formulas for ammonia and water.
4 Shakespeare, *King Lear*, 3.4.21.
5 Samoa
6 Native American ceremonial pipe.
7 Ritual infant sacrifice in India's sacred Ganga River.
8 Shakespeare, *Richard III*, 1.2.71.
9 Human evolution by natural selection.
10 Romans 8:22.
11 Stevenson describes "the perennial war among [the] members" in *Strange Case of Dr. Jekyll and Mr. Hyde* published two years earlier.
12 Galatians 6:9.
13 Paul Maixner identifies an allusion to Edward Fitzgerald's Rubáiyát of Omar Khayyám (1859): "Surely not in vain / My Substance from the common Earth was ta'en" (390).

38

A CHRISTMAS SERMON

By the time this paper appears, I shall have been talking for twelve months; and it is thought I should take my leave in a formal and seasonable manner.[1] Valedictory eloquence is rare. Even death-bed sayings have not often hit the mark of the occasion; and perhaps there are but three that may be profitably cited. Charles Second, wit and sceptic, a man whose life had been one long lesson in human incredulity, an easy-going comrade, a manœuvring king—remembered and embodied all his wit and scepticism along with more than his usual good humor in the famous "I am afraid, gentlemen, I am an unconscionable time a-dying." Marcus Aurelius in that last passage did not forget that he was Cæsar: "*Vale vobis dico, vos precedens.*"[2] And there is yet another passing-word: "Father, forgive them, for they know not what they do."[3]

I

The attitude and the words of Charles Second are what best become humanity. An unconscionable time a-dying—there is the picture ("I am afraid, gentlemen,") of your life and of mine. The sands run out, and the hours are "numbered and imputed," and the days go by; and when the last of these finds us, we have been a long time dying, and what else? The very length is something, if we reach that hour of separation undishonored; and to have lived at all is doubtless (in the soldierly expression) to have served. There is a tale in Tacitus of how the veterans mutinied in the German wilderness; of how they mobbed Germanicus, clamoring to go home; and of how, seizing their general's hand, these old, war-worn exiles passed his finger along their toothless gums.[4] *Sunt lacrymæ rerum*[5]: this was the most eloquent of the songs of Simeon.[6] And when a man has lived to a fair age, he bears his marks of service. He may have never been remarked upon the breach at the head of the army; at least he shall have lost his teeth on the camp bread.

The idealism of serious people in this age of ours is of a noble character. It never seems to them that they have served enough; they have a fine impatience of their virtues. It were perhaps more modest to be singly thankful that we are no worse. It is not only our enemies, those desperate characters—it is we ourselves who know not what we do;—thence springs the glimmering hope that perhaps we do better than we think: that to scramble through this random business with hands reasonably clean, to have played the part of a man or woman with some reasonable fulness, to have often resisted the diabolic, and at the end to be still resisting it, is for the poor human soldier to have done right well. To ask to see some print of our endeavor is but a transcendental way of serving for reward; and what we take to be contempt of self is only greed of hire.

And again if we require so much of ourselves, shall we not require much of others? If we do not genially judge our own deficiencies, is it not to be feared we shall be even stern to the trespasses of others? And he who (looking back upon his own life) can see no more than that he has been unconscionably long a-dying, will he not be tempted to think his neighbor unconscionably long of getting hanged? It is probable that nearly all who think of conduct at all think of it too much; it is certain we all think too much of sin. We are not damned for doing wrong, but for not doing right; Christ would never hear of negative morality; *thou shalt* was ever his word, with which he superseded *thou shalt not*. To make our idea of morality centre on forbidden acts is to defile the imagination and to introduce into our judgments of our fellow-men a secret element of gusto. If a thing is wrong for us, we should not dwell upon the thought of it; or we shall soon dwell upon it with inverted pleasure. If we cannot drive it from our minds—one thing of two: Either our creed is in the wrong and we must more indulgently remodel it; or else, if our morality be in the right, we are criminal lunatics and should place our persons in restraint. A mark of such unwholesomely divided minds is the passion for interference with others: the Fox without the Tail was of this breed, but had (if his biographer is to be trusted) a certain antique civility now out of date.[7] A man may have a flaw, a weakness, that unfits him for the duties of life, that spoils his temper, that threatens his integrity, or that betrays him into cruelty. It has to be conquered; but it must never be suffered to engross his thoughts. The true duties lie all upon the farther side, and must be attended to with a whole mind so soon as this preliminary clearing of the decks has been effected. In order that he may be kind and honest, it may be needful he should become a total abstainer; let him become so then, and the next day let him forget the circumstance. Trying to be kind and honest will require all his thoughts; a mortified appetite is never a wise companion; in so far as he has had to mortify an appetite, he will still be the worse man; and of such an one a great deal of cheerfulness will be required in judging life, and a great deal of humility in judging others.

It may be argued again that dissatisfaction with our life's endeavor springs in some degree from dulness. We require higher tasks, because we do not recognize the height of those we have. Trying to be kind and honest seems an affair too simple and too inconsequential for gentlemen of our heroic mould; we had rather set ourselves to something bold, arduous, and conclusive; we had rather found a schism or suppress a heresy, cut off a hand or mortify an appetite. But the task before us, which is to co-endure with our existence, is rather one of microscopic fineness, and the heroism required is that of patience. There is no cutting of the Gordian knots of life; each must be smilingly unravelled.[8]

To be honest, to be kind—to earn a little and to spend a little less, to make upon the whole a family happier for his presence, to renounce when that shall be necessary and not to be embittered, to keep a few friends but these without capitulation—above all, on the same grim condition, to keep friends with himself—here is a task for all that a man has of fortitude and delicacy. He has an ambitious soul who would ask more; he has a hopeful spirit who should look in such an enterprise to be successful. There is indeed one element in human destiny that not blindness itself can controvert: whatever else we are intended to do, we are not intended to succeed; failure is the fate allotted. It is so in every art and study; it is so above all in the continent art of living well. Here is a pleasant thought for the year's end or for the end of life: Only self-deception will be satisfied, and there need be no despair for the despairer.

II

But Christmas is not only the mile-mark of another year, moving us to thoughts of self-examination: it is a season, from all its associations, whether domestic or religious, suggesting thoughts of joy. A man dissatisfied with his endeavors is a man tempted to sadness. And in the midst of the winter, when his life runs lowest and he is reminded of the empty chairs of his beloved, it is well he should be condemned to this fashion of the smiling face. Noble disappointment, noble self-denial are not to be admired, not even to be pardoned, if they bring bitterness. It is one thing to enter the kingdom of heaven maim; another to maim yourself and stay without.[9] And the kingdom of heaven is of the childlike, of those who are easy to please, who love and who give pleasure. Mighty men of their hands, the smiters and the builders and the judges, have lived long and done sternly and yet preserved this lovely character; and among our carpet interests and twopenny concerns, the shame were indelible if *we* should lose it. Gentleness and cheerfulness, these come before all morality; they are the perfect duties. And it is the trouble with moral men that they have neither one nor other. It was the moral man, the pharisee, whom Christ could not away with. If your morals make you dreary, depend upon it they are wrong. I do not say "give them up," for they may be all you have; but conceal them like a vice, lest they should spoil the lives of better and simpler people.

A strange temptation attends upon man: to keep his eye on pleasures, even when he will not share in them; to aim all his morals against them. This very year a lady (singular iconoclast!) proclaimed a crusade against dolls;[10] and the racy sermon against lust is quite a feature of the age. I venture to call such moralists insincere. At any excess or perversion of a natural appetite, their lyre sounds of itself with relishing denunciations; but for all displays of the truly diabolic—envy, malice, the mean lie, the mean silence, the calumnious truth, the backbiter, the petty tyrant, the peevish poisoner of family life—their standard is quite different. These are wrong, they will admit, yet somehow not so wrong; there is no zeal in their assault on them, no secret element of gusto warms up the sermon; it is for things not wrong in themselves that they reserve the choicest of their indignation. A man may naturally disclaim all moral kinship with the Reverend Mr. Zola[11] or the hobgoblin old lady of the dolls; for these are gross and naked instances. And yet in each of us some similar element resides. The sight of a pleasure in which we cannot or else will not share moves us to a particular impatience. It may be because we are envious, or because we are sad, or because we dislike noise and romping—being so refined, or because—being so philosophic—we have an over-weighing sense of this life's gravity: at least, as we go on in years, we are all tempted to frown upon our neighbor's pleasures. People are nowadays so fond of resisting temptations; here is one to be resisted. They are fond of self-denial; here is a propensity that cannot be too peremptorily denied. There is an idea abroad among moral people that they should make their neighbors good. One person I have to make good: myself. But my duty to my neighbor is much more nearly expressed by saying that I have to make him happy—if I may.

III

Happiness and goodness, according to canting moralists, stand in the relation of effect and cause. There was never anything less proved or less probable: our happiness is never in our own hands; we inherit our constitution; we stand buffet among friends and enemies; we may be so built as to feel a sneer or an aspersion with unusual keenness, and so circumstanced as to be unusually exposed to them; we may have nerves very sensitive to pain, and be afflicted with a disease very painful. Virtue will not help us, and it is not meant to help us. It is not even its own reward, except for the self-centred and—I had almost said—the unamiable. No man can pacify his conscience; if quiet be what he want, he shall do better to let that organ perish from disuse. And to avoid the penalties of the law, and the minor *capitis diminutio*[12] of social ostracism, is an affair of wisdom—of cunning, if you will—and not of virtue.

In his own life, then, a man is not to expect happiness, only to profit by it gladly when it shall arise. He is on duty here; he knows not how or why, and does not need to know; he knows not for what hire, and must not ask. Somehow or other, though he does not know what goodness is, he must try to be good; somehow or other, though he cannot tell what will do it, he must try to give happiness to others. And no doubt there comes in here a frequent clash of duties. How far is he to make his neighbor happy? How far must he respect that smiling face, so easy to cloud, so hard to brighten again? And how far, on the other side, is he bound to be his brother's keeper[13] and the prophet of his own morality? How far must he resent evil?

The difficulty is that we have little guidance; Christ's sayings on the point being hard to reconcile with each other, and (the most of them) hard to accept. But the truth of his teaching would seem to be this: in our own person and fortune, we should be ready to accept and to pardon all; it is *our* cheek we are to turn, *our* coat that we are to give away to the man who has taken *our* cloak.[14] But when another's face is buffeted, perhaps a little of the lion will become us best. That we are to suffer others to be injured, and stand by, is not conceivable and surely not desirable. Revenge, says Bacon, is a kind of wild justice; its judgments at least are delivered by an insane judge, and in our own quarrel we can see nothing truly and do nothing wisely.[15] But in the quarrel of our neighbor, let us be more bold. One person's happiness is as sacred as another's; when we cannot defend both, let us defend one with a stout heart. It is only in so far as we are doing this, that we have any right to interfere: the defence of B is our only ground of action against A. A has as good a right to go to the devil, as we to go to glory; and neither knows what he does.

The truth is that all these interventions and denunciations and militant mongerings of moral half-truths, though they be sometimes needful, though they are often enjoyable, do yet belong to an inferior grade of duties. Ill temper and envy and revenge find here an arsenal of pious disguises; this is the playground of inverted lusts. With a little more patience and a little less temper, a gentler and wiser method might be found in almost every case; and the knot that we cut by some fine heady quarrel-scene in private life, or, in public affairs, by some denunciatory act against what we are pleased to call our neighbor's vices, might yet have been unwoven by the hand of sympathy.

IV

To look back upon the past year, and see how little we have striven and to what small purpose; and how often we have been cowardly and hung back, or temerarious and rushed unwisely in; and how every day and all day long we have transgressed the law of kindness;—it may seem a paradox, but in the bitterness of these discoveries, a certain consolation resides. Life is not designed to minister to a man's vanity. He goes upon his long business most of the time with a hanging head, and all the time like a blind child. Full of rewards and pleasures as it is—so that to see the day break or the moon rise, or to meet a friend, or to hear the dinner-call when he is hungry, fills him with surprising joys—this world is yet for him no abiding city. Friendships fall through, health fails, weariness assails him; year after year, he must thumb the hardly varying record of his own weakness and folly. It is a friendly process of detachment. When the time comes that he should go, there need be few illusions left about himself. *Here lies one who meant well, tried a little, failed much:*—surely that may be his epitaph, of which he need not be ashamed. Nor will he complain at the summons which calls a defeated soldier from the field: defeated, ay, if he were Paul or Marcus Aurelius![16]—but if there is still one inch of fight in his old spirit, undishonored. The faith which sustained him in his life-long blindness and life-long disappointment will scarce even be required in this last formality of laying down his arms. Give him a march[17] with his old bones; there, out of the glorious sun-colored earth, out of the day and the dust and the ecstasy—there goes another Faithful Failure!

From a recent book of verse, where there is more than one such beautiful and manly poem, I take this memorial piece: it says better than I can, what I love to think; let it be our parting word.

A late lark twitters from the quiet skies;
And from the west,
Where the sun, his day's work ended,
Lingers as in content,
There falls on the old, gray city
An influence luminous and serene,
A shining peace.

The smoke ascends
In a rosy-and-golden haze. The spires
Shine, and are changed. In the valley
Shadows rise. The lark sings on. The sun,
Closing his benediction,
Sinks, and the darkening air
Thrills with a sense of the triumphing night—
Night, with her train of stars
And her great gift of sleep.

So be my passing!
My task accomplished and the long day done,
My wages taken, and in my heart
Some late lark singing,
Let me be gathered to the quiet west,
The sundown splendid and serene,
Death.[18]

Notes

1 Published in Dec. 1888, "A Christmas Sermon" was the last of 12 essays Stevenson published in a monthly series for *Scribner's Magazine* that year.
2 Stevenson quotes the final sentence of Marcus Aurelius's Stoic reflection on death at the end of his *Meditations*: "Why then should it be grievous unto thee, if . . . the same nature that brought thee in, doth now send thee out of the world? . . . Go thy ways then well pleased and contented: for so is He that dismisseth thee."
3 Christ's words on the cross (Luke 23:34).
4 Tacitus, *The Annals of Imperial Rome* (1. ch. 2).
5 "There are tears for things" or there is pity for misfortune (Virgil, *The Aeneid* 1.462).
6 "Lord, now lettest thou thy servant depart in peace, according to thy word" (Luke 2:29).
7 From *Aesop's Fables*. After losing his own tail in a trap, the fox tries to convince the other foxes of the dangers of tails, encouraging them to cut theirs off.

8 Gordian knot: a proverbial term for a complex problem requiring bold action, which comes from an account of Alexander the Great (356–323 BC) in Gordion on his march through Anatolia. The chariot of the city's ancient founder, Gordius, was tied to a pole by an intricate knot with hidden ends. Tradition held that only the future conqueror of Asia could untie it, and Alexander sliced through the knot with his sword.

9 Matthew 18:8.

10 Frances Willard (1839–1898), American educator, reformer, suffragette, and president of the Woman's Christian Temperance Union. She argued in her pamphlet "Dress and Vice" that "wretched, heathenish dolls" help socialize girls into a superficial focus on beauty. The magazine *Babyhood* ran a quotation in March of 1888, which was reprinted in many periodicals, along with a host of disparaging letters in response. Willard later clarified her position distinguishing "simple, modest, 'old-fashioned'" dolls from fancy French dolls, arguing that boys and girls should play with the same toys and that boys needed to cultivate parental instincts more than girls (*Babyhood,* vol. 9, no. 40, p. 126; no. 47, pp. 345–346).

11 Émile Zola's 1887 novel *Le Terre* (The Soil) is one of the most graphically violent and sexually explicit books of the century. The novel's English translator, Henry Vizetelly, was imprisoned for obscenity.

12 "Diminished capacity" in Roman law: a lowering of a person's legal or social status.

13 Genesis 4:9.

14 Matthew 5:39–40.

15 From the opening lines of Francis Bacon's fourth essay "On Revenge" in *Essayes or Counsels, Civill and Morall* (1625).

16 Probably a reference to Paul's statement, "For the good that I would I do not: but the evil which I would not, that I do" (Romans 7:19). In his *Meditations*, Marcus Aurelius seeks to combat his own faults and acknowledges the distance between his conduct and Stoic beliefs: "it is clear to many others and to you yourself that you are far from philosophy. . . . For your experience tells you how much you have strayed" (VIII.I).

17 Military funeral procession.

18 William Ernest Henley's "Margaritæ Sorori" from *A Book of Verses* (1888).

UNCOLLECTED PUBLISHED ESSAYS

39

ROADS

No amateur will deny that he can find more pleasure in a single drawing, over which he can sit a whole quiet forenoon and so gradually study himself into humour with the artist, than he can ever extract from the dazzle and accumulation of incongruous impressions that send him, weary and stupefied, out of some famous picture-gallery. But what is thus admitted with regard to art, is not extended to the (so-called) natural beauties: no amount of excess in sublime mountain outline or the graces of cultivated lowland can do anything, it is supposed, to weaken or degrade the palate. We are not at all sure, however, that moderation, and a regimen tolerably austere, even in scenery, are not healthful and strengthening to the taste; and that the best school for a lover of nature is not to be found in one of those countries where there is no stage effect—nothing salient or sudden; but a quiet spirit of orderly and harmonious beauty pervades all the details, so that we can patiently attend to each of the little touches that strike in us, all of them together, the subdued note of the landscape. It is in scenery such as this that we find ourselves in the right temper to seek out small sequestered lovelinesses. The constant recurrence of similar combinations of colour and outline gradually forces upon us a sense of how the harmony has been built up, and we become familiar with something of nature's mannerism. This is the true pleasure of your "rural voluptuary,"[1]—not to remain awe-stricken before a Mount Chimborazo;[2] not to sit deafened over the big drum in the orchestra, but day by day to teach himself some new beauty—to experience some new vague and tranquil sensation that has before evaded him. It is not the people who "have pined and hungered after nature many a year, in the great city pent," as Coleridge said in the poem that made Charles Lamb so much ashamed of himself[3]—it is not those who make the greatest progress in this intimacy with her, or who are most quick to see and have the greatest gusto to enjoy. In this, as in everything else, it is minute knowledge and long-continued loving industry that make the true dilettante. A man must have thought much over scenery before he begins fully to enjoy it. It is no youngling enthusiasm on hill-tops that can possess itself of the last essence of beauty. Probably most people's heads are growing bare before they can see all in a landscape that they have the capability of seeing; and, even then, it will be only for one little moment of consummation before the faculties are again on the decline, and they that look out of the windows begin to be darkened and restrained in sight. Thus the study of nature should be carried forward thoroughly and with system. Every gratification should be rolled long under the tongue, and we should be always eager to analyse and compare, in order that we may be able to give some plausible reason for our admirations. True, it is difficult to put even approximately into words the kind of feelings thus called into play. There is a dangerous vice inherent in any such intellectual refining upon vague sensation. The analysis of such satisfactions lends itself very readily to literary affectations; and we can all think of instances where it has shown itself apt to exercise a morbid influence, even upon an author's choice of language and the turn of his sentences. And yet there is much that makes the attempt attractive; for any expression, however imperfect, once given to a cherished feeling, seems a sort of legitimation of the pleasure we take in it. A common sentiment is one of those great goods that make life palatable and ever new. The knowledge that another has felt as we have felt, and seen things, even if they are little things, not much otherwise than we have seen them, will continue to the end to be one of life's choicest pleasures.

Let the reader, then, betake himself in the spirit we have recommended to some of the quieter kinds of English landscape. In those homely and placid agricultural districts, familiarity will bring into relief many things worthy of notice, and urge them pleasantly home to him by a sort of loving repetition; such as the wonderful life-giving speed of windmill sails above the stationary country; the occurrence and recurrence of the same church tower at the end of one long vista after another: and, conspicuous among these sources of quiet pleasure, the character and variety of the road itself, along which he takes his way. Not only near at hand, in the lithe contortions with which it adapts itself to the interchanges of level and slope, but far away also, when he sees a few hundred feet of it upheaved against a hill and shining in the afternoon sun, he will find it an object so changeful and enlivening, that he can always pleasurably busy his mind about it. He may leave the river-side or fall out of the way of villages, but the road he has always with him; and, in the true humour of observation, will find in that sufficient company. From its subtle windings and changes of level there arises a keen and continuous interest, that keeps the attention ever alert and cheerful. Every sensitive adjustment to the contour of the ground, every little dip and swerve, seems instinct with life and an exquisite sense of balance and beauty. The road rolls upon the easy slope of the country, like a long ship in the hollows of the sea. The very margins of waste ground, as they trench a little further on the beaten way or recede again to the shelter of the hedge, have something of the same free delicacy of line—of the same swing and wilfulness. You might think for a whole summer's day (and not have thought it any nearer an end by evening), what concourse and succession of circumstances has produced the least of these deflections; and it is, perhaps, just in this that we should look for the secret of their interest. A footpath across a meadow—in all its human waywardness and unaccountability, in all the *grata protervitas*[4] of its varying direction—will always be more to us than a railroad, well engineered through a difficult country.[5] No reasoned sequence is thrust upon our attention: we seem to have slipped, for one lawless little moment, out of the iron rule of cause and effect; and so we revert at once to some of the pleasant old heresies of personification, always poetically orthodox, and attribute a sort of free will, an active and spontaneous life, to the white riband of road that lengthens out, and bends, and cunningly adapts itself to the inequalities of the land before our eyes. We remember, as we write, some miles of fine wide highway laid out with conscious æsthetic artifice through a broken and richly-cultivated tract of country. It is said that the engineer had Hogarth's line of beauty in his mind, as he laid them down.[6] And the result is striking. One splendid satisfying sweep passes, with easy transition, into another, and there is nothing to trouble or dislocate the strong continuousness of the main line of the road. And yet there is something wanting. There is here no saving imperfection, none of those secondary curves and little trepidations of direction that carry, in natural roads, our curiosity actively along with them. One feels at once that this road has not grown, like a natural road, but has been laboriously made to pattern; and that, while a model may be academically correct in outline, it will always be inanimate and cold. The traveller is also aware of a congruity of mood between himself and the road he travels. We have all seen ways that have wandered into heavy sand near the sea coast, and trail wearily over the dunes like a trodden serpent: here we too must plod forward at a dull, laborious pace; and so a sympathy is preserved between our frame of mind and the expression of the relaxed, heavy curves of the roadway. Such a phenomenon, indeed, our reason might perhaps resolve with a little trouble. We might reflect that the present road had been developed out of a tract spontaneously followed by generations of primitive wayfarers; and might see in its expression a testimony that those generations had been affected at the same ground, one after another, in the same manner as we are affected to-day. Or we might carry the reflection further, and remind ourselves that where the air is invigorating and the ground firm under the traveller's foot, his eye is quick to take advantage of small undulations, and he will turn carelessly aside from the direct way wherever there is anything beautiful to examine or some promise of a wider view; so that even a bush of wild roses may permanently bias and deform the straight path over the meadow; whereas, where the soil is heavy, one is preoccupied with the labour of mere progression and goes with a bowed head heavily and unobservantly forward. Reason, however, will not carry us the whole way; for the sentiment often recurs in situations where it is very hard to imagine any possible explanation; and indeed, if we drive briskly along a good well-made road in an open vehicle, we shall experience this sympathy almost at its fullest. We feel the sharp settle of the springs at some curiously twisted corner; after a steep ascent, the fresh air dances in our faces as we rattle precipitately down the other side, and we find it difficult to avoid attributing something headlong, a sort of sudden *abandon*, to the road itself.

The mere winding of the path is enough to enliven a long day's walk in even a commonplace or dreary country-side. Something that we have seen from miles back, upon an eminence, is so long hid from us, as we wander through folded valleys or among woods, that our expectation of seeing it again is sharpened into a violent appetite, and as we draw nearer we impatiently quicken our steps and turn every corner with a beating heart. It is through these prolongations of expectancy, this succession of one hope to another, that we live out long seasons of pleasure in a few hours' walk. It is in following these capricious sinuosities that we learn, only bit by bit and through one coquettish reticence after another, much as we learn the heart of a friend, the whole loveliness of the country. This disposition preserves always something new to be seen, and takes us, like a careful cicerone,[7] to many different points of distant view before it allows us finally to approach the hoped-for destination.

In its connexion with the traffic and whole friendly intercourse of the country, there is something very pleasant in that succession of saunterers and brisk and business-like passers by, that peoples our ways and helps to build up what Walt Whitman calls "the cheerful voice of the public road, the gay, fresh sentiment of the road."[8] But out of the great network of ways, that binds all life together from the hill farm to the city, there is something individual to most, and on the whole, nearly as much choice on the score of company as on the score of beauty or easy travel. On some, we are never long without the sound of wheels, and folk pass us by so thickly that we lose the sense of their number. But on others, about little-frequented districts, a meeting is an affair of moment; we have the sight far off of some one coming towards us, the growing definiteness of the person, and then the brief passage and salutation, and the road left empty in front of us for perhaps a great while to come. Such encounters have a wistful interest that can hardly be understood by the dweller in places more populous. We remember standing beside a countryman once, in the mouth of a quiet by-street in a city that was more than ordinarily crowded and bustling; he seemed stunned and bewildered by the con-tinual passage of different faces; and after a long pause, during which he appeared to search for some suitable expression, he said timidly that there seemed to be *a great deal of meeting thereabouts*. The phrase is significant. It is the expression of town life in the language of the long, solitary, country highways. A meeting of one with one was what this man had been used to in the pastoral uplands from which he came; and the concourse of the streets was in his eyes only an extraordinary multiplication of such "meetings."

And now we come to that last and most subtle quality of all, to that sense of prospect, of outlook, that is brought so powerfully to our minds by a road. In real Nature as well as in old landscapes, beneath that impartial daylight in which a whole variegated plain is plunged and saturated, the line of the road leads the eye forth with the vague sense of desire up to the green limit of the horizon. Travel is brought home to us, and we visit in spirit every grove and hamlet that tempts us in the distance. *Sehnsucht*—the passion for what is ever beyond—is livingly expressed in that white riband of possible travel that severs the uneven country; not a ploughman following his plough up the shining furrow, not the blue smoke of any cottage in a hollow, but is brought to us with a sense of nearness and attainability by this wavering line of junction. There is a passionate paragraph in *Werther* that strikes the very key.[9] "When I came hither," he writes, "how the beautiful valley invited me on every side, as I gazed down into it from the hill-top! There the wood—ah, that I might mingle in its shadows! there the mountain-summits—ah, that I might look down from them over the broad country! the interlinked hills! the secret valleys! Oh to lose myself among their mysteries! I hurried into the midst, and came back without finding aught I hoped for. Alas! the distance is like the future. A vast whole lies in the twilight before our spirit; sight and feeling alike plunge and lose themselves in the prospect, and we yearn to surrender our whole being and let it be filled full with all the rapture of one single glorious sensation; and alas! when we hasten to the fruition, when *there* is changed to *here*, all is afterwards as it was before, and we stand in our indigent and cramped estate, and our soul thirsts after a still ebbing elixir." It is to this wandering and uneasy spirit of anticipation that roads minister. Every little vista, every little glimpse that we have of what lies before us, gives the impatient imagination rein, so that it can outstrip the body and already plunge into the shadow of the woods, and overlook from the hill-top the plain beyond it, and wander in the windings of the valleys that are still far in front. The road is already there—we shall not be long behind. It is as if we were marching with the rear of a great army, and, from far before, heard the acclamation of the people as the vanguard entered some friendly and jubilant city. Would not every man, through all the long miles of march, feel as if he also were within the gates?[10]

Notes

1 Washington Irving, "Stratford-on-Avon," *The Sketch Book* (1820).
2 Chimborazo: Ecuadorian mountain peak over 20,000 feet high.
3 Samuel Taylor Coleridge, "This Lime-Tree Bower My Prison" (28–30). The poem addresses the essayist Charles Lamb three times as "gentle-hearted CHARLES" (28, 68, 75). Lamb pleaded with Coleridge in his letters, which were later published in 1837, "don't make me ridiculous any more by terming me gentle-hearted Charles in print" (*The Letters of Charles and Mary Anne Lamb* 1:217–218).
4 An attractively flirtatious manner (Horace, *Odes* 1.19.7).
5 RLS: Compare Blake, in the "Marriage of Heaven and Hell;" "Improvement makes straight roads: but the crooked roads, without improvement, are roads of Genius."
6 William Hogarth (1697–1764), English painter and aesthetic theorist. Hogarth's "line of beauty" was a serpentine or s-shaped line that he argued in *The Analysis of Beauty* (1753) captured the variety and expressiveness of nature, excited the viewer's attention, and signified liveliness and activity.
7 A guide who shows a place to sightseers and explains its features, named for the Roman orator Cicero.
8 "Song of the Open Road" (4.4).
9 Johann Wolfgang von Goethe's Romantic German novel *The Sorrows of Young Werther* (1774). Translation unknown.
10 In *The Portfolio*, Stevenson signed the essay "L.S. Stoneven."

40

NOTES ON THE MOVEMENTS OF
YOUNG CHILDREN

I wish to direct the reader's attention to a certain quality in the movements of children when young, which is somehow lovable in them, although it would be even unpleasant in any grown person. Their movements are not graceful, but they fall short of grace by something so sweetly humorous that we only admire them the more. The imperfection is so pretty and pathetic, and it gives so great a promise of something different in the future, that it attracts us more than many forms of beauty. They have something of the merit of a rough sketch by a master, in which we pardon what is wanting or excessive for the sake of the very bluntness and directness of the thing. It gives us pleasure to see the beginning of gracious impulses and the springs of harmonious movement laid bare to us with innocent simplicity.

One night, some ladies formed a sort of impromptu dancing-school in the drawing-room of an hôtel in France. One of the ladies led the ring, and I can recall her as a model of accomplished, cultured movement. Two little girls, about eight years old, were the pupils; that is an age of great interest in girls, when natural grace comes to its consummation of justice and purity, with little admixture of that other grace of forethought and discipline that will shortly supersede it altogether. In these two, particularly, the rhythm was sometimes broken by an excess of energy, as though the pleasure of the music in their light bodies could endure no longer the restraint of regulated dance. So that, between these and the lady, there was not only some beginning of the very contrast I wish to insist upon in these notes, but matter enough to set one thinking a long while on the beauty of motion. I do not know that, here in England, we have any good opportunity of seeing what that is; the generation of British dancing men and women are certainly more remarkable for other qualities than for grace: they are, many of them, very conscientious artists, and give quite a serious regard to the technical parts of their performance; but the spectacle, somehow, is not often beautiful, and strikes no note of pleasure. If I had seen no more, therefore, this evening might have remained in my memory as a rare experience. But the best part of it was yet to come. For after the others had desisted, the musician still continued to play, and a little button between two and three years old came out into the cleared space and began to figure before us as the music prompted. I had an opportunity of seeing her, not on this night only but on many subsequent nights; and the wonder and comical admiration she inspired was only deepened as time went on. She had an admirable musical ear; and each new melody, as it struck in her a new humour, suggested wonderful combinations and variations of movement. Now it would be a dance with which she would suit the music, now rather an appropriate panto-mime, and now a mere string of disconnected attitudes. But whatever she did, she did it with the same verve and gusto. The spirit of the air seemed to have entered into her, and to possess her like a passion; and you could see her struggling to find expression for the beauty that was in her against the inefficacy of the dull, half-informed body. Though her footing was uneven and her gestures often ludicrously helpless, still the spectacle was not merely amusing; and though subtile inspira-tions of movement miscarried in tottering travesty, you could still see that they had been inspirations; you could still see that she had set her heart on realising something just and beautiful, and that, by the discipline of these abortive efforts, she was making for herself in the future a quick, supple and obedient body. It was grace in the making. *Elle s'efforçait d'être belle.*[1] She was not to be daunted by any merriment of people looking on critically; the music said something to her, and her whole spirit was intent on what the music said: she must carry out its sug-gestions, she must do her best to translate its language into that other dialect of the modulated body into which it can be translated most easily and fully.

Just the other day I was witness to a second scene, in which the motive[2] was something similar; only this time with quite common children, and in the familiar neighbourhood of Hampstead. A little congregation had formed itself in the lane underneath my window, and was busy over a skipping-rope. There were two sis-ters, from seven to nine perhaps, with dark faces and dark hair, and slim, lithe, little figures, clad in lilac frocks. The elder of these two was a mistress of the art of skipping. She was just and adroit in every movement; the rope passed over her black head and under her scarlet-stockinged legs with a precision and regularity that was like machinery; but there was nothing mechanical in the infinite variety and sweetness of her inclinations, and the spontaneous agile flexure of her lean waist and hips. There was one variation favourite with her, in which she crossed her hands before her with a motion not unlike that of weaving, which was admira-bly intricate and complete. And when the two took the rope together and whirled in and out with occasional interruptions, there was something Italian in the type of both—in the length of nose, in the slimness and accuracy of the shapes—and something gay and harmonious in the double movement, that added to the whole scene a southern element, and took me over sea and land into distant and beauti-ful places. Nor was this impression lessened when the elder girl took in her arms a fair-haired baby, and while the others held the rope for her, turned and gyrated, and went in and out over it lightly, with a quiet regularity that seemed as if it might go on for ever. Somehow, incongruous as was the occupation, she reminded me of Italian Madonnas.[3] And now, as before in the hôtel drawing-room, the humorous element was to be introduced; only this time it was in broad farce. The funniest little girl with a mottled complexion and a big, damaged nose, and looking for all the world like any dirty broken-nosed doll in a nursery lumber-room, came forward to take her turn. While the others swung the rope for her as gently as it could be done—a mere mockery of movement—and playfully taunted her timidity, she passaged backwards and forwards in a pretty flutter of indecision, putting up her shoulders and laughing with the embarrassed laughter of children by the water's edge, eager to bathe and yet fearful. There never was anything at once so droll and so pathetic. One did not know whether to laugh or to cry. And when at last she had made an end of all her deprecations and drawings back, and summoned up heart enough to straddle over the rope, one leg at a time, it was a sight to see her ruffle herself up like a peacock and go away down the lane with her damaged nose, seeming to think discretion the better part of valour, and rather uneasy lest they should ask her to repeat the exploit. Much as I had enjoyed the grace of the older girls, it was now just as it had been before in France, and the clumsiness of the child seemed to have a significance and a sort of beauty of its own, quite above this grace of the others in power to affect the heart. I had looked on with a certain sense of balance and completion at the silent, rapid, masterly evolutions of the eldest; I had been pleased by these in the way of satisfaction. But when little broken-nose began her pantomime of indecision I grew excited. There was something quite fresh and poignant in the delight I took in her imperfect movements. I remember, for instance, that I moved my own shoulders, as if to imitate her; really, I suppose, with an inarticulate wish to help her out.

Now, there are many reasons why this gracelessness of young children should be pretty and sympathetic to us. And, first, there is an interest as of battle. It is in travail and laughable *fiasco* that the young school their bodies to beautiful expression, as they school their minds. We seem, in watching them, to divine antagonists pitted one against the other; and, as in other wars, so in this war of the intelligence against the unwilling body, we do not wish to see even the cause of progress triumph without some honourable toil; and we are so sure of the ultimate result, that it pleases us to linger in pathetic sympathy over these reverses of the early campaign, just as we do over the troubles that environ the heroine of a novel on her way to the happy ending. Again, people are very ready to disown the pleasure they take in a thing merely because it is big, as an Alp, or merely because it is little, as a little child; and yet this pleasure is surely as legitimate as another. There is much of it here; we have an irrational indulgence for small folk; we ask but little where there is so little to ask it of; we cannot overcome our astonishment that they should be able to move at all, and are interested in their movements somewhat as we are interested in the movements of a puppet. And again, there is a prolongation of expectancy when, as in these movements of children, we are kept continually on the very point of attainment and ever turned away and tantalised by some humorous imperfection. This is altogether absent in the secure and accomplished movements of persons more fully grown. The tight-rope walker does not walk so freely or so well as any one else can walk upon a good road; and yet we like to watch him for the mere sake of the difficulty; we like to see his vacillations; we like this last so much even, that I am told a really artistic tight-rope walker must feign to be troubled in his balance, even if he is not so really. And again, we have in these baby efforts an assurance of spontaneity that we do not have often. We know this at least certainly, that the child tries to dance for its own pleasure and not for any by-end of ostentation and conformity. If we did not know it we should see it. There is a sincerity, a directness, an impulsive truth, about their free gestures that shows throughout all imperfection, and it is to us as a reminiscence of primitive festivals and the Golden Age. Lastly, there is in the sentiment much of a simple human compassion for creatures more helpless than ourselves. One nearly ready to die is pathetic; and so is one scarcely ready to live. In view of their future, our heart is softened to these clumsy little ones. They will be more adroit when they are not so happy.

Unfortunately, then, this character that so much delights us is not one that can be preserved in any plastic art. It turns, as we have seen, upon considerations not really æsthetic. Art may deal with the slim freedom of a few years later; but with this fettered impulse, with these stammering motions, she is powerless to do more than stereotype what is ungraceful, and, in the doing of it, lose all pathos and humanity. So these humorous little ones must go away into the limbo of beautiful things that are not beautiful for art, there to await a more perfect age before they sit for their portraits.

Notes

1 She was striving to be beautiful (French).
2 Motif: a distinctive feature or dominant idea of an artistic composition.
3 Artistic representations of the Virgin Mary.

41

ON THE ENJOYMENT OF
UNPLEASANT PLACES

It is a difficult matter to make the best of any given place; and we have much in our own power. Things looked at patiently from one side after another, generally end by showing a side that is beautiful. A few months ago some words were said in the *Portfolio* as to an "austere regimen in scenery;" and such a discipline was then recommended as "healthful and strengthening to the taste."[1] That is the text, so to speak, of the present essay. This discipline in scenery, it must be understood, is something more than a mere walk before breakfast to whet the appetite. For when we are put down in some unsightly neighbourhood, and especially if we have come to be more or less dependent on what we see, we must set ourselves to hunt out beautiful things with all the ardour and patience of a botanist after a rare plant. Day by day we perfect ourselves in the art of seeing nature favourably. We learn to live with her, as people learn to live with fretful or violent spouses: to dwell lovingly on what is good, and shut our eyes against all that is bleak or inharmonious. We learn, also, to come to each place in the right spirit. The traveller, as Brantôme[2] quaintly tells us, "fait des discours en soi pour se soutenir en chemin;"[3] and into these discourses he weaves something out of all that he sees and suffers by the way: they take their tone greatly from the varying character of the scene; a sharp ascent brings different thoughts from a level road; and the man's fancies grow lighter, as he comes out of the wood into a clearing. Nor does the scenery any more affect the thoughts, than the thoughts affect the scenery. We see places through our humours as through differently coloured glasses. We are ourselves a term in the equation, a note of the chord, and make discord or harmony almost at will. There is no fear for the result, if we can but surrender ourselves sufficiently to the country that surrounds and follows us, so that we are ever thinking suitable thoughts or telling ourselves some suitable sort of story as we go. We become thus, in some sense, a centre of beauty; we are provocative of beauty, much as a gentle and sincere character is provocative of sincerity and gentleness in others. And even where there is no harmony to be elicited by the quickest and most obedient of spirits, we may still embellish a place with some attraction of romance. We may learn to go far afield for associations, and handle them lightly when we have found them. Sometimes an old print comes to our aid; I have seen many a spot lit up at once with picturesque imaginations, by a reminiscence of Callot, or Sadeler, or Paul Brill.[4] Dick Turpin[5] has been my lay figure for many an English lane. And I suppose the Trossachs would hardly be the Trossachs for most tourists, if a man of admirable romantic instinct had not peopled it for them with harmonious figures, and brought them thither with minds rightly prepared for the impression.[6] There is half the battle in this preparation. For instance: I have rarely been able to visit, in the proper spirit, the wild and inhospitable places of our own Highlands. I am happier where it is tame and fertile, and not readily pleased without trees. I understand that there are some phases of mental trouble that harmonise well with such surroundings, and that some persons, by the dispensing power of the imagination, can go back several centuries in spirit and put themselves into sympathy with the hunted, houseless, unsociable way of life, that was in its place upon these savage hills. Now, when I am sad, I like nature to charm me out of my sadness, like David before Saul;[7] and the thought of these past ages strikes nothing in me but an unpleasant pity; so that I can never hit on the right humour for this sort of landscape, and lose much pleasure in consequence. Still, even here, if I were only let alone, and time enough were given, I should have all manner of pleasures, and take many clear and beautiful images away with me when I left. When we cannot think ourselves into sympathy with the great features of a country, we learn to ignore them, and put our head among the grass for flowers, or pore, for long times together, over the changeful current of a stream. We come down to the sermons in stones,[8] when we are shut out from any poem in the spread landscape. We begin to peep and botanise,[9] we take an interest in birds and insects, we find many things beautiful in miniature. The reader will recollect the little summer scene in "Wuthering Heights"[10]—the one warm scene, perhaps, in all that powerful, miserable novel—and the great figure that is made therein by grasses and flowers and a little sunshine: this is in the spirit of which I now speak. And, lastly, we can go indoors; interiors are sometimes as beautiful, often more picturesque, than the shows of the open air, and they have that quality of shelter of which I shall presently have more to say.

With all this in mind, I have often been tempted to put forth the paradox that any place is good enough to live a life in, while it is only in a few, and those highly favoured, that we can pass a few hours agreeably. For if we only stay long enough, we become at home in the neighbourhood. Reminiscences spring up, like flowers, about uninteresting corners. We forget to some degree the superior loveliness of other places, and fall into a tolerant and sympathetic spirit which is its own reward and justification. Looking back the other day on some recollections of my own, I was astonished to find how much I owed to such a residence; six weeks in one unpleasant country-side[11] had done more, it seemed, to quicken and educate my sensibilities than many years in places that jumped more nearly with my inclination.

The country to which I refer was a level and treeless plateau, over which the winds cut like a whip. For miles on miles it was the same. A river, indeed, fell into the sea near the town where I resided; but the valley of the river was shallow and bald, for as far up as ever I had the heart to follow it. There were roads certainly, but roads that had no beauty or interest; for as there was no timber and but little irregularity of surface, you saw your whole walk exposed to you from the beginning: there was nothing left to fancy, nothing to expect, nothing to see by the wayside, save here and there an unhomely-looking homestead, and here and there a solitary, spectacled stone-breaker; and you were only accompanied, as you went doggedly forward, by the gaunt telegraph-posts and the hum of the resonant wires in the keen sea wind. To one who had learned to know their song in warm pleasant places by the Mediterranean, it seemed to taunt the country, and make it still bleaker by suggested contrast. Even the waste places by the side of the road were not, as Hawthorne liked to put it, "taken back to Nature" by any decent covering of vegetation.[12] Wherever the land had the chance, it seemed to lie fallow. There is a certain tawny nudity of the South, bare sunburnt plains, coloured like a lion, and hills clothed only in the blue transparent air; but this was of another description—this was the nakedness of the North; the earth seemed to know that it was naked, and was ashamed and cold.

It seemed to me to be always blowing on that coast. Indeed this had passed into the speech of the inhabitants, and they saluted each other when they met with "Breezy, breezy," instead of the customary "Fine day" of further South. These continual winds were not like the harvest breeze, that just keeps an equable pressure against your face as you walk, and serves to set all the trees talking over your head, or bring round you the smell of the wet surface of the country after a shower. They were of the bitter, hard, persistent sort, that interferes with sight and respiration, and makes the eyes sore. Even such winds as these have their own merit in proper time and place. It is splendid to see them brandish great masses of shadow. And what a power they have over the colour of the world! How they ruffle the solid woodlands in their passage, and make them shudder and whiten like a single willow! There is nothing more vertiginous than a wind like this among the woods, with all its sights and noises; and the effect gets between some painters and their sober eyesight, so that, even when the rest of their picture is calm, the foliage is coloured like foliage in a gale. There was nothing, however, of this sort to be noticed in a country where there were no trees, and hardly any shadows, save the passive shadows of clouds or those of rigid houses and walls. But the wind was nevertheless an occasion of pleasure; for nowhere could you taste more fully the pleasure of a sudden lull, or a place of opportune shelter. The reader knows what I mean; he must remember how, when he has sat himself down behind a dike on a hill-side, he delighted to hear the wind hiss vainly through the crannies at his back; how his body tingled all over with warmth, and it began to dawn upon him, with a sort of slow surprise, that the country was beautiful, the heather purple, and the far-away hills all marbled with sun and shadow. Wordsworth, in a beautiful passage of the "Prelude," has used this as a figure for the feeling struck in us by the quiet by-streets of London after the uproar of the great thoroughfares; and the comparison may be turned the other way with as good effect:—

Meanwhile the roar continues, till at length,
Escaped as from an enemy, we turn
Abruptly into some sequestered nook,
Still as a sheltered place when winds blow loud![13]

316

I remember meeting a man once, in a train, who told me of what must have been quite the most perfect instance of this pleasure of escape. He had gone up one sunny, windy morning, to the top of a great cathedral somewhere abroad; I think it was Cologne Cathedral, the great unfinished marvel by the Rhine;[14] and after a long while in dark stairways, he issued at last into the sunshine, on a platform high above the town. At that elevation, it was quite still and warm; the gale was only in the lower strata of the air, and he had forgotten it in the quiet interior of the church and during his long ascent; and so you may judge of his surprise when resting his arms upon the sunlit balustrade and looking over into the *Place*[15] far below him, he saw the good people holding on their hats and leaning hard against the wind as they walked. There is something, to my fancy, quite perfect in this little experience of my fellow-traveller's. The ways of men seem always very trivial to us, when we find ourselves alone on a church top with the blue sky and a few tall pinnacles, and see far below us the steep roofs and foreshortened buttresses, and the silent activity of the city streets; but how much more must they not have seemed so to him as he stood, not only above other men's business, but above other men's climate, in a golden zone like Apollo's!

This was the sort of pleasure I found in the country of which I write. The pleasure was to be out of the wind, and to keep it in memory all the time, and hug oneself upon the shelter. And it was only by the sea that any such sheltered places were to be found. Between the black worm-eaten headlands there are little bights and havens, well screened from the wind and the commotion of the external sea, where the sand and weeds look up into the gazer's face from a depth of tranquil water, and the sea-birds, screaming and flickering from the ruined crags, alone disturb the silence and the sunshine. One such place has impressed itself on my memory beyond all others. On a rock by the water's edge, old fighting-men of the Norse breed has planted a double castle; the two stood wall to wall like semi-detached villas; and yet feud had run so high between their owners, that one, from out of a window, shot the other as he stood in his own doorway. There is something in the juxtaposition of these two enemies full of tragic irony. It is grim to think of bearded men and bitter women taking hateful counsel together about the two hall-fires at night, when the sea boomed against the foundations and the wild winter wind was loose over the battlements. And in the study, we may reconstruct for ourselves some pale figure of what life then was. Not so when we are there; when we are there such thoughts come to us only to intensify a contrary impression, and association is turned against itself. I remember walking thither three afternoons in succession, my eyes weary with being set against the wind, and how, dropping suddenly over the edge of the down, I found myself in a new world of warmth and shelter. The wind, from which I had escaped, "as from an enemy," was seemingly quite local. It carried no clouds with it, and came from such a quarter that it did not trouble the sea within view. The two castles, black and ruinous as the rocks about them, were still distinguishable from these by something more insecure and fantastic in the outline, something that the last storm had left imminent and the next would demolish entirely. It would be difficult to render in words the sense of peace that took possession of me on these three afternoons. It was helped out, as I have said, by the contrast. The shore was battered and bemauled by previous tempests; I had the memory at heart of the insane strife of the pigmies, who had erected these two castles and lived in them in mutual distrust and enmity; and knew I had only to put my head out of this little cup of shelter, to find the hard wind blowing in my eyes; and yet there were the two great tracts of motionless blue air and peaceful sea looking on, unconcerned and apart, at the turmoil of the present moment and the memorials of the precarious past. There is ever something transitory and fretful in the impression of a high wind under a cloudless sky; it seems to have no root in the constitution of things; it must speedily begin to faint and wither away like a cut flower. And on those days the thought of the wind and the thought of human life came very near together in my mind. Our noisy years did indeed seem moments in the being of the eternal silence:[16] and the wind, in the face of that great field of stationary blue, was as the wind of a butterfly's wing. The placidity of the sea was a thing likewise to be remembered. Shelley speaks of the sea as "hungering for calm,"[17] and in this place one learned to understand the phrase. Looking down into these green waters from the broken edge of the rock, or swimming leisurely in the sunshine, it seemed to me that they were enjoying their own tranquillity; and when now and again it was disturbed, by a wind-ripple on the surface or the quick black passage of a fish far below, they settled back again (one could fancy) with relief.

On shore, too, in the little nook of shelter, everything was so subdued and still, that the least particular struck in me a pleasurable surprise. The desultory crackling of the whin-pods[18] in the afternoon sun usurped the ear. The hot, sweet breath of the bank, that had been saturated all day long with sunshine and now exhaled it into my face, was like the breath of a fellow-creature. I remember that I was haunted by two lines of French verse; in some dumb way they seemed to fit my surroundings and give expression to the contentment that was in me; and I kept repeating to myself—

Mon cœur est un luth suspendu,
Sitôt qu'on le touche, il résonne.[19]

I can give no reason why these lines came to me at this time; and for that very cause I repeat them here. For all I know, they may serve to complete the impression in the mind of the reader, as they were certainly a part of it for me.

And this happened to me in the place of all others where I liked least to stay. When I think of it I grow ashamed of my own ingratitude. "Out of the strong came forth sweetness."[20] There, in the bleak and gusty North, I received, perhaps, my strongest impression of peace. I saw the sea to be great and calm; and the earth, in that little corner, was all alive and friendly to me. So, wherever a man is, he will find something to please and pacify him: in the town he will meet pleasant faces of men and women, and see beautiful flowers at a window, or hear a cage-bird singing at the corner of the gloomiest street; and for the country, there

318

is no country without some amenity—let him only look for it in the right spirit, and he will surely find.

Notes

1 *The Portfolio* was a literary magazine founded by art critic Philip Gilbert Hamerton (1834–1894), who published several of Stevenson's essays, including this one and "Roads," quoted here.
2 Pierre de Bourdeille, Abbé de Brantôme (1540–1614), French historian, cleric, and soldier.
3 "Talks to himself to lift his spirits on the road" (French).
4 Jacques Callot (1592–1632), French printmaker; Aegidius Sadeler (1570–1629), Flemish engraver; Paul Bril (1554–1626), Flemish landscape painter.
5 Dick Turpin (1705–1739), famous, often romanticized, English highwayman.
6 Walter Scott's *The Lady of the Lake* (1810) and *Rob Roy* (1817) are set in Scotland's picturesque Trossachs.
7 David's harp lifts Saul's spirits (1 Samuel 16:23).
8 Shakespeare, *As You Like It*, 2.1.17.
9 Wordsworth, "A Poet's Epitaph" (18–20).
10 Chapter 24 of Emily Brontë's *Wuthering Heights* (1847).
11 Stevenson was in northern Scotland's Wick in the autumn of 1868 for his engineering training.
12 In his travel book on England *Our Old Home* (1863), for instance, Hawthorne writes of Blenheim Palace in Oxfordshire, "the lapse of a century has softened the harsh outline of man's labors, and has given the place back to Nature again" (ch. 7).
13 Wordsworth, *The Prelude* 7.168–71 (1850).
14 Construction on Cologne Cathedral first began in 1248 and was not completed until 1880.
15 The Square.
16 Wordsworth, "Ode: Intimations" (159–60).
17 *Prometheus Unbound* (3.2.49).
18 Gorse seedpods.
19 "My heart is a lute newly strung, / Just one touch, and it resounds" (French). Pierre-Jean de Béranger's "Le Refus" or "The Refusal" (1830).
20 Judges 14:14.

42

AN AUTUMN EFFECT[1]

"Nous ne décrivons jamais mieux la nature que lorsque nous nous efforçons
d'exprimer sobrement et simplement l'impression que nous en avons reçue.—M.
André Theuriet, "L'Automne dans les bois," *Revue des Deux Mondes*, 1st Oct.
1874, p. 562.[2]

A country rapidly passed through under favourable auspices, may leave upon
us a unity of impression that would only be disturbed and dissipated if we stayed
longer. Clear vision goes with the quick foot. Things fall for us into a sort of
natural perspective, when we see them for a moment in going by; we generalise
boldly and simply, and are gone before the sun is overcast, before the rain falls,
before the season can steal like a dial hand from his figure, before the lights
and shadows, shifting round towards nightfall, can show us the other sides of
things, and belie what they showed us in the morning. We expose our mind to
the landscape (as we would expose the prepared plate in the camera) for the
moment only during which the effect endures; and we are away before the effect
can change. Hence we shall have in our memories a long scroll of continuous
wayside pictures, all imbued already with the prevailing sentiment of the season,
the weather, and the landscape, and certain to be unified more and more, as time
goes on, by the unconscious processes of thought. So that we who have only
looked at a country over our shoulder, so to speak, as we went by, will have a
conception of it far more memorable and articulate, than a man who has lived
there all his life from a child upwards, and had his impression of to-day modified
by that of to-morrow, and belied by that of the day after, till at length the stable
characteristics of the country are all blotted out from him behind the confusion
of variable effect.

That is one remark I desired to make before beginning to describe my little
pilgrimage; because, from such a point of view, this pilgrimage was especially
fortunate: the effect was simple and continuous throughout. One more remark,
however, I desire to make; and it is one on which I lay great stress. I have spoken
in a previous essay of how "we saw places through our humours as through differently coloured glasses," and just indicated some of the subjective conditions that
modify the sight we have of scenery. This is not the place to develope the theory
of the matter; and it will be enough to say that there goes to the building up of any

general idea of a country, besides the question of good or bad temper, an infinity of infinitesimal conditions; that no man knows what these conditions are, or which of them at any moment is effective; and hence, if I want to communicate to others the very complex impression given to me by a tract of variegated country as I went over it for three days in succession, I shall do best if I follow instinct simply, and chronicle, in good faith, all that I vividly remember. Observe, it is not the aspect of the country, but the impression only, that I can hope to reproduce; and there went to the making of this impression many things that I should certainly omit if I were trying to describe the country, myself abstracted, but which I must as certainly preserve and accentuate, if I am to try this humbler and wiser task of reproducing the impression. The action and reaction of our own moods upon scenery, and the scenery upon our moods, is so constant and subtle that no man can follow it out intelligently to an end; and we cannot tell where the influence of our surroundings ceases, or which of our thoughts is not, in some deepest sense, suggested from without.

And so it should first be noticed that I began my little pilgrimage in the most enviable of all humours: that in which a person, with a sufficiency of money and a knapsack, turns his back on a town and walks forward into a country of which he knows only by the vague report of others. Such an one has not surrendered his will and contracted for the next hundred miles, like a man on a railway. He may change his mind at every finger-post, and where ways meet, follow vague preferences freely and go the low road or the high, choose the shadow or the sunshine, suffer himself to be tempted by the lane that turns immediately into the woods, or the broad road that lies open before him a long way into the blue distance, and shows him the far-off spires of some great city, or a range of faint mountain-tops, or a rim of sea, perhaps, along the low horizon. In short, he may gratify his every whim and fancy, without a pang of reproving conscience, or the least jostle to his self-respect. It is true, however, that most men do not possess the faculty of free action, the priceless gift of being able to live for the moment only; and as they begin to go forward on their journey, they will find that they have made for themselves new fetters. Slight projects they may have entertained for a moment, half in jest, become iron laws to them, they know not why. They will be led by the nose by these vague reports of which I spoke above; and the mere fact that their informant mentioned one village and not another, will compel their footsteps with inexplicable power. And yet a little while, yet few days of this fictitious liberty, and they will begin to hear imperious voices calling on them to return; and some passion, some duty, some worthy or unworthy expectation, will set its hand upon their shoulder and lead them back into the old paths. Once and again, we have all made the experiment. We know the end of it right well. And yet if we make it for the hundredth time to-morrow, it will have the same charm as ever; our heart will beat and our eyes will be bright, as we leave the town behind us, and we shall feel once again (as we have felt before so often) that we are cutting ourselves loose for ever from our whole past life, with all its sins and follies and circumscriptions, and go forward as a new creature into a new world.

It was well, perhaps, that I had this first enthusiasm to encourage me up the long hill above High Wycombe; for the day was a bad day for walking at best, and now began to draw towards afternoon, dull, heavy, and lifeless. A pall of grey cloud covered the sky, and its colour reacted on the colour of the landscape. Near at hand, indeed, the hedgerow trees were still fairly green, shot through with bright autumnal yellows, bright as sunshine. But a little way off, the solid bricks of woodland that lay squarely on slope and hilltop were not green, but russet and grey, and ever less russet and more grey as they drew off into the distance. As they drew off into the distance, also, the woods seemed to mass themselves together, and lay thin and straight, like clouds, upon the limit of one's view. Not that this massing was complete, or gave the idea of any extent of forest, for every here and there the trees would break up and go down into a valley in open order, or stand in long Indian file along the horizon, tree after tree relieved, foolishly enough, against the sky. I say foolishly enough, although I have seen the effect employed cleverly in art, and such long line of single trees thrown out against the custom-ary sunset of a Japanese picture with a certain fantastic effect that was not to be despised; but this was over water and level land, where it did not jar, as here, with the soft contour of hills and valleys. The whole scene had an indefinable look of being painted, the colour was so abstract and correct, and there was something so sketchy and merely impressional about these distant single trees on the horizon that one was forced to think of it all as of a clever French landscape. For it is rather in nature that we see resemblances to art, than in art to nature; and we say a hundred times, "How like a picture!" for once that we say, "How like the truth!" The forms in which we learn to think of landscape are forms that we have got from painted canvas. Any man can see and understand a picture; it is reserved for the few to separate anything out of the confusion of nature, and see that distinctly and with intelligence. Thus, I know one who has a magical faculty of understanding, and reproducing in words, the gestures of people within picture-frames, or hung on the wall in tapestry; and yet ask him to describe the action of the live man who has just passed him in the street, and he cannot—he has not seen it, it has been nothing to him, and is gone for ever. So that most of us, when they look abroad over a landscape, go merely peeping for what they have already seen reproduced in pictures.

The sun came out before I had been long on my way; and as I had got, by that time, to the top of the ascent, and was now threading a labyrinth of confined bye-roads, my whole view brightened considerably in colour; for it was the distance only that was grey and cold, and the distance I could see no longer. Overhead, there was a wonderful carolling of larks, which seemed to follow me as I went. Indeed, during all the time I was in that country the larks did not desert me; the air was alive with them from High Wycombe to Tring; and as, day after day, their "shrill delight"[3] fell upon me out of the vacant sky, they began to take such a prominence over other conditions, and form so integral a part of my concep-tion of the country, that I could have baptized it "The Country of Larks." This, of course, might just as well have been in early spring; but everything else was deeply imbued with the sentiment of the later year. There was no stir of insects in the grass. The sunshine was more golden, and gave less heat than summer sunshine: and the shadows under the hedge were somewhat blue and misty. It was only in autumn that you could have seen the mingled green and yellow of the elm foliage; and the fallen leaves that lay about the road, and covered the surface of wayside pools so thickly that the sun was reflected only here and there from little joints and pinholes in that brown coat of proof;[4] or that your ear would have been troubled, as you went forward, by the occasional report of fowling-pieces from all directions and all degrees of distance.

For a long time this dropping fire was the one sign of human activity that came to disturb me as I walked. The lanes were profoundly still. They would have been sad but for the sunshine and the singing of the larks. And as it was, there came over me at times a feeling of isolation that was not disagreeable, and yet was enough to make me quicken my steps eagerly when I saw some one before me on the road. This fellow-voyager proved to be no less a person than the parish-constable. It had occurred to me that in a district which was so little populous and so well wooded, a criminal of any intelligence might play hide-and-seek with the authorities for months; and this idea was strengthened by the aspect of the portly constable, as he walked by my side with deliberate dignity and turned-out toes. But a few minutes' converse set my heart at rest. These rural criminals were very tame birds, it appeared. If my informant did not immediately lay his hand on an offender, he was content to wait: some evening after nightfall there would come a tap at his door; and the outlaw, weary of outlawry, would give himself quietly up to undergo sentence, and resume his position in the life of the country-side. Married men caused him no disquietude whatever; he had them fast by the foot; sooner or later they would come back to see their wives, a peeping neighbour would pass the word, and my portly constable would walk quietly over and take the bird sitting. And if there were a few who had no particular ties in the neighbourhood and preferred to shift into another county when they fell into trouble, their departure moved the placid constable in no degree. He was of Dogberry's opinion; and if a man would not stand in the Prince's name, he took no note of him, but let him go, and thanked God he was rid of a knave.[5] And surely the crime and the law were in admirable keeping: rustic constable was well met with rustic offender; the officer sitting at home over a bit of fire until the criminal came to visit him, and the criminal coming—it was a fair match. One felt as if this must have been the order in that delightful seaboard Bohemia, where Florizel and Perdita courted in such sweet accents, and the Puritan sang psalms to horn-pipes, and the four-and-twenty shearers danced with nosegays in their bosoms and chanted their three songs apiece at the old shepherd's festival;[6] and one could not help picturing to oneself what havoc among good people's purses, and tribulation for benignant constable, might be worked here by the arrival, over stile and footpath, of a new Autolycus.[7]

Bidding good-morning to my fellow-traveller, I left the road and struck across country. It was rather a revelation to pass from between the hedgerows and find quite a bustle on the other side, a great coming and going of school-children upon bye-paths, and, in every second field, lusty horses and stout country folk a-ploughing. The way I followed took me through many fields thus occupied, and through many strips of plantation, and then over a little space of smooth turf, very pleasant to the feet, set with tall fir-trees and clamorous with rooks making ready for the winter, and so back again into the quiet road. I was now not far from the end of my day's journey. A few hundred yards farther, and, passing through a gap in the hedge, I began to go down hill through a pretty extensive tract of young beeches. I was soon in shadow myself, but the afternoon sun still coloured the upmost boughs of the wood, and made a fire over my head in the autumnal foliage. A little faint vapour lay among the slim tree stems in the bottom of the hollow; and from farther up I heard from time to time an outburst of gross laughter, as though clowns were making merry in the bush. There was something about the atmosphere that brought all sights and sounds home to one with a singular purity; so that I felt as if my senses had been washed with water. After I had crossed the little zone of mist, the path began to remount the hill; and just as I, mounting along with it, had got back again, from the head downwards, into the thin golden sunshine, I saw in front of me a donkey tied to a tree. Now, I have a certain liking for donkeys, principally, I believe, because of the delightful things that Sterne has written of them. But this was not after the pattern of the ass at Lyons.[8] He was of a white colour, that seemed to fit him rather for rare festal occasions than for constant drudgery. Besides, he was very small, and of the daintiest proportions you can imagine in a donkey. And so, sure enough, you had only to look at him to see he had never worked. There was something too roguish and wanton in his face, a look too like that of a schoolboy or a street Arab, to have survived much cudgelling. It was plain that these feet had kicked off sportive children oftener than they had plodded with a freight through miry lanes. He was altogether a fine-weather, holiday sort of donkey; and though he was just then somewhat solemnized and rueful, he still gave proof of the levity of his disposition by impudently wagging his ears at me as I drew near. I say he was somewhat solemnised just then; for with the admirable instinct of all men and animals under restraint, he had so wound and wound the halter about the tree, that he could go neither back nor forwards, nor so much as put down his head to browse. There he stood, poor rogue, part puzzled, part angry, part, I believe, amused. He had not given up hope, and dully revolved the problem in his head, giving ever and again another jerk at the few inches of free rope that still remained unwound. A humorous sort of sympathy for the creature took hold upon me; I went up, and, not without some trouble on my part and much distrust and resistance on the part of Neddy,[9] got him forced backward until the whole length of the halter was set loose, and he was once more as free a donkey as I dared to make him. I was pleased (as people are) with this friendly action to a fellow-creature in tribulation; and glanced back over my shoulder to see how he was profiting by his freedom. The brute was looking after me; and, no sooner did he catch my eye, then he put up his long white face into the air, pulled an impudent mouth at me, and began to bray derisively. If ever any one person made

a grimace at another, that donkey made a grimace at me. And the hardened ingratitude of his behaviour and the inimitable impertinence that inspired his whole face,
as he curled up his lip, and showed his teeth, and began to bray, so tickled me, and
was so much in keeping with what I had imagined to myself about his character,
that I could not find it in my heart to be angry, and burst into a peal of hearty
laughter. This seemed to strike the ass as a repartee; so he brayed at me again, by
way of rejoinder; and we went on for a while, braying and laughing, until I began
to grow a-weary of it, and, shouting a derisive farewell, turned to pursue my way.
In so doing—it was like going suddenly into cold water—I found myself face to
face with a prim little old maid. She was all in a flutter, the poor old dear! She had
concluded beyond question that this must be a lunatic, who stood laughing aloud
at a white donkey in the placid beech-woods. I was sure, by her face, that she had
already recommended her spirit most religiously to Heaven, and prepared herself
for the worst. And so, to reassure her, I uncovered and besought her, after a very
staid fashion, to put me on my way to Great Missenden. Her voice trembled a
little to be sure, but I think her mind was set really at rest; and she told me, very
explicitly, to follow the path until I came to the end of the wood, and then I should
see the village below me in the bottom of the valley. And, with mutual courtesies,
the little old maid and I went on our respective ways.

Nor had she misled me. Great Missenden was close at hand, lying, as she had
said, in the trough of a gentle valley, with many great elms about it. The smoke
from its chimneys went up pleasantly in the afternoon sunshine. The sleepy hum
of a threshing-machine filled the neighbouring fields, and hung about the quaint
street corners. A little above, the church sits well back on its haunches against the
hill-side: an attitude for a church, you know, that makes it look as if it could be
ever so much higher if it liked; and the trees grew about it thickly, so as to make
a density of shade in the churchyard. A very quiet place it looks; and yet I saw
many boards and posters about, threatening dire punishment against those who
broke the church-windows or defaced the precinct, and offering rewards for the
apprehension of those who had done the like already. It was fair-day in Great
Missenden: there were three stalls set up *sub jove*, for the sale of pastry and cheap
toys; and a great number of holiday children thronged about the stalls, and noisily
invaded every corner of the straggling village. They came round me by coveys,
blowing simultaneously upon penny trumpets, as though they imagined I should
fall to pieces like the battlements of Jericho.[10] I noticed one among them who
could make a wheel of himself like a London boy, and seemingly enjoyed a grave
pre-eminence upon the strength of the accomplishment. By-and-by, however, the
trumpets began to weary me, and I went indoors, leaving the fair, I fancy, at its
height.

Night had fallen before I ventured forth again. It was pitch-dark in the village
street, and the darkness seemed only the greater for a light here and there in an
uncurtained window or from an open door. Into one such window I was rude
enough to peep, and saw within a charming *genre* picture. In a room, all white
wainscot and crimson wall-paper, a perfect gem of colour after the black empty

325

darkness in which I had been groping, a pretty girl was telling a story, as well as I could make out, to an attentive child upon her knee, while an old woman sat placidly dozing over the fire. You may be sure I was not behindhand with a story for myself—a good old story, after the good old manner of G. P. R. James[11] and the village melodramas, with a wicked squire, and poachers, and an attorney, and a very virtuous young man with a decided genius for mechanics, who should love, and protect, and ultimately marry the girl in the crimson room. Baudelaire[12] has a few dainty sentences on the fancies that we are inspired with, when we look through a window into other people's lives; and I think Dickens has somewhere enlarged on the same text in his own wild, imaginative way:[13] the subject, at least, is one that I am seldom weary of entertaining. I remember, night after night, at Brussels, watching a good family sup together, and make merry, and retire to rest; and night after night I waited to see the candles lit, and the salad made, and the last salutations dutifully exchanged, without any abatement of interest: night after night I found the scene rivet my attention and keep me awake in bed with all manner of quaint imaginations. Much of the pleasure of the "Arabian Nights" hinges upon this Asmodean[14] interest; and we are not weary of lifting other people's roofs, and going about behind the scenes of life with the Caliph and the serviceable Giaffar. It is a salutary exercise, besides: it is salutary to get out of ourselves, and see people living together in perfect unconsciousness of our existence, as they will live when we are gone. If to-morrow the blow falls, and the worst of our ill fears is realised, the girl will none the less tell stories to the child on her lap in the cottage at Great Missenden, nor the good Belgians light their candle, and mix their salad, and go orderly to bed. The foundations of the universe will not be shaken after all. It is but a storm in a teapot: in an hour this storm will have blown over, and the world will still be fair about our path, and people will meet us as before, with pleasant countenances and kind words; and with patience and courage, we may yet rebuild the ruined pleasure-house of fancy.[15]

The next morning was sunny overhead and damp underfoot, with a thrill in the air like a reminiscence of frost. I went up into the sloping garden behind the inn and smoked a pipe pleasantly enough, to the tune of my landlady's lamentations over sundry cabbages and cauliflowers that had been spoiled by caterpillars. She had been so much pleased in the summer time, she said, to see the garden all hovered over by white butterflies. And now, look at the end of it! She could nowise reconcile this with her moral sense. And, indeed, unless these butterflies are created with a side-look to the composition of improving apologues, it is not altogether easy, even for people who have read Hegel and Dr. M'Cosh,[16] to decide intelligibly upon the issue raised. Then I fell into a long and abstruse calculation with my landlord; having for object to compare the distance driven by him during eight years' service on the box of the Wendover coach, with the girth of the round world itself. We tackled the question most conscientiously, made all necessary allowance for Sundays and leap years, and were just coming to a triumphant conclusion of our labours when we were stayed by a small lacuna in my information. I did not know the circumference of the earth. The landlord knew it, to be sure—plainly he had made the same calculation twice and once before,—but he wanted confidence in his own figures, and from the moment I showed myself so poor a second seemed to lose all interest in the result.

Wendover (which was my next stage) lies in the same valley with Great Missenden, but at the foot of it, where the hills trend off on either hand like a coastline, and a great hemisphere of plain lies, like a sea, before one. I went up a chalky road, until I had a good outlook over the place. The vale, as it opened out into the plain, was shallow, and a little bare perhaps, but full of graceful convolutions. From the level to which I had now attained the fields were exposed before me like a map, and I could see all that bustle of autumn field-work which had been hid from me yesterday behind the hedge-rows, or shown to me only for a moment as I followed the foot-path. Wendover lay well down in the midst, with mountains of foliage about it. The great plain stretched away to the northward, variegated near at hand with the quaint pattern of the fields, but growing even more and more indistinct, until it became a mere hurly-burly of trees and bright crescents of river and snatches of slanting road, and finally melted into the ambiguous cloudland over the horizon. The sky was an opal-gray, touched here and there with blue, and with certain faint russets that looked as if they were reflections of the colour of the autumnal woods below. I could hear the ploughmen shouting to their horses, the uninterrupted carol of larks innumerable overhead; and from a field where the shepherd was marshalling his flock, a sweet tumultuous tickle of sheep-bells. All these noises came to me very thin and distinct in the clear air. There was a wonderful sentiment of distance and atmosphere about the day and the place.

I mounted the hill yet farther by a rough staircase of chalky footholds cut in the turf. The hills about Wendover and, as far as I could see, all the hills in Buckinghamshire, wear a sort of hood of beech-plantation; but in this particular case the hood had been suffered to extend itself into something more like a cloak, and hung down about the shoulders of the hill in wide folds, instead of lying flatly along the summit. The trees grew so close and their boughs were so matted together, that the whole wood looked as dense as a bush of heather. The prevailing colour was a dull, smouldering red, touched here and there with vivid yellow. But the autumn had scarce advanced beyond the outworks; it was still almost summer in the heart of the wood; and as soon as I had scrambled through the hedge, I found myself in a dim green forest atmosphere under eaves of virgin foliage. In places where the wood had itself for a background and the trees were massed together thickly, the colour became intensified and almost gem-like: a perfect fire of green, that seemed none the less green for a few specks of autumn gold. None of the trees were of any considerable age or stature; but they grew well together, I have said; and as the road turned and wound among them, they fell into pleasant groupings and broke the light up pleasantly. Sometimes there would be a colonnade of slim, straight tree-stems, with the light running down them as down the shafts of pillars, that looked as if it ought to lead to something and led only to a corner of sombre and intricate jungle. Sometimes a spray of delicate foliage would be thrown out flat, the light lying flatly along the top of it, so that against a dark background it

327

seemed almost luminous. There was a great hush over the thicket (for, indeed, it was more of a thicket than a wood); and the vague rumours that went among the tree-tops, and the occasional rustling of big birds or hares among the undergrowth, had in them a note of almost treacherous stealthiness, that put the imagination on its guard and made me walk warily on the russet carpeting of last year's leaves. The spirit of the place seemed to be all attention; the wood listened as I went, and held its breath to number my footfalls. One could not help feeling that there ought to be some reason for this stillness; whether, as the bright old legend goes, Pan lay somewhere near in a siesta,[17] or whether perhaps the heaven was meditating rain and the first drops would soon come pattering through the leaves. It was not unpleasant, in such an humour, to catch sight, ever and anon, of large spaces of the open plain. This happened only where the path lay much upon the slope, and there was a flaw in the solid leafy thatch of the wood at some distance below the level at which I chanced myself to be walking; then, indeed, little scraps of foreshortened distance, miniature fields, and Lilliputian[18] houses and hedgerow-trees, would appear for a moment in the aperture, and grow larger and smaller, and change, and melt one into another, as I continued to go forward and so shift my point of view.

For ten minutes, perhaps, I had heard from somewhere before me in the wood a strange, continuous noise, as of clucking, cooing, and gobbling, now and again interrupted by a harsh scream. As I advanced towards this noise, it began to grow lighter about me, and I caught sight, through the trees, of sundry gables and enclosure walls, and something like the tops of a rickyard. And sure enough, a rickyard it proved to be, and a neat little farm-steading, with the beech-woods growing almost to the door of it. Just before me, however, as I came up the path, the trees drew back and let in a wide flood of daylight on to a circular lawn. It was here that the noises had their origin. More than a score of peacocks (there are altogether thirty at the farm), a proper contingent of peahens, and a great multitude that I could not number of more ordinary barn-door fowls, were all feeding together on this little open lawn among the beeches. They fed in a dense crowd, which swayed to and fro and came hither and thither as by a sort of tide, and of which the surface was agitated like the surface of a sea as each bird guzzled his head along the ground after the scattered corn. The clucking, cooing noise that had led me thither, was formed by the blending together of countless expressions of individual contentment into one collective expression of contentment, or general grace during meat. Every now and again, a big peacock would separate himself from the mob and take a stately turn or two about the lawn, or perhaps mount for a moment upon the rail, and there shrilly publish to the world his satisfaction with himself and what he had to eat. It happened, for my sins, that none of these admirable birds had anything beyond the merest rudiment of a tail. Tails, it seemed, were out of season just then. But they had their necks for all that; and by their necks alone they do as much surpass all the other birds of our gray climate as they fall in quality of song below the blackbird or the lark. Surely the peacock, with its incomparable parade of glorious colour and the scrannel voice of it issuing forth, as in mockery, from its painted throat, must, like my landlady's butterflies at Great Missenden, have been invented by some skilful fabulist for the consolation and support of homely virtue: or rather, perhaps, by a fabulist not quite so skilful, who made points for the moment without having a studious enough eye to the complete effect; for I thought these melting greens and blues so beautiful that afternoon, that I would have given them my vote just then before the sweetest pipe in all the spring woods. I spoke of greens and blues. Now the reader must recollect a time, and not so long ago, when he was told—nay, even believed, after a dim, uncertain fashion—that green and blue were colours altogether incompatible and discordant. Perhaps people in those days had a knack of choosing blues and greens to bear their theory out: but what I want to know is, whether none of us, during all those deluded years, ever looked by any chance upon a peacock's neck; and, if we did, how we contrive to reconcile this wonder of perfect colouring with our obnoxious preconceptions? For indeed there is no piece of colour of the same extent in nature, that will so flatter and satisfy the lust of a man's eyes; and to come upon so many of them after these acres of stone-coloured heavens and russet woods and gray-brown ploughlands and white roads, was like going three whole days' journey to the southward, or a month back into the summer.

I was sorry to leave *Peacock Farm*—for so the place is called, after the name of its splendid pensioners—and go forward again in the quiet woods. It began to grow both damp and dusk under the beeches; and as the day declined the colour faded out of the foliage; and shadow, without form and void, took the place of all the fine tracery of leaves and delicate gradations of living green that had before accompanied my walk. I had been sorry to leave *Peacock Farm*, but I was not sorry to find myself once more in the open road under a pale and somewhat troubled-looking evening sky, and put my best foot foremost for the inn at Wendover.

Wendover, in itself, is a straggling, purposeless sort of place. Everybody seems to have had his own opinion as to how the street should go; or rather, every now and then a man seems to have arisen with a new idea on the subject, and led away a little sect of neighbours to join him in his heresy. It would have somewhat the look of an abortive watering-place, such as we may now see them here and there along the coast, but for the age of the houses, the comely quiet design of some of them, and the look of long habitation, of a life that is settled and rooted, and makes it worth while to train flowers about the windows and otherwise shape the dwelling to the humour of the inhabitant. The church, which might perhaps have served as rallying-point for these loose houses and pulled the township into something like intelligible unity, stands some distance off among great trees; but the inn (to take the public buildings in order of importance) is in what I understand to be the principal street: a pleasant old house, with bay windows, and three peaked gables, and many swallows' nests plastered about the eaves.

The interior of the inn was answerable to the outside: indeed I never saw any room much more to be admired than the low wainscoted parlour in which I spent the remainder of the evening. It was a short oblong in shape, save that the fireplace was built across one of the angles so as to cut it partially off, and the opposite angle was similarly truncated by a corner cupboard. The wainscoat was white;

and there was a Turkey carpet on the floor, so old that it might have been imported by Walter Shandy before he retired, worn almost through in some places, but in others making a good show of blues and oranges, none the less harmonious for being somewhat faded. The corner cupboard was agreeable in design; and there were just the right things upon the shelves—decanters and tumblers, and blue plates, and one red rose in a glass of water. The furniture was old-fashioned and stiff. Everything was in keeping down to the ponderous leaden inkstand on the round table. And you may fancy how pleasant it looked, all flushed and flickered over by the light of a brisk companionable fire, and seen, in a strange, tilted sort of perspective, in the three compartments of the old mirror above the chimney. As I sat reading in the great arm-chair, I kept looking round with the tail of my eye at the quaint bright picture that was about me, and could not help some pleasure and a certain childish pride in forming part of it. The book I read was about Italy in the early Renaissance, the pageantries and the light loves of princes, the passion of men for learning and poetry and art; but it was written, by good luck, after a solid prosaic fashion, that suited the room infinitely more nearly than the matter; and the result was, that I thought less, perhaps, of Lippo Lippi, or Lorenzo, or Politian,[19] than of the good Englishman who had written in that volume what he knew of them, and taken so much pleasure in his solemn polysyllables.

I was not left without society. My landlord had a very pretty little daughter, whom we shall call Lizzie. If I had made any notes at the time, I might be able to tell you something definite of her appearance. But faces have a trick of growing more and more spiritualised and abstract in the memory, until nothing remains of them but a look, a haunting expression; just that secret quality in a face that is apt to slip out somehow under the cunningest painter's touch, and leave the portrait dead for the lack of it. And if it is hard to catch with the finest of camel's-hair pencils, you may think how hopeless it must be to pursue after it with clumsy words. If I say, for instance, that this look, which I remember as Lizzie, was something wistful that seemed partly to come of slyness and in part of simplicity, and that I am inclined to imagine it had something to do with the daintiest suspicion of a cast in one of her large eyes, I shall have said all that I can, and the reader will not be much advanced towards comprehension. I had struck up an acquaintance with this little damsel in the morning, and professed much interest in her dolls and an impatient eagerness to see the large one which was kept locked away somewhere for great occasions. And so, I had not been very long in the parlour before the door opened, and in came Miss Lizzie with two dolls tucked clumsily under her arm. She was followed by her brother John, a year or so younger than herself, not simply to play propriety at our interview, but to show his own two whips in emulation of his sister's dolls. I did my best to make myself agreeable to my visitors; showing much admiration for the dolls and dolls' dresses, and, with a very serious demeanour, asking many questions about their age and character. I do not think that Lizzie distrusted my sincerity, but it was evident that she was both bewildered and a little contemptuous. Although she was ready herself to treat her dolls as if they were alive, she seemed to think rather poorly of any grown person who could fall heartily into the spirit of the fiction. Sometimes she would look at me with gravity and a sort of disquietude, as though she really feared I must be out of my wits. Sometimes, as when I inquired too particularly into the question of their names, she laughed at me so long and heartily that I began to feel almost embarrassed. But when, in an evil moment, I asked to be allowed to kiss one of them, she could keep herself no longer to herself. Clambering down from the chair on which she sat perched to show me, Cornelia-like,[20] her jewels, she ran straight out of the room and into the bar—it was just across the passage—and I could hear her telling her mother in loud tones, but apparently more in sorrow than in merriment, that *the gentleman in the parlour wanted to kiss Dolly*. I fancy she was determined to save me from this humiliating action even in spite of myself, for she never gave me the desired permission. She reminded me of an old dog I once knew, who would never suffer the master of the house to dance, out of an exaggerated sense of the dignity of that master's place and carriage.

After the young people were gone there was but one more incident ere I went to bed. I heard a party of children go up and down the dark street for a while, singing together sweetly. And the mystery of this little incident was so pleasant to me that I purposely refrained from asking who they were and wherefore they went singing at so late an hour. One can rarely be in a pleasant place without meeting with some pleasant accident. I have a conviction that these children would not have gone singing before the inn, unless the inn-parlour had been the delightful place it was. At least, if I had been in the customary public-room of the modern hotel, with all its disproportions and discomforts, my ears would have been dull, and there would have been some ugly temper or other uppermost in my spirit, and so they would have wasted their sweet songs upon an unworthy hearer.

Next morning early I went along to visit the church. It is a long-backed, red-and-white building, very much restored, and stands in a pleasant graveyard among those great trees of which I have spoken already. The sky was drowned in mist. Now and again pulses of cold wind went about the enclosure, and set the branches busy overhead, and the dead leaves scurrying into the angles of the church buttresses. Now and again, also, I could hear the dull sudden fall of a chestnut among the grass—the dog would bark before the rectory door—or there would come a clinking of pails from the stable-yard behind. But in spite of these occasional interruptions, in spite, also, of the continuous autumn twittering that filled the trees, the chief impression somehow was one as of utter silence, insomuch that the little greenish bell that peeped out of a window in the tower disquieted me with a sense of some possible and more inharmonious disturbance. The grass was wet, as if with a hoar-frost that had just been melted. I do not know that ever I saw a morning more autumnal. As I went to and fro among the graves, I saw some flowers set reverently before a recently erected tomb, and, drawing near, was almost startled to find they lay on the grave of a man seventy-two years old when he died. We are accustomed to strew flowers only over the young, where love has been cut short untimely, and great possibilities have been restrained by death. We strew them there in token that these possibilities, in some deeper sense,

331

shall yet be realised, and the touch of our dead loves remain with us and guide us to the end. And yet there was more significance, perhaps, and perhaps a greater consolation, in this little nosegay on the grave of one who had died old. We are apt to make so much of the tragedy of death, and think so little of the enduring tragedy of some men's lives, that we see more to lament for in a life cut off in the midst of usefulness and love, than in one that miserably survives all love and usefulness, and goes about the world the phantom of itself, without hope or joy or any consolation. These flowers seemed not so much the token of love that survived death, as of something yet more beautiful—of love that had lived a man's life out to an end with him, and been faithful and companionable, and not weary of loving, throughout all these years.

The morning cleared a little, and the sky was once more the old stone-coloured vault over the sallow meadows and the russet woods, as I set forth on a dog-cart[21] from Wendover to Tring. The road lay for a good distance along the side of the hills, with the great plain below on one hand, and the beechwoods above upon the other. The fields were busy with people ploughing and sowing: every here and there a jug of ale stood in the angle of the hedge, and I could see many a team wait smoking in the furrow as ploughman or sower stepped aside for a moment to take a draught. Over all the brown ploughlands, and under all the leafless hedgerows, there was a stout spirit of labour abroad, and, as it were a spirit of pic-nic. The horses smoked and the men laboured and shouted and drank in the sharp autumn morning; so that one had a strong effect of large, open-air existence. The fellow who drove me was something of a humourist; and his conversation was all in praise of an agricultural labourer's way of life. It was he who called my attention to these jugs of ale by the hedgerow; he could not sufficiently express the liberality of these men's wages; he told me how sharp an appetite was given by breaking up the earth in the morning air, whether with plough or spade, and cordially admired this provision of nature. He sang *O fortunatos agricolas!*[22] indeed, in every possible key, and with many cunning inflections; till I began to wonder what was the use of such people as Mr. Arch,[23] and to sing the same air myself in a more diffident manner.

Tring was reached, and then Tring railway station; for the two are not very near, the good people of Tring having held the railway, of old days, in extreme apprehension, lest some day it should break loose in the town and work mischief. I had a last walk, among russet beeches as usual, and the air filled, as usual, with the carolling of larks; I heard shots fired in the distance, and saw, as a new sign of the fulfilled autumn, two horsemen exercising a pack of fox-hounds. And then the train came and carried me back to London.

Notes

1 This essay recounts a walking tour Stevenson took of the Chiltern Hills in Buckinghamshire in October of 1874.

2 "We never describe nature better than when we strive to express soberly and simply the impression we have received." *The Revue des deux Mondes* (Review of the Two

Worlds)—a French magazine on literature and culture established in 1829. **RLS:** "I had nearly finished the transcription of the following pages, when I saw on a friend's table the number containing the piece from which this sentence is extracted, and, struck with a similarity of title, took it home with me and read it with indescribable satisfaction. I do not know whether I more envy M. Theuriet the pleasure of having written this delightful article, or the reader the pleasure, which I hope he has still before him, of reading it once and again, and lingering over the passages that please him most."

3 P.B. Shelley, "To a Skylark" (20).

4 Impenetrability or invulnerability.

5 Dogberry is the bumbling constable in Shakespeare's *Much Ado About Nothing* (3.3.21–27).

6 Shakespeare, *The Winter's Tale*, 4.3.34–45.

7 A thief in *The Winter's Tale*.

8 Laurence Sterne, *Tristram Shandy* (ch. 32).

9 Slang for donkey.

10 Joshua 6:1–21.

11 George Payne Rainsford James (1799–1860), popular English author of historical romance novels.

12 Charles Baudelaire's "Les Fenêtres" or "Windows" (1869).

13 *A Christmas Carol* (1843).

14 Asmodeus is the demon or genie released from imprisonment in a bottle in Alain Rene le Sage's 1707 novel *Le Diable boiteux* (*Asmodeus, the Lame Devil* or *The Devil on Two Sticks*). He repays his liberator by lifting house roofs so he can look into hidden scandals and write a satire on Paris society.

15 This essay was published in two parts in April and May of 1875 in *The Portfolio*. The first installment ends here.

16 Georg Wilhelm Friedrich Hegel (1770–1831), German idealist philosopher suspected of atheism and associated with the later theological debates of "higher criticism" (n. 6, p. 455). James McCosh (1811–1894), Scottish philosopher and President of Princeton University who attempted to reconcile Darwinian evolution with Christianity.

17 See "Pan's Pipes" (p. 113).

18 Small, of Lilliput: the kingdom of tiny people in Jonathan Swift's *Gulliver's Travels* (1726).

19 Painters of the Italian Renaissance: Filippo Lippi (1406–1469), depicted in Robert Browning's "Fra Lippo Lippi," and Lorenzo Costa (1460–1535). Agnolo Poliziano (Politian) (1454–1494), poet and classical scholar.

20 Cornelia (97–69 BC), wife of Julius Caesar.

21 An open carriage with back-to-back seats, one of which originally converted into a box for dogs.

22 "O fortunatos nimium sua si bona norint, agricolas" (Latin): The farmers would count themselves lucky, if they only knew how good they had it.—Virgil, *Georgics* (2.458).

23 Joseph Arch (1826–1919), activist for agricultural workers, founding president of the National Agricultural Labourers' Union in the U.K., and MP.

43

FOREST NOTES

On the Plain

Perhaps the reader knows already the aspect of the great levels of the Gâtinais, where they border with the wooded hills of Fontainebleau.[1] Here and there, a few grey rocks creep out of the forest as if to sun themselves. Here and there, a few apple-trees stand together on a knoll. The quaint undignified tartan of a myriad small fields dies out into the distance; the strips blend and disappear; and the dead flat lies forth open and empty, with no accident[2] save perhaps a thin line of trees or faint church-spire against the sky. Solemn and vast at all times, in spite of pettiness in the near details, the impression becomes more solemn and vast towards evening. The sun goes down, a swollen orange, as it were, into the sea. A blue-clad peasant rides home, with a harrow smoking behind him among the dry clods. Another still works with his wife in their little strip. An immense shadow fulfils the plain; these people stand in it up to their shoulders; and their heads, as they stoop over their work and rise again, are relieved from time to time against the golden sky.

These peasant farmers are well off now-a-days, and not by any means overworked; but somehow you always see in them the historical representative of the serf of yore, and think not so much of present times, which may be prosperous enough, as of the old days when the peasant was taxed beyond possibility of payment, and lived, in Michelet's image, like a hare between two furrows.[3] These very people now weeding their patch under the broad sunset, that very man and his wife, it seems to us, have suffered all the wrongs of France. It is they who have been their country's scapegoat for long ages; they who, generation after generation, have sowed and not reaped, reaped and another has garnered; and who have now entered into their reward, and enjoy their good things in their turn. For the days are gone by when the Seigneur[4] ruled and profited. "Le Seigneur," says the old formula, "enferme ses manants comme sous porte et gonds, du ciel à la terre. Tout est à lui, forêt chenue, oiseau dans l'air, poisson dans l'eau, bête au buisson, l'onde qui coule, la cloche dont le son au loin roule."[5] Such was his old state of sovereignty, a local god rather than a mere king. And now you may ask yourself where he is, and look round for vestiges of my late lord, and in all the countryside

334

there is no trace of him but his forlorn and fallen mansion. At the end of a long avenue, now sown with grain, in the midst of a close full of cypresses and lilacs, ducks and crowing chanticleers and droning bees, the old château[6] lifts its red chimneys and peaked roofs and turning vanes into the wind and sun. There is a glad spring bustle in the air perhaps, and the lilacs are all in flower, and the creepers green about the broken balustrade; but no spring shall revive the honour of the place. Old women of the people, little children of the people, saunter and gambol in the walled court or feed the ducks in the neglected moat. Plough horses, mighty of limb, browse in the long stables. The dial-hand on the clock waits for some better hour. Out on the plain, where hot sweat trickles into men's eyes and the spade goes in deep and comes up slowly, perhaps the peasant may feel a movement of joy at his heart, when he thinks that these spacious chimneys are now cold which have so often blazed and flickered upon gay folk at supper, while he and his hollow-eyed children watched through the night with empty bellies and cold feet. And perhaps, as he raises his head and sees the forest lying like a coast-line of low hills along the sea-like level of the plain, perhaps forest and château hold no unsimilar place in his affections. If the château was my lord's, the forest was my lord the king's; neither of them for this poor Jacques. If he thought to eke out his meagre way of life by some petty theft of wood for the fire, or for a new roof-tree, he found himself face to face with a whole department from the Grand Master of the Woods and Waters, who was a high-born lord, down to the common sergeant, who was a peasant like himself, and wore stripes or a bandoleer by way of uniform. For the first offence, by the Salic law,[7] there was a fine of fifteen sols; and should a man be taken more than once in fault, or circumstances aggravate the colour of his guilt, he might be whipped, branded, or hanged. There was a hangman over at Melun, and I doubt not a fine tall gibbet hard by the town gate, where Jacques might see his fellows dangle against the sky as he went to market.

And then, if he lived near so great a cover, there would be the more hares and rabbits to eat out his harvest and the more hunters to trample it down. My lord has a new horn from England. He has laid out seven francs in decorating it with silver and gold, and fitting it with a silken leash to hang about his shoulder. The hounds have been on a pilgrimage to the shrine of Saint Mesmer, or Saint Hubert in the Ardennes,[8] or some other holy intercessor who has made a specialty of the health of hunting dogs. In the grey dawn, the game was turned and the branch broken by our best piqueur. A rare day's hunting is before us. Wind a jolly flourish, sound the *bien-aller*[9] with all your lungs! Jacques must stand by, hat in hand, while quarry and hound and huntsman sweep across his field, and a year's sparing and labouring is as though it had not been. If he can see the ruin with a good enough grace, who knows but he may fall in favour with my lord; who knows but his son may become the last and least among the servants at his lordship's kennel—one of the two poor varlets[10] who get no wages, and sleep at night among the hounds?

For all that, the forest has been of use to Jacques, not only warming him with fallen wood, but giving him shelter in days of sore trouble, when my lord of the château, with all his troopers and trumpets, had been beaten from field after field into some ultimate fastness, or lay over-seas in an English prison. In these dark days, when the watch on the church steeple saw the smoke of burning villages on the sky-line, or a clump of spears and fluttering pennon[11] drawing nigh across the plain, these good folk gat them up, with all their household gods, into the wood, whence, from some high spur, their timid scouts might overlook the coming and going of the marauders, and see the harvest ridden down, and church and cottage go up to heaven all night in flame. It was but an unhomely refuge that the woods afforded, where they must abide all change of weather and keep house with wolves and vipers. Often there was none left alive, when they returned, to show the old divisions of field from field. And yet, as times went, when the wolves entered at night into depopulated Paris, and perhaps De Retz[12] was passing by with a company of demons like himself, even in these caves and thickets there were glad hearts and grateful prayers.

Once or twice, as I say, in the course of the ages, the forest may have served the peasant well, but at heart it is a royal forest, and noble by old association. These woods have rung to the horns of all the Kings of France, from Philip Augustus downwards. They have seen Saint Louis exercise the dogs he brought with him from Egypt; Francis I. go a-hunting with ten thousand horses in his train; and Peter of Russia following his first stag.[13] And so they are still haunted for the imagination by royal hunts and progresses, and peopled with the faces of memorable men of yore. And this distinction is not only in virtue of the pastime of dead monarchs. Great events, great revolutions, great cycles in the affairs of men, have here left their note, here taken shape in some significant and dramatic situation. It was hence that Guise and his leaguers led Charles the Ninth a prisoner to Paris.[14] Here, booted and spurred, and with all his dogs about him, Napoleon met the Pope beside a woodland cross. Here, on his way to Elba not so long after, he kissed the eagle of the Old Guard, and spoke words of passionate farewell to his soldiers. And here, after Waterloo, rather than yield its ensign to the new power, one of his faithful regiments burned that memorial of so much toil and glory on the Grand Master's table, and drank its dust in brandy, as a devout priest consumes the remnants of the Host.[15]

In the Season

Close in to the edge of the forest, so close that the trees of the *bornage*[16] stand pleasantly about the last houses, sits a certain small and very quiet village. There is but one street, and that, not long ago, was a green lane, where the cattle browsed between the door-steps. As you go up this street, drawing ever nearer the beginning of the wood, you will arrive at last before an inn where artists lodge. To the door (for I imagine it to be six o'clock on some fine summer's even), half-a-dozen, or maybe half-a-score, of people have brought out chairs, and now sit sunning themselves and waiting the omnibus from Melun. If you go on into the court you will find as many more, some in the billiard-room over absinthe and a match of corks, some without over a last cigar and a vermout. The doves coo and flutter from the dovecot; Hortense is drawing water from the well; and as all the rooms open into the court, you can see the white-capped cook over the furnace in the kitchen, and some idle painter, who has stored his canvases and washed his brushes, jangling a waltz on the crazy tongue-tied piano in the salle-à-manger. "*Edmond, encore un vermout*," cries a man in velveteen, adding in a tone of apologetic after-thought, "*un double, s'il vous plaît.*"[17] "Where were you working?" asks one in pure white linen from top to toe. "At the Carrefour de l'Epine,"[18] returns another in corduroy (they are all gaitered, by the way). "I couldn't do a thing to it. I ran out of white. Where were you?" "I wasn't working, I was looking for motives." Here is an outbreak of jubilation, and a lot of men clustering together about some new-comer with outreached hands; perhaps the "correspondence" has come in and brought So-and-so from Paris, or perhaps it is only So-and-so who has walked over from Chailly to dinner.

"*A table, Messieurs!*" cries M. Siron, bearing through the court the first tureen of soup. And immediately the company begins to settle down about the long tables, in the dining-room framed all round with sketches of all degrees of merit and demerit. There is the big picture of the huntsman winding a horn, with a dead boar between his legs, and his legs—well, his legs in stockings. And here is the little picture of a raw mutton-chop, in which Such-a-one knocked a hole last summer with no worse a missile than a plum from the dessert. And under all these works of art so much eating goes forward, so much drinking, so much jabbering in French and English, that it would do your heart good merely to peep and listen at the door. One man is telling how they all went last year to the Fête[19] at Fleury, and another how well So-and-so would sing of an evening; and here are a third and fourth making plans for the whole future of their lives; and there is a fifth imitating a conjuror and making faces on his clenched fist, surely of all arts the most difficult and admirable! A sixth has eaten his fill, lights a cigarette, and resigns himself to digestion. A seventh has just dropped in, and calls for soup. Number eight, meanwhile, has left the table, and is once more trampling the poor piano under powerful and uncertain fingers.

Dinner over, people drop outside to smoke and chat. Perhaps we go along to visit our friends at the other end of the village, where there is always a good welcome and a good talk, and perhaps some pickled oysters and white wine to close the evening. Or a dance is organized in the dining-room, and the piano exhibits all its paces under manful jockeying, to the light of the three or four candles and a lamp or two, while the waltzers move to and fro upon the wooden floor, and sober men, who are not given to such light pleasures, get up on the table or the sideboard and sit there looking on approvingly, over a pipe and a tumbler of wine. Or sometimes—suppose my lady moon looks forth, and the court from out the half-lit dining-room seems nearly as bright as by day, and the light picks out the window-panes, and makes a clear shadow under every vine-leaf on the wall—sometimes a picnic is proposed, and a basket made ready, and a good procession formed in front of the hotel. The two trumpeters in honour go before; and as we file down the long alley, and up through devious footpaths among rocks and pine-trees, with every here and there a dark passage of shadow, and every here and there a spacious outlook over moonlit woods, these two precede us and sound many a jolly flourish as they walk. We gather ferns and dry boughs into the cavern, and soon a good blaze flutters the shadows of the old bandits' haunt, and shows shapely beards and comely faces and toilettes ranged about the wall. The bowl is lit, and the punch burned and sent around in scalding thimblefuls. So a good hour or two may pass with song and jest. And then we go home in the moonlight morning, straggling a good deal among the birch-tufts and the boulders, but ever called together again, as one of our leaders winds his horn. Perhaps some one of the party will not heed the summons, but chooses out some by-way of his own. As he follows the winding sandy road, he hears the flourishes grow fainter and fainter in the distance, and die finally out, and still walks on in the strange coolness and silence and between the crisp lights and shadows of the moonlit woods, until suddenly the bell rings out the hour from far away Chailly, and he starts to find himself alone. No surf-bell on forlorn and perilous shores, no passing knoll over the busy market-place, can speak with a more heavy and disconsolate tongue to human ears. Each stroke calls up a host of ghostly reverberations in his mind. And as he stands rooted, it has grown once more so utterly silent that it seems to him he might hear the church bells ring the hour out all the world over, not at Chailly only, but in Paris, and away in outlandish cities, and in the village on the river, where his childhood passed between the sun and flowers.

Idle Hours

The woods by night, in all their uncanny effect, are not rightly to be understood until you can compare them with the woods by day. The stillness of the medium, the floor of glittering sand, these trees that go streaming up like monstrous seaweeds and waver in the moving winds like the weeds in submarine currents, all these set the mind working on the thought of what you may have seen off a foreland or over the side of a boat, and make you feel like a diver, down in the quiet water, fathoms below the tumbling, transitory surface of the sea. And yet in itself, as I say, the strangeness of these nocturnal solitudes is not to be felt fully without the sense of contrast. You must have risen in the morning and seen the woods as they are by day, kindled and coloured in the sun's light; you must have felt the odour of innumerable trees at even, the unsparing heat along the forest roads and the coolness of the groves.

And on the first morning, you will doubtless rise betimes. If you have not been wakened before by the visit of some adventurous pigeon, you will be wakened as soon as the sun can reach your window—for there are no blinds or shutters to keep him out—and the room, with its bare wood floor and bare whitewashed walls, shines all round you in a sort of glory of reflected lights. You may doze a while longer by snatches, or lie awake to study the charcoal-men and dogs and horses with which former occupants have defiled the partitions; Thiers,[20] with wily profile; local celebrities, pipe in hand; or maybe a romantic landscape, splashed in oil. Meanwhile artist after artist drops into the salle-à-manger[21] for coffee, and then shoulders easel, sunshade, stool, and paint-box, bound into a faggot, and sets off for what he calls his "motive." And artist after artist, as he goes out of the village, carries with him a little following of dogs. For the dogs, who belong only nominally to any special master, hang about the gate of the forest all day long, and whenever any one goes by, who hits their fancy, profit by his escort, and go forth with him to play an hour or two at hunting. They would like to be under the trees all day. But they cannot go alone. They require a pretext. And so they take the passing artist as an excuse to go into the woods, as they might take a walking-stick as an excuse to bathe. With quick ears, long spines, and bandy legs, or perhaps as tall as a greyhound and with a bulldog's head, this company of mongrels will trot by your side all day and come home with you at night, still showing white teeth and wagging stunted tail. Their good humour is not to be exhausted. You may pelt them with stones, if you please, and all they will do is to give you a wider berth. If once they come out with you, to you they will remain faithful, and with you return; although if you meet them next morning in the street, it is as like as not they will cut you with a countenance of brass.

The forest—a strange thing for an Englishman—is very destitute of birds. This is no country where every patch of wood among the meadows gives up an incense of song, and every valley, wandered through by a streamlet, rings and reverberates from side to side with a profusion of clear notes. And this rarity of birds is not be regretted on its own account only. For the insects prosper in their absence, and become as one of the plagues of Egypt.[22] Ants swarm in the hot sand; mosquitoes drone their nasal drone; wherever the sun finds a hole in the roof of the forest you see a myriad transparent creatures coming and going in the shaft of light; and even between whiles, even where there is no incursion of sun-rays into the dark arcade of the wood, you are conscious of a continual drift of insects, an ebb and flow of infinitesimal living things between the trees. Nor are insects the only evil creatures that haunt the forest. For you may plump into a cave among the rocks, and find yourself face to face with a wild boar; or see a crooked viper slither across the road.

Perhaps you may set yourself down in the bay between two spreading beech-roots with a book on your lap, and be awakened all of a sudden by a friend: "I say, just keep where you are, will you? You make the jolliest motive." And you reply: "Well, I don't mind, if I may smoke." And thereafter the hours go idly by. Your friend at the easel labours doggedly, a little way off, in the wide shadow of the tree; and yet farther, across a strait of glaring sunshine, you see another painter, encamped in the shadow of another tree, and up to his waist in the fern. You cannot watch your own effigy growing out of the white trunk, and the trunk beginning to stand forth from the rest of the wood, and the whole picture getting dappled over with the flecks of sun, that slip through the leaves overhead, and as a wind goes by and sets the trees a-talking, flicker hither and thither like butterflies of light. But you know it is going forward; and, out of emulation with the painter, get ready your own palette and lay out the colour for a woodland scene in words.

Your tree stands in a hollow paved with fern and heather, set in a basin of low hills, and scattered over with rocks and junipers. All the open is steeped in pitiless sunlight. Everything stands out as though it were cut in cardboard, every colour is strained into its highest key. The boulders are some of them upright and dead like monolithic castles, some of them prone like sleeping cattle. The junipers—looking, in their soiled and ragged mourning, like some funeral procession that has gone seeking the place of sepulture three hundred years and more in wind and rain—are daubed in, forcibly against the glowing ferns and heather. Every tassel of their rusty foliage is defined with præ-Raphaelite[23] minuteness. And a sorry figure they make out there in the sun, like misbegotten yew-trees! The scene is all pitched in a key of colour so peculiar, and lit up with such a discharge of violent sunlight as a man might live fifty years in England and not see.

Meanwhile at your elbow some one tunes up a song, words of Ronsard[24] to a pathetic tremulous air, of how the poet loved his mistress long ago, and pressed on her the flight of time, and told her how white and quiet the dead lay under the stones, and how the boat dipped and pitched as the shades embarked for the passionless land. Yet a little while, sang the poet, and there shall be no more love; only to sit, and remember loves that might have been. There is a falling flourish in the air that remains in the memory and comes back in incongruous places, on the seat of hansoms or in the warm bed at night, with something of a forest savour.

"You can get up now," says the painter; "I'm at the background."

And so up you get, stretching yourself, and go your way into the wood, the daylight becoming richer and more golden, and the shadows stretching further into the open. A cool air comes along the highways, and the scents awaken. The fir-trees breathe abroad their ozone. Out of unknown thickets comes forth the soft, secret, aromatic odour of the woods, not like a smell of the free heaven, but as though court ladies, who had known these paths in ages long gone by, still walked in the summer evenings, and shed, from their brocades, a breath of musk or bergamot upon the woodland winds. One side of the long avenues is still kindled with the sun, the other is plunged in transparent shadow. Over the trees, the west begins to burn like a furnace; and the painters gather up their chattels, and go down, by avenue or footpath, to the plain.

A Pleasure Party

As this excursion is a matter of some length, and moreover we go in force, we have set aside our usual vehicle, the pony cart, and ordered a large wagonette from Lejosne's.[25] It has been waiting for near an hour, while one went to pack a knapsack, and t'other hurried over his toilette and coffee; but now it is filled from end to end with merry folk in summer attire, the coachman cracks his whip, and amid much applause from round the inn door, off we rattle at a spanking trot. The way lies through the forest, up hill and down dale, and by beech and pine wood, in the cheerful morning sunshine. The English get down at all the ascents and walk on a-head for exercise; the French are mightily entertained at this, and keep coyly

340

underneath the tilt. As we go we carry with us a pleasant noise of laughter and light speech, and some one will be always breaking out into a bar or two of opera bouffe.[26] Before we get to the Route Ronde[27] here comes Desprez, the colourman from Fontainebleau, trudging across on his weekly peddle with a case of merchandise; and it is, "Desprez, leave me some malachite green;" "Desprez, leave me so much canvas;" "Desprez, leave me this, or leave me that;" M. Desprez standing the while in the sunlight with grave face and many salutations. The next interruption is more important. For some time back we have had the sound of cannon in our ears; and now, a little past Franchard, we find a mounted trooper holding a led horse, who brings the wagonette to a stand. The artillery is practising in the Quadrilateral,[28] it appears; passage along the Route Ronde formally interdicted for the moment. There is nothing for it but to draw up at the glaring cross-roads, and get down to make fun with the notorious Cocardon, the most ungainly and ill-bred dog of all the ungainly and ill-bred dogs of Barbizon, or clamber about the sandy banks. And meanwhile the Doctor, with sun umbrella, wide panama, and patriarchal beard, is busy wheedling and (for ought the rest of us know) bribing the too facile sentry. His speech is smooth and dulcet, his manner dignified and insinuating. It is not for nothing that the Doctor has voyaged all the world over, and speaks all languages, from French to Patagonian. He has not come home from perilous journeys to be thwarted by a corporal of horse. And so we soon see the soldier's mouth relax, and his shoulders intimate a relenting heart. "En voiture, Messieurs, Mesdames,"[29] sings the Doctor; and on we go again at a good round pace, for black care follows hard after us, and discretion prevails not a little over valour in some timorous spirits of the party. At any moment we may meet the sergeant, who will send us back. At any moment we may encounter a flying shell, which will send us somewhere further off than Grez.

Grez—for that is our destination—has been highly recommended for its beauty. "Il y a de l'eau,"[30] people have said, with an emphasis, as if that settled the question, which, for a French mind, I am rather led to think it does. And Grez, when we get there, is indeed a place worthy of some praise. It lies out of the forest, a cluster of houses, with an old bridge, an old castle in ruin, and a quaint old church. The inn garden descends in terraces to the river; stable-yard, kail-yard, orchard, and a space of lawn, fringed with rushes and embellished with a green arbour. On the opposite bank there is a reach of English-looking plain, set thickly with willows and poplars. And between the two lies the river, clear and deep and full of reeds and floating lilies. Water-plants cluster about the starlings of the long low bridge, and stand half-way up upon the piers in green luxuriance. They catch the dipped oar with long antennæ, and chequer the slimy bottom with the shadow of their leaves. And the river wanders hither and thither among the islets, and is smothered and broken up by the weeds, like an old building in the lithe hardy arms of the climbing ivy. You may watch the box where the good man of the inn keeps fish alive for his kitchen, one oily ripple following another over the top of the yellow deal. And you can hear a splashing and a prattle of voices from the shed under the old kirk, where the village women wash and wash all day, among the fish and water-lilies. It seems as if linen washed there should be specially cool and sweet.

We have come here for the river. And no sooner have we all bathed than we board the two shallops,[31] and push off gaily, and go gliding under the trees and gathering a great treasure of water-lilies. Some one sings; some trail their hands in the cool water; some lean over the gunwale, to see the image of the tall poplars far below, and the shadow of the boat with the balanced oars and their own head protruded, glide smoothly over the yellow floor of the stream. At last, the day declining—all silent and happy, and up to the knees in the wet lilies—we punt slowly back again to the landing-place beside the bridge. There is a wish for solitude on all. One hides himself in the arbour with a cigarette; another goes a walk in the country with Cocardon; a third inspects the church. And it is not till dinner is on the table, and the inn's best wine goes round from glass to glass, that we begin to throw off the restraint and fuse once more into a jolly fellowship.

Half the party are to return to-night with the wagonette, and some of the others, loth to break up good company, will go with them a bit of the way and drink a stirrup-cup at Marlotte. It is dark in the wagonette, and not so merry as it might have been. The coachman loses the road. So-and-so tries to light fireworks with the most indifferent success. Some sing, but the rest are too weary to applaud; and it seems as if the festival were fairly at an end:

Nous avons fait la noce,
Rentrons à nos foyers![32]

And such is the burthen, even after we have come to Marlotte and taken our places in the court at Mother Antonine's. There is punch on the long table out in the open air, where the guests dine in summer weather. The candles flare in the night wind, and the faces around the punch are lit up, with shifting emphasis, against a background of complete and solid darkness. It is all picturesque enough; but the fact is, we are aweary. We yawn; we are out of the vein; we have made the wedding, as the song says, and now, for pleasure's sake, let's make an end on't. When here comes striding into the court, booted to mid thigh, spurred and splashed, in a jacket of green cord, the great famous and redoubtable Blank;[33] and in a moment the fire kindles again, and the night is witness of our laughter as he imitates Spaniards, Germans, Englishmen, picture-dealers, all eccentric ways of speaking and thinking, with a possession, a fury, a strain of mind and voice, that would rather suggest a nervous crisis than a desire to please. We are as merry as ever when the trap sets forth again, and say farewell noisily to all the good folk going further. Then, as we are far enough from thoughts of sleep, we visit Blank in his quaint house, and sit an hour or so in a great tapestried chamber, laid with furs, littered with sleeping hounds, and lit up, in fantastic shadow and shine, by a wood fire in a mediæval chimney. And then we plod back through the darkness to the inn beside the river.

342

How quick bright things come to confusion! When we arise next morning, the grey showers fall steadily, the trees hang limp, and the face of the stream is spoiled with dimpling raindrops. Yesterday's lilies encumber the garden walk, or begin, dismally enough, their voyage towards the Seine and the salt sea. A sickly shimmer lies upon the dripping house roofs, and all the colour is washed out of the green and golden landscape of last night, as though an envious man had taken a water-colour sketch and blotted it together with a sponge. We go out a-walking in the wet road; but the roads about Grez have a trick of their own: they go on for a while among clumps of willows and patches of vine, and then, suddenly and without any warning, cease and determine in some miry hollow or upon some bald knowe; you have a short period of hope, then right about face, and back the way you came! So we draw about the kitchen fire and play a round game of cards for ha'pence, or go to the billiard-room for a match at corks; and by one consent, a messenger is sent over for the wagonette—Grez shall be left to-morrow.

To-morrow dawns so fair that two of the party agree to walk back for exercise,[34] and let their knapsacks follow by the trap. I need hardly say they are neither of them French; for of all English phrases, the phrase "for exercise" is the least comprehensible across the straits of Dover. All goes well for a while with the pedestrians. The wet woods are full of scents in the noontide. At a certain cross, where there is a guard-house, they make a halt, for the forester's wife is the daughter of their good host at Barbizon. And so there they are hospitably received by the comely woman, with one child in her arms and another prattling and tottering at her gown, and drink some syrup of quince in the back parlour, with a map of the forest on the wall, and some prints of love affairs and the great Napoleon hunting. As they draw near the Quadrilateral, and hear once more the report of the big guns, they take a by-road to avoid the sentries, and go on a while somewhat vaguely, with the sound of the cannon in their ears and the rain beginning to fall. The ways grow wider and sandier; here and there there are real sand-hills as though by the sea-shore; the firwood is open and grows in clumps upon the hillocks, and the race of sign-posts is no more. One begins to look at the other doubtfully. "I am sure we should keep more to the right," says one; and the other is just as certain they should hold to the left. And now, suddenly, the heavens open and the rain falls "sheer and strong and loud,"[35] as out of a shower-bath. In a moment, they are as wet as shipwrecked sailors; they cannot see out of their eyes for the drift, and the water churns and gurgles in their boots. They leave the track, and try across country with a gambler's desperation; for it seems as if it were impossible to make the situation worse; and, for the next hour, go scrambling from boulder to boulder, or plod along paths that are now no more than rivulets, and across waste clearings where the scattered shells and broken fir-trees tell all too plainly of the cannon in the distance. And meantime the cannon grumble out responses to the grumbling thunder. There is such a mixture of melodrama and sheer discomfort about all this, it is at once so gray and so lurid, that it is far more agreeable to read and write about by the chimney-corner, than to suffer in the person. At last, they chance on the right path, and make Franchard in the early evening, the sorriest pair of wanderers that ever welcomed English ale. Thence, by the Bois d'Hyver, the Ventes-Alexandre, and the Pins Brulés,[36] to the clean hostelry, dry clothes, and dinner.

The Woods in Spring

I think you will like the forest best in the sharp early springtime, when it is just beginning to reawaken and innumerable violets peep from among the fallen leaves; when two or three people at most sit down to dinner; and, at table, you will do well to keep a rug across your knees, for the nights are chill, and the salle-à-manger opens on the court. There is less to distract the attention for one thing, and the forest is more itself; it is not bedotted with artists' sunshades as with unknown mushrooms, nor bestrewn with the remains of English picnics. The hunting still goes on, and at any moment your heart may be brought into your mouth as you hear far-away horns, or you may be told by an agitated peasant that the Vicomte[37] has gone up the avenue, not ten minutes since, "à fond de train, monsieur, et avec douze piqueurs."[38]

If you go up to some coign of vantage in the system of low hills that permeates the forest, you will see many different tracts of country, each of its own cold and melancholy neutral tint, and all mixed together and mingled one into the other at the seams. You will see tracts of leafless beeches of a faint yellowish gray, and leafless oaks a little ruddier in the hue. Then zones of pine of a solemn green, and, dotted among the pines or standing by themselves in rocky clearings, the delicate snow-white trunks of birches, spreading out into snow-white branches yet more delicate, and crowned and canopied with a purple haze of twigs. And then a long bare ridge of tumbled boulders, with bright sandbreaks between them, and wavering sandy roads among the bracken and brown heather. It is all rather cold and unhomely; it has not the perfect beauty, not the gemlike colouring, of the wood in the later year, when it is no more than one vast colonnade of verdant shadow, tremulous with insects, intersected here and there by lanes of sunlight set in purple heather. The loveliness of the woods in March is not, assuredly, of this blowsy, rustic type. It is made sharp with a grain of salt, with a touch of ugliness; it has a sting like the sting of bitter ale; you acquire the love of it as men acquire a taste for olives. And the wonderful clear, pure air wells into your lungs the while, by voluptuous inhalations, and makes the eyes bright, and sets the heart ticking to a new tune. Or rather, to an old tune; for you remember in your boyhood something akin to this spirit of adventure, this thirst for exploration, that now takes you masterfully by the hand, plunges you into many a deep grove and drags you over many a stony crest. It is as though the whole wood were full of friendly voices calling you farther in, and you turn from one side to another, like Buridan's donkey,[39] in a maze of pleasure.

Comely beeches send up their white, straight, clustered branches, barred with green moss, like so many fingers from a half-clenched hand. Mighty oaks stand to the ankles in a fine tracery of underwood; thence, the tall shaft climbs upward, and the great forest of stalwart boughs spreads out into the golden evening sky, where the rooks are flying and calling. On the sward of the Bois d'Hyver, the firs stand well asunder with outspread arms, like fencers saluting; and the air smells of resin all around, and the sound of the axe is rarely still. But strangest of all, and in appearance oldest of all, are the dim and wizard upland districts of young wood. The ground is carpeted with fir-tassel, and strewn with fir-apples and flakes of fallen bark. Rocks lie crouching in the thicket, guttered with rain, tufted with lichen, white with years and the rigours of the changeful seasons. Brown and yellow butterflies are sown and carried away again by the light air—like this-tledown. The loneliness of these coverts is so excessive, that there are moments when pleasure draws to the verge of fear. You listen and listen for some noise to break the silence, till you grow half mesmerised by the intensity of the strain; your sense of your own identity is troubled; your brain reels, like that of some gymnosophist[40] poring on his own nose in Asiatic jungles; and should you see your own outspread feet, you see them, not as anything of yours, but as a feature of the scene around you.

Still the forest is always, but the stillness is not always unbroken. You can hear the wind pass in the distance over the tree-tops; sometimes briefly, like the noise of a train; sometimes with a long steady rush, like the breaking of waves. And sometimes, close at hand, the branches move, a moan goes through the thicket, and the wood thrills to its heart. Perhaps you may hear a carriage on the road to Fontainebleau, a bird gives a dry continual chirp, the dead leaves rustle underfoot, or you may time your steps to the steady recurrent strokes of the woodman's axe. From time to time, over the low grounds, a flight of rooks goes by; and from time to time, the cooing of wild doves falls upon the ear, not sweet and rich and near at hand as in England, but a sort of voice of the woods, thin and far away, as fits these solemn places. Or you hear suddenly the hollow, eager, violent barking of dogs; scared deer flit past you through the fringes of the wood; then a man or two run-ning, in green blouse, with gun and game-bag on a bandoleer; and then, out of the thick of the trees, comes the jar of rifle-shots. Or perhaps the hounds are out, and horns are blown, and scarlet-coated huntsmen flash through the clearings, and the solid noise of horses galloping passes below you, where you sit perched among the rocks and heather. The boar is afoot, and all over the forest and in all neigh-bouring villages, there is a vague excitement and a vague hope; for who knows whither the chase may lead? and even to have seen a single piqueur[41] or spoken to a single sportsman, is to be a man of consequence for the night.

Besides men who shoot and men who ride with the hounds, there are few people in the forest, in the early spring, save woodcutters plying their axes steadily, and old women and children gathering wood for the fire. You may meet such a party coming home in the twilight: the old woman laden with a faggot of chips, and the little ones hauling a long branch behind them in her wake. That is the worst of what there is to encounter; and if I tell you of what once happened to a friend of mine, it is by no means to tantalize you with false hopes; for the adventure was unique. It was on a very cold, still, sunless morning, with a flat grey sky and a frosty tingle in the air, that this friend (who shall here be nameless)[42] heard the notes of a key-bugle played with much hesitation, and saw the smoke of a fire spread out along the green pine-tops, in a remote uncanny glen, hard by a hill of naked boulders. He drew near warily, and beheld a picnic party seated under a tree in an open. The old father knitted a sock, the mother sat staring at the fire. The eldest son, in the uniform of a private of dragoons, was choosing out notes on a key-bugle. Two or three daughters lay in the neighbourhood picking violets. And the whole party as grave and silent as the woods around them! My friend watched for a long time, he says; but all held their peace; not one spoke or smiled; only the dragoon kept choosing out single notes upon the bugle, and the father knitted away at his work, and made strange movements the while with his flexible eyebrows. They took no notice whatever of my friend's presence, which was disquieting in itself, and increased the resemblance of the whole party to mechanical waxworks. Certainly, he affirms, a wax figure might have played the bugle with more spirit than that strange dragoon. And as this hypothesis of his became more certain, the awful insolubility of why they should be left out there in the woods with nobody to wind them up again when they ran down, and a growing disquietude as to what might happen next, became too much for his courage, and he turned tail, and fairly took to his heels. It might have been a singing in his ears, but he fancies he was followed, as he ran, by a peal of Titanic laughter. Nothing has ever transpired to clear up the mystery; it may be they were automata; or it may be (and this is the theory to which I lean myself), that this is all another chapter for Heine's "Gods in Exile;"[43] that the upright old man with the eyebrows was no other than Father Jove, and the young dragoon with the taste for music either Apollo or Mars.

Morality

Strange indeed is the attraction of the forest for the minds of men. Not one nor two only, but a great chorus of grateful voices have arisen to spread abroad its fame. Half the famous writers of modern France have had their word to say about Fontainebleau. Chateaubriand, Michelet, Béranger, George Sand, de Sènancour, Flaubert, Murger, the brothers Goncourt, Théodore de Banville, each of these has done something to the eternal praise and memory of these woods.[44] Even at the very worst of times, even when the picturesque[45] was anathema in the eyes of all Persons of Taste, the forest still preserved a certain reputation for beauty. It was in 1730 that the Abbé Guilbert[46] published his *Historical Description of the Palace, Town, and Forest of Fontainebleau*. And very droll it is to see him, as he tries to set forth his admiration in terms of what was then permissible. The monstrous rocks, &c., says the Abbé, "sont admirées avec surprise des voyageurs qui s'écrient aussitôt avec Horace: Ut mihi devio rupes et vacuum nemus mirari libet."[47] The good man is not exactly lyrical in his praise; and you see how he sets his back against Horace as against a trusty oak. Horace, at any rate, was classical. For the rest, however, the Abbé likes places where many alleys meet; or which, like the Belle-Etoile,[48] are kept up "by a special gardener," and admires at the Table du Roi[49] the labours of the Grand Master of Woods and Waters, the Sieur de la Falure, "qui a fait faire ce magnifique endroit."[50]

But indeed it is not so much for its beauty that the forest makes a claim upon men's hearts, as for that subtle something, that quality of the air, that emanation from the old trees, that so wonderfully changes and renews a weary spirit. Disappointed men, sick Francis Firsts and vanquished Grand Monarchs, time out of mind have come here for consolation. Hither perplexed folk have retired out of the press of life, as into a deep bay-window on some night of masquerade, and here found quiet and silence, and rest, the mother of wisdom. It is the great moral spa; this forest without a fountain is itself the true fountain of Juventius.[51] It is the best place in the world to bring an old sorrow that has been a long while your friend and enemy; and if, like Béranger's, your gaiety has run away from home and left open the door for sorrow to come in, of all covers in Europe, it is here you may expect to find the truant hid. With every hour you change. The air penetrates through your clothes, and nestles to your living body. You love exercise and slumber, long fasting and full meals. You forget all your scruples and live awhile in peace and freedom, and for the moment only. For here, all is absent that can stimulate to moral feeling. Such people as you see may be old, or toilworn, or sorry; but you see them framed in the forest, like figures on a painted canvas; and for you, they are not people in any living and kindly sense. You forget the grim contrariety of interests. You forget the narrow lane where all men jostle together in unchivalrous contention, and the kennel, deep and unclean, that gapes on either hand for the defeated. Life is simple enough, it seems, and the very idea of sacrifice becomes like a mad fancy out of a last night's dream.

Your ideal is not perhaps high, but it is plain and possible. You become enamoured of a life of change and movement and the open air, where the muscles shall be more exercised than the affections. When you have had your will of the forest, you may visit the whole round world. You may buckle on your knapsack and take the road on foot. You may bestride a good nag, and ride forth, with a pair of saddle-bags, into the enchanted East. You may cross the Black Forest, and see Germany widespread before you, like a map, dotted with old cities, walled and spired, that dream all day on their own reflections in the Rhine or Danube. You may pass the spinal cord of Europe, and go down from Alpine glaciers to where Italy extends her marble moles and glasses her marble palaces in the midland sea. You may sleep in flying trains or wayside taverns. You may be wakened at dawn by the scream of the express or the small pipe of the robin in the hedge. For you the rain should allay the dust of the beaten road; the wind dry your clothes upon you as you walked. Autumn should hang out russet pears and purple grapes along the lane; inn after inn proffer you their cups of raw wine; river by river receive your body in the sultry noon. Wherever you went warm valleys and high trees and pleasant villages should compass you about; and light fellowships should take you by the arm, and walk with you an hour upon your way. You may see, from afar off, what it will come to in the end—the weather-beaten red-nosed vagabond, consumed by a fever of the feet, cut off from all near touch of human sympathy, a waif, an Ishmael,[52] and an outcast. And yet it will seem well—and yet, in the air of the forest, this will seem the best—to break all the network bound about your feet by birth and old companionship and loyal love, and bear your shovelful of phosphates to and fro, in town and country, until the hour of the great dissolvent.

Or, perhaps, you will keep to the cover. For the forest is by itself, and forest life owns small kinship with life in the dismal land of labour. Men are so far sophisticated that they cannot take the world as it is given to them by the sight of their eyes. Not only what they see and hear, but what they know to be behind, enter into their notion of a place. If the sea, for instance, lie just across the hills, sea-thoughts will come to them at intervals, and the tenor of their dreams from time to time will suffer a sea-change. And so here, in this forest, a knowledge of its greatness is for much in the effect produced. You reckon up the miles that lie between you and intrusion. You may walk before you all day long, and not fear to touch the barrier of your Eden, or stumble out of fairyland into the land of gin and steam-hammers. And there is an old tale that enhances for the imagination the grandeur of the woods of France, and secures you in the thought of your seclusion. When Charles VI. hunted in the time of his wild boyhood near Senlis, there was captured an old stag, having a collar of bronze about his neck, and these words engraved on the collar: "Cæsar mihi hoc donavit."[53] It is no wonder if the minds of men were moved at this occurrence, and they stood aghast to find themselves thus touching hands with forgotten ages, and following an antiquity with hound and horn. And even for you, it is scarcely in an idle curiosity that you ponder how many centuries this stag had carried its free antlers through the wood, and how many summers and winters had shone and snowed on the imperial badge. If the extent of solemn wood could thus safeguard a tall stag from the hunters' hounds and horses, might not you also play hide and seek, in these groves, with all the pangs and trepidations of man's life, and elude Death, the mighty hunter, for more than the span of human years? Here, also, crash his arrows; here, in the farthest glade, sounds the gallop of the pale horse. But he does not hunt this cover with all his hounds, for the game is thin and small: and if you were but alert and wary, if you lodged ever in the deepest thickets, you too might live on into later generations, and astonish men by your stalwart age and the trophies of an immemorial success.

For the forest takes away from you all excuse to die. There is nothing here to cabin or thwart your free desires. Here all the impudencies of the brawling world reach you no more. You may count your hours, like Endymion,[54] by the strokes of the lone woodcutter, or by the progression of the lights and shadows, and the sun wheeling his wide circuit through the naked heavens. Here shall you see no enemies but winter and rough weather. And if a pang comes to you at all, it will be a pang of healthful hunger. All the puling sorrows, all the carking repentance, all this talk of duty that is no duty, in the great peace, in the pure daylight of these woods, fall away from you like a garment. And if perchance you come forth upon an eminence, where the wind blows upon you large and fresh, and the pines knock their long stems together, like an ungainly sort of puppet, and see far away over the plain a factory chimney defined against the pale horizon—it is for you, as for the staid and simple peasant when, with his plough, he upturns old arms and harness from the furrow of the glebe.[55] Ay, sure enough, there was a battle there in the old times; and, sure enough, there is a world out yonder where men strive together with a noise of oaths and weeping and clamorous dispute. So much you apprehend by an athletic act of the imagination. A faint far-off rumour as of Merovingian[56] wars: a legend as of some dead religion.

Notes

1 Stevenson repeatedly visited France's Fontainebleau, Barbizon, and Grez-sur-Loing between 1875 and 1878.
2 A variation of landscape.
3 Jules Michelet, *The Bird* (1856, Part II, ch. 7 "The Song").
4 Feudal lord.
5 The Lord shut up his peasants as under doors and hinges, from heaven to earth. Everything is his, oak forest, bird in the air, fish in the water, beast in the bush, the flowing wave, the bell whose sound far off rolls (French).
6 Palace or manor house.
7 Frankish legal code, compiled by the first Frankish King Clovis around 500 AD, that formed the basis of early medieval law.
8 Franz Anton Mesmer (1734–1815), German physician who popularized therapeutic hypnosis or *mesmerism* through animal magnetism. Saint Hubertus or Hubert (656–727), Belgian bishop and the patron saint of hunters, known as "the Apostle of the Ardennes."
9 "Going fine": A horn signal indicating that the hunt is going well.
10 A menial servant or groom caring for animals—a quotation from Aimé Louis Champollion-Figeac's *Louis et Charles d'Orléans* (1844).
11 A narrow flag carried on a lance as a knight's ensign or cavalry's banner.
12 Gilles de Rais (1405–1440), French lord and military leader convicted of molesting and murdering many children.
13 French monarchs: Philip Augustus or Philip II (1165–1223), Louis IX (1214–1270), and Francis I (1494–1547). Peter the Great (1682–1725), Russian Tsar and Emperor who went to France to seek allies against the Ottoman Empire in 1697.
14 In 1562, Francis, Duke of Guise and head of the Catholic League (1519–1563) took the Catholic King Charles IX (1550–1574) and his mother Catherine de' Medici (1519–1589) as prisoners in the religious war against the Calvinist Huguenots to demonstrate that they would change the monarch if he changed his religion.
15 After Pope Pius VII (1742–1823) excommunicated Napoleon in 1809, Napoleon had him arrested and brought over the Alps to Fontainebleau despite his poor health in the spring of 1812. Imprisoned in the Palace of Fontainebleau for two more years, Pope Pius was forced to sign the Concordat of Fontainebleau in January of 1813, relinquishing his temporal sovereignty. Napoleon abdicated in 1814 and was exiled to the Tuscan island of Elba. The French Imperial Eagle was the battle standard of Napoleon's army. After reclaiming power, Napoleon was defeated by the British allied forces under the Duke of Wellington at the Battle of Waterloo on 18 June 1815.
16 Boundary.
17 Another vermouth. A double, please.
18 "Crossroads of the Thorn" in Fontainebleau.
19 Party.

20 Adolphe Thiers (1797–1877), President of France 1871–1873.
21 Dining room.
22 Exodus 7–11.
23 Pre-Raphaelites: a group of Victorian painters who valued the direct, detailed, and vibrant representation of nature.
24 Pierre de Ronsard (1524–1585), preeminent poet of the French Renaissance.
25 A local omnibus company.
26 A French comic opera.
27 A local road through the forest of Fontainebleau.
28 Napoleon established a military school at the Palace of Fontainebleau in 1803.
29 By wagon, gentlemen, ladies (French).
30 There is water.
31 A rowboat for shallow waters.
32 "We made the wedding, let's go back to our homes!"
33 Most likely Olivier de Penne (1831–1897), who painted hunting scenes and kept dogs.
34 RLS and Bob Stevenson (*Letters* 2.156).
35 William Ernest Henley's "Rain" (5) in "Bric-A-Brac Ballades" from *A Book of Verses* (1891).
36 Local roads.
37 French nobleman (Viscount).
38 At full speed, sir, and with twelve biters (dogs).
39 A philosophical illustration that imagines a donkey, equally hungry and thirsty precisely midway between water and hay, who is unable to decide between the two and dies. The thought experiment favors free will over the determinism of the 14th-century philosopher Jean Buridan.
40 Member of an ascetic sect of ancient Hindu philosophers who wore little clothing, didn't eat meat, and devoted themselves to contemplation.
41 An attendant who directs the hounds during a hunt.
42 Stevenson himself.
43 1854 essay "The Gods in Exile" by Heinrich Heine (1797–1856), German poet and critic who emigrated to France. The essay imagines the Greek gods living obscurely in contemporary Christian societies.
44 François-René de Chateaubriand (1768–1848), politician and leading figure in French Romanticism; Pierre-Jean de Béranger (1780–1857), poet and songwriter—see also Stevenson's essay "Pierre-Jean de Béranger" (1876); Gustave Flaubert (1821–1880), novelist best known for *Madame Bovary* (1857); Henri Murger (1822–1861), poet and novelist best known for *Scènes de la vie de bohème* or *Scenes of Bohemian Life* (1851); Edmond de Goncourt (1822–1896) and Jules de Goncourt (1830–1870), brothers and collaborating authors of naturalistic novels and nonfiction; Théodore de Banville (1823–1891), poet, critic, and fiction writer whose work was important for French Symbolism; Étienne Pivert de Senancour (1770–1846), French essayist and novelist best known for his novel *Obermann* (1804); Jules Michelet (1798–1874), French philosopher and historian; George Sand, penname of French novelist Amantine Dupin (1804–1876).
45 An aesthetic ideal popular in the late eighteenth and early nineteenth centuries meant to guide the supposedly optimal viewing and appreciation of landscapes.
46 Pierre Guilbert (1697–1759), French abbot and historian.
47 "Are admired with surprise by travelers who cry out immediately with Horace: 'I take delight in the lovely solitude of the surrounding woods and rock formations'" (Horace, *Odes*, Book III, Ode 25).

48 "Beautiful star" (French)—an allusion to Marie-Catherine d'Aulnoy's French fairytale *La Princesse Belle-Étoile* (1698), in which the eponymous character is watched over by fairies.

49 King's table.

50 Who made this beautiful place.

51 Fountain of youth.

52 Abraham's son by Hagar, an outcast (Genesis 16:11–12).

53 "Caesar gave me this [life]" or saved me (Latin)—a legend associated with many rulers since the Middle Ages.

54 Stevenson alludes to a passage in John Keats's *Endymion* (2.51–53) based on the Greek myth of the shepherd who loves the moon goddess Selene.

55 Field.

56 Ruling family of the Franks from the mid-fifth century to 751.

44

IN THE LATIN QUARTER I

A Ball at Mr Elsinare's

Mr Elsinare's studio lies in a long, rambling, silent street not a hundred miles from the Boulevard Mont-Parnasse—a quarter of Paris which is cheap, airy, and free from the visitation of tourists.[1] The house presents to the thoroughfare a modest gable, a rickety carriage-gate, and a sort of cottage on the other side of it, which looks as if it was meant for the porter. The wicket stands open as we arrive, but there is no sign of life. We venture in, as we might venture after nightfall into a farm-steading, with a kind of beware-of-the-dog feeling at heart. The court is long and narrow like a bit of a country lane; the ground descends, the pavement is of the roughest; and ladies with high heels, on their way to Mr Elsinare's, stumble in the darkness over all manner of heights and hollows, and have to pilot their drapery through many dangers.

The studio is up several pair of stairs; it has been arranged with much art for the occasion. The floor is cleaned; Elsinare and his partner, Smiler,[2] have been rubbing it with candle-ends all the morning, until now it is as shiny and as slippery as heart could wish. Two Chinese lanterns and a couple of bronze lamps illuminate the ballroom from the rafters. There is a piano against the wall, and casts make a great figure on the shelves.

A door stands open on one side, and gives entrance into a small closet which is to do duty on the present occasion as a buttery and a lady's cloak-room. Here a French *bonne*,[3] lent for the evening by the lady patroness, mixes glasses of syrup and water and lays out sweet biscuits for distribution. She is surrounded by cloaks and hats and great-coats, and from time to time examines her own face critically in the mirror. Even in the cloak-room, the eye is scared by unexpected and inharmonious details. An iron bedstead leaning against the wall strikes rather a homely note for the ante-chambers of a festival. One corner is occupied by a lay figure with an air of glaring immorality. From another, a death's-head,[4] jauntily accoutred with a helmet, scowls down upon the syrup and sweet biscuits, and catches the young ladies' eyes wickedly in the mirror, as if to remind them of the vanity of balls. Truly, this Egyptian refinement is but little in key with the mild and innocent diversions of the evening. Syrup and water is scarcely the right sort of beverage to quaff among the emblems of mortality.

The company is mixed as to nationality, and varied in attire. The chaperon is an Austrian Countess, who seems to have had all the Austria taken out of her by a prolonged sojourn in New York. There are many Americans, a sprinkling of French, a Swede,[5] and some Britishers. Most of the men are in evening dress, and one or two in costume. Elsinare appears as Hamlet, and makes a very graceful host. Dear Smiler, the best of men, has waxed his moustaches until he is nearly off the face of the earth, and radiates welcome and good happiness as though he had six thousand a year and an island in the Aegæn. The floor is just a trifle too much waxed for his free, Californian style of dancing; and, as he goes round in the last figure of the quadrille, he falls into the arms of all the ladies in succession. It makes no difference, however, for they are mostly bigger than he is, and he carries it off with a good humour that is more beautiful than grace. Shaun O'Shaughnessy[6] also bites the dust repeatedly with true Hibernian[7] *aplomb*. George Rowland, dressed as a Yorkshire farmer of the old school, makes his entrance in character, to the unfeigned alarm of all the French.[8] They evidently think the scalping is going to begin. But it is just Rowland's way, and they are reassured by the laughter of the rest. Willie MacIntyre, in the national costume, brings with him a powerful atmosphere of sporran.[9] He does not dance from motives of delicacy, and tries as far as possible to keep the sporran in unfrequented corners. A sporran, like a bag-pipe, is most agreeable in the extreme distance, and in breezy, mountainous places.

Almost all the young ladies are in costume. There are some pretty Italian dresses round the room, to say nothing of their wearers. But Belle Bird is not to be passed over among the rest. She is a Californian girl, and has spent her childhood among Bret Harte's stories,[10] petted by miners, and gamblers, and trappers, and ranche-men, and all the *dramatis personæ* of the new romance; and, I must say, they seem to spoil people in the right direction, for Belle is frank and simple and not at all like an American miss. She looks like a Russian—a South Russian, I mean. The pleasant gentlemen, old and young, who make it their business to accost ladies on the streets of Paris, had a favorite phrase by way of endeavouring to open a friendly understanding with her:—"Quelle jolie, gentille petite Russe!"[11] they would remark. Belle says it was by mistake she hit one of these intelligent young men over the mouth last winter; but, of course, we all have our own ideas; I am glad, at least, it was the intelligent young man who got the buffet, instead of you or me. For a young lady of sixteen, to employ her own idiom, you bet your sweet life she'd fetch him! Tonight she is dressed in gilt, like a stage fairy, and her hair is full of gold powder; her dark face is flushed, and her eyes shine with happiness. She and Smiler are quite the features of the evening; Smiler looks so gratified with everybody else, and she looks so pleased with herself. Upon my word, it is impossible to say which is the more becoming sentiment. You cannot set eyes on either of them without solid satisfaction. Your heart gives a bounce and a thrill; and, like the Ancient Mariner with the watersnakes, you want badly to bless them.[12] I know I keep blessing little Smiler all night long.

George Rowland considers syrup and water an unwholesome, if not an impertinent, beverage. He eyes the tray dejectedly; and so I draw near and begin to
conjure up divine drinks before his thirsty imagination. I ask him what he would
think of a pint of stout? "I should look upon it with a very friendly eye," answers
George, in a tragic voice. "Or a bottle of the Cluny Pommard?" I go on, referring
to the crack café of the Quarter. George passes his hand waterily over his mouth,
and his eyes wink and look suffused. "Or even one of Laverne's Fleury?" He begs
me to stop, and we drink to each other dispiritedly in syrup and water.

Willie MacIntyre is only a passing visitor in town. He has the eccentricity to
remain all winter at one of those artistic villages, which are the Brighton and
Scarborough of the Latin Quarter. Hence he is an object of interest; and old frequenters of G—[13] draw near the sporran gingerly to hear the news. The landlord's
daughter has been unwell; the captain of the *pompiers*[14] has been exceptionally
drunk. MacIntyre, being a man of means, is going to build a studio at the back of
the inn, entering out of the room Reake Yetton had last summer. It is to be more of
a menagerie than a studio, as is to be expected from the man in question; and he
has come up to town to buy pigeons, a cat, a monkey, and another dog—Taureau,
his bull terrier, having succumbed to natural laws on a diet of absinthe, vermouth,
coffee, champagne, and mutton cutlets.

There is another topic of interest. Shaun O'Shaughnessy, MacIntyre, and
another Scotchman, happily absent from Paris and still ignorant of his misfortune, are in a fair way to lose all their furniture for another man's debts, owing to
some infamous chink in the French Code. MacIntyre looks stiff and smiles evilly
when the subject is broached. Rowland offers burlesque counsel in a graveyard
tone of voice, and relapses into his character part of the Yorkshire farmer fitfully
and rather feebly; for the syrup has done its work. Shaun comes into the corner between the dances, and denunciates the whole French nation in a sweeping
organ-roll[15] of brogue.

It is strange to think that almost all these good folk are daubers of canvas; even
Belle has a maul-stick[16] with which she will break your head if you are impolite;
and yet, while they all diligently paint and paint by the month together, and wash
their brushes with quite as knowing an air as any R.A.[17] in England, and send
really quite a considerable extent of canvas into different exhibitions—there is not
one painter that ever you heard of in the party; they are all as unknown as if they
were dead, and the most of them have never sold a pennyworth of their productions. You may hear of them some day for all that; and, in the meantime, I am sure
they enjoy their evening rarely.

Notes

1 For Stevenson in France, see n. 1, p. 231. The Latin Quarter is an intellectual and
artistic hub near the former University of Paris, established in the 12th century, where
students traditionally spoke Latin. The ball took place in January 1877 (*Letters* 2:199).
"Mr. Elsinare" is Carolus-Duran (1837–1917), French painter and studio instructor to

several of the artists in Stevenson's circle, including Bob Stevenson, Will Low, and John Singer Sargent. The studio is on the Rue Notre Dame des Champs near the Boulevard du Montparnasse in Paris. The British illustrator and author George Du Maurier worked in the studio years earlier and used it as the setting for his popular novel *Trilby* (1894).

2 Hiram Reynolds Bloomer (1845–1908), American landscape painter.

3 Housemaid.

4 Skull and crossbones.

5 Swedish painter Carl Fredrik Hill (1849–1911).

6 Probably Stevenson's friend Frank O'Meara (1853–1888): an Irish painter who studied in Paris, lived at Grez, and had a romantic relationship with Fanny's daughter Belle Osbourne (1858–1953), also described here.

7 Irish.

8 Probably Olivier de Penne (1831–1897) who painted hunting scenes and kept dogs.

9 Willie Simpson (1850–1911), younger brother of Stevenson's close friend Walter Simpson (n. 1, p. 242); Sporran: the pouch traditionally worn with the kilt of the Scottish Highlander.

10 Bret Harte (1836–1902), American writer of fiction on the California Gold Rush.

11 What a pretty, kind little Russian girl (French).

12 Coleridge, "The Ancient Mariner" (4.272–291).

13 Grez.

14 Firefighters.

15 A roll of paper used to operate a mechanical organ, which records and plays music with perforations.

16 A padded stick used to support the painter's hand.

17 Member of the British Royal Academy of Arts.

45

IN THE LATIN QUARTER II
A Studio of Ladies

Students of Art in Paris are usually attached to some painter of name, in whose wake they humbly follow. The master gives them so much of his time for criticism and advice, and when he is occupied on a work of any magnitude, employs the most capable to lay it in. The pupils pay by subscription for the models and the large studio in which they work. Some learn to forge the master's touch with great nicety; others recoil to the opposite extreme, and take pleasure in producing battle-pieces under the tuition of a painter of sheep; but all, when they come to exhibit in the Salon,[1] sign themselves as the pupil of M. Couture, or M. Gérome, or M. Carolus Duran, as the case may be.[2] This is an arrangement honourable and useful to both parties.

In the case of lady students there is one little difference. The peculiar chivalry of the male sex comes strongly to the front. It is a question of money. Thews and sinews ruled the world of yore; it was "none but the brave, none but the brave, none but the brave deserve the fair;"[3] and the prize-fighter came swelling into the arena to the sound of trumpets. And in those days men had the advantage because they were strong. Now a pocketful of yellow sovereigns makes sweeter music than Joachim's fiddle;[4] and the bald and peak-faced banker, sitting humped up in a brougham and two,[5] is, for most practical purposes, stronger and more beautiful than Hercules or Apollo. And we still have the pull, because we carry the purse. The ball is still at our feet. But we are aware of peril; we know we must keep the money greedily to ourselves; for we are fonder of women than they are of us; we must bribe them to come to us, as we bribe a child with a sugar almond for a kiss; and if once they have all our sugar almonds, they will leave us like a pack of Satyrs, sitting in dim oak-coverts, and hearing only afar off the voices and swift feet of Artemis's maidens.[6] Hence we cozen them by law; studiously making account of their greater longevity in the case of annuities, where it takes something out of their pocket; and slily omitting that consideration in cases of insurance, where it would put something into it. Hence, also, painters will not accept female students without mulcting them in a smart fee.

M. Concert, a heavy-shouldered French painter,[7] with a sneering countenance, a long nose, and a most seductive deportment, had thrown open his *atelier*[8] to ladies, and pocketed their money with great sweetness. To him flocked quite a troop of English, Americans, and French, and a knot of indefatigable Swedes.

Now, however hard the other women work, the Swedes outdo them. This Swedish cohort at M. Concert's had many things in common: there were thin Swedes and fat Swedes, the Swede who always had her jaw tied up for toothache, and the Swede who came day about in curl-papers and in curls; and yet they all had the same profile, so that you could only distinguish them from the front, and they were all the early birds on Monday morning. Monday morning is an epoch in studio existence; it is then that a new model begins a sitting, and those who arrive first have the first choice of places for the week. At Carolus Duran's, the other year, there were one or two fellows who lived in the same building with the studio. These would arise wilily at three or four on Monday morning, and, after having inscribed their names upon the board, return cozily to roost. You may imagine the discomfiture of early students from all parts of Paris, when they dropped in as soon as the studio was opened, and found a whole company of names already registered. At last the trick got wind. The porter was found to be venal; through his connivance Shaun O'Shaughnessy[9] and the whole ruck of out-students made their entrance on Sunday evening; and when their tricksy comrades crept down before daybreak with a bit of candle and their finger to their nose, they found the tables turned, and had to inscribe themselves humbly in the fag-end[10] of the class. The Swedes, as I said, were invariably the first of M. Concert's pupils; and not just by ones or twos, but in a body. Adventurous girls would rise very early; it would be freezing weather; the lamps would still burn along the streets of Paris, now in belated midnight, now jostling with a blink of dawn; but there would be all the Swedes—the lean and the corpulent, she with the toothache and she with the curl-papers—seated in awful guise upon the *atelier* doorstep; and there would be all the Swedish names, chalked up with shivering fingers on the jamb of the *atelier* door. This began in time to take legendary proportions; whisperers broached strange theories; and the street has a doubtful reputation in Paris to this day.

Time of work at M. Concert's was remarkable for a good deal of talk and some unlovely singularities. The conversation ran generally in two lines—those who could not paint, spoke of their conquests and admirers; those who could, discoursed exclusively upon cheap clothing. I wish it had been the other way, I am sure, and the women of talent had talked all day long about the excellence of men, only it wasn't so, and it is just another proof of our precarious situation. Oh, my brothers! let us stand back to back, and keep the women poor; raise your fees, if necessary. Already I wander in fancy upon dismal hill-tops, and my heart quivers as Dian's hunt goes by below me in the woods. I raise my streaming eyes towards the stars, and accuse the gods vainly; for I must go for ever without a mate! As I was saying, the clever ones spoke of cheap clothing, and where to buy shoes, and where a dress might be dyed and yet look like new. Mrs Nero and another talked scandal in a feminine strain, small, and false, and deadly; and a prim American girl might be overheard by her neighbours in a placid running commentary on the scandal. "That's a lie," she would remark, in a grave undertone. "That's another; I ain't so. Oh, you Spanish wretch!" On the whole, a capital American girl.

I have spoken of unlovely singularities among M. Concert's lady pupils; these were connected with the models, whom they used disgracefully. Women generally prefer to *pose* to men, and men to women; but in this studio, where they treated all badly, they treated the men like brutes. It may be as well to explain to the mercantile British mind that there is no such thing as delicacy about a model. The Briton would have seen this for himself with stupefaction had he been an hour in Concert's. The Swedes, from where they sat in the first places, used to arrange the model's hair, and generally poke him up and make him look lively with the end of their maul-sticks. An old Frenchwoman with false hair would scuttle forward among the easels, and measure him all over with a bit of tape. In sharp wintry weather they kept one poor fellow bringing coal from a distant cellar during his intervals of repose, to save them the trouble of going into the next room and calling down a tube. He not unnaturally developed a smart catarrh, and whenever he sneezed or had to blow his nose, the Swedes and Mrs. Nero would cry out upon him as if he had done it on purpose.

These were the sharpest persecutors. With the Swedes it was done in the way of business. The model should take an arduous position, because they wished to draw it; he should rest little, because they wanted as much as possible for their money; and they shoved him about with their maul-sticks, because it was the handiest way to straighten him up. There was no ill-will about these denizens of the pensive North; they merely drove their slave. Mrs. Nero, on the other hand, was a pretty, curly French-American, fond of ices and flirtation; and I suspect a certain inverted element of sex prompted and intensified her cruelty to men. She did not misuse them in callousness, but out of an evil-minded sensibility. I think I can see her by Faustina's elbow, above the confusion of the amphitheater; I think I can see the little thumb turned down, and the curly head look forth in a luxurious horror on the carnival of death.[11]

One day a splendid, brawny Hercules of a fellow came to M. Concert's, and the Swedes, who always carried their point, decided he should pose in the attitude of the Dying Gladiator.[12] Women models have an interval of rest every thirty minutes; men only once in the hour. An hour on end in the attitude of the Dying Gladiator is no joke, and the man soon began to give the most distressing tokens of exhaustion; his muscles quivered, great drops stood upon him; it was the spectacle of an agony. Murmurs arose among the better-natured members of the class; but as long as any one person insists on his going on, the model must finish his hour or forfeit his money, and Mrs. Nero would hear of no compromise. "It is our business to paint," she said; "it is his to *pose* for an hour at a time; he has been paid to do so, and I mean he shall." "Don't you see the man is suffering?" they asked. She took some color off her *palette*, and laid it on deliberately. "I just love to see him suffer," said she. It appears the model had a smattering of English, for he understood this remark, or perhaps the tone in which it was uttered, and, raising his head, he gave Mrs. Nero a murderous stare between the eyes. With that the class broke out

358

into revolt. Mrs. Wycherley and many more would stay no longer in the room. But Mrs. Nero and the Swedes—those conscientious artists—finished their hour with great deliberation.

The model would not stay out the week; it was the first time he had ever *posed* for women, he said, and he vowed horribly it would be the last.

Notes

1 The prestigious annual exhibit of the Academy of Fine Arts in Paris.
2 French painters and teachers: Thomas Couture (1815–1879), Jean-Léon Gérôme (1824–1904), and Carolus-Duran (1837–1917), who taught several of Stevenson's friends (n. 1, p. 354).
3 John Dryden, "Alexander's Feast" (1697, 13–15).
4 Joseph Joachim (1831–1907), famous Hungarian violinist.
5 An enclosed horse-drawn carriage with two doors and a front window.
6 Artemis is the Greek goddess of chastity, whose handmaidens the nymphs are traditionally depicted fleeing the amorous, half-animal satyrs.
7 Rodolphe Julian (1839–1907), established the Académie Julian in 1868 just north of the Latin Quarter. Women students, generally excluded from art education in Paris, worked in a separate studio but received the same training as the men, including working with nude male models. Upon arriving in Pairs, Fanny Osbourne and her daughter Belle enrolled there in Nov. 1875.
8 Studio.
9 The Irish painter Frank O'Meara (1853–88). See n. 6, p. 355.
10 The very end; the last and least desirable part.
11 Faustina the Younger (130–175/76 CE), the Roman empress and wife of Marcus Aurelius had affairs with gladiators. The exhibitor signaled with the thumb whether defeated gladiators would live or die.
12 Sculpture also known as "The Dying Gaul": a Roman copy of the lost Hellenistic sculpture.

46

THE PARIS BOURSE

Now and again, of a morning, an idle person may do worse than drop into the Bourse at Paris[1] for a snatch of meditation. Nothing very high, if you like, will be the result; nothing about the North Pole, or the Dog Star, or the Battle of Armageddon.[2] Nor will you have too much of it for personal convenience; but, as it were, a before-dinner cigarette's worth of morality to give you an appetite for entertainment.

The building, if you make allowance for the roof, may figure very well for a Greek temple. You can put it, in imagination, on some agreeable promontory, girt about with olive-yards, and looking out over the sea; whither you may come, with some votive doves over your arm, in a basket covered with a white napkin, to find the fane[3] quite empty and silent, and kneel awhile before immortal statues. As a matter of fact, its base is shaded by nothing more rural than a stand of hackney-coaches; and unless the arcade of the Rue des Colonnes[4] is to be considered an exception, the neighbourhood is not remarkable for romantic scenery. Moreover, the roof is not quite in keeping with these Hellenic fancies. And still there is something solemn, austere, and antique about the building which inclines a man towards contemplation as he ascends the steps.

This predisposition is somewhat rudely assailed upon entrance. The rites of the god of Mammon[5] are conducted with a confusion, fervent perhaps, but verging on the indecorous. The temple reverberates with profane clamour. Conversation is only possible at the pitch of the voice. Nowhere out of the Inferno[6] had one conceived it possible to hear so sustained and dismal an uproar. One is led to understand that the French Assembly is a somewhat noisy gathering. The priests of Baal are supposed to have kicked up a fair row on the occasion of their conflict with Elijah.[7] The inhabitants of Ephesus must have made the ears ring when they called out all together in praise of their many-breasted goddess.[8] But to hear the Parisian devotees of Mammon at their exercises is to exhaust and outstrip all that imagination can conceive in the way of stupefying sound. Shrill or sullen, cracked or jovial, bawl or shriek, every form of human outcry is massed together into one solid object of offence. The ears crack and tingle; the brain shrinks in the brain-pan; the heart doubles time, as if at the call of drums. It is hideous and hateful; it wounds, mangles, and obliterates; it hurts like the toothache, and irritates like an insult. You feel like a wild animal when the wake is full of horns and beagles; you wish to wreak your misery on some one; if you were but Samson, and the pillars were near enough together, there would be no more than a heave and a crash, and silence would be re-established.[9]

You go up to the gallery and look over; the scene becomes simpler. There is an intricate figure of railings described upon the floor. I think I have seen just such an enclosure made with loose hurdles in a pleasant country place upon a hillside; that was a kind of sheepfold, where sheep with Roman noses are clipped and dipped, and subjected to all manner of commercial and hygienic indignities. The centre of the figure is a circle, and this is surrounded by various other pens, some closed and some open, on whose shape, at this distance from Euclid's elements,[10] I should not care to put a name. The whole enclosures together, when you see them on a by-day and quite empty, form a curious hieroglyphic, an abracadabra,[11] the symbol and emblem of Finance. In and about these railings miserable human beings are pressed as tight as herrings in a barrel. The upper surface is violently agitated, as though you had a bird's-eye view of a forest in a tornado. Arms, and notebooks, and hats, and the countenances of agonised financiers surge and eddy, appear and disappear, below you. They shake their heads wildly; they scribble on flying notebooks at arm's length over their heads—Heaven knows how they can decipher what they have written; their faces are all distorted and deformed in a desperate effort to be heard. Now you think a man's eye is out; now you are sure that little phthysical[12] broker has gone under, and is being trampled callously to death. It is like a scene in a madhouse, when there has been a successful revolt against the keepers; it is like a hideous tumult in the Faubourg St. Antoine;[13] it is like some disreputable part of the Inferno. Any quiet-minded person would refuse quite a hatful of money before he adventured his frail limbs in such a ferment. He would think twice of such an exploit even if it were to hear a crack singer, and for one evening only; but to undergo this pulling and hauling day by day and all day long, to keep his brain working in this deplorable confusion, to howl with all these famished wolves, to dance and elbow in this sanguinary burlesque of the "Devil among the Brokers," and all for a fortune, all to be a little more thought of when he's bald and broken-down—the game, he would tell you, is not worth the candle,[14] and with a polite obeisance go his way.

And the strangest part of it is to see the men in the holy of holies[15]—the little central ring—fenced about from the profane vulgar for the exclusive use of the *Agents de Change*. Some of them are young and handsome; some are old and have surely earned their repose; some are decorated. They are all wealthy, or they could not be *Agents de Change*.[16] And yet there they are, bawling with puffed cheeks all day long and day by day in the very heart of Babel.[17]

Addison[18] when he wished to indulge a thoughtful humour walked among the tombs at Westminster; for my part, I like to lean over the gallery at the Bourse, and moralise on the bald heads of these uneasy Crœsuses.[19]

Do they not know that there are great forests full of deer and boars, and pleas-ant trout-streams running from all the hills? Do they never picture themselves smoking a pipe in a rustic portico, with a nice long glass by their elbow? The wind blows steady at sea; could they not affod a yacht? The booksellers' shops are full of delightful novels; how about a sofa and a pair of slippers? Do they not know that the overwhelming majority of their fellow-men would think their present capital a thousand times more than enough? Red-faced peasants in blouses are sitting even now in farm doors, smiling widely to themselves because they have amassed in a lifetime a tenth part of what these indefatigable brokers had to start with. Penniless young painters, over in the Latin Quarter,[20] are idling and sunning themselves in their pennilessness with the highest contentment. All manner of men are taking their ease, and going about life deliberately, as if there was no such thing as an Exchange on earth. And yet there they go at it, and cry themselves hoarse in their railed enclosure all day long and day by day, until some fine morning—tol-de-rol-de-rol[21]—down comes the edifice, and behold a hasty passenger for Belgium with a carpet-bag!

Indeed, it is a problem worthy of some thought. Consider the *Agents de Change*, and be wise. You stand in the gallery, and stare and stare; you seem them maniacally striving in the broker-pens; you hear the noise boiling up to you, as if out of a place of torture. Did you ever know money was so dear? Did you ever know men were so frenzied? What does it matter if your *concierge* regards you somewhat sourly, and permits himself little observations about the custom of the establishment in the matter of the monthly bill? At least you do not have to descend into the arena and fight all day long and day by day with wild beasts in the shape of brokers!

Notes

1 The French securities market or stock exchange of France. For Stevenson in France, see n. 1, p. 231.
2 Sirius or Alpha Canis Majoris: the night sky's brightest star.
3 Temple.
4 A street lined with successive arches between the Bourse and the Opera of Paris.
5 Money (Hebrew), associated with idolatrous greed in the Bible.
6 Hell (Italian), the first part of Dante's *Divine Comedy* (1472).
7 1 Kings 18.
8 Silversmiths who made shrines for the goddess Diana objected to Paul's preaching (Acts 19).
9 Judges 16:23–30.
10 Euclid's *Elements*: a foundational geometry text written around 300 BC and commonly taught in the 19th century.
11 Obscure or mystifying language; nonsense, gibberish.
12 Tubercular.
13 The chaotic Fronde Battle of the Faubourg St. Antoine on 2 Jul. 1652 in France.
14 When the effort required outweighs the benefit, referring to a card game in which the stakes are less than the cost of the candle needed to light it.
15 The restricted inner sanctuary of the biblical tabernacle reserved for God's presence.
16 Stock agents.

17 Biblical city where God confounded humanity's language (Genesis 11).
18 Joseph Addison (1672–1719), English essayist, poet, and playwright.
19 Croesus (595–546 BC), King of Lydia renowned for his great wealth, prompting the expression "rich as Croesus."
20 The Latin Quarter is an intellectual and artistic hub near the former University of Paris, established in the 12th century, where students traditionally spoke Latin.
21 A nonsense refrain of old folk songs.

47

HEALTH AND MOUNTAINS[1]

There has come a change in medical opinion, and a change has followed in the lives of sick folk. A year or two ago and the wounded soldiery of mankind were all shut up together in some basking angle of the Riviera, walking a dusty promenade or sitting in dusty olive-yards within earshot of the interminable and unchanging surf—idle among spiritless idlers; not perhaps dying, yet hardly living either; and aspiring, sometimes fiercely, after livelier weather and some vivifying change.[2] These were certainly beautiful places to live in, and the climate was wooing in its softness. Yet there was a latent shiver in the sunshine; you were not certain whether you were being wooed; and these mild shores would sometimes seem to you to be the shores of death. There was a lack of a manly element; the air was not reactive; you might write bits of poetry and practise resignation, but you did not feel that here was a good spot to repair your tissue or regain your nerve. And it appears, after all, that there was something just in these appreciations. The invalid is now asked to lodge on wintry Alps; a ruder air shall medicine him; the demon of cold is no longer to be fled from, but bearded in his den. For even Winter has his "dear domestic cave," and in those places where he may be said to dwell for ever tempers his austerities.[3]

Any one who has travelled westward by the great transcontinental railroad of America must remember the joy with which he perceived, after the tedious prairies of Nebraska and across the vast and dismal moorlands of Wyoming, a few snowy mountain summits along the southern sky. It is among these mountains, in the new State of Colorado, that the sick man may find, not merely an alleviation of his ailments, but the possibility of an active life and an honest livelihood. There, no longer as a lounger in a plaid,[4] but as a working farmer, sweating at his work, he may prolong and begin anew his life. Instead of the bath-chair, the spade; instead of the regulated walk, rough journeys in the forest; and the pure, rare air of the open mountains for the miasma[5] of the sick-room—these are the changes offered him, with what promise of pleasure and of self-respect, with what a revolution in all his hopes and terrors, none but an invalid can know. Resignation, the cowardice that apes a kind of courage and that lives in the very air of health resorts, is cast aside at a breath of such a prospect. The man can open the door; he can be up and doing; he can be a kind of a man after all and not merely an invalid.

But it is a far cry to the Rocky Mountains. We cannot all of us go farming in Colorado; and there is yet a middle term, which combines the medical benefits of the new system with the moral drawbacks of the old. Again the invalid has to lie aside from life and its wholesome duties; again he has to be an idler among idlers; but this time at a great altitude, far among mountains, with the snow piled before his door and the frost-flowers every morning on his window. The mere fact is tonic to his nerves. His choice of a place of wintering has somehow to his own eyes the air of an act of bold conduct; and, since he has wilfully sought low temperatures, he is not so apt to shudder at a touch of chill. He came for that, he looked for it, and he throws it from him with the thought.

A long straight reach of valley, wall-like mountains upon either hand that rise higher and higher and shoot up new summits the higher you climb; a few noble peaks seen even from the valley; a village of hotels; a world of black and white— black pinewoods clinging to the sides of the valley, and white snow flouring it, and papering it between the pinewoods, and covering all the mountains with a dazzling curd; add a few score invalids marching to and fro upon the snowy road, or skating on the ice-rinks, possibly to music, or sitting under sunshades by the door of the hotel—and you have the larger features of a mountain sanatorium. A certain furious river runs curving down the valley; its pace never varies, it has not a pool for as far as you can follow it; and its unchanging, senseless hurry is strangely tedious to witness. It is a river that a man could grow to hate. Day after day breaks with the rarest gold upon the mountain spires, and creeps, growing and glowing, down into the valley. From end to end the snow reverberates the sun shine; from end to end the air tingles with the light, clear and dry like crystal. Only along the course of the river, but high above it, there hangs far into the noon one waving scarf of vapour. It were hard to fancy a more engaging feature in a landscape; perhaps it is harder to believe that delicate, long-lasting phantom of the atmosphere a creature of the incontinent stream whose course it follows. By noon the sky is arrayed in an unrivalled pomp of colour—mild and pale and melting in the north, but towards the zenith dark with an intensity of purple blue. What with this darkness of heaven and the intolerable lustre of the snow space is reduced again to chaos. An English painter, coming to France late in life, declared with natural anger that "the values were all wrong."[6] Had he got among the Alps on a bright day he might have lost his reason. And even to anyone who has looked at landscape with any care, and in any way through the spectacles of representative art, the scene has a character of insanity. The distant shining mountain peak is here beside your eye; the neighbouring dull-coloured house in comparison is miles away; the summit, which is all of splendid snow, is close at hand; the nigh slopes, which are black with pine trees, bear it no relation, and might be in another sphere. Here there are none of those delicate gradations, those intimate, misty joinings-on and spreadings-out into the distance, nothing of that art of air and light by which the face of nature explains and veils itself in climes which we may be allowed to think more lovely. A glaring piece of crudity, where everything that is not white is a solecism and defies the judgment of the eyesight; a scene of blinding definition; a parade of daylight, almost scenically vulgar, more than scenically trying, and yet hearty and healthy, making the nerves to tighten and the mouth to smile: such is the winter daytime in the Alps. With the approach of evening all is changed. A mountain will suddenly intercept the sun; a shadow fall upon the valley; in ten minutes the thermometer will drop as many degrees; the peaks that are no longer shone upon dwindle into ghosts; and meanwhile, overhead, if the weather be rightly characteristic of the place, the sky fades towards night through a surprising key of colours. The latest gold leaps from the last mountain. Soon, perhaps, the moon shall rise, and in her gentler light the valley shall be mellowed and misted, with here and there a wisp of silver cloud upon a hilltop, and here and there a warmly glowing window in a house, between fire and starlight, kind and homely in the fields of snow.

But the valley is not seated so high among the clouds to be eternally exempt from changes. The clouds gather, black as ink; the wind bursts rudely in; day after day the mists drive overhead, the snow-flakes flutter down in blinding disarray; daily the mail comes in later from the top of the pass; people peer through their windows and foresee no end but an entire seclusion from Europe and death by gradual dry-rot, each in his indifferent inn; and when at last the storm goes, and the sun comes again, behold a world of unpolluted snow, glossy like fur, bright like daylight, a joy to wallowing dogs and cheerful to the souls of men. Or perhaps, from across storied and malarious Italy, a wind cunningly winds about the mountains and breaks, warm and unclean, upon our mountain valley. Every nerve is set ajar: the conscience recognises, at a gust, a load of sins and negligences hitherto unknown; and the whole invalid world huddles into its private chambers, and silently recognises the empire of the *Föhn*.[7]

Notes

1 Stevenson spent his winters in Davos, Switzerland for his health from 1880 to 1882. Alpine sanatoriums touted the benefits of clean, cold, mountain air for tuberculosis. "Health and Mountains," "Davos in Winter," "Alpine Diversions," "The Stimulation of the Alps," and "The Misgivings of Convalescence" are based on his time there.
2 See "Ordered South" (p. 70).
3 Wordsworth, "Song for the Wandering Jew" (14).
4 Scottish woolen cloth with a tartan pattern used as a blanket.
5 *Miasma*—the Greek word for pollution or bad air—was a medical theory predating germ theory that attributed diseases to noxious vapors from rotting organic matter.
6 Value—the relative lightness or darkness of a color in painting.
7 A warm dry south wind which blows down the valleys on the north side of the Alps.

48

DAVOS IN WINTER

A mountain valley has, at the best, a certain prison-like effect on the imagination; but a mountain valley, an Alpine winter, and an invalid's weakness make up among them a prison of the most effective kind. The roads indeed are cleared, and at least one footpath dodging up the hill; but to these the health-seeker is rigidly confined. There are for him no cross cuts over the field, no following of streams, no unguided rambles in the wood. His walks are cut and dry. In five or six different directions he can push as far, and no farther, than his strength permits; never deviating from the line laid down for him and beholding at each repetition the same field of wood and snow from the same corner of the road. This, of itself, would be a little trying to the patience in the course of months; but to this is added, by the heaped mantle of the snow, an almost utter absence of detail and an almost unbroken identity of colour. Snow, it is true, is not merely white. The sun touches it with roseate and golden lights. Its own crushed infinity of crystals, its own richness of tiny sculpture, fills it, when regarded near at hand, with wonderful depths of coloured shadow, and, though wintrily transformed, it is still water, and has watery tones of blue. But, when all is said, these fields of white and blots of crude black forest are but a trite and staring substitute for the infinite variety and pleasantness of the earth's face. Even a boulder, whose front is too precipitous to have retained the snow, seems, if you come upon it in your walk, a perfect gem of colour, reminds you almost painfully of other places, and brings into your head the delights of more Arcadian[1] days—the path across the meadow, the hazel dell, the lilies on the stream, and the scents, the colours, and the whisper of the woods. And scents here are as rare as colours. Unless you get a gust of kitchen in passing some hotel, you shall smell nothing all day long but the faint and choking odour of frost. Sounds, too, are absent: not a bird pipes, not a bough waves, in the dead, windless atmosphere. If a sleigh goes by, the sleigh bells ring, and that is all; you work all winter through to no other accompaniment but the crunching of your steps upon the frozen snow.

It is the curse of Alpine valleys to be each one village from one end to the other. Go where you please, houses will still be in sight, before and behind you, and to the right and left. Climb as high as an invalid is able, and it is only to spy new habitations nested in the wood. Nor is that all; for about the health resort the walks are besieged by single people walking rapidly with plaids about their shoulders, by sudden troops of German boys trying to learn to *jodel*,[2] and by German couples silently and, as you venture to fancy, not quite happily, pursuing love's young dream. You may perhaps be an invalid who likes to make bad verses as he walks abroad. Alas! no muse will suffer this imminence of interruption—and at the second stampede of jodellers you find your modest inspiration fled. Or you may only have a taste for solitude: it may try your nerves to have someone always in front whom you are visibly overtaking, and someone always behind who is audibly over taking you, to say nothing of a score or so who brush past you in an opposite direction. It may annoy you to take your walks and seats in public view. Alas! there is no help for it among the Alps. There are no recesses, as in Gorbio Valley by the oil-mill; no sacred solitude of olive gardens on the Roccabruna-road; no nook upon Saint Martin's Cape, haunted by the voice of breakers, and fragrant with the threefold sweetness of the rosemary and the sea-pines and the sea.[3]

For this publicity there is no cure and no alleviation; but the storms, of which you will complain so bitterly while they endure, chequer and by their contrast brighten the sameness of fair-weather scenes. When sun and storm contend together—when the thick clouds are broken up and pierced by arrows of golden daylight—there will be startling rearrangements and transfigurations of the mountain summits. A sun-dazzling spire of alps hangs suspended in mid-sky among awful glooms and blackness; or perhaps the edge of some great mountain shoulder will be designed in living gold, and appear for the duration of a glance bright like a constellation, and alone "in the unapparent."[4] You may think you know the figure of these hills; but when they are thus revealed, they belong no longer to the things of earth—meteors we should rather call them, appearances of sun and air that endure but for a moment and return no more. Other variations are more lasting, as when, for instance, heavy and wet snow has fallen through some windless hours, and the thin, spiry, mountain pine-trees stand each stock-still and loaded with a shining burthen. You may drive through a forest so disguised, the tongue-tied torrent struggling silently in the cleft of the ravine, and all still except the jingle of the sleigh bells and you shall fancy yourself in some untrodden northern territory—Lapland, Labrador,[5] or Alaska.

Or, possibly, you arise very early in the morning; totter downstairs in a state of somnambulism; take the simulacrum of a meal by the glimmer of one lamp in the deserted coffee-room; and find yourself by seven o'clock outside in a belated moonlight and a freezing chill. The mail-sleigh takes you up and carries you on, and you reach the top of the ascent in the first hour of the day. To trace the fires of the sun rise as they pass from peak to peak, to see the unlit tree-tops stand out soberly against the lighted sky, to be for twenty minutes in a wonderland of clear, fading shadows, disappearing vapours, solemn blooms of dawn, hills half-glorified already with the day and still half-confounded with the greyness of the western heaven—these will seem to repay you for the discomforts of that early start; but as the hour proceeds, and these enchantments vanish, you will find yourself upon the further side in yet another Alpine valley, snow-white and coal-black, with such another long-drawn congeries of hamlets and such another senseless watercourse bickering along the foot. You have had your moment; but you have not changed the scene. The mountains are about you like a trap; you cannot foot it up a hillside and behold the sea as a great plain, but live in holes and corners, and can change only one for another.

Notes

1 Idyllic, utopian.
2 Yodel (German).
3 Gorbio, Roccabruna, and St. Martin's: small villages in the mountains of southeastern France, northwestern Italy, and eastern Canada, respectively.
4 Percy Bysshe Shelley, "Adonais" (45. 3).
5 Lapland—The multinational region forming the most northerly portion of the Scandinavian peninsula. Labrador—Atlantic Canada's northernmost region.

49

ALPINE DIVERSIONS

There will be no lack of diversion in an Alpine sanitarium.[1] The place is half Englished to be sure, the local sheet appearing in double column, text and translation; but it still remains half German; and hence we have a band which is able to play, and a company of actors able, as you will be told, to act. This last you will take on trust, for the players, unlike the local sheet, confine themselves to German; and though at the beginning of winter they come with their wig-boxes to each hotel in turn, long before Christmas they will have given up the English for a bad job. There will follow, perhaps, a skirmish between the two races; the German element seeking, in the interest of their actors, to raise a mysterious item, the *Kur-taxe*,[2] which figures heavily enough already in the weekly bills, the English element stoutly resisting. Meantime, in the English hotels home-played farces, *tableaux-vivants*,[3] and even balls enliven the evenings; a charity bazaar sheds genial consternation; Christmas and New Year are solemnized with Pantagruelian[4] dinners, and from time to time the young folks carol and revolve untunefully enough through the figures of a singing quadrille. A magazine club supplies you with everything, from the *Quarterly* to the *Sunday at Home*.[5] Grand tournaments are organized at chess, draughts, billiards, and whist. Once and again wandering artists drop into our mountain valley, coming you know not whence, going you cannot imagine whither, and belonging to every degree in the hierarchy of musical art, from the recognized performer who announces a concert for the evening, to the comic German family or solitary long-haired German baritone who surprises the guests at dinner-time with songs and a collection. They are all of them good to see; they, at least, are moving; they bring with them the sentiment of the open road; yesterday, perhaps, they were in Tyrol, and next week they will be far in Lombardy, while all we sick folk still simmer in our mountain prison. Some of them, too, are welcome as the flowers in May for their own sake; some of them may have a human voice; some may have that magic which transforms a wooden box into a song-bird, and what we jeeringly call a fiddle into what we mention with respect as a violin. From that grinding lilt, with which the blind man, seeking pence, accompanies the beat of paddle wheels across the ferry, there is surely a difference rather of kind than of degree to that unearthly voice of singing that bewails and praises the destiny of man at the touch of the true virtuoso. Even that you may perhaps enjoy; and if you do so, you will own it impossible to enjoy it more keenly than here, "im Schnee der Alpen."[6] A hyacinth in a pot, a handful of primroses packed in moss, or a piece of music by some one who knows the way to the heart of a violin, are things that, in this invariable sameness of the snows and frosty air, surprise you like an adventure. It is droll, moreover, to compare the respect with which the invalids attend a concert, and the ready contempt with which they greet the dinner-time performers. Singing which they would hear with real enthusiasm—possibly with tears—from a corner of a drawing-room, is listened to with laughter when it is offered by an unknown professional and no money has been taken at the door.

Of skating little need be said; in so snowy a climate the rinks must be intelligently managed; their mismanagement will lead to many days of vexation and some petty quarrelling; but when all goes well, it is certainly curious, and perhaps rather unsafe, for the invalid to skate under a burning sun and walk back to his hotel in a sweat, through long tracts of glare and passages of freezing shadow. But the peculiar outdoor sport of this district is tobogganing. A Scotchman may remember the low flat board, with the front wheels on a pivot, which was called a "hurlie;" he may remember this contrivance, laden with boys, as, laboriously started, it ran rattling down the brae, and was, now successfully now unsuccessfully, steered round the corner at the foot; he may remember scented summer evenings passed in this diversion, and many a grazed skin, bloody cockscomb,[7] and neglected lesson. The toboggan is to the hurlie what the sled is to the carriage; it is a hurlie upon runners; and if for a grating road you substitute a long declivity of beaten snow you can imagine the giddy career of the tobogganist. The correct position is to sit; but the fantastic will sometimes sit hind-foremost, or dare the descent upon their belly or their back. A few steer with a pair of pointed sticks, but it is more classical to use the feet. If the weight be heavy and the track smooth the toboggan takes the bit between its teeth; and to steer a couple of full-sized friends in safety requires not only judgment but desperate exertion. On a very steep track, with a keen evening frost, you may have moments almost too appalling to be called enjoyment; the head goes, the world vanishes; your blind steed bounds below your weight; you reach the foot, with all the breath knocked out of your body, jarred and bewildered as though you had just been subjected to a railway accident. Another element of joyful horror is added by the formation of a train; one toboggan being tied to another, perhaps to the number of half a dozen, only the first rider being allowed to steer, and all the rest pledged to put up their feet and follow their leader, with heart in mouth, down the mad descent. This, particularly if the track begins with a headlong plunge, is one of the most exhilarating follies in the world, and the tobogganing invalid is early reconciled to somersaults.

There is all manner of variety in the nature of the tracks, some miles in length, others but a few yards, and yet, like some short rivers, furious in their brevity. All degrees of skill and courage and taste may be suited in your neighbourhood. But perhaps the true way to toboggan is alone and at night. First comes the tedious climb, dragging your instrument behind you. Next a long breathing space, alone with snow and pine woods, cold, silent, and solemn to the heart. Then you push off; the toboggan fetches way; she begins to feel the hill, to glide, to swim, to gallop. In a breath you are out from under the pine trees, and a whole heavenful of stars reels and flashes overhead. Then comes a vicious effort; for by this time your wooden steed is speeding like the wind, and you are spinning round a corner, and the whole glittering valley and all the lights in all the great hotels lie for a moment at your feet; and the next you are racing once more in the shadow of the night, with close-shut teeth and beating heart. Yet a little while and you will be landed on the high road by the door of your own hotel. This, in an atmosphere tingling with forty degrees of frost, in a night made luminous with stars and snow, and girt with strange white mountains, teaches the pulse an unaccustomed tune and adds a new excitement to the life of man upon his planet.

Notes

1 See n. 1, p. 366.
2 Tourist tax (German).
3 *Tableau vivant* "living picture" (French): a static scene with posed models, costumes, props, and scenery often performed live and photographed.
4 Enormous, excessive.
5 London magazines: *The Sunday at Home: A Family Magazine for Sabbath Reading* (1854–1940), a religious weekly, and *The Quarterly Review* (1809–1967), a well-known literary and political publication.
6 In the snow of the Alps (German).
7 Head.

50

THE STIMULATION OF THE ALPS

To any one who should come from a southern sanitarium to the Alps, the row of sunburned faces round the table would present the first surprise. He would begin by looking for the invalids, and he would lose his pains, for not one out of five of even the bad cases bears the mark of sickness on his face. The plump sunshine from above and its strong reverberation from below colour the skin like an Indian climate; the treatment, which consists mainly of the open air, exposes even the sickliest to tan, and a tableful of invalids comes, in a month or two, to resemble a tableful of hunters. But although he may be thus surprised at the first glance, his astonishment will grow greater as he experiences the effects of the climate on himself. In many ways it is a trying business to reside upon the Alps: the stomach is exercised, the appetite often languishes, the liver may at times rebel; and, because you have come so far from metropolitan advantages, it does not follow that you shall recover. But one thing is undeniable—that in the rare air, clear, cold, and blinding light of Alpine winters, a man takes a certain troubled delight in his existence which can nowhere else be paralleled. He is perhaps no happier, but he is stingingly alive. It does not, perhaps, come out of him in work or exercise, yet he feels an enthusiasm of the blood unknown in more temperate climates. It may not be health, but it is fun.

There is nothing more difficult to communicate on paper than this baseless ardour, this stimulation of the brain, this sterile joyousness of spirits. You wake every morning, see the gold upon the snow peaks, become filled with courage, and bless God for your prolonged existence. The valleys are but a stride to you; you cast your shoe over the hill-tops; your ears and your heart sing; in the words of an unverified quotation from the Scotch psalms, you feel yourself fit "on the wings of all the winds" to "come flying all abroad."[1] Europe and your mind are too narrow for that flood of energy. Yet it is notable that you are hard to root out of your bed; that you start forth singing, indeed, on your walk, yet are unusually ready to turn home again; that the best of you is volatile; and that although the restlessness remains till night, the strength is early at an end. With all these heady jollities, you are half conscious of an underlying languor in the body; you prove not to be so well as you had fancied; you weary before you have well begun; and though you mount at morning with the lark, that is not precisely a song-bird's heart that you bring back with you when you return with aching limbs and peevish temper to your inn.

It is hard to say wherein it lies, but this joy of Alpine winters is its own reward. Baseless, in a sense, it is more than worth more permanent improvements. The dream of health is perfect while it lasts; and if, in trying to realize it, you speedily wear out the dear hallucination, still every day, and many times a day, you are conscious of a strength you scarce possess, and a delight in living as merry as it proves to be transient. The brightness—heaven and earth conspiring to be bright—the levity and quiet of the air; the odd, stirring silence—more stirring than a tumult; the snow, the frost, the enchanted landscape: all have their part in the effect and on the memory, "tous vous tapent sur la tête;"[2] and yet when you have enumerated all, you have gone no nearer to explain or even to qualify the delicate exhilaration that you feel—delicate, you may say, and yet excessive, greater than can be said in prose, almost greater than an invalid can bear. There is a certain wine of France, known in England in some gaseous disguise, but when drunk in the land of its nativity still as a pool, clean as river water, and as heady as verse.[3] It is more than probable that in its noble natural condition this was the very wine of Anjou so beloved by Athos in the "Musketeers."[4] Now, if the reader has ever washed down a liberal second breakfast with the wine in question, and gone forth, on the back of these dilutions, into a sultry, sparkling noontide, he will have felt an influence almost as genial, although strangely grosser, than this fairy titillation of the nerves among the snow and sunshine of the Alps. That also is a mode, we need not say of intoxication, but of insobriety. Thus also a man walks in a strong sunshine of the mind, and follows smiling, insubstantial meditations. And, whether he be really so clever or so strong as he supposes, in either case he will enjoy his chimera while it lasts.

The influence of this giddy air displays itself in many secondary ways. A certain sort of laboured pleasantry has already been recognized, and may perhaps have been remarked in these papers, as a sort peculiar to that climate. People utter their judgments with a cannonade of syllables; a big word is as good as a meal to them; and the turn of a phrase goes further than humour or wisdom. By the professional writer many sad vicissitudes have to be undergone. At first, he cannot write at all. The heart, it appears, is unequal to the pressure of business, and the brain, left without nourishment, goes into a mild decline. Next, some power of work returns to him, accompanied by jumping head-aches. Last, the spring is opened, and there pours at once from his pen a world of blatant, hustling polysyllables, and talk so high as, in the old joke, to be positively offensive in hot weather. He writes it in good faith and with a sense of inspiration; it is only when he comes to read what he has written that surprise and disquiet seize upon his mind. What is he to do, poor man? All his little fishes talk like whales. This yeasty inflation, this stiff and strutting architecture of the sentence has come upon him while he slept; and it is not he, it is the Alps, who are to blame. He is not, perhaps, alone, which somewhat comforts him. Nor is the ill without a remedy. Some day, when the Spring returns, he shall go down a little lower in this world, and remember quieter inflections and more modest language. But here, in the meantime, there seems to swim up some outline of a new cerebral hygiene and a good time coming, when experienced advisers shall send a man to the proper measured level for the ode, the biography, or the religious tract; and a nook may be found, between the sea and Chimborazo,[5] where Mr. Swinburne shall be able to write more continently, and Mr. Browning somewhat slower.[6]

Is it a return of youth, or is it a congestion of the brain? It is a sort of congestion, perhaps, that leads the invalid, when all goes well, to face the new day with such a bubbling cheerfulness. It is certainly congestion that makes night hideous with visions, all the chambers of a many-storeyed caravanserai[7] haunted with vociferous nightmares, and many wakeful people come down late for breakfast in the morning. Upon that theory the cynic may explain the whole affair—exhilaration, nightmares, pomp of tongue and all. But, on the other hand, the peculiar blessedness of boyhood may itself be but a symptom of the same complaint, for the two effects are strangely similar; and the frame of mind of the invalid upon the Alps is a sort of intermittent youth, with periods of lassitude. The fountain of Juventus[8] does not play steadily in these parts; but there it plays, and possibly nowhere else.

Notes

1 Thomas Sternhold's metrical adaptation of Psalm 18 in *The Book of Common Prayer* (1561).
2 It all hits you on the head (French).
3 Coteaux Champenois, or champagne without bubbles.
4 One of the three musketeers in Alexandre Dumas's 1844 novel.
5 Chimborazo: Ecuadorian mountain peak over 20,000 feet high.
6 English Victorian poets: Robert Browning (1812–1889) and Algernon Charles Swinburne (1837–1909).
7 Roadside inns along commercial trade routes in the Eastern world.
8 Fountain of youth.

51

THE MISGIVINGS OF
CONVALESCENCE

There is no problem more difficult, in view of modern thought upon morality, than to make a decent and human-hearted convalescence. Many elements are questionable. It may be open to doubt whether the man will or will not make an ultimate recovery, or whether it might or might not be better for humanity that he should die. A little while ago, and such inquiries would have been fantastic; but the weathercock has gone about; opinion tends to lie, if not in the direction of more modesty, at least in that of more self-consciousness; and between wisdom and folly, any young man, not yet riveted to life by years and complications, comes to regard the question of the importance of his own survival with a critical eye. In all this mass of rights and duties in which we find ourselves involved no right and no duty seem more doubtful, in hours of sickness and depression, than those that have to do with our own continued existence. A question, perhaps essentially impertinent, but yet continually recurring and almost as old as the art of logical speech—it is hardly imperative to state it: *cui bono?*[1]—haunts any phthisical[2] young man like his own shadow, and, in many instances, steps between him and the beginning of recovery. The world is too much with us, not only in getting and spending, but in our dank and downhearted speculations.[3] Truths of social complexity and instant, personal obligation, which we may be proud to call noble, have yet their sickly and sophisticated side. A considerable body of lugubrious prose and some verses, worthy at best of a tooth-comb for *obbligato*,[4] teach a proportion of the human race to feel a pride in self-abasement; and even political economy, read with a generous spirit, leads the same class of people to grudge perhaps too bitterly the expenses of their sickness. If you asked them the highest purpose to which humanity might apply its hoarded treasures, they would tell you to alleviate the pains and combat the dangers of sickness. But in their own case they cannot see the application. Yet a few natural tears, and they will lay them down with dignity to die. Existences that have not yet begun to be efficient among men, names that have not been writ even in water,[5] who is to mourn, who to suffer by their loss? And ten to one, there is some old parent to whom the world will be clean darkened by that death.

There is a mixture of the hero and of Mawworm[6] in this attitude, which makes it neither beautiful nor ugly; only superlatively young. The true heroic lies the other way. The man who has father, mother, wife, sister, friend, an honourable work to live for, cannot tamely die without, one need not say dishonor, but defeat. It is an uphill work to fight the sapping malady with one hand, the failing courage with the other; its difficulty alone would lend it some nobility; but when we reflect upon the prize of that contention, and how the man holds up against outward assaults and inward failings, not for the love of life, which is a feeble passion, but that he may bear and forbear, help and serve, and love and let himself be loved for some years longer in this rugged world, it will be clear there are few fights more worthy to be fought and few victories more to be lauded, than what are fought and won against disease. To those who fall, we say Farewell! theirs is the better part. From all our dangers and dissentions they escape; they leave us, when our time shall come, to follow through the same unknown and agonising pass; and to those who love them they bequeath no portion of their part in this world's happiness, only a continual blank and slowly diminishing pang. There is sense in pity for the dying: pity for the dead is false to nature and reason. We have spoken of the true heroic; the true pathetic, at least, is to conquer; to return again into the strife among our fellows, and take our share, with a sound spirit, in giving and receiving charities. There are many, it is more than possible, who will do no good, but only harm, in what remains to them of a career; but to recognise yourself for one of these is to do your utmost to ensure the fact that it shall be so. Perpetual previous failure should make a man, who is a man at all, nigh desperate to retrieve some part of such a past.

To keep up the braver, to encourage the feebler of these spirits, is a great end in medicine as well as in morality. Whatever tends to do so makes in the first place for recovery, and in the second supports and improves the tone of the recovering invalid. Never to have despaired is ground for a just satisfaction with oneself, and is second best to never having lost one's health. Hence, even if the directly medical effect were equal, that health resort would still be preferable where the moral influence is stronger and more brisk.

Now, if anywhere there was an emasculated air and an effeminate loveliness in nature that unstrung and dispirited the sick for vigorous resistance, it was to that place they would be sent in the old days of treatment.[7] We cannot say that it was bad, since they avoided many obvious dangers and had an opportunity to heal them of their wounds; yet there is certainly a sense in which the influence of such a climate and surroundings was not good. A swoon descended on the mind. Tender and dreamy not enterprising thoughts, resignation not rebellion, the quiet of peace not the ardour and glory of exercise, were the suggestions of that languorous land. Active memories came to the invalid only at long intervals, and veiled in a poetic haze; not otherwise than, from time to time about sundown, Corsica would swim for a little into view—farther, it would seem, and softer than a star, fainter and more immaterial than a cloud. Flowers and scents and phantom islands, delicate, tearful fancies, and deliquescence of the radical man, beauty over all, and nowhere any strength—such was the discipline in the older kind of sanitarium; and when suddenly a mistral[8] struck along the hills and sent a living shiver through the olive gardens, there would be such a panic among the sunshades and the respirators as though fleet-foot Achilles had burst in panoply upon the lotus-eaters' island.[9]

For each case, of course, there is a different rule. But *similia similibus*;[10] a man who puts his pleasure in activity, who desires a stirring life or none at all, will be certain to do better in the Alps. The continual, almost painful bracing, the boisterous inclemencies, the rough pleasure of tobogganing, the doctor exciting him to be up and walking, and to walk daily further, the glittering, unhomely landscape, the glare of day, the solemn splendours of the night, spur him to the gallop in his quest of health. He takes a risk; he makes an effort; action is in all his thoughts. The very sameness of his prison valley bids him make a push to recover and escape. The ground is deep with snow; and he cannot lounge on violets. The frost flutters his heart and tingles in his nerves; today, if not yesterday, he will gain the summit of that hill. And, in a word, if pluck, vigour, and the desire of living at all help or speed the invalid in his recovery, it is here upon the Alps, and not among the perfumed valleys of Liguria, that he will find the stimulus required. Cold he may dismiss from his consideration; he will rarely feel it. Dulness at first he must endure; his eagerness will be so vastly greater than his strength. And it is never pleasant to be ill nor easy to recover. But here he will be free from morbid weakness on his own part; he will be eager, human, decently mirthful, at least rationally hopeful; he will work briskly at his own recovery like a piece of business; and, even if he shall not succeed, he makes a better figure in defeat and is a shorter time a-dying.

Notes

1 "To whom is it a benefit?" A Latin phrase used to identify criminal suspects with a possible motive.
2 Phthisis—tuberculosis.
3 Wordsworth, "The World is Too Much With Us" (1–2).
4 *Obbligato*—a distinctive, integral, instrumental part of a musical piece.
5 Per his instructions, John Keats's epitaph reads, "Here lies One Whose Name was writ in Water."
6 A sanctimonious hypocrite, named for the character in Isaac Bickerstaff's play *The Hypocrite* (1768).
7 See "Ordered South" (n. 1, p. 77).
8 A strong, cold, northwesterly wind blowing through southern France into the Mediterranean.
9 Achilles—hero of the Trojan War and protagonist of Homer's *Iliad*; lotus-eaters—mythological people who ate lotus fruit, which made them lethargic and apathetic.
10 *Similia similibus curantur* (Latin): Like is cured by like: a disease may be cured by something that can cause similar symptoms.

52

THE MORALITY OF THE
PROFESSION OF LETTERS

The profession of letters has been lately debated in the public prints; and it has
been debated, to put the matter mildly, from a point of view that was calculated to
surprise high-minded men, and bring a general contempt on books and reading.
Some time ago, in particular, a lively, pleasant, popular writer devoted an essay,
lively and pleasant like himself, to a very encouraging view of the profession.[1]
We may be glad that his experience is so cheering, and we may hope that all
others, who deserve it, shall be as handsomely rewarded; but I do not think we
need be at all glad to have this question, so important to the public and ourselves,
debated solely on the ground of money. The salary in any business under heaven
is not the only, nor indeed the first, question. That you should continue to exist is
a matter for your own consideration; but that your business should be first honest,
and second useful, are points in which honour and morality are concerned. If the
writer to whom I refer succeeds in persuading a number of young persons to adopt
this way of life with an eye set singly on the livelihood, we must expect them in
their works to follow profit only, and we must expect in consequence, if he will
pardon me the epithets, a slovenly, base, untrue, and empty literature. Of that
writer himself I am not speaking; he is diligent, clean, and pleasing; we all owe
him periods of entertainment, and he has achieved an amiable popularity which
he has adequately deserved. But the truth is, he does not, or did not when he first
embraced it regard his profession from this purely mercenary side. He went into
it, I shall venture to say, if not with any noble design, at least in the ardour of a
first love; and he enjoyed its practice long before he paused to calculate the wage.
The other day an author was complimented on a piece of work, good in itself
and exceptionally good for him, and replied in terms unworthy of a commercial
traveller, that as the book was not briskly selling he did not give a copper farthing
for its merit. It must not be supposed that the person to whom this answer was
addressed received it as a profession of faith; he knew, on the other hand, that it
was only a whiff of irritation; just as we know, when a respectable writer talks of
literature as a way of life, like shoemaking, but not so useful, that he is only debating one aspect of a question, and is still clearly conscious of a dozen others more
important in themselves and more central to the matter in hand. But while those
who treat literature in this penny-wise and virtue-foolish spirit are themselves

379

truly in possession of a better light, it does not follow that the treatment is decent or improving, whether for themselves or others. To treat all subjects in the highest, the most honourable, and the pluckiest spirit, consistent with the fact, is the first duty of a writer. If he be well paid, as I am glad to hear he is, this duty becomes the more urgent, the neglect of it the more disgraceful. And perhaps there is no subject on which a man should speak so gravely as that industry, whatever it may be, which is the occupation or delight of his life; which is his tool to earn or serve with; and which, if it be unworthy, stamps himself as a mere incubus of dumb and greedy bowels on the shoulders of labouring humanity. On that subject alone even to force the note might lean to virtue's side. It is to be hoped that a numerous and enterprising generation of writers will follow and surpass the present one; but it would be better if the stream were stayed, and the roll of our old, honest, English books were closed, than that esurient bookmakers should continue and debase a brave tradition and lower, in their own eyes, a famous race. Better that our serene temples were deserted than filled with trafficking and juggling priests.

There are two just reasons for the choice of any way of life: the first is inbred taste in the chooser; the second some high utility in the industry selected. Literature, like any other art, is singularly interesting to the artist; and in a degree peculiar to itself among the arts, it is useful to mankind. These are the sufficient justifications for any young man or woman who adopts it as the business of his life. I shall not say much about the wages. A writer can live by his writing. If not so luxuriously as by other trades, then less luxuriously. The nature of the work he does all day will more affect his happiness than the quality of his dinner at night. Whatever be your calling, and however much it brings you in the year, you could still, you know, get more by cheating. We all suffer ourselves to be too much concerned about a little poverty; but such considerations should not move us in the choice of that which is to be the business and justification of so great a portion of our lives; and like the missionary, the patriot, or the philosopher, we should all choose that poor and brave career in which we can do the most and best for mankind. Now nature, faithfully followed, proves herself a careful mother. A lad, for some liking to the jingle of words, betakes himself to letters for his life; by-and-by, when he learns more gravity, he finds that he has chosen better than he knew; that if he earns little, he is earning it amply; that if he receives a small wage, he is in a position to do considerable services; that it is in his power, in some small measure, to protect the oppressed and to defend the truth. So kindly is the world arranged, such great profit may arise from a small degree of human reliance on oneself, and such, in particular, is the happy star of this trade of writing, that it should combine pleasure and profit to both parties, and be at once agreeable, like fiddling, and useful, like good preaching.

This is to speak of literature at its highest; and with the four great elders[2] who are still spared to our respect and admiration, with Carlyle, Ruskin, Browning, and Tennyson before us, it would be cowardly to consider it at first in any lesser aspect. But while we cannot follow these athletes, while we may none of us, perhaps, be very vigorous, very original, or very wise, I still contend that, in the humblest sort of literary work, we have it in our power either to do great harm or great good. We may seek merely to please; we may seek, having no higher gift, merely to gratify the idle nine-days' curiosity of our contemporaries; or we may essay, however feebly, to instruct. In each of these we shall have to deal with that remarkable art of words which, because it is the dialect of life, comes home so easily and powerfully to the minds of men; and since that is so, we contribute, in each of these branches, to build up the sum of sentiments and appreciations which goes by the name of Public Opinion or Public Feeling. The total of a nation's reading, in these days of daily papers, greatly modifies the total of the nation's speech; and the speech and reading, taken together, form the efficient educational medium of youth. A good man or woman may keep a youth some little while in clearer air; but the contemporary atmosphere is all powerful in the end on the average of mediocre characters. The copious Corinthian[3] baseness of the American reporter or the Parisian *chroniqueur*,[4] both so lightly readable, must exercise an incalculable influence for ill; they touch upon all subjects, and on all with the same ungenerous hand; they begin the consideration of all, in young and unprepared minds, in an unworthy spirit; on all, they supply some pungency for dull people to quote. The mere body of this ugly matter overwhelms the rarer utterances of good men; the sneering, the selfish, and the cowardly are scattered in broad sheets on every table, while the antidote, in small volumes, lies unread upon the shelf. I have spoken of the American and the French, not because they are so much baser, but so much more readable, than the English; their evil is done more effectively, in America for the masses, in French for the few that care to read; but with us as with them, the duties of literature are daily neglected, truth daily perverted and suppressed, and grave subjects daily degraded in the treatment. The journalist is not reckoned an important officer; yet judge of the good he might do, the harm he does; judge of it by one instance only: that when we find two journals on the reverse sides of politics each, on the same day, openly garbling a piece of news for the interest of its own party, we smile at the discovery (no discovery now!) as over a good joke and pardonable stratagem. Lying so open is scarce lying, it is true; but one of the things that we profess to teach our young is a respect for truth; and I cannot think this piece of education will be crowned with any great success, so long as some of us practise and the rest openly approve of public falsehood.

There are two duties incumbent upon any man who enters on the business of writing: truth to the fact and a good spirit in the treatment. In every department of literature, though so low as hardly to deserve the name, truth to the fact is of importance to the education and comfort of mankind, and so hard to preserve, that the faithful trying to do so will lend some dignity to the man who tries it. Our judgments are based upon two things: first, upon the original preferences of our soul; but, second, upon the mass of testimony to the nature of God, man, and the universe which reaches us, in divers manners, from without. For the most part these divers manners are reducible to one, all that we learn of past times and much that we learn of our own reaching us through the medium of books or papers, and even he who cannot read learning from the same source at second hand and by the report of him who can. Thus the sum of the contemporary knowledge or ignorance of good and evil is, in large measure, the handiwork of those who write. Those who write have to see that each man's knowledge is, as near as they can make it, answerable to the facts of life; that he shall not suppose himself an angel or a monster; nor take this world for a hell; nor be suffered to imagine that all rights are concentred in his own caste or country, or all veracities in his own parochial creed. Each man should learn what is within him, that he may strive to mend; he must be taught what is without him, that he may be kind to others. It can never be wrong to tell him the truth; for, in his disputable state, weaving as he goes his theory of life, steering himself, cheering or reproving others, all facts are of the first importance to his conduct; and even if a fact shall discourage or corrupt him, it is still best that he should know it; for it is in this world as it is, and not in a world made easy by educational suppressions, that he must win his way to shame or glory. In one word, it must always be foul to tell what is false; and it can never be safe to suppress what is true. The very fact that you omit may be what somebody was wanting, for one man's meat is another man's poison, and I have known a person who was cheered by the perusal of *Candide*.[5] Every fact is a part of that great puzzle we must set together; and none that comes directly in a writer's path but has some nice relations, unperceivable by him, to the totality and bearing of the subject under hand. Yet there are certain classes of fact eternally more necessary than others, and it is with these that literature must first bestir itself. They are not hard to distinguish, nature once more easily leading us; for the necessary, because the efficacious, facts are those which are most interesting to the natural mind of man. Those which are coloured, picturesque, human, and rooted in morality, and those, on the other hand, which are clear, indisputable, and a part of science, are alone vital in importance, seizing by their interest, or useful to communicate. So far as the writer merely narrates, he should principally tell of these. He should tell of the kind and wholesome and beautiful elements of our life; he should tell unsparingly of the evil and sorrow of the present, to move us with instances; he should tell of wise and good people in the past, to excite us by example; and of these he should tell soberly and truthfully, not glossing faults, that we may neither grow discouraged with ourselves nor exacting to our neighbours. So the body of contemporary literature, ephemeral and feeble in itself, touches in the minds of men the springs of thought and kindness, and supports them (for those who will go at all are easily supported) on their way to what is true and right. And if, in any degree, it does so now, how much more might it do so if the writers chose! There is not a life in all the records of the past but, properly studied, might lend a hint and a help to some contemporary. There is not a juncture in to-day's affairs but some useful word may yet be said of it. Even the reporter has an office, and, with clear eyes and honest language, may unveil injustices and point the way to progress. And for a last word: in all narration there is only one way to be clever, and that is to be exact. To be vivid is a secondary quality which must presuppose the first; for vividly to convey a wrong impression is only to make failure conspicuous.

But a fact may be viewed on many sides; it may be chronicled with rage, tears, laughter, indifference, or admiration, and by each of these the story will be transformed to something else. The newspapers that told of the return of our representatives from Berlin,[6] even if they had not differed as to the facts, would have sufficiently differed by their spirit; so that the one description would have been a second ovation, and the other a prolonged insult. The subject makes but a trifling part of any piece of literature, and the view of the writer is itself a fact more important because less disputable than the others. Now this spirit in which a subject is regarded, important in all kinds of literary work, becomes all important in works of fiction, meditation, or rhapsody; for there it not only colours but itself chooses the facts; not only modifies but shapes the work. And hence, over the far larger proportion of the field of literature, the health or disease of the writer's mind or momentary humour forms not only the leading feature of his work, but is, at bottom, the only thing he can communicate to others. In all works of art, widely speaking, it is first of all the author's attitude that is narrated, though in the attitude there be implied a whole experience and a theory of life. An author who has begged the question and reposes in some narrow faith, cannot, if he would, express the whole or even many of the sides of this various existence; for his own life being maim, some of them are not admitted in his theory, and were only dimly and unwillingly recognised in his experience. Hence the smallness, the triteness, and the inhumanity in works of merely sectarian religion; and hence we find equal although unsimilar limitations in works inspired by the spirit of the flesh or the despicable taste for high society. So that the first duty of any man who is to write is intellectual. Designedly or not, he has so far set himself up for a leader of the minds of men; and he must see that his own mind is kept supple, charitable, and bright. Everything but prejudice should find a voice through him; he should see the good in all things; where he has even a fear that he does not wholly understand, there he should be wholly silent; and he should recognise from the first that he has only one tool in his workshop, and that tool is sympathy.[7]

The second duty, far harder to define, is moral. There are a thousand different humours in the mind, and about each of them, when it is uppermost, some literature tends to be deposited. Is this to be allowed? not certainly in every case, and yet perhaps in more than rigourists would fancy. It were to be desired that all literary work, and chiefly works of art, issued from sound, human, healthy, and potent impulses, whether grave or laughing, humorous, romantic, or religious. Yet it cannot be denied that some valuable books are partially insane; some, mostly religious, partially inhuman; and very many tainted with morbidity and impotence. We do not loathe a masterpiece although we gird against its blemishes. We are not, above all, to look for faults but merits. There is no book perfect, even in design; but there are many that will delight, improve, or encourage the reader. On the one hand, the Hebrew Psalms are the only religious poetry on earth; yet they contain sallies that savour rankly of the man of blood. On the other hand, Alfred de Musset had a poisoned and a contorted nature; I am only quoting that generous and frivolous giant, old Dumas, when I accuse him of a bad heart;[8] yet, when the impulse under which he wrote was purely creative, he could give us works like *Carmosine* or *Fantasio*, in which the lost note of the romantic comedy seems to have been found again to touch and please us. When Flaubert wrote *Madame Bovary*,[9] I believe he thought chiefly of a somewhat morbid realism; and behold! the book turned in his hands into a masterpiece of appalling morality. But the truth is, when books are conceived under a great stress, with a soul of ninefold power, nine times heated and electrified by effort, the conditions of our being are seized with such an ample grasp, that, even should the main design be trivial or base, some truth and beauty cannot fail to be expressed. Out of the strong comes forth sweetness; but an ill thing poorly done is an ill thing top and bottom. And so this can be no encouragement to knock-knee'd, feeble-wristed scribes, who must take their business conscientiously or be ashamed to practise it.

Man is imperfect; yet, in his literature, he must express himself and his own views and preferences; for to do anything else, is to do a far more perilous thing than to risk being immoral: it is to be sure of being untrue. To ape a sentiment, even a good one, is to travesty a sentiment; that will not be helpful. To conceal a sentiment, if you are sure you hold it, is to take a liberty with truth. There is probably no point of view possible to a sane man but contains some truth and, in the true connection, might be profitable to the race. I am not afraid of the truth, if any one could tell it me, but I am afraid of parts of it impertinently uttered. There is a time to dance and a time to mourn;[10] to be harsh as well as to be sentimental; to be ascetic as well as to glorify the appetites; and if a man were to combine all these extremes into his work, each in its place and proportion, that work would be the world's masterpiece of morality as well as of art. Partiality is immorality; for any book is wrong that gives a misleading picture of the world and life. The trouble is that the weakling must be partial; the work of one proving dank and depressing; of another, cheap and vulgar; of a third, epileptically sensual, of a fourth, sourly ascetic. In literature as in conduct, you can never hope to do exactly right. All you can do is to make as sure as possible; and for that there is but one rule. Nothing should be done in a hurry that can be done slowly. It is no use to write a book and put it by for nine or even ninety years; for in the writing you will have partly convinced yourself; the delay must precede any beginning; and if you meditate a work of art, you should first long roll the subject under the tongue to make sure you like the flavour, before you brew a volume that shall taste of it from end to end; or if you propose to enter on the field of controversy, you should first have thought upon the question under all conditions, in health as well as in sickness, in sorrow as well as in joy. It is this nearness of examination necessary for any true and kind writing, that makes the practice of the art a prolonged and noble education for the writer.

There is plenty to do, plenty to say, or to say over again, in the meantime. Any literary work which conveys faithful facts or pleasing impressions is a service to the public. It is even a service to be thankfully proud of having rendered. The slightest novels are a blessing to those in distress, not chloroform itself a greater. Our fine old sea-captain's life was justified when Carlyle soothed his mind with *The King's Own* or *Newton Forster*.[11] To please is to serve; and so far from its being difficult to instruct while you amuse, it is difficult to do the one thoroughly without the other. Some part of the writer or his life will crop out in even a vapid book; and to read a novel that was conceived with any force, is to multiply experience and to exercise the sympathies. Every article, every piece of verse, every essay, every *entre-filet*,[12] is destined to pass, however swiftly, through the minds of some portion of the public, and to colour, however transiently, their thoughts. When any subject falls to be discussed, some scribbler on a paper has the invaluable opportunity of beginning its discussion in a dignified and human spirit; and if there were enough who did so in our public press, neither the public nor the parliament would find it in their minds to drop to meaner thoughts. The writer has the chance to stumble, by the way, on something pleasing, something interesting, something encouraging, were it only to a single reader. He will be unfortunate, indeed, if he suit no one. He has the chance, besides, to stumble on something that a dull person shall be able to comprehend; and for a dull person to have read anything and, for that once, comprehended it, makes a marking epoch in his education.

Here then is work worth doing and worth trying to do well. And so, if I were minded to welcome any great accession to our trade, it should not be from any reason of a higher wage, but because it was a trade which was useful in a very great and in a very high degree; which every honest tradesman could make more serviceable to mankind in his single strength; which was difficult to do well and possible to do better every year; which called for scrupulous thought on the part of all who practised it, and hence became a perpetual education to their nobler natures; and which, pay it as you please, in the large majority of the best cases will still be underpaid. For surely, at this time of day in the nineteenth century, there is nothing that an honest man should fear more timorously than getting and spending[13] more than he deserves.

Notes

1 James Payn (1830–1898), successful novelist, essayist, poet, and editor of *Chambers's Journal* (1859–1874) and *Cornhill Magazine* (1882–1896). His essay on "Penny Fiction" appeared in *Nineteenth Century* in 1881.
2 **RLS:** "Since this article was written, only three of these remain. But the other, being dead, yet speaketh." Thomas Carlyle (b. 1795) died on 5 Feb. 1881. John Ruskin (1819–1900), Robert Browning (1812–1889), and Alfred Tennyson (1809–1892).
3 Libertine.
4 Columnist (French).
5 Voltaire's satire on optimism *Candide* (1759).
6 The Congress of Berlin—an important gathering of European diplomats in 1878. Prime Minister Benjamin Disraeli triumphantly claimed "peace with honour" on his return.
7 **RLS:** "A footnote, at least, is due to the admirable example set before all young writers in the width of literary sympathy displayed by Mr. [Algernon Charles] Swinburne. He runs forth to welcome merit, whether in Dickens or Trollope, whether in Villon, Milton, or Pope. This is, in criticism, the attitude we should all seek to preserve, not only in that, but in every branch of literary work."

8 Before the French Romantic writer Alfred de Musset (1810–1847) died of heart failure in 1857, his head bobbed—a condition caused by aortic regurgitation now called "de Musset's sign."

9 Gustave Flaubert's sexually explicit novel *Madame Bovary* (1857).

10 Ecclesiastes 3:1.

11 *The King's Own* (1830) and *Newton Forster* (1832) are popular novels by the naval officer Captain Frederick Marryat (1792–1848).

12 Paragraph.

13 Wordsworth, "The World Is Too Much With Us" (1–2).

53

A MODERN COSMOPOLIS[1]

The Pacific coast of the United States, as you may see by the map, and still better in that admirable book, "Two Years Before the Mast," by Dana,[2] is one of the most exposed and shelterless on earth. The trade-wind blows fresh; the huge Pacific swell booms along degree after degree of an unbroken line of coast. South of the joint firth of the Columbia and Williamette, there flows in no considerable river; south of Puget Sound there is no protected inlet of the ocean. Along the whole seaboard of California there are but two unexceptionable anchorages, the bight of the bay of Monterey, and the inland sea that takes its name from San Francisco.

Whether or not it was here that Drake[3] put in in 1597,[4] we cannot tell. There is no other place so suitable; and yet the narrative of Francis Pretty[5] scarcely seems to suit the features of the scene. Viewed from seaward, the Golden Gates should give no very English impression to justify the name of a New Albion.[6] On the west, the deep lies open; nothing near but the still vexed Farralones. The coast is rough and barren. Tamalpais, a mountain of a memorable figure, springing direct from the sea-level, over-plumbs the narrow entrance from the north. On the south, the loud music of the Pacific sounds along beaches and cliffs, and among broken reefs, the sporting place of the sea-lion. Dismal, shifting sand-hills, wrinkled by the wind, appear behind. Perhaps, too, in the days of Drake, Tamalpais would be clothed to its peak with the majestic redwoods.

Within the memory of persons not yet old, a mariner might have steered into these narrows—not yet the Golden Gates—opened out the surface of the bay— here girt with hills, there lying broad to the horizon—and beheld a scene as empty of the presence, as pure from the handiwork of man, as in the days of our old sea-commander. A Spanish mission, fort, and church[7] took the place of those "houses of the people of the country" which were seen by Pretty, "close to the water-side." All else would be unchanged. Now, a generation later, a great city covers the sand-hills on the west, a growing town lies along the muddy shallows of the east; steamboats pant continually between them from before sunrise till the small hours of the morning; lines of great sea-going ships lie ranged at anchor; colours fly upon the islands; and from all around the hum of corporate life, of beaten bells, and steam, and running carriages, goes cheerily abroad in the sunshine. Choose a place on one of the huge, throbbing ferry-boats, and, when you are midway between the city and the suburb, look around. The air is fresh and salt as if you were at sea. On the one hand is Oakland, gleaming white among its gardens. On the other, to seaward, hill after hill is crowded and crowned with the palaces of San Francisco; its long streets lie in regular bars of darkness, east and west, across the sparkling picture; a forest of masts bristles like bulrushes about its feet; nothing remains of the days of Drake but the faithful trade-wind scattering the smoke, the fogs that will begin to muster about sundown, and the fine bulk of Tamalpais looking down on San Francisco, like Arthur's Seat on Edinburgh.[8]

Thus, in the course of a generation only, this city and its suburb have arisen. Men are alive by the score who have hunted all over the foundations in a dreary waste. I have dined, near the "punctual centre"[9] of San Francisco, with a gentleman (then newly married) who told me of his former pleasures, wading with his fowling-piece in sand and scrub, on the site of the house where we were dining. In this busy, moving generation, we have all known cities to cover our boyish playgrounds, we have all started for a country walk and stumbled on a new suburb; but I wonder what enchantment of the Arabian Nights can have equalled this evocation of a roaring city, in a few years of a man's life, from the marshes and the blowing sand. Such swiftness of increase, as with an overgrown youth, suggests a corresponding swiftness of destruction. The sandy peninsula of San Francisco, mirroring itself on one side in the bay, beaten, on the other, by the surge of the Pacific, and shaken to the heart by frequent earthquakes, seems in itself no very durable foundation. According to Indian tales, perhaps older than the name of California, it once rose out of the sea in a moment, and some time or other shall, in a moment, sink again. No Indian, they say, cares to linger on that doubtful land. "The earth hath bubbles as the water has, and this is of them."[10] Here, indeed, all is new, nature as well as towns. The very hills of California have an unfinished look; the rains and the streams have not yet carved them to their perfect shape. The forests spring like mushrooms from the unexhausted soil; and they are mown down yearly by forest fires. We are in early geological epochs, changeful and insecure; and we feel, as with a sculptor's model, that the author may yet grow weary of and shatter the rough sketch.

Fancy apart, San Francisco is a city beleaguered with alarms. The lower parts, along the bay side, sit on piles: old wrecks decaying, fish dwelling unsunned, beneath the populous houses; and a trifling subsidence might drown the business quarters in an hour. Earthquakes are not only common, they are sometimes threatening in their violence; the fear of them grows yearly on a resident; he begins with indifference, ends in sheer panic; and no one feels safe in any but a wooden house. Hence it comes that, in that rainless clime, the whole city is built of timber—a woodyard of unusual extent and complication; that fires spring up readily, and, served by the unwearying trade-wind, swiftly spread; that all over the city there are fire-signal boxes; that the sound of the bell, telling the number of the threatened ward, is soon familiar to the ear; and that nowhere else in the world is the art of the fireman carried to so nice a point.

Next, perhaps, in order of strangeness to the speed of its appearance, is the mingling of the races that combine to people it. The town is essentially not Anglo-Saxon; still more essentially not American. The Yankee and the Englishman find themselves alike in a strange country. There are none of these touches—not of nature, and I dare scarcely say of art—by which the Anglo-Saxon feels himself at home in so great a diversity of lands. Here, on the contrary, are airs of Marseilles and of Pekin.[11] The shops along the street are like the consulates of different nations. The passers-by vary in feature like the slides of a magic-lantern.[12] For we are here in that city of gold to which adventurers congregated out of all the winds of heaven;[13] we are in a land that till the other day was ruled and peopled by the countrymen of Cortés;[14] and the sea that laves the piers of San Francisco is the ocean of the east and of the isles of summer. There goes the Mexican, unmistakable; there the blue-clad Chinaman with his white slippers; there the soft-spoken, brown Kanaka,[15] or perhaps a waif from far-away Malaya.[16] You hear French, German, Italian, Spanish, and English indifferently. You taste the food of all nations in the various restaurants; passing from a French *prix-fixe*, where every one is French, to a roaring German ordinary[17] where every one is German; ending, perhaps, in a cool and silent Chinese tea-house. For every man, for every race and nation, that city is a foreign city, humming with foreign tongues and customs; and yet each and all have made themselves at home. The Germans have a German theatre and innumerable beer-gardens. The French Fall of the Bastille is celebrated with squibs and banners, and marching patriots, as noisily as the American Fourth of July.[18] The Italians have their dear domestic quarter, with Italian caricatures in the windows, Chianti and polenta in the taverns. The Chinese are settled as in China. The goods they offer for sale are as foreign as the lettering on the signboard of the shop: dried fish from the China seas; pale cakes and sweetmeats—the like, perhaps, once eaten by Badroubadour;[19] nuts of unfriendly shape; ambiguous, outlandish vegetables, misshapen, lean or bulbous—telling of a country where the trees are not as our trees, and the very back garden is a cabinet of curiosities. The joss-house[20] is hard by, heavy with incense, packed with quaint carvings and the paraphernalia of a foreign ceremonial. All these you behold, crowded together in the narrower arteries of the city, cool, sunless, a little mouldy, with the unfamiliar faces at your elbow, and the high, musical sing-song of that alien language in your ears. Yet the houses are of Occidental build; the lines of a hundred telegraphs pass, thick as a ship's rigging, overhead, a kite hanging among them perhaps, or perhaps two, one European, one Chinese, in shape and colour; mercantile Jack,[21] the Italian fisher, the Dutch merchant, the Mexican vaquero[22] go hustling by; at the sunny end of the street, a thoroughfare roars with European traffic; and meanwhile high and clear, out breaks, perhaps, the San Francisco fire alarm, and people pause to count the strokes, and in the stations of the double fire-service you know that the electric bells are ringing, the traps opening and clapping to, and the engine, manned and harnessed, being whisked into the street, before the sound of the alarm has ceased to vibrate on your ear. Of all romantic places for a boy to loiter in, that Chinese quarter is the most romantic. There, on a half-holiday, three doors from home, he may visit an actual foreign land, foreign in people, language, things, and customs. The very barber of the Arabian Nights[23] shall be at work before him, shaving heads; he shall see Aladdin playing on the streets; who knows, but among those nameless vegetables, the fruit of the nose-tree[24] itself may be exposed for sale? And the interest is heightened with a chill of horror. Below, you hear, the cellars are alive with mystery; opium dens, where the smokers lie one above another, shelf above shelf, close-packed and grovelling in deadly stupor; the seats of unknown vices and cruelties, the prisons of unacknowledged slaves and the secret lazarettos[25] of disease.

With all this mass of nationalities, crime is common. Amid such a competition of respectabilities, the moral sense is confused; in this camp of gold-seekers, speech is loud and the hand ready.[26] There are rough quarters where it is dangerous o' nights; cellars of public entertainment which the wary pleasure-seeker chooses to avoid. Concealed weapons are unlawful, but the law is continually broken. One editor was shot dead while I was there; another walked the streets accompanied by a bravo,[27] his guardian angel. I have been quietly eating a dish of oysters in a restaurant, where, not more than ten minutes after I had left, shots were exchanged and took effect; and one night about ten o'clock, I saw a man standing watchfully at a street-corner with a long Smith-and-Wesson glittering in his hand behind his back. Somebody had done something he should not, and was being looked for with a vengeance. It is odd, too, that the seat of the last vigilance committee[28] I know of—a mediæval *Vehmgericht*[29]—was none other than the Palace Hotel,[30] the world's greatest caravanserai,[31] served by lifts and lit with electricity; where, in the great glazed court, a band nightly discourses music from a grove of palms. So do extremes meet in this city of contrasts: extremes of wealth and poverty, apathy and excitement, the conveniences of civilisation and the red justice of Judge Lynch.[32] The streets lie straight up and down the hills, and straight across at right angles, these in sun, those in shadow, a trenchant pattern of gloom and glare; and what with the crisp illumination, the sea-air singing in your ears, the chill and glitter, the changing aspects both of things and people, the fresh sights at every corner of your walk—sights of the bay, of Tamalpais, of steep, descending streets, of the outspread city—whiffs of alien speech, sailors singing on shipboard, Chinese coolies toiling on the shore, crowds brawling all day in the street before the Stock Exchange—one brief impression follows and obliterates another, and the city leaves upon the mind no general and stable picture, but a profusion of airy and incongruous images, of the sea and shore, the east and west, the summer and the winter.

In the better parts of the most interesting city there is apt to be a touch of the commonplace. It is in the slums and suburbs that the city dilettante finds his game. And there is nothing more characteristic and original than the outlying quarters of San Francisco. The Chinese district is the most famous; but it is far from the only truffle in the pie. There is many another dingy corner, many a young antiquity, many a *terrain vague*[33] with that stamp of quaintness that the city lover seeks and dwells on; and the indefinite prolongation of its streets, up hill and down dale, makes San Francisco a place apart. The same street in its career visits and unites so many different classes of society, here echoing with drays,[34] there lying decorously silent between the mansions of Bonanza millionaires, to founder at last among the drifting sands beside Lone Mountain cemetery,[35] or die out among the sheds and lumber of the north. Thus you may be struck with a spot, set it down for the most romantic of the city, and, glancing at the name-plate, find it is on the same street that you yourself inhabit in another quarter of the town.

The great net of straight thoroughfares lying at right angles, east and west and north and south, over the shoulders of Nob Hill, the hill of palaces, must certainly be counted the best part of San Francisco. It is there that the millionaires are gathered together, vying with each other in display; and you may see by our first illustration something of how they look down upon the business wards of the city. That is California Street. Far away down you may pick out a building with a little belfry; and that is the Stock Exchange, the heart of San Francisco: a great pump we might call it, continually pumping up the savings of the lower quarters into the pockets of the millionaires upon the hill. But these same thoroughfares that enjoy for awhile so elegant a destiny have their lines prolonged into more unpleasant places. Some meet their fate in the sands; some must take a cruise in the ill-famed China quarters; some run into the sea; some perish unwept among pig-stys and rubbish-heaps.

Nob Hill comes, of right, in the place of honour; but the two other hills of San Francisco are more entertaining to explore. On both there are a world of old wooden houses snoozing together all forgotten. Some are of the quaintest design, others only romantic by neglect and age. Some have been almost undermined by new thoroughfares, and sit high up on the margin of the sandy cutting, only to be reached by stairs. Some are curiously painted, and I have seen one at least with ancient carvings panelled in its wall. Surely they are not of Californian building, but far voyagers from round the stormy Horn,[36] like those who sent for them and dwelt in them at first. Brought to be the favourites of the wealthy, they have sunk into these poor, forgotten districts, where, like old town toasts,[37] they keep each other silent countenance. Telegraph Hill and Rincon Hill, these are the two dozing quarters that I recommend to the city dilettante. There stand these forgotten houses, enjoying the unbroken sun and quiet. There, if there were such an author, would the San Francisco Fortuné de Boisgobey[38] pitch the first chapter of his mystery. But the first is the quainter of the two. It is from Telegraph Hill or the near neighborhood of North Reach, that our three last illustrations have been taken; but the camera and the graver are unromantic tools, and the strangeness and interest have been somehow lost between the pair. Visited under the broad natural daylight, and with the relief and accent of reality, these scenes have a quality of dreamland and of the best pages of Dickens. Telegraph Hill, besides, commands a noble view; and as it stands at the turn of the bay, its skirts are all waterside, and round from North Reach to the Bay Front you can follow doubtful paths from one quaint corner to another. Everywhere the same; tumble-down decay and sloppy progress, new things yet unmade, old things tottering to their fall; everywhere the same out-at-elbows,[39] many-nationed loungers at dim, irregular grog-shops; everywhere the same sea-air and isletted sea-prospect; and for a last and more romantic note, you have on the one hand Tamalpais standing high in the blue air, and on the other the tail of that long alignment of three-masted, full-rigged, deep-sea ships that make a forest of spars along the eastern front of San Francisco. In no other port is such a navy congregated. For the coast trade is so trifling, and the ocean trade from round the Horn so large, that the smaller ships are swallowed up, and can do nothing to confuse the majestic order of these merchant princes. In an age when the ship-of-the-line[40] is already a thing of the past, and we can never again hope to go coasting in a cock-boat[41] between the "wooden walls" of a squadron at anchor, there is perhaps no place on earth where the power and beauty of sea architecture can be so perfectly enjoyed as in this bay.

Notes

1 Stevenson lived in California (Monterey, San Francisco, and Napa Valley) from 30 Aug. 1879 to 29 July 1880. He went in pursuit of the still married Fanny Osbourne, who divorced her husband in Dec. 1879 and married Stevenson on 19 May 1880.

2 Richard Henry Dana Jr. (1815–1882), American memoirist, lawyer, and politician.

3 Francis Drake (1540–1596), privateer and naval captain.

4 1579.

5 *Sir Francis Drake's Famous Voyage Round the World* (1580).

6 Drake named North America "New Albion" after Britain's ancient name.

7 The Spanish established Mission Dolores in 1776.

8 A hill just east of the center of Edinburgh.

9 The Stock Exchange with its large clock.

10 Shakespeare, *Macbeth*, 1.3.79–80.

11 Peking: modern Beijing.

12 An early image projector.

13 Shakespeare, *Hamlet*, 1.2.141.

14 Spanish Conquistador Hernán Cortés (1485–1587).

15 Native of the South Sea Islands.

16 Malaysia.

17 *Prix-fixe*—A restaurant that serves a multi-course meal at a fixed price; an *ordinary*.

18 French state prison famously seized by revolutionaries on 14 July 1789. July 4, 1776—America's Declaration of Independence.

19 Badroulbadour—Chinese princess who marries Aladdin in *The Arabian Nights*.

20 Chinese shrine or temple.

21 Sailor.

22 Cowboy.

23 The Barber of Baghdad.

24 A German folktale about a magic tree's apples that enlarge the eater's nose until it's restored by magic pears.

25 Quarantine stations.

26 Stevenson later removed this sentence.

27 Bodyguard.

28 A vigilante body (n. 19, p. 219).

29 Extralegal Vehmic courts for secret criminal trials in 12th-century feudal warfare, por-
    trayed in Walter Scott's *Anne of Geierstein* (1829).
30 A luxury hotel in San Francisco's financial district.
31 Roadside inns along commercial trade routes in the Eastern world.
32 Charles Lynch (1736–1796), a Virginia justice whose extralegal court punished British
    loyalists and gave rise to the term *lynching*.
33 Waste ground or vacant lot.
34 Dray: a flat-bed wagon generally used for transporting beer.
35 Now central San Francisco, Lone Mountain was the site of a cemetery at its western
    edge.
36 Cape Horn.
37 Drunks.
38 Fortuné du Boisgobey, penname of Fortuné Hippolyte Auguste Abraham-Dubois
    (1821–1891), a prolific and popular French novelist.
39 Shabbily dressed.
40 Large warships on the front line.
41 Small boat used to service large ships.

54

BOOKS WHICH HAVE
INFLUENCED ME

The Editor has somewhat insidiously laid a trap for his correspondents, the question put appearing at first so innocent, truly cutting so deep.[1] It is not, indeed, until after some reconnaissance and review that the writer awakes to find himself engaged upon something in the nature of autobiography, or, perhaps worse, upon a chapter in the life of that little, beautiful brother whom we once all had, and whom we have all lost and mourned, the man we ought to have been, the man we hoped to be. But when word has been passed (even to an editor), it should, if possible, be kept; and if sometimes I am wise and say too little, and sometimes weak and say too much, the blame must lie at the door of the person who entrapped me.

The most influential books, and the truest in their influence, are works of fiction. They do not pin the reader to a dogma, which he must afterwards discover to be inexact; they do not teach him a lesson, which he must afterwards unlearn. They repeat, they rearrange, they clarify the lessons of life; they disengage us from ourselves, they constrain us to the acquaintance of others; and they show us the web of experience, not as we can see it for ourselves, but with a singular change—that monstrous, consuming *ego* of ours being, for the nonce, struck out. To be so, they must be reasonably true to the human comedy; and any work that is so serves the turn of instruction. But the course of our education is answered best by those poems and romances where we breathe a magnanimous atmosphere of thought and meet generous and pious characters. Shakespeare has served me best. Few living friends have had upon me an influence so strong for good as Hamlet or Rosalind. The last character, already well beloved in the reading, I had the good fortune to see, I must think, in an impressionable hour, played by Mrs. Scott Siddons.[2] Nothing has ever more moved, more delighted, more refreshed me; nor has the influence quite passed away. Kent's brief speech over the dying Lear had a great effect upon my mind, and was the burthen of my reflections for long, so profoundly, so touchingly generous did it appear in sense, so overpowering in expression. Perhaps my dearest and best friend outside of Shakespeare is D'Artagnan—the elderly D'Artagnan of the "Vicomte de Bragelonne." I know not a more human soul, nor, in his way, a finer; I shall be very sorry for the man who is so much of a pedant in morals that he cannot learn from the Captain of

Musketeers.[3] Lastly, I must name the "Pilgrim's Progress," a book that breathes of every beautiful and valuable emotion.

But of works of art little can be said; their influence is profound and silent, like the influence of nature; they mould by contact; we drink them up like water, and are bettered, yet know not how. It is in books more specifically didactic that we can follow out the effect, and distinguish and weigh and compare. A book which has been very influential upon me fell early into my hands, and so may stand first, though I think its influence was only sensible later on, and perhaps still keeps growing, for it is a book not easily outlived: the "Essais" of Montaigne. That temperate and genial picture of life is a great gift to place in the hands of persons of to-day; they will find in these smiling pages a magazine of heroism and wisdom, all of an antique strain; they will have their "linen decencies" and excited orthodoxies fluttered, and will (if they have any gift of reading) perceive that these have not been fluttered without some excuse and ground of reason; and (again if they have any gift of reading) they will end by seeing that this old gentleman was in a dozen ways a finer fellow, and held in a dozen ways a nobler view of life, than they or their contemporaries.

The next book, in order of time, to influence me, was the New Testament, and in particular the Gospel according to St. Matthew. I believe it would startle and move any one if they could make a certain effort of imagination and read it freshly like a book, not droningly and dully like a portion of the Bible. Any one would then be able to see in it those truths which we are all courteously supposed to know and all modestly refrain from applying. But upon this subject it is perhaps better to be silent.

I come next to Whitman's "Leaves of Grass,"[4] a book of singular service, a book which tumbled the world upside down for me, blew into space a thousand cobwebs of genteel and ethical illusion, and, having thus shaken my tabernacle of lies, set me back again upon a strong foundation of all the original and manly virtues. But it is, once more, only a book for those who have the gift of reading. I will be very frank—I believe it is so with all good books, except, perhaps, fiction. The average man lives, and must live, so wholly in convention, that gunpowder charges of the truth are more apt to discompose than to invigorate his creed. Either he cries out upon blasphemy and indecency, and crouches the closer round that little idol of part-truths and part-conveniences which is the contemporary deity, or he is convinced by what is new, forgets what is old, and becomes truly blasphemous and indecent himself. New truth is only useful to supplement the old; rough truth is only wanted to expand, not to destroy, our civil and often elegant conventions. He who cannot judge had better stick to fiction and the daily papers. There he will get little harm, and, in the first at least, some good.

Close upon the back of my discovery of Whitman, I came under the influence of Herbert Spencer.[5] No more persuasive rabbi exists, and few better. How much of his vast structure will bear the touch of time, how much is clay and how much brass, it were too curious to inquire. But his words, if dry, are always manly and honest; there dwells in his pages a spirit of highly abstract joy, plucked naked like an algebraic symbol, but still joyful; and the reader will find there a *caput-mortuum*[6] of piety, with little indeed of its loveliness, but with most of its essentials; and these two qualities make him a wholesome, as his intellectual vigour makes him a bracing, writer. I should be much of a hound if I lost my gratitude to Herbert Spencer.

"Goethe's Life," by Lewes,[7] had a great importance for me when it first fell into my hands—a strange instance of the partiality of man's good and man's evil. I know no one whom I less admire than Goethe; he seems a very epitome of the sins of genius, breaking open the doors of private life, and wantonly wounding friends, in that crowning offence of "Werther," and in his own character a mere pen-and-ink Napoleon, conscious of the rights and duties of superior talents as a Spanish inquisitor was conscious of the rights and duties of his office. And yet in his fine devotion to his art, in his honest and serviceable friendship for Schiller, what lessons are contained! Biography, usually so false to its office, does here for once perform for us some of the work of fiction, reminding us, that is, of the truly mingled tissue of man's nature, and how huge faults and shining virtues cohabit and persevere in the same character. History serves us well to this effect, but in the originals, not in the pages of the popular epitomiser, who is bound, by the very nature of his task, to make us feel the difference of epochs instead of the essential identity of man, and even in the originals only to those who can recognise their own human virtues and defects in strange forms, often inverted and under strange names, often interchanged. Martial is a poet of no good repute, and it gives a man new thoughts to read his works dispassionately, and find in this unseemly jester's serious passages the image of a kind, wise, and self-respecting gentleman.[8] It is customary, I suppose, in reading Martial, to leave out these pleasant verses; I never heard of them, at least, until I found them for myself; and this partiality is one among a thousand things that help to build up our distorted and hysterical conception of the great Roman empire.

This brings us by a natural transition to a very noble book—the "Meditations" of Marcus Aurelius. The dispassionate gravity, the noble forgetfulness of self, the tenderness of others, that are there expressed and were practised on so great a scale in the life of its writer, make this book a book quite by itself. No one can read it and not be moved. Yet it scarcely or rarely appeals to the feelings—those very mobile, those not very trusty parts of man. Its address lies farther back: its lesson comes more deeply home; when you have read, you carry away with you a memory of the man himself; it is as though you had touched a loyal hand, looked into brave eyes, and made a noble friend; there is another bond on you thenceforward, binding you to life and to the love of virtue.

Wordsworth should perhaps come next. Every one has been influenced by Wordsworth, and it is hard to tell precisely how. A certain innocence, a rugged austerity of joy, a sight of the stars, "the silence that there is among the hills,"[9] something of the cold thrill of dawn, cling to his work and give it a particular address to what is best in us. I do not know that you learn a lesson; you need not—Mill did not—agree with any one of his beliefs;[10] and yet the spell is cast.

Such are the best teachers: a dogma learned is only a new error—the old one was perhaps as good; but a spirit communicated is a perpetual possession. These best teachers climb beyond teaching to the plane of art; it is themselves, and what is best in themselves, that they communicate.

I should never forgive myself if I forgot "The Egoist."[11] It is art, if you like, but it belongs purely to didactic art, and from all the novels I have read (and I have read thousands) stands in a place by itself. Here is a Nathan for the modern David;[12] here is a book to send the blood into men's faces. Satire, the angry picture of human faults, is not great art; we can all be angry with our neighbour; what we want is to be shown not his defects, of which we are too conscious, but his merits, to which we are too blind. And "The Egoist" is a satire; so much must be allowed; but it is a satire of a singular quality, which tells you nothing of that obvious mote which is engaged from first to last with that invisible beam. It is yourself that is hunted down; these are your own faults that are dragged into the day and numbered, with lingering relish, with cruel cunning and precision. A young friend of Mr. Meredith's (as I have the story) came to him in an agony. "This is too bad of you," he cried. "Willoughby is me!" "No, my dear fellow," said the author, "he is all of us." I have read "The Egoist" five or six times myself, and I mean to read it again; for I am like the young friend of the anecdote—I think Willoughby an unmanly but a very serviceable exposure of myself.

I suppose, when I am done, I shall find that I have forgotten much that was most influential, as I see already I have forgotten Thoreau, and Hazlitt, whose paper "On the Spirit of Obligations" was a turning point in my life, and Penn, whose little book of aphorisms had a brief but strong effect on me, and Mitford's "Tales of Old Japan," wherein I learned for the first time the proper attitude of any rational man to his country's laws—a secret found, and kept, in the Asiatic islands.[13] That I should commemorate all is more than I can hope or the editor could ask. It will be more to the point, after having said so much upon improving books, to say a word or two about the improvable reader. The gift of reading, as I have called it, is not very common, nor very generally understood. It consists, first of all, in a vast intellectual endowment—a free grace, I find I must call it—by which a man rises to understand that he is not punctually right, nor those from whom he differs absolutely wrong. He may hold dogmas; he may hold them passionately; and he may know that others hold them but coldly, or hold them differently, or hold them not at all. Well, if he has the gift of reading, these others will be full of meat for him. They will see the other side of propositions and the other side of virtues. He need not change his dogma for that, but he may change his reading of that dogma, and he must supplement and correct his deductions from it. A human truth, which is always very much a lie, hides as much of life as it displays. It is men who hold another truth, or, as it seems to us, perhaps, a dangerous lie, who can extend our restricted field of knowledge, and rouse our drowsy consciences. Something that seems quite new, or that seems insolently false or very dangerous, is the test of a reader. If he tries to see what it means, what truth excuses it, he has the gift, and let him read. If he is merely hurt, or offended, or exclaims upon his author's folly, he had better take to the daily papers; he will never be a reader.

And here, with the aptest illustrative force, after I have laid down my part-truth, I must step in with its opposite. For, after all, we are vessels of a very limited content. Not all men can read all books; it is only in a chosen few that any man will find his appointed food; and the fittest lessons are the most palatable, and make themselves welcome to the mind. A writer learns this early, and it is his chief support; he goes on unafraid, laying down the law; and he is sure at heart that most of what he says is demonstrably false, and much of a mingled strain, and some hurtful, and very little good for service; but he is sure besides that when his words fall into the hands of any genuine reader, they will be weighed and winnowed, and only that which suits will be assimilated; and when they fall into the hands of one who cannot intelligently read, they come there quite silent and inarticulate, falling upon deaf ears, and his secret is kept as if he had not written.

Notes

1 This essay was published as part of a series in *The British Weekly: A Journal of Social and Christian Progress* on 13 May 1887.
2 British actor and dramatic reader Mary Frances Scott-Siddons (1844–1896) visited Edinburgh's Theatre Royal in 1874.
3 Alexandre Dumas's *Vicomte de Bragelonne* (1850)—the third and final volume of *The d'Artagnan Romances*, which began with *The Three Musketeers* (1844).
4 Whitman's *Leaves of Grass* (1855). See Stevenson's essay "The Gospel According to Walt Whitman" (1878).
5 Herbert Spencer (1820–1913), philosopher and evolutionary biologist.
6 Dead-head (Latin): a thing that no longer has value.
7 G.H. Lewes's *Life of Goethe* (1855).
8 Martian, Latin epigrammatist whose work Stevenson translated in Davos in 1881–1882.
9 William Wordsworth, "Song at the Feast of Brougham Castle" (1807, 167–168).
10 John Stuart Mill famously described the effect Wordsworth's poetry had on him during a nervous breakdown in his *Autobiography* (1873).
11 George Meredith's novel *The Egoist* (1879).
12 Nathan, biblical prophet and adviser to David.
13 See Stevenson's essay "Henry David Thoreau: His Character and Opinions" (1880). Hazlitt's "On the Spirit of Obligations" (1826), William Penn's collection of aphorisms *Some Fruits of Solitude* (1693), and Algernon Bertram Freeman-Mitford's *Tales of Old Japan* (1871).

55

GENTLEMEN

What do we mean today by that common phrase, a gentleman? By the lights of history, from *gens, gentilis*, it should mean a man of family, "one of a kent house," one of notable descent: thus embodying an ancient stupid belief and implying a modern scientific theory.[1] The ancient and stupid belief came to the ground, with a prodigious dust and the collapse of several polities, in the latter half of the last century. There followed upon this an interregnum, during which it was believed that all men were born "free and equal,"[2] and that it really did not matter who your father was. Man has always been nobly irrational, bandaging his eyes against the facts of life, feeding himself on the wind of ambitious falsehood, counting his stock to be the children of the gods; and yet perhaps he never showed in a more touching light than when he embraced this boyish theory. Freedom we now know for a thing incompatible with corporate life and a blessing probably peculiar to the solitary robber; we know besides that every advance in richness of existence, whether moral or material, is paid for by a loss of liberty; that liberty is man's coin in which he pays his way; that luxury and knowledge and virtue, and love and the family affections, are all so many fresh fetters on the naked and solitary freeman. And the ancient stupid belief having come to the ground and the dust of its fall subsided, behold the modern scientific theory beginning to rise very nearly on the old foundation; and individuals no longer (as was fondly imagined) springing into life from God knows where, incalculable, untrammelled, abstract, equal to one another—but issuing modestly from a race; with virtues and vices, fortitudes and frailties, ready made; the slaves of their inheritance of blood; eternally unequal. So that we in the present, and yet more our scientific descendants in the future, must use, when we desire to praise a character, the old expression, gentleman, in nearly the old sense: one of a happy strain of blood, one fortunate in descent from brave and self-respecting ancestors, whether clowns or counts.

And yet plainly this is of but little help. The intricacy of descent defies prediction; so that even the heir of a hundred sovereigns may be born a brute or a vulgarian. We may be told that a picture is an heirloom; that does not tell us what the picture represents. All qualities are inherited, and all characters; but which are the qualities that belong to the gentleman? what is the character that earns and deserves that honorable style?

II

The current ideas vary with every class, and need scarce be combated, need scarce be mentioned save for the love of fun. In one class, and not long ago, he was regarded as a gentleman who kept a gig. He is a gentleman in one house who does not eat peas with his knife; in another, who is not to be discountenanced by any created form of butler. In my own case I have learned to move among pompous menials without much terror, never without much respect. In the narrow sense, and so long as they publicly tread the boards of their profession, it would be difficult to find more finished gentlemen; and it would often be a matter of grave thought with me, sitting in my club, to compare the bearing of the servants with that of those on whom they waited. There could be no question which were the better gentlemen. And yet I was hurried into no democratic theories; for I saw the members' part was the more difficult to play, I saw that to serve was a more graceful attitude than to be served, I knew besides that much of the servants' gentility was *ad hoc*[3] and would be laid aside with their livery jackets; and to put the matter in a nutshell, that some of the members would have made very civil footmen and many of the servants intolerable members. For all that, one of the prettiest gentlemen I ever knew was a servant. A gentleman he happened to be, even in the old stupid sense, only on the wrong side of the blanket;[4] and a man besides of much experience, having served in the Guards' Club,[5] and been valet to old Cooke of the *Saturday Review*, and visited the States with Madame Sinico (I think it was) and Portugal with Madame Someone-else, so that he had studied, at least from the chair-backs, many phases of society. It chanced he was waiter in a hotel where I was staying with my mother; it was midwinter and we were the only guests; all afternoons, he and I passed together on a perfect equality in the smoking-room; and at mealtime, he waited on my mother and me as a servant. Now here was a trial of manners from which few would have come forth successful. To take refuge in a frozen bearing would have been the timid, the inelegant, resource of almost all. My friend was much more bold; he joined in the talk, he ventured to be jocular, he pushed familiarity to the nice margin, and yet still preserved the indefinable and proper distance of the English servant, and yet never embarrassed, never even alarmed, the comrade with whom he had just been smoking a pipe. It was a masterpiece of social dexterity—on artificial lines no doubt, and dealing with difficulties that should never have existed, that exist much less in France, and that will exist nowhere long—but a masterpiece for all that, and one that I observed with despairing admiration, as I have watched Sargent paint.[6]

I say these difficulties should never have existed; for the whole relation of master and servant is to-day corrupt and vulgar. At home in England it is the master who is degraded; here in the States, by a triumph of inverted tact, the servant often so contrives that he degrades himself. He must be above his place; and it is the mark of a gentleman to be at home. He thinks perpetually of his own dignity; it is the proof of a gentleman to be jealous of the dignity of others. He is ashamed of his trade, which is the essence of vulgarity. He is paid to do certain services, yet he does them so gruffly that any man of spirit would resent them if they were gratuitous favors; and this (if he will reflect upon it tenderly) is so far from the genteel as to be not even coarsely honest. Yet we must not blame the man for these mistakes; the vulgarity is in the air. There is a tone in popular literature much to be deplored; deprecating service, like a disgrace; honoring those who are ashamed of it; honoring even (I speak not without book) such as prefer to live by the charity of poor neighbors instead of blacking the shoes of the rich. Blacking shoes is counted (in these works) a thing specially disgraceful. To the philosophic mind, it will seem a less exceptionable trade than to deal in stocks, and one in which it is more easy to be honest than to write books. Why, then, should it be marked out for reprobation by the popular authors? It is taken, I think, for a type; inoffensive in itself, it stands for many disagreeable household duties; disagreeable to fulfil, I had nearly said shameful to impose; and with the dulness of their tribe, the popular authors transfer the shame to the wrong party. Truly, in this matter there seems a lack of gentility somewhere; a lack of refinement, of reserve, of common modesty; a strain of the spirit of those ladies in the past, who did not hesitate to bathe before a footman. And one thing at least is easy to prophesy, not many years will have gone by before those shall be held the most "elegant" gentlemen, and those the most "refined" ladies, who wait (in a dozen particulars) upon themselves. But the shame is for the masters only. The servant stands quite clear. He has one of the easiest parts to play upon the face of earth; he must be far misled, if he so grossly fails in it.

III

It is a fairly common accomplishment to behave with decency in one character and among those to whom we are accustomed and with whom we have been brought up. The trial of gentility lies in some such problem as that of my waiter's, in foreign travel, or in some sudden and sharp change of class. I once sailed on the emigrant side from the Clyde[7] to New York; among my fellow-passengers I passed generally as a mason, for the excellent reason that there was a mason on board *who happened to know*; and this fortunate event enabled me to mix with these working people on a footing of equality. I thus saw them at their best, using their own civility; while I, on the other hand, stood naked to their criticism. The workmen were at home, I was abroad, I was the shoe-black in the drawing-room, the Huron at Versailles;[8] and I used to have hot and cold fits, lest perchance I made a beast of myself in this new environment. I had no allowances to hope for; I could not plead that I was "only a gentleman after all," for I was known to be a mason; and I must stand and fall by my transplanted manners on their own intrinsic decency. It chanced there was a Welsh blacksmith on board, who was not only well-mannered himself and a judge of manners, but a fellow besides of an original mind. He had early diagnosed me for a masquerader and a person out of place; and as we had grown intimate upon the voyage, I carried him my troubles. How did I behave? Was I, upon this crucial test, at all a gentleman? I might

401

have asked eight hundred thousand blacksmiths (if Wales or the world contain so many) and they would have held my question for a mockery; but Jones was a man of genuine perception, thought a long time before he answered, looking at me comically and reviewing (I could see) the events of the voyage, and then told me that "on the whole" I did "pretty well." Mr. Jones was a humane man and very much my friend, and he could get no further than "on the whole" and "pretty well." I was chagrined at the moment for myself; on a larger basis of experience, I am now only concerned for my class. My coëquals would have done but little better, and many of them worse. Indeed, I have never seen a sight more pitiable than that of the current gentleman unbending; unless it were the current lady! It is these stiff-necked condescensions, it is that graceless assumption, that make the diabolic element in times of riot. A man may be willing to starve in silence like a hero; it is a rare man indeed who can accept the unspoken slights of the unworthy, and not be embittered. There was a visit paid to the steerage quarters on this same voyage, by a young gentleman and two young ladies; and as I was by that time pretty well accustomed to the workman's standard, I had a chance to see my own class from below. God help them, poor creatures! As they ambled back to their saloon, they left behind, in the minds of my companions, and in my mind also, an image and an influence that might well have set them weeping, could they have guessed its nature. I spoke a few lines past of a shoe-black in a drawing-room; it is what I never saw; but I did see that young gentleman and these young ladies on the forward deck, and the picture remains with me, and the offence they managed to convey is not forgotten.

IV

And yet for all this ambiguity, for all these imperfect examples, we know clearly what we mean by the word. When we meet a gentleman of another class, though all contrariety of habits, the essentials of the matter stand confessed: I never had a doubt of Jones. More than that, we recognize the type in books; the actors of history, the characters of fiction, bear the mark upon their brow; at a word, by a bare act, we discern and segregate the mass, this one a gentleman, the others not. To take but the last hundred years, Scott, Gordon, Wellington in his cold way, Grant in his plain way, Shelley for all his follies, these were clearly gentlemen; Napoleon, Byron, Lockhart, these were as surely cads, and the two first cads of a rare water.[9]

Let us take an anecdote of Grant and one of Wellington. On the day of the capitulation, Lee wore his presentation sword; it was the first thing Grant observed, and from that moment he had but one thought: how to avoid taking it. A man, who should perhaps have had the nature of an angel, but assuredly not the special virtues of the gentleman, might have received the sword, and no more words about it: he would have done well in a plain way. One who wished to be a gentleman, and knew not how, might have received and returned it: he would have done infamously ill, he would have proved himself a cad; taking the stage for himself,

402

leaving to his adversary confusion of countenance and the ungraceful posture of the man condemned to offer thanks. Grant, without a word said, added to the terms this article: "All officers to retain their side-arms;" and the problem was solved and Lee kept his sword, and Grant went down to posterity, not perhaps a fine gentleman, but a great one. And now for Wellington. The tale is on a lower plane, is elegant rather than noble; yet it is a tale of a gentleman too, and raises besides a pleasant and instructive question. Wellington and Marshal Marmont[10] were adversaries (it will not have been forgotten) in one of the prettiest recorded acts of military fencing, the campaign of Salamanca: it was a brilliant business on both sides, just what Count Tolstoï[11] ought to study before he writes again upon the inutility of generals; indeed, it was so very brilliant on the Marshal's part that on the last day, in one of those extremes of cleverness that come so near stupidity, he fairly overreached himself, was taken "in flagrant delict,"[12] was beaten like a sack, and had his own arm shot off as a reminder not to be so clever the next time. It appears he was incurable; a more distinguished example of the same precipitate, ingenious blundering will be present to the minds of all—his treachery in 1814;[13] and even the tale I am now telling shows, on a lilliputian scale, the man's besetting weakness. Years after Salamanca, the two generals met, and the Marshal (willing to be agreeable) asked the Duke his opinion of the battle. With that promptitude, wit, and willingness to spare pain which make so large a part of the armory of the gentleman, Wellington had his answer ready, impossible to surpass on its own ground: "I early perceived your excellency had been wounded." And you see what a pleasant position he had created for the Marshal, who had no more to do than just to bow and smile and take the stage at his leisure. But here we come to our problem. The Duke's answer (whether true or false) created a pleasant position for the Marshal. But what sort of position had the Marshal's question created for the Duke? and had not Marmont the manœuvrer once more manœuvred himself into a false position? I conceive so. It is the man who has gained the victory, not the man who has suffered the defeat, who finds his ground embarrassing. The vanquished has an easy part, it is easy for him to make a handsome reference; but how hard for the victor to make a handsome reply! An unanswerable compliment is the social bludgeon; and Marmont (with the most graceful intentions in the world) had propounded one of the most desperate. Wellington escaped from his embarrassment by a happy and courtly inspiration. Grant, I imagine, since he had a genius for silence, would have found some means to hold his peace. Lincoln, with his half-tact and unhappy readiness, might have placed an appropriate anecdote and raised a laugh; not an unkindly laugh, for he was a kindly man; but under the circumstances the best-natured laugh would have been death to Marmont. Shelley (if we can conceive him to have gained a battle at all) would have blushed and stammered, feeling the Marshal's false position like some grossness of his own; and when the blush had communicated itself to the cheeks of his unlucky questioner, some stupid, generous word (such as I cannot invent for him) would have found its way to his lips and set them both at ease. Byron? well, he would have managed to do wrong; I have too little sympathy for that unmatched vulgarian

403

to create his part. Napoleon? that would have depended: had he been angry, he would have left all competitors behind in cruel coarseness: had he been in a good humor, it might have been the other way. For this man, the very model of a cad, was so well served with truths by the clear insight of his mind, and with words by his great though shallow gift of literature, that he has left behind him one of the most gentlemanly utterances on record: "*Madame, respectez le fardeau.*"[14] And he could do the right thing too, as well as say it; and any character in history might envy him that moment when he gave his sword, the sword of the world subduer, to his old, loyal enemy, Macdonald. A strange thing to consider two generations of a Skye family, and two generations of the same virtue, fidelity to the defeated: the father braving the rains of the Hebrides with the tattered beggar-lad that was his rightful sovereign; the son, in that princely house of Fontainebleau, himself a marshal of the Empire, receiving from the gratitude of one whom he had never feared and who had never loved him, the tool and symbol of the world's most splendid domination.[15] I am glad, since I deal with the name of gentlemen, to touch for one moment on its nobler sense, embodied, on the historic scale and with epic circumstance, in the lives of these Macdonalds. Nor is there any man but must be conscious of a thrill of gratitude to Napoleon, for his worthy recognition of the worthiest virtue. Yes, that was done *like* a gentleman; and yet in our hearts we must think that it was done by a performer. For to feel precisely what it is to be a gentleman and what it is to be a cad, we have but to study Napoleon's attitude after Trafalgar, and compare it with that beautiful letter of Louis the Fourteenth's in which he acknowledges the news of Blenheim.[16] We hear much about the Sun-king nowadays, and Michelet[17] is very sad reading about his government, and Thackeray was very droll about his wig;[18] but when we read this letter from the vainest king in Europe smarting under the deadliest reverse, we know that at least he was a gentleman. In the battle, Tallard had lost his son, Louis the primacy of Europe; it is only with the son the letter deals. Poor Louis! if his wig had been twice as great, and his sins twice as numerous, here is a letter to throw wide the gates of Heaven for his entrance. I wonder what would Louis have said to Marshal Marmont? Something infinitely condescending; for he was too much of a king to be quite a gentleman. And Marcus Aurelius, how would he have met the question? With some reference to the gods no doubt, uttered not quite without a twang; for the good emperor and great gentleman of Rome was of the methodists of his day and race.

And now to make the point at which I have been aiming. The perfectly straightforward person who should have said to Marmont, "I was uncommonly glad to get you beaten," would have done the next best to Wellington who had the inspiration of graceful speech; just as the perfectly straightforward person who should have taken Lee's sword and kept it, would have done the next best to Grant who had the inspiration of the truly graceful act. Lee would have given up his sword and preserved his dignity; Marmont might have laughed, his pride need not have suffered. Not to try to spare people's feelings is so much kinder than to try in a wrong way; and not to try to be a gentleman at all is so much more gentlemanly than to try and fail! So that this gift, or grace, or virtue, resides not so much in conduct as in knowledge; not so much in refraining from the wrong, as in knowing the precisely right. A quality of exquisite aptitude marks out the gentlemanly act; without an element of wit, we can be only gentlemen by negatives.

V

More and more, as our knowledge widens, we have to reply to those who ask for a definition: "I can't give you that, but I will tell you a story." We cannot say what a thing will be, nor what it ought to be; but we can say what it has been, and how it came to be what it is: History instead of Definition. It is this which (if we continue teachable) will make short work of all political theories; it is on this we must fall back to explain our word, gentleman.

The life of our fathers was highly ceremonial; a man's steps were counted; his acts, his gestures were prescribed; marriage, sale, adoption, and not only legal contracts, but the simplest necessary movements, must be all conventionally ordered and performed to rule. Life was a rehearsed piece; and only those who had been drilled in the rehearsals could appear with decency in the performance. A gentile man, one of a dominant race, hereditary priest, hereditary leader, was, by the circumstances of his birth and education, versed in this symbolic etiquette. Whatever circumstance arose, he would be prepared to utter the sacramental word, to perform the ceremonial act. For every exigence of family or tribal life, peace or war, marriage or sacrifice, fortune or mishap, he stood easily waiting, like the well-graced actor for his cue. The clan that he guided would be safe from shame, it would be ensured from loss; for the man's attitude would be always becoming, his bargains legal, and his sacrifices pleasing to the gods. It is from this gentile man, the priest, the chief, the expert in legal forms and attitudes, the bulwark and the ornament of his tribe, that our name of gentleman descends. So much of the sense still clings to it, it still points the man who, in every circumstance of life, knows what to do and how to do it gracefully; so much of its sense it has lost, for this grace and knowledge are no longer of value in practical affairs; so much of a new sense it has taken on, for as well as the nicest fitness, it now implies a punctual loyalty of word and act. And note the word loyalty; here is a parallel advance from the proficiency of the gentile man to the honor of the gentleman, and from the sense of legality to that of loyalty. With the decay of the ceremonial element in life, the gentleman has lost some of his prestige, I had nearly said some of his importance; and yet his part is the more difficult to play. It is hard to preserve the figures of a dance when many of our partners dance at random. It is easy to be a gentleman in a very stiff society, where much of our action is prescribed; it is hard indeed in a very free society where (as it seems) almost any word or act must come by inspiration. The rehearsed piece is at an end; we are now floundering through an impromptu charade. Far more of ceremonial remains (to be sure) traditional in the terms of our association, far more hereditary in the texture of brains, than is dreamed by the superficial; it is our fortress against many perils, the cement of states, the meeting ground of classes. But much of life comes up for the first time, unrehearsed, and must be acted on upon the instant. Knowledge there can here be none; the man must invent an attitude, he must be inspired with speech; and the most perfect gentleman is he who, in these irregular cases, acts and speaks with most aplomb and fitness. His tact simulates knowledge; to see him so easy and secure and graceful, you would think he had been through it all before; you would think he was the gentile man of old, repeating for the thousandth time, upon some public business, the sacramental words and ceremonial gestures of his race.

Lastly, the club footman, so long as he is in his livery jacket, appears the perfect gentleman and visibly outshines the members; and the same man, in the public house, among his equals, becomes perhaps plain and dull, perhaps even brutal. He has learned the one part of service perfectly; there he has knowledge, he shines in the prepared performance; outside of that he must rely on tact, and sometimes flounders sadly in the unrehearsed charade. The gentleman, again, may be put to open shame as he changes from one country, or from one rank of society to another. The footman was a gentleman only *ad hoc*; the other (at the most) *ad hæc*;[19] and when he has got beyond his knowledge, he begins to flounder in the charade. Even so the gentile man was only gentile among those of his own gens and their subordinates and neighbors; in a distant city, he too was peregrine and inexpert, and must become the client of another, or find his bargains insecure and be excluded from the service of the gods.

Notes

1 *Gens*: race or family (Latin); *gentil*: high-born, noble (Old French); *gentilis*: belonging to the same race or family (Latin); *kent*: known (Scottish).
2 "Declaration of the Rights of Man" (Article 1), National Assembly of France (1789).
3 *To this* (Latin): for a particular purpose; when necessary or as needed.
4 Out of wedlock.
5 An elite London gentlemen's club for officers of the Army's Guards Division.
6 John Singer Sargent (1856–1925), famous American expatriate portrait artist. Sargent painted Stevenson in 1884, 1885, and 1887.
7 Scotland's River Clyde.
8 A reference to Voltaire's novel *L'Ingénu* (1767) or "The Huron." Hurons or Wyandots are Iroquoian people native to Ontario. The novel follows a Huron called "Child of Nature" to France, satirizing French culture through his misunderstandings and mishaps.
9 Sir Walter Scott (1771–1832), eminent Scottish novelist and poet; Major-General Charles George Gordon (1833–1885), British Army Officer and Administrator in Crimea, China, and Sudan; Arthur Wellesley, 1st Duke of Wellington (1769–1852), British military commander and Prime Minister best known for defeating French Emperor Napoleon (1769–1821) at Waterloo in 1815; Ulysses S. Grant (1822–1885) leader of the Union Army in the American Civil War and 18th President of the United States; Percy Bysshe Shelley (1792–1822) and George Gordon, Lord Byron (1788–1824), English Romantic poets; Sir George Lockhart (1673–1731), Scottish Tory MP and secret Jacobite informant.
10 Auguste de Marmont (1744–1802), Marshal of France in the Napoleonic Wars.

11 Count Lev Nikolayevich Tolstoy or Leo Tolstoy (1828–1910), famous Russian novelist, author of *War and Peace* (1869) on the French invasion of Russia.

12 *In flagrante delicto* (Latin) "in blazing offence," a term describing someone caught in the act.

13 To end the war, Marmont secretly agreed to march his troops where they were quickly surrounded by Allied troops and surrendered. Known afterwards as the man who betrayed Napoleon, his title, Duke of Ragusa, became the verb *raguser*, colloquially meaning "to betray."

14 "Respect the burden, madam" was Napoleon's reported response to an English lady who told slaves carrying a heavy load to step out of his path.

15 Jacques Macdonald (1765–1840), A Scottish commander in Napoleon's army. The son of an exiled Jacobite, he was discharged because of ties with anti-Bonapartist intrigues in 1804, called back to active duty in 1809, and appointed Marshal of the Empire by Napoleon. For distinguished service and loyalty to the war's end, Napoleon gave Macdonald the saber of Egyptian ruler Murad Bey and directed him to support the new regime.

16 Louis XIV (1638–1715), King of France for 72 years; The Battle of Blenheim, a major French defeat in the War of Spanish Succession on 13 Aug. 1704.

17 Jules Michelet (1798–1874), French philosopher, historian and author of *Histoire de France* (1867).

18 In *The Paris Sketch Book* (1840), Thackeray notes that Louis XIV powdered his wig with gold dust and wore high-heeled shoes to add a foot to his stature.

19 Ad hoc—To This. Ad hœc—For these (Latin).

56

MY FIRST BOOK

Treasure Island

It was far indeed from being my first book, for I am not a novelist alone. But I am well aware that my paymaster, the Great Public, regards what else I have written with indifference, if not aversion; if it call upon me at all, it calls on me in the familiar and indelible character; and when I am asked to talk of my first book, no question in the world but what is meant is my first novel.

Sooner or later, somehow, anyhow, I was bound to write a novel. It seems vain to ask why. Men are born with various manias: from my earliest childhood, it was mine to make a plaything of imaginary series of events; and as soon as I was able to write, I became a good friend to the paper-makers. Reams upon reams must have gone to the making of *Rathillet, The Pentland Rising,*[1]* *The King's Pardon* (otherwise *Park Whitehead*), *Edward Daven, A Country Dance,* and *A Vendetta in the West;*[2] and it is consolatory to remember that these reams are now all ashes, and have been received again into the soil. I have named but a few of my ill-fated efforts, only such indeed as came to a fair bulk ere they were desisted from; and even so they cover a long vista of years. *Rathillet* was attempted before fifteen, *The Vendetta* at twenty-nine, and the succession of defeats lasted unbroken till I was thirty-one. By that time, I had written little books and little essays and short stories; and had got patted on the back and paid for them—though not enough to live upon. I had quite a reputation, I was the successful man; I passed my days in toil, the futility of which would sometimes make my cheek to burn—that I should spend a man's energy upon this business, and yet could not earn a livelihood: and still there shone ahead of me an unattained ideal: although I had attempted the thing with vigour not less than ten or twelve times, I had not yet written a novel. All—all my pretty ones—had gone for a little, and then stopped inexorably like a schoolboy's watch. I might be compared to a cricketer of many years' standing who should never have made a run. Anybody can write a short story—a bad one, I mean—who has industry and paper and time enough; but not everyone may hope to write even a bad novel. It is the length that kills. The accepted novelist may take his novel up and put it down, spend days upon it in vain, and write not any more than he makes haste to blot. Not so the beginner. Human nature has certain rights; instinct—the instinct of self-preservation—forbids that any man (cheered and supported by the consciousness of no previous victory) should endure the miseries of unsuccessful literary toil beyond a period to be measured in weeks. There must be something for hope to feed upon. The beginner must have a slant of wind, a lucky vein must be running, he must be in one of those hours when the words come and the phrases balance of themselves—*even to begin*. And having begun, what a dread looking forward is that until the book shall be accomplished! For so long a time, the slant is to continue unchanged, the vein to keep running, for so long a time you must keep at command the same quality of style: for so long a time your puppets are to be always vital, always consistent, always vigorous! I remember I used to look, in those days, upon every three-volume novel with a sort of veneration, as a feat—not possibly of literature—but at least of physical and moral endurance and the courage of Ajax.[3]

In the fated year I came to live with my father and mother at Kinnaird, above Pitlochry. Then I walked on the red moors and by the side of the golden burn[4]; the rude, pure air of our mountains inspirited, if it did not inspire us, and my wife and I projected a joint volume of bogie stories, for which she wrote *The Shadow on the Bed*, and I turned out *Thrawn Janet* and a first draft of the *Merry Men*.[5] I love my native air, but it does not love me; and the end of this delightful period was a cold, a fly-blister, and a migration by Strathairdle and Glenshee to the Castleton of Braemar. There it blew a good deal and rained in a proportion; my native air was more unkind than man's ingratitude, and I must consent to pass a good deal of my time between four walls in a house lugubriously known as the Late Miss McGregor's Cottage. And now admire the finger of predestination. There was a schoolboy in the Late Miss McGregor's Cottage, home from the holidays, and much in want of "something craggy to break his mind upon."[6] He had no thought of literature; it was the art of Raphael[7] that received his fleeting suffrages; and with the aid of pen and ink and a shilling box of water colours, he had soon turned one of the rooms into a picture gallery. My more immediate duty towards the gallery was to be showman; but I would sometimes unbend a little, join the artist (so to speak) at the easel, and pass the afternoon with him in a generous emulation, making coloured drawings. On one of these occasions, I made the map of an island; it was elaborately and (I thought) beautifully coloured; the shape of it took my fancy beyond expression; it contained harbours that pleased me like sonnets; and with the unconsciousness of the predestined, I ticketed my performance *Treasure Island*. I am told there are people who do not care for maps, and find it hard to believe. The names, the shapes of the woodlands, the courses of the roads and rivers, the prehistoric footsteps of man still distinctly traceable up hill and down dale, the mills and the ruins, the ponds and the ferries, perhaps the *Standing Stone* or the *Druidic Circle* on the heath; here is an inexhaustible fund of interest for any man with eyes to see or twopence worth of imagination to understand with! No child but must remember laying his head in the grass, staring into the infinitesimal forest and seeing it grow populous with fairy armies. Somewhat in this way, as I pored upon my map of *Treasure Island*, the future characters of the book began to appear there visibly among imaginary woods; and their brown faces and bright weapons peeped out upon me from unexpected quarters, as they passed to and fro, fighting and hunting treasure, on these few square inches of a flat projection. The next thing I knew I had some papers before me and was writing out a list of chapters. How often have I done so, and the thing gone no further! But there seemed elements of success about this enterprise. It was to be a story for boys; no need of psychology or fine writing; and I had a boy at hand to be a touchstone. Women were excluded. I was unable to handle a brig (which the *Hispaniola* should have been), but I thought I could make shift to sail her as a schooner without public shame.[8] And then I had an idea for John Silver from which I promised myself funds of entertainment; to take an admired friend of mine (whom the reader very likely knows and admires as much as I do),[9] to deprive him of all his finer qualities and higher graces of temperament, to leave him with nothing but his strength, his courage, his quickness, and his magnificent geniality, and to try to express these in terms of the culture of a raw tarpaulin. Such psychical surgery is, I think, a common way of "making character"; perhaps it is, indeed, the only way. We can put in the quaint figure that spoke a hundred words with us yesterday by the wayside; but do we know him? Our friend, with his infinite variety and flexibility, we know—but can we put him in? Upon the first, we must engraft secondary and imaginary qualities, possibly all wrong; from the second, knife in hand, we must cut away and deduct the needless arborescence of his nature, but the trunk and the few branches that remain we may at least be fairly sure of.

On a chill September morning, by the cheek of a brisk fire, and the rain drumming on the window, I began *The Sea Cook*, for that was the original title. I have begun (and finished) a number of other books, but I cannot remember to have sat down to one of them with more complacency. It is not to be wondered at, for stolen waters are proverbially sweet.[10] I am now upon a painful chapter. No doubt the parrot once belonged to Robinson Crusoe.[11] No doubt the skeleton is conveyed from Poe.[12] I think little of these, they are trifles and details; and no man can hope to have a monopoly of skeletons or make a corner in talking birds. The stockade, I am told, is from *Masterman Ready*.[13] It may be, I care not a jot. These useful writers had fulfilled the poet's saying: departing, they had left behind them Footprints on the sands of time, Footprints which perhaps another—and I was the other![14] It is my debt to Washington Irving that exercises my conscience, and justly so, for I believe plagiarism was rarely carried farther. I chanced to pick up the *Tales of a Traveller*[15] some years ago with a view to an anthology of prose narrative, and the book flew up and struck me: Billy Bones, his chest, the company in the parlour, the whole inner spirit, and a good deal of the material detail of my first chapters—all were there, all were the property of Washington Irving. But I had no guess of it then as I sat writing by the fireside, in what seemed the springtides of a somewhat pedestrian inspiration; nor yet day by day, after lunch, as I read aloud my morning's work to the family. It seemed to me original as sin; it seemed to belong to me like my right eye. I had counted on one boy, I found I had two in my audience. My father caught fire at once with all the romance and childishness of his original nature. His own stories, that every night of his life he put himself

410

to sleep with, dealt perpetually with ships, roadside inns, robbers, old sailors, and commercial travellers before the era of steam. He never finished one of these romances; the lucky man did not require to! But in *Treasure Island* he recognised something kindred to his own imagination; it was *his* kind of picturesque; and he not only heard with delight the daily chapter, but set himself acting to collaborate. When the time came for Billy Bones's chest to be ransacked, he must have passed the better part of a day preparing, on the back of a legal envelope, an inventory of its contents, which I exactly followed; and the name of "Flint's old ship"—the *Walrus*—was given at his particular request. And now who should come dropping in, *ex machinâ*, but Dr. Japp, like the disguised prince who is to bring down the curtain upon peace and happiness in the last act; for he carried in his pocket, not a horn or a talisman, but a publisher—had, in fact, been charged by my old friend, Mr. Henderson,[16] to unearth new writers for *Young Folks*.[17] Even the ruthlessness of a united family recoiled before the extreme measure of inflicting on our guest the mutilated members of *The Sea Cook*; at the same time, we would by no means stop our readings; and accordingly the tale was begun again at the beginning, and solemnly re-delivered for the benefit of Dr. Japp. From that moment on, I have thought highly of his critical faculty; for when he left us, he carried away the manuscript in his portmanteau.

Here, then, was everything to keep me up, sympathy, help, and now a positive engagement. I had chosen besides a very easy style. Compare it with the almost contemporary *Merry Men*; one reader may prefer the one style, one the other—'tis an affair of character, perhaps of mood; but no expert can fail to see that the one is much more difficult, and the other much easier to maintain. It seems as though a full-grown experienced man of letters might engage to turn out *Treasure Island* at so many pages a day, and keep his pipe alight. But alas! this was not my case. Fifteen days I stuck to it, and turned out fifteen chapters; and then, in the early paragraphs of the sixteenth, ignominiously lost hold. My mouth was empty; there was not one word of *Treasure Island* in my bosom; and here were the proofs of the beginning already waiting me at the *Hand and Spear*![18] Then I corrected them, living for the most part alone, walking on the heath at Weybridge in dewy autumn mornings, a good deal pleased with what I had done, and more appalled than I can depict to you in words at what remained for me to do. I was thirty-one; I was the head of a family; I had lost my health; I had never yet paid my way, never yet made £200 a year; my father had quite recently bought back and cancelled a book that was judged a failure: was this to be another and last fiasco? I was indeed very close on despair; but I shut my mouth hard, and during the journey to Davos, where I was to pass the winter, had the resolution to think of other things and bury myself in the novels of M. de Boisgobey.[19] Arrived at my destination, down I sat one morning to the unfinished tale; and behold! it flowed from me like small talk; and in a second tide of delighted industry, and again at a rate of a chapter a day, I finished *Treasure Island*. It had to be transacted almost secretly; my wife was ill; the schoolboy remained alone of the faithful; and John Addington Symonds (to whom I timidly mentioned what I was engaged on) looked on me askance. He was at that time very eager I should write on the characters of Theophrastus: so far out may be the judgments of the wisest men.[20] But Symonds (to be sure) was scarce the confidant to go for sympathy in a boy's story. He was large-minded; "a full man," if there ever was one;[21] but the very name of my enterprise would suggest to him only capitulations of sincerity and solecisms of style. Well! he was not far wrong.

Treasure Island—it was Mr. Henderson who deleted the first title, *The Sea Cook*—appeared duly in the story paper, where it figured in the ignoble midst, without woodcuts, and attracted not the least attention. I did not care. I liked the tale myself, for much the same reason as my father liked the beginning: it was my kind of picturesque. I was not a little proud of John Silver, also; and to this day rather admire that smooth and formidable adventurer. What was infinitely more exhilarating, I had passed a landmark; I had finished a tale, and written *The End* upon my manuscript, as I had not done since *The Pentland Rising*, when I was a boy of sixteen not yet at college. In truth it was so by a set of lucky accidents; had not Dr. Japp come on his visit, had not the tale flowed from me with singular ease, it must have been laid aside like its predecessors, and found a circuitous and unlamented way to the fire. Purists may suggest it would have been better so. I am not of that mind. The tale seems to have given much pleasure, and it brought (or was the means of bringing) fire and food and wine to a deserving family in which I took an interest. I need scarcely say I mean my own.

But the adventures of *Treasure Island* are not yet quite at an end. I had written it up to the map. The map was the chief part of my plot. For instance, I had called an islet *Skeleton Island*, not knowing what I meant, seeking only for the immediate picturesque, and it was to justify this name that I broke into the gallery of Mr. Poe and stole Flint's pointer. And in the same way, it was because I had made two harbours that the *Hispaniola* was sent on her wanderings with Israel Hands. The time came when it was decided to republish, and I sent in my manuscript, and the map along with it, to Messrs. Cassell. The proofs came, they were corrected, but I heard nothing of the map. I wrote and asked; was told it had never been received, and sat aghast. It is one thing to draw a map at random, set a scale in one corner of it at a venture, and write up a story to the measurements. It is quite another to have to examine a whole book, make an inventory of all the allusions contained in it, and, with a pair of compasses, painfully design a map to suit the data. I did it; and the map was drawn again in my father's office, with embellishments of blowing whales and sailing ships, and my father himself brought into service a knack he had of various writing, and elaborately *forged* the signature of Captain Flint, and the sailing directions of Billy Bones. But somehow it was never *Treasure Island* to me.

I have said the map was the most of the plot. I might almost say it was the whole. A few reminiscences of Poe, Defoe, and Washington Irving, a copy of Johnson's *Buccaneers*, the name of the Dead Man's Chest from Kingsley's *At Last*, some recollections of canoeing on the high seas, and the map itself, with its infinite, eloquent suggestion, made up the whole of my materials.[22] It is, perhaps, not often that a map figures so largely in a tale, yet it is always important. The author must know his countryside, whether real or imaginary, like his hand; the distances, the points of the compass, the place of the sun's rising, the behaviour of the moon, should all be beyond cavil. And how troublesome the moon is! I have come to grief over the moon in *Prince Otto*, and so soon as that was pointed out to me, adopted a precaution which I recommend to other men—I never write now without an almanack. With an almanack, and the map of the country, and the plan of every house, either actually plotted on paper or already and immediately apprehended in the mind, a man may hope to avoid some of the grossest possible blunders. With the map before him, he will scarce allow the sun to set in the east, as it does in *The Antiquary*.[23] With the almanack at hand, he will scarce allow two horsemen, journeying on the most urgent affair, to employ six days, from three of the Monday morning till late in the Saturday night, upon a journey of, say, ninety or a hundred miles, and before the week is out, and still on the same nags, to cover fifty in one day, as may be read at length in the inimitable novel of *Rob Roy*.[24] And it is certainly well, though far from necessary, to avoid such "croppers." But it is my contention—my superstition, if you like—that he who is faithful to his map, and consults it, and draws from it his inspiration, daily and hourly, gains positive support, and not mere negative immunity from accident. The tale has a root there; it grows in that soil; it has a spine of its own behind the words. Better if the country be real, and he has walked every foot of it and knows every milestone. But even with imaginary places, he will do well in the beginning to provide a map; as he studies it, relations will appear that he had not thought upon; he will discover obvious, though unsuspected, short-cuts and footpaths for his messengers; and even when a map is not all the plot, as it was in *Treasure Island*, it will be found to be a mine of suggestion.

Notes

1 **RLS:** "*Ne pas confondre* [do not confuse]. Not the slim green pamphlet with the imprint of Andrew Elliott, for which (as I see with amazement from the book-lists) the gentlemen of England are willing to pay fancy prices; but its predecessor, a bulky historical romance without a spark of merit, and now deleted from the world."

2 At 14, Stevenson began writing a novel called *Rathillet* on David Hackston, the militant Scottish Covenanter who murdered Archbishop James Sharp of St. Andrews. *The King's Pardon* was to be a five-act tragedy in collaboration with Henley. Stevenson worked on *A Vendetta in the West*, which he later abandoned and probably destroyed, in Monterey in the autumn of 1879. At his father's expense, Stevenson published his research for the aborted novel "The Pentland Rising" as the historical essay: *The Pentland Rising: A Page of History, 1666* in 1866 at 16 years old.

3 Ajax the Greater, second in strength and courage only to Achilles, whose body he rescued from the Trojans in *The Aeneid*.

4 Stream or river.

5 Stevenson was at Kinnaird from 2 June to 2 Aug. 1881. "Thrawn Janet" (Oct. 1881) and "The Merry Men" (June 1882) appeared in *Cornhill*.

6 Fanny's son, Samuel (Lloyd) Osbourne (1868–1947), with whom Stevenson would later collaborate on three books: *The Wrong Box*, *The Ebb-Tide*, and *The Wrecker*.

Byron studied Armenian because his "mind wanted something craggy to break upon" (Letter to Mr. Moore, 17 Nov. 1816).

7 Raphael (1483–1520), a leading painter of the Italian Renaissance.

8 A brig is generally much larger than a schooner, and their masts are configured differently.

9 Stevenson's friend William Ernest Henley (1849–1903), playwright, journalist, and poet. He wore a wooden leg following an amputation and is best remembered for "Invictus."

10 Proverbs 9:17.

11 Daniel Defoe's novel *Robinson Crusoe* (1719).

12 Most likely refers to Edgar Allan Poe's "The Premature Burial" or "The Cask of Amontillado." See also Stevenson's review of "*The Works of Edgar Allan Poe*" (1875).

13 Frederick Marryat, *Masterman Ready, or the Wreck of the Pacific* (1841).

14 Henry Wadsworth Longfellow, "A Psalm of Life" (28–29).

15 Washington Irving's 1824 story collection published under the pseudonym Geoffrey Crayon.

16 James Henderson, proprietor of *Young Folks*, which published *Treasure Island, Kidnapped,* and *The Black Arrow.*

17 *Deus ex machinâ* (God from the machine): a plot device in which a difficult, apparently unsolvable problem is resolved through a sudden, unlikely occurrence. The term originally referred to a contrivance of Greek drama in which actors playing gods were lowered onto the stage or entered from a trap door in the floor. Alexander Hay Japp (1837–1905), Scottish author, journalist, and publisher who negotiated Stevenson's contract with *Young Folks* and later wrote *Robert Louis Stevenson: A Record, an Estimate, and a Memorial* (1905).

18 Hotel and pub in Weybridge, Surrey.

19 Fortuné du Boisgobey, penname of Fortuné Hippolyte Auguste Abraham-Dubois (1821–1891), a prolific and popular French novelist.

20 John Addington Symonds (1840–1893), critic, translator, historian, and biographer.

21 "Reading maketh a full man, conference a ready man, and writing an exact man" (Francis Bacon, Essay L "Of Studies"). Theophrastus (371–287 BC), Greek philosopher and author of the influential *Characters* on negative types of people in Athens.

22 Captain Charles Johnson, *A General History of the Robberies and Murders of the Most Notorious Pyrates* (1724). Charles Kingsley, *At Last: A Christmas in the West Indies* (1871).

23 Walter Scott's 1816 novel.

24 Walter Scott's novel *Rob Roy* (1817).

414

UNPUBLISHED AND EARLY ESSAYS

57

NIGHT OUTSIDE THE WICK MAIL

The Wick Mail then, my dear fellow, is the last Mail-Coach within Great Britain, whence there comes a romantic interest that few could understand.[1] To me, on whose imagination positively nothing took so strong a hold as the Dick Turpins and Claude Duvals of last Century, a Mail was an object of religious awe. I pictured the long, dark highways, the guard's blunderbuss, the passengers with three-cornered hats above a mummery of great coat and cravat; and the sudden "Stand and deliver!,"—the stop, the glimmer of the coach lamp upon the horseman—Ah! We shall never get back to Wick.[2]

All round that northern capital of stink and storm there stretches a succession of flat and dreary moors absolutely treeless, with the exception of above a hundred bour-trees[3] beside Wick, and a stunted plantation at Stirkoke, for the distance of nearly twenty miles south. When we left to cross this tract, it was cloudy and dark. A very cold and pertinacious wind blew with unchecked violence, across these moorlands. I was sick sleepy, and drawing my cloak over my face set myself to doze. Mine was the box-seat, desirable for the apron[4] and the company of the coachman, a person, in this instance, enveloped in that holy and tender interest that hangs about the *Last of the Mohicans* or the *Derniers Bretons*.[5] And, as this example of the loquacious genus coachman was more than ordinarily loquacious I put down my hood again and talked with him. He had a philosophy of his own, I found, and a philosophy eminently suited to the needs of his position. The most fundamental and original doctrine of this, was as to what constitutes a gentleman. It was in speaking of Lockyer of Wenbury[6] that I found it out. This man is an audacious quack and charlatan, destined for aught, I know, to be the Cagliostro of the British Revolution;[7] and, as such, Mr. Lockyer is no favourite of mine: I hate quacks, not personally (for are they not men of imagination like ourselves?) but because of their influence; so I was rather struck in hearing the following. "Well, sir," said the coachman, "Mr. Lockyer has always shown himself a perfect gentleman to me, sir—*his hand as open as you'll see, sir!*" In other words, half-a-crown to the coachman! As the pleasures of such philosophical talk rather diminished and the slumber increased, I buried my face again. The coach swayed to and fro. The wind battled and roared about us. I observed the difference in sounds—the rhythmic and regular beat of the hoofs as the horses cantered up some incline, and

417

the ringing, merry, irregular clatter as they slung forward, at a merry trot, along the level.

First stage: Lybster. A Roman Catholic priest travelling within, knowing that I was delicate, made me take his seat inside for the next stage. I dozed. When I woke, the moon was shining brightly. We were off the moors and up among the high grounds near the Ord of Caithness. I remember seeing a curious thing: the moon shone on the ocean, and on a river swollen to a great pool and between stretched a great black mass of rock: I wondered dimly how the river got out and then to doze again. When next I wake, we have passed the lone Church of Berriedale, standing sentinel on the heathery plateau northward of the valley, and are descending the steep road past the Manse: I think it was about one: the moon was frosty but gloriously clear. In another minute—

Second stage: Berriedale. And of all lovely places, one of the loveliest. Two rivers run from the inner hills, at the bottom of two deep, Killiecrankie-like[8] gorges, to meet in a narrow bare valley close to the grey North Ocean. The high Peninsula between and the banks, on either hand until they meet, are thickly wooded— birch and fir. On one side is the bleak plateau with the lonesome little church, on the other the bleaker, wilder mountain of the Ord. When I and the priest had lit our pipes, we crossed the streams, now speckled with the moonlight that filtered through the trees, and walked to the top of the Ord. There the coach overtook us and away we went for a stage, over great, bleak mountains, with here and there a hanging wood of silver birches and here and there a long look of the moonlit sea, the white ribbon of the road marked far in front by the newly erected telegraph posts. We were all broad awake with our walk, and made very merry outside, proffering "fills" of tobacco and pinches of snuff and dipping surreptitiously into aristocratic flasks and plebeian pint bottles.

Third stage: Helmsdale. Round a great promontory with the gleaming sea far away in front, and rattling through some sleeping streets that shone strangely white in the moonlight, and then we pull up beside the Helmsdale posting-house, with a great mountain valley behind. Here I went in to get a glass of whisky and water. A very broad, dark commercial said: "Ha! do you remember me? Anstruther?" I had met him five years before in the Anstruther commercial room, when my father was conversing with an infidel and put me out of the room to be away from contamination; whereupon I listened outside and heard the man say he had not sinned for seven years, and declare that he was better than his maker. I did not remember him: nor did he my face, only my voice. He insisted on "standing me the whisky 'for auld lang syne'"; and he being a bagman, it was useless to refuse.[9] Then away again. The coachman very communicative this stage, telling us about the winter before, when the mails had to be carried through on horseback and how they left one of their number sticking in the snow, bag and all I suppose. The country here was softer; low, wooded hills running along beside the shore, and all inexpressibly delightful to me after my six months of Wick barrenness and storm.

Fourth stage: name unknown. O sweet little spot, how often have I longed to be back to you! A lone farm-house on the sea-shore shut in on three sides by the same, low, wooded hills. Men were waiting for us by the roadside, with the horses—sleepy, yawning men. What a peaceful place it was! Everything *steeped* in the moonlight, and the gentle plash of the waves coming to us from the beach. On again. Through Brora, where we stopped at the Post-office, and exchanged letter-bags through a practicable window-pane, as they say in stage directions. Then on again. Near Golspie now, and breakfast, and the roaring railway. Passed Dunrobin, the dew-steeped, tree-dotted park, the princely cluster of its towers, rising from bosky plantations and standing out against the moon-shimmering sea— all this sylvan and idyllic beauty so sweet and new to me! Then the Golspie Inn, and breakfast and another pipe, as the morning dawned, standing in the verandah. And then round to the station to fall asleep in the train.

Notes

1 Four days after turning 18, Stevenson included this essay in his 17 Nov. 1868 letter to his cousin Bob Stevenson (*Letters* 1.167–72). Stevenson spent the autumn of 1868 in Wick as part of his lighthouse engineering training. The essay describes Stevenson's journey on the mail coach from Wick in the far north of Scotland's eastern coast to the village of Golspie fifty miles south. The Highland Railway reached Wick in 1874, ending the mail coach era.
2 Dick Turpin (1705–1739) and Claude Duval (1643–1670) were famous, often romanticized, highwaymen in England. "Stand and deliver" was the highwayman's command to his victims to stop and surrender their belongings.
3 Elder trees (Scottish).
4 A leather covering for the legs in an open carriage.
5 James Fenimore Cooper's 1826 novel and probably Stevenson's memory of Balzac's novel *Le Dernier Chouan* (1829), subsequently titled *Les Chouans* (*Letters* 1.170).
6 Lionel Lockyer (1600–1672), English quack doctor who sold cure-all pills.
7 Giuseppe Balsamo (1743–1795), who called himself Count Cagliostro, was an Italian charlatan who enjoyed great success posing as a physician, alchemist, and magician for the Parisian elite. Stevenson may have read Alexandre Dumas's novels about him: *Mémories d'un Médecin: Joseph Balsamo* (1846–1848) and *Le Collier de la Reine* (1849–1850).
8 Killiecrankie, a village in central Scotland's Perthshire on the River Garry, was the site of a rebel victory over government forces in the 1689 Jacobite Rising—the first in a series of attempts to restore James VII and later his descendants of the House of Stuart to the throne of Scotland following the Glorious Revolution of 1688. Redcoat soldier Donald MacBane was said to jump 18 feet over the gorge while fleeing the Jacobites.
9 Stand: to pay for a present or treat. For *auld lang syne*: in consideration or regard for old friendship or loyalty, for old time's sake. Literal Scottish translation: times long past. Bagman: a somewhat depreciative term for a traveling salesman.

58

REMINISCENCES OF COLINTON MANSE[1]

Every young man, as M. St. Beuve says, has somewhere in the bottom of his heart, a reminiscence of the golden age.[2] Certainly, I should be the last to contradict it. I have not only one, but a thousand. I seem to have lived under Saturn;[3] and the name of my Arcadia[4] stands most fitly at the head of these pages, in which I mean to chronicle my recollections of happier days. I am not at all sure let it be understood that they were any happier; but the dross has been sifted out in the passage of many years, and nothing is left but the superlatives, the brightest and the darkest. Possibly hereafter, I may look back upon the present time with as much love and regret; but for the present, my childhood is the only part of my life that I can really be said to grasp. None of the rest is out of limbo yet: I have not yet been able to detach it from its homely background of weariness and commonplace; but the older recollections have been turned over with delight for the running of many an hour glass, have been my solace in hours of wakefulness and pain, and are now fairly graven upon my heart in their true proportion and beauty. They are the first-fruits of my life: the only things that I am sure about: the corn already harvested and laid by in the grange of my memory. It is little wonder, therefore, that I take pleasure in writing them down, not because I fear to forget them, but because I wish to renew and to taste more fully the satisfaction that they have afforded me already. Nor do I altogether despair of taking the reader along with me; for surely I should be able to describe and well describe, memories which I love so much and which have been so long simmering at the bottom of my heart. And to begin with, as I do not know who may chance to read these lines, I had better give a sketch of the old manse—not as it is, I promise you, but as it was when my grandfather was minister of the parish.

The water of L—, after passing under C—[5] bridge, moves a curve, following the line of the high, steep, wooded bank on the convex, but on the concave enclosing a round flat promontory, which was once, I suppose, a marsh and then a riverside-meadow. Now-a-days, however, this plateau, dominated by the church and the churchyard, is principally occupied by two enclosures—one the garden of the snuff-mill, and one the garden of the manse. In this way, my old Arcadia occupies the central band of the little flat space and stands between the snuff-mill and the flour-mill. Immediately after crossing the bridge, the roadway forks into two; one branch whereof tends upward to the entrance of the churchyard; while the other, green with grass, slopes downward, between two blank walls and past the cottage of the snuff-mill, to the gate of the manse. And since I shall refer to it again, I may as well notice that, just before the high wall of the churchyard hides the one road from the other, they are joined by a ruinous flight of steps.

There were two ways of entering the manse-garden: one the two-winged gate that admitted the old phaeton; and the other a door for pedestrians on the side next the kirk, which was held shut by a long tapering rod of iron, working by a spring, or a weight, or some other infernal mechanism. One day, having drawn this formidable arm backward and (in the innocence of my heart) let it go again, I remember my doleful yell, as the end of it in flying back to its place just shaved my cheek and left a ribbon of raw flesh for its memorial. But, once bitten, twice shy, such an accident, I promise you, would not twice occur; and so we may pass onward without further delay. On the left hand (church-yard side) were the stable, coachhouse and washing houses, clustered round a small paven court. For the interior of these buildings, as abutting behind on the place of sepulture, I had always considerable terror, perhaps fostered by John[6] out of regard for curry-combs and harness; but the court has one pleasant memento of its own. When the grass was cut and stacked against the wall, do you not remember, my friends, making round holes in the cool green herb and calling ourselves birds? It did not take a great height, in those days, to lift our feet off the ground; so when we shut our eyes we were free to imagine ourselves in the fork of an elm-bough, or halfway down a cliff among a colony of gulls and gannets.

Once past the stable, you were now fairly within the garden; but with this reservation, the outer garden. From the end of the stable, the carriageway—by courtesy, avenue—ran down in a graceful curve towards the river and the back of the manse, having on one side a beech-hedge of the most stalwart dimensions,—a very Goliath among hedges. Inside of this, was the inner garden. Outside of it, the roadway leaves a corner of lawn, sloping towards the river, overlooked and shut in by the steep, wooded "banks," and hidden from all view of the water by a regular cincture of evergreens. Right in the midst of the little pleasance, grew a young Deodar in a ring of fence, which, like the border of Sinai, it was treason even to touch.[7] I do not know from whence it came; but I know that on summer afternoons, it could not have regretted its old home upon the plea of heat. The sloping lawn was literally *steeped* in sunshine; and all the day long, from the impending wood, there came the sweetest and fullest chorus of merles and thrushes and all manner of birds, that it ever was my lot to hear. The lawn was just the centre of all this—a perfect goblet for sunshine, and the Dionysius-ear[8] for a whole forest of bird-songs. This lawn was a favourite playground; and, in consequence, is connected with many pleasant memories. A lilac that hung its scented blossom out of the glossy semicirque of laurels, was identified by my playmates and myself as that tree whose very shadow was death. In the great laurel at the corner, I have often lain perdu, with my toy gun in my hand, waiting for a herd of antelopes to defile past me down the carriage drive, and waiting (need I add?) in vain. I remember, also, as a very striking incident, the day when we managed to scramble up upon the snuff-mill wall (it formed one side of the lawn, you understand, but hidden by the line of evergreens) and looked down upon its bright and close-like garden, basking in the sunshine around the mill itself. It was a glimpse into a new world; and perhaps was as great a thing to us, as was the first glimpse of the far bright Pacific to the happy leader,

Silent upon a peak in Darien.[9] But alas! before I leave the lawn, I must proceed to chronicle a most shameful incident in my childhood. In general, I am inclined to feel, with Elia,[10] equal scorn for what I now am and love for the child that I used to be; but some incidents of snobbery and falsehood (and this among the number) dismally suggest that

The time when I
Shined in my angel infancy[11]

owes some of its lustre to distance, and more of it still, perhaps, to the want of that self-examination which is at once the pleasure and the curse of riper years. Judge for yourselves: I find myself standing among a circle of young cousins on the carriage-drive, and humming a good deal of that inarticulate nonsense with which children will sometimes amuse themselves for hours, under pretext of some "alien tongue." Now it happened that I had a new coat with pockets at the side into which I could thrust my hands and swagger with almost as good an effect as if I had the orthodox continuations.[12] Only a very little later, I was cured of my conceit by a rude little girl calling out: "Sh! there's a laddie in a bloose and trimmin' troosers!"; but in the meantime I was naturally elate, and thirsting for further applause. Accordingly, I told my cousins that I was singing a French song, and was awfully bothered when one of them asked me to sing it over again, as both nonsense-words and nonsense tune had most appropriately taken *French* leave of me.

I am glad to leave the atmosphere of deceit and take you to see one other and, with me most favourite, spot before we leave the outer garden. Down at the corner of the lawn next the snuff-mill wall, there was a practicable passage through the evergreens and a door in the wall, which let you out on a small patch of sand, four feet long perhaps, left in the corner by the river. Just across the woods rose like a wall into the sky; and their lowest branches trailed in the black waters. Naturally it was very sunless; and there hung about that beach an indescribable odour of moistened sand with a smack of soap suds, which I can recall to my nostrils as I write the words. A prosaic friend says that it came from the paper mills—an assertion which I refuse to admit, and that it was very nasty—a piece of unappreciative criticism which I indignantly deny. A little lower down, the river was damned up for the service of the flour-mill; but the outward curve of the ruinous garden wall, with the laurels hanging over it and the white willows wedging their roots into the sand at its base, hid the weir from you entirely. There was nothing, around and above you, but the shadowy foliage of trees. It seemed a marvel how they clung to the steep slope on the other side; and indeed they were forced to grow far apart, and showed you the ground between them hid by an undergrowth of butterbur, hemlock and nettle. I have said that the river was black; but where it neared the sand it was black no more, but a beautiful, rich, oily brown. And alway, as its strings of bubbles defiled past me, I would stand by the edge and wait for the larger craft. Sometimes there came a great, quivering castle of yellow foam like trifle, great lumps of which adhered to the grass and roots on the opposite side. Sometimes a dead leaf glided past on the smooth surface. And sometimes it was a great agglomeration of twigs and sticks and leaves. Often such a passenger would be caught, like an aquatic Absalom,[13] in the pendant boughs of the opposite wood; and there it would remain tugging feebly and regularly; until at last it was either enfranchised altogether, or, going in twain, one half of it went onward and left the other still tugging to be after it.

I wish I could give you an idea of this place, of the gloom, of the black slow water, of the strange wet smell, of the draggled vegetation on the far side whither the current took everything, and of the incomparably fine, smooth, rich-yellow sand, without a grit in the whole of it and moving below your feet with scarcely more resistance than a liquid. Talking of the sand, I remember climbing down one day, a good bit farther on and past the lawn altogether, to a place where we discovered an island of this treacherous material. O the great discovery! On we leapt in a moment; but, on feeling the wet, sluicy island flatten out into a level with the river and the brown water gathering about our feet, we were off it again as quickly. It was a "quicksand," we said; and thenceforward the island was held in much the same regard as the lilac tree on the lawn.

So much for the outer garden; and now let me introduce you to the inner. There was no means of passing the beech-hedge but two quite small doorways within its green thickness; so that he who drove out of town in a wet day, needed either to leave the phaeton and make a run for it under dripping boughs, or condescend to the humiliating expedient of the kitchen entrance. But in fine weather, the approach was all the more pleasant as it went in between the two lignum-vitae trees, whose leaves W— and I called snuff and carried about in our pockets.

You remember that I talked of the wall of the churchyard. This wall faces to the manse. Only it is necessary to explain that the churchyard is on a level with the top of the wall that is to say some eight or ten feet above the garden so that the lean rank grapes hang over it and the tombstones are visible from the enclosure of the manse. The church with its campanile was near the edge, so that on Sundays we could also see the cluster of people about the door. Under the retaining wall, which I have been so long in describing, was a somewhat dark pathway, extending from the stable to the far end of the garden and called the Witches Walk from a game we used to play in it. At the stable end it took its rise under a yew, which is one of the glories of the village. It must, I should think, be sæcular. Under the circuit of its wide black branches, it was always dark and cool; and there was a green scurf[14] over all the trunk among which glistened the round bright drops of resin, which, standing on the rotten seat below, it was my especial pleasure to collect. This was a sufficiently gloomy commencement for the Witches Walk; but its chief horror was the retaining wall of the kirkyard itself, about which we were always hovering at even with the strange attraction of fear. This it was that supplied our Arcady with its Gods; and in place of classic fauns and the split hooves of satyrs, we were full of homely Scottish superstitions of grues[15] and ghosts and goblins. These poor Greeks, what pleasures they lost! It was not dark enough in their climate to have a proper phantom or anything worthy the name of an apparition. Theirs were essentially daylight phantasies. But, as I said before, my superstitions were of a different kind. Often after nightfall, have I looked long and eagerly from the manse windows to see the "*spunkies*"[16] playing among the graves; and by the bye this very name of spunkie, recalls to me the most important of our discoveries in the supernatural walk; for I first heard it in a solemn discussion with H—, when she, W— and[17] I, just about dusk, discovered a burning eye looking out from a hole in the retaining wall, in the corner where it joins the back of the stable. In hushed tones we debated the question: whether it was some bird of ill omen roosting in the cranny of the wall; or whether the hole pierced right through into a grave, and it was some dead man who was sitting up in his coffin and watching us with that strange fixed eye. If you will remember the level of the churchyard, you will see that this explanation suited pretty well; so we drew a wheelbarrow into the corner; one after another, got up and looked in; and when, the last, was satisfied, turned round, took to our heels and never stopped till we were in the shelter of the house. We ourselves, in our after discussions, thought it might have been the bird, though we preferred the more tremendous explanation. A sceptical reader on the other hand might be apt to suggest a piece of bottle glass. But for my own part, I simply believe that we saw nothing at all. The fact is we would have given anything to see a ghost, or to persuade ourselves that we had seen a ghost, or lastly perhaps to be able to persuade others that we had seen a ghost. The dread for our innocent laurel first arose from a conscious myth to feed this thirst for the unnatural, though by degrees it grew into a real, horrible belief. Nor is such a disposition at all uncommon among children. See how the dark rooms and passages attract them, how they will always go so far into them, feeding each other's alarm by pretending to hear noises and see sights, until at last they have reached the exquisite pitch of terror and run away, only to return again and repeat the manœuvre. I remember going down into the cellars of our own house in town (in company with another, *bien entendu*[18]) and persuading myself that I saw a face looking at me from around a corner; and though I did run away, I must say that the apparition was hailed with unmingled delight. I may even confess since the laws against sorcery have been for some while in abeyance, that I essayed at sundry times to call up the devil, founding my incantations on no more abstruse a guide than "Skelt's Juvenile Drama of *Der Freischütz*."[19] It is little wonder perhaps that my spells were unavailing; but it was a great disappointment; and it was not till the other day that the following words of Sir Thomas Browne consoled me a little, by throwing a new light on the cause of my failure. "Those that, to confute their incredulity, desire to see apparitions, shall, questionless, never behold any, nor have the power to be so much as witches. The devil hath them already in a heresy as capital as witchcraft; and to appear to them were but to convert them."[20] So that the failure of my half-doubting sorceries, according to the worthy doctor, need not breed in me any of that flat and frigid scepticism which eats the marrow out of a ghost story and robs us of the pleasures of alarm.

I am about the end of horrors now: even out of the Witches Walk, you saw the manse facing toward you with its back to the river and the wooded bank, and the bright flower plots and stretches of comfortable vegetables in front and on each side of it. Flower plots and vegetable borders, by the way, on which it was almost death to set foot, and about which we held a curious belief:—namely, that my grandfather went round and measured any prints that he saw to compare the measurement at night with the boots put out for brushing; to avoid which, we were accustomed, by a strategic wriggling of the foot to make the mark larger. Only, to the honour of childhood be it told, I remember having conscientious scruples in the matter lest some the thunders of the law should fall on some larger person; over which question I had as fine a self-conflict as I once had, apropos of my abortive sorceries, whether I should say the Lord's Prayer backward[21] or not; and, let me add, that in both cases I came to what I still think a just conclusion: I continued to deform my footprint; and I adhered to the legitimate order of the prayer.

The house was at the very extremity of the curve; and so the garden on the farther side looked upon the mill, the weir and the farther course of the river, which were all hidden from my little beach by the convex shape of the garden. Leaning between the row of poplars, I used to watch the still black waters rushing, with rapidly increasing speed, into the few feet of lade[22]; and there I saw my rafts of twigs spinning round the corner, rolling in the waves which began to form themselves, and finally caught, amidst a great palpitating mass of foam and drift upon the grating that protects the wheel. The sound of the mill was the only noise in the valley but the ceaseless music of the birds. Nor was it less interesting to watch the stone slope of the weir, dry atop, and with ever more fountains and threads of running water the lower you followed it down. Below the weir, our own bank rose as steep and high as the other one had been the whole time: the wood coped the water and covered both slopes; and the farther course of the stream disappears down a dark, winding and tree-shadowed valley. Just before I leave the poplars. I shall give one other recollection. Upon a day of wind and rain, about ten or eleven in the forenoon I should think, my father carried me out enveloped in shawls to see the great red flood waters pour over the weir and rush wildly down the valley; and, in return, I was seized with a shivering fit and a feverish attack whenever I got back into the house. So much for the garden: now, kind reader, will you follow me into the house.

On entering by the front door, you find before you a stone paved lobby, with doors on either hand that extended the whole length of the house. There stood a case of foreign birds, two or three marble deities from India and a lily of the Nile in a pot; and at the far end the stairs shut in the view.[23] Seated on these stairs, one morning, with hold of the bannisters and thinking of what I do not know, there occurred to me a somewhat comical event. I heard a quick rustling behind: next moment I was enveloped in darkness; and the moment after, as the reef might see the wave rushing on past it towards the beach, I saw my aunt below rushing downward. I know that she denies this; but she has no right to do so; and her well known habit of literally precipitating herself from one flat to another throws a strong light on the truth of my anecdote.

Leaving the lobby, we shall go into the dining room. A long low room, with two windows looking out on the garden, and one at the end on the poplar row. What an atmosphere of joy and festivity there was about this room, I cannot explain. How many people have been feasted in its somewhat narrow limits, no one alive or dead can say. If the statistics that I have received be true, some such miracle as Satan performed must have been necessary before the guests could

> in narrow room
> Throng numberless.[24]

How many faces of Uncles, Aunts and Cousins (of which the present writer's family has a larger assortment than has ever before been exhibited in this country) have I seen in that pleasant room! And how many games of tig, or brick building in the forenoon is it connected with in my mind. I remember one afternoon about Easter and all its incidents as well as if it were yesterday. It was spent in that dining room; and of course H— and W— were there with me. First as in duty bound in honour of the season, we boiled at the dining room fire three eggs which were to turn out mysteriously green or red or blue. Next, we played mysteriously on the sofa with my toy-gun. W— was fed on military literature; while I was full of backwoods and African deserts through the intervention of Mayne Reid.[25] Accordingly, he said he was in the trenches; and I declared that I was stalking deer—an amusement in which the most of my time was spent in those days; and it is like to be the only shooting I shall ever have. But the cup of my scorn for his abilities was filled to overflowing, when he called my weapon a musket.

> "It is not a musket," I said with dignity. "It's a rifle."
> "Soldiers always have muskets," he answered.
> "Ah but Hendrik and Basil" (characters from Mayne Reid who divided
> my worship between them) "and all hunters have rifles."[26]

Whether he found an answer to this I do not know; but I recollect that they took away with them that evening a volume of Mayne Reid for their nurse to read to them; and from thenceforward W— was converted to the rifle. Perhaps this discussion broke up our game for I next remember us building houses together behind the sofa with the bricks. About four o'clock, however, there came on a thunderstorm. The gun was put away and everything metallic followed in the same cause; while we crouched below the table, having heard that you are safest in the middle of the room. After the storm, tea upstairs; and the usual trial who would get first to the bottom of the cup and see the blue dragons or blue hieroglyphics that resembled dragons, with which the set was beautified.

But the dining room is principally dear to me, from memories of the time when I, sickly child, stayed there alone. First, in the forenoon about eleven how my aunt used to open the storeroom at the one end and give me out three Albert biscuits and some calf-foot jelly in a black pot with a sort of raised white pattern over it. That storeroom was a most voluptuous place let me remark, with its piles of biscuit boxes and spice tins, the rack for buttered eggs, the little window that let in sunshine and the flickering shadow of leaves, and the strong sweet odour of everything that pleaseth the taste of man. But after my biscuits were eaten and my pot emptied (I am supposing one of those many days when I was not allowed to cross the threshold) what did there remain to do? Well, there was every now and then a making of calf-foot jelly, when a great, loathsome, woollen bag strained by the liquid jelly into the form of an inverted cone, and dripping with the nectar at the foot, was suspended in front of the fire. Sometimes this operation was discreetly relegated to the kitchen, but, when my aunt must have it under her own eye, and the whole baggage of strainer and bowl was introduced into the dining room, there was always a feeble attempt to conceal the inherent loathsomeness of the operation, by leaning a two-winged fire screen against the mantel piece. Many a time have I peeped in behind the screen at the great, yellow hairy bag and the suspicious drops that fell regularly from its point, wondering how a process so horrible could produce results so comfortable both to eye and palate. Again, were there no calf's foot jelly on hand, I would often get some one for amanuensis[27] and write divers pleasant and instructive narratives which, in the march of refinement, have fallen some degree into unjust oblivion. One, I remember, had for scene the Witches Walk, and for heroine a kitten. It was intended to be something very thrilling and spectral; but I can only now recall the intense satisfaction (for I illustrated my works) with which I contemplated the effects of three coats of gamboge upon the cat's supper of pease-brose. By another of these romantic narrations, I was led into the only other low trick which I shall have to chronicle in these pages. It was entitled I remember *The Adventures of Basil*, and consisted mainly of bungling adaptations from Mayne Reid, to whom as you will observe I was indebted even for my hero's name; but I introduced the further attraction of a storm at sea, where the captain cried out, "All hands to the pumps." Now, when the work was being read to Aunt J—,[28] I listening, blown up with silly conceit, she objected to this speech of the captain's. It was not the order that a captain would have given, she said. Whereupon I entered into a long and laborious explanation to the effect that the words were not intended as the captain's and that the passage should read thus: "The captain said" (*elision*: "that") "all hands" (*elision*: "were to go") "to the pumps." I could not bear even this little fall from my idiotic pedestal, you see; but, as I have now somewhat lost the high opinion that I had of that juvenile production and can bear to hear it called in question with greater equanimity, I may confess that this explanation was as false as it was clumsy.

One winter forenoon (this recollection is not connected with the dining room, but I wish to make an end of the forenoon) my mother charged me with divers packages of tea and sugar which she was going to give to poor women in the village, and I trotted away by her side, very well pleased with my mission and my self. As we crossed the bridge the parcels under my arm bothered me as I tried to pull on my little gloves onto little hands that are now some small degree expanded.

Well, to finish with the forenoon and go forward to the dinner hour, I shall next describe what was to me a most important incident. My aunt had brought me a large box of soldiers from Town. I had only to drop the smallest hint of what I wanted and I had it the next time the phaeton went in; which was the phrase for a journey to Edinburgh. Once I remember I indicated admiration for a toy-gun with a green breast-strap which I had seen in C—'s[29] possession; and next day, not only did I receive my oft-mentioned "rifle," but a humble apology for the absence of the green bandoleer or whatever the thing may be called. So, after dinner on the first day of my new acquisition, I was told to exhibit my soldiers to Grandpapa. The idea of this great and somewhat alarming dignitary stooping to examine my toys, was a new one; and I ranged my wooden militia with excessive care upon the broad mahogany, while my Grandfather took his usual nuts and port wine. Not only was he pleased to approve of the manner in which I had "marshalled my array"; but he also gave a new light to me on the subject of "*playing with soldiers*,"—a technical term, you observe. He told me to make the battle of Coburg.[30] Now Waterloo I knew; and Crimean battle-fields I knew (for they were within my own memory); but this Coburg was a new and grand idea—a novel vista of entertainment—an addition to my vocabulary of warlike sports; and so I have never forgotten it.

But now I come to the crown of my dining-room reminiscences; for after dinner when the lamp was brought in and shaded and my aunt sat down to read in the rocking chair, there was a great open space behind the sofa left entirely in the shadow. This was my especial domain: once round the corner of the sofa I had left the lightsome, merry indoors and was out in the cool, dark night: I could almost see the stars. I looked out of the back window at the bushes outside. I lay in the darkest corners, rifle in hand, like a hunter in a lonely bivouac. I crawled about stealthily watching the people in the circle of lamplight, with some vague remembrance of a novel that my aunt had read to me, where some fellow went out from the "heated ball-room" and moralized in the "Park." Down in the corner beside the bricks, whether on the floor or in a book shelf I do not remember, were four volumes of Joanna Baillie's Plays. Now as C—[31] always expatiated on the wickedness of everything "theetrical," I supposed these books to be forbidden, and took every sly opportunity of reading them. Two of the plays I remember; for they took a powerful hold on my imagination. One was about a man who had committed a murder, and was going to be married when it was found out: just as the executioner lifted his axe, a reprieve arrived; but when they tried to raise the victim, he was already dead.[32] The other (called *Montfort* or *De Montfort*) was remarkable for a starry night and people arriving one after the other in the chapel of a convent, who had all been startled by something horrible in the forest: one had seen a murdered body: a second had seen the murderer flying in the distance; and a third (most terrified of all) was the murderer himself. But I don't think I ever read one through: my chief satisfaction was puzzling out, in the obscurity, the scenes—"a convent in a forest: the chapel lit: organ playing a solemn chant"—"a passage in a Saxon Castle"—and the like; and then transforming my dark place behind the sofa, into one and all of these.

The study was next door to the dining room—mysterious apartment with a book-case and talc-pictures (from India) ranged inside the glasses. I remember going in here one Sunday night to repeat to my grandfather the Psalm—a very awful ordeal, but which was passed with credit.

Opposite the study, the parlour. A small room crammed full of furniture and covered with portraits, with a cabinet at the one side full of shells, and foreign curiosities and a sort of anatomical trophy on the top. During a grand cleaning out of this apartment, I remember all the furniture was ranged on the circular grass plot between the churchyard and the house. It was a lovely still summer evening; and I stayed out climbing among the chairs and sofas. Falling on a large bone or skull I asked what it was. Part of an Albatross, Auntie told me. "What is an Albatross?" I asked. And then she described to me this great bird, nearly as big as a house, that you saw out miles away from land, sleeping above the waste and desolate Ocean; raised my respect for Uncle John a piece higher (if that were pos-sible; for he it was who had sent home almost all these wonders) by saying that he had shot it; told me that the Ancient Mariner was all about one; and quoted with great verve (she had a duster in her hand I recollect)

> With my cross-bow
> I shot the Albatross.[33]

Wonderful visions did all this raise in my imagination, so wonderful that when, many years later, I came to read the poem, my only feeling was one of utter dis-appointment. W— had a cross-bow; but up till this date, I had never envied him its possession. After this, however, it became one of the objects of my life. It has never been satisfied: time has laid its healing balm upon the wound; and my ambi-tion sleeps.

Notes

1 The manse was the home of Stevenson's grandfather, Reverend Lewis Balfour (1777–1860), minister of the village Colinton southwest of Edinburgh. Stevenson visited the manse often as a child and played there with his many cousins.
2 Charles Augustin Sainte-Beuve (1804–1869), French critic and literary historian.
3 Saturn, Roman god of plenty, peace, and liberty, who presided over the Golden Age.
4 Region of Greece named for the mythic Arcas traditionally celebrated as utopia: an unspoiled, rustic paradise.
5 Leith and Colinton.

6 Stevenson's maternal uncle John Balfour (1809–1886).
7 Exodus 19:11–12.
8 Natural acoustic amplification named for an Italian cave purportedly used by the Greek tyrant of Syracuse Dionysius I (432–367 BCE) to spy on his captives.
9 Conquistador Hernán Cortés (1485–1587) in John Keats's "On First Looking Into Chapman's Homer" (14).
10 Charles Lamb, *Essays of Elia* (1823).
11 Henry Vaughan, "The Retreat" (1–2).
12 The gaiters worn continuous with "shorts" or knee-breeches by bishops and deans.
13 King David's rebellious son Absalom was caught in the boughs of an oak tree after riding his mule under it in battle. He was killed against orders by David's men (2 Samuel 18: 8–15).
14 Mold.
15 A shiver or shudder (Scottish).
16 A will-o'-the-wisp or *ignis fatuus*: a phosphorescent light seen flickering over marshy ground at night. In folklore, a misleading ghost light.
17 Henrietta and Willie: Stevenson's favorite maternal cousins. See "To Willie and Henrietta" in *A Child's Garden of Verses*.
18 It is well understood; of course (French).
19 In Carl Maria von Weber's opera *Der Freischütz* (1821) or *The Marksman,* the protagonist invokes satanic forces to cast magic bullets to win a marksmanship contest, become head forester, and win the heroine's hand.
20 *Religio Medici* (1643). Sir Thomas Browne (1605–1682), scholar of science, religion, and the occult.
21 Reciting the Lord's Prayer (Matthew 6: 9–13) backwards supposedly summoned the devil.
22 A channel constructed for leading water to a mill-wheel (Scottish).
23 In *Memoirs of Himself,* Stevenson notes "the Indian curiosities with which my uncles had stocked the house"—*The Works of Robert Louis Stevenson. Vailima Edition.* vol. 26, 211 (1921–23, Doubleday Page & Co.).
24 Milton, *Paradise Lost* 1.779–780.
25 Thomas Mayne Reid (1818–1883), Scots-Irish American adventure novelist who served in the Mexican-American War and wrote novels set in the American West, Latin America, Africa, the Caribbean, and the Himalayas.
26 Reid's novels *The Bush Boys* (1856) and *The Boy Hunters* (1853).
27 A literary assistant who takes dictation.
28 Jane Balfour.
29 Lewis Charles Balfour (1851–1903), Stevenson's cousin.
30 The Battle of Neerwinden (18 March 1793) in the French Revolutionary Wars. The Prince of Coburg led coalition forces to victory over the French Republican army.
31 Stevenson's childhood nurse Alison "Cummy" Cunningham (1822–1913). See "Nurses" and n. 29, p. 439.
32 *The Dream: A Tragedy, in Prose, in Three Acts* (1812).
33 Samuel Taylor Coleridge, "The Rime of the Ancient Mariner" (1834, 81–82).

59

SKETCHES

I

The Satirist

My companion enjoyed a cheap reputation for wit and insight. He was, by habit and repute, a satirist.[1] If he did occasionally condemn anything or anybody who richly deserved it and whose demerits had hitherto escaped, it was simply because he condemned everything and everybody. While I was with him he disposed of St. Paul with an epigram, shook my reverence for Shakespeare in a neat antithesis, and fell foul of the Almighty himself, on the score of one or two out of the ten commandments.

Nothing escaped his blighting censure. At every sentence he overthrew an idol, or lowered my estimation of a friend. I saw every thing with new eyes, and could only marvel at my former blindness. How was it possible that I had not before observed A's false hair, B's selfishness or C's boorish manners? I and my companion, methought, walked the streets like a couple of Gods, among a swarm of vermin; for every one we saw seemed to bear openly upon his brow, the mark of the apocalyptic beast.[2] I half expected that these miserable beings, like the people of Lystra, would recognize their betters and force us to the altar; in which case, warned by the fate of Paul and Barnabas, I do not know that my modesty would have prevailed upon me to decline.[3] But there was no need for such churlish virtue. More blinded than the Lycaonians, the people saw no divinity in our gait; and as our temporary godhead lay more in the way of observing than healing their infirmities, we were content to pass them by in scorn.

I could not leave my companion, not from regard or even from interest, but from a very natural feeling, inseparable from the case. To understand it, let us take a simile. Suppose yourself walking down the street with a man, who continues to sprinkle the crowd out of a flask of vitriol. You would be much diverted with the grimaces and contortions of his victims; and at the same time you would fear to leave his arm, until his bottle was empty, knowing that, when once among the crowd, you would run a good chance yourself of baptism with his biting liquor. Now, my companion's vitriol was inexhaustible.

431

It was perhaps the consciousness of this, the knowledge that I was being anointed already out of the vials of his wrath, that made me fall to criticising the critic, whenever we had parted.

After all, I thought, our satirist has just gone far enough into his neighbours to find that the outside is false, without caring to go farther and discover what is really true. He is content to find that things are not what they seem; and broadly generalizes from it, that they do not exist at all. He sees our virtues are not what they pretend they are; and, on the strength of that, he denies us the possession of virtue altogether. He has learned the first lesson, that no man is wholly good; but he has not even suspected that there is another equally true, to wit, that no man is wholly bad. Like the inmate of a coloured star, he has eyes for one colour alone. He has a keen scent after evil, but his nostrils are plugged against all good, as people plugged their nostrils before going about the streets of the plague-struck city.

Why does he do this? It is most unreasonable to flee the knowledge of good like the infection of a horrible disease, and batten[4] and grow fat in the real atmosphere of a lazar house.[5] This was my first thought; but my second was not like unto it,[6] and I saw that our satirist was wise, wise in his generation like the unjust steward.[7] He does not want light, because the darkness is more pleasant. He does not wish to see the good, because he is happier without it. I recollect that when I walked with him, that I was in a state of divine exaltation, such as Adam and Eve must have enjoyed when the savour of the fruit was still unfaded between their lips; and I recognize that this must be the man's habitual state. He has the forbidden fruit in his waistcoat pocket, and can make himself a God as often and as long as he likes. He has raised himself upon a glorious pedestal above his fellows, he has touched the summit of ambition; and he envies neither King nor Kaiser, Prophet nor Priest, content in an elevation as high as theirs and much more easily attained. Yes, certes,[8] much more easily attained. He has not risen by climbing himself, but by pushing others down. He has grown great in his own estimation, not by blowing himself out, and risking the fate of Æsop's frog,[9] but simply by the habitual use of a diminishing glass on everybody else. And I think altogether that his is a better, a safer and a surer recipe than most others.

After all, however, looking back on what I have written, I detect a spirit suspiciously like his own. All through, I have been comparing myself with our satirist, and all through, I have had the best of the comparison. Well, well, contagion is as often mental as physical; and I do not think my readers, who have all been under his lash, will blame me very much for giving the headsman a mouthful of his own saw-dust.

II

Nuits Blanches[10]

If any one should know the pleasure and pain of a sleepless night, it should be I. I remember, so long ago, the sickly child that woke from his few hours' slumber with the sweat of a nightmare on his brow, to lie awake and listen and long for the first signs of life among the silent streets. These nights of pain and weariness are graven on my mind; and so when the same thing happened to me again, everything that I heard or saw was rather a recollection than a discovery.

Weighed upon by the opaque and almost sensible darkness, I listened eagerly for anything to break the sepulchral quiet. But nothing came save, perhaps, an emphatic crack from the old cabinet that was made by Deacon Brodie[11] or the dry rustle of the coals on the extinguished fire. It was a calm; or I know that I should have heard in the roar and clatter of the storm, as I have not heard it for so many years, the wild career of a horseman, always scouring up from the distance and passing swiftly below the window; yet always returning again from the place whence first he came, as though, baffled by some higher power, he had retraced his steps to gain impetus for another and another attempt.

As I lay there, there arose out of the utter stillness, the rumbling of a carriage a very great way off, that drew near, and passed within a few streets of the house, and died away as gradually as it had arisen. This, too, was as a reminiscence.

I rose and lifted a corner of the blind. Over the black belt of the garden, I saw the long line of Queen Street,[12] with here and there a lighted window. How often before had my nurse lifted me out of bed and pointed them out to me, while we wondered together if, there also, there were children that could not sleep and if these lighted oblongs were signs of those that waited like us for the morning.

I went out into the lobby, and looked down into the great deep well of the staircase. For what cause I know not, just as it used to be in the old days that the feverish child might be the better served, a peep of gas illuminated a narrow circle far below me. But where I was, all was darkness and silence, save the dry monotonous ticking of the clock that came ceaselessly up to my ear.

The final crown of it all, however, the last touch of reproduction on the pictures of my memory, was the arrival of that time for which, all night through, I waited and longed of old. It was my custom, as the hours dragged on, to repeat the question "When will the carts come in?"; and repeat it again and again until at last those sounds arose in the street that I have heard once more this morning. The road before our house is a great thoroughfare for early carts. I know not, and I never have known, what they carry, whence they come or whither they go. But I know that, long ere dawn and for hours together, they stream continuously past, with the same rolling and jerking of wheels and the same clink of horses' feet. It was not for nothing that they made the burthen of my wishes all night through. They are really the first throbbings of life, the harbingers of day; and it pleases you as much to hear them, as it must please a shipwrecked seaman once again to grasp a hand of flesh and blood after years of miserable solitude. They have the freshness of the daylight life about them. You can hear the carters cracking their whips and crying hoarsely to their horses or to one another; and sometimes even a peal of healthy, harsh horse-laughter comes up to you through the darkness. There is now an end of mystery and fear. Like the knocking at the door in *Macbeth*[13] or the cry of the watchman in the *Tour du Nesle*,[14] they show that the horrible cæsura is over and the nightmares have fled away, because the day is breaking and the ordinary life of men is beginning to bestir itself among the streets.

In the middle of it all, I fell asleep, to be wakened by the officious knocking at my door and find myself twelve years older than I had dreamed myself all night.

III

The Wreath of Immortelles

It is all very well to talk of death as "a pleasant potion of immortality"[15] but the most of us I suspect are of "queasy stomachs," and find it none of the sweetest. The graveyard may be cloak-room to Heaven; but we must admit that it is a very ugly and offensive vestibule in itself, however fair may be the life to which it leads. And though Enoch and Elias went into the temple through a gate which certainly may be called Beautiful, the rest of us have to find our way to it, through Ezekiel's low-bowed door and the vault full of creeping things and all manner of abominable beasts.[16] Nevertheless, there is a certain frame of mind, to which a cemetery is, if not an antidote, at least an alleviation. If you are in a fit of the blues, go nowhere else. It was in obedience to this wise regulation, that the other morning found me lighting my pipe at the entrance to Old Greyfriars, thoroughly sick of the town, the country and myself.

Two of the men were talking at the gate, one of them carrying a spade in hands still crusted with the soil of graves. Their very aspect was delightful to me; and I crept nearer to them, thinking to pick up some snatch of sexton-gossip, some "talk fit for a charnel,"[17] something in fine worthy of that fastidious logician, that adept in coroner's law, who has come down to us as the patron of Yaughan's liquor and the very prince of gravediggers.[18] Scotch people in general are so much wrapped up in their profession, that I had a good chance of overhearing such conversation: the talk of fishmongers running usually on stock-fish and haddocks; while of the Scotch sexton I could repeat stories and speeches that positively smell of the graveyard. But on this occasion, I was doomed to disappointment. My two friends were far into the region of generalities. Their profession was forgotten in their electorship. Politics had engulfed the narrower economy of gravedigging. "Na, na," said the one, "ye're a' wrang." "The English and Irish churches," answered the other, in a tone as if he had made the remark before and it had been called in question—"The English and Irish churches have *impoverised* the country."

"Such are the results of education," thought I, as I passed beside them and came fairly forth among the tombs. Here, at least, there were no commonplace politics, no diluted this-morning's leader,[19] to distract or offend me. The old shabby church showed, as usual, its quaint extent of roofage and the relievo[20] skeleton on one gable still blackened with the fire of thirty years ago. A chill dank mist lay over all. The Old Greyfriars[21] churchyard was in perfection that morning; and one could go round and reckon up the associations, with no fear of vulgar interruption. On this stone, the Covenant was signed. In that vault, as the story goes, John Knox took hiding in some Reformation broil.[22] From that window Burke the murderer[23] looked out many a time across the tombs, and perhaps o' nights, let himself down over the sill to rob some new-made grave. Certainly he would have a selection here. The very walks have been carried over forgotten resting places; and the whole ground is uneven, because (as I was once quaintly told) "when the wood rots, it stands to reason the soil should fall in"; which from the law of gravitation, is certainly beyond denial. But, it is round the boundary that there are the finest tombs. The whole irregular space is as it were fringed with quaint old monuments, rich in deaths-heads and scythes and hour-glasses, and doubly rich in pious epitaphs and Latin mottoes—rich in them to such an extent that their proper space has run over, and they have crawled end-long up the shafts of columns and ensconced themselves in all sorts of odd corners among the sculpture. These tombs raise their backs against the rubble of squalid dwelling houses; and, every here and there, a clothespole projects, between two monuments, its fluttering trophy of white and yellow and red. With a grim irony, they recall the banners in the Invalides,[24] banners as appropriate perhaps over the sepulchres of tailors and weavers, as these others above the dust of armies. Why they put things out to dry on that particular morning, it was hard to imagine. The grass was grey with drops of rain, the headstones black with moisture. Yet, in despite of weather and common-sense, there they hung between the tombs; and beyond them I could see through open windows into miserable rooms where whole families were born and fed, and slept and died. At one a girl sat singing merrily with her back to the graveyard; and from another came the shrill tones of a scolding woman. Every here and there, was a town garden full of sickly flowers, or a pile of crockery inside upon the window seat. But you do not grasp the connexion between these houses of the dead and the living, the unnatural marriage of stately sepulchres and squalid houses, till, lower down, where the road has sunk far below the surface of the cemetery and the very roofs are scarcely on a level with its wall, you observe that a proprietor has taken advantage of a tall monument and trained a chimney stack against its back. It startles you to see the red, modern pots, peering over the shoulder of the tomb.

A man was at work on a grave, his spade clinking away the drift of bones that permeates the thin brown soil; but my first disappointment had taught me to expect little from Greyfriars sextons, and I passed him by in silence. A slater on the slope of a neighbouring roof eyed me curiously. A lean black cat, looking as if it had battened[25] on strange meats, slipped past me. A little boy at a window, put his finger to his nose, in so offensive a manner that I was put upon my dignity and turned grandly off to read old epitaphs and peer through the gratings into the shadow of vaults.

Just then, I saw two women coming down a path, one of them old, and the other younger with a child in her arms. Both had faces eaten with famine and hardened with sin, and both had reached that stage of degradation, much lower in a woman than a man, when all care for dress is lost. As they came down, they neared a grave, where some pious friend or relative had laid a wreath of immortelles,[26] and put a bell glass over it, as is the custom. The effect of that ring of dull yellow among so many blackened and dusty sculptures, was more pleasant than it is in modern cemeteries, where every second mound can boast a similar coronal; and here, where it was the exception and not the rule, I could even fancy the drops of moisture that dimmed the covering, were the tears of those who laid it where it was. As the two women came up to it, one of them kneeled down on the wet grass and looked long and silently through the clouded shade, while the second stood above her, gently oscillating to and fro to lull the muling baby. I was struck a great way off with something religious in the attitude of these two unkempt and haggard women; and I drew near faster, but still cautiously, to hear what they were saying. Surely on them the spirit of death and decay had descended: I had no education to dread here: should I not have a chance of seeing nature? Alas! a pawnbroker could not have been more practical and commonplace; for this was what the kneeling woman said to the woman upright—this and nothing more: "Eh what Extravagance!"

O nineteenth century, wonderful art thou indeed—wonderful, but wearisome in thy stale and deadly uniformity. Thy men are more like numerals than men. They must bear their idiosyncrasies or their professions written on a placard about their neck, like the scenery in Shakespeare's theatre.[27] Thy precepts of economy have pierced into the lowest ranks of life; and there is now a decorum in vice, a respectability among the disreputable, a pure spirit of Philistinism among the waifs and strays of thy Bohemia.[28] For lo! thy very gravediggers talk politics; and thy castaways kneel upon new graves, to discuss the cost of the monument and grumble at the improvidence of love.

Such was the elegant apostrophe that I made, as I went out of the gates again, happily satisfied in myself, and feeling that I alone of all whom I had seen, was able to profit by the silent poem of these green mounds and blackened headstones.

IV

Nurses[29]

I knew one once, and the room where, lonely and old, she waited for death. It was pleasant enough, high up above the lane, and looking forth upon a hillside, covered all day with sheets and yellow blankets, and with long lines of underclothing fluttering between the battered posts. There were any number of cheap prints and a drawing by one of "her children," and there were flowers in the window, and a sickly canary withered into consumption in an ornamental cage. The bed, with its checked coverlid, was in a closet.[30] A great bible lay on the table; and her drawers were full of *scones* which it was her pleasure to give to young visitors such as I was then.

You may not think this a melancholy picture; but the canary, and the cat, and the white mouse that she had for a while and that died, were all indications of the want that ate into her heart. I think I know a little of what that old woman felt; and I am as sure as if I had seen her, that she sat many an hour in silent tears, with the big bible open before her clouded eyes.

If you could look back upon her life, and feel the great chain that had linked her to one child after another, sometimes to be wrenched suddenly through, and sometimes which is infinitely worse, to be torn gradually off through years of growing neglect, or perhaps growing dislike. She had like the mother overcome that natural repugnance—repugnance which no man can conquer—towards the infirm and helpless mass of putty of the earlier stage. She had spent her best and happiest years in tending, watching and learning to love like a mother this child, with which she has no connexion and to which she has no tie. Perhaps she refused some sweetheart (such things have been) or put him off and off, until he lost heart and turned to some one else, all for fear of leaving this creature that had wound itself about her heart. And the end of it all, her month's warning, and a present perhaps, and the rest of the life to vain regret. Or, worse still, to see the child gradually forgetting and forsaking her, fostered in disrespect and neglect on the plea of growing manliness, and at last beginning to treat her as a servant whom he had treated a few years before as a mother. She sees the bible or the psalm book, which with gladness and love unutterable in her heart, she had bought for him years ago out of her slender savings, neglected for some newer gift of his father, lying in dust in the lumber room or given away to a poor child, and the act applauded for its unfeeling charity. Little wonder if she becomes hurt and angry, and attempts to tyrannize and to grasp her old power back again. We are not all patient Grizzels,[31] by good fortune, but the most of us human beings with feelings and tempers of our own.

And so in the end, behold her in the room that I described. Very likely and very naturally, in some fling of feverish misery or recoil of thwarted love, she has quarrelled with her old employers and the children are forbidden to see her or to speak to her; or at best, she gets her rent paid and a little to herself, and now and then, her late charges are sent up (with another nurse perhaps) to pay her a short visit. How bright these visits seem as she looks forward to them on her lonely bed! How unsatisfactory their realisation, when the forgetful child, half wondering, checks with every word and action, the outpouring of her maternal love! How bitter and restless the memories that they leave behind! And for the rest, what else has she? to watch them with eager eyes as they go to school, to sit in church where she can see them every Sunday, to be passed some day unnoticed in the street or deliberately *cut* because the great man or the great woman are with friends before whom they are ashamed to recognize the old woman that loved them.

When she goes home that night, how lonely will the room appear to her! Perhaps the neighbours may hear her sobbing to herself in the dark, with the fire burnt out for want of fuel, and the candle still unlit upon the table.

And it is for this that they live, these quasi-mothers—mothers in everything but the travail and the thanks. It is for this, that they have remained virtuous in youth, living the dull life of a household servant. It is for this, that they refused the old sweetheart and have no fireside or offspring of their own.

I believe in a better state of things, that there will be no more nurses, and that every mother will nurse her own offspring; for what can be more hardening and demoralizing than to call forth the tenderest feelings of a woman's heart and cherish them yourself as long as you need them, as long as your children require a nurse to love them, and then, to blight and thwart and destroy them, whenever your own use for them is at an end. This may be Utopian; but it is always a little thing, if one mother or two mothers can be brought to feel more tenderly to those who share their toil and have no part in their reward.[32]

Notes

The Satirist

1 The unidentified satirist must have been Stevenson's friend James Walter Ferrier (1850–1883). Prior to Ferrier's disgrace and struggle to reform himself, Stevenson describes in the more sympathetic "Old Mortality," "something soulless in our friend. He would astonish us by sallies, witty . . . and inhumane; and by a misapplied Johnsonian pleasantry, demolish honest sentiment." Stevenson portrays Ferrier "following vanity and incredulous of good" (140). See also n. 16, p. 142.
2 Revelation 13.
3 After seeing Paul and Barnabas heal a crippled man, the people of Lystra tried to worship and sacrifice to them as Mercurius and Jupiter before the apostles stopped them (Acts 14).
4 To thrive at another's expense.
5 A place to quarantine people with infectious diseases, named for the leprous beggar Lazarus in Jesus' parable (Luke 16:19–31).
6 Matthew 22:37–39.
7 Luke 16: 1–8.
8 Assuredly.
9 In one of Aesop's fables, a frog bursts after trying to rival an ox by inflating itself.

Nuits Blanches

10 Sleepless nights (French).
11 William Brodie (1741–1788), Edinburgh cabinetmaker and city councilor who was convicted of burglary and hanged. Brodie was the inspiration for Stevenson's play, co-authored with W.E. Henley, *Deacon Brodie* (1888).
12 Stevenson's family moved to Edinburgh's Heriot Row across from Queen Street Gardens when he was six.
13 **RLS:** "See a short Essay of De Quincey's." In Shakespeare's *Macbeth,* the sound of knocking interrupts the conspiring of Macbeth and Lady Macbeth: "Whence is that knocking? / How is 't with me, when every noise appalls me?" (2.2.56–57). In "On the Knocking at the Gate in *Macbeth*" (1823), Thomas de Quincey (1785–1859) analyzes why the audience, who should want to see Macbeth brought to justice, is also unnerved by the knocking. He argues that our horror of death subconsciously makes us sympathize with a murderer more easily than with a victim.
14 In Frédéric Gaillardet and Alexandre Dumas' play *La Tour de Nesle* (1832), based on the scandal of 1314 in which the daughters-in-law of Philip IV were tried for adultery, Margaret of Burgundy had her lovers killed after copulation.

The Wreath of Immortelles

15 "We all labour against our owne cure, for death is the cure of all diseases . . . which though nauseous to queasie stomachs, yet to prepared appetites is Nectar and a pleasant potion of immortality" (Sir Thomas Browne, *Religio Medici* 2.9).
16 Enoch and Elias (Elijah) were taken by God rather than dying (Genesis 5:24, 2 Kings 2:11). Refers to the "beautiful gate of the temple" (Acts 3:10) and Ezekiel's vision (Ezekiel 8:7–10).
17 John Webster, *The Duchess of Malfi* 4.2.163.
18 Gravedigger in Shakespeare's *Hamlet* who asks for liquor from Yaughan (Johan) (5.1.55–56).
19 Leading article: a newspaper editorial.
20 Molding, carving, or stamping in which the design stands out from the surface.
21 Parish Kirk of the Church of Scotland in Old Town Edinburgh includes Old Greyfriars, built in 1614, and New Greyfriars, erected in 1718.
22 John Knox (1513–1572), leader of the Scottish Protestant Reformation and founder of the Presbyterian Church of Scotland (see Stevenson's 1875 essay "John Knox and His Relations to Women"). National Covenant—a compact signed by Scottish "Covenanters" 28 Feb. 1638 maintaining Presbyterian church and civil government against Episcopalianism, escalating a conflict into the Scottish Civil War in 1644–1645 and extending to the 3rd English Civil War.
23 Grave robbers William Burke and William Hare murdered 16 people and sold their corpses to the Edinburgh anatomy researcher Robert Knox in 1828, inspiring Stevenson's story "The Body Snatcher."
24 Les Invalides, or Hôtel des Invalides: a Paris museum and monument of French military history containing tombs of France's war heroes, most notably Napoleon, along with a hospital and retirement home for war veterans. In the veterans' chapel, Cathédrale Saint-Louis-des-Invalides, flags captured in military campaigns hang as war trophies.
25 Grown fat.
26 A durable floral arrangement of dried flowers or plaster for graves, typically under glass.
27 A placard on the stage pillar indicated the setting in Shakespeare's Globe Theatre.
28 Philistinism: lack of enlightenment and aesthetic sophistication; indifference or hostility to art and culture. Bohemia: unconventional or countercultural community of free spirits, artists, and writers.

Nurses

29 Alison "Cummy" Cunningham (1822–1913) became Stevenson's nurse in 1852 and stayed in the household for twenty years. She was a strict Calvinist, raising Stevenson on biblical Presbyterianism and stories of Covenanters. He corresponded with her throughout his life and dedicated *A Child's Garden of Verses* (1885) to her.
30 Alcove.
31 Grizzel Clay is a good-tempered dairymaid in Ellen Wood's novel *Johnny Ludlow* (1874).
32 The fifth section "A Character" is a brief portrait of a passerby Stevenson imagines as evil. More of a sketch than a personal essay, it is omitted here.

60

A RETROSPECT[1]

If there is anything that delights me in Hazlitt[2] beyond the charm of style and the unconscious portrait of a vain and powerful spirit which his works present, it is the loving and tender way in which he returns again to the memory of the past. These little recollections of bygone happiness were too much a part of the man to be carelessly or poorly told. The imaginary landscapes and visions of the most ecstatic dreamer can never rival such recollections, told simply perhaps, but still told, (as they could not fail to be) with precision, delicacy and evident delight. They are too much loved by the author not to be palated by the reader. But beyond the mere felicity of pencil, the nature of the piece could never fail to move my heart. Whenever I read his essay "On the Past and Future," every word seemed to be something I had said myself. I could have thought he had been eavesdropping at the doors of my heart, so entire was the coincidence between his writing and my thought. It is a sign perhaps of a somewhat vain disposition. The future is nothing; but the past is myself, my own history, the seed of my present thoughts, the mould of my present disposition. It is not in vain that I return to the nothings of my childhood; for every one of them has left some stamp upon me or put some fetter on my boasted free-will. In the past is my present fate; and in the past also, is my real life. It is not the past only but the past that has been many years in that tense. The doings and actions of last year are as uninteresting and vague to me, as the blank gulph of the future, the tabula rasa[3] that may never be anything else. I remember a confused hotch-potch of unconnected events, a "chaös without form and void"; but nothing salient or striking rises from the dead level of "flat, stale and unprofitable" generality.[4] When we are looking at a landscape we think ourselves pleased; but it is only when it comes back upon us by the fire o' nights that we can disentangle the main charm from the thick of particulars. It is just so with what is lately past. It is too much loaded with detail to be distinct; and the canvass is too large for the eye to encompass. But this is no more the case when our recollections have been strained long enough through the hourglass of time, when they have been the burthen of so much thought, the charm and comfort of so many a merry vigil. All that is worthless has been sieved and sifted out of them. Nothing remains but the brightest lights and the darkest shadows. When we were near at hand, the spurs and haunches crowded up in eager rivalry, and the whole range seemed to have shrugged its shoulders to its ears, till we could not tell the higher from the lower; but when we are far off, these lesser prominences are melted back into the bosom of the rest or have set behind the round horizon of the plain, and the supreme mountain peaks stand forth in lone and sovereign dignity against the sky. It is just the same with our recollections. We require to draw back and shade our eyes before the picture dawns upon us in full breadth and outline. Late years are still in limbo to us; but the more distant past is all that we possess in life, the corn already harvested and stored for ever in the grange of memory. The doings of today at some future time will gain the required offing, I shall learn to love the things of my adolescence, as Hazlitt loved them, and as I love already the recollections of my childhood. They too will surge in prominence from the "chaos dire"[5] in which they still lie wombed. They will gather interest with every year. They will ripen in forgotten corners of my memory; and someday I shall waken and find them vested with new glory and new pleasantness.

It is for stirring the chords of memory, then, that I love Hazlitt's essays, and for the same reason (I remember) he himself threw in his allegiance to Rousseau,[6] saying of him, what was so true of his own writings: "He seems to gather up the past moments of his being like drops of honey dew to distil some precious liquor from them; his alternate pleasures and pains are the bead-roll that he tells over and piously worships; he makes a rosary of the flowers of hope and fancy that strewed his earliest years."[7] How true are these words when applied to himself! and how much I thank him that it was so! All my childhood is a golden age to me. I have no recollection of bad weather. Except one or two storms whose grandeur had impressed itself on my mind, the whole time seems steeped in sunshine. "Et ego in Arcadia vixi"[8] would be no empty boast upon my grave. If I desire to live long, it is that I may have the more to look back upon. Even to one, like the unhappy Duchess,

Acquainted with sad misery
As the tanned galley slave is with his oar,[9]

and seeing over the night of troubles no "lily-wristed morn"[10] of hope appear, a retrospect of even chequered and doubtful happiness in the past may sweeten the bitterness of present tears. And here, I may be excused if I quote a passage from an unpublished drama (the unpublished is perennial I fancy) which the author believed was not all devoid of the flavour of our elder dramatists. However this may be, it expresses better than I could, some further thoughts on this same subject. The heroine is taken by a minister to the grave, where already some have been recently buried, and where her sister's lover is destined to rejoin them on the following day.

What led me to the consideration of this subject and what has made me take up my pen tonight, is the rather strange coincidence of two very different accidents— a prophecy of my future and a return into my past. No later than yesterday, seated in the coffee room here there came into the tap of the hotel, a poor mad highland woman. The noise of her strained, thin voice brought me out to see her. I could conceive that she had been pretty once; but that was many years ago. She was now withered and fallen looking. Her hair was thin and straggling; her dress poor and scanty. Her moods changed as rapidly as a weathercock before a thunderstorm. One moment she said her "mutch"[11] was the only thing that gave her comfort; and the next, she slackened the strings and let it back upon her neck, in a passion at it, for making her too hot. Her talk was a wild, somewhat weird farrago, of utterly meaningless balderdash, mere inarticulate gibber, snatches of old Jacobite[12] ballads and exaggerated phrases from the drama, to which she suited equally exaggerated action. She "babbled of green fields"[13] and highland glens: she prophesied "the drawing of the claymore"[14], with a lofty disregard of cause or commonsense; and she broke out suddenly, with uplifted hands and eyes, into ecstatic "Heaven bless hims!" and "Heaven forgive hims!" She had been a camp follower in her younger days; and she was never tired of expatiating on the gallantry, the fame, and the beauty of the 42nd Highlanders.[15] Her patriotism knew no bounds, and her prolixity was much in the same scale. This witch of Endor[16] offered to tell my fortune, with much dignity and proper oracular enunciation. But on my holding forth my hand, a somewhat ludicrous incident occurred. "Na, na," she said, "wait till I have a draw of my pipe." Down she sate in the corner, puffing vigorously and regaling the lady behind the counter with conversation more remarkable for stinging satire than prophetic dignity. The person in question had "mair weeg than hair on her head"—(did not the chignon plead guilty at these words?)—"wad be better if she had less tongue"—and would come at last to the grave, a goal which, in a few words, she invested with "warning circumstance" enough to make a stoic shudder. Suddenly, in the midst of this, she rose up and beckoned me to approach. The oracles of my highland sorceress had no claim to consideration except in the matter of obscurity. In "question hard and sentence intricate" she beat the priests of Delphi[17] or the . . . . . In bold unvarnished falsity (as regards the past) even spirit rapping was a child to her.[18] All that I could gather may be thus summed up shortly: that I was to visit America, that I was to be very happy, and that I was to be much upon the sea, predictions, which in consideration of an uneasy stomach, I can scarcely think agreeable with one another. Two incidents alone relieved the dead level of idiocy and incomprehensible gabble. The first was the comical announcement that "when I drew fish to the Marquis of Bute,[19] I should take care of my sweetheart," from which I deduce the fact that at some period of my life I shall drive a fishmonger's cart. The second, in the middle of such nonsense, had a touch of the tragic. She suddenly looked at me with an eager glance, and dropped my hand saying, in what were either tones of misery or a very good affectation of them, "Black eyes!" A moment after she was noisily at work again. It is as well to mention that I have not black eyes.[20]

This incident, strangely blended of the pathetic and the ludicrous, set my mind at work upon the future; but I could find little interest in the study. Even the predictions of my sibyl. . . .

I started on a cold bright morning for my long promised excursion. Vast irregular masses of white and purple cumulus drifted rapidly over the sky. The great
hills, brown with heather, were here and there buried in blue shadows, here and
there streaked with sharp bands of sunlight. The new-fired larches were green in
the glens; and the "pale primroses"[21] hid themselves in marish[22] hollows and under
the hawthorn roots. I had not in my former days, observed the beauties, the larch-
woods, the winding road edged in between field and flood, or the broad ruffled
bosom of the hill surrounded loch.[23] It was above all the height of these hills that
astonished me. Hills I remembered; but the picture in my memory was low and
featureless. They seemed to have kept pace with me in growth. The villas which
I remembered as half way up the slopes, had been left behind in the process of
time and merely ringed their eternal feet, white among the newly kindled woods.

As I felt myself on the road at last that I had been dreaming of for these many
days before, a perfect intoxication of joy took hold upon me; and I was so pleased
at my own happiness that I could let none past me, till I had taken them into my
confidence. I asked my way from everyone, and took good care to let them all
know, before they left me, what my object was and how many years had elapsed
since my last visit. I wonder what the good folk thought of me and my communications—not that it matters much to me. At last, however, after much enquiry,
I arrive at the place, make my peace with the gardener and enter. My disillusion
dates from the opening of the garden door. I repine, I find a reluctation of spirit
against believing that this is the place. What, is this kailyard, that inexhaustible
paradise of a garden in which M— and I found "elbow-room," and expatiated
together without sensible constraint? Is that little turfed slope, the huge and perilous green bank, down which I counted it a feat and the gardener a sin, to run? Are
these two squares of stone, some two feet high, the pedestals on which I walked
with such a penetrating sense of dizzy elevation and which I had expected to find
on a level with my eyes? Aye, the place is no more like what I expected than this
bleak April day is like the glorious September with which it is incorporated in my
memory. I look at the gardener, disappointment in my face, and tell him that the
place seems sorrily shrunken from the high estate that it had held in my remembrance; and he returns, with quiet laughter, by asking me how long it is since
I was there. I tell him; and he remembers me. Ah! I say, I was a great nuisance,
I believe. But no, my good gardener will plead guilty to having kept no record of
my evildoings; and I find myself much softened toward the place and willing to
take a kinder view and pardon its shortcomings, for the sake of the gardener and
his pretended recollection of myself. And it is just at this stage (to complete my
reëstablishment) that I see a little boy—the gardener's grandchild—just about
the same age and the same height that I must have been in the days when I was
here last. My first feeling is one of almost anger, to see him playing on the gravel
where I had played before, as if he had usurped something of my identity; but,
next moment, I feel a softening and a sort of rising and qualm of the throat accompanied by a pricking heat in the eyeballs. I hastily join conversation with the child
and inwardly felicitate myself that the gardener is opportunely gone for the key

443

of the house. But the child is a sort of homily to me. He is perfectly quiet and resigned, an unconscious hermit. I ask him jocularly if he gets as much abused as I used to do for running down the bank; but the child's perfect seriousness of answer staggers me—O no, grandpapa doesn't allow it—why should he? I feel caught: I stand abashed at the reproof: I must not expose my childishness again to this youthful disciplinarian, and so I ask him very stately what he is going to be—a good serious practical question, out of delicacy for his parts. He answers that he is going to be a missionary to China; and tells me how a missionary once took him on his knee and told him about missionary work and asked him if he, too, would not like to become one; to which the child had simply answered in the affirmative. The child is altogether so different from what I have been, is so absolutely complementary to what I now am, that I turn away not a little abashed from the conversation; for there is always something painful in sudden contact with the good qualities that we do not possess. Just then, the grandfather returns; and I go with him to the summerhouse where I used to learn my catechism, to the wall on which M—and I thought it no small exploit to walk upon, and all the other places that I remembered.[24]

In fine the matter being ended, I turn and go my way home to the hotel, where, in the cold afternoon, I write these notes with the table and chair drawn as near the fire as the rug and the French polish will permit.

One other thing I may as well make a note of; and that is how there arises that strange contradiction of the hills being higher than I had expected; and everything near at hand being so ridiculously smaller. This is a question I think easily answered. The very terms of the problem suggest the solution. To everything near at hand I applied my own stature, as a sort of natural unit of measurement, so that I had no actual image of their dimensions, but their ratio to myself; so, of course, as one term of the proportion changed, the other changed likewise, and as my own height increased my notion of things near at hand became equally expanded. But the hills, mark you, were out of my reach: I could not apply myself to them: I had an actual, instead of a proportional, eidolon of their magnitude; so that of course (my eye being larger and flatter now a days and so the image presented to me then being in sober earnest smaller than the image presented to me now) I found the hills nearly as much too great, as I had found the other things too small.

Notes

1 This unfinished essay is based on Stevenson's visit to Dunoon on the outer Firth of Clyde in the spring of 1870, during which visit he went to a house where he once stayed in childhood.
2 William Hazlitt (1778–1830), English Romantic essayist.
3 *Scraped tablet* (Latin) or blank slate, commonly associated with John Locke's empiricist *Essay Concerning Human Understanding* (1689).
4 Genesis 1:2; *Hamlet* 1.2.133.
5 Seneca, *Phaedra* 5.1239–1240.

6 Jean-Jacque Rousseau (1712–1778), Genevan writer and philosopher influential in Romanticism and the French Revolution.
7 Hazlitt, "The Past and Future" (1821).
8 Arcadia—region of Greece named for the mythic Arcas traditionally celebrated as utopia: an unspoiled, rustic paradise. "Et in Arcadia ego"—*I have lived in Arcadia* (Latin)—the title of a 1638 painting depicting shepherds around a tomb by the French Baroque artist Nicolas Poussin.
9 John Webster, *The Duchess of Malfi* 4.2.26–27.
10 Robert Herrick, "The Country Life" (20).
11 Nightcap.
12 A supporter of James II, his son, and the Stuart Dynasty after the Revolution of 1688.
13 *Henry V* 2.3.15–16.
14 Broadsword used by Scottish Highlanders.
15 Scottish infantry regiment of the British Army in the Napoleonic Wars, Crimean War, and the Indian Rebellion of 1857.
16 A biblical witch who summons the deceased prophet Samuel, foretells Saul's death, and prophesizes the defeat of Israel by the Philistines (1 Samuel 28).
17 In the ancient Greek Temple of Apollo at Delphi, priests purportedly turned the frenzied, incomprehensible sayings of the oracle Pythia into enigmatic prophecies in poetry.
18 Victorian spiritualists claimed the spirits of the dead tapped and knocked on tables in séances to communicate. Such methods were later exposed as fraudulent in high-stakes, public demonstrations of the Society for Psychical Research.
19 John Patrick Crichton-Stuart (1847–1900), Scottish aristocrat, industrialist, scholar and the 3rd Marquess of Bute, reportedly the richest man in the world.
20 Reviewing this abandoned essay seven years after writing it, Stevenson added the following note to the manuscript: "And very strange it is: the old pythoness was right: I have been happy, I did go to America (am even going again—unless—) and I have been twice and once upon the deep. Moreover I have (and had) black eyes. R.L.S 1887." Stevenson's eyes were dark brown.
21 Shakespeare, *The Winter's Tale* 4.4.143.
22 Marshy.
23 Lake (Scots).
24 Possibly Stevenson's mother, Margaret Balfour Stevenson (1829–1897), or an unknown childhood playmate.

61

THE PHILOSOPHY OF UMBRELLAS

It is wonderful to think what a turn has been given to our whole Society, by the fact that we live under the sign of Aquarius[1],—that our climate is essentially wet. A mere arbitrary distinction, like the walking-swords of yore might have remained the symbol of foresight and respectability, had not the raw mists and dropping showers of our island pointed the inclination of Society to another exponent of those virtues. A ribbon of the Legion of Honour[2] or a string of medals may prove a person's courage; a title may prove his birth; a professorial chair his study and acquirement; but it is the habitual carriage of the umbrella that is the stamp of Respectability. The umbrella has become the acknowledged index of social position.

Robinson Crusoe[3] presents us with a touching instance of the hankering after them, inherent in the civilized and educated mind. To the superficial, the hot suns of Juan Fernandez[4] may sufficiently account for his quaint choice of a luxury; but surely one who had borne the hard labour of a seaman under the tropics for all these years, could have supported an excursion after goats or a peaceful *constitutional* arm in arm with the nude Friday. No, it was not this: the memory of a vanished respectability called for some outward manifestation, and the result was—an umbrella. A pious castaway might have rigged up a belfry and solaced his Sunday mornings with the mimicry of church-bells; but Crusoe was rather a moralist than a pietist, and his leaf umbrella is as fine an example of the civilized mind striving to express itself under adverse circumstances, as we have ever met with.

It is not for nothing, either, that the umbrella has become the very foremost badge of modern civilization—the Urim and Thummim[5] of respectability. Its pregnant symbolism has taken its rise in the most natural manner. Consider, for a moment, when umbrellas were first introduced into this country, what manner of men would use them, and what class would adhere to the useless but ornamental cane. The first, without doubt, would be the hypochondriacal out of solicitude for their health, or the frugal out of care for their raiment; the second, it is equally plain, would include the fop, the fool and the Bobadil.[6] Any one acquainted with the growth of Society, and knowing out of what small seeds of cause are produced great revolutions, and wholly new conditions of intercourse, sees from this simple thought, how the carriage of an umbrella came to indicate frugality, judicious

THE PHILOSOPHY OF UMBRELLAS

regard for bodily welfare, and scorn for mere outward adornment; and, in one word, all those homely and solid virtues implied in the term *respectability*. Not that the umbrella's costliness has nothing to do with its great influence. Its possession, besides symbolizing (as we have already indicated) the change from wild Esau to plain Jacob dwelling in tents, implies a certain comfortable provision of fortune.[7] It is not every one that can expose twenty-six shillings' worth of property to so many chances of loss and theft. So strongly do we feel on this point indeed, that we are almost inclined to consider all who possess really well-conditioned umbrellas as worthy of the Franchise. They have a qualification standing in their lobbies—they carry a sufficient stake in the common-weal below their arm. One who bears with him an umbrella—such a complicated structure of whalebone, of silk, and of cane, that it becomes a very microcosm of modern industry—is necessarily a man of peace. A half-crown cane may be applied to an offender's head on very moderate provocation; but a six and twenty shilling silk is a possession too precious to be adventured in the shock of war.

These are but a few glances at how umbrellas (in the general) came to their present high estate. But the true Umbrella-Philosopher meets with far stranger applications as he goes about the streets.

Umbrellas, like faces, acquire a certain sympathy with the individual who carries them: indeed, they are far more capable of betraying his trust; for—whereas a face is given to us so far ready-made, and all our power over it is in frowning and laughing and grimacing, during the first three or four decades of life—each umbrella is selected from a whole shopful, as being most consonant to the purchaser's disposition. An undoubted power of diagnosis rests with the practised Umbrella-philosopher. O you who lisp, and amble, and change the fashion of your countenances—you, who conceal all these, how little do you think that you left a proof of your weakness openly in our umbrella-stand,—that even now, as you shake out the folds to meet the thickening snow, we read in its ivory handle the outward and visible sign of your snobbery, or from the exposed gingham of its cover detect, through coat and waistcoat, the hidden hypocrisy of the "*dickey*"![8] But alas! even the umbrella is no certain criterion. The falsity and the folly of the human race have degraded that graceful symbol to the ends of dishonesty; and while some umbrellas, from carelessness in selection, are not strikingly characteristic—(for it is only in what a man loves that he displays his real nature)—others, from certain prudential motives, are chosen directly opposite to the person's disposition. A mendacious umbrella is a sign of great moral degradation. Hypocrisy naturally shelters itself below a silk; while the fast youth goes to visit his religious friends armed with the decent and reputable gingham. May it not be said of the bearers of these inappropriate umbrellas that they go about the streets "with a lie in their right hand?"[9]

The kings of Siam, as we read, besides having a graduated social scale of umbrellas (which was a good thing), prevented the great bulk of their subjects from having any at all, which was as certainly a bad thing.[10] We should be sorry to believe that this Eastern legislator was a fool—(the idea of an aristocracy of umbrellas is too philosophic to have originated in a nobody); and we have accordingly taken exceeding pains to find out the reason of this harsh restriction. We think we have succeeded; but while admiring the principle at which he aimed, and while cordially recognizing in the Siamese potentate the only man before ourselves who had taken a real grasp of the umbrella, we must be allowed to point out how unphilosophically the great man acted in this particular. His object, plainly, was to prevent any unworthy persons from bearing the sacred symbol of domestic virtues. We cannot excuse his limiting these virtues to the circle of his court. We must only remember that such was the feeling of the age in which he lived. Liberalism had not yet raised the war-cry of the working classes. But here was his mistake,—it was a needless regulation. Except in a very few cases of hypocrisy joined to powerful intellect, men, not by nature *umbrellarians*, have tried again and again to become so by art, and yet have failed—have expended their patrimony in the purchase of umbrella after umbrella, and yet have systematically lost them—and have finally, with contrite spirits and shrunken purses, given up their vain struggle and relied on theft and borrowing for the remainder of their lives. This is the most remarkable fact that we have had occasion to notice; and yet we challenge the candid reader to call it in question. Now, as there cannot be any *moral selection* in a mere dead piece of furniture,—as the umbrella cannot be supposed to have an affinity for individual men, equal and reciprocal to that which men certainly feel toward individual umbrellas—we took the trouble of consulting a scientific friend,[11] as to whether there was any possible physical explanation of the phenomenon. He was unable to supply a plausible theory, or even hypothesis; but we extract from his letter, the following interesting passage relative to the physical peculiarities of umbrellas:—"Not the least important and by far the most curious property of the umbrella is the energy which it displays in affecting the atmospheric strata. There is no fact in meteorology better established—indeed it is almost the only one on which meteorologists are agreed—than that the carriage of an umbrella produces dessication of the air; while, if it be left at home, aqueous vapour is largely produced, and is soon deposited in the form of rain. No theory," my friend continues, "competent to explain this hygrometric law, has yet been given (as far as I am aware) by Herschel, Dove, Glaisher, Tait, Buchan,[12] or any other writer; nor do I pretend to supply the defect. I venture, however, to throw out the conjecture that it will be ultimately found to belong to the same class of natural laws, as that, agreeable to which a slice of toast always descends with the buttered surface downwards."

But it is time to draw to a close. We could expatiate much longer upon this topic; but want of space constrains us to leave unfinished these few desultory remarks—slender contributions towards a subject, which has fallen sadly backward, and which, we grieve to say, was better understood by the King of Siam in 1686, than by all the philosophers of to-day. If, however, we have awakened in any rational mind an interest in the symbolism of umbrellas,—in any generous heart a more complete sympathy with the dumb companion of his daily walk,—or in any grasping spirit, a pure notion of respectability strong enough to make him expend his six and twenty shillings—we shall have deserved well of the world, to say nothing of the many industrious persons employed in the manufacture of the article.

Stevenson's note: "This paper was written in collaboration with James Walter Ferrier,[13] and if reprinted this is to be stated, though his principal collaboration was to lie back in an easy-chair and laugh."

Notes

1 The eleventh astrological sign of the zodiac, meaning water-bearer and represented by Ganymede—cupbearer to the gods—pouring water from a jug.

2 The highest civil and military French order of merit, established by Napoleon in 1802.

3 The protagonist of Daniel Defoe's *Robinson Crusoe* (1719) is shipwrecked on a deserted island for 28 years.

4 Island group off the coast of Chile where marooned sailor Alexander Selkirk lived from 1704 to 1708, which may have inspired Defoe's novel. The island is now called Robinson Crusoe.

5 Sacred divination stones in the breastplate of the High Priest of the Biblical Israelites.

6 A pretentious braggart named for the character in Ben Jonson's play *Every Man in His Humour* (1598).

7 The biblical sons of Rebecca and Isaac. Esau, a hunter, gives his birthright to his tent-dwelling brother Jacob in exchange for pottage or stew (Genesis 25).

8 A detachable shirt front worn by a man as part of formal evening dress.

9 Matthew Henry and Thomas Scott, *A Commentary Upon the Holy Bible* (1835, 105). "Their Right Hand Is A Right Hand of Falsehood" (Psalms 144:8).

10 Only the elite of Siam (Thailand) were reportedly permitted to use an umbrella; the king's nine-tiered umbrella was sacred royal regalia.

11 Stevenson's father (*Letters* 8.308).

12 Astronomer William Herschel (1738–1822), physicist and meteorologist Heinrich Wilhelm Dove (1803–1879), aeronaut and astronomer James Glaisher (1809–1903), physicist and pioneer in thermodynamics Peter Tait (1831–1901), and meteorologist, oceanographer, and botanist Alexander Buchan (1829–1907).

13 James Walter Ferrier (1850–1883). n. 16, p. 142.

62

THE MODERN STUDENT
CONSIDERED GENERALLY

We have now reached the difficult portion of our task. *Mr Tatler*, for all that we care, may have been as virulent as he liked about the students of a former day;[1] but for the iron to touch our sacred selves—for a brother of the Guild to betray its most privy infirmities—let such a Judas look to himself as he passes on his way to the Scots Law or the Diagnostic,[2] below the solitary lamp at the corner of the dark quadrangle. We confess that this idea alarms us. We enter a protest. We bind ourselves over verbally to keep the peace. We hope, moreover, that having thus made you secret to our misgivings, you will excuse us if we be dull, and set that down to caution which you might before have charged to the account of stupidity.

The natural tendency of civilization is to obliterate those distinctions which are the best salt of life. All the fine old professional flavour in language has evaporated. Your very grave-digger has forgotten his avocation in his electorship, and would quibble on the Franchise over Ophelia's grave,[3] instead of more appropriately discussing the duration of bodies under ground. From this tendency—from this gradual attrition of life, in which everything pointed and characteristic is being rubbed down, till the whole world begins to slip between our fingers in smooth undistinguishable sands—from this, we say, it follows that we must not attempt to join *Mr Tatler* in his simple division of students into *Law*, *Divinity*, and *Medical*. Now-a-days, the Faculties may shake hands over their follies; and, like Mrs Frail and Mrs Foresight (in *Love for Love*) they may stand in the doors of opposite classrooms, crying: "Sister, Sister—Sister everyway!"[4] A few restrictions, indeed, remain to influence the followers of individual branches of study. The *Divinity*, for example, must be an avowed believer; and as this, in the present day, is unhappily considered by many as a confession of weakness, he is fain to choose one of two ways of gilding the distasteful orthodox bolus. Some swallow it in a thin jelly of metaphysics; for it is even a credit to believe in God on the evidence of some crack-jaw[5] philosopher, although it is a decided slur to believe in Him on His own authority. Others again (and this we think the worst method) finding German grammar somewhat dry a morsel,[6] run their own little heresy as a proof of independence; and deny one of the cardinal doctrines that they may hold the others without being laughed at.

450

Besides, however, such influences as these, there is little more distinction between the faculties than the traditionary ideal, handed down through a long sequence of students and getting rounder and more featureless at each successive session. The plague of uniformity has descended on the College. Students (and indeed all sorts and conditions of men) now require their faculty and character hung round their neck on a placard, like the scenes in Shakespeare's Theatre. And in the midst of all this weary sameness, not the least common feature, is the gravity of every face. No more does the merry medical run eagerly, in the clear winter morning, up the rugged sides of Arthur's Seat,[7] and hear the church-bells begin and thicken and die away below him among the gathered smoke of the city. He will not break Sunday to so little purpose. He no longer finds pleasure in the mere output of his surplus energy. He husbands his strength, and lays out walks, and reading, and amusement with deep consideration, so that he may get as much work and pleasure out of his body as he can, and waste none of his energy on mere impulse, or such flat enjoyment as an excursion in the country.

See the quadrangle in the interregnum of classes, in those two or three minutes when it is full of passing students, and we think you will admit that, if we have not made it "an habitation of dragons," we have at least transformed it into "a court for owls."[8] Solemnity broods heavily over the enclosure; and wherever you seek it, you will find a dearth of merriment, and absence of real youthful enjoyment. You might as well try "To move wild laughter in the throat of death," as to excite any healthy stir among the bulk of this staid company.[9]

The studious congregate about the doors of the different classes, debating the matter of the lecture, or comparing note-books. A reserved rivalry sunders them. Here are some deep in Greek particles: there, others are already inhabitants of that land

> Where entity and quiddity,
> Like ghosts of defunct bodies fly–
> Where Truth in person does appear
> Like words congealed in northern air.[10]

But none of them seem to find any relish for their studies—no pedantic love of this subject or that lights up their eyes—science and learning are only means for a livelihood, which they have considerately embraced and which they solemnly pursue. "Labour's pale priests," their lips seem incapable of laughter, except in the way of politic recognition of professional wit. The stains of ink are chronic on their meagre fingers. They walk like Saul among the asses.[11]

The dandies are not less subdued. In 1824 there was a noisy dapper dandyism abroad. Vulgar, as we should now think, but yet genial—a matter of white greatcoats and loud voices—strangely different from the stately foppery that is rife at present. These men are out of their element in the quadrangle. Even the small remains of boisterous humour, which still clings to any collection of young men, jars painfully on their morbid sensibilities; and they beat a hasty retreat to resume their perfunctory march along Princes Street. Flirtation is to them a great social duty, a painful obligation, which they perform on every occasion in the same chill official manner, and with the same common-place advances, the same dogged observance of traditional behaviour. The shape of their raiment is a burden almost greater than they can bear, and they halt in their walk to preserve the due adjustment of their trouser knees, till one would fancy he had mixed in a procession of Jacobs.[12] We speak, of course, for ourselves; but we would as soon associate with a herd of sprightly apes as with these gloomy modern beaux. Alas, that our Mirabels, our Valentines, even our Brummels,[13] should have left their mantle upon nothing more amusing!

Nor are the fast men less constrained. Solemnity even in dissipation is the order of the day; and they go to the devil with a perverse seriousness, a systematic rationalism of wickedness that would have surprised the simpler sinners of old. Some of these men whom we see gravely conversing on the steps, have but a slender acquaintance with each other. Their intercourse consists principally of mutual bulletins of depravity; and, week after week, as they meet, they reckon up their items of transgression, and give an abstract of their downward progress for approval and encouragement. These folk form a free-masonry of their own. An oath is the shibboleth of their sinister fellowship. Once they hear a man swear, it is wonderful how their tongues loosen and their bashful spirits take enlargement, under the consciousness of brotherhood. There is no folly, no pardoning warmth of temper about them: they are as steady going and systematic in their own way as the studious in theirs.

Not that we are without merry men. No. We shall not be ungrateful to those, whose grimaces, whose ironical laughter, whose active feet in the "*College Anthem*" have beguiled so many weary hours and added a pleasant variety to the strain of close attention. But, even these, are too evidently professional in their antics. They go about cogitating puns and inventing tricks. It is their avocation, Hal.[14] They are the gratuitous jesters of the class-room; and, like the clown when he leaves the stage, their merriment too often sinks as the bell rings the hour of liberty, and they pass forth by the Post-Office, grave and sedate, and meditating fresh gambols for the morrow.

This is the impression left on the mind of any observing student by too many of his fellows. They seem all frigid old men; and one pauses to think how such an unnatural state of matters is produced. We feel inclined to blame for it the unfortunate absence of *University feeling*, which is so marked a characteristic of our Edinburgh students. Academical interests are so few and far between—students, as students, have so little in common, except a peevish rivalry—there is such an entire want of broad college sympathies and ordinary college friendships, that we fancy no University in the kingdom is in so poor a plight. Our system is full of anomalies. A who cut B, whilst he was the shabby student, curries sedulously up to him and cudgels his memory for anecdotes about him, when he becomes the great so-and-so. Let there be an end of this shy, proud reserve on the one hand and this shuddering fine-ladyism on the other; and we think we shall find both ourselves and the College bettered. Let it be a sufficient reason for intercourse, that two men sit together on the same benches. Let the great A be held excused for nodding to the shabby B in Princes Street, if he can say, "That fellow is a student." Once this could be brought about, we think you would find the whole heart of the University beat faster. We think you would find a fusion among the students, a growth of common feelings, an increasing sympathy between class and class, whose influence (in such a heterogeneous company as ours) might be of incalculable value in all branches of politics and social progress. It would do more than this. If we could find some method of making the University a real mother to her sons—something beyond a building full of class-rooms, a senatus[15] and a lottery of somewhat shabby prizes—we should strike a death blow at the constrained and unnatural attitude of our Society. At present we are not a united body but a loose gathering of individuals, whose inherent attraction is allowed to condense them into little knots and coteries. Our last snow-ball riot read us a plain lesson on our condition. There was no party-spirit—no unity of interests. A few, who were mischievously inclined, marched off to the College of Surgeons in a pretentious file; but even before they reached their destination, the feeble inspiration had died out in many, and their numbers were sadly thinned. Some followed strange gods in the direction of Drummond Street; and others slunk back to meek good-boyism at the feet of the Professors. The same is visible in better things. As you send a man to an English University that he may have his prejudices rubbed off, you might send him to Edinburgh that he may have them engrained—rendered indelible—fostered by sympathy into living principles of his spirit. And the reason of it is quite plain. From this absence of University feeling, it comes that a man's friendships are always the direct and immediate results of these very prejudices. A common weakness is the best master of ceremonies in our quadrangle: a mutual vice is the readiest introduction. The studious associate with the studious alone— the dandies with the dandies. There is nothing to force them to rub shoulders with the others; and so they grow day by day more wedded to their own original opinions and affections. They see through the same spectacles continually. All broad sentiments, all real Catholic humanity expires; and the mind gets gradually stiffened into one position—becomes so habituated to a contracted atmosphere, that it shudders and withers under the least draught of the free air that circulates in the general field of mankind.

Specialism in Society then, is, we think, one cause of our present state. Specialism in study is another. We doubt whether this has ever been a good thing since the world began; but we are sure it is much worse now than it was. Formerly, when a man became a specialist, it was out of affection for his subject. With a somewhat grand devotion, he left all the world of Science, to follow his true love; and he contrived to find that strange pedantic interest which inspired the man, who

Settled *Hoti's* business—let it be—
Properly based *Oun*—
Gave us the Doctrine of the enclitic *De*,
Dead from the waist down.[16]

Now-a-days it is quite different. Our pedantry wants even the saving clause of Enthusiasm. The election is now matter of necessity and not of choice. Knowledge is now too broad a field for your Jack-of-all-Trades; and from beautifully utilitarian reasons, he makes his choice, draws his pen through a dozen branches of study, and behold—John the Specialist. That this is the way to be wealthy, we shall not deny; but we hold that it is *not* the way to be healthy or wise.[17] The whole mind becomes narrowed and circumscribed to one "punctual spot"[18] of knowledge. A rank unhealthy soil breeds an harvest of prejudices. Feeling himself above others in his one little branch—in the classification of toad-stools, or Carthaginian history—he waxes great in his own eyes and looks down on others. Having all his sympathies educated and fostered in one way, they die out in every other; and he is apt to remain a peevish, narrow, and intolerant bigot. Dilettante is now a term of reproach; but there is a certain form of dilletantism to which no one can object. It is this that we want among our students. We wish them to abandon no subject until they have seen and felt its merit—to act under a general interest in all branches of knowledge, not a commercial eagerness to excel in one.

In both these directions our sympathies are constipated. We are apostles of our own caste and our own subject of study, instead of being, as we should, true men and *loving* students. Of course both of these could be corrected by the students themselves; but this is nothing to the purpose: it is more important to ask whether the Senatus or the body of alumni could do nothing toward the growth of better feeling and wider sentiments. Perhaps, in another paper, we may say something upon this head.

One other word, however, before we have done. What shall we be when we grow really old? Of yore, a man was thought to lay on restrictions and acquire new dead-weight of mournful experience with every year, till he looked back on his youth as the very summer of impulse and freedom. We please ourselves with thinking that it can not be so with us. We would fain hope that, as we have begun in one way, we may end in another; and that when we *are* in fact the octogenarians that we *seem* at present, there shall be no merrier men on earth. It is pleasant to picture us, sunning ourselves in Princes Street of a morning, or chirping over our evening cups, with all the merriment that we wanted in youth.

Notes

1 "The Modern Student Considered Generally," published in the *Edinburgh University Magazine*, Feb. 1871, followed Stevenson's "Edinburgh Students in 1824" in the magazine's inaugural issue the previous month. The earlier article compares the new magazine with an older college magazine: *Lapsus Linguae; or, the College Tatler*, which ran for three months in 1824.

2 Originally established as the Dialectic Society in 1787 and reconstituted in 1816, the Diagnostic Society is Edinburgh's oldest society and the UK's first debating society. Scots Law was Stevenson's course of study.

3 Shakespeare, *Hamlet* 5.1.

4 Mrs. Frail's words just before reconciling with her sister Mrs. Foresight after a fight involving hairpins in William Congreve's 1695 comedy *Love for Love* (2.9).

5 Difficult to pronounce.

6 A reference to the "higher criticism" of nineteenth-century German scholars such as David Friedrich Strauss (1808–1874) and Ludwig Feuerbach (1804–1872), whose historical and literary analysis of the Bible undermined its status as divine revelation.

7 A hill just east of the center of Edinburgh.

8 Isaiah 34:13.

9 Shakespeare, *Love's Labour's Lost* 5.2.832.

10 A paraphrase of the satirical description of Sir Hudibras's philosophical skill in Samuel Butler's 1684 mock-heroic epic *Hudibras* (1.1.145–148).

11 1 Samuel 9.

12 The funeral procession of Israel (Jacob) went from Egypt to Canaan (Genesis 50).

13 Mirabel, the romantic protagonist of William Congreve's comedy *The Way of the World* (1700); Valentine, romantic hero of Shakespeare's *The Two Gentlemen of Verona*; George Bryan "Beau" Brummell (1778–1840), a fashion icon of Regency England.

14 2 Henry IV.1.2.90.

15 *Senatus academicus*: the university's governing body.

16 Robert Browning, "A Grammarian's Funeral" (129–132). *Hoti, Oun, De*: Greek particles meaning "that," "then," and "towards" respectively. The "enclitic *De*" is a suffix-forming particle.

17 "Early to bed and early to rise, makes a man healthy, wealthy, and wise" (Benjamin Franklin, *Poor Richard's Almanac*).

18 John Milton, *Paradise Lost* 8.23.

63

DEBATING SOCIETIES

A debating society[1] is at first somewhat of a disappointment. You do not often find the youthful Demosthenes chewing his pebbles in the same room with you;[2] or, even if you do, you will probably think the performance little to be admired. As a general rule, the members speak shamefully ill. The subjects of debate are heavy; and so are the fines. The Ballot Question—oldest of dialectic nightmares—is often found astride of a somnolent sederunt. The Greeks and Romans, too, are reserved as sort of *general utility* men, to do all the dirty work of illustration; and they fill as many functions as the famous water-fall scene at the *Princess's*,[3] which I found doing duty on one evening as a gorge in Peru, a haunt of German robbers, and a peaceful vale in the Scottish borders. There is a sad absence of striking argument or real lively discussion. Indeed you feel a growing contempt for your fellow members; and it is not until you rise yourself to hawk and hesitate and sit shamefully down again, amid eleemosynary applause, that you begin to find your level and value others rightly. Even then, even when failure has damped your critical ardour, you will see many things to be laughed at in the deportment of your rivals.

   Most laughable, perhaps, are your indefatigable strivers after eloquence. They are of those who "pursue with eagerness the phantoms of hope," and who, since they expect "that the deficiencies of last sentence will be supplied by the next," have been recommended by Dr Samuel Johnson to "attend to *The History of Rasselas, Prince of Abyssinia*."[4] They are characterized by an hectic hopefulness. Nothing damps them. They rise from the ruins of one abortive sentence, to launch forth into another with unabated vigour. They have all the manner of an orator. From the tone of their voice, you would expect a splendid period—and lo! a string of broken-backed, disjointed clauses, eked out with stammerings and throat clearings. They possess the art (learned from the pulpit) of rounding an uneuphonious sentence by dwelling on a single syllable—of striking a balance in a top-heavy period, by lengthening out a word into a melancholy quaver. Withal, they never cease to hope. Even at last, even when they have exhausted all their ideas, even after the would-be peroration has finally refused to perorate, they remain upon their feet with their mouths open, waiting for some further inspiration, like Chaucer's widow's son in the dung-hole, after "His throat was kit unto the nekké bone," in vain expectation of the seed that was to be laid upon his tongue, and give him renewed and clearer utterance.[5]

These men may have something to say, if they could only say it—indeed they generally have; but the next class are people who, having nothing to say, are cursed with a facility and an unhappy command of words, that makes them the prime nuisances of the society they affect. They try to cover their absence of matter, by an unwholesome vitality of delivery. They look triumphantly round the room, as if courting applause, after a torrent of diluted truism. They talk in a circle, harping on the same dull round of argument and returning again and again to the same remark, with the same sprightliness, the same irritating appearance of novelty.

After this set, any one is tolerable; so we shall merely hint at a few other varieties. There is your man, who is pre-eminently conscientious, whose face beams with sincerity as he opens on the negative, and who votes on the affirmative at the end, looking round the room with an air of chastened pride. There is also the irrelevant speaker, who rises, emits a joke or two, and then sits down again, without ever attempting to tackle the subject of debate. Again we have men who ride pick a-back[6] on their family reputation, or, if their family have none, identify themselves with some well known statesman, use his opinions and lend him their patronage on all occasions. This is a dangerous plan; and serves oftener, I am afraid, to point a difference, than to adorn a speech.

But alas! a striking failure may be reached, without tempting Providence by any of these ambitious tricks. Our own stature will be found high enough for shame. The success of three simple sentences lures us into a fatal parenthesis in the fourth, from whose shut brackets we may never disentangle the thread of our discourse. A momentary flush tempts us into a quotation; and we may be left helpless in the middle of one of Pope's couplets, a white film gathering before our eyes, and our kind friends charitably trying to cover our disgrace by a feeble round of applause. *Amis lecteurs,*[7] this is a painful topic. It is possible that we too, we the "potent grave and reverend"[8] editor, may have suffered these things and drunk as deep as any of the cup of shameful failure. Let us dwell no longer on so delicate a subject.

In spite, however, of these disagreeables, I should recommend any student to suffer them with Spartan courage, as the benefits he receives should repay him an hundred fold for them all. The life of the debating society is a handy antidote to the life of the class-room and quadrangle. Nothing could be conceived more excellent as a weapon against many of those *peccant humours* that we have been railing against in the Jeremiad of our last *College Paper,*—particularly in the field of intellect.[9] It is a sad sight to see our heather-scented students, our boys of seventeen, coming up to College with determined views—*roués* in speculation—having gaged the vanity of philosophy or learned to shun it as the middle-man of heresy—a company of determined, deliberate opinionists, not to be moved by all the sleights of logic. What have such men to do with study? If their minds are made up irrevocably, why burn the "studious lamp"[10] in search of further confirmation?

Every set opinion I hear a student deliver I feel a certain lowering of my regard. He who studies, he who is yet employed in groping for his premises, should keep his mind fluent and sensitive, keen to mark flaws and willing to surrender untenable positions. He should keep himself teachable, or cease the expensive farce of being taught. It is to further this docile spirit that we desire to press the claims of debating societies. It is as a means of melting down this museum of premature petrifactions into living and impressionable soul that we insist on their utility. If we could once prevail on our students to feel no shame in avowing an uncertain attitude toward any subject, if we could teach them that it was unnecessary for every lad to have his *opinionette* on every topic, we should have gone a far way towards bracing the intellectual tone of the coming race of thinkers; and this it is which debating societies are so well fitted to perform.

We there meet people of every shade of opinion, and make friends with them. We are taught to rail against a man the whole session through, and then hob-a-nob with him at the concluding entertainment. We find men of talent far exceeding our own, whose conclusions are widely different from ours; and we are thus taught to distrust ourselves. But the best means of all toward catholicity, is that wholesome rule which some folk are most inclined to condemn,—I mean the law of *obliged speeches*. Your senior member commands; and you must take the affirmative or the negative, just as suits his best convenience. This tends to the most perfect liberality. It is no good hearing the arguments of an opponent; for in good verity, you rarely follow them; and even if you do take the trouble to listen, it is merely in a captious search for weaknesses. This is proved, I fear, in every debate; when you hear each speaker arguing out his own prepared *specialité* (he never intended speaking, of course, until some remarks of, etc.)—arguing out, I say, his own *coached-up* subject without the least attention to what has gone before, as utterly at sea about the drift of his adversary's speech as Panurge when he argued with Thaumaste,[11] and merely linking his own prelection to the last by a few flippant criticisms. Now as the rule stands, you are saddled with the side you disapprove, and so you are forced, by regard for your own fame, to argue out—to feel with— to elaborate completely—the case as it stands against yourself; and what a fund of wisdom do you not turn up in this idle digging of the vineyard! How many new difficulties take form before your eyes—how many superannuated arguments cripple finally into limbo, under the glance of your enforced eclecticism!

Nor is this the only merit of Debating Societies. They tend also to foster taste, and to promote friendship between University men. This last, as we have had occasion before to say, is the great requirement of our student life; and it will therefore be no waste of time if we devote a paragraph to this subject in its connexion with Debating Societies. At present they partake too much of the nature of a *clique*. Friends propose friends, and mutual friends second them; until the society degenerates into a sort of family party. You may confirm old acquaintances, but you can rarely make new ones. You find yourself in the atmosphere of your own daily intercourse. Now, this is an unfortunate circumstance which it seems to me might readily be rectified. Our Principal has shown himself so friendly towards all college improvements, that I cherish the hope of seeing shortly realized a certain suggestion, which is not a new one with me, and which must often have been proposed and canvassed heretofore,—I mean, a real *University Debating Society*, patronized by the Senatus, presided over by the Professors, to which every one might gain ready admittance on sight of his matriculation ticket, where it would be a favour and not a necessity to speak, and where the obscure student might have another object for attendance besides the mere desire to save his fines: to wit, the chance of drawing on himself the favourable consideration of his teachers. This would be merely following in the good tendency, which has been so noticeable during all this session, to increase and multiply student societies and clubs of every sort. Nor would it be a matter of much difficulty. The united societies would form a nucleus: one of the class-rooms at first, and perhaps afterward the great hall above the Library, might be the place of meeting. There would be no want of attendance or enthusiasm, I am sure; for it is a very different thing to speak under the bushel of a private club on the one hand, and on the other, in a public place, where a happy period or a subtle argument may do the speaker permanent service in after life. Such a club might end, perhaps, by rivaling the "Union" at Cambridge or the "Union" at Oxford.

Notes

1 The Speculative Society is a debate club of students at the University of Edinburgh founded in 1764. Members were elected, paid an annual subscription, and subjected to fines for absence and lateness. Stevenson was elected to the Society on 16 Feb. 1869.

2 Demosthenes (384–322 BC), a Greek politician and orator who reportedly practiced speaking with pebbles in his mouth to overcome his "inarticulate and stammering pronunciation" (Plutarch, *Parallel Lives*).

3 Princess's Theatre in Oxford Street, London (1836–1902), known for lavish stage productions.

4 Stevenson paraphrases the opening sentence of Johnson's *Rasselas* (1759), a philosophical tale following Rasselas's unsuccessful pursuit of happiness.

5 Geoffrey Chaucer, "The Prioress's Tale," *The Canterbury Tales*.

6 Piggyback.

7 Friendly readers (French).

8 *Othello* 1.3.76.

9 See "The Modern Student Considered Generally" (p. 450).

10 *The Satires of Lodovico Ariosto* 7.52.

11 François Rabelais's *Pantagruel* (1532) depicts a farcical debate between the scholar Thaumaste and the trickster Panurge conducted entirely with gestures and inarticulate sounds.

459

64

THE PHILOSOPHY OF
NOMENCLATURE

"How many Cæsars and Pompeys, by mere inspiration of the names, have been rendered worthy of them? And how many are there, who might have done exceeding well in the world, had not their characters and spirits been totally depressed and Nicodemus'd into nothing?"

– Tristram Shandy, vol. i. chap. xix.

Such were the views of the late Walter Shandy, Esq., Turkey Merchant.[1] To the best of my belief, Mr Shandy is the first who fairly pointed out the incalculable influence of nomenclature upon the whole life—who seems first to have recognised the one child, happy in an heroic appellation, soaring upward on the wings of Fortune, and the other, like the dead sailor in his shotted hammock, haled down by sheer weight of name, into the abysses of social failure. Solomon possibly had his eye on some such theory, when he said that "a good name is better than precious ointment;"[2] and perhaps we may trace a similar spirit in the compilers of the English Catechism and the affectionate interest with which they linger round the Catechumen's name at the very threshold of their work.[3] But, be these as they may, I think no one can censure me, for appending, in pursuance of the expressed wish of his son, the Turkey merchant's name to his system, and announcing without further preface, a short epitome of the *Shandean Philosophy of Nomenclature*.

To begin, then, the influence of our name makes itself felt from the very cradle. As a schoolboy I remember the pride with which I hailed Robin Hood, Robert Bruce, and *Robert Le Diable*[4], as my name fellows; and the feeling of sore disappointment that fell on my heart when I found a freebooter[5] or a general who did not share with me a single one of my numerous praenomena.[6] Look at the delight with which two children find they have the same name—they are friends from that moment forth—they have a bond of union stronger than exchange of nuts and sweetmeats. This feeling, I own, wears off in later life—our names lose their freshness and interest—become trite and indifferent. But this, dear reader, is merely one of the sad effects of those "shades of the prison house"[7] which come gradually betwixt us and nature with advancing years: it affords no weapon against the philosophy of names.

In after life, although we fail to trace its working, that name which careless god-fathers lightly applied to your unconscious infancy, will have been moulding your character, and influencing with irresistible power the whole course of your earthly fortunes. But the last name, overlooked by Mr Shandy, is no whit less important as a condition of success. Family names, we must recollect, are but inherited nicknames; and if the *soubriquet* were applicable to the ancestor, it is most likely applicable to the descendant also. You would not expect to find Mr M'Phun acting as a mute, or Mr M'Lumpha excelling as a professor of dancing. Therefore, in what follows we shall consider names, independent of whether they are first or last. And to begin with, look what a pull *Cromwell*[8] had over *Pym*[9]—the one name full of a resonant imperialism; the other, mean, pettifogging, and unheroic to a degree. Who would expect eloquence from *Pym*—who would read poems by *Pym*—who would bow to the opinion of *Pym*? He might have been a dentist, but he should never have aspired to be a statesman. I can only wonder that he succeeded as he did. Pym and Habakkuk[10] stand first upon the roll of men who have triumphed by sheer force of genius, over the most unfavourable appellations; but even these have suffered; and, had they been more fitly named—the one might have been Lord Protector, and the other have shared the laurels with Isaiah. In this matter we must not forget that all our great poets have borne great names. Chaucer, Spenser, Shakespeare, Milton, Pope, Wordsworth, Shelley—what a constellation of lordly words! Not a single commonplace name among them—not a Brown, not a Jones, not a Robinson—they are all names that one would stop and look at on a door-plate. Now, imagine if *Pepys* had tried to clamber somehow into the inclosure of poetry, what a blot would that word have made upon the list! The thing was impossible. In the first place, a certain natural consciousness that men have, would have held him down to the level of his name—would have prevented him from rising above the Pepsine standard, and so haply withheld him altogether from attempting verse. Next, the booksellers would refuse to publish, and the world to read them, on the mere evidence of the fatal appellation. And now, before I close this section, I must say one word as to *punnable* names—names that stand alone—that have a significance and life apart from him that bears them. These are the bitterest of all. One friend of mine goes bowed and humbled through life, under the weight of this misfortune; for it is an awful thing when a man's name is a joke—when he can not be mentioned without exciting merriment, and when even the intimation of his death bids fair to carry laughter into many a home.

So much for people who are badly named. Now for people who are *too well* named, who go top-heavy from the font, who are baptized into a false position, and find themselves beginning life eclipsed under the fame of some of the great ones of the past. A man, for instance, called William Shakespeare, could never dare to write plays. He is thrown into too tumbling an apposition with the author of *Hamlet*. His own name coming after is such an anti-climax. "The Plays of William

Shakespeare?" says the reader—"O no! The plays of William Shakespeare *Cockerill*," and he throws the book aside. In wise pursuance of such views, Mr John Milton Hengler, who not long since delighted us in this favoured town, has never attempted to write an epic, but has chosen a new path, and has excelled upon the tight-rope. A marked example of triumph over this, is the case of Mr Dante Gabriel Rossetti.[11] On the face of the matter, I should have advised him to imitate the pleasing modesty of the last-named gentleman, and confine his ambition to the sawdust. But Mr Rossetti has triumphed. He has even dared to translate from his mighty name-father; and the voice of fame supports him in his boldness.

Dear readers, one might write a year upon this matter. A lifetime of comparison and research could scarce suffice for its elucidation. So here, if it please you, we shall let it rest. Slight as these notes have been, I would that the great founder of the system had been alive to see them—how he had warmed and brightened—how his persuasive eloquence would have fallen on the ears of Toby; and what a letter of praise and sympathy would not the editor have received before the month was out.[12] Alas, the thing was not to be. Walter Shandy died and was duly buried, while yet his theory lay forgotten and neglected by his fellow-countrymen. But, reader, the day will come, I hope, when a paternal government will stamp out, as seeds of national weakness, all depressing patronymics, and when Godfathers and Godmothers will soberly and earnestly debate the interest of the nameless one, and not rush blindfold to the Christening. In these days, there shall be written a "God-father's assistant," in shape of a dictionary of names, with their concomitant virtues and vices; and this book shall be scattered broad-cast through the land, and shall be on the table of every one eligible for God-fathership, until such a thing as a vicious or untoward appellation shall have ceased from off the face of the earth.

Notes

1 The father of the narrator and title character in Laurence Sterne's *Tristram Shandy* (1767) considered Tristram the worst of all possible names. He intended to name his ill-favored son Trismegistus after the purported author of the *Hermetic Corpus*, founder of arithmetic, geometry, astronomy, and letters, "the greatest . . . of all earthly beings," but Susannah the chambermaid bungles the name in her instructions to the curate, and he is christened Tristram.

2 Ecclesiastes 7:1.

3 The first two questions in the Catechism of the Church of England are "What is your name?" and "Who gave you that name?"

4 Robert Le Diable, knight and protagonist of the 1831 French opera by Giacomo Meyerbeer. One of Stevenson's closest lifelong friends was his cousin, Robert "Bob" Stevenson.

5 Pirate.

6 First personal name given to Roman children.

7 Wordsworth, "Ode: Intimations" (68).

8 Oliver Cromwell (1599–1658), British Lord Protector and leader of parliamentary forces in the Civil War.

9 John Pym (1583/84–1643), leader of Parliament's victory over Charles I in the English Civil Wars.

10 Minor Old Testament prophet whose poetic writings form the short book bearing his name.
11 Dante Gabriel Rossetti (1828–1882), English painter and poet named for Dante Alighieri (1265–1321) author of the classic Italian epic *The Divine Comedy*. Rossetti translated some of Dante's poetry in *The Early Italian Poets* (1861). Rossetti was a leading member of the Pre-Raphaelite Brotherhood aesthetic group. Inspired and championed by the eminent art critic by John Ruskin (1819–1900), they valued representing nature with vividness and realism.
12 Toby is Tristram Shandy's uncle in Sterne's novel.

65

COCKERMOUTH AND KESWICK[1]

Very much as a painter half-closes his eyes so that some salient unity may disengage itself from among the crowd of details and what he sees may thus form itself into a whole; very much on the same principle, I may say, I allow a considerable lapse of time to intervene between any of my little journeyings and the attempt to chronicle them. I cannot describe a thing that is before me at the moment, or that has been before me only a very little while before; I must allow my recollections to get thoroughly strained free from all chaff till nothing be except the pure gold; I allow my memory to choose out what is truly memorable by a process of natural selection and I piously believe that, in this way, I ensure the Survival of the Fittest.[2] If I make notes for future use, or if I am obliged to write letters during the course of my little excursion, I so interfere with the process that I can never again find out what is worthy of being preserved, or what should be given in full length, what in torso, or what merely in profile. This process of incubation may be unreasonably prolonged; and I am somewhat afraid that I have made this mistake with the present journey. Like a bad daguerreotype,[3] great part of it has been entirely lost; I can tell you nothing about the beginning and nothing about the end; but the doings of some fifty or sixty hours about the middle, remain quite distinct and definite, like a little patch of sunshine on a long, shadowy plain, or the one spot on an old picture that has been restored by the dexterous hand of the cleaner. I remember a tale of an old Scotch minister, called upon suddenly to preach, who had hastily snatched an old sermon out of his study and found himself in the pulpit before he noticed that the rats had been making free with his manuscript and eaten the first two or three pages away; he gravely explained to the congregation how he found himself situated; "and now," said he, "let us just begin where the rats have left off." I must follow the divine's example and take up the thread of my discourse, where it first distinctly issues from the limbo of forgetfulness.

Cockermouth

I was lighting my pipe, as I stepped out of the Inn at Cockermouth, and did not raise my head until I was fairly in the street. When I did so, it flashed upon me that I was in England; the evening sunlight lit up English houses, English faces, an English conformation of street; as it were, an English atmosphere blew against my face. There is nothing perhaps more puzzling (if one thing in Sociology can ever really be more unaccountable than another) than the great gulph that is set between England and Scotland; a gulf so easy in appearance, in reality so difficult, to traverse. Here are two people almost identical in blood; pent up together on one small island so that their intercourse (one would have thought) must be as close as that of prisoners who shared one cell of the Bastille;[4] the same in language and religion; and yet a few years of quarrelsome isolation—a mere forenoon's tiff, as one may call it, in comparison with the great historical cycles—has so separated their thoughts and ways, that not unions, nor mutual dangers, nor steamers, nor railways, nor all the King's horses and men,[5] seem able to obliterate the broad distinction. In the trituration of another century or so, the corners may disappear; but in the meantime, in the Year of Grace 1871, I was as much in a new country, as if I had been walking out of the Hotel St. Antoine at Antwerp. I felt a little thrill of pleasure at my heart, as I realised the change, and strolled away up the street with my hands behind my back, noting in a dull, sensual way, how foreign, and yet how friendly, were the slopes of the gables, and the colour of the tiles, and even the demeanour and voices of the gossips round about me.

Wandering in this aimless humour, I turned up a lane and found myself fol-lowing the course of the bright little river. I passed, first one and then another, and a third, several couples out lovemaking in the Spring evening; and a con-sequent feeling of loneliness was beginning to grow upon me, when I came to a dam across the river and a mill—a great, gaunt promontory of building, half on dry ground and half arched over the stream. The road here drew in its shoulders and crept through between the landward extremity of the mill and a little garden enclosure, with a small house and a large signboard within its privet-hedge. I was pleased to fancy this an inn and drew little etchings in fancy of a sanded parlour, and three-cornered spittoons, and a society of parochial gossips seated within over their churchwardens; but as I drew near the board displayed its superscription and I could read the name of Smethurst, and the designation of "Canadian Felt Hat Manufacturs." There was no more hope of evening fellowship, and I could only stroll on by the riverside, under the trees. The water was dappled with slanting sunshine, and dusted all over with a little mist of flying insects. There were some amorous ducks, also, whose love-making reminded me of what I had seen a little farther down. But the road grew sad, and I grew weary; and, as I was perpetually haunted with the terror of a return of the tic[6] that had been playing such ruin in my head a week ago, I turned and went back to the inn, and supper, and my bed.

The next morning at breakfast, I communicated to the smart waitress my inten-tion of continuing down the Coast and through Whitehaven to Furness; and, as I might have expected, I was instantly confronted by that last and most worrying form of interference, that chooses to introduce tradition and authority into the choice of a man's own pleasures. I can excuse a person combatting my religious or philosophical heresies, because them I have deliberately accepted and am ready to justify by present argument. But I do not seek to justify my pleasures; if I prefer tame scenery to grand—a little hot sunshine over lowland parks and woodlands to the war of the elements round the summit of Mont Blanc; or if I prefer a pipe of mild tobacco and the company of one or two chosen companions to a ball where I feel myself very hot, awkward and weary; I merely state these preferences as facts and do not seek to establish them as principles. This is not the general rule, however; and accordingly the waitress was shocked, as one might be at a heresy, to hear the route that I had sketched out for myself; everybody who came to Cockermouth for pleasure, it appeared, went on to Keswick. It was in vain that I put up a little plea for the liberty of the subject; it was in vain that I said I should prefer to go to Whitehaven. I was told that there was "nothing to see there"—that weary, hackneyed, old falsehood; and at last as the handmaiden began to look really concerned, I gave way, as men always do in such circumstances and agreed that I was to leave for Keswick by a train in the early evening.

An Evangelist

Cockermouth itself, on the same authority, was a place with "nothing to see"; nevertheless I saw a good deal and retain a pleasant, vague picture of the town and all its surroundings. I might have dodged happily enough all day about the main street and up to the castle and in and out of byeways; but the curious attraction that leads a person in a strange place to follow, day after day, the same round and to make set habits for himself in a week or ten days, led me half unconsciously up the same road that I had gone the evening before. When I came up to the hat manufactory, Smethurst himself was standing in the garden gate; he was brushing one Canadian felt hat, and several others had been put to await their turn one above the other on his own head; so that he looked something like the typical Jew old-clothesman.[7] As I drew near, he came sidling out of the doorway to accost me with so curious an expression on his face, that I instinctively prepared myself to apologise for some unwitting trespass. His first question rather confirmed me in this belief; for it was whether, or not, he had seen me going up this way, last night; and after having answered in the affirmative, I waited in some alarm for the rest of my indictment. But the good man's heart was full of peace; and he stood there brushing his hats and prattling on about fishing, and walking, and the pleasures of convalescence, in a bright, shallow stream that kept me pleased and interested, I could scarcely say how. As he went on, he warmed to his subject, and laid his hats aside to go along the waterside and show me where the large fish commonly lay, underneath an overhanging bank; and he was much disappointed, for my sake, that there were none visible just then. Then he wandered off onto another tack, and stood a great while out in the middle of a meadow in the hot sunshine, trying to make out that he had known me before or, if not me, some friend of mine; merely, I believe, out of a desire that we should feel more at our ease with one another. At last, he made a little speech to me, of which I wish I could recollect the very words; for they were so simple and unaffected that they put all the best writing and speaking to the blush; as it is, I can recall only the sense, and that perhaps imperfectly. He began by saying that he had little things in his past life that it gave him especial pleasure to recall, and that the faculty of receiving such sharp impressions had now died out in himself, but must at my age be still quite lively and active. Then he told me that he had a little raft afloat on the river above the dam, which he was going to lend to me; in order that I might be able to look back, in after years, upon having done so and get great pleasure from the recollection. Now I have a friend of my own, who will forego present enjoyments and suffer much present inconvenience, for the sake of manufacturing "a reminiscence" for himself;[8] but there was something singularly refined in this pleasure that the hat-maker found, in making reminiscences for others; surely no more simple or unselfish luxury can be imagined. After he had unmoored his little embarkation and seen me safely shoved off into mid-stream, he ran away back to his hats, with the air of a man who had just recollected that he had anything to do.

I did not stay very long on the raft; it ought to have been very nice punting about there in the cool shade of the trees or sitting moored to an overhanging root; but perhaps the very notion that I was bound in gratitude specially to enjoy my little cruise and cherish its recollection, turned the whole thing from a pleasure into duty. Be that as it may, there is no doubt that I soon wearied and came ashore again, and that it gives me more pleasure to recall the man himself and his simple, happy conversation, so full of gusto and sympathy, than anything possibly connected with his crank, insecure embarkation. In order to avoid seeing him (for I was not a little ashamed of myself for having failed to enjoy his treat sufficiently), I determined to continue up the river and, at all prices, to find some other way back into the town in time for dinner. As I went, I was thinking of Smethurst with admiration: a look into that man's mind was like a retrospect over the smiling champaign of his past life, and very different from the Sinai-Gorges[9] up which one looks for a terrified moment into the dark souls of many good, many wise and many prudent men. I cannot be very grateful to such men for their excellence and wisdom and prudence. I find myself facing as stoutly as I can a hard, combative existence, full of doubt, difficulties, defeats, disappointments and dangers; quite a hard enough life without their dark countenances at my elbow; so that what I want is a happy minded Smethurst placed here and there at ugly corners of my life's wayside, preaching his gospel of quiet and contentment.

Another

I was shortly to meet with an evangelist of another stamp. After I had forced my way through a gentleman's grounds, I came out on the high road and sat down to rest myself on a heap of stones at the top of a long hill with Cockermouth lying snugly at the bottom. An Irish beggar woman, with a beautiful little girl by her side, came up to ask for alms and gradually fell to telling me the little tragedy of her life. Her own sister, she told me, had seduced her husband from her after many years of married life; and the pair had fled, leaving her destitute, with the little girl upon her hands. She seemed quite hopeful and cheery and, though she was unaffectedly sorry for the loss of her husband's earnings, she made no pretence of despair at the loss of his affection; some day, she would meet the fugitives and the law would see her duly righted, and in the meantime the smallest contribution was gratefully received. While she was telling me all this, in the most matter of fact way, I had been noticing the approach of a tall man, with a high white hat and darkish clothes. He came up the hill at a rapid pace, and joined our little group with a sort of half-salutation. Turning at once to the woman, he asked her in a business-like way whether she had anything to do, whether she were a Catholic or a Protestant, whether she could read, and so forth; and then, after a few kind words and some sweeties to the child, he despatched the mother with some tracts about Biddy and the Priest,[10] and the Orangemen's Bible.[11] I was a little amused at his abrupt manner; for he was still a young man and had somewhat the air of a navy officer; but he tackled me with great solemnity. I could make fun of what he said, for I do not think it was very wise; but the subject does not appear to me just now in a jesting light; so I shall only say that he related to me his own conversion, which had been effected (as is very often the case) through the agency of a gig-accident, and that, after having examined me and diagnosed my case, he selected some suitable tracts from his repertory, gave them to me and, bidding me God speed, went on his way.

Last of Smethurst

That evening, I got into a third class carriage on my way for Keswick, and was followed almost immediately by a burly man in brown clothes. This fellow passenger was seemingly ill at ease; and kept continually putting his head out of the window and asking the bystanders if they saw him coming. At last, when the train was already in motion, there was a commotion on the platform and a way was left clear to our carriage door. He had arrived. In the hurry I could just see Smethurst, red and panting, thrust a couple of clay pipes into my companion's outstretched hand, and hear him crying his farewell after us as we slipped out of the station at an ever accelerating pace. I said something about its being a close run; and the broad man, already engaged in filling one of the pipes, assented and went on to tell me of his own stupidity in forgetting a necessary and of how his friend had good-naturedly gone down town, at the last moment to supply the omission. I mentioned that I had seen Mr. Smethurst already and that he had been very polite to me; and we fell into a discussion of the hatter's merits that lasted some time and left us quite good friends at its conclusion. The topic was productive of good will. We exchanged tobacco and talked about the season; and agreed at last that we should go to the same hotel at Keswick and sup in company. As he had some business in the town which would occupy him some hour or so, on our arrival, I was to improve the time and go down to the lake, that I might see a glimpse of the promised wonders.

The night had fallen already, when I reached the water-side at a place where many pleasure-boats are moored and ready for hire; and as I went along a stony path, between wood and water, a strong wind blew in gusts from the far end of the lake. The sky was covered with flying scud;[12] and, as this was ragged, there was quite a wild chase of shadow, and moon-glimpse over the surface of the shudder-ing water. I had to hold my hat on, and was growing rather tired and inclined to go back in disgust, when a little incident occurred to break the tedium. A sudden and violent squall of wind sundered the low underwood, and at the same time there came one of those brief discharges of moonlight which leaped into the opening thus made and showed me three girls in the prettiest flutter and disorder. It was as though they had sprung out of the ground. I accosted them very politely in my capacity of stranger and requested to be told the names of all manner of hills and woods and places that I did not wish to know; and we stood together for a while and had an amusing little talk. The wind, too, made himself of the party, brought the colour into their faces, and gave them enough to do to repress their drapery; and one of them, amid much giggling, had to pirouette round and round upon her toes (as girls do) when some specially strong gust had got the advantage over her. They were just high enough up in the social order, not to be afraid to speak to a gentleman; and just low enough, to feel a little tremor, a nervous consciousness of wrongdoing—of stolen waters, that gave a considerable zest to our most innocent interview.[13] They were as much discomposed and fluttered, indeed, as if I had been a wicked baron proposing to elope with the whole trio; but they showed no inclination to go away, and I had managed to get them off hills and waterfalls and onto more promising subjects, when a young man was descried coming along the path from the direction of Keswick. Now whether he was the young man of one of my friends, or the brother of one of them, or indeed the brother of all, I do not know; but they incontinently said that they must be going and went away up the path with friendly salutations. I need not say, that I found the lake and the moonlight rather dull after their departure, and speedily found my way back to potted herrings and whiskey and water in the commercial room with my late fel-low traveller. In the smoking room, there was a tall, dark man with a moustache, in an ulster coat, who had got the best place and was monopolising most of the talk; and, as I came in, a whisper came round to me from both sides, that this was the manager of a London theatre; the presence of such a man was a great event for Keswick and I must own that the manager showed himself equal to his position. He had a large fat pocket-book, from which he produced poem after poem, written on the backs of letters or hotel bills; and nothing could be more humourous than his recitation of these elegant extracts, except perhaps the anecdotes with which he varied the entertainment. Seeing I suppose something less countrified in my appearance than in most of the company, he singled me out to corroborate some statements as to the depravity and vice of the aristocracy, and when he went on to describe some gilded-saloon experiences, I am proud to say that he honoured my sagacity with one little covert wink before a second time appealing to me for confirmation. The wink was not thrown away; I went in up to the elbows with the manager, until I think that some of the glory of that great man settled by reflexion upon me and that I was as noticeably the second person in the smoking room as he was the first. For a young man, this was a position of some distinction, I think you will admit.

Notes

1 Neighboring towns in England's Lake District. Cockermouth is the birthplace of Romantic poet William Wordsworth (1770–1850). Stevenson visited in 1871 and composed this unfinished essay in July of 1873.
2 Natural selection: the central evolutionary theory of Charles Darwin's *On the Origin of Species* (1859). The phrase "survival of the fittest" first appeared in Herbert Spencer's *The Principles of Biology* (1863) and was later adopted by Darwin.
3 One of the earliest photographic processes employing an iodine-sensitized silvered plate and mercury vapor.
4 French state prison famously seized by revolutionaries on 14 July 1789.
5 A quotation from the English nursery rhyme "Humpty Dumpty," which figured memorably in Lewis Carroll's *Through the Looking-Glass* (1872) published a year earlier.
6 Short for *tic douloureux* (French) or "painful twitching": neuralgia characterized by spasmodic twitching of facial muscles.
7 Second-hand clothes dealer, stereotypically Jewish.
8 Charles Baxter (1848–1919), model for Charles Butler "who manufactures reminiscences" in Stevenson's story "The Edifying Letters of the Rutherford Family" (1876–1877). *An Old Song and . . . Edifying Letters of the Rutherford Family* (1982), ed. Roger G. Swearingen, 97.
9 Mt. Sinai: a steep, deeply-gorged granite peak in Egypt where God delivered the Ten Commandments to Moses (Exodus 20).
10 Bridget Ellen "Biddy" Early (1798–1872), Irish herbalist, healer, and clairvoyant. Local Catholic priests accused her of witchcraft.
11 Orange Order or the Orangemen: an Irish religious and political society that promoted Protestantism and opposed Catholic Emancipation. The society is named for the Protestant William of Orange (King William III) and still commemorates his defeat of the Roman Catholic King James II at the Battle of the Boyne in 1690.
12 Soot from coal mining. A large coalfield surrounds Cockermouth and Keswick. Scud also means sail and *The Flying Scud* is the name of the ship in Stevenson's *The Wrecker*.
13 Proverbs 9:17.

66

A WINTER'S WALK IN CARRICK
AND GALLOWAY[1]

At the famous bridge of Doon, Kyle, the central district of the shire of Ayr, marches with Carrick, the most southerly. On the Carrick side of the river, rises a hill of somewhat gentle conformation, cleft with shallow dells and sown here and there with farms and tufts of wood. Inland, it loses itself, joining, I suppose, the great herd of similar hills that occupies the centre of the Lowlands. Towards the sea, it swells out the coast line into a protuberance, like a bay-window in a plan, and is fortified against the surf behind bold crags. This hill is known as the Brown Hill of Carrick, or, more shortly, Brown Carrick.

It had snowed over night. The fields were all sheeted up; they were tucked in among the snow, and their shape was modelled through the pliant counterpane, like children tucked in by a fond mother. The wind had made ripples and folds upon the surface, like what the sea, in quiet weather, leaves upon the sand. There was a frosty stifle in the air. An effusion of coppery light on the summit of Brown Carrick showed where the sun was trying to look through; but along the horizon, clouds of cold fog had settled down, so that there was no distinction of sky and sea. Over the white shoulders of the headlands, or in the opening of bays, there was nothing but a great vacancy and blackness; and the road, as it drew near the edge of the cliff, seemed to skirt the shores of creation and void space.

The snow crunched underfoot, and, at farms, all the dogs broke out barking as they smelt a passer-by upon the road. I met a fine old fellow, who might have sat as the father in "The Cotter's Saturday Night,"[2] and swore most heathenishly at a cow he was driving. And a little after, scraped acquaintance with a poor body, tramping out to gather cockles. His face was wrinkled by exposure; it was broken up into flakes and channels, like mud beginning to dry, and weathered in two colours, an incongruous pink and gray. He had a faint air of being surprised—which, God knows, he might well be—that life had gone so ill with him. The shape of his trousers was in itself a jest, so strangely were they bagged and ravelled about his knees; and his coat was all bedaubed with clay, as though he had lain in a rain dub during the New Year's festivity. I will own I was not sorry to think he had had a merry new year, and been young again for an evening; but I was sorry to see the mark still there. One could not expect such an old gentleman to be much of a dandy, or a great student of respectability in dress; but there might have been

471

a wife at home, who had brushed out similar stains after fifty new years, now become old; or a round-armed daughter, who would wish to have him neat, were it only out of self respect and for the ploughman sweet-heart when he looks round at night. Plainly there was nothing of this in his life; and years and loneliness hung heavily on his old arms. He was seventy-six, he told me; and nobody would give a day's work to a man that age; they would think he couldn't do it. "And deed," he went on, with a sad little chuckle, "deed, I doubt if I could." He said good-bye to me at a footpath, and crippled wearily off to his work. It will make your heart ache, if you think of his old fingers groping in the snow.

He told me I was to turn down beside the schoolhouse for Dunure. And so when I found a lone house among the snow, and heard a babble of childish voices from within, I struck off into a steep road leading downwards to the sea. Dunure lies close under the hill: a haven among the rocks, a breakwater in consummate disrepair, much apparatus for drying nets and a score or so of fishers' houses. Hard by, a few shards of ruined castle overhang the sea, a few vaults and one tall gable honeycombed with windows. The snow lay on the beach to the tidemark. It was daubed onto the sills of the ruin; it roosted in the crannies of the rock like white seabirds; even on outlying reefs, there would be a little cock of snow, like a toy lighthouse. Everything was gray and white in a cold and dolorous sort of shepherd's plaid. In the profound silence, broken only by the noise of oars at sea, a horn was sounded twice; and I saw the postman, girt with two bags, pause a moment at the end of the clachan for letters. It is perhaps characteristic of Dunure, that none were brought him.

The people at the public house did not seem well pleased to see me and, though I would fain have stayed by the kitchen fire, sent me "ben the hoose"[3] into the guest-room. This guest-room at Dunure was painted in quite æsthetic fashion. There are rooms in the same taste not a hundred miles from London, where persons of an extreme sensibility meet together without embarrassment. It was all in a fine dull bottle-green and black; a grave harmonious piece of colouring, with nothing, so far as coarser folk can judge, to hurt the better feelings of the most exquisite purist. A cherry-red half window blind kept up an imaginary warmth in the cold room, and threw quite a glow on the floor. Twelve cockle shells and a half-penny china figure were ranged solemnly along the mantel-shelf. Even the spittoon was an original note; and instead of sawdust, contained sea shells. And as for the hearthrug, it would merit an article to itself, and a coloured diagram to help the text. It was patchwork, but the patchwork of the poor; no glowing shreds of old brocade and Chinese silk, shaken together in the kaleidoscope of some tasteful housewife's fancy; but a work of art in its own way, and plainly a labour of love. The patches came exclusively from people's raiment. There was no colour more brilliant than a heather mixture. "My Johnnie's grey breeks,"[4] well polished over the oar on the boat's thwart, entered largely into its composition. And the spoils of an old black cloth coat, that had been many a Sunday to church, added something of preciousness to the material.

While I was at luncheon, four carters came in, long, limber, muscular Ayrshire Scots, with lean, intelligent faces. Four quarts of stout were ordered; they kept filling the tumbler with the other hand as they drank; and in less time than it takes me to write these words, the four quarts were finished—another round was proposed, discussed, and negatived—and they were creaking out of the village with their carts.

The ruins drew you towards them. You never saw any place look more desolate from a distance, nor one that less belied its promise near at hand. Some crows and gulls flew away croaking, as I scrambled in. The snow had drifted into the vaults. The clachan dabbled with snow, the white hills, the black sky, the sea marked in the coves with faint circular wrinkles, the whole world, as it looked from a loop-hole in Dunure, was cold, wretched and out-at-elbows. If you had been a wicked baron and compelled to stay there all the afternoon, you would have had a rare fit of the remorse. How you would have heaped up the fire and gnawed your fingers! I think it would have come to homicide before the evening—if it were only for the pleasure of seeing something red! And the masters of Dunure, it is to be noticed, were remarkable of old for inhumanity. One of these vaults where the snow had drifted, was that "black voute" where "Mr. Alane Stewart commendatour of Crossraguel" endured his fiery trials. On the first and seventh September 1570 (ill dates for Mr. Alan!), Gilbert, Earl of Cassilis, his chaplain, his baker, his cook, his pantryman and another servant, bound the poor Commendator "betwix an iron chimlay and a fire," and there cruelly roasted him until he signed away his abbacy. It is one of the ugliest stories of an ugly period, but not, somehow, without such a flavour of the ridiculous as makes it hard to sympathise quite seriously with the victim. And it is consoling to remember, that he got away at last, and kept his abbacy, and, over and above, had a pension from the earl until he died.[5]

Some way beyond Dunure, a wide bay, of somewhat less unkindly aspect, opened out. Colzean plantations lay all along the steep shore, and there was a wooded hill towards the centre, where the trees made a sort of shadowy etching over the snow. The road went down and up, and past a blacksmith's cottage that made fine music in the valley. Three compatriots of Burns drove up to me in a cart. They were all drunk, and asked me jeeringly if this was the way to Dunure. I told them it was; and my answer was received with unfeigned merriment. One gentle-man was so much tickled, he nearly fell out of the cart; indeed he was only saved by a companion, who either had not so fine a sense of humour, or had drunken less.

"The toune of Mayboll," says the inimitable Abercrummie,[6] "stands upon an ascending ground from east to west, and lyes open to the south. It hath one prin-cipall street, with houses upon both sides, built of freestone; and it is beautifyed with the situation of two castles, one at each end of this street. That on the east belongs to the Erle of Cassilis. On the west end is a castle, which belonged some-time to the laird of Blairquan, which is now the tolbuith, and is adorned with a pyremide" (conical roof), "and a row of ballesters round it raised from the top

473

of the staircase, into which they have mounted a fyne clock. There be four lanes which pass from the principall street; one is called the Back Venall, which is steep, declining to the south-east, and leads to a lower street, which is far larger than the high chiefe street, and it runs from the Kirkland to the Well Trees, in which there have been many pretty buildings, belonging to the severall gentry of the countrey, who were wont to resort thither in winter, and divert themselves in converse together at their owne houses. It was once the principall street of the town; but many of these houses of the gentry having been decayed and ruined, it has lost much of its ancient beautie. Just opposite to this vennel, there is another that leads north-west from the chiefe street to the green, which is a pleasant plott of ground, enclosed round with an earthen wall, wherein they were wont to play football, but now at the Gowff and byasse-bowls. The houses of this towne, on both sides of the street, have their several gardens belonging to them; and in the lower street there be some pretty orchards, that yield store of good fruit." As Patterson says, this description is near enough even today, and is mighty nicely written to boot. I am bound to add of my own experience, that Maybole is tumble-down and dreary. Prosperous enough in reality, it has an air of decay; and though the population has increased, a roofless house, every here and there, seems to protest the contrary. The women are more than well-favoured, and the men fine, tall fellows; but they look slipshod and dissipated. As they slouched at street corners, or stood about gossiping in the snow, it seemed they would have been more at home in the slums of a large city, than here, in a country place betwixt a village and a town. I heard a great deal about drinking, and a great deal about religious revivals: two things in which the Scottish character is emphatic and most unlovely. In particular, I heard of clergymen who were employing their time in explaining, to a delighted audience, the physics of the Second Coming. It is not very likely, any of us will be asked to help; if we were, it is likely we should receive instructions for the occasion, and that on more reliable authority; and so I can only figure to myself a congregation truly curious in such flights of theological fancy, as one of saintly veterans, who have fought the good fight to an end and outlived all worldly passion, and are to be regarded rather as a part of the Church Triumphant than the poor, imperfect company on earth. And yet I saw some young fellows about the smoking room, who seemed, in the eyes of one who cannot count himself strait-laced, in need of some more practical sort of teaching. They seemed only eager to get drunk, and to do so speedily. It was not much more than a week after the new year; and to hear them return on their past bouts, with gusto unspeakable, was not altogether pleasing. Here is one snatch of talk, for the accuracy of which I can vouch.

"Ye had a spree here last Thursday?"
"We had that!"
"I wasnae able to be oot o' my bed. Man, I was awful bad on Wednesday!"
"Aye, ye were gey bad."[7]

And you should have seen the bright eyes, and heard the sensual accents! They recalled their doings with devout gusto, and a sort of rational pride. Schoolboys, after their first drunkenness, are not more boastful; a cock does not plume himself with a more unmingled satisfaction, as he paces forth among his harem; and yet these were grown men, and by no means short of wit. It was hard to suppose they were very eager about the second coming; it seemed as if some elementary notions of temperance for the men, and comeliness for the women, would have gone nearer the mark. And yet, as it seemed to me typical of much that is evil in Scotland, Maybole is also typical of much that is best. Some of the factories which have taken the place of weaving in the town's economy, were originally founded and are still possessed by self-made men of the sterling, stout old breed; fellows who made some little bit of an invention, borrowed some little pocketful of capital, and then, step by step, in courage, thrift and industry, fought their way upward to an assured position.

Abercrummie has told you enough of the Tolbooth;[8] but, as a bit of spelling, this inscription on the Tolbooth bell seems too delicious to withhold. "This bell is founded at Maiboll Bi Danel Geli, a Frenchman, the 6th November, 1696, Bi appointment of the heritors of the parish of Maiyboll." The Castle deserves more notice. It is a large and shapely tower, plain from the ground upward, but with a zone of ornamentation running about the top. In a general way, this adornment is perched on the very summit of the chimney stacks; but there is one corner more elaborate than the rest. A very heavy string-course runs round the upper story; and just above this, facing up the street, the tower carries a small oriel window, fluted and corbelled and carved about with stone heads. It is so ornate it has somewhat the air of a shrine. And it was, indeed, the casket of a very precious jewel; for in the room to which it gives light lay, for long years, the heroine of the sweet old ballad of "Johnnie Faa"—she who, at the call of the gipsies' songs, "came tripping down the stair, and all her maids before her."[9] Some people say the ballad has no basis in fact, and have written, I believe, unanswerable papers to the proof. But in the face of all that, the very look of that high oriel window convinces the imagination; and we enter into all the sorrows of the imprisoned dame. We conceive the burthen of the long, lacklustre days, when she leaned her sick head against the mullions, and saw the burghers loafing in Maybole High-street, and the children at play, and ruffling gallants riding by from hunt or foray. We conceive the passion of odd moments, when the wind threw up to her some snatch of song, and her heart grew hot within her, and her eyes overflowed, at the memory of the past. And even if the tale be not true of this or that lady, or this or that old tower, it is true, in the essence, of all men and women. For all of us, some time or other, hear the gipsies singing; over all of us is the glamour cast. Some resist and sit resolutely by the fire. Most go and are brought back again, like Lady Cassilis. A few, of the tribe of Waring, go and are seen no more; only, now and again, at springtime, when the gipsies' song is afloat in the amethyst evening, we can catch their voices in the glee.

By night, it was clearer and Maybole more visible than during the day. Clouds coursed over the sky in great masses; the full moon battled the other way, and lit up the snow with gleams of flying silver. The town came down the hill in a cascade of brown gables, bestridden by smooth white roofs, and spangled here and there with lighted windows. At either end, the snow stood high up in the darkness, on the peak of the Tolbooth and among the chimneys of the Castle. As the moon flashed a bull's-eye glitter across the town, between the racing clouds, the white roofs leaped into relief over the gables, and the chimney-stalks and their shadows over the white roofs. In the town itself, the lit face of the clock peered down the street; an hour was hammered out on M. Geli's bell; and from behind the red curtains of a public house, some one trolled out—a compatriot of Burns again!—"The saut tear blin's my e'e."[10]

Next morning, there were sun and a flapping wind. From the street corners of Maybole, I could catch breezy glimpses of green fields. The road underfoot was wet and heavy, part ice, part snow, part water; and anyone I met greeted me, by way of salutation, with "A fine thowe" (thaw). My way lay among rather bleak hills, and passed bleak ponds and dilapidated castles and monasteries, to the Highland-looking village of Kirkoswald. It has little claim to notice; save that Burns came there to study surveying in the summer of 1777 and there also, in the kirkyard, the original of Tam o' Shanter sleeps his last sleep.[11] It is worth noticing, however, that this was the first place I thought "Highland-looking." Over the hill from Kirkoswald, a farm road leads to the coast. As I came down above Turnberry, the sea view was indeed strangely different from the day before. The cold fogs were all blown away; and there was Ailsa Craig, like a refraction, magnified and deformed, of the Bass Rock; and there were the chiselled mountain tops of Arran, veined and tipped with snow; and, behind and fainter, the low blue land of Cantyre. Cottony clouds stood, in a great castle, over the top of Arran, and blew out in long streamers to the south. The sea was bitten all over with white; little ships, tacking up and down the Firth, lay over at different angles in the wind. On Shanter, they were ploughing lea; and a cart foal, all in a field by himself, capered and whinnied as if the Spring were in him.

The road from Turnberry to Girvan lies along the shore, among sand hills and by wildernesses of tumbled bent. Every here and there, a few cottages stood together beside a bridge. They had one odd feature not easy to describe in words. A triangular porch projected from above the door, supported at the apex by a single upright post. A secondary door was hinged to the post, and could be hasped on either cheek of the real entrance; so, whether the wind was north or south, the cotter could make himself a triangular bight of shelter, where to set his chair and finish a pipe with comfort. There is one objection to this device; for, as the post stands in the middle of the fairway, anyone precipitately issuing from the cottage, must run his chance of a broken head. So far as I am aware, it is peculiar to the little corner of country about Girvan. And that corner is noticeable for more reasons; it is certainly one of the most characteristic districts in Scotland. It has this movable porch, by way of architecture; it has, as we shall see, a sort of remnant of provincial costume; and it has the handsomest population in the Lowlands.

Notes

1 This unfinished essay reports Stevenson's walking tour of about 70 miles in southwest Scotland for his health in January of 1876.
2 Robert Burns, "The Cotter's Saturday Night" (1785).
3 In or towards the inner part of a house (*Dictionary of the Scots Language*).
4 "Johnie's Gray Breeks"—a traditional Scottish song in which Johnie's lover compares his worn trousers with his love and resolves, "We'll make them hale between us yet."
5 Kennedy of Bargany led a large force to help Stewart and take the castle of Dunure. Stewart reported the Earl of Cassilis to the Privy Council, which sent him to Dumbarton Castle until he paid a £ 2,000 security.
6 William Abercrombie, minister at Maypole from 1673 to 1690, recorded in *Fasti Ecclesiae Scoticanae*.
7 Spree: a lively and prolonged bout of drinking; gey: very or pretty.
8 Rev. William Abercrummie, Minister of Maybole from 1683 to 1722, describes a castle repurposed as a jail and tollbooth in *A Description of Carrick*.
9 From the ballad, "Johnie Faa, The Gypsy Laddie" (Robert Chambers, *The Scottish Ballads*, 1829, 144). The ballad is based on the seduction of Lady Cassilis by the wandering gypsy Faa. According to Chambers, Sir John Faa of Dunbar disguised as a gypsy and eloped with his old lover, the wife of the Covenanter John, sixth Earl of Cassilis when he was at Westminster. They were caught and Sir John and his companions were hanged.
10 "The teir blinded his ee" from the ballad "Sir Patrick Spens" (verse 4).
11 Douglas Graham (1738?–1811), a farmer from Shanter and the model for Robert Burns's "Tam o' Shanter." He is buried at Kirkoswald churchyard.

67

ON THE CHOICE OF A
PROFESSION, IN A LETTER TO A
YOUNG GENTLEMAN

You write to me, my dear sir, requesting advice at one of the most momentous epochs in a young man's life. You are about to choose a profession; and with a diffidence highly pleasing at your age, you would be glad, you say, of some guidance in the choice. There is nothing more becoming than for youth to seek counsel; nothing more becoming to age than to be able to give it; and in a civilization, old and complicated like ours, where practical persons boast a kind of practical philosophy superior to all others, you would very naturally expect to find all such questions systematically answered. For the dicta of the Practical Philosophy,[1] you come to me. What, you ask, are the principles usually followed by the wise in the like critical junctures? There, I confess, you pose me on the threshold. I have examined my own recollections; I have interrogated others; and with all the will in the world to serve you better, I fear I can only tell you that the wise, in these circumstances, act upon no principles whatever. This is disappointing to you; it was painful to myself; but if I am to declare the truth as I see it, I must repeat that wisdom has nothing to do with the choice of a profession.

We all know what people say, and very foolish it usually is. The question is to get inside of these flourishes, and discover what it is they think and ought to say: to perform, in short, the Socratic Operation.[2] The more ready-made answers there are to any question, the more abstruse it becomes; for those of whom we make the enquiry have the less need of consideration before they reply. The world being more or less beset with Anxious Enquirers of the Socratic persuasion, it is the object of a Liberal Education to equip people with a proper number of these answers by way of passport; so that they can pass swimmingly to and fro on their affairs without the trouble of thinking. How should a banker know his own mind? It takes him all his time to manage his bank. If you saw a company of pilgrims, walking as if for a wager, each with his teeth set;[3] and if you happened to ask them one after another: Whither they were going? and from each you were to receive the same answer: that Positively they were all in such a hurry, they had never found leisure to inquire into the nature of their errand:—confess, my dear sir, you would be startled at the indifference they exhibited. Am I going too far, if

I say that this is the condition of the large majority of our fellow men and almost all our fellow women?

I stop a banker.
"My good fellow," I say, "give me a moment."
"I have not a moment to spare," says he.
"Why?" I enquire.
"I must be banking," he replies. "I am so busily engaged in banking all day long that I have hardly leisure for my meals."
"And what," I continue my interrogatory, "is banking?"
"Sir," says he, "it is my business."
"Your business?" I repeat. "And what is a man's business?"
"Why," cries the banker, "a man's business is his duty."
And with that he breaks away from me, and I see him skimming to his avocations.

But this is a sort of answer that provokes reflection. Is a man's business his duty? or perhaps should not his duty be his business? If it is not my duty to conduct a bank (and I contend that it is not) is it the duty of my friend the banker? Who told him it was? Is it in the Bible? Is he sure that banks are a good thing? Might it not have been his duty to stand aside, and let some one else conduct the bank? Or perhaps ought he not to have been a ship-captain instead? All these perplexing queries may be summed up under one head: the grave problem which my friend offers to the world: Why is he a Banker?

Well, why is it? There is one principal reason, I conceive: That the man was trapped. Education, as practised, is a form of hocussing with the friendliest intentions. The fellow was hardly in trousers before they whipt him into school; hardly done with school before they smuggled him into an office; it is ten to one they have had him married into the bargain. And all this before he has had time so much as to imagine that there may be any other practicable course. Drum, drum, drum; you must be in time for school; you must do your Cornelius Nepos;[4] you must keep your hands clean; you must go to parties—a young man should make friends; and finally—you must take this opening in a bank. He has been used to caper to this sort of piping from the first; and he joins the regiment of bank clerks for precisely the same reason as he used to go to the nursery at the stroke of eight. Then at last, rubbing his hands with a complacent smile, the parent lays his conjuring pipe aside. The trick is performed, ladies and gentlemen; the wild ass's colt is broken in, and now sits diligently scribing. Thus it is, that, out of men, we make bankers.

You have doubtless been present at the washing of sheep, which is a brisk, high-handed piece of manœuvring in its way; but what is it, as a subject for contemplation, to the case of the poor young animal, Man, turned loose into this roaring world, herded by robustious guardians, taken with the panic before he has wit enough to apprehend its cause, and soon flying with all his heels in the van of the general stampede? It may be that in after years, he shall fall upon a train of reflection, and begin narrowly to scrutinise the reasons that decided his path and his continued, mad activity in that direction. And perhaps he may be very well pleased at the retrospect, and see fifty things that might have been worse, for one that would have been better; and even supposing him to take the other cue, bitterly to deplore the circumstances in which he is placed and bitterly to reprobate the jockeying that got him into them, the fact is, it is too late to indulge such whims. It is too late, after the train has started, to debate the needfulness of this particular journey: the door is locked, the express goes tearing overland at sixty miles an hour; he had better betake himself to sleep or the daily paper, and discourage unavailing thought. He sees many pleasant places out of the window: cottages in a garden, anglers by the riverside, balloons voyaging the sky; but as for him, he is hooked for all his natural days, and must remain a banker to the end.

If the juggling only began with schooltime, if even the domineering friends and counsellors had made a choice of their own, there might still be some pretension to philosophy in the affair. But no. They too were trapped; they are but tame elephants unwittingly ensnaring others, and were themselves ensnared by tame elephants of an older domestication. We have all learned our tricks in captivity, to the spiriting of Mrs. Grundy[5] and a system of rewards and punishments. The crack of the whip and the trough of fodder: the cut direct and an invitation to dinner: the gallows and the Shorter Catechism[6]: a pat upon the head and a stinging lash on the reverse: these are the elements of education and the principles of the Practical Philosophy. Sir Thomas Browne,[7] in the earlier part of the seventeenth century, had already apprehended the staggering fact that geography is a considerable part of orthodoxy; and that a man who, when born in London, makes a conscientious protestant, would have made an equally conscientious Hindu if he had first seen daylight in Benares. This is but a small part, however important, of the things that are settled for us by our place of birth. An Englishman drinks beer and tastes his liquor in the throat; a Frenchman drinks wine and tastes it in the front of the mouth. Hence, a single beverage lasts the Frenchman all afternoon; and the Englishman cannot spend above a very short time in a café, but he must swallow half a bucket. The Englishman takes a cold tub every morning in his bedroom; the Frenchman has an occasional hot bath. The Englishman has an unlimited family and will die in harness; the Frenchman retires upon a competency with three children at the outside. So this imperative national tendency follows us through all the privacies of life, dictates our thoughts and attends us to the grave. We do nothing, we say nothing, we wear nothing, but it is stamped with the Queen's Arms. We are English down to our boots and into our digestions. There is not a dogma of all those by which we lead young men, but we got it ourselves, between sleep and waking, between death and life, in a complete abeyance of the reasoning part.

"But how, sir" (you will ask) "is there then no wisdom in the world? and when my admirable father was this day urging me, with the most affecting expressions, to decide on an industrious, honest and lucrative employment—?" Enough, sir;

I follow your thoughts, and will answer them to the utmost of my ability. Your father, for whom I entertain a singular esteem, is I am proud to believe a profess-ing Christian: the Gospel, therefore, is or ought to be his rule of conduct. Now, I am of course ignorant of the terms employed by your father; but I quote here from a very urgent letter, written by another parent, who was a man of sense, integrity, great energy and a Christian persuasion, and who has perhaps set forth the common view with a certain innocent openness of his own: "You are now come to that time of life," he writes to his son, "and have reason within yourself to consider the absolute necessity of making provision for the time when it will be asked Who is this man? Is he doing any good in the world? Has he the means of being "One of Us?" I beseech you," he goes on, rising in emotion, and appeal-ing to his son by name, "I beseech you do not trifle with this till it actually comes upon you. Bethink yourself and bestir yourself as a man. This is the time—" And so forth. This gentleman has candour; he is perspicacious, and has to deal appar-ently with a perspicacious picklogic of a son; and hence the startling perspicuity of the document. But, my dear sir, what a principle of life! To "do good in the world" is to be received in a society, apart from personal affection. I could name many forms of evil vastly more exhilarating, whether in prospect or enjoyment. If I scraped money, believe me, it should be for some more cordial purpose. And then, scraping money? It seems to me as if he had forgotten the Gospel. This is a view of life not quite the same as the Christian, which the old gentleman professed and sincerely studied to practise. But upon this point, I dare dilate no farther. Suf-fice it to say, that looking round me on the manifestations of this Christian society of ours, I have been often tempted to exclaim: What, then, is Antichrist?[8]

A wisdom, at least, which professes one set of propositions and yet acts upon another, can be no very entire or rational ground of conduct. Doubtless, there is much in this question of money; and for my part, I believe no young man ought to be at peace till he is self-supporting, and has an open, clear life of it on his own foundation. But here a consideration occurs to me, of, as I must consider, startling originality. It is this:—that there are two sides to this question as well as to so many others. Make more?—Aye, or Spend less? There is no absolute call upon a man to make any specific income, unless indeed he has set his immortal soul on being "One of us." A thoroughly respectable income is As much as a man spends. A luxurious income, or true opulence, is Something more than a man spends. Raise the income, lower the expenditure, and, my dear sir, surprising as it seems, we have the same result. But I hear you remind me, with pursed lips of privations— of hardships. Alas! sir, there are privations upon either side; the banker has to sit all day in his bank, a serious privation; can you not conceive that the landscape painter, whom I take to be the meanest and most lost among contemporary men, truly and deliberately *prefers* the privations upon his side—to wear no gloves, to drink beer, to live on chops or even on potatoes, and lastly not to be "One of us"— truly and deliberately prefers his privations to those of the banker? I can. Yes, sir, I repeat the words; I can. Believe me, there are Rivers in Bohemia![9]—But there is nothing so hard to get people to understand as this: That they *pay for their money*;

481

and nothing so difficult to make them remember as this: That money, when they have it, is, for most of them at least, only a cheque to purchase pleasure with. How then if a man gets pleasure in following an art? he might gain more cheques by following another; but then, although there is a difference in cheques, the amount of pleasure is the same. He gets some of his directly; unlike the bank clerk, he is having his fortnight's holiday, and doing what delights him, all the year.

All these patent truisms have a very strange air, when written down. But that, my dear sir, is no fault of mine or of the truisms. There they are. I beseech you do not trifle with them. Bethink yourself like a man. This is the time.

But, you say, all this is very well; it does not help me to a choice. Once more, sir, you have me; it does not. What shall I say? A choice, let us remember, is almost more of a negative than a positive. You embrace one thing; but you refuse a thousand. The most liberal profession imprisons many energies and starves many affections. If you are in a bank, you cannot be much upon the sea. You cannot be both a first rate violinist and a first rate painter: you must lose in the one art if you persist in following both. If you are sure of your preference, follow it. If not—nay, my dear sir, it is not for me or any man, to go beyond this point. God made you; not I. I cannot even make you over again. I have heard of a schoolmaster, whose speciality it was to elicit the bent of each pupil: poor schoolmaster, poor pupils! As for me, if you have nothing indigenous in your own heart, no living preference, no fine, human scorn, I leave you to the tide; it will sweep you somewhere. Have you but a grain of inclination, I will help you. If you wish to be a costermonger, be it, shame the devil; and I will stand the donkey.[10] If you wish to be nothing, once more I leave you to the tide.

I regret profoundly, my dear young sir, not only for you, in whom I see such a lively promise of the future but for the sake of your admirable and truly worthy father and your no less excellent mama, that my remarks should seem no more conclusive. I can give myself this praise, that I have kept back nothing; but this alas! is a subject on which there is little to put forward. It will probably not much matter what you decide upon doing; for most men seem to sink at length to the degree of stupor necessary for contentment in their different estates. Yes, sir, this is what I have observed. Most men are happy, and most men dishonest. Their mind sinks to the proper level; their honour easily accepts the custom of the trade. I wish you may find degeneration no more painful than your neighbours, soon sink into apathy, and be long spared, in a state of respectable somnambulism, from the grave to which we haste.

Notes

1 Practical or moral philosophy, as opposed to theoretical philosophy (logic and meta-physics), emphasizes values, morality, attitudes, and behavior. The University of Edin-burgh divides these studies into two different departments.
2 Socrates's method of instruction, as portrayed in Plato's dialogues, involving ques-tioning and cross-examining students to show the inadequacy of their answers.
3 Resolute or determined.

4 Cornelius Nepos (110–24 BCE), Roman historian and author of moralistic biographical sketches of distinguished figures.
5 Mrs. Grundy, fictional English character who first appears in Thomas Morton's 1798
play *Speed the Plough* and represents conventional opinion and social pressure.
6 The Presbyterian Westminster Shorter Catechism was approved by England's Parliament in 1648 and abandoned with the restoration of the monarchy in 1660. The Church
of Scotland adopted it in 1648 and the Scottish Parliament authorized it in 1649.
7 Sir Thomas Browne (1605–1682), scholar of science and religion.
8 Christ's opposite and enemy, mentioned in the Epistles of John, who will reign in the
period prior to the final judgment according to Christian tradition.
9 Bohemia: unconventional or countercultural community of free spirits, artists, and
writers.
10 A costermonger: a merchant selling produce in the street from a handcart or animal-
drawn cart. *Stand*: to pay for or buy as a present. "Tell the truth and shame the devil"
appears in Shakespeare's *1 Henry IV* (3.1.59), though it was a common proverb at least
50 years earlier.

68

LAY MORALS

Chapter I

(1) What a man makes of this world for himself, and what view of it he teaches to aspiring youth, gives the measure of what we may hope from him in thought or conduct, and constitutes what we call that man's religion. But the problem of education is twofold: first, to know and then to utter. Every one who lives any semblance of an inner life thinks more nobly and profoundly than he speaks; and the best of teachers can impart only broken images of the truth which they perceive. Speech which goes from one to another, between two natures and, what is worse, between two experiences, is doubly relative. The speaker buries his meaning; it is for the hearer to dig it up again; and all speech, written or spoken, is in a dead language until it finds a willing and prepared hearer. Such, moreover, is the complexity of life, that when we condescend upon details in our advice, we may be sure we condescend on error; and the best of education is to throw out some magnanimous hints. No man was ever so poor that he could express all that he has in him by words or looks or actions; his true knowledge is eternally incommunicable, for it is a knowledge of himself; and his best wisdom comes to him by no process of the mind, but in a supreme self-dictation, which keeps varying from hour to hour in its dictates with the variation of events and circumstances.

A few men of picked nature, full of faith, courage and contempt for others, try earnestly to set forth as much as is tangible of this inner law; but the vast majority when they come to advise the young, must be content to retail certain doctrines which have been already retailed to them in their own youth. Every generation has to educate another which it has brought unreflectingly upon the stage. People who ruddily accept the responsibility of parentship, having very different matters in their eye, are apt to feel rueful when that responsibility falls due. What are they to tell the child about life and conduct, subjects on which they have themselves so few and such confused opinions? Indeed, I do not know; the least said, perhaps, the soonest mended; and yet the child keeps asking, and the parent must find some words to say in his own defence. Where does he find them? and what are they when found?

(2) As a matter of experience, and in nine hundred and ninety nine cases out of a thousand, he will instill into his wide-eyed brat three bad things, the terror of public opinion, and flowing from that as a fountain, the desire of wealth and desire of applause. Besides these, or what might be deduced as corollaries from these, he will teach not much else of any effective value: some dim notions of divinity, perhaps, and book-keeping, and how to walk through a quadrille.

(3) But, you may tell me, the young people are taught to be Christians. It may be want of penetration, but I have not yet been able to perceive it. As an honest man, whatever we teach and be it good or evil, it is not the doctrine of Christ. What he taught (and in this he is like all other teachers worthy of the name) was not a code of rules, but a ruling spirit; not truths, but a spirit of truth; not views, but a view. What he showed us was an Attitude of mind. Towards the many considerations on which conduct is built, each man stands in a certain relation. He takes life on a certain principle. He has a compass in his spirit which points in a certain direction. It is the attitude, the relation, the point of the compass, that is the whole body and gist of what he has to teach us; in this, the details are comprehended; out of this, the specific precepts issue and by this, and this only, can they be explained and applied. And thus, to learn aright from any teacher, we must first of all, like an historical artist, think ourselves into sympathy with his position and, in the technical phrase, create his character. An historian confronted with some ambiguous politician or an actor charged with a part, have but one preoccupation; they must search all round and upon every side, and grope for some central conception which is to explain and justify the most extreme details; until that is found, the politician is an enigma or perhaps a quack, and the part a tissue of fustian sentiment and big words; but once that is found, all enters into a plan, a human nature appears, the politician or the stage king is understood from point to point, from end to end. This is a degree of trouble which will be gladly taken by a very humble artist; but not even the terror of eternal fire, can teach a business man to bend his imagination to such athletic efforts. Yet without this, all is vain; until we understand the whole, we shall understand none of the parts; and otherwise we have no more than broken images and scattered words; the meaning remains buried; and the language in which our prophet speaks to us is a dead language in our ears.

(4) Take a few of Christ's sayings and compare them with our current doctrines.

"*Ye cannot,*" he says, "*serve God and Mammon.*"[1] Cannot? And our whole system is to teach us how we can!

"*The children of this world are wiser in their generation than the children of light.*"[2] Are they? I had been led to understand the reverse: that the Christian merchant, for example, prospered exceedingly in his affairs; that honesty was the best policy; that one Binney had written a conclusive treatise "How to make the best of both worlds." Of both worlds indeed! Which am I to believe then—Christ or Binney?[3]

"*Take no thought for the morrow.*"[4] Ask Binney; ask Budgett the Successful Merchant;[5] interrogate your own heart; and you will have to admit that this is not only a silly but an immoral position. All we believe, all we hope, all we honour in ourselves or our contemporaries, stands condemned in this one sentence, or if you take the other view, condemns the sentence as unwise and inhumane. We are not then of the "same mind that was in Christ."[6] We disagree with Christ. Either Christ meant nothing, or else he or we must be in the wrong. Well, says Thoreau, speaking of some texts from the New Testament, and finding a strange echo of another style which the reader may recognise: "Let but one of these sentences be rightly read from any pulpit in the land, and there would not be left one stone of that meetinghouse upon another."

(5) It may be objected that these are what are called "hard sayings";[7] and that a man, or an education, may be very sufficiently Christian although it leave some of these sayings upon one side. But this is a very gross delusion. Although truth is difficult to state, it is both easy and agreeable to receive, and the mind runs out to meet it ere the phrase be done. The universe, in relation to what any man can say of it, is plain patent and staringly comprehensible. In itself, it is a great and travailing ocean, unsounded, unvoyageable, an eternal mystery to man; or let us say, it is a monstrous and impassable mountain, one side of which and a few near slopes and foothills, we can dimly study with these mortal eyes. But what any man can say of it, even in his highest utterance, must have relation to this little and plain corner, which is no less visible to us than to him. We are looking on the same map; it will go hard if we cannot follow the demonstration. The longest and most abstruse flight of a philosopher, becomes clear and shallow, in the flash of a moment, when we suddenly perceive the aspect and drift of his intention. The longest argument is but a finger pointed; once we get our own finger rightly parallel, we see what the man meant, whether it be a new star or an old street lamp. And briefly, if a saying is hard to understand, it is because we are thinking of something else.

But to be a true disciple, is to think of the same things as our prophet, and to think of different things in the same order. To be of the same mind with another is to see all things in the same perspective; it is not to agree in a few indifferent matters near at hand and not much debated; it is to follow him in his farthest flights, to see the force of his hyperboles, to stand so exactly in the centre of his vision that whatever he may express, your eyes will light at once on the original, that whatever he may see to declare, your mind will at once accept. You do not belong to the school of any philosopher, because you agree with him that theft is, on the whole, objectionable, or that the sun is overhead at noon. It is by the hard sayings that discipleship is tested. We are all agreed about the middling and indifferent parts of knowledge and morality; even the most soaring spirits too often take them tamely upon trust. But the man, the philosopher or the moralist, does not stand upon these chance adhesions; and the purpose of any system looks towards those extreme points where it steps valiantly beyond tradition and returns with some covert hint of things outside. Then only can you be certain that the words are not words of course, nor mere echoes of the past; then only are you sure that if he be indicating anything at all, it is a star and not a street-lamp; then only do you touch the heart of the mystery, since it was for these that the author wrote his book.

Now every now and then, and indeed surprisingly often, Christ finds a word that transcends all commonplace morality; every now and then he quits the beaten track to pioneer the unexpressed, and throws out a pregnant and magnanimous hyperbole; for it is only by some bold poetry of thought that men can be strung up above the level of everyday conceptions to take a broader look upon experience or accept some higher principle of conduct. To a man who is of the same mind that was in Christ, who stands at some centre not too far from his and looks at the world and conduct from some not dissimilar or, at least, not opposing attitude,—or shortly to a man who is of Christ's philosophy,—every such saying should come home with a thrill of joy and corroboration; he should feel each one below his feet as another sure foundation in the flux of time and chance; each should be another proof that in the torrent of the years and generations, where doctrines and great armaments and empires are swept away and swallowed, he stands immovable, holding by the eternal stars. But alas! at this juncture of the ages it is not so with us; on each and every such occasion, our whole fellowship of Christians falls back in disapproving wonder and implicitly denies the saying. Christians! The farce is impudently broad. Let us stand up in the sight of heaven and confess. The ethics that we hold are those of Benjamin Franklin. *Honesty is the best Policy*,[8] is perhaps a hard saying; it is certainly one by which a wise man of these days will not too curiously direct his steps; but I think it shows a glimmer of meaning to even our most dimmed intelligences; I think we perceive a principle behind it; I think, without hyperbole, we are of the same mind that was in Benjamin Franklin.

Chapter II

But, I may be told, we teach the ten commandments,[9] where a world of morals lies condensed, the very pith and epitome of all ethics and religion; and a young man with these precepts engraved upon his mind, must follow after profit with some conscience and Christianity of method. A man cannot go very far astray, who neither dishonours his parents, nor kills, nor commits adultery, nor steals, nor bears false witness; for these things, rightly thought out, cover a vast field of duty.

(6) Alas! what is a precept? It is at best an illustration; it is case law at the best, which can be learned by precept. The letter is not only dead, but killing; the spirit which underlies and cannot be uttered, alone is true and helpful. This is trite to sickness; but familiarity has a cunning disenchantment; in a day or two, she can steal beauty from the mountain tops; and the most startling words, begin to fall dead upon the ear after several repetitions. (If you see a thing too often, you no longer see it; if you hear a thing too often, you no longer hear it. Our attention requires to be surprised; and to carry a fort by assault or to gain a thoughtful hearing from the ruck[10] of mankind, are feats of about an equal difficulty and must be tried by not dissimilar means.) The whole bible has thus lost its message for the common run of hearers; it has become mere words of course; and the parson may bawl himself scarlet and beat the pulpit like a thing possessed, but his hearers will continue to nod; they are strangely at peace; they know all he has to say; ring the

old bell as you choose, it is still the old bell and it cannot startle their composure. And so with this byword about the letter and the spirit.[11] It is quite true, no doubt; but it has no meaning in the world to any man of us. Alas! it has just this meaning, and neither more nor less: that while the spirit is true, the letter is eternally false.

The shadow of a great oak lies abroad upon the ground at noon, perfect, clear and stable like the earth. But let a man set himself to mark out the boundary with cords and pegs, and were he never so nimble and never so exact, what with the multiplicity of the leaves and the progression of the shadow as it flees before the travelling sun, long ere he has made the circuit, the whole figure will have changed. Life may be compared, not to a single tree, but to a great and complicated forest; circumstance is more swiftly changing than a shadow, language much more inexact than the tools of a surveyor; from day to day, the trees fall and are renewed; the very essences are fleeting as we look; and the whole world of leaves is swinging tempest-tossed among the winds of time. Look now for your shadows. O man of formulæ, is this a place for you? Have you fitted the spirit to a single case? alas, in the cycle of the ages when shall such another be proposed for the judgement of man? Now when the sun shines and the winds blow, the wood is filled with an innumerable multitude of shadows, tumultuously tossed and changing; and at every gust the whole carpet leaps and becomes new. Can you, or your heart, say more?

Look back now, for a moment on your own brief experience of life; and although you lived it feelingly in your own person, and had every step of conduct burned in by pains and joys upon your memory, tell me what definite lesson does experience hand on from youth to manhood or from both to age? The settled tenor which first strikes the eye, is but the shadow of a delusion. This is gone; that never truly was; and you yourself are altered beyond recognition. Times and men and circumstances change about your changing character, with a speed of which no earthly hurricane affords an image. What was the best yesterday, is it still the best in this changed theatre of a tomorrow? Will your own Past truly guide you in your own violent and unexpected Future? And if this be questionable, with what humble, with what hopeless eyes, should we not watch other men driving beside us on their unknown careers, seeing with unlike eyes, impelled by different gales, doing and suffering in another sphere of things?

(7) And as the authentic clue to such a labyrinth and scene of change, do you offer me these two score words? these five bald prohibitions? For there are no more than five; the first four are religious; the tenth, *Thou shalt not covet*, stands upon another basis and shall be spoken of ere long. The Jews, to whom they were first given, in the course of years began to find these precepts insufficient; and made an addition of no less than six hundred and fifty others! They hoped to make a pocket book of reference on morals, which should stand to life as Hoyle to the scientific game of whist.[12] The comparison is just and condemns the design; for those who play by rule will never be more than tolerable players; and you and I would like to play our game in life to the noblest and the most divine advantage. Yet if the Jews took a petty and huckstering view of conduct, what view do we

take ourselves, who callously leave youth to go forth into the enchanted forest, full of spells and dire chimeras, with no better guidance than five dry chips of insignificant precept?

Honour thy father and thy mother. Yes, but does that mean to obey? and if so, how long and how far? *Thou shalt not kill*. Yet the very intention and purport of the prohibition, may be best fulfilled by killing. *Thou shalt not commit adultery*. But some of the ugliest adulteries are committed in the bed of marriage and under the sanction of religion and law. *Thou shalt not bear false witness*. How? by speech? or by silence also? or even by a smile? *Thou shalt not steal*. Ah, that indeed! But what is *to steal*?

(8) To steal? It is another word to be construed; and who is to be our guide? The police will give us one construction, leaving the word only that least minimum of meaning without which society would fall in pieces; but surely we must take some higher sense than this; surely we hope more than a bare subsistence for mankind; surely we wish mankind to prosper and go on from strength to strength, and ourselves to live rightly in the eye of some more exacting potentate than a policeman. The approval or the disapproval of the police must be eternally indifferent to a man who is both valorous and good. There is extreme discomfort, but no shame, in the condemnation of the law. The law represents that modicum of morality which can be squeezed out of the ruck of mankind; but what is that to me, who aim higher and seek to be my own more stringent judge? I observe with pleasure that no brave man has ever given a rush for such considerations. The Japanese have a nobler and more sentimental feeling for this social bond into which we all are born when we come into the world, and whose comforts and protection we all indifferently share throughout our lives; but even to them, no more than to our western saints and heroes, does the law of the state supersede the higher law of duty. Without hesitation and without remorse, they transgress the stiffest enactments rather than abstain from doing right. But the accidental duty being thus fulfilled, they at once return in allegiance to the common duty of all citizens; hasten to denounce themselves; and value at an equal rate their just crime and their equally just submission to its punishment.

The reading of the police will not long satisfy an active conscience or a thoughtful head. But to show you how one or the other may trouble a man, and what a vast extent of frontier is left unridden by this invaluable eighth commandment, let me tell you a few pages out of a young man's life.

(9) He was a friend of mine;[13] a young man like others; generous, flighty, as variable as youth itself, but always with some high motions and on the search for higher thoughts of life. I should tell you at once that he thoroughly agreed with the eighth commandment. But he got hold of some unsettling works, the New Testament among others, and this loosened his views of life and led him into many perplexities. As he was the son of a man in a certain position and well off, my friend had enjoyed from the first the advantages of education, nay, he had been kept alive through a sickly childhood by constant watchfulness, comforts and change of air; for all of which he was indebted to his father's wealth.

At college, he met other lads more diligent than himself, who followed the plough in summer-time to pay their college fees in winter; and this inequality struck him with some force. He was at that age of a conversible temper and insatiably curious in the aspects of life; and he spent much of his time scraping acquaintance with all classes of man and woman-kind. In this way he came upon many depressed ambitions an d many intelligences stunted for want of opportunity; and this also struck him. He began to perceive that life was a handicap upon strange, wrongsided principles, and not, as he had been told, a fair and equal race. He began to tremble lest he himself had been unjustly favoured, when he saw all the avenues of wealth and power and comfort closed against so many of his superiors and equals, and held unwearyingly open before so idle, so desultory and so dissolute a being as himself. There sat a youth beside him on the college benches, who had only one shirt to his back and, at intervals sufficiently far apart, must stay at home to have it washed. It was my friend's principle to stay away as often as he durst; for I fear he was no friend to learning. But there was something that came home to him sharply, in this fellow who had to give over study till his shirt was washed, and the scores of others who had never an opportunity at all. *If one of these could take his place*, he thought; and the thought tore away a bandage from his eyes. He was eaten by the shame of his discoveries and despised himself as an unworthy favourite and a creature of the back stairs of Fortune. He could no longer see without confusion one of these brave young fellows battling up-hill against adversity. Had he not filched that fellow's birthright? At best was he not coldly profiting by the injustice of society, and greedily devouring Stolen Goods? The money belonged to his father, who had worked and thought and given up his liberty to earn it; but by what justice could the money belong to my friend, who had as yet done nothing but help to squander it? A more sturdy honesty, joined to a more even and impartial temperament, would have drawn from these considerations a new force of industry, that this equivocal position might be brought as swiftly as possible to an end, and some good services to mankind justify the appropriation of expense. It was not so with my friend, who was only unsettled and discouraged, and filled full of that trumpeting anger with which young men regard injustices in the first blush of youth; although in a few years, they will tamely acquiesce in their existence and knowingly profit by their complications. Yet all this while, he suffered many indignant pangs. And once when he put on his boots, like many another unripe donkey, to run away from home, it was his best consolation that he was now, at a single plunge to free himself from the responsibility of this wealth that was not his, and do battle equally against his fellows in the warfare of life.

Some time after this, falling into ill health, he was sent at great expense to a more favourable climate; and then I think his perplexities were thickest. When he thought of all the other young men of singular promise, upright, good, the prop of families, who must remain at home to die and with all their possibilities be lost to life and mankind; and how he, by one more unmerited favour, was chosen out from all these others to survive; he felt as if there were no life, no labour, no

490

devotion of soul and body, that could repay and justify these partialities. A religious lady, to whom he communicated these reflexions, could see no force in them whatever. "It was God's will," said she. But he knew, it was by God's will that Joan of Arc was burned at Rouen, which cleared neither Bedford nor Bishop Cauchon,[14] and again by God's will that Christ was crucified outside Jerusalem, which excused neither the rancour of the priests nor the timidity of Pilate. He knew moreover that although the possibility of this favour he was now enjoying issued from his circumstances, its acceptance was the act of his own will; and he had accepted it greedily, longing for rest and sunshine. And hence this allegation of God's providence did little to relieve his scruples. I promise you he had a very troubled mind. And I would not laugh if I were you, though while he was thus making mountains out of what you think molehills, he were still (as perhaps he was) contentedly practising many other things that to you seem black as hell. Every man is his own judge and mountain guide through life. There is an old story of a mote and a beam,[15] apparently not true, but worthy perhaps of some consideration. I should, if I were you, give some consideration to these scruples of his, and if I were him, I should do the like by yours; for it is not unlikely that there may be something under both. In the meantime, you must hear how my friend acted. Like many invalids, he supposed that he would die. Now should he die, he saw no means of repaying this huge loan which, by the hands of his father, mankind had advanced him for his sickness. In that case, it would be lost money. So he determined that the advance should be as small as possible; and so long as he continued to doubt his recovery, lived in an upper room and grudged himself all but necessaries. But so soon as he began to perceive a change for the better, he felt justified in spending more freely to speed and brighten his return to health, and trusted in the future to lend a help to mankind, as mankind, out of its treasury, had lent a help to him.

I do not say but that my friend was a little too curious and partial in his view; nor thought too much of himself and too little of his parents. But I do say that here are some scruples which tormented my friend in his youth, and still perhaps at odd times give him a prick in the midst of his enjoyments, and which may after all have some foundation in justice, and point, in their confused way, to some more honourable honesty within the reach of man. And at least, is not this an unusual gloss upon the eighth commandment? and what sort of comfort, guidance or illumination did that precept afford my friend throughout these contentions?

Thou shalt not steal. With all my heart! But *am* I stealing?

(10) The truly quaint materialism of our view of life disables us from pursuing any transaction to an end. You can make no one understand that his bargain is anything more than a bargain, whereas in point of fact it is a link in the policy of mankind, and either a good or an evil to the world. We have a sort of blindness which prevents us from seeing anything but sovereigns. If one man agrees to give another so many shillings for so many hours of work, and then wilfully gives him a certain proportion of the price in bad money and only the remainder in good, we can see with half an eye that this man is a thief. But if the other spends a certain

proportion of the hours in smoking a pipe of tobacco, and a certain other proportion in looking at the sky, or the clock, or trying to recall an air, or in meditation on his own past adventures, and only the remainder in downright work such as he is paid to do, is he, because the theft is one of time and not of money,—is he any the less a thief? The one gave a bad shilling, the other an imperfect hour; but both broke the bargain and each is a thief. In piece work, which is what most of us do, the case is none the less plain for being even less material. If you forge a bad knife, you have wasted some of mankind's iron, and then, with unrivalled cynicism, you pocket some of mankind's money for your trouble. Is there any man so blind, who cannot see that this is theft? Again, if you carelessly cultivate a farm, you have been playing fast and loose with mankind's resources against hunger; there will be less bread in consequence, and for lack of that bread somebody will die next winter: a grim consideration. And you must not hope to shuffle out of blame because you got less money for your less quantity of bread; for although a theft be partly punished, it is none the less a theft for that. You took the farm against competitors; there were others ready to shoulder the responsibility and be answerable for the tale of loaves; but it was you who took it. By the act, you came under a tacit bargain with mankind to cultivate that farm with your best endeavour; you were under no superintendence, you were on parole; and you have broke your bargain, and to all who look closely, and yourself among the rest if you have moral eyesight, you are a thief. Or take the case of men of letters. Every piece of work which is not as good as you can make it, which you have palmed off imperfect, meagrely thought, niggardly in execution, upon mankind who is your paymaster on parole and, in a sense, your pupil, every hasty or slovenly or untrue performance, should rise up against you in the court of your own heart and condemn you for a thief. Have you a salary? if you trifle with your health, and so render yourself less capable for duty, and still touch, and still greedily pocket the emolument—what are you but a thief? Have you double accounts? do you by any time-honoured juggle, deceit or hocus pocus, gain more from those who deal with you, than if you were bargaining and dealing face to face in front of God?—you are a thief. Lastly, if you fill an office, or produce an article, which, in your heart of hearts, you think a delusion and a fraud upon mankind, and still draw your salary and go through the sham manœuvres of this office, or still book your profits and keep on flooding the world with these injurious goods?—though you were old, and bald, and the first at church, and a baronet, what are you but a thief? These may seem hard words and mere curiosities of the intellect, in an age when the spirit of honesty is so sparingly cultivated, that all business is conducted upon lies and so-called customs of the trade, that not a man bestows two thoughts on the utility or honourableness of his pursuit; and that some workmen, having laid aside the last rag of self-respect, organise a secondary trade and pay a clumsy workman to cloke their brutal idleness and theft. I would say less, if I thought less. But looking to my own reason and the right of things, I can only avow that I am a thief myself and that I passionately suspect my neighbours of the same guilt.

Where did you hear that it was easy to be honest? Do you find that in your bible? Easy? It's easy to be an ass and follow the multitude like a blind, besotted bull in a stampede; and that, I am well aware is what you and Mrs. Grundy mean by being honest.[16] But it will not bear the stress of time nor the scrutiny of conscience. Even before the lowest of all tribunals,—before a court of law, whose business it is, not to keep men right or within a thousand miles of right, but to withhold them from going so tragically wrong that they will pull down the whole jointed fabric of society by their misdeeds—even before a court of law, as we begin to see in these last days, our easy view of following at each other's tails alike to good and evil, is beginning to be reproved, and punished, and declared no honesty at all, but open theft and swindling; and simpletons who have gone on through life with a quiet conscience, may learn suddenly, from the lips of a judge, that the custom of the trade may be a custom of the devil. You thought it was easy to be honest. Did you think it was easy to be just and kind and truthful? Did you think the whole duty of aspiring man was as simple as a hornpipe? and you could walk through life like a gentleman and a hero, with no more concern than it takes to go to church or to address a circular?[17] And yet all this time you had the eighth commandment! and what makes it richer, you would not have broken it for the world!

(11) The truth is that these commandments are of no use in private judgement. They are as senseless as Lord Burleigh's words without the commentary.[18] If compression is what you want, you have their whole spirit compressed into the golden rule; and yet there expressed with more significance, since the law is there spiritually and not materially stated. And in truth, four out of these ten commands from the sixth to the ninth, are rather legal than ethical. The police court is their proper home. A magistrate cannot tell whether you love your neighbour as yourself, but he can tell more or less whether you have murdered, or stolen or committed adultery, or held up your hand and testified to that which was not; and these things, for rough practical tests, are as good as can be found. And perhaps, therefore, the best condensation of the Jewish moral law is in the maxims of the Jurists: "neminem lædere" and "suum cuique tribuere."[19]

But all this granted, it becomes only the more plain that they are out of place in the sphere of personal morality; that while they tell the magistrate roughly when to punish, they can never direct an anxious sinner what to do. Only Polonius, or the like solemn sort of ass, can offer us a succinct proverb by way of advice, and not burst out blushing in our faces.[20] We grant them one and all and for all that they are worth; it is something above and beyond, that we desire. Christ was in general a great enemy to such a way of teaching; we rarely find him meddling with any of these plump commands, but it was to open them out, and lift his hearers from the letter to the spirit. For morals are a personal affair; in the war of righteousness, every man fights for his own hand; all the six hundred precepts of the Mishna[21] cannot shake my private judgement; my magistracy of myself is an indefeasible charge, and my decisions absolute for the time and case. The moralist is not a judge of appeal, but an advocate who pleads at my tribunal. He has to show not the law, but that the law applies. Can he convince me? then he gains the cause. And thus you find Christ giving various counsels to varying people, and often jealously careful to avoid definite precept. Is he asked for example to divide a heritage? He refuses; and the best advice that he will offer is but a paraphrase of that tenth commandment which figures so strangely among the rest. *Take heed, and beware of covetousness.* If you complain that this is vague, I have failed to carry you along with me in my argument. For no definite precept *can be more* than an illustration, though its truth were resplendent like the sun, and it was announced from heaven by the voice of God. And life is so intricate and changing, that perhaps not twenty times or perhaps not twice in the ages, shall we find that nice consent of circumstances to which alone it can apply.

Chapter III

Although the world and life have in a sense become commonplace to our experience;'tis but in an external torpor; the true sentiment slumbers within us; and we have but to reflect on ourselves or our surroundings to rekindle our astonishment. No length of habit can blunt our first surprise. Of the world I have but little to say in this connection; a few strokes shall suffice. We inhabit a dead ember swimming wide in the blank of space, dizzily spinning as it swims, and lighted up from several million miles away by a more horrible hell-fire than was ever conceived by the theological imagination. Yet the dead ember is a green, commodious dwelling place; and the reverberation of this hell-fire ripens flower and fruit and mildly warms us on summer eves upon the lawn. Far off on all hands other dead embers, other flaming suns, wheel and race in the apparent void; the nearest is out of call, the farthest so far that the heart sickens in the effort to conceive the distance. Shipwrecked seamen on the deep, though they bestride but the truncheon of a boom, are safe and near at home compared with mankind on its bullet. Even to us who have known no other, it seems a strange, if not an appalling, place of residence. But far stranger is the resident, man, a creature compact of wonders that, after centuries of custom, are still wonderful to himself. He inhabits a body, which he is continually outliving, discarding and renewing. Food and sleep, by an unknown alchemy, restore his spirits and the freshness of his countenance. Hair grows on him like grass; his eyes, his brain, his sinews, thirst for action; he joys to see and touch and hear, to partake the sun and wind, to sit down and intently pore on his astonishing attributes and situation, to rise up and run, to perform the strange and revolting round of physical functions. The sight of a flower, the note of a bird, will often move him deeply; yet he looks unconcerned on the impassable distances and portentous bonfires of the universe. He comprehends, he designs, he tames nature, rides the sea, ploughs, climbs the air in a balloon, makes vast inquiries, begins interminable labours, joins himself into federations and populous cities, spends his days to deliver the ends of the earth or to benefit unborn posterity; and yet knows himself for a piece of unsurpassed fragility and the creature of a few days. His sight, which conducts him, which takes notice of the furthest stars, which is miraculous in every way and a thing defying explanation or belief, is yet lodged in a piece of jelly and can be extinguished with a touch. His heart which all through life so indomitably, so athletically labours, is but a capsule and may be stopped with a pin. His whole body, for all its savage energies, its leaping and its wing'd desires, may yet be tamed and conquered by a draught of air or a sprinkling of cold dew. What he calls death, which is the seeming arrest of everything and the ruin and hateful transformation of the visible body, lies in wait for him outwardly in a thousand accidents, and grows up in secret diseases from within. He is still learning to be a man when his faculties are already beginning to decline; he has not yet understood himself or his position, before he inevitably dies. And yet this mad, chimerical creature can take no thought of his last end, lives as though he were eternal, plunges with his vulnerable body into the shock of war, and daily affronts death with unconcern.

He cannot take a step without pain or pleasure. His life is a tissue of sensations, which he distinguishes as they seem to come more directly from himself or his surroundings. He is conscious of himself as a joyer or a sufferer, as that which craves, chooses and is satisfied; conscious of his surroundings as it were of an inexhaustible purveyor, the source of aspects, inspirations, wonders, cruel knocks and transporting caresses. Thus he goes on his way, stumbling among delights and agonies.

Matter is a far-fetched theory, and materialism is without a root in man. To him, everything is important in the degree to which it moves him. The telegraph wires and posts, the electricity speeding from clerk to clerk, the clerks, the glad or sorrowful import of the message, and the paper on which it is finally brought to him at home, are all equally facts, all equally exist for man. A word or a thought can wound him as acutely as a knife of steel. If he thinks he is loved, he will rise up and glory to himself, although he be in a distant land and short of necessary bread. Does he think he is not loved?—he may have the woman at his beck, and there is not a joy for him in all the world. Indeed if we are to make any account of this figment of reason, the distinction between material and immaterial, we shall conclude that the life of each man as an individual is immaterial, although the continuation and prospects of mankind as a race turn upon material conditions. The physical business of each man's body is transacted for him; like a sybarite, he has attentive valets in his own viscera; he breathes, he sweats, he digests without an effort, or so much as a consenting volition; for the most part he even eats, not with a wakeful consciousness, but as it were between two thoughts. His life is centred among other and more important considerations; touch him in his honour or his love, creatures of the imagination which attach him to mankind or to an individual man or woman; cross him in his piety which connects his soul with heaven; and he turns from his food, he loathes his breath, and with a magnanimous emotion cuts the knot of his existence and frees himself at a blow from the web of pains and pleasures.

It follows that man is twofold at least; that he is not a rounded and autonomous empire; but that in the same body with him there dwell other powers, tributary but independent. If I now behold one walking in a garden, curiously coloured and illuminated by the sun, digesting his food with elaborate chemistry, breathing, circulating blood, directing himself by the sight of his eyes, accommodating his body by a thousand delicate balancings to the wind and the uneven surface of the path, and all the time perhaps with his mind engaged about America or the dog star[22] or the attributes of God—what am I to say or how am I to describe the thing I see? Is that truly a man, in the rigorous meaning of the word? or is it not a man and something else? What then are we to count the centrebit and axle of a being so variously compounded? It is a question much debated. Some read his history in a certain intricacy of nerve and the success of successive digestions; others find him an exiled piece of heaven blown upon and determined by the breath of God; and both schools of theorist will scream like scalded children at a word of doubt. Yet either of these views, however plausible, is beside the question; either may be right, and I care not; I ask a more particular answer and to a more immediate point. What is the man? There is something that was before hunger and that remains behind after a meal. It is what we always find between affections. It may or may not be engaged in any act or passion, but when it is, it changes, heightens and certifies. Thus it is not engaged in lust, where satisfaction ends the chapter; and it is engaged in love where no satisfaction can blunt the edge of the desire, and where age, sickness or alienation may deface what was desirable without diminishing the sentiment. This, which is the man, is a permanence which abides through the vicissitudes of passion, now overwhelmed and now triumphant, now unconscious of itself in the immediate distress of appetite or pain, now rising unclouded above all. So, to the man, his own central self fades and grows clear again amid the tumult of the senses, like a revolving Pharos[23] in the night. It is forgotten; it is hid, it seems, forever; and yet in the next calm hour, he shall behold Himself once more, shining and unmoved among changes and storm.

Mankind, as the creeping mass that is born and eats, that generates and dies, is but the aggregate of the outer and lower sides of man. This inner consciousness, this lantern alternately obscured and shining, to and by which the individual exists and must order his conduct, is something special to himself and not common to the race. His joys delight, his sorrows wound him, according as *this* is interested or indifferent in the affair; according as they arise in an imperial war or in a broil conducted by the tributary chieftains of the mind. He may lose all, and *this* not suffer; he may lose what is materially a trifle, and *this* leap in his bosom with a cruel pang. I do not speak of it to hardened theorists; the living man knows keenly what it is I mean.

"Perceive at last that thou hast in thee something better and more divine than the things which cause the various affects, and as it were pull thee by the strings. What is there now in thy mind? is it fear, or suspicion, or desire or anything of that kind?"[24] Thus far Marcus Aurelius in one of the most notable passages in any book. Here is a question worthy to be answered. What is in thy mind? What is the utterance of your inmost self when, in a quiet hour, it can be heard intelligibly? It is something beyond the compass of your thinking, inasmuch as it is yourself; but it is of a higher spirit than you had dreamed betweenwhiles, and erect above all base considerations. This soul seems hardly touched with our infirmities; we can find certainly no fear, suspicion or desire; we are only conscious, and that as though we read it in the eyes of some one else, of a great and unqualified readiness. A readiness to what? to pass over and look beyond the objects of desire and fear, for something else. And this something else? this something which is apart from desire and fear, to which all the kingdoms of the world and the immediate death of the body are alike indifferent and beside the point, and which yet regards conduct—by what name are we to call it? It may be the love of God; or it may be an inherited and certainly well concealed instinct to preserve self and propagate the race; I am not for the moment, averse to either theory; but it will save time to call it Righteousness. By so doing I intend no subterfuge to beg a question; I am indeed ready and more than willing to accept the rigid consequence, and lay aside, as far as the treachery of the reason will permit, all former meanings attached to the word, Righteousness. What is right is that for which a man's central self is ever ready to sacrifice immediate or distant interests; what is wrong is what the central self discards or rejects as incompatible with its fixed design of righteousness.

To make this admission, is to lay aside all hope of definition. That which is right upon this theory, is intimately dictated to each man by himself, but can never be rigorously set forth in language and never, above all, imposed upon another. The conscience has, then, a vision like that of the eyes, which is incommunicable and for the most part illuminates none but its possessor. When many people perceive the same or any cognate facts, they agree upon a word as symbol; and hence we have such words as *tree, star, love, honour* or *death*; hence also, we have this word, *right*, which, like the others, we all understand, most of us understand differently, and none can express succinctly otherwise. Yet even on the straitest view, we can make some steps towards comprehension of our own superior thoughts. For it is an incredible and most bewildering fact that a man, through life, is on variable terms with himself; he is aware of tiffs and reconciliations; the intimacy is at times almost suspended, at times it is renewed again with joy. As we said before, his inner self or soul appears to him by successive revelations, and is frequently obscured. It is from a study of these alternations that we can alone hope to discover, even dimly, what seems right and what seems wrong to this veiled prophet of ourself.

All that is in the man in the larger sense, what we call impression as well as what we call intuition, so far as my argument looks, we must accept. It is not wrong to desire food, or exercise, or beautiful surroundings, or the love of sex, or interest which is the food of the mind. All these are craved; all these should be craved; to none of these in itself, does the soul demur; where there comes an undeniable want, we recognise a demand of nature. Yet we know that these natural demands may be superseded; for the demands which are common to mankind make but a shadowy consideration in comparison to the demands of the individual soul. Food is almost the first prerequisite; and yet a high character will go without food to the ruin and death of the body, rather than gain it in a manner which the spirit disavows. Pascal laid aside mathematics; Origen doctored his body with a knife; every day, some one is thus mortifying his dearest interests and desires and, in Christ's words, entering maim into the kingdom of heaven.[25] This is to supersede the lesser and less harmonious affections by a renunciation; and though by this ascetic path, we may get to heaven, we cannot get thither a whole and perfect man. But there is another way, to supersede by reconciliation, in which the soul and all the faculties and senses pursue a common route and share in one desire. Thus, man is tormented by a very imperious physical desire; it spoils his rest, it is not to be denied; the doctors will tell you, not I, how it is a physical need like the want of food or slumber. In the satisfaction of this desire, as it first appears, the soul sparingly takes part; nay, it oft unsparingly regrets and disapproves the satisfaction. But let the man learn to love a woman as far as he is capable of love; and for this random affection of the body, there is substituted a steady determination and consent of all his powers and faculties, which supersedes, adopts and commands the other. The desire survives, strengthened perhaps, but taught obedience and changed in scope and character. Life is no longer a tale of betrayals and regrets; for the man now lives as a whole; his consciousness now moves on uninterrupted like a river; through all the extremes and ups and downs of passion, he remains approvingly conscious of himself.

Now to me, this seems a type of that rightness which the soul demands. It demands that we shall not live alternately with our opposing tendencies in a continual see-saw of passion and disgust, but seek some path on which the tendencies shall no longer oppose but serve each other to a common end. It demands that we shall not pursue broken ends but great and comprehensive purposes in which soul and body may unite like notes in a harmonious chord. That were indeed a way of peace and pleasure; that were indeed a heaven upon earth. It does not demand, however, or, to speak in measure, it does not demand of me, that I should starve my appetites for no purpose under heaven but as a purpose in itself; or in a weak despair, pluck out the eye[26] that I have not yet learned to guide and enjoy with wisdom. The soul demands unity of purpose, not the dismemberment of man; it seeks to roll up all his strength and sweetness, all his passion and wisdom, into one, and make of him a perfect man exulting in perfection. To conclude ascetically, is to give up and not to solve the problem. The ascetic and the creeping hog, although they are at different poles, have equally failed in life. The one has sacrificed his crew; the other brings back the seamen in a cockboat, and has lost the ship. I believe there are not many sea captains who would plume themselves on either result as a success.

But if it is righteousness thus to fuse together our divisive impulses and march with one mind through life, there is plainly one thing more unrighteous than all others, and one declension which is irretrievable and draws on the rest. And this is to lose consciousness of oneself. In the best of times, it is but by flashes, when our whole nature is clear, strong and conscious, and events conspire to leave us free, that we enjoy communion with our soul. At the worst, we are so fallen and passive, that we may say shortly we have none. An arctic torpor seizes upon men. Although built of nerves, and set adrift in a stimulating world, they develope a tendency to go bodily to sleep; consciousness becomes engrossed among the reflex and mechanical parts of life; and soon loses both the will and power to look higher considerations in the face. This is ruin; this is the last failure in life; this is temporal damnation, damnation on the spot and without the form of judgement. "What shall it profit a man if he gain the whole world and *lose himself*?"[27]

It is to keep a man awake, to keep him alive to his own soul and its fixed design of righteousness, that the better part of moral and religious education is directed; not only that of words and doctors, but the sharp ferule[28] of calamity under which we are all God's scholars till we die. If, as teachers, we are to say anything to the purpose, we must say what will remind the pupil of his soul; we must speak that soul's dialect; we must talk of life and conduct as his soul would have him think of them. If, from some conformity between us and the pupil, or perhaps among all men, we do in truth speak in such a dialect and express such views, beyond question we shall touch in him a spring; beyond question, he will recognise the dialect as one that he himself has spoken in his better hours; beyond question, he will cry, "I had forgotten, but now I remember; I too have eyes, and I had forgot to use them! I have a soul of my own, arrogantly upright, and to that I will listen and conform." In short, say to him anything that he has once thought, or been upon the point of thinking, or show him any view of life that he has once clearly seen, or been upon the point of clearly seeing; and you have done your part and may leave him to complete the education for himself.

Now the view taught at the present time, seems to me to want greatness; and the dialect in which alone it can be intelligibly uttered, is not the dialect of my soul. It is a sort of postponement of life; nothing quite is, but something different is to be; we are to keep our eyes upon the indirect from the cradle to the grave. We are to regulate our conduct, not by desire, but by a politic eye upon the future; and to value acts as they will bring us money or good opinion; as they will bring us, in one word, *profit*. We must be what is called respectable and offend no one by our carriage; it will not do to make oneself conspicuous—who knows? even in virtue? says the Christian parent! And we must be what is called prudent and make money; not only because it is pleasant to have money, but because that also is a part of respectability, and we cannot hope to be received in society without decent possessions. Received in society! as if that were the kingdom of heaven! There is dear Mr. So-and-so—look at him!—so much respected—so much looked up to—quite the Christian merchant! And we must cut our conduct as strictly as possible after the pattern of Mr. So-and-so; and lay out our whole lives to make money and be strictly decent. Besides these holy injunctions which form by far the greater part of a youth's training in our Christian homes, there are at least two other doctrines. We are to live just now as well as we can, but scrape at last into heaven where we shall be good. We are to worry through the week in a lay, disreputable way, but to make matters square, live a different life on Sunday.

The train of thought we have been following, gives us a key to all these positions, without stepping aside to justify them on their own ground. It is because we have been disgusted fifty times with physical squalls and fifty times torn between conflicting impulses, that we teach people this indirect and tactical procedure in life and to judge by remote consequences instead of the immediate face of things. The very desire to act as our own souls would have us, coupled with a pathetic disbelief in ourselves, moves us to follow the example of others; perhaps, who knows? they may be on the right track; and the more our patterns are in number, the better seems the chance; until if we be acting in concert with a whole civilised nation, there are surely a majority of chances that we must be acting right. And again, how true it is that we can never behave as we wish in this tormented sphere, and can only aspire in different and more favourable circumstances, to stand out and be ourselves wholly and rightly! And yet once more, if in the hurry and pressure of affairs and passions you tend to nod and become drowsy, here are twenty four hours of Sunday set apart for you to hold counsel with your soul and look around you on the possibilities of life.

This is not, of course, all that is, or even should be, said for these doctrines. Only, in the course of this chapter, the reader and I have agreed upon a few catchwords, and been looking at morals on a certain system; it was a pity to lose an opportunity of testing the catchwords, and seeing whether, by this system as well as by others, current doctrines could show any probable justification. If the doctrines had come too badly out of the trial, it would have condemned the system. Our sight of the world is very narrow; the mind but a pedestrian instrument; there's nothing new under the sun, as Solomon says,[29] except the man himself; and though that changes the aspect of everything else, yet he must see the same things as other people, only from a different side.

And now, having admitted so much, let us turn to criticism.

If you teach a man to keep his eyes upon what others think of him, unthinkingly to lead the life and hold the principles of the majority of his contemporaries, you must discredit in his eyes the one authoritative voice of his own soul. He may be a docile citizen; he will never be a man. It is ours, on the other hand, to disregard this babble and chattering of other men better and worse than we are, and to walk straight before us by what light we have. They may be right; but so, before heaven, are we. They may know; but we know also, and by that knowledge we must stand or fall. There is such a thing as loyalty to a man's own better self; and from those who have not that, God help me, how am I to look for loyalty to others? The most dull, the most imbecile, at a certain moment turn round, at a certain point will hear no further argument, but stand unflinching by their own dumb, irrational sense of right. It is not only by steel or fire, but through contempt and blame, that the martyr fulfils the calling of his dear soul. Be glad if you are not tried by such extremities. But although all the world ranged themselves in one line to tell you "this is wrong," be you your own faithful vassal and the ambassador of God—throw down the glove and answer "this is right." Do you think you are only declaring yourself? Perhaps in some dim way, like a child who delivers a message not fully understood, you are opening wider the straits of prejudice and preparing mankind for some truer and more spiritual grasp of truth; perhaps, as you stand forth for your own judgement, you are covering a thousand weak ones with your body; perhaps, by this declaration alone, you have avoided the guilt of false witness against humanity and the little ones unborn. It is good, I believe, to be respectable; but much nobler to respect oneself and utter the voice of God. God, if there be any God, speaks daily in a new language by the tongues of men; the thoughts and habits of each fresh generation and each new-coined spirit, throw another light upon the universe and contain another commentary on the printed Bibles; every scruple, every true dissent, every glimpse of something new, is a letter of God's alphabet; and though there is a grave responsibility for all who speak, is there none for those who unrighteously keep silence and conform? Is not that also to conceal and cloak God's counsel? And how should we regard the man of science who suppressed all facts that would not tally with the orthodoxy of the hour?

Wrong? You are as surely wrong as the sun rose this morning round the revolving shoulder of the world. Not truth, but truthfulness, is the goal of your endeavour. For when will men receive that first part and prerequisite of truth, that, by the order of things, by the greatness of the universe, by the darkness and partiality of man's experience, by the inviolate secrecy of God kept close in his most open revelations, every man is, and to the end of the ages must be, wrong? Wrong to the universe; wrong to mankind; wrong to God. And yet in another sense, and that plainer and nearer, every man of men who wishes truly, must be right. He is right to himself and in the measure of his sagacity and candour. That let him do in all sincerity and zeal, not sparing a thought for contrary opinions; that, for what it is worth, let him proclaim. Be not afraid; although he be wrong, so also is the dead, stuffed Dagon[30] he insults. For the voice of God, whatever it is, is not that stammering, inept tradition which the people holds. These truths survive in travesty, swamped in a world of spiritual darkness and confusion; and what a few comprehend and faithfully hold, the many, in their dead jargon, repeat, degrade and misinterpret.

So far Respectability: what the Covenanters[31] used to call "rank conformity": the deadliest gag and wet blanket that can be laid on men. And now of Profit. And this doctrine is perhaps the more redoubtable, because it harms all sorts of men; not only the heroic and self reliant, but the obedient, cowlike squadrons. A man by this doctrine, looks to consequences at the second, or third, or fiftieth turn. He chooses his end, and for that, with wily turns and through a great sea of tedium, steers this mortal bark. There may be political wisdom in such a view; but I am persuaded there can spring no great moral zeal. To look thus obliquely upon life, is the very recipe for moral slumber. Our intention and endeavour should be directed, not on some vague end of money or applause, which shall come to us by a ricochet in a month or a year, or twenty years, but on the act itself; not on the approval of others, but on the rightness of that act. At every instant, at every step in life, the point has to be decided, our soul has to be saved, Heaven has to be gained or lost. At every step, our spirits must applaud. At every step, we must set down the foot and sound the trumpet. "This have I done," we must say; "right or wrong, this have I done, in unfeigned honour of intention, as to myself and God."

The profit of every act should be this, that it was right for us to do it. Any other profit than that, if it involved a kingdom or the woman I love, ought, if I were God's upright soldier, to leave me untempted.

It is the mark of what we call a righteous decision, that it is made directly and for its own sake. The whole man, mind and body, having come to an agreement, tyrannically dictates conduct. There are two dispositions eternally opposed: that in which we recognise that one thing is wrong and another right, and that in which, not seeing any clear distinction, we fall back on the consideration of consequences. The truth is, by the scope of our present teaching nothing is thought very wrong and nothing very right, except a few actions which have the disadvantage of being disrespectable when found out; the more serious part of men inclining to think all things *rather wrong*, the more jovial to suppose them *right enough for practical purposes*. I will engage my head, they do not find that view in their own hearts; they have taken it up in a dark despair; they are but troubled sleepers talking in their sleep. The soul, or my soul at least, thinks very distinctly upon many points of right and wrong, and often differs flatly with what is held out as the thought of corporate humanity in the code of society or the code of law. Am I to suppose myself a monster? I have only to read books, the Christian gospels for example, to think myself a monster no longer; and instead I think the mass of people are merely speaking in their sleep.

It is a commonplace, enshrined, if I mistake not, even in school copy books, that honour is to be sought and not fame. I ask no other admission; we are to seek honour, upright walking with our own conscience every hour of the day, and not fame, the consequence, the far off reverberation, of our footsteps. The walk, not the rumour of the walk, is what concerns righteousness. Better disrespectable honour, than dishonourable fame. Better useless or seemingly hurtful honour, than dishonour ruling empires and filling the mouths of thousands. For the man must walk by what he sees, and leave the issue with God who made him and taught him by the fortune of his life. You would not dishonour yourself for money; which is at least tangible; would you do it, then, for a doubtful forecast in politics, or another person's theory of morals?

So intricate is the scheme of our affairs, that no man can calculate the bearing of his own behaviour even on those immediately around him, how much less upon the world at large or on succeeding generations! To walk by external prudence and the rule of consequences, would require, not a man, but God. All that we know to guide us in this changing labyrinth, is our soul with its fixed design of righteousness, and a few old precepts, which commend themselves to that; the precepts are vague when we endeavour to apply them; consequences are more entangled than a wisp of string, and their confusion is unrestingly in change; we must hold to what we know and walk by it. We must walk by faith, indeed, and not by knowledge.[32]

You do not love another because he is wealthy or wise or eminently respectable; you love him because you love him; that is love, and any other only a derision and grimace. It should be the same with all our actions. If we were to conceive a perfect man, it should be one who was never torn between conflicting impulses,

502

but who, in the absolute consent of all his parts and faculties, submitted in every action of his life to a self-dictation as absolute and unreasoned as that which bids him love one woman and be true to her till death. But we should not conceive him as sagacious, ascetical, playing off his appetites against each other, turning the wing of public respectable immorality instead of riding it directly down, or advancing toward his end through a thousand sinister compromises and considerations. The one man might be wily, might be adroit, might be wise, might be respectable, might be gloriously useful; it is the other man who would be good.

The soul asks honour and not fame; to be upright not to be successful; to be good not prosperous; to be essentially not outwardly respectable. Does your soul ask profit? Does it ask money? Does it ask the approval of the indifferent herd? I believe not. For my own part, I want but little money, I hope; and I do not want to be decent at all, but to be good.

Chapter IV

We have spoken of that supreme self-dictation which keeps varying from hour to hour in its dictates with the variation of events and circumstances. Now, for us, that is ultimate. It may be founded on some reasonable process, but it is not a process which we can follow or comprehend. And moreover the dictation is not continuous, or not continuous except in very lively and well-living natures; and betweenwhiles we must brush along without it. Practice is a more intricate and desperate business than the toughest theorising; Life an affair of cavalry, where rapid judgement and prompt action are alone possible and right. As a matter of fact, there is no one so upright but he is influenced by the world's chatter; and no one so headlong but he requires to consider consequences and to keep an eye on profit. For the soul adopts all affections and appetites without exception, and cares only to combine them for some common purpose which shall interest all. Now respect for the opinion of others, the study of consequences and the desire of power and comfort, are all undeniably factors in the nature of man; and the more undeniably since we find that, in our current doctrines, they have swallowed up the others and are thought to conclude in themselves all the worthy parts of man. These, then, must also be suffered to affect conduct in the practical domain; much or little according as they are forcibly or feebly present to the mind of each.

Now a man's view of the universe is mostly a view of the civilised society in which he lives. Other men and women are so much more grossly and so much more intimately palpable to his perceptions, that they stand between him and all the rest; they are larger to his eye than the sun, he hears them more plainly than thunder; with them, by them and for them, he must live and die. And hence the laws that affect his intercourse with his fellow men, although merely customary and the creatures of a generation, are more clearly and continually before his mind, than those which bind him into the eternal system of things, support him in his upright progress on this whirling ball, or keep up the fire of his bodily life. And hence it is, that money stands in the first rank of considerations and so powerfully affects the choice. For our society is built with money for mortar; money is present in every joint of circumstance; it might be named the social atmosphere, since, in society, it is by that alone that men continue to live and only through that or chance that they can reach or affect one another. It would take an essay as long as this to indicate even roughly how money enters into the structure of our lives; but by good or evil fortune, that is a point on which our generation has been completely educated, and a few hints will set the dullest on the key. Money gives us food, shelter and privacy; it permits us to be clean in person, opens for us the doors of the theatre, gains us books for study or pleasure, enables us to help the distresses of others, and puts us above necessity so that we can choose the best in life. If we love, it enables us to meet and live with the loved one, or even to prolong her health and life; if we have scruples, it gives us an opportunity to be honest; if we have any bright designs, here is what will smooth the way to their accomplishment. Penury is the worst slavery, and will soon lead to death.

But money is only a mean; it presupposes a man to use it. The rich can go where he pleases, but perhaps pleases himself nowhere. He can buy a library or visit the whole world, but perhaps has neither patience to read nor intelligence to see. The table may be loaded and the appetite wanting; the purse may be full, and the heart empty. He may have gained the world and lost himself; and with all his wealth around him, in a great house and spacious and beautiful demesne, he may live as blank a life as any tattered ditcher. Without an appetite, without an aspiration, void of appreciation, bankrupt of desire and hope, there, in his great house, let him sit and look upon his fingers. It is perhaps a more fortunate destiny to have a taste for collecting shells than to be born a millionaire. Although neither is to be despised, it is always better policy to learn an interest than to make a thousand pounds; for the money will soon be spent, or perhaps you may feel no joy in spending it; but the interest remains imperishable and ever new. To become a botanist, a geologist, a social philosopher, an antiquary or an artist, is to enlarge one's possessions in the universe by an incalculably higher degree and by a far surer sort of property, than to purchase a farm of many acres. You had perhaps two thousand a year before the transaction; perhaps you have two thousand five hundred after it. That represents your gain in the one case. But in the other, you have thrown down a barrier which concealed significance and beauty. The blind man has learned to see. The prisoner has opened up a window in his cell and beholds enchanting prospects; he will never again be a prisoner as he was; he can watch clouds and changing seasons, ships on the river, travellers on the road, and the stars at night; happy prisoner! his eyes have broken jail! And again he who has learned to love an art or science, has wisely laid up riches against the day of riches; if prosperity come, he will not enter poor into his inheritance; he will not slumber and forget himself in the lap of money or spend his hours in counting idle treasures, but be up and briskly doing; he will have the true alchemic touch, which is not that of Midas,[33] but which transmutes dead money into living delight and satisfaction. *Être et pas avoir*—to be not to possess—that is the problem of life. To be wealthy, a rich nature is the first requisite and money but the second. To be of a quick and healthy blood, to share in all honourable curiosities, to be rich in admiration and free from envy, to rejoice greatly in the good of others, to love with such generosity of heart that your love is still a dear possession in absence or unkindness—these are the gifts of fortune which money cannot buy and without which money can buy nothing. For what can a man possess, or what can he enjoy, except himself? If he enlarge his nature, it is then that he enlarges his estates. If his nature be happy and valiant, he will enjoy the universe as if it were his park and orchard.

But money is not only to be spent; it has also to be earned. It is not merely a convenience or a necessary in social life; but it is the coin in which mankind pays his wages to the individual man. And from this side, the question of money has a very different scope and application. For no man can be honest who does not work. Service for service. If the farmer buys corn, and the labourer ploughs and reaps, and the baker sweats in his hot bakery, plainly you who eat, must do something in your turn. It is not enough to take off your hat, or to thank God upon your knees for the admirable constitution of society and your own convenient situation in its upper and more ornamental stories. Neither is it enough to buy the loaf with a sixpence; for then you are only changing the point of the inquiry; and you must first have bought *the sixpence*. Service for service: how have you bought your sixpences? A man of spirit desires certainty in a thing of such a nature; he must see to it that there is some reciprocity between him and mankind; that he pays his expenditure in service; that he has not a lion's share in profit and a drone's in labour; and is not a sleeping partner and mere costly incubus on the great mercantile concern of mankind.

Services differ so widely with different gifts, and some are so inappreciable to external tests, that this is not only a matter for the private conscience, but one which even there must be leniently and trustfully considered. For remember how many serve mankind who do no more than meditate; and how many are precious to their friends for no more than a sweet and joyous temper. To perform the function of a man of letters, it is not necessary to write, nay it is perhaps better to be a living book. So long as we love, we serve; so long as we are loved by others, I would almost say that we are indispensable; and no man is useless while he has a friend. The true services of life are inestimable in money and are never paid. Kind words and caresses, high and wise thoughts, humane designs, tender behaviour to the weak and suffering, and all the charities of man's existence, are neither bought nor sold.

Yet the dearest and readiest, if not the most just, criterion of a man's services, is the wage that mankind pays him, or, briefly, what he earns. There at least, there can be no ambiguity. St. Paul is fully and freely entitled to his earnings as a tentmaker, and Socrates[34] fully and freely entitled to his earnings as a sculptor, although the true business of each was not only something different but something which remained unpaid. A man cannot forget that he is not superintended, and serves mankind on parole. He would like, when challenged by his own conscience, to reply: "I have done so much work and no less with my own hands and brain, and taken so much profit and no more for my own personal delight."

And though St. Paul, if he had possessed a private fortune, would probably have scorned to waste his time in making tents, yet of all sacrifices to public opinion, none can be more easily pardoned than that by which a man, already spiritually useful to the world, should restrict the field of his chief usefulness to perform services more apparent and possess a livelihood that neither stupidity nor malice could call in question. Like all sacrifices to public opinion and mere external decency, this would certainly be wrong; for the soul should rest contented with its own approval and undissuadably pursue its own calling. Yet, so grave and delicate is the question, that a man may well hesitate before he decides it for himself; he may well fear that he sets too high a valuation on his own endeavours after good; he may well condescend upon a humbler duty where others than himself shall judge the service and proportion the wage.

And yet it is to this very responsibility that the rich are born. They can shuffle off the duty on no other; they are their own paymasters on parole; and must pay themselves fair wages and no more. For I suppose that in the course of ages, and through reform and civil war and invasion, mankind was pursuing some other and more general design, than to set one or two Englishmen of the nineteenth century beyond the reach of needs and duties. Society was scarce put together and defended with so much eloquence and blood, for the convenience of two or three millionaires and a few hundred other persons of wealth and position. It is plain that if mankind thus acted and suffered during all these generations, they hoped some benefit, some ease, some well-being, for themselves and their descendants; that if they supported law and order, it was to secure fair play for all; that if they denied themselves in the present, they must have had some designs upon the future. Now a great hereditary fortune is a miracle of man's wisdom and mankind's forbearance; it has not only been amassed and handed down, it has been suffered to be amassed and handed down; and surely in such a consideration as this, its possessor should find only a new spur to activity and honour, that with all this power of service he should not prove unserviceable, and that this mass of treasure should return in benefits upon the race. If he had twenty or thirty or a hundred thousand at his bankers, or if all Yorkshire or all California were his to manage or to sell, he would still be morally penniless, and have the world to begin like Whittington,[35] until he had found some way of serving mankind. His wage is physically in his own hand; but in honour, that wage must still be earned. He is only steward on parole of what is called his fortune. He must honourably perform his stewardship. He must estimate his own services and allow himself a salary in proportion, for that will be one among his functions. And while he will then be free to spend that salary, great or little, on his own private pleasures, the rest of his fortune he but holds and disposes under trust for mankind; it is not his, because he has not earned it; it cannot be his, because his services have already been paid; but year by year it is his to distribute, whether to help individuals whose birthright and outfit have been swallowed up in his, or to further public works and institutions.

At this rate, short of inspiration, it seems hardly possible to be both rich and honest; and the millionaire is under a far more continuous temptation to thieve, than the labourer who gets his shilling daily for despicable toils. Are you surprised? It is even so. And you repeat it every Sunday in your churches. "It is easier for a camel to pass through the eye of a needle than for a rich man to enter the Kingdom of God."[36] I have heard this and similar texts ingeniously explained away and brushed from the path of the aspiring Christian by the tender Greatheart[37] of the parish. One excellent clergyman told us that the "eye of a needle" meant a low, oriental postern through which camels could not pass till they were unloaded—which is very likely just; and then went on, bravely confounding the "Kingdom of God" with heaven, the future paradise to show that of course no rich person could expect to carry his riches beyond the grave—which, of course, he could not and never did. Various greedy sinners of the congregation drank in the comfortable doctrine with relief. It was worth the while, having come to church that Sunday morning! All was plain. The Bible, as usual, meant nothing in particular; it was merely an obscure and figurative school-copybook; and if a man were only respectable, he was a man after God's own heart.

Alas! I fear not. And though this matter of a man's services is one for his own conscience, there are some cases in which it is difficult to restrain the mind from judging. Thus I shall be very easily persuaded that a man has earned his daily bread; and if he has but a friend or two to whom his company is delightful at heart, I am more than persuaded at once. But it will be very hard to persuade me that any one has earned an income of a hundred thousand. What he is to his friends, he still would be if he were made penniless tomorrow; for as to the courtiers of luxury and power, I will neither consider them friends, nor indeed consider them at all. What he does for mankind, there are most likely hundreds who would do the same, as effectually for the race and as pleasurably to themselves, for the merest fraction of this monstrous wage. Why it is paid, I am, therefore, unable to conceive. And as the man pays it himself, out of funds in his detention, I have a certain backwardness to think him honest.

At least, we have gained a very obvious point: that *what a man spends upon himself, he shall have earned by services to the race.* Thence flows a principle for the outset of life, which is a little different from that taught in the present day. I am addressing the middle and the upper classes; those who have already been fostered and prepared for life at some expense; those who have some choice before them, and can pick professions; and above all, those who are what is called independent, and need do nothing unless pushed by honour or ambition. In this particular the poor are happy; among them, when a lad comes to his strength, he must take the work that offers, and can take it with an easy conscience. But in the richer classes, the question is complicated by the number of opportunities and a variety of considerations. Here then, this principle of ours comes in helpfully. The young man has to seek, not a road to wealth, but an opportunity of service; not money, but honest work. If he has some strong propensity, some calling of nature, some overweening interest in any special field of industry, inquiry or art, he will do right to obey the impulse; and that for two reasons: the first external, because there he will render the best services; the second personal, because a demand of his own nature is to him without appeal whenever it can be satisfied with the consent of his other faculties and appetites. If he has no such elective taste, by the very principle on which he chooses any pursuit at all, he must choose the most honest and serviceable, and not the most highly remunerated. We have here an external problem, not from or to ourself, but flowing from the constitution of society; and we have our own soul with its fixed design of righteousness. All that can be done is to present the problem in proper terms, and leave it to the soul of the individual. Now the problem to the poor is one of necessity: to earn wherewithal to life, they must find remunerative labour. But the problem to the rich is one of honour: having the wherewithal, they must find serviceable labour. Each has to earn his daily bread: the one, because he has not yet got it to eat; the other, who has already eaten it, because he has not yet earned it.

Of course, what is true of bread is true of luxuries and comforts, whether for the body or the mind. But the consideration of luxuries, leads us to a new aspect of the whole question, and to a second proposition no less true, and maybe no less startling, than the last.

At the present day, we, of the easier classes, are in a state of surfeit and disgrace after meat. Plethora has filled us with indifference; and we are covered from head to foot with the callosities of habitual opulence. Born into what is called a certain rank, we live, as the saying is, up to our station. We squander without enjoyment, because our fathers squandered. We eat of the best, not from delicacy, but from brazen habit. We do not keenly enjoy or eagerly desire the presence of a luxury; we are unaccustomed to its absence. And not only do we squander money from habit, but still more pitifully waste it in ostentation. I can think of no more melancholy disgrace for a creature who professes either reason or pleasure for his guide, than to spend the smallest fraction of his income upon that which he does not desire; and to keep a carriage in which you do not wish to drive or a butler of whom you are afraid is a pathetic kind of folly. Money, being a means of happiness, should make both parties happy when it changes hands; rightly disposed, it should be twice blessed[38] in its employment; and buyer and seller should alike have their twenty shillings worth of profit out of every pound. Benjamin Franklin went through life an altered man, because he once paid too dearly for a penny whistle.[39] My concern springs usually from a deeper source, to wit from having bought a whistle when I did not want one. I find I regret this, or would regret it if I gave myself the time, not only on personal but on moral and philanthropical considerations. For first in a world where money is wanting to buy books for eager students and food and medicine for pining children, and where a large majority are starved in their most immediate desires, it is surely base, stupid and cruel to squander money when I am pushed by no appetite and enjoy no return of genuine satisfaction. My philanthropy is wide enough in scope to include myself; and when I have made myself happy, I have at least one good argument that I have acted rightly; but where that is not so, and I have bought and not enjoyed, my mouth is closed, and I conceive that I have robbed the poor. And second anything I buy or use which I do not sincerely want or cannot vividly enjoy, disturbs the balance of supply and demand, and contributes to remove industrious hands from the production of what is useful or pleasurable and to keep them busy upon ropes of sand and things that are a weariness to the flesh. That extravagance is truly sinful, and a very silly sin to boot, in which we impoverish mankind and ourselves. It is another question for each man's heart. He knows if he can enjoy what he buys and uses; if he cannot, he is a dog in the manger;[40] nay, if he cannot, I contend he is a thief, for nothing really belongs to a man which he cannot use. Proprietor is connected with propriety; and that only is the man's which is proper to his wants and faculties.

A youth, in choosing a career, must not be alarmed by poverty. Want is a sore thing, but poverty does not imply want. It remains to be seen whether with half his present income, or a third, he cannot, in the most generous sense, live as fully as at present. He is a fool who objects to luxuries; but he is also a fool who does not protest against the waste of luxuries on those who do not desire and cannot enjoy them. It remains to be seen, by each man who would live a true life to himself and not a merely specious life to society, how many luxuries he truly wants and to how many he merely submits as to a social propriety; and all these last he will immediately forswear. Let him do this, and he will be surprised to find how little money it requires to keep him in complete contentment and activity of mind and senses. Life at any level among the easy classes, is conceived upon a principle of rivalry, where each man and each household must ape the tastes and emulate the display of others. One is delicate in eating, another in wine, a third in furniture or works of art or dress; and I, who care nothing for any of these refinements, who am perhaps a plain athletic creature and love exercise, beef, beer, flannel shirts and a camp bed, am yet called upon to assimilate all these other tastes and make these foreign occasions of expenditure my own. It may be cynical; I am sure I shall be told it is selfish; but I will spend my money as I please and for my own intimate personal gratification, and should count myself a nincompoop indeed to lay out the colour of a halfpenny on any fancied social decency or duty. I shall not wear gloves unless my hands are cold, or unless I am born with a delight in them. Dress is my own affair, and that of one other in the world; that, in fact and for an obvious reason, of any woman who shall chance to be in love with me. I shall lodge where I have a mind. If I do not ask society to live with me, they must be silent; and even if I do, they have no further right but to refuse the invitation.

The true Bohemian,[41] a creature lost to view under the imaginary Bohemians of literature, is exactly described by such a principle of life. The Bohemian of the novel, who drinks more than is good for him, prefers anything to work, and wears strange clothes, is for the most part, a respectable Bohemian, respectable in disrespectability, living for the outside and an adventurer. But the man, I mean, lives wholly to himself, does what he wishes and not what is thought proper, buys what he wants for himself and not what is thought proper, works at what he believes he can do well and not at what will bring in money or favour. You may be the most respectable of men, and yet a true Bohemian. And the test is this: a Bohemian, for as poor as he may be, is always openhanded to his friends; he knows what he can do with money and how he can do without it, a far rarer and more useful knowledge; he has had less and continued to live in some contentment; and hence he cares not to keep more, and shares his sovereign or his shilling with a friend. The poor, if they are generous, are Bohemian in virtue of their birth. Do you know where beggars go? Not to the great houses where people sit dazed among their thousands, but to the doors of poor men who have seen the world; and it was the widow who had only two mites, who cast half her fortune into the treasury.[42]

But a young man who elects to save on dress or on lodging, or who in any way falls out of the level of expenditure which is common to his level in society, falls out of society altogether. I suppose the young man to have chosen his career on honourable principles; he finds his talents and instincts can be best contented in a certain pursuit; in a certain industry, he is sure that he is serving mankind with a healthy, and becoming service; and he is not sure that he would be doing so, or doing so equally well, in any other industry within his reach. Then that is his true sphere in life; not the one in which he was born to his father, but the one which is proper to his talents and instincts. And suppose he does fall out of society, is that a cause of sorrow? Is your heart beat so dead that you prefer the recognition of many to the love of a few? Do you think society loves you? Put it to the proof. Decline in material expenditure, and you will find they care no more for you than for the Khan of Tartary.[43] You will lose no friends. If you had any, you will keep them. Only those who were friends to your coat and equipage, will disappear; the smiling faces will disappear as by enchantment; but the kind hearts will remain steadfastly kind. Are you so lost, are you so dead, are you so little sure of your own soul and your own footing upon solid fact, that you prefer before goodness and happiness the countenance of sundry diners-out, who will flee from you at a report of ruin, who will drop you with insult at a shadow of disgrace, who do not know you and do not care to know you but by sight, and whom you in your turn neither know nor care to know in a more human manner? Is it not the principle of society, openly avowed, that friendship must not interfere with business? which being paraphrased, means simply that a consideration of money goes before any consideration of affection known to this cold-blooded gang, that they have not even the honour of thieves, and will rook[44] their nearest and dearest as readily as a stranger. I hope I would go as far as most to serve a friend; but I declare openly I would not put on my hat to do a pleasure to society. I may starve my appetites and control my temper for the sake of those I love; but society shall take me as I choose to be, or go without me. Neither they nor I will lose; for where there is no love, it is both laborious and unprofitable to associate.

But it is obvious that if it is only right for a man to spend money on that which he can truly and thoroughly enjoy, the doctrine applies with equal force to the rich and to the poor, to the man who has amassed many thousands as well as to the youth precariously beginning life. And it may be asked, is not this merely preparing misers who are not the best of company? But the principle was this: that which a man has not fairly earned and, further, that which he cannot fully enjoy, does not belong to him but is a part of mankind's treasure which he holds as steward on parole. To mankind, then, it must be made profitable; and how this should be done is, once more, a problem which each man must solve for himself and about which none has a right to judge him. Yet there are a few considerations which are very obvious and may here be stated. Mankind is not only the whole in general, but every one in particular. Every man or woman is one of mankind's dear possessions; to his just brain, in his kind heart, in his active hands, mankind entrusts some of her hopes for the future; he or she is a possible well spring of good acts and source of blessings to the race. This money which you do not need, which, in a rigid sense, you do not want, may therefore be returned not only in public benefactions to the race, but in private kindnesses. Your wife, your children, your friends stand nearest to you, and should be helped the first. There at least there can be little imposture, for you know their necessities of your own knowledge. And consider, if all the world did as you did, and according to their means extended help in the circle of their affections, there would be no more crying want in times of plenty and no more cold, mechanical charity given with a doubt and received with confusion. Would not this simple rule make a new world out of the old and cruel one which we inhabit? Have you more money after this is done? are you so wealthy in gold, so poor in friends who need your help, that having done all you can among your own circle, you have still much of mankind's treasure undisposed upon your hands? There are still other matters to be done where you need not fear imposition; and what is over you may hand over without fear to the children whom you have taught; they may be unfaithful to the trust, but you will have done your best and told them on what a solemn responsibility, they must accept and deal with this money.

And now, let us look back and see what we have reached upon this practical point of money.

1st That wealth should not be the first object in life.
2nd That only so much money as he has earned by services to mankind, can a man honestly spend on his own comfort or delight.
3rd That of what he has earned, only so much as he can spend for his own comfort or delight, is his to spend at all; and that whatever is spent by carelessness or through habit or for ostentation, is spent dishonestly and to the hurt of mankind.
4th That whatever we have in our hands which we have not earned, or which we cannot spend to profit or sincere pleasure on ourselves, we must return in principal or interest, to mankind at large; to some other persons to whom it will be profitable or sincerely pleasurable.
And 5th That this may be best done by helping our own friends.

Is not this a very natural, easy, and plain-sailing scheme of life? Wealth should not be the first object in life; but how can it, except in arid and contented natures, or after some violence has been done to the mind externally in the misused name of Prudence? We have a thousand instincts, and a man who begins life wisely must consider them all, and not only that which leads us to desire wealth. Is it natural to buy things we have no mind to? to eat or drink till we are sick? And is it not the natural motion of the soul to communicate wealth among our friends and make them all happy in our prosperity.

Notes

1 Matthew 6:24.

2 Luke 16:8.

3 Thomas Binney (1798–1874), English Congregationalist minister and author of *Is It Possible to Make the Best of Both Worlds* (1853), which attempted to reconcile material success with Christianity.

4 Matthew 6:34.

5 Samuel Budgett (1794–1851), considered the model of a respectable Christian businessman and the subject of William Arthur's popular book *The Successful Merchant: Sketches of the Life of Mr. Samuel Budgett* (1852).

6 Philippians 2:5.

7 John 6:60.

8 Though often associated with Franklin, this proverb predates him by at least a century.

9 Exodus 20:1–17.

10 Fight or brawl.

11 2 Corinthians 3:6.

12 Edmond Hoyle (1672–1769), author of rule books for games, including *A Short Treatise on the Game of Whist* (1742). The phrase "according to Hoyle" means strictly according to the rules.

13 Stevenson himself.

14 John of Lancaster, 1st Duke of Bedford (1389–1435), English prince, military commander, brother of Henry V, and acting regent of France who oversaw the trial of Joan of Arc. The French Catholic Bishop Pierre Cauchon (1371–1442) supported the English cause and conducted the trial.

15 Matthew 7:3–5.

16 Mrs. Grundy, fictional English character who first appears in Thomas Morton's 1798 play *Speed the Plough* and represents conventional opinion and social pressure.

17 Letter of financial credit.

18 *A Collection of State Papers* (1759) of William Cecil, Lord Burleigh (1520–1598), chief advisor to Queen Elizabeth I, is printed with the marginal explanatory gloss of its editor, William Murdin.

19 *Not to harm anyone* and *To each his own due* (Latin).

20 The character in Shakespeare's *Hamlet* who states, "to thine own self be true" (1.3.564).

21 The first major collection of Jewish oral tradition and rabbinic literature, known as the "Oral Torah."

22 Sirius or Alpha Canis Majoris: the night sky's brightest star.

23 Lighthouse.

24 *The Meditations of Marcus Aurelius* (12.19).

25 Blaise Pascal (1623–1662), influential French mathematician and physicist who wrote Catholic theology following his conversion. Origen of Alexandria (184–253), early Christian scholar and ascetic who allegedly castrated himself "for the sake of the kingdom of heaven" (Matthew 19:12). "Entering maim" (Matthew 18:8–9).

26 Matthew 5:29.

27 Luke 9:25.

28 A flat wooden rod used to punish school children.

29 Ecclesiastes 1:9.
30 God of the Philistines in the Hebrew Bible.
31 Scottish Presbyterians of the 17th century who pledged and fought to maintain their church government (n. 22, p. 439).
32 2 Corinthians 5:7.
33 King in Greek mythology who asked the god Dionysus to make everything he touched turn to gold and lost the ability to enjoy food, drink, or human contact.
34 Socrates (470–399 BC), the first moral philosopher, was the son of a sculptor or stone-mason. St. Paul was a tentmaker before converting and becoming an apostle (Acts 18:1–3).
35 Dick Whittington is the protagonist of an English folk tale adapted as a seventeenth-century play called *The History of Richard Whittington, of his lowe byrth, his great fortune* and a popular nineteenth-century pantomime *Dick Whittington and His Cat.* Loosely based on the historical Richard Whittington (1354–1423), merchant, philanthropist, and Lord Mayor of London, the folktale turns Whittington's wealthy gentry origins into a self-made man's rags to riches story.
36 Mark 10:25.
37 The guide and protector of Christian pilgrims in Part II of Bunyan's *Pilgrim's Progress.*
38 Shakespeare, *The Merchant of Venice*, 4.1.179, 181.
39 "The Whistle," *The Life of Benjamin Franklin, written by Himself* (1874).
40 A phrase originating in a Greek fable meaning someone who has no use for something but selfishly prevents others from having it.
41 Bohemia: unconventional or countercultural community of free spirits, artists, and writers.
42 Luke 21:1–4.
43 The title of Chingīz Khan's successors: medieval rulers of the Turkish, Tartar, and Mongol tribes.
44 Cheat or swindle.

69

THE IDEAL HOUSE[1]

Two things are necessary in any neighbourhood where we propose to spend a life: a desert and some living water.

There are many parts of the earth's face which offer the necessary combination of a certain wildness with a kindly variety. A great prospect is desirable but the want may be otherwise supplied; even greatness can be found on the small scale; and the mind and the eye measure differently. Bold rocks near hand are more inspiriting than distant Alps, and the thick fern upon a Surrey heath makes a fine forest for the imagination, and the dotted yew trees noble mountains. A Scottish moor with birches and firs grouped here and there upon a knoll, or one of those rocky sea side deserts of Provence overgrown with rosemary and thyme and smoking with aroma, are places where the mind is never weary. Forests, being more enclosed, are not at first sight so attractive, but they exercise a spell; they must, however, be diversified with either heath or rock, and are hardly to be considered perfect without conifers. Even sand hills, with their intricate plan, and their gulls and rabbits, will stand well for the necessary desert.

The house must be within hail of either a little river or the sea. A great river is more fit for poetry than to adorn a neighbourhood; its sweep of waters increases the scale of the scenery and the distance of one notable object from another; and a lively burn[2] gives us in the space of a few yards, a greater variety of promontory and islet, of cascade, shallow, goil[3] and boiling pool, with answerable changes both of song and colour, than a navigable stream in many hundred miles. The fish, too, make a more considerable feature of the brookside, and the trout plumping in the shadow takes the ear. A stream should, besides, be narrow enough to cross, or the burn hard by a bridge, or we are at once shut out of Eden. The quantity of water need be of no concern, for the mind sets the scale, and can enjoy a Niagara Fall of thirty inches. Let us approve the singer of

> Shallow rivers by whose falls
> Melodious birds sing madrigals.[4]

If the sea is to be our ornamental water, choose an open seaboard with a heavy beat of surf; one much broken in outline, with small havens and dwarf headlands;

if possible a few islets; and as a first necessity, rocks reaching out into deep water. Such a rock on a calm day is a better station than the top of Teneriffe or Chimborazo.[5] In short, both for the desert and the water, the conjunction of many near and bold details is bold scenery for the imagination and keeps the mind alive.

Given these two prime luxuries, the nature of the country where we are to live is I had almost said indifferent; or, after that, inside the garden, we can construct a country of our own. Several old trees, a considerable variety of level, several well grown hedges to divide our garden into provinces, a good extent of old well-set turf, and thickets of shrubs and evergreens to be cut into and cleared at the new owner's pleasure, are the qualities to be sought for in your chosen land. Nothing is more delightful than a succession of small lawns, opening one out of the other through tall hedges; these have all the charm of the old bowling green repeated, do not require the labour of many trimmers, and afford a series of changes. You must have much lawn against the early summer, so as to have a great field of daisies, the year's morning frost; as you must have a wood of lilacs, to enjoy to the full the period of their flowering. Hawthorn is another of the Spring's ingredients; but it is even best to have a rough public lane at one side of your enclosure which, at the right season, shall become an avenue of bloom and odour. The old flowers are the best and should grow carelessly in corners. Indeed, the ideal fortune is to find an old garden, once very richly cared for, since sunk into neglect, and to tend not repair that neglect; it will thus have a smack of nature and wildness which skillful dispositions cannot overtake. The gardener should be an idler, and have a gross partiality to the kitchen plots: an eager or toilful gardener misbecomes the garden landscape; a tasteful gardener will be ever meddling, will keep the borders raw, and take the bloom off nature. Close adjoining, if you are in the south, an olive-yard, if in the north, a swarded apple orchard reaching to the stream, completes your miniature domain; but this is perhaps best entered through a door in the high fruit-wall; so that you close the door behind you on your sunny plots, your hedges and evergreen jungle, when you go down to watch the apples falling in the pool. It is a golden maxim to cultivate the garden for the nose, and the eyes will take care of themselves. Nor must the ear be forgotten: without birds, a garden is a prison yard. There is a garden near Marseilles on a steep hill side, walking by which, upon a sunny morning, your ear will suddenly be ravished with a burst of small and very cheerful singing: some score of cages being set out there to sun their occupants. This is a heavenly surprise to any passer-by; but the price paid, to keep so many ardent and winged creatures from their liberty, will make the luxury too dear for any thoughtful pleasure-lover. There is only one sort of bird that I can tolerate caged, though even then I think it hard, and that is what is called in France the Bec-d'Argent.[6] I once had two of these pigmies in captivity; and in the quiet, bare house upon a silent street where I was then living, their song which was not much louder than a bee's, but airily musical, kept me in a perpetual good humour. I put the cage upon my table when I worked, carried it with me when I went for meals, and kept it by my head at night: the first thing in the morning, these maëstrini[7] would pipe up. But these, even if you can pardon their imprisonment, are for the house. In the garden the wild birds must plant a colony, a chorus of the lesser warblers that should be almost deafening, a blackbird in the lilacs, a nightingale down the lane, so that you must stroll to hear it, and yet a little farther, treetops populous with rooks.

Your house should not command much outlook; it should be set deep and green though upon rising ground or if possible crowning a knoll for the sake of drainage. Yet it must be open to the east, or you will miss the sunrise; sunset, occurring so much later, you can go a few steps and look the other way. A house of more than two stories is a mere barrack; indeed the ideal is of one story, raised upon cellars. If the rooms are large, the house may be small: a single room, lofty, spacious, and lightsome, is more palatial than a castleful of cabinets and cupboards. Yet size in a house, and some extent and intricacy of corridor is certainly delightful to the flesh. The reception room should be if possible a place of many recesses which are "pretty retiring places for conference";[8] but it must have one long wall with a divan: for a day spent upon a divan, among a world of cushions, is as full of diversion as to travel. The eating-room, in the French mode, should be *ad hoc*: unfurnished but with a buffet, the table, necessary chairs, one or two of Canaletto's etchings,[9] and a tile fire-place for the winter. In neither of these public places should there be anything beyond a shelf or two of books; but the passages may be one library from end to end, and the stair, if there be one, lined with volumes in old leather, very brightly carpeted, and leading half way up, and by way of landing, to a windowed recess with a fire place: this window, almost alone in the house, should command a handsome prospect. Husband and wife must each possess a studio; on the woman's sanctuary, I hesitate to dwell, and turn to the man's. The walls are shelved waist-high for books, and the top thus forms a continuous table running round the wall. Above are prints, a large map of the neighbourhood, a Corot and a Claude[10] or two. The room is very spacious, and the five tables and two chairs are but as islands. One table is for actual work, one close by for references in use; one, very large, for M.S.S.[11] or proofs that wait their turn; one kept clear for an occasion; and the fifth is the map table, groaning under a collection of large scale maps and charts. Of all books these are the least wearisome to read and the richest in matter; the course of roads and rivers, the contour lines and the forests in the maps—the reefs, soundings, anchors, sailing marks and little pilot-pictures, in the charts—and in both, the bead-roll of names—make them of all printed matter the most fit to stimulate and satisfy the fancy. The chair in which you write is very low and easy, and backed into a corner; at one elbow the fire twinkles; close at the other, if you are a little inhumane, your cage of Silver-Bills are twittering into song.

Joined along a passage, you may reach the great, sunny, glass-roofed and tiled gymnasium; at the far end of which, lined with bright marble, is your plunge and swimming bath, fitted with a capacious boiler.

The whole loft of the house from end to end makes one undivided chamber; here are set forth tables on which to model imaginary or actual countries, in putty or plaster, with tools and hardy pigments; a carpenter's bench; and a spared corner for photography, while at the far end a space is kept clear for playing soldiers. Two boxes contain the two armies of some five hundred horse and foot; two others, the ammunition of each side and a fifth the foot rules and the three colours of chalk, with which you lay down, or after a day's play, refresh the outlines of the country: red or white for the two kinds of road (according as they are suitable or not for the passage of ordnance) and blue for the course of the obstructing rivers. Here I foresee that you may pass much happy time; against a good adversary a game may well continue for a month; for with armies so considerable three moves will occupy an hour. It will be found to set an excellent edge on this diversion, if one of the players shall, every day or so, write a report of the operations in the character of army correspondent.

I have left to the last the little room for winter evenings. This should be furnished in warm positive colours, and, the sofas and floor thick with rich furs. The hearth, where you burn wood of aromatic quality on silver dogs, tiled round about with Bible pictures; the seats deep and easy; a single Titian[12] in a gold frame; a white bust or so upon a bracket; a rack for the journals of the week; a table for the books of the year, and close in a corner the three shelves full of eternal books that never weary: Shakespeare, Molière, Montaigne, Lamb, Sterne, De Musset's comedies (the one volume open at *Carmosine* and the other at *Fantasio*), the *Arabian Nights* and kindred stories in Weber's solemn volumes, Borrow's *Bible in Spain*, the *Pilgrim's Progress, Guy Mannering* and *Rob Roy, Monte Cristo* and the *Vicomte de Bragelonne*, immortal Boswell sole among biographers, Chaucer, Herrick, and the *State Trials*.[13]

The bedrooms are large, airy, with almost no furniture, floors of varnished wood and at the bed-head, in case of insomnia, one shelf of books of a particular and dippable order; such as *Pepys*, the *Paston Letters*, Burt's *Letters from the Highlands*, or the *Newgate Calendar*. . . .

Notes

1 Stevenson wrote this essay—a parody of advice-for-living magazine articles and Francis Bacon's essay "Of Building"—in April 1884 in Hyères, France. Four months later, he and Fanny moved to Bournemouth. In July of 1885, they moved into a house Stevenson's father bought for them as a wedding present. Stevenson named the house Skerryvore after the famous lighthouse his uncle Alan Stevenson designed.
2 A small stream or brook.
3 A channel (Scottish).
4 Christopher Marlowe, "The Passionate Shepherd to His Love" (7–8).
5 Mount Teide: a volcano on the Spanish island Tenerife, the highest point in the Atlantic islands. Chimborazo: Ecuadorian mountain peak over 20,000 feet high.
6 Silverbill.
7 Little musical masters: a variation on maestro (Italian).
8 Francis Bacon, "Essay 45. Of Building"
9 Canaletto (1697–1768), Venetian landscape artist.
10 French landscape painters, Jean-Baptiste-Camille Corot (1796–1875) and Claude Lorrain (1600–1682).

11 Manuscripts.
12 Titian (1490–1576), leading Italian Renaissance painter of the Venetian school.
13 Molière, Jean-Baptiste Poquelin (1622–1673), French dramatist and poet, widely considered one of the greatest writers in French; Michel de Montaigne (1533–1592), French author of the *Essais*, which established the essay form; Charles Lamb (1775–1834), English essayist and critic; Laurence Sterne (1713–1768), Irish novelist, author of *Tristram Shandy*; Alfred de Musset (1810–1847), French Romantic writer, author of the poem *Carmoisine* (1850) and the play *Fantasio* (1834); Georg Weber (1808–1888) philologist, historian, and professor at Heidelberg; George Borrow's travel memoir *The Bible in Spain* (1843); John Bunyan's *The Pilgrim's Progress* (1678); Walter Scott's novels *Guy Mannering* (1815) and *Rob Roy* (1817); Alexandre Dumas's *The Count of Monte Cristo* (1844) and *Vicomte de Bragelonne* (1850)—the third and final volume of *The d'Artagnan Romances*, which began with *The Three Musketeers* (1844); James Boswell's *The Life of Samuel Johnson* (1791); *State Trials at Large. The Whole Proceedings on the Trials of Col. Despard, and the other State Prisoners . . . Original and Authentic Memoirs of Col. Despard* (1803). Colonel Edward Marcus Despard (1751–1803), Irish-born revolutionary executed for high treason on charge of an attempted plot to assassinate George III; Robert Herrick (1591–1674) lyric poet; Samuel Pepys (1633–1703), English naval administrator and MP whose famous *Diary and Correspondence* was published in 1825; *The Paston Letters: 1429–1509*, edited by James Gairdner (1872–1875); Edward Burt's *Letters from a Gentleman in the North of Scotland to his Friend in London* (1754). Edward Burt (d. 1755), civil servant who worked with General George Wade building a network of military roads in the Highlands; Andrew Knapp and William Baldwin's *The Newgate Calendar; comprising Interesting Memoirs of the Most Notorious Characters who have been Convicted of Outrages on the Laws of England since the Commencement of the Eighteenth Century* (1824–1828).

70

ROSA QUO LOCORUM[1]

Through what little channels, by what hints and premonitions, the consciousness of the man's art dawns first upon the child, it should be not only interesting but instructive to inquire. A matter of curiosity today, it will become the ground of science tomorrow. From the mind of childhood there is more history and more philosophy to be fished up than from all the printed volumes in a library. The child is conscious of an interest, not in literature but in life; a taste for the precise, the adroit or the comely in the use of words, comes late; and long before that he has enjoyed in books a delightful dress rehearsal of experience. He is first conscious of this material—I had almost said this practical—preoccupation; it does not follow that it really came the first. I have some old fogged negatives in my collection that would seem to imply a prior stage. "The Lord is gone up with a shout, and God with the sound of a trumpet"[2]—memorial version, I know not where to find the text—rings still in my ear from my first childhood, and perhaps with something of my nurse's[3] accent. There was possibly some sort of image written in my mind by these loud words, but I believe the words themselves were what I cherished. I had about the same time, and under the same influence—that of my dear nurse, a favourite author: it is possible the reader has not heard of him— Dr Robert Murray M'Cheyne. My nurse and I admired his name exceedingly, so that I must have been taught the love of beautiful sounds before I was breeched; and I remember two specimens of his muse until this day.

> Behind the hills of Naphtali
> The sun went slowly down,
> Leaving on mountain, tower and tree,
> A tinge of golden brown.[4]

There is imagery here, and I set it on one side. The other—it is but a verse— not only contains no image, but is quite unintelligible even to my comparatively instructed mind, and I know not even how to spell the outlandish vocable that charmed me in my childhood.

> Jehovah Tschidkenu is nothing to her.[5]

519

I may say, without flippancy, that he was nothing to me either, since I had no ray of a guess of what he was about; yet the verse, from then to now, a longer interval than the life of a generation, has continued to haunt me. I have said that I should set a passage distinguished by obvious and pleasing imagery, however faint; for the child thinks much in images, words are very live to him, phrases that imply a picture eloquent beyond their value. Rummaging in the dusty pigeonholes of memory, I came once upon a graphic version of the famous psalm: "The Lord's my Shepherd:"[6] and from the places employed in its illustration which are all in the immediate neighbourhood of a house then occupied by my father, I was able to date it before the seventh year of my age: though it was probably earlier in fact. The pastures green were a certain suburban stubble field, where I had once walked with my nurse, under an autumnal sunset, on the banks of the Water of Leith: the place is long ago built up: no pastures now, no stubble fields; only a maze of little streets and smoking chimneys, and shrill children. Here in the fleecy person of a sheep, I seemed to myself to follow something unseen, unrealised and yet benignant; and close by the sheep, in which I was incarnated—as if for greater security—rustled the skirts of my nurse. "Death's dark vale" was a certain archway in the Warriston Cemetery: a formidable, yet beloved spot; for children love to be afraid in measure, as they love all experience of vitality. Here I beheld myself (some paces ahead—seeing myself—I mean from behind) utterly alone in that uncanny passage: on the one side of me a rude, nobbly shepherd's staff, such as cheers the heart of the cockney tourist, on the other a rod like a billiard cue, appeared to accompany my progress: the staff sturdily upright, the billiard cue inclined confidentially, like one whispering, towards my ear. I was aware—I will never tell you how—that the presence of these articles afforded me encouragement. The third and last of my pictures illustrated the words:

> My table thou hast furnished in presence of my foes;
> My head thou dost with oil anoint and my cup overflows

and this was perhaps the most interesting of the series. I sat in a kind of open stone summer house at table; over my shoulder a hairy, bearded, and robed presence anointed me from an authentic shoe-horn; the summer house was part of the green court of a ruin, and from the far side of the court black and white imps discharged against me ineffectual arrows. The picture appears arbitrary, but I can trace every detail to its source, as Mr Brock analysed the dream of Alan Armadale.[7] The summer house and court were muddled together out of Billings's *Antiquities of Scotland*;[8] the imps conveyed from Bagster's *Pilgrim's Progress*;[9] the bearded and robed figure from any one of a thousand bible pictures; and the shoe horn plagiarised from an old illustrated bible, where it figured in the hand of Samuel anointing Saul,[10] and had been pointed out to me as a jest by my father. It was shown me for a jest, remark; but the serious spirit of infancy adopted it in earnest. Children are all classics; a bottle would have seemed an intermediary too trivial for that divine refreshment—of whose meaning I had no guess; and I seized on the idea of that mystic shoehorn with delight, even as a little later I should have written flagon, chalice, hanaper beaker, or any word that might have appealed to me at the moment as least contaminate with mean associations. In this string of pictures I believe the gist of the psalm to have consisted; I believe it had no more to say to me; and the result was consolatory. I would go to sleep dwelling with restfulness upon these images; they passed before me, besides, to an appropriate music; for I had already singled out from that rude psalm, the one lovely verse which dwells in the minds of all, not growing old, not disgraced by its association with long Sunday tasks, a scarce conscious joy in childhood, in age a companion thought:

> In Pastures green thou leadest me
> The quiet waters by.

The remainder of my childish recollections are all of the matter of what was read to me, and not of any manner in the words. If these pleased me, it was unconsciously; I listened for news of the great vacant world upon whose edge I stood; I listened for delightful plots that I might reënact in play, and romantic scenes and circumstances that I might call up before me, with closed eyes, when I was weary of Scotland, and home, and that weary prison of the sickchamber in which I lay so long in durance. *Robinson Crusoe*, some of the books of that cheerful, ingenious, romantic soul, Mayne Reid,[11] and a work (rather gruesome and bloody for a child but very picturesque) called *Paul Blake*,[12] are the three strongest impressions I remember: *The Swiss Family Robinson* came next, *longo intervallo*.[13] At these I played, conjured up their scenes, and delighted to hear them rehearsed unto seventy times seven. I am not sure but what *Paul Blake* came after I could read. It seems connected with a visit to the country, and an experience unforgettable. The day had been warm; H—[14] and I had played together charmingly all day in a sandy wilderness across the road; then came the evening with a great flush of colour and a heavenly sweetness in the air. Somehow my playmate had vanished; or is out of the story, as the sagas say, but I was sent into the village on an errand; and taking a book of fairy tales, went down alone through a fir wood, reading as I walked. How often since then, has it befallen me to be happy even so; but that was the first time: the shock of that pleasure I have never since forgot, and if my mind serves me to the last, I never shall; for it was then that I knew I loved reading.

II

To pass from hearing literature to reading it, is to take a great and dangerous step. With not a few, I think a large proportion of this pleasure there determines; "the malady of not marking"[15] overtakes them, they read thenceforward by the eye alone; and hear never again the chime of fair words or the march of the stately period. *Non ragioniam*[16] of these. But to all the step is dangerous; it involves coming of age; it is even a kind of second weaning. In the past all was at the choice of others; they chose, they digested, they read aloud for us and sang to their own tune the books of childhood. In the future, we are to approach the silent inexpressive type alone, like pioneers; and the choice of what we are to read is in our own hands thenceforward. For instance—in the passages already adduced, I detect and applaud the ear of my old nurse; they were of her choice, and she imposed them on my infancy; reading the works of others, as a poet would scarce dare to read his own; gloating on the rhythm, dwelling with delight on assonances and alliterations. I know very well my mother must have been all the while trying to educate my taste upon more secular authors; but the vigour and the continual opportunities of my nurse triumphed, and after a long search, I can find in these earliest volumes of my autobiography, no mention of anything but nursery rhymes, the bible, and Dr M'Cheyne.

I suppose all children agree in looking back with delight on their school readers. We might not now find so much pathos in "Bingen on the Rhine—" a soldier of the legion lay dying in Algiers,[17] or in "The Soldier's Funeral,"[18] in the declamation of which I was held to have surpassed myself. "Robert's voice," said the master on this memorable occasion, "is not strong but impressive": an opinion which I was fool enough to carry home to my father; who roasted me for years in consequence. I am sure one should not be so deliciously tickled by the humorous pieces:

"What, crusty?" cries Will in a taking
"Who would not be crusty with half a year's baking?"[19]

I think this quip would leave us cold. "The Isles of Greece"[20] seem rather tawdry too; but on the "Address to the Ocean," or on "The Dying Gladiator," "time has writ no wrinkle":[21]

Tis the morn, but dim & dark.
Whither flies the silent lark?[22]

Does the reader recall the moment when his eye first fell upon these lines in the Fourth Reader;[23] and "Surprised with joy, impatient as the wind,"[24] he plunged into the sequel? And there was another piece, this time in prose, which none can have forgotten; many like me must have searched Dickens with zeal to find it again, and in its proper context, and have perhaps been conscious of some inconsiderable measure of disappointment, that it was only Tom Pinch who drove, in such a pomp of poetry, to London.[25]

But in the Reader, we are still under guides, what a boy turns out for himself, as he rummages the bookshelves, is the real test and pleasure. My father's library was a spot of some austerity: the proceedings of learned societies, some Latin divinity, Cyclopedias, physical science and above all optics, held the chief place upon the shelves, and it was only in holes and corners that anything really legible existed as by accident. *The Parent's Assistant*,[26] *Rob Roy*, *Waverley*, and *Guy Mannering*,[27] the *Voyages* of Captain Woodes Rogers,[28] Fuller's and Bunyan's *Holy Wars*,[29] *The Reflections of Robinson Crusoe*, *The Female Blue Beard*[30], (Sue's

Morne-au-Diable—how came it in that grave assembly?) Ainsworth's *Tower of London* and four old volumes of *Punch*—these were the chief exceptions. In these latter, which almost as soon as I could spell the words made for years the chief of my diet, I very early fell in love with the *Snobs Papers*,[31] I knew them almost by heart, particularly the visit to the Pontos; and I remember my surprise when I found, long afterwards, that they were famous and signed with a famous name; to me, as I read and admired them, they were the works of Mr Punch. Time and again I tried to read *Rob Roy*, with whom of course I was acquainted from the *Tales of a Grandfather*;[32] time and again the early part, with Rashleigh and (think of it!) the adorable Diana, choked me off; and I shall never forget the pleasure and surprise with which, lying on the floor one summer evening, I struck of a sudden into the first scene with Andrew Fairservice. "The worthy Dr Lightfoot— mistrysted with a bogle—a wheen green trash—Jenny, lass, I think I hae her": from that day to this the phrases have been unforgotten. I read on, I need scarce say; I came to Glasgow, I bided tryst on Glasgow Bridge, I met Rob Roy and the Bailie in the Toll-booth,—all with transporting pleasure, and then the clouds gathered once more about my path; and I dozed and skipped until I stumbled half asleep into the clachan of Aberfoyle and the voices of Iverach and Galbraith recalled me to myself. With that scene and the defeat of Captain Thornton, the book concluded; Helen and her sons shocked even the little schoolboy of nine or ten with their unreality; I read no more, or I did not grasp what I was reading; and years elapsed before I consciously met Diana and her father among the hills, or saw Rashleigh sit dying in the chair. When I think of that novel, and that evening, I am impatient with all others; they seem but shadows and impostors; they cannot satisfy the appetite which this awakened: and I dare be known to think it the best of Sir Walter's by nearly as much as Sir Walter is the best of novelists. Perhaps Mr Lang is right, and our first friends in the land of fiction are always the most real.[33] And yet I had read before this *Guy Mannering*, and some of *Waverley*, with no such delighted sense of truth and humour, and I read immediately after the greater part of the Waverley novels, and was never moved again in the same way or to the same degree. One circumstance is suspicious; my critical estimate of the Waverley novels has scarce changed at all since I was ten. *Rob Roy*, *Guy Mannering* and *Redgauntlet* first; then, a little lower, *The Fortunes of Nigel*; then, after a huge gulf, *Ivanhoe* and *Anne of Geierstein*; the rest nowhere: such was the verdict of the boy. Since then *The Antiquary, Saint Ronan's Well, Kenilworth*, and *The Heart of Midlothian*, have gone up in the scale; perhaps *Ivanhoe* and *Anne of Geierstein*, though I still think them fine pieces of swash bucklery, have gone a trifle down; Diana Vernon has been added to my admirations in that enchanted world of *Rob Roy*; I think more of the letters in *Redgauntlet*, and Peter Peebles, that dreadful piece of realism, I can now read about with equanimity, interest and I had almost said pleasure, while to the critic often he caused unmixed distress. But the rest is the same; I could not finish *The Pirate* when I was a child, I have never finished it yet; *Peveril of the Peak* dropped half way through from my schoolboy hands, and though I have since waded to an end in a kind of wager with myself, the exercise was quite without enjoyment. There is something disquieting in these considerations. I still think the visit to Ponto's the best part of *The Book of Snobs*: does that mean that I was right when I was a child, or does it mean that I have never grown since then, that the child is not the man's father,[34] but the man? and that I came into the world with all my faculties complete and have only learned sinsyne[35] to be more tolerant of boredom?

Notes

1 "Mitte sectari, rosa quo locorum / sera moretur": stop searching places where the last rose may linger (Horace, *Odes* 1.38.3–4). Stevenson composed this unfinished essay in Aug. 1890.
2 Psalms 47:5.
3 Alison "Cummy" Cunningham (1822–1913) became Stevenson's nurse in 1852 and stayed in the household for twenty years. She was a strict Calvinist, raising Stevenson on biblical Presbyterianism and stories of Covenanters. He corresponded with her throughout his life and dedicated *A Child's Garden of Verses* (1885) to her. See "Nurses" (p. 436).
4 From the hymn "To Yonder Side" (1–4) by Robert Murray M'Cheyne (1813–1843), religious poet and Church of Scotland minister.
5 M'Cheyne's poem is titled "Jehovah Tschidkenu: 'The Lord Our Righteousness' (The Watchword of the Reformers)" from Jeremiah 23:5–6. The line reads, "Jehovah Tschidkenu was nothing to me" (4).
6 Psalm 23.
7 Characters in Wilkie Collins's novel *Armadale* (1866).
8 Robert William Billings's illustrated, four-volume *The Baronial and Ecclesiastical Antiquities of Scotland* (1845–1852).
9 The Samuel Bagster and Sons 1857 edition of John Bunyan's *Pilgrim's Progress*, illustrated by Eunice Bagster. See Stevenson's essay "Byways of Book Illustration: Bagster's Pilgrim's Progress" (1882).
10 1 Samuel 9–10.
11 Thomas Mayne Reid (1818–1883), Scots-Irish American adventure novelist who served in the Mexican-American War and wrote novels set in the American West, Latin America, Africa, the Caribbean, and the Himalayas.
12 Alfred Elwes's *Paul Blake; or, The Story of a Boy's Peril in the Islands of Corsica and Monte Cristo* (1859).
13 After a long interval (Latin).
14 Stevenson's maternal cousin Henrietta.
15 Shakespeare, *Henry IV Part II* 1.2.108–109.
16 From Canto III of Dante's *Inferno*: "do not reason." The line reads, "non ragioniam di lor, ma guarda e passa" or "let us not talk of them, but look and pass." The quoted phrase is used to avoid discussing persons deemed unworthy of attention.
17 Caroline Norton, "Bingen on the Rhine."
18 Letitia Elizabeth Landon's 1824 poem.
19 George Colman's "Lodgings for Single Gentlemen" from his comic poetry collection *My Night-Gown and Slippers* (1797). In the poem, a young fat man rents a room from a baker, gets a fever, and becomes thin only to discover that his bed is directly above the oven. He becomes crusty in both senses: baked like bread and (consequently) short-tempered and curt.
20 A poem praising Greece's glorious heritage and lamenting its subjection by the court poet in the third canto of Byron's *Don Juan* (1819).

524

21 From the fourth canto of Byron's *Childe Harold's Pilgrimage*: "The Dying Gladiator" (1252–1269) and "The Address to the Ocean" (1603–1656). "Time writes no wrinkle on thine azure brow" (1637).
22 Byron's *The Deformed Transformed* 2.1.1–2.
23 *The Chambers's Graduated Readers*: a series of grammar school textbooks edited and published by William (1800–1883) and Robert Chambers (1802–1871). The most advanced volumes were literary anthologies of canonical authors, including Byron.
24 William Wordsworth, "Surprised by Joy" (1815, 1).
25 In Dickens's *Martin Chuzzlewit* (1844), Tom Pinch travels to London to seek new employment after being exploited by the greedy and unscrupulous architect Seth Pecksniff.
26 Maria Edgeworth's 1796 collection of children's stories.
27 Novels by Walter Scott.
28 *The Voyage of Captain Woodes Rogers to the South Seas and Round the World* (1790): the account of Woodes Rogers (1679–1732), English sea captain and privateer known for successful expeditions against the Spanish and rescuing the marooned Alexander Selkirk, who was thought to be the inspiration for Defoe's *Robinson Crusoe* (1719).
29 Thomas Fuller's *The Historie of the Holy Warre* (1651) and John Bunyan's allegorical novel *The Holy War* (1682).
30 Eugène Sue's *The Female Bluebeard: or, Le Morne-au-Diable* (1845); William Harrison Ainsworth's *The Tower of London: A Historical Romance* (1840); *Punch*: a satirical British magazine established in 1841.
31 William Makepeace Thackeray's satirical weekly series "The Snobs of England, by one of themselves," published in *Punch* and later as *The Book of Snobs* (1848).
32 Walter Scott's four-volume collection of children's stories from Scottish history (1828–1831).
33 Stevenson's friend Andrew Lang (1844–1912) published his first volume of edited fairy tales *The Blue Fairy Book* in 1889.
34 "The Child is father of the Man" (Wordsworth, "My Heart Leaps Up," 7).
35 Since then or from that time (Scottish).

EMENDATIONS LIST

The following emendations are corrections of clear errors in the original copy text, which appears in brackets following the modified version.

"Virginibus Puerisque": "What a pity!" he exclaims [What a pity?] p. 25.
– Imagine Consuelo as Mrs. Samuel Budgett [Budget] p. 27.
"Virginibus Puerisque II": rags of honour [rays of honour] p. 37.
"Virginibus Puerisque III. On Falling in Love": In *Adelaide*, in Tennyson's *Maud*, and in some of Heine's songs [Maud] p. 41.
– fourth act of *Antony and Cleopatra* [Antony and Cleopatra] p. 43.
"Virginibus Puerisque IV. Truth of Intercourse": the truth which makes love possible and mankind happy [makes mankind unhappy] p. 46.
"Crabbed Age and Youth": She says, I am *too witty*; Anglicè [Angelicè] p. 52.
– *Si Jeunesse savait, si Vieillesse pouvait* [*Si Feunesse*] p. 55.
– what sorry and pitiful quibbling all this is! [all this is?] p. 83.
"The English Admirals": It is warm work, and this day may be the last to any of us at a moment [It is warm work, and this may be the last to any of us at any moment] p. 92–93.
"Walking Tours": pleasure leads on to pleasure in an endless chain [to an endless chain] p. 107.
– that I sat down to a volume of the *New Héloïse* [new *Héloïse*] p. 110.
– surly weather imprisons you [imprison you] p. 111.
"A College Magazine": the other, originally known as *Semiramis: a Tragedy* [originally know as] p. 144.
– there still shines beyond the student's reach [byond tehe] p. 145.
– in this volume of *Memories and Portraits* [Memories and Portraits] p. 148.
"An Old Scotch Gardener": labyrinths of walk and wildernesses [windernesses] p. 150–151.
"Talk and Talkers II": wisdom's simple, plain considerations [wisdom's simples] p. 187.
"Fontainebleau: Village Communities of Painters": to think of his material and nothing else, is, for a while at least, the king's highway of progress. [awhile] p. 222.

"An Epilogue to *An Inland Voyage*": *je suppose qu'il faut lâcher votre cama-rade* [*votre camarades*] p. 240.

"Contributions to the History of Fife": and I like to think of him standing back upon the bridge [I live to think of him] p. 248.

"Roads": *Werther* [Werther] p. 308.

"On the Enjoyment of Unpleasant Places": *Portfolio* [Portfolio] p. 314.

"An Autumn Effect": an old woman sat placidly dozing over the fire [set placidly] p. 326.

– Lilliputian [Liliputian] p. 328.

"Forest Notes": And there is an old tale that enhances [old tale enhances] p. 348.

– like an ungainly sort of puppet [puppets] p. 348.

"The Morality of the Profession of Letters": lost note of the romantic comedy [last note] p. 384.

– This is, in criticism, the attitude we should all seek to preserve, not only in that, but in every branch of literary work [not only in taht] p. 385, n. 7.

"A Modern Cosmopolis": an unbroken line of coast [line of eoast] p. 387.

"Gentlemen": those shall be held the most "elegant" gentlemen, and those the most "refined" ladies [gentleman] p. 401.

"My First Book: *Treasure Island*": Somewhat in this way, as I pored upon my map of *Treasure Island*, the future characters of the book began to appear there visibly among imaginary woods; and their brown faces and bright weapons peeped out upon me from unexpected quarters [paused upon my map . . . the future character of the book] p. 409.

– projected a joint volume of bogie stories [logic stories] p. 409.

– It had to be transacted almost secretly; my wife was ill; the schoolboy remained alone of the faithful [transcribed almost exactly] p. 411.

– He was large-minded; "a full man," if there ever was one [if there was one] p. 412.

– short-cuts and footpaths for his messengers [short-cuts and footprints] p. 413.

– that he who is faithful to his map [that who is faithful] p. 413.

"The Modern Student": Dilettante is now a term of reproach [Dilletante] p. 454.

"Debating Societies": *roués* in speculation [*roué* in speculation] p. 457.

"Philosophy of Nomenclature": I found a freebooter or a general [as a general] p. 460.

– How many Cæsars and Pompeys, by mere inspiration of the names . . . have been Nicodemus'd into nothing? [Nicodemus'd into nothing.] p. 460.

– and if the *soubriquet* were applicable to the ancestor [*soubiquet*] p. 461.

– Pym and Habakkuk [Habbakuk] p. 461.

– apposition with the author of *Hamlet* [Hamlet] p. 461.

"The Ideal House": The reception room should be if possible a place of many recesses which are "pretty retiring places for conference" [petty retiring places] p. 516.

END-OF-LINE HYPHENS

Listed below by page number are the "hard" end-of-line hyphens, not produced accidentally by typesetting but included in the copy text. These should be retained in reproduction and quotation.

p. 29 sea-sick
p. 34 ticket-of-leave
p. 42 Joan-of-Arc's
p. 63 lack-lustre
p. 73 olive-garden
p. 82 poetry-books
p. 84 full-blooded
p. 100 well-being
p. 123 Cornish-speaking
p. 126 Bible-quoting
p. 126 self-sufficiency
p. 127 public-house
p. 140 red-hot
p. 145 Senatus-consults
p. 145 humble-minded
p. 147 ear-wigging
p. 147 fellow-men
p. 155 peat-smoke
p. 164 one-quarter
p. 167 bare-legged
p. 168 rock-habit
p. 177 counter-assertion
p. 178 cross-lights
p. 180 arm-in-arm
p. 189 dining-room
p. 201 home-coming
p. 202 to-day
p. 203 powder-horn

p. 217 Smith-and-Wesson
p. 218 waiting-rooms
p. 220 river-side
p. 221 girl-student
p. 235 country-side
p. 237 *Voyez-vous*
p. 239 semi-darkness
p. 246 sea-wood
p. 259 fisher-wives
p. 262 lantern-bearer
p. 262 bull's-eyes
p. 272 drawing-room
p. 280 first-class-passenger
p. 282 belly-god
p. 285 dining-room
p. 289 to-morrow
p. 299 over-weighing
p. 300 sun-colored
p. 309 mountain-summits
p. 311 half-informed
p. 317 semi-detached
p. 322 bye-roads
p. 323 parish-constable
p. 327 coast-line
p. 329 fire-place
p. 331 red-and-white
p. 334 blue-clad
p. 334 over-worked
p. 337 window-panes
p. 338 sea-weeds
p. 339 beech-roots
p. 344 salle-à-manger
p. 346 key-bugle
p. 348 steam-hammers
p. 360 hackney-coaches
p. 360 brain-pan
p. 368 tongue-tied
p. 368 half-glorified
p. 370 *tableaux-vivants*
p. 371 full-sized
p. 380 by-and-by
p. 387 sea-commander
p. 389 Anglo-Saxon
p. 390 nose-tree

p. 392 deep-sea
p. 420 first-fruits
p. 420 riverside-meadow
p. 422 nonsense-words
p. 428 toy-gun
p. 435 head-stones
p. 456 top-heavy
p. 468 gig-accident
p. 474 strait-laced
p. 515 olive-yard
p. 516 pilot-pictures

Printed in the USA
CPSIA information can be obtained
at www.ICGtesting.com
LVHW012257190524
780793LV00027B/516